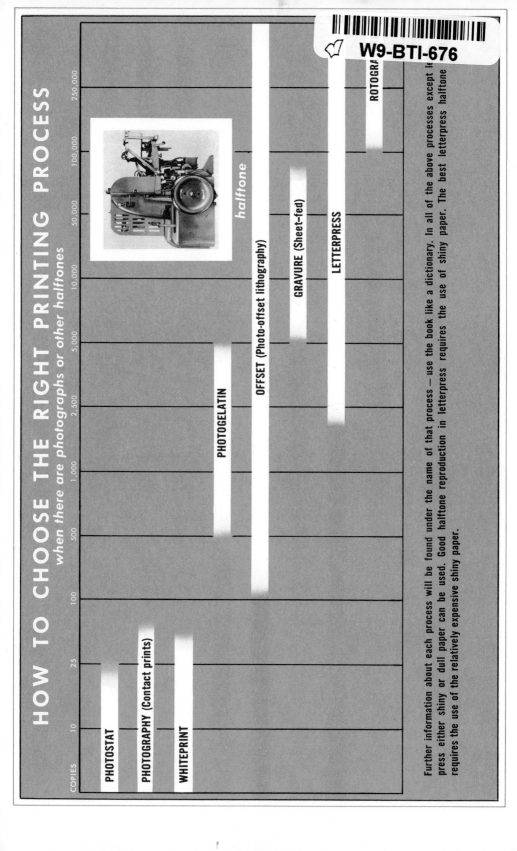

HOW TO CHOOSE THE RIGHT PRINTING PROCESS
when there are photographs or other halftones

COPIES   10   25   100   500   1,000   2,500   5,000   10,000   50,000   100,000   250,000

PHOTOSTAT

PHOTOGRAPHY (Contact prints)

WHITEPRINT

PHOTOGELATIN

OFFSET (Photo-offset lithography)

halftone

GRAVURE (Sheet–fed)

LETTERPRESS

ROTOGRA

Further information about each process will be found under the name of that process — use the book like a dictionary. In all of the above processes except le press either shiny or dull paper can be used. Good halftone reproduction in letterpress requires the use of shiny paper. The best letterpress halftone requires the use of the relatively expensive shiny paper.

**Printing and
Promotion Handbook**

OTHER McGRAW-HILL HANDBOOKS OF INTEREST

ABBOTT AND RIDER *Handbook of Broadcasting*

AMERICAN SOCIETY OF TOOL AND MANUFACTURING ENGINEERS *Manufacturing Planning and Estimating Handbook*

ARKIN *Handbook of Sampling for Auditing and Accounting*

BRADY *Materials Handbook*

CONDON AND ODISHAW *Handbook of Physics*

DICHTER *Handbook of Consumer Motivations*

DUNN *International Handbook of Advertising*

FACTORY MUTUAL ENGINEERING DIVISION *Handbook of Industrial Loss Prevention*

HEYEL *The Foreman's Handbook*

HUSKEY AND KORN *Computer Handbook*

JURAN *Quality Control Handbook*

KNOWLTON *Standard Handbook for Electrical Engineers*

KORN AND KORN *Mathematical Handbook for Scientists and Engineers*

LANGE *Handbook of Chemistry*

LASSER *Business Management Handbook*

LASSER *Standard Handbook for Accountants*

MAGILL, HOLDEN, AND ACKLEY *Air Pollution Handbook*

MANAS *National Plumbing Code Handbook*

MARKS AND BAUMEISTER *Mechanical Engineers' Handbook*

MAYNARD *Industrial Engineering Handbook*

MAYNARD *Top Management Handbook*

MERRITT *Building Construction Handbook*

MORROW *Maintenance Engineering Handbook*

PERRY *Engineering Manual*

ROSSNAGEL *Handbook of Rigging*

STANIAR *Plant Engineering Handbook*

STANLEY *Handbook of International Marketing*

STEPHENSON *Handbook of Public Relations*

URQUHART *Civil Engineering Handbook*

YODER, HENEMAN, TURNBULL, AND STONE *Handbook of Personnel Management and Labor Relations*

Printing and Promotion Handbook

HOW TO PLAN, PRODUCE, AND USE PRINTING, ADVERTISING, AND DIRECT MAIL

Daniel Melcher

Nancy Larrick

THIRD EDITION

McGRAW-HILL BOOK COMPANY

New York   San Francisco   Toronto
London   Sydney

ACKNOWLEDGMENTS

The authors wish to acknowledge their great indebtedness to the many people who read and criticized sections of the manuscript of this book. Literally hundreds of individuals helped check it for accuracy.

Special thanks are given to the following for their invaluable assistance:

Irving B. Simon, author of The Story of Printing, *and free-lance consultant on publishing and printing problems*

Lawrence Creshoff, former Executive Editor of the Television Information Office, now consultant on communications

Norman Dolph of Columbia Records, and

Ann Clayton, R. R. Bowker Co., Inc., who researched, typed, checked and rechecked at every stage.

Z
118
M4
1966

HOW TO USE THIS BOOK

The *Printing and Promotion Handbook* consists of an A-to-Z encyclopedia followed by four appendixes: Appendix 1, Type Faces; Appendix 2, Bibliography; and Appendix 3, Postal Information.

In the A-to-Z arrangement of the main body of the book, you will find many rather detailed articles on such all-embracing subjects as PAMPHLETS; ADVERTISING; DUPLICATING; SHIPPING INFORMATION; and CAMPAIGN PLANNING. You will also find many brief, but highly specific, entries on procedures, techniques, services, and materials that are basic in various segments of the field of printing and promotion. Scattered throughout, in the appropriate alphabetical spot, there are definitions, references, and cross references.

This material has been arranged and cross-referenced to help the reader in many ways:

1. To look up answers to specific questions quickly and easily.
2. To ensure that no detail or possibility has been overlooked in a promotion or publicity campaign.
3. To explore the various facets of many related fields of information, just as you would use a primer or take a refresher course in a particular subject.

For example, if you have a general pamphlet problem, you can turn to the entry on PAMPHLETS and find a check list of factors that you should consider

in planning a pamphlet as well as practical suggestions for efficient production and buying. This article will also refer you to other entries which will give specific details about such possibilities as the use of cold type, reverse plates, and even label printers. If you need to know more about paper for your pamphlet, you can refer to the entry on PAPER or that on PAPER SIZES AND WEIGHTS. And if you are concerned with the selection of type, you can turn to the entry on TYPE or to Appendix 1, Type Faces, which is a convenient type specimen book of text type and display faces.

When you look up POSTER, the authors assume you are saying, "Tell me all about posters." The handbook answers, "Well, how many of what kind? You say you need 1,000 posters in a few simple colors? Then consider silk screen." You then look up SILK SCREEN which will tell you how silk-screen printing works, about how much it costs, when to use it, and where to buy it.

We believe it will be unnecessary to follow up more than three or four cross references at most to get the answer to a single problem. In many cases, the first reference will answer your question.

For the Expert or the Beginner

The *Printing and Promotion Handbook* has been written for people—including beginners—who have to buy printing and direct mail services; for those who have to plan or prepare advertising, publicity, or information material of any kind, from covering letters to bound books; for anyone, in fact, who attempts to influence others by the printed or duplicated word. It also discusses films, recordings, radio, and television as intrinsic parts of a complete publicity or information program.

Unlike so many existing books, the *Printing and Promotion Handbook* is not primarily for the printer or the specialist. It assumes that most editors may also have to grapple with production and distribution problems. It further assumes that the reader who is considering a *printed* circular may also be interested in alternate ways and costs of achieving the same results—for example, by using a form letter or advertisement.

For these reasons, there are several entries which are particularly recommended as preliminary reading. They include CAMPAIGN PLANNING; ESTIMATING COSTS; SAVING MONEY; PRINTING; and DISTRIBUTION. In the Table of Contents, you will find many other basic entries grouped under general topics. A check of such entries will serve as a guide to the beginner who needs to build a good basic fund of information and as a form of insurance to the old hand who wants to be sure he has considered every possibility.

What Information Will You Find?

We have assumed that the readers of this handbook are busy people in search of specific information and practical details. Therefore, we have given where-to-buy-it information for every type of service and product, typical current prices (1965–1966), suggestions on where to get additional information on specialized subjects, complete shipping information including postal information (Appendix 3) as well as comparative rates, regulations, and services of REA Express (surface and air), freight (motor, rail and air), and parcel service. Type specimens showing complete alphabets and character counts are given in Appendix 1, Type Faces. Books for further reading are listed and described in Appendix 2. They are referred to under appropriate entries throughout the handbook.

Firms listed in this handbook are not necessarily recommended in preference to firms not listed. Space does not permit a full listing. The authors have mentioned a few names as a service to readers without in any way vouching for the quality of their work or for the reasonableness of their prices. Some of the firms listed are those with whom the authors have dealt personally. Some have been recommended by friends. Some have been listed solely on the strength of information originating with those firms themselves.

No firm has paid to be listed in this handbook. The authors would appreciate hearing from any reader who has had bad luck with any listed firm, so that the name may be dropped in future editions.

The prices mentioned in these pages were included only after careful consideration. It would be easy to rely too heavily upon them unless they are used comparatively (see ESTIMATING COSTS). However, the authors felt that readers would want to know, for example, that rotogravure jobs are never priced under four figures, or that 1,000 8 × 11 leaflets *can* be bought for $8 or so in combination run offset, etc.

Choosing the Right Printing Process and the Right Printer

Cross references are used very generously within the various entries, particularly under such far-reaching entries as PRINTING. This seemed especially desirable in view of the fact that "printing" is not one process, or three processes, but a whole host of specialized processes. There is one "best" process for practically any given job.

In fact, one of the first things that the beginner needs to know about printing is that *printing is a specialized business.* The first rule for getting professional and economical results is to go to the printer who specializes in the kind of work you want.

Any well-equipped printer *can* do practically anything; but he cannot necessarily do it economically. For instance, almost any printer can print a book. But a book printer is more likely to produce a professional-looking book. Almost any printer can print a poster or a label; but in certain circumstances a silk-screen printer can offer better posters for less money.

When a printer is offered a job that he is not very well equipped to handle, one of several things may happen:

1. He may suggest that the inquirer take the work where it can be done best.
2. He may accept the job, but subcontract it.

3. He may quote a price high enough to cover the cost of doing the job on his own not-quite-appropriate equipment, reasoning that it is the buyer's lookout if he does not know that he could get the work done more cheaply elsewhere.
4. He may not even know or admit that the work can be done better or less expensively elsewhere.

The best printers will follow the first or second course. When they subcontract work, they charge a commission for doing so but may nevertheless save the customer's time and money by knowing where to take the work and by being able to purchase it at "trade" rates.

Unfortunately, some job printers proceed along line 3 or 4. It is, therefore, well worth while for any buyer of printing or duplicating service to check with this handbook to make sure that he is asking for quotations from the right kind of printer.

CHECK THIS LIST BEFORE GOING AHEAD WITH ANY PRINTING AND PROMOTION JOB

Purposes: What results are sought? Is the objective to change habits of thought, or secure action, create good will, or what?

Audience: Who must be reached with this information or message? Will the material get their interest, claim their confidence, answer their doubts, and be completely understandable to them?

Means: Might there be a better way to attain the desired result? (Pamphlet *versus* letter, advertising, radio, television, film, exhibit, etc.)

Competition: What competition for attention will this message be up against? Will the message be able to compete successfully for reader attention? Most messages compete against comics, picture magazines, sports pages and television. There are millions of people who just do not read solid type. Some do not read at all.

Time requirements: Does the day-by-day schedule for this job assure time for editing, printing, addressing, and shipping? Or must the job and the specifications be altered to permit delivery on time?

Mechanical requirements: Do the specifications take account of

1. Space requirements at point of use? (Bulletin board, pocket, wallet, handbag, etc.)
2. Shipping method (envelopes, tubes, cartons, etc.)? Postal regulations?
3. Inserting or binding machine requirements?
4. Economic cutting of paper?
5. Size of printing presses?

Delivery instructions: Have accurate instructions been made up covering both shipping and receiving bulk lots? Have samples been ordered sent to all the proper people? Are labels or envelopes addressed for shipping single copies?

CONTENTS

The *Printing and Promotion Handbook* consists of an encyclopedia (with articles arranged in alphabetical order) and three appendixes: Appendix 1, Type Faces; Appendix 2, Bibliography; and Appendix 3, Postal Information.

Below, the important basic articles are grouped much as they might have been if the book had been divided into chapters. By referring to this listing, you may use the book for general study as easily as for spot reference. No page numbers are given since each entry will be found in its proper alphabetical place in the body of the book or in the proper appendix.

HOW TO PLAN A COMPLETE CAMPAIGN

See entries on CAMPAIGN PLANNING; ESTIMATING COSTS; SAVING MONEY; SCHEDULING; DELIVERY; DISTRIBUTION; ADVERTISING; RADIO; TELEVISION; MOTION PICTURES; FILMSTRIPS; RECORDINGS; ADVERTISING AGENCIES; PUBLIC-RELATIONS CONSULTANTS

HOW TO CHOOSE THE RIGHT PROCESS AND PRINTER

See entries on PRINTING; PRINTERS: HOW TO CHOOSE; and the charts inside the covers of this book

HOW TO PLAN AND PRODUCE SPECIFIC PRINTED MATERIALS

See entries on PAMPHLETS; CIRCULARS; LETTERS; POSTERS; NEWSPAPERS; PERIODICALS; HOUSE ORGANS; DISPLAYS; SIGNS; OUTDOOR ADVERTISING; TRANSIT ADVERTISING; LABELS; ENVELOPES; BOOKS; JACKETS; CATALOGS; BUSINESS FORMS; BLOTTERS; CALENDARS

THE MAJOR PRINTING PROCESSES

See entries on PRINTING; RELIEF PRINTING; PLANOGRAPHY; INTAGLIO; STENCIL; LETTERPRESS; OFFSET; LITHOGRAPHY; PHOTOGELATIN; GRAVURE; ROTOGRAVURE; ENGRAVING; SILK SCREEN; PRESSWORK; COLOR PRINTING; PHOTOGRAPHY: AS A PRINTING PROCESS

OFFICE DUPLICATING PROCESSES

See entries on DUPLICATING; OFFSET DUPLICATING; PHOTOCOPYING; MIMEOGRAPH; SPIRIT DUPLICATING; HECTOGRAPH; LETTERS; XEROX; VERIFAX; THERMO-FAX; WHITEPRINT; BLUEPRINT; AUTOMATIC TYPEWRITER

USE OF CUTS AND PLATES

See entries on CUT; LINECUT; HALFTONE; COMBINATION HALFTONE AND LINE-CUT; PLATES; REVERSE PLATES; DUPLICATE PLATES; ELECTRO; STEREO; WOOD ENGRAVINGS; PROCESS COLOR

SETTING TYPE, TYPING, HAND-LETTERING

See entries on TYPE; TYPE MEASUREMENTS; INTERTYPE; LINOTYPE; MONOTYPE; LUDLOW; FOUNDRY TYPE; LETTER SPACING; LEADING; TYPEWRITERS; COLD TYPE; VARITYPER; PHOTOTYPESETTING; COMPUTER TYPESETTING; FOTOTYPE; LETTERING; *and also* Appendix 1, Type Faces

PHOTOGRAPHY

See entries on PHOTOGRAPHY; PHOTOGRAPHY: AS A PRINTING PROCESS; PHOTO-COPYING; PHOTOGRAPHS: CARE IN HANDLING; PHOTOGRAPHS: HOW TO SELECT; PHOTOGRAPHERS; PHOTO AGENCIES; COLOR PHOTOGRAPHY; BLEED; CROP; ENLARG-ING; NEGATIVE; RETOUCHING; MONTAGE; SCALING; STRIPPING

EDITING AND PROOFREADING

See entries on EDITORIAL PLANNING; EDITORIAL WORK; COPY PREPARATION; COPY EDITING; COPYFITTING; COPYWRITING; PROOFS; DUMMY; PASTE-UP DUMMY; MAKEUP; INDEXING; CAPTIONS; COPYRIGHT; PROOFREADING

DESIGNING AND ILLUSTRATING

See entries on DESIGN; DESIGNERS; LAYOUT; LETTERING; ARTWORK; ARTISTS; ART SERVICES; DRAWING TECHNIQUES; SHADING TINTS; MARGINS; ILLUSTRATIONS; CARTOONS; SCALING

SELECTING PAPER

See entries on PAPER; PAPER SIZES AND WEIGHTS; CARDBOARD

FOLDING, BINDING, AND FINISHING

See entries on MOUNTING AND FINISHING; FOLDING; SELF-COVER; BINDING; BOOK-BINDING; MECHANICAL BINDINGS; DIE CUTTING; STAPLING; PERFORATING; PEB-BLING; VARNISHING

HOW TO UTILIZE DIRECT MAIL ADVERTISING

See entries on DIRECT MAIL ADVERTISING; MAIL ORDER; LETTERSHOPS; MAILING LISTS; ADDRESSING; ADDRESSOGRAPH; ELLIOTT ADDRESSING; CHESHIRE; HEYER ADDRESSER. *Also* Appendix 3, Postal Information, *see entry on* MAILING-LIST CORRECTIONS

POSTAL AND SHIPPING INFORMATION

See entries on REA EXPRESS; FREIGHT; SHIPPING INFORMATION; UNITED PARCEL SERVICES; WRAPPING AND PACKING. *Also* Appendix 3, Postal Information, in which entries are arranged alphabetically

SPECIALIZED PRINTING

See entries on NOVELTY PRINTING; IMPRINTING; EMBOSSING; MARBLING; FOREIGN-LANGUAGE PRINTING; MUSIC PRINTING; CONTAINER PRINTING; PACKAGES; CLOTH PRINTING; MAPS; TICKETS; NUMBERING; BADGES; GREETING CARDS; TAGS; BALLOONS; MATCHES; SEALS; DECALCOMANIAS; FLOCK PRINTING; LUMINESCENT PRINTING; THERMOGRAPHY

ADDITIONAL INFORMATION

See Appendix 2, Bibliography

A | a

A.A.'s Abbreviation for author's alterations. (See AUTHOR'S ALTERATIONS.)

abbreviations In this book abbreviations are listed alphabetically among the regular headings. (For the use of abbreviations in editorial work, see PROOFREADING and COPY PREPARATION.)

ABC Abbreviation for Audit Bureau of Circulations. (See ADVERTISING.)

adcut See LOGOTYPE.

addressing See also ADDRESSOGRAPH; ELLIOTT ADDRESSING; HEYER ADDRESSER; CHESHIRE ADDRESSING; LETTERSHOP; MAILING LISTS; MASTER ADDRESSER.

Envelopes can be hand-addressed by pen or typewriter at rates ranging from $10 to $15 per thousand or can be machine-addressed from prepared plates at rates as low as $2.50 to $4 per thousand. Typing is generally no more expensive than pen addressing and tends to look neater. In fact, unless there is a substantial difference in the hourly wage, typing is noticeably cheaper. In almost every city there are lettershops equipped to handle addressing. In New York, one addressing firm which offers daily pickup and delivery service is De Groodt & Associates, Inc., 88–20 95 Ave., Ozone Park, N.Y. For typing perforated gummed labels and supplying an original and two carbons of each address, their rate is about $3 per thousand above their ordinary base rate.

Machine addressing may be done from embossed metal plates (Addressograph, Speedaumat, Pitney Bowes), from stencils (Elliott, Nord), from cards (Scriptomatic), or from paper rolls (Master Addresser). In all the foregoing methods, the information is stored in the form of a small metal or paper printing plate, capable of duplicating its address directly onto an envelope.

It is also possible to store address information in the form of punched cards, punched tape, magnetic (computer) tape, etc., in which case the information is re-created rather than "printed" during the addressing process. Almost any kind of data-processing equipment can be adapted to addressing work, provided that labeling equipment is available to transfer the resulting "print-out" to the mailing pieces. For example, it is possible to print out addresses two, three, four, and even five abreast on an

1

IBM 1403 impact printer and then transfer the addresses to mailing pieces by means of machines such as the Cheshire. (See CHESHIRE ADDRESSING.) Such machines will also accept address labels produced on other types of addressing equipment, in wide or narrow rolls, packs, single-cut labels, etc.

The principal methods of direct addressing (which, of course, can also produce address labels) are Addressograph, Elliott, and Scriptomatic.

For small users, there is also an addressing machine which sells for $31 with enough supplies to handle 500 names. This is called the "Master Addresser" and works on the spirit-duplicator principle. (See MASTER ADDRESSER.) The addresses are typed, with special carbon paper, on a paper tape. The tape can be used for addressing envelopes up to 200 times before the work becomes too faint to be legible. The speed of addressing is about 15 to 20 envelopes per minute.

Addressing costs are of four kinds: (1) the cost of installing and maintaining the equipment, (2) the cost of preparing the nameplates, (3) the cost of mailing-list maintenance, such as making corrections, additions, and deletions (see MAILING LISTS), and (4) the cost of doing the actual addressing.

Equipment costs. Elliott equipment tends to require a smaller investment in machinery. Minimum equipment for handling a mailing list of about 500 names costs about $139. The lowest-cost office machine is about $295, as against $160 for the Addressograph. Elliott address cards can be cut on an office typewriter: in contrast to a price of over $500 for much slower Addressograph embossing equipment. Elliott trays and cabinets cost less and take less space. A standard, heavy-duty Elliott addressing machine costs $500 to $900, against about $1,000 for the comparable Addressograph machine.

Running costs. When a large volume of work is to be handled, first costs may not be nearly so important as running costs. A comparison of the cost per thousand of preparing the nameplates is given in the accompanying table. (Figures are based on estimates supplied by the companies.)

In general, more work goes into the Addressograph plates. Making a so-called "CB" Addressograph plate (in two parts) requires (1) embossing a metal strip, (2) inserting this strip in a frame, (3) taking a proof, and (4) trimming and inserting the proof in the frame. Whether or not a more useful address plate results is for the user to decide.

Comparative costs on list maintenance are hard to measure. Elliott address cards are lighter and more compact. A drawer containing 250 Elliott addresses weighs 2¼ lb, as against a similar drawer holding 175 Addressograph plates weighing 14 lb. Running costs do not seem to show much variation one way or the other. Speeds of addressing are comparable on comparable models for Addressograph and Elliott.

Comparison of quality. There are a few things that Addressograph machines will do particularly well, e.g., make carbon copies, cut mimeograph stencils, print in two colors through a two-color ribbon, and print with special ink on paper offset (Multilith) plates and Ditto (spirit-duplicating) masters.

A comparison between Elliott and Addressograph as to quality of work is a matter of opinion. Both processes are capable of producing both superior and inferior work.

Both processes can be used for striking in a name, address, and salutation at the head of a form letter. An Elliott fill-in of this sort is closer in appearance to a mimeographed form letter, since both are done by a stencil process; an Addressograph fill-in is closer to a Multigraphed letter, since both are done through a ribbon. However, a perfectly matched fill-in is difficult if not impossi-

Preparation costs per thousand	Elliott	Addressograph
Cost of address cards or plates	$20.00	$ 6.00–30.00
Cost for preparing these cards or plates with three-line address, plus index line or proof for identification	24.00	35.00–50.00
Cost of materials for making changes or substitutions on these cards or plates	20.00	5.00 up

ble to get in either way. (See LETTERS and PROCESS LETTERS.)

Selective addressing is possible in all processes. The addressing machines can be set either to accept or to reject any stencil with a hole punched at any given position in its frame, or a plate with a notch or tab at any given position.

The "keying" or "tabbing" of address plates is a feature that needs to be used with care. There is little economy in running 10,000 plates through a machine in order to address 100 envelopes. Small lists should not be merged into one big keyed list if the small lists will be used more often separately than together. If, however, the usual practice is to use them all together, then it pays to merge the plates into one big, geographically arranged list to simplify the problem of getting the mailings sorted and tied geographically in a form acceptable to the post office.

Magazines key their mailing lists so that each month the machine will automatically drop from the list those whose subscriptions expire. One big book club punches the address card when a book is shipped to a subscriber and again when it is paid for. This permits automatic billing.

In general, if a mailing list is likely to be used as many as eight to twelve times within two years, it may pay to put it on stencils or plates. This, however, depends on the rate of annual change in the list. A 20 percent annual change is common.

Addressing done by lettershop. Lettershops are usually glad to maintain and run off lists of plates, although some firms often prefer to do this themselves, both in the interests of greater accuracy and for greater speed in emergencies. Where magazines are concerned, the printer may maintain the mailing list himself, or he may receive in advance of each issue addressed wrappers, envelopes, or labels.

In making arrangements for outside maintenance of a mailing list, one big user recommends getting both hourly rates and piecework rates. The same user gets new bids at intervals to keep prices right.

There are several methods of using IBM or Remington punched cards as addressing masters. One puts an aniline-dye carbon image of the address right on the card, from which impressions can be taken directly by the spirit duplicating method. (See SCRIPTO-MATIC.) The Addressograph electronic addressing system uses an electronic eye to scan a typed address on the card and transfer it to a paper tape intended for direct pasting on magazines, envelopes, etc., or to a tape intermediary from which, with heat and pressure, the address image only can be transferred to envelopes or other surfaces. Both IBM and Remington card printers of the kind used in accounting work have been adapted for writing addresses from information punched into cards, at rates of 3,000 or so per hour. A limitation here is that columns used for coding in the address (one column per character) are no longer available for coding in other information—and there are only 80 or 90 columns.

Companies which have access to computers of any kind may find it advantageous to look into methods of maintaining their mailing lists on magnetic tape, for print-out in the form of address labels. Much flexibility and selectivity can be built into such a system, and sometimes the otherwise burdensome job of keeping the addresses up-to-date can be shared with another department such as the billing or credit department.

Addresses to be placed in magnetic storage must, of course, first be prepared in a form suitable for computer "input." This input usually takes the form of punched cards or punched paper tape. Considerable economies can be made if the creation of the input record can be a by-product of some other operation. Such would be the case, for example, if customer invoices were being addressed on tape-punching Flexowriters, the tape being later available for updating the mailing lists.

Some mailing lists exist only in a single sequence of plates, stencils, or cards. Others are maintained in duplicate, e.g., a file of Addressograph plates and a matching file of 3 by 5 cards. This permits list maintenance work to be done in one place while the plates are maintained in another. Of course, it can also double the number of motions involved in an address change—and the chances for error.

The need for a duality of files increases when the address plates must be kept in postal-zone sequence and it is desired to keep a separate file arranged strictly by customers' names.

When lists are maintained by computer, parallel files (e.g., the punched cards used for original input) may or may not be kept. Rather than keep card files for "look-up," lists in any desired sequence can be printed out by the computer at intervals—in duplicate or multiple copies if desired.

Computer lists almost always rely for their sequence on customer numbers rather than customer names. Addresses are killed by number, corrected by number, and inserted by number. The numbers are therefore normally printed out along with the address to minimize the need for look-up. Magazine subscribers are urged to send in an old address label when reporting a new address. Promotional mailings may use a combination of window envelope and addressed order-reply card on which both the customer address and his account number will be printed.

Another approach to the problem of assigning a number to each name on a list is the so-called "match-code" technique, under which an alphanumeric code is derived from the address information, consisting perhaps of the ZIP-Code number plus certain numbers or letters from the street address and name. This is somewhat analogous to the policy of reducing all first names to initials to avoid the possibility of confusion resulting from having A. B. Smith duplicated in the file under Andrew B. Smith. This technique makes unnecessary much of the look-up involved in finding or assigning arbitrary account numbers, although it poses certain problems of its own. The IBM Corporation publishes a reference manual, "Subscription Fulfillment on Magnetic Tape Processing Systems," in which reference is made to systems used by such publications as *Look Magazine, Reader's Digest, McCall's Magazine, Newsweek, Esquire,* and *Parents' Magazine.*

Addressograph See also ADDRESSING.

Addressograph machines, using several different sizes and styles of plates, are made in a number of models for addressing and for many other uses where information must be repetitively written.

Metal plates are used. Characters are embossed on these plates in a special machine called a "graphotype." The embossing produces raised letters, which print through a wide inked ribbon to

A tray of Addressograph plates. The embossed metal plate from which the printing is done slides into the lower portion of the frame. A proof of this embossed area slides into the upper portion of the frame. The plates shown carry metal tabs.

give results closely duplicating typewritten addressing.

The information on each Addressograph plate can be keyed through the use of special metal tabs affixed to the top of the plate. Thus the machine can be set either to print only plates having a tab in, say, position 2 or to print all plates except those having a tab in that position.

Plates can carry a paper proof of all or part of the embossed lettering to facilitate reading, filing, and finding. This card-index feature of the Addressograph plate, combined with the tabs, provides the user with a filing system, often used as a master file for reference as well as for reproduction purposes.

Recent prices on Addressograph machines start at $160 for a hand-operated model with an automatic plate feed. The company has introduced many new developments in specialized single-plate imprinter models at prices ranging downward to under $50 per unit. Electrically operated machines range up to several thousand dollars, the price depending upon the production requirements of a given installation.

The name "Speedaumat" identifies the line of Addressograph machines that use the low-cost Speedaumat plate, which has certain features particularly adaptable to the publishing business and to certain types of large lists. This plate is coded by notching instead of tabbing.

Graphotype machines for embossing the plates are priced at just over $500 and up—but it is not necessary to purchase one of these machines. Addressograph field offices and many lettershops maintain an embossing service.

Addressograph plate costs range from approximately $6 per thousand for Speedaumat plates in large quantities to

An Addressograph plate.

$30 and more for multiple-unit combinations of frame, printing plates, and index cards. The latter represent original requirements. The frames represent a capital investment because they can be used over and over again when changes occur. Blank replacement plates in many popular styles are priced from around $6 a thousand for complete inserts to less than $5 a thousand for many sectional inserts. There are more than 100 styles, and many variations within each style can be worked out to suit the individual requirements of a given problem.

The embossing of the metal plates is a process akin to typing but somewhat slower. An experienced graphotype operator can produce from 30 to 100 three-line plates per hour. This rate is dependent largely upon whether the operator is using a hand-operated or the more expensive keyboard machine. Two graphotype models feature automatic plate feed and discharge, eliminating many hand operations. There is also a completely automatic graphotype machine which operates from a punched tape. The tape is prepared as a by-product of another typing operation on such machines as a Flexowriter or teletype. All the operator has to do is to insert the tape and start the machine. As many as 10 of these automatic graphotype machines can be attended by one person.

There are two major contenders in the field of addressing machines: Addressograph and Elliott. (See ELLIOTT ADDRESSING.) Special advantages claimed for Addressograph are that embossed metal plates give more consistently uniform results (stencils can be cut well or badly); mistakes are easier to correct because the graphotype operator simply backspaces and either blanks out or embosses over; the plate can be identified with a printed proof of itself mounted right in the frame and an index card and so is easier to read, file, and handle; keys or tabs on plates

can be changed at any time without making new plates; metal frames on multipart plates can be reused at a cost of less than a penny for newly embossed metal area; and the metal plate is fire-resistant and able to withstand water and fire-fighting chemicals.

In addition to addressing envelopes and labels, Addressograph machines can be used for making out monthly bills, timecards, payrolls, checks, etc., and for signing, numbering, and dating business records. In fact, for short messages, Addressograph plates and the same machine can be used for duplicating or imprinting.

Among the new models now on the market are accounting Addressograph units that not only perform all the traditional Addressograph functions, but also do certain types of accounting work. These machines operate from the familiar embossed Addressograph metal plates. The accounting information is carried in the form of punched holes in these plates. In certain of the larger accounting models, the holes from the plates are automatically interpreted and punched into tabulating cards as a by-product of the regular Addressograph imprinting run. Some Addressograph models start an operation with blank paper either in rolls or in flat sheets. The actual business form is duplicated automatically while the regular Addressograph run is being made.

Adherography A duplicating technique similar in principle to the process described under IMAGIC.

advertisements See also ADVERTISING; ADVERTISING AGENCIES; MAT SERVICES.

The problems involved in writing, designing, and ordering a printed advertisement are very similar to those involved in producing pamphlets, letters, posters, etc. However, once the advertising medium has been chosen, this choice usually determines the nature of the printing process to be used and sets up some limitations on size, the nature of illustrations, and perhaps the use of color.

The easiest way to place an advertisement is through an advertising agency. The use of an agency need cost the advertiser no money since each agency receives a 15 percent commission direct from the newspaper or magazine on all space purchased through that agency. Agencies do charge the client for special services beyond general advice on placement and on copy. (See ADVERTISING AGENCIES.)

Newspapers and magazines stand ready to set type and even to advise advertisers on layout without charge other than regular space rates. However, advertisers who place ads in a variety of media usually prefer to get them set up in one independent composition house so that they will have a uniformity of style. The advertisers supply plates, mats, or proofs to the periodical.

Periodicals that are printed by letterpress, including practically all newspapers and most magazines, print from cuts or type or plates. The advertiser must supply copy, or a duplicate plate made from his own type, and also supply, or at least pay for, any cuts required. Some periodicals, however, are printed by the offset or rotogravure process and, therefore, have no use for cuts or plates. They want reproduction proofs and artwork from which to make their own printing plates.

Before planning an ad, one should learn the following things about the periodical:

1. By what process is it printed? That is, are cuts needed or perhaps artwork and reproduction proofs? Are mats acceptable? Should electros or other duplicate plates be blocked or unblocked?

2. Can halftones be used? Of what screen?

3. What is the exact size of the area being purchased?

4. What kind of competition for reader attention will the ad probably be up against, and what can be done to meet this competition successfully?

5. If the periodical is to set the ad in type, what type styles are available? In what sizes?

The answers to questions 1, 2, and 3 can be found quickly on the advertising rate card of the publication or from the guides published by Standard Rate and Data Service, Inc., 5201 Old Orchard Rd., Skokie, Ill. The answers to questions 4 and 5 can be found best by looking over a few numbers of the publication.

It cannot be assumed that any type style used in a publication is available to an advertiser; it may have been supplied by another advertiser in plate form. However, display type styles used editorially are generally available for advertising use. An easy way to specify type for a simple ad is to snip out lines of the type style desired and paste these to the layout. (See LAYOUT; DESIGN; COPYWRITING.)

advertising See also ADVERTISEMENTS; ADVERTISING AGENCIES; OUTDOOR ADVERTISING; RADIO; TELEVISION; DIRECT MAIL ADVERTISING; MAIL ORDER; DISPLAYS; COPYWRITING; LAYOUT; CAMPAIGN PLANNING.

This whole book is about, or applies to, advertising in one form or another, but the emphasis is on the planning, writing, editing, and production of material that the purchaser will distribute himself.

However, in order to choose intelligently among the many ways of moving ideas and information from here to there, it is necessary to know something about all the channels of communication that are available. Hence this overly brief entry on the purchase of space in newspapers, general magazines, and business papers. For information about radio and television advertising see RADIO and TELEVISION. For some excellent books on every aspect of advertising, consult Appendix 2, Bibliography.

The purchaser of newspaper or magazine advertising is buying more than just printing; he is buying distribution. He is paying for a chance to put his message before so many thousand or so many million people.

Whether or not advertising will pay depends primarily upon the proportion of the audience who are really prospects for the advertiser's product or service. If only 10,000 *Life* readers are really prospects for an advertised product that is inexpensive, a page in *Life* may be a rather expensive way to reach them. If every *Life* reader is a potential buyer, then a page in *Life* may be an exceedingly good investment.

Advertising rates are, of course, obtainable on request to publications or radio and TV stations. The advertising manager of each medium can usually supply not only rates, but also useful market-analysis material.

Circulation figures are usually quoted as ABC, BPA, or VAC figures. This means that they have been audited and certified as correct by the Audit Bureau of Circulations, the Business Publications Audit of Circulation, or the Verified Audit Circulation Corporation. Smaller publications may issue their figures as "Publishers' Sworn Statements."

The ABC audits only circulations that are at least 50 percent paid. Magazines with a controlled free circulation may be audited by the BPA or VAC.

All newspapers and magazines will put the advertiser's message into type at no cost above the regular space charge if they receive copy in time to permit this. Large advertisers, however, almost invariably make their own arrangements for typesetting, since this gives them a broader variety of types to choose from and greater control over appearance. They supply the publication with a complete plate ready for printing. (See also ADVERTISEMENTS.)

Data on circulation may be found in Ayer's "Directory of Newspapers & Periodicals" (N. W. Ayer & Son, Philadelphia 6, $30).

Monthly advertising rate guides are published by Standard Rate and Data Service, Inc., 5201 Old Orchard Rd., Skokie, Ill. These include: *Newspaper Rates and Data,* $32.50 a year; *Consumer Magazines and Farm Publications Rates and Data,* $30; *Business Publications Rates and Data,* $35; *Spot Radio Rates and Data,* $37.50; and *Spot Television Rates and Data,* $32.50.

Magazine advertising. Magazine rates run upward from about $3.50 per black-and-white page per thousand circulation. Circulation and page rates in

Circulation and Page Rates of 10 National Magazines

Magazine	Net paid circulation (6-month average)	Page size (nonbleed)	Page rate (black and white)	Rate per M circulation
Reader's Digest	14,500,000	$4\frac{3}{8}$ x $6\frac{1}{2}$	$49,800	$ 3.43
McCall's Magazine	8,250,000	$9\frac{3}{8}$ x $12\frac{1}{8}$	31,000	3.76
Look	7,500,000	$9\frac{3}{8}$ x $12\frac{1}{8}$	34,035	4.53
Life	7,200,000	$9\frac{3}{8}$ x $12\frac{1}{8}$	35,200	4.88
The New Yorker	463,700	7 x $10\frac{3}{16}$	3,500	7.55
Business Week	433,826	7 x 10	5,250	12.13
Fortune	408,541	$8\frac{7}{8}$ x 11	5,980	14.65
Saturday Review	345,000	$7\frac{1}{8}$ x 10	2,835	8.22
Harper's	275,000	7 x 10	2,250	8.18
The Reporter	180,000	$7\frac{1}{16}$ x 10	1,375	7.63

Circulation and Line Rates in Five Large Daily Newspapers

Newspaper	Daily circulation	Weekly line rate	Sunday circulation	Sunday line rate
Chicago Tribune	836,702	$2.30	1,151,995	$3.15
Los Angeles Times	817,087	2.10	1,144,326	2.75
The New York Times	652,135	2.50	1,355,614	3.10
Atlanta Journal (morning and evening)	445,541	1.20	496,588	1.25
Washington Post & Times Herald	438,741	1.44	536,647	1.48

a few media are shown in the table on page 8.

Plates are, of course, required only by periodicals that are printed by the letterpress process. Magazines that are printed by offset or by rotogravure want artwork, not plates. Weeklies usually want advertising plates three to ten days ahead of publication. Monthlies may need them three to six weeks ahead of publication, with color plates still further in advance.

Newspaper advertising. Newspaper rates run upward from about $2.50 per agate line per million of circulation. This is known as the "milline" rate. Another term, the "Marline" rate, is the cost per agate line per billion dollars of retail sales in the market area covered. An agate line is an area one column wide by $\frac{1}{14}$ in. deep. The minimum milline rate quoted above converts (for comparison with magazine rates) to about $6 per large newspaper page per thousand circulation.

A full newspaper page is usually billed as about 2,400 agate lines. A common advertising rate in newspapers of small circulation is about 10 cents per agate line, or $1.40 per column inch.

Rates for national advertisers are usually higher than for local advertisers, a fact that has led many national advertisers to encourage their local outlets to advertise.

Newspaper rates may vary between different lines of merchandise or service and also between preferred positions and run of paper (rop).

Daily newspapers will accept complete advertising plates up to a late hour the day preceding publication. Weeklies may require advertising plates one to three days ahead of publication date.

advertising agencies See also ADVERTISING; CAMPAIGN PLANNING; PUBLIC-RELATIONS CONSULTANTS.

The privilege of working with a good advertising agency is a very real one. All large advertisers use agencies, and most small advertisers use them or wish they could.

A real agency-client relationship with continuity (as distinct from the kind of piecework relationship which may be satisfactory with an art agency or printer) can hardly begin until the account can yield for the agency at least one full-time salary. However, if your advertising budget is small, it may yet pay you to look into the possibilities of working with an agency. A good agency may well be able to show you how you can gain handsome returns by increasing your present budget.

The stock-in-trade of an advertising agency is, of course, know-how in the techniques of advertising. Depending on the agency, this know-how may or may not extend to direct mail, public relations, product development, market research, merchandising, customer service, fund raising, editing house organs, using posters, planning exhibits, etc. In choosing an agency, it is well to remember that it is likely to have a bias in favor of the techniques it knows best. Agencies do specialize, and often an advertiser will use one agency for space and broadcast advertising, another for direct mail, and a third for public relations.

Advertising agencies get a 15 percent commission from magazines and newspapers on the space advertising that they place. They get a like discount from radio and TV stations in the larger cities. This is generally regarded as compensation only for their professional advice on media selection, copy, layout, etc. They bill the client for the cost of space and time and for specific extra items like artwork, typography, and program talent. When they procure for the client printed literature and other items on which they get no commission, they charge the client both for the money paid out and for the agency's own services.

A good agency can relieve you of jobs that are not your meat and can thus free you for the important things you cannot delegate. It can apply to your problems experience gained in other industries or organizations and can give you access to top skills in marketing, media selection, layout, copywriting, direct mail, public relations, etc., beyond what you could or should attempt to obtain from people on your own staff.

For further information on the selection of an agency and ways to work with an agency, consult the books listed in Appendix 2, Bibliography.

agate line Newspaper advertising space is bought by the agate line. There are 14 agate lines to the column inch. Thus, an advertisement two columns wide by 2 in. deep would occupy 56 agate lines of space.

The following paragraph has been set in 5½ pt (agate) type.

It is actually possible for an advertiser to get 14 lines of type into 1 in. of advertising space by using agate type (5 1/2 pt.). However, this is rarely done, except in legal notices and classified advertisements. The agate line is a measure of area, 1/14 in. high and one standard newspaper column wide, and has nothing to do with the size of type that may be printed in that space.

airbrush An airbrush is an implement for spraying liquids, especially a film of color, by means of a blast of air. It permits tone blending and soft effects almost impossible to achieve by any other method. Artists use the airbrush extensively for retouching photographs, as well as for producing original artwork. Not all artists have airbrush equipment, which is relatively expensive. Although the airbrush is deceptively easy to use, it is hard to use well and with restraint.

Airbrush and holder.

A good book on the subject is "Airbrush Techniques for Commercial Art," by Henri A. Fluchère, John B. Musacchia, and Melvis J. Grainger (New York, Reinhold Publishing Corporation, $6.65).

air express See REA EXPRESS.

air freight See FREIGHT.

airmail See Appendix 3, Postal Information.

air parcel post See Appendix 3, Postal Information.

All-Purpose Linotype   See LUDLOW.

alphabet length   The alphabet length of any style and size of type is a measure of that type's compactness. It is the length (usually measured in points) of the alphabet as set in that style of type, abcdefghijklmnopqrstuvwxyz. Alphabet length can be converted easily into characters per pica (c.p.p.). (See TYPE.)

Alphatype   A keyboard photocomposing system for producing both text and display typography of graphic-arts quality. It consists of three units: an electric typewriter, a recorder for putting the keyboarded information on magnetic tape, and a printer which produces fully justified type on photographic paper or film from the magnetic tape. An Alphatype installation, complete with a selection of type fonts, costs about $18,000. The printer unit can set type at the rate of about 600 characters per minute, in sizes from 6 to 18 pt and in lines up to 60 picas long, with interline spacing up to 40 pt.

Each font consists of 168 characters and can include roman with italic, roman with bold, etc. Each character can have from 4 to 18 units of width. Justification is by means of uniform interword spacing. One font must be ordered for each size desired, and the fonts cost $65 each. The type can also be blown up photographically when larger sizes are required. Special fonts are obtainable on request. Decisions about leading can be made or changed after the keyboarding has been done. The magnetic tapes can be stored or erased and reused.

The Alphatype keyboard will look familiar to any typist, except that a single keystroke will "kill" a faulty line, and it is possible to code in signals to "quad right," "quad left," and "center." (The carriage-return key itself conveys

Alphatype printer.

The Alphatype keyboard and recorder.

the information required to enable a line to be justified.) The Alphatype is compact, quiet in operation. It does not require special power supplies or air conditioning. For further information, write to The Alphatype Corporation, 7500 McCormick Blvd., Skokie, Ill.

ampersand The name of the symbol "&" used for the word "and."

anchoring To anchor or "sweat" a printing plate or cut onto its block means to solder it on. Cuts can be soldered to wood blocks by inserting metal plugs in the wood. This used to be necessary wherever a cut had to be blocked close all around and had neither shoulders nor nonprinting areas through which nails could be driven. Anchoring is less common now that many engravers are blocking cuts with adhesives requiring neither shoulders nor nails.

aniline printing See FLEXOGRAPHIC PRINTING.

antique Books are commonly printed on an antique wove or antique laid paper, unless halftones are to be printed on the same paper as the text. Paper

with an antique finish has no shine and bulks thicker than paper that has been calendered to a smooth finish. Eggshell paper is a relatively smooth antique.

APL Abbreviation for All-Purpose Linotype. (See LUDLOW.)

art agencies See ART SERVICES.

artists See also ARTWORK; ART SERVICES; DESIGN; DESIGNERS; PHOTOGRAPHERS.

Many buyers of printing seem to find it much easier to procure ten thousand words than one good picture. They grant the effectiveness of pictures, but they do not know any artists, and besides they have the idea that artists cost a lot of money.

Artists exist in almost every town, and a good one is generally worth more than he is paid. A couple of attractive drawings or an excellent layout (see DESIGN and DESIGNERS) can easily double the effectiveness of any piece of printing.

Popular impressions to the contrary, most artists are just ordinary people trying to make a living. They are not eccentrics. The top men make big money, but many competent artists earn less than $150 a week and can turn out a lot of work in that time.

A free-lance artist has to charge more than a salaried artist, of course, to tide him over between jobs and to cover his overhead.

$10 is a minimum price for a small spot drawing when a lot are ordered at once. For a single small drawing, prices of $15 and up are common minimums.

To keep his average income up to a reasonable level, a free-lance artist needs to average at least $50 a day. The result is that an artist frequently sets a minimum price for any job, whether the assignment is one drawing or several. This is to reimburse him for the time spent in consultation.

Prices for artwork are hard to pin down because they vary according to what the traffic will bear. If it is worth an advertiser's while to spend $50,000 to put a painting before the public, $1,000 for the artist does not seem so much. On the other hand, $100 for a book-jacket design is about all that a publisher can afford on a book with advertising appropriations that total less than $1,000. There may be as much work on a book jacket as on any poster or ad.

To find artists (1) inquire of local schools or colleges that teach art; (2) ask advertisers where they get the art that they use; (3) try the classified advertising columns; (4) go to an art agency or art services. (See ART SERVICES.)

Artists specialize. A man who can do the Disney type of caricatures may be quite unable to draw "straight," and vice versa. A good designer and mechanical draftsman may be poor on faces and figures. An illustrator showing complete ads as samples of his work may or may not be capable of doing the layout that frames the illustrations. He may not even have been responsible for the composition of his own illustrations—an art director may have roughed them out for him. To be safe,

ask artists to use only those techniques in which they are demonstrably skilled, regardless of their assurance that they can work in any technique.

Some art buyers maintain a file of artists under such headings as letterers; layout men who can make "roughs," "visuals," and "comprehensives"; designers (packages, etc.); illustrators (figures, heads); general, all-around artists; and cartoonists.

Artists who cannot show any samples of the type of work under consideration may reasonably be asked to submit rough sketches on speculation. Otherwise, it is customary and fair to pay something for preliminary sketches made to definite order even though no order for finished artwork is placed.

An art buyer should have his ideas well thought out before he goes to an artist. Good artists are not necessarily also good gag men or promotion experts. If the buyer has been unable to decide just what he wants the drawings to say, the artist may have no better luck.

Artists may quote lower prices if relieved of the task of research. For instance, suppose a drawing calls for a farm scene. Try to get photos showing the kind of cow, the kind of silo, the kind of barn roof, etc., that should go in the picture. Such research may take hours in the picture collection of a library or searching old magazines or purchasing photos from stock photo houses. If the artist has to do the research, he charges for it.

Art buyers should read "Careers and Opportunities in Commercial Art," by J. I. Biegeleisen (Dutton, $4.95). It was written to give vocational guidance to would-be artists, but it offers the art buyer invaluable guidance on how artists specialize and what they charge.

art services See also ARTISTS; ART-WORK.

Art services are an important source of help for advertisers and editors.

They fall into two classes: artists' representatives and art studios.

Artists' representatives are essentially salesmen who relieve their artist clients from the need of peddling their skills.

Art studios may also represent certain free-lance artists. In addition, they employ staff artists on a permanent basis and usually a competent art director or studio manager, perhaps the head of the studio, whose own skill and advice are at the disposal of art buyers. Both kinds of art services can help an art buyer find the right artist or artists for a job.

Sometimes, however, a customer's problem plus an artist's skill are not enough to produce superior results. Something else must be added, namely, the ability of a good art director to visualize an answer to the problem and to prepare a layout ready for the artist to fill in. The best art services can solve such problems and, if an illustrator is weak at lettering, they can have the lettering done by another man.

The great advantage of working with an art service is its ability to relieve a client of such details as securing models, having photographs taken, retouching, having type set, ordering photostats and Velox prints, and pasting up.

Dealing with an art service costs more than dealing with the artist direct, because there is a commission to be paid. However, if the agency is able to suggest a competent but little-known artist in place of a big-name artist and get good results, the total cost may be less in the end.

Two useful guides to firms and individuals specializing in art services are "The Literary Market Place" and the "Buyers' Guide" of *Art Direction*, 19 W. 44 St., New York 36.

art techniques See DRAWING TECHNIQUES.

artwork See also ARTISTS; DRAWING TECHNIQUES; PHOTOGRAPHS; ILLUSTRATIONS.

Artwork is an omnibus term used by layout men and printers to cover photographs, drawings, paintings, hand-lettering, etc. Three things must be assembled in preparation for ordering a printing job: manuscript, artwork, and layout.

The destiny of most artwork is to be photographed—to be tacked up in front of a copying camera and transferred to film as the first step in making printing plates. The exceptions are when it is to be traced, transferred, or copied, as in mimeographing, hectograph work, etc.

Artwork must, therefore, be kept scrupulously clean and flat (no folds). It is usually protected by a paper or transparent plastic flap and by mounting on heavy cardboard. Care in wrapping for mailing is particularly necessary.

Artwork should never be prepared without foreknowledge of its intended use. The size to which it will be reduced, the method of reproduction, the paper to be used, and the likes and dislikes of the proposed audience—all these factors must be known to the artist if he is to do his work well. Whenever possible, artist and printer should discuss the work in advance. Otherwise, each may blame the other when results are disappointing.

Help in ordering, selecting, and evaluating artwork may be obtained from excellent books on the subject listed in Appendix 2, Bibliography.

Artype Artype is a product that permits the setting of display type in the office or art department. A sheet of Artype, costing $1, consists of a 10- by 14-in. sheet of cellophane mounted temporarily on a paper backing. From three to eight impressions of each letter of the alphabet are printed on the underside of the cellophane. Under each is a horizontal line (later cut off), which helps to align the letters.

The letters to be used are cut out, one by one, with a knife or razor, peeled from the backing sheet, and arranged in the desired order. Tweezers help in positioning. When rubbed down, the letters stick firmly, since they carry their own adhesive. It is easy to align them by first ruling a faint blue guideline. Since the printing is underneath, they cannot be smudged. Since they are transparent, they can be run across other artwork, thus eliminating extra printers' or engravers' charges for doing this by stripping. Artype is available in black or white and in more than 800 stock items of type faces, hand-lettered alphabets, arrows, numbers, symbols, and borders. The letters are sharp. Correct letterspacing and perfect joining of script letters are not difficult. Symbols, accents, adcuts, musical notes, etc., of your own choice will be made up to order. For free catalog, write Artype, Inc., 127 S. Northwest Highway, Barrington, Ill., 60010. Similar alphabets are made under the name "Craf-Type" by the Craftint Manufacturing Co., 18501 Euclid Ave., Cleveland 12, Ohio.

ascender The part of a small or lowercase (lc) letter that extends above the body of the letter, as in "b" and "d."

A descender extends below the body of the letter, as in "p," "q," and "y." The size of a type face is measured from the top of the tallest character—whether a capital letter or a small letter with ascender—to the bottom of the lowest descender. (See illustrations under TYPE.)

asterisk A star-shaped symbol (*) used for reference to footnotes where the preferred superior numbers [1,2] might cause confusion, as in material containing figures. The dagger (†) and the double dagger (‡) may be used when a second and a third footnote occur on the same page. The full series is * † ‡ § ‖ ¶.

ATF Abbreviation for American Type Founders, leading makers of foundry or hand-set type. (See TYPE.)

ATF typesetter ATF's Model B and Model B-8 keyboard phototypesetting machines are designed to handle text composition at speeds up to about 300 characters a minute. They are priced in the $15,000 to $20,000 range.

ATF's Model B-8 tape-driven phototypesetter.

ATF MODEL B TYPESETTER AND PHOTOGRAPHIC UNIT

1. Manuscript is marked for type styles and sizes, line widths, leading, necessary instructions of any kind.

2. After setting the measures, the operator types until a panel light warns that the justification zone has been reached.

3. Errors caught at once are immediately corrected by deleting wrong codes, or by deleting the whole line.

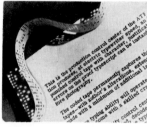  

4. The control tape and the compositor's proof. Errors noted after proofreading are easily corrected before the composition is photoset.

5. After inserting the control tape into the properly set-up photographic unit, the operator can return to the keyboard.

6. Sharp smear-proof type images are produced on inexpensive photographic paper, or on film.

7. The ATF-Fotorite Processor is a table-top unit that replaces conventional darkroom processing steps and produces dryprint positives in normal room-light.

8. Whether the end product is on paper for immediate paste-up or on film for positive or negative platemaking, the image is sharp and clear.

Both are two-unit systems, consisting of a typewriter keyboard with tape perforator and a separate tape-actuated photo unit. The photo unit is of the disk type, each disk carrying two fonts, usually roman with italic or roman with bold, in a size from 5 to 14 pt. Extra disks sell for about $150.

Both models offer proportional spacing, but only the B-8 offers full flexibility of letter widths, to an 18-unit base. Wire-service tapes can be converted for use on the photo units. Model B disks can intermix 168 characters; Model B-8 disks can intermix 176 characters.

ATF also offers a Model KD-84 display typesetting machine that is keyboard-actuated. It can set display lines up to 84 pt, using master alphabets on interchangeable disks.

author's alterations See also COPY PREPARATION; PROOFS; PROOFREADING.

Author's alterations, abbreviated "AA's," mean corrections in proofs which are not caused by any printer's error. On any bill for type composition there is likely to appear an item for author's alterations which is over and above the original estimate. When an incautious editor or author starts making proof changes that he should have made in manuscript, the charge for AA's may easily exceed the cost of composition.

Printers are responsible for any failure to follow copy. They are not responsible for AA's and will charge for them on a time basis. Making any change in any line usually involves resetting that line and perhaps the rest of the paragraph, getting out the galley of type in which the change occurs, pulling out the old lines, inserting the new, and then proofreading the change. The resetting alone may mean as much adjusting on the typesetting machine as was necessary in preparation for setting the whole job.

Some AA's are almost inevitable.

Book publishers usually allow their authors to make them without charge up to 10 percent of the amount of the bill for typesetting. However, AA's betray careless preparation of manuscript—a kind of carelessness for which there is a high monetary penalty.

automatic typewriter Automatic electric typewriters can operate either manually or unattended. In the latter case, the keys are depressed electromechanically in accordance with information "read" from a tape or in obedience to electric impulses generated at a remote keyboard, within a computer, etc.

Many automatic typewriters can also create punched tape as well as read it and thus capture for subsequent reuse all or selected parts of what is typed on them.

One common application of automatic typewriters is in the typing of personal letters containing much repetitive information. The first letter is typed in the usual way, but the repetitive portions are recorded on the punched tape. The tape is then made into a loop and placed in "read" position. The typing of the second letter proceeds in the usual way through the salutation, but after that, the operator simply pushes the "read" key and the machine will type at top speed the first repetitive portion of the original letter, stopping only when a personalized fill-in has been signaled by a "stop-read" code or when the letter is completed.

Since the machines do most of the work, one typist can sometimes triple her output by attending three machines at once.

One widely used automatic typewriter is the Friden Flexowriter, illustrated, which begins at about $2,200 and can be had with almost any desired combination of capabilities. An adaptation called the "Justowriter" can even provide the proportionally spaced types

The Friden Flexowriter.

used on IBM Executive typewriters and can automatically justify the lines. (See JUSTOWRITER.)

The mechanism of the IBM Selectric typewriter is at the heart of the Dura and Letteriter automatic typewriters (see DURA and LETTERITER) and makes these machines somewhat quieter than typebar machines.

Actually, any electric typewriter can be modified for automatic operation. See AUTO-TYPIST for an illustration of an installation using four standard IBM electrics in connection with the Auto-typist's own memory system.

Automatic typewriters make possible many refinements in data handling. For example, while the operator is typing the name and address on a letterhead, another "slave" machine can be automatically addressing the envelope—and, if desired, punching a tape for use in future mailing-list applications.

If the names and addresses and salutations are already available on tape, perhaps together with certain informa-

tion *about* the addresses, it may be possible to produce unmistakably personalized letters without personal attention at all. For example, fund-raising letters can mention the amount of the addressee's last contribution; collection letters can mention the exact amount due; sales-promotion letters can refer back to the nature and date of the prospect's last purchase.

Other uses for automatic electric typewriters include: input to, and read-out from, computers and accounting machines in general; over-the-wire transmission; input to automatic address plate-cutting equipment; and "data capture" of all kinds. (See DATA CAPTURE.)

The first automatic typewriter was the Hooven, and personalized letters produced on automatic typewriters are still sometimes referred to as "Hooven letters," though the Hooven equipment is no longer being made.

Autopositive A method for converting a negative into a positive during the de-

An Auto-typist installation.

velopment process, so that in effect a positive is made directly from a positive. Suitable materials are available from Eastman Kodak.

Autoscreen film The Eastman Kodak Company offers lithographers a Kodalith Autoscreen Ortho Film with which it is possible to make high-quality halftone negatives from photographic originals without either a ruled screen or a contact screen. This is available in only 133 lines and in standard cut sizes from 4 by 5 through 11 by 14. The film itself is of such variable sensitivity that, if it is exposed to a pure white surface and developed, a dot pattern will be revealed, varying in its density with the length of the exposure. Less time is required to make halftone negatives with this material than by conventional methods.

Auto-typist The illustration shows an Auto-typist installation that permits a single operator to supervise and personalize the work of four automatic typewriters. Standard office electric typewriters are used together with Auto-typist equipment in which repetitive information is stored on perforated paper rolls. A special perforator is required, either on the premises or accessible through a service bureau. Some models permit push-button selection from up to 100 different paragraphs, thus speeding the answering of multi-question letters. The Auto-typist is made by the American Automatic Typewriter Company, 2323 N. Pulaski Rd., Chicago, 60639. See also AUTOMATIC TYPEWRITER.

Azograph See SPIRIT DUPLICATOR.

B | b

backbone See SPINE.

backing A binder's term. In binding a 320-page book made up of ten 32-page units, for example, the units are gathered in the correct order (see GATHERING), sewed, and then backed (or perhaps rounded and backed).

The operation of backing consists of spreading the back edge of the book (before the cover is applied) so that the width of the spine will be as wide as the thickness of the pages plus the thickness of the boards used in the cover. Backing provides a sort of shoulder against which the cover of the book fits and is hinged. This shoulder is called the "joint." The backed book is then lined up with pieces of coarse crash and paper. The lined book is then "cased into" the cover by paste, pressure, and drying. (See illustration under BOOK-BINDING).

back up To back up a sheet of paper that has already been printed on one side is to print on the other side of it. Ink has to dry before a sheet can be backed up, so usually a job is printed one day and is not backed up until the next. Perfector presses can print a sheet and back it up in one operation.

20

badges Paper, ribbon, celluloid, plastic, enamel, and metal devices for the lapel are obtainable for campaign, convention, membership, and identification purposes at rates ranging from less than 1 cent to relatively high jewelry prices. The printing is part of the manufacturing process.

See the Classified Telephone Directory under Badges and Advertising Specialties for the names of local suppliers.

It is advisable to consult several firms, since prices vary widely. The 2-cent product of one firm may actually be more appropriate for the business in hand than the 12-cent item of some other firm.

Large manufacturers of badges, lapel buttons, and insignia have agents in the major cities and will have their local representative call on request. Two such firms are Bastian Brothers Co., 1600 Clinton Ave., N., Rochester 1, N.Y.; and Whitehead and Hoag, 622 Valley Rd., Upper Montclair, N.J.

balloons Toy balloons can be imprinted with advertising messages. For best results, the printing must be done when they are inflated. It can be done either from type and stock cuts or from specially made, deep-routed, zinc engravings.

Some suppliers of imprinted advertising balloons are The Van Dam Rubber Co., Inc., 1299 Jerome Ave., Bronx 52, N.Y.; and Sterling Rubber Co., 4914 W. Wrightwood Ave., Chicago 39.

basic weight, basis weight See also PAPER SIZES AND WEIGHTS.

Many books are printed on paper of "basis weight" or "basic substance weight" 60 lb. This means that a ream (500 sheets) 25 by 38 in. in size weighs 60 lb. A 50-lb paper is lighter; a 70-lb paper is heavier.

The practice is also growing of referring to the weight *per thousand* sheets. Thus, substance 60 would be the same as substance 120/M.

To buy 60-lb paper 35 by 45 in size, it is not necessary to figure out that 500 sheets of the larger size will weigh 99 lb. It is sufficient to order a ream of 35 by 45 paper in "substance 60." The bill will read "One ream, 35 × 45, substance 60, 99 lb at — cents per pound."

Book-paper substance weights are based on the 25 by 38 size. Bond-paper substance weights are figured on a 17 by 22 basis. Cover-paper substance weights are figured on a 20 by 26 basis. Bristolboard substance weights are figured on a 22½ by 28½ or 22 by 28 basis. (See table under PAPER SIZES AND WEIGHTS.)

A 20-lb bond is about the equivalent of 50-lb book paper.

Baskerville See Appendix 1, Type Faces.

batter Battered type is damaged type. A pressman reports a "press batter" when a cut, say, works loose from its mounting and gets crushed into adjoining matter.

bearers See also FOUNDRY PROOFS; PROOFS.

Type-high strips of metal placed around the pages of type to protect their edges during the molding of electrotype or other duplicate plates. (See DUPLICATE PLATES.)

bed The surface of a printing press against which the typeform is clamped. When the type is in the press ready for printing, a publication is said to have been "put to bed."

benday See SHADING TINTS.

bf Proofreader's abbreviation for boldface. (See BOLDFACE; PROOFREADING.)

billboards See OUTDOOR ADVERTISING.

bimetal plates Bimetal plates give the offset printer a printing surface from which he can run a million or more copies with the last copy being almost indistinguishable from the first.

One bimetal plate can outlast a whole series of conventional deep-etched plates and thus easily justify its extra cost on long runs.

Several different kinds of bimetal plates have been introduced, but the principle is much the same for all: The printing areas are surfaced with a grease-receptive metal, and the non-printing areas are surfaced with a water-receptive metal. (Conventional plates are made of the same metal throughout, treated to make it grease-receptive or water-receptive as desired.)

The International Printing Ink Corporation calls its version of these long-life offset plates the "Trimetal plate." The "Lithure" and "Lithengrave" plates are developments of Time-Life-Fortune. A Danish version, now in use in the United States, is called the "Aller plate."

binder's board See also CARDBOARD.

A stiff, high-grade composition board used in bookbinding, usually inside the cloth. (See illustration under BOOKBIND-

ING.) Cheaper products used in the same way are chipboard and pasted chipboard.

bindery See also BINDING.

Many printers have no facilities of their own for the binding of books or pamphlets and send out their work to independent binderies.

Some binderies specialize in book or "edition" work. Others handle folders and pamphlets and sometimes offer additional mounting and finishing services, such as perforating, punching, round-cornering, eyeleting, tabbing, creasing, varnishing, easeling, gumming, etc. (See MOUNTING AND FINISHING.)

On small jobs it is often advisable to make the printer responsible for finished delivery, even though he has no binding facilities of his own and will add his own overhead charges to what the binder will charge.

On very large jobs, it may pay to deal separately with a binder. However, the printer must know who is going to bind the job, since he must print to suit the equipment of that bindery.

binding See also BOOK MANUFACTURING; BOOKBINDING; MECHANICAL BINDINGS; FOLDING; TRIM; DIE CUTTING; MOUNTING AND FINISHING; PADDING; VARNISHING.

Binding begins after a printer has laid the ink on the paper. It includes cutting, folding, trimming, gathering, stitching, pasting, insetting, casing-in, etc.

Since binding can easily cost more than all preceding operations, a knowledge of what each step costs is invaluable in planning printing to achieve the greatest effectiveness most economically.

The simplest and cheapest binding is none at all, e.g., the poster or one- or two-page leaflet that is finished the moment it comes off the press. Next is the simple folded job, done either on a folding mechanism attached to the press or on a separate folding machine.

If a four-page, six-page, or French fold (uncut eight-page) job can be accepted as it comes from the folding machine, the expense of an additional edge-trimming operation can be saved. (See FRENCH FOLD.)

However, pamphlets and books of eight pages and up first must be folded, then stitched and trimmed. The trimming both opens the pages so they can be turned and evens up the slightly uneven edges produced in the folding operation. Some folding machinery, such as that used for newspapers and newspaper supplements, will do rough trimming, producing serrated edges, as a part of the folding operation, thus eliminating the need for a separate trimming operation. Some folders also do slitting. (See SERRATED EDGES.)

Note that the two sides of an unfolded sheet of paper make two pages. When folded, a sheet of paper gives the following results:

One fold—4 pages
Two folds—6 or 8 pages
Three folds—12 or 16 pages
Four folds—24 or 32 pages

Pamphlets and books should be designed around these units. Departure from them will necessitate the use of inserts or cancels. (See INSERTS; CANCEL.)

Before trimming folded sheets, the pages are usually fastened together by saddle-wire stitching, by side-wire stitching, or, for thicker booklets that must open flat, by thread sewing and/or gluing. Stitching is usually a separate operation. Some folding machines are equipped to insert wire staples as a part of the folding operation. Many apply a thin line of paste along the fold in 8-page or 12-page jobs, thus eliminating the need for stapling. (See STITCHING.)

A self-cover pamphlet is one with its cover on the same kind of paper as the text and printed along with the text. (See illustration.) This is always cheaper than a pamphlet having a cover of different paper and is often as satis-

THESE LEAFLETS NEED NOT BE TRIMMED

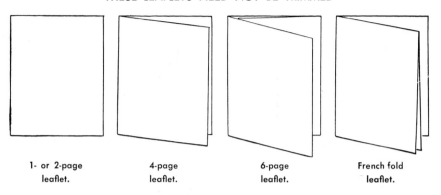

| 1- or 2-page | 4-page | 6-page | French fold |
| leaflet. | leaflet. | leaflet. | leaflet. |

THESE LEAFLETS MUST BE TRIMMED

| 8 pages | 8 pages | 12 pages | 16 pages |
| after trim. | before trim. | before trim. | before trim. |

SPECIAL FOLDS

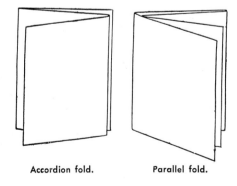

Accordion fold.   Parallel fold.

Note: The last fold should always be parallel to the grain of the paper (see *grain*). Otherwise booklets may handle badly during folding and may spring open. Paper must be ordered with grain the right way.

STYLES OF BINDING

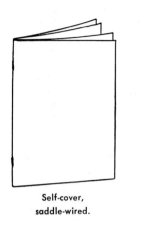

Self-cover,
saddle-wired.

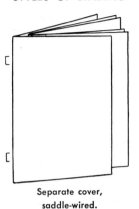

Separate cover,
saddle-wired.

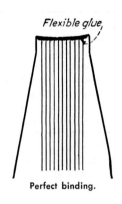

Flexible glue

Perfect binding.

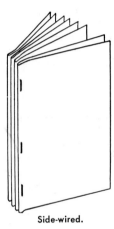

Side-wired.

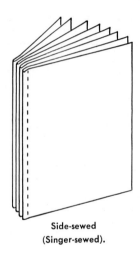

Side-sewed
(Singer-sewed).

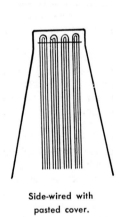

Side-wired with
pasted cover.

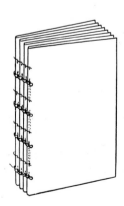

The Smyth-sewed binding (*left* and *above*) lets a thick book open flat. It consists of two or more separate signatures which are saddle-sewed and at the same time sewed to each other. "Perfect" bindings also open flat. Saddle-wiring is most used for pamphlets under ¼ in. thick. Sidestitching is strong but will not open as flat as a Smyth-sewed binding. Steps in binding a book are shown in the illustrations under *bookbinding*.

factory. Many small pamphlets can be run in two colors throughout for less than the cost of a one-color text and a separate cover. Larger booklets are often given stiff covers for both appearance and durability. The larger the booklet, the stronger the cover should be.

The steps in binding one 6- by 9-in. 64-page-plus-cover pamphlet follow: The text was run on 38- by 50-in. paper, printed both sides, and slit on the press into two 38- by 25-in. sections, each containing 32 pages. One section contained pages 1–16 and 49–64. The other contained pages 17–48. The four-page cover was run separately on a small press, on 9½- by 12½-in. cover paper.

The 25- by 38-in. flat sheets and the cover were folded to 6¼ by 9½ in. Then the first and second sections, or "signatures," were gathered inside the cover and all were saddle-wired together. They were then stacked and trimmed on three sides to 6 by 9 in. The gathering and saddle-wiring could have been done on a machine known as an "inserter," some of which have built-in trimmers. (See SIGNATURE; GATHERING; TRIM.)

The above job might have been bound as four 16's and a 4, instead of two 32's and a 4, but it would not have been handled as a 64 and a 4, since so large a signature folds awkwardly. It might also have been handled as a side-wired job, with the signatures laid on top of each other instead of inside each other, stitched together about ³⁄₁₆ in. from the fold, and then pasted inside the cover. This is usually an integrated machine operation.

Books are generally printed in signatures of 16 or 32 pages, gathered, Smyth-sewed, smashed, furnished with endpapers, trimmed on three sides, rounded and backed, and cased in. (See BOOK MANUFACTURING.) The binding of a cloth-covered standard novel costs 25 to 30 cents.

The so-called "perfect" binding, used on telephone books (see illustration) is a glued binding, which can be much cheaper than other binding methods on large jobs. The technique has been improved in recent years, thanks to developments in plastic adhesives. The low-cost binding of paperback books incorporates many interesting features, including stained edges and occasionally a laminated cover. (For information on spiral, plastic, and loose-leaf bindings, see MECHANICAL BINDINGS.)

Simple, standard binding operations are comparatively cheap. Putting one, two, or three folds into a piece of paper may cost no more than $3 per thousand. Putting two wire staples through an ordinary pamphlet may cost another $3 per thousand. Gathering (e.g., putting one 16-page unit or signature inside another, and both inside a cover, preparatory to stitching) may cost another $4 per thousand. Trimming pamphlets of 8 to 64 pages may cost from $2 to $4 per thousand.

On the other hand, trick folds can run into more money. Some can be done only by hand; others have to be sent through the folding machine a separate time for each fold. Mechanical bindings are always more expensive than wire stitching. (See MECHANICAL BINDINGS.)

black-and-white prints See WHITE-PRINTS.

blackface See also BOLDFACE.

This line is set in blackface type, usually called "boldface," as distinct from lightface.

black letter See also Appendix 1, Type Faces.

𝔗𝔥𝔦𝔰 𝔰𝔢𝔫𝔱𝔢𝔫𝔠𝔢 𝔦𝔰 𝔰𝔢𝔱 𝔦𝔫 𝔞 𝔟𝔩𝔞𝔠𝔨-𝔩𝔢𝔱𝔱𝔢𝔯 𝔱𝔶𝔭𝔢, 𝔪𝔬𝔯𝔢 𝔠𝔬𝔪𝔪𝔬𝔫𝔩𝔶 𝔠𝔞𝔩𝔩𝔢𝔡 "𝔒𝔩𝔡 𝔈𝔫𝔤𝔩𝔦𝔰𝔥" 𝔬𝔯 "𝔱𝔢𝔵𝔱."

In Germany, this kind of type is still widely used, especially in a lighter version called "Fraktur."

bleed See also CROP, CROPPING.

A photograph or piece of artwork is said to bleed when it extends to the very edge of the printed page. To achieve this effect the page is trimmed right

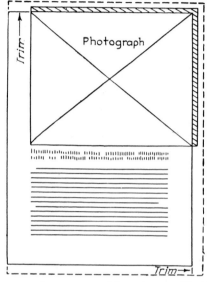

Layout for page containing photo to bleed top and right. Dotted lines show the edge of the paper before trim. Shaded part of the photo is lost in the trimming.

through the picture. When a picture occupies the entire page of a magazine or pamphlet, with no margins at all, it is said to bleed on three sides and run flush to the gutter on the fourth side.

After being printed and folded, booklets of eight pages and over must be trimmed to open folds that would otherwise require the reader to use a paper knife. (See illustration under BINDING.) For example, a pamphlet that folds to 6¼ by 9½ in. must be trimmed to 6⅛ by 9¼ merely to open the pages. If there are bleed photos, it must usually be trimmed to 6 by 9 in. to make sure that all photos actually will bleed.

If a photograph is to bleed, one must specify that it be reproduced ⅛ in. or 1 pica wider on the side or sides to bleed, and one must crop and scale it accordingly. (See illustration above. *Warning:* see also GRIPPER EDGE.)

blind stamping Pressing a design into a book cover with tools or dies, without the use of ink or gold leaf. It is also called "blind tooling" and "blocking."

block See also CUT.

The word "block" is used in England synonymously with cut and engraving, e.g., line block, halftone block, and linoleum block.

To block a cut means to mount it on a wood or metal base. To block a cut type-high means to make its printing surface the same height as that of printing type.

block printing Printing from hand-carved linoleum or wooden blocks. This is essentially a handicraft, not to be considered in the same category with the photomechanical, chemical, and power-driven processes used in commercial printing.

Its value is in its simplicity, its individuality, and its cheapness. A child can make a block print and use it quite effectively. On the other hand, the best block prints are the work of skilled artists of long experience.

A block print is made up of relatively heavy lines and solid areas as contrasted with the fine hairlines of an etching or engraving. The wood or linoleum will permit only the bolder, stronger lines.

A block is made for relief printing, carrying ink on the uncut surfaces and no ink in the depressions that have been carved out. (See RELIEF.)

To make a block print the design must first be drawn on tracing paper in the exact size and proportions desired in the final print. This design is transferred (by means of carbon paper) from the paper to the block in reverse so that the printed proof will be identical with the original.

Then with the tools appropriate for wood or linoleum block carving, the areas that are not to print are carved or routed out. The block is inked, proofs are taken, and with necessary improvements the block is ready to be run. The best effects are obtained when soft papers are used.

In comparison with metal plates the woodcut or linoleum block is very soft and hence impractical for long runs. For a short run, such as a program for a small club or the senior class play, it is both inexpensive and effective. Wood or linoleum blocks may be printed alongside type in a regular printing press.

To print in two colors, two blocks may be made and printed separately. Highly skilled artists sometimes make many blocks, each to reproduce a different color in a multicolor print. Interesting effects may also be obtained by painting on the inks, several colors side by side, and thus getting several colors from a single impression.

blotters Advertising blotters, like calendars, have a chance of remaining within view of the prospective customer for a long time.

Photos cannot be printed on plain blotting paper. But almost anything can be printed on coated paper, which can be laminated to one side of blotting paper.

Practically any printer is equipped to produce advertising blotters economically. The letterpress process is perhaps used more often than offset.

Stock blotters are worth investigating. These come already printed with eye-catching illustrations in color and can be imprinted with any sales message and are obtainable from such firms as Brown & Bigelow, 1286 University Ave., St. Paul 4, Minn.; Lutz and Sheinkman, 421 Hudson St., New York 14.

blowup A blowup of a photograph or an advertisement is an enlargement of it.

blue-penciling According to tradition, editors use a blue pencil when they cut, correct, or rewrite material. Many a reporter has complained that the rewrite man blue-penciled the best part of his story.

blueprint The blueprint method is used primarily for duplicating mechanical and architectural drawings. It does not permit enlarging or reducing.

For best results the original drawing is prepared in black ink on translucent paper. It is placed in contact with sensitized blueprint paper and exposed to strong light. The exposed paper is then washed. The result is that the paper turns blue wherever the light hits it and remains white where shielded by the black ink on the original drawing.

Blueprints can be made quickly and cheaply. They cost as little as 5 cents a square foot, with a minimum charge, and are usually procurable in any width up to 42 in., and in any length at all. They can be made from a relatively opaque master drawing, provided there is nothing on the back of it. Blueprints are always approximately the same size as the original—approximately, since the paper may stretch or shrink a little in the washing as in photostating.

The so-called "whiteprints" made by the Ozalid and Bruning processes (see WHITEPRINT) are now displacing ordinary blueprints. They provide a more legible print, showing black lines or colored lines on a white background like the original. They can be made about as cheaply as blueprints. Because they are developed dry, there is a minimum of difficulty about changes in dimensions during the developing.

The blueprint process is the oldest in the field, and for some time to come the word "blueprint" will probably be applied to any method of same-size photocopying from translucent originals.

Blueprints are made from the "flats" (the assembled films) used in making offset or other plates, to provide an advance check of how the plates will print. (See also VANDYKE.)

A same-size copy made in permanent printer's ink (as if lithographed) may be be obtained at 20 cents per square foot from the Lithoprint Company, 145 Hudson St., New York 13. The process resembles both photogelatin and the hectograph.

boards See CARDBOARD.

Bodoni See Appendix 1, Type Faces.

body The body of a type character or slug is the piece of metal on which the letter or letters are cast. 10-pt type can be cast on a 10-pt body; it can also be cast on an 11-pt, 12-pt, or larger body to avoid the need for inserting one, two, or more points of leading between the lines as a separate operation.

The letter "W" must be cast on a wider body than the letter "i," but both are cast on bodies of equal height.

The term "body type" is sometimes used to mean small type, or text type, as opposed to headlines and display lettering. (See TYPE.)

boiler plate Stereotyped news and feature material prepared centrally and supplied to small newspapers for use as filler.

boldface See also Appendix 1, Type Faces.

This sentence is set in bold type or boldface, abbreviated bf.

When a manuscript is marked for the printer, a wavy line under certain words indicates that they should be set in boldface. Many kinds of type have boldface counterparts. Some boldface type has no corresponding lightface.

The well-known Bodoni series of types comes in four weights: **Bodoni**

Book, Bodoni, Bodoni Bold, Ultra Bodoni (also called Poster Bodoni).

Unfortunately for the designer, the same words sometimes mean different things. For instance, the Linotype Spartan series includes Spartan Light, Spartan Medium, **Spartan Heavy**, and **Spartan Black**. The identical faces, when put out by Intertype are called Futura Light, Futura Medium, Futura Demibold, and Futura Bold, respectively.

See charts entitled "The Futura Family" in Appendix 1.

A Linotype matrix will hold two faces, but not three. It is more common for printers to have roman and italic paired than roman and boldface.

bond paper See also PAPER.

Bond paper is made to present a good surface for pen and ink and is used for writing paper, typewriter paper, and miscellaneous leaflet work. It is suitable for offset printing.

Bond paper comes in basic substance weights (see BASIC WEIGHT) of 13, 16, 20, and 24 lb to the ream of 500 17- by 22-in. sheets. Heavier papers of the same sort are called "ledger" papers. Sulfite bond is made of chemically treated wood pulp. Rag-content bonds contain 25, 50, 75, or 100 percent of pulp made from cotton rags and offer somewhat greater strength and "snap" if well made.

Bond papers come in colors as well as in white.

book See BOOK MANUFACTURING.

bookbinding See also BINDING; BOOK MANUFACTURING.

The basic steps in bookbinding are outlined in the accompanying illustration.

A remarkably clear and detailed demonstration of bookbinding is given in the 16mm sound film *Bound to Last,* which runs 18 min and is available on loan from Association Films, Inc., 347 Madison Ave., New York 17.

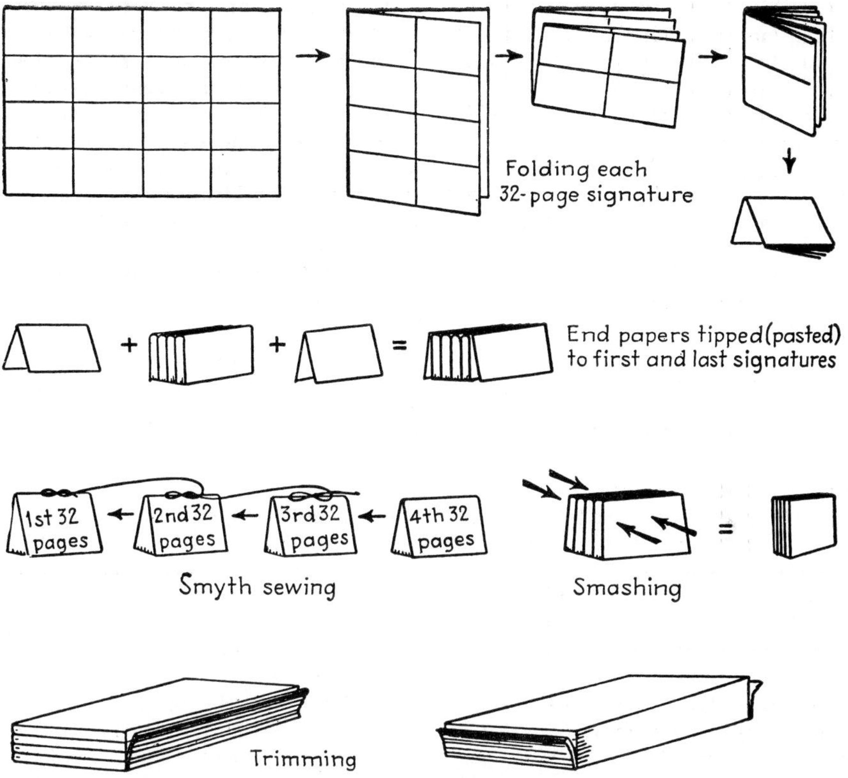

Folding each
32-page signature

End papers tipped(pasted)
to first and last signatures

1st 32 pages ← 2nd 32 pages ← 3rd 32 pages ← 4th 32 pages

Smyth sewing   Smashing

Trimming

Steps in binding a 128-page book, as shown above, include (1) folding (signatures could also have 8, 16, 24, 48, or 64 pages), (2) adding endpapers and inserts, if any, (3) gathering in proper order (not shown), (4) sewing, (5) smashing, and (6) trimming. The next step, not shown, is to apply a thin coat of glue to the sewn edges, preliminary to the rounding and backing shown on the next page.

book cloth See also BOOK MANUFAC-TURING.

Cloth for binding books falls into three main categories: starch-filled cloth, used for novels, etc.; pyroxylin-impregnated cloth; and pyroxylin-coated cloth or imitation leather, much used for textbooks.

Starch-filled cloth is least expensive but is vulnerable to water spotting and soiling. It cannot be wiped clean as can impregnated or coated cloths. It is not suited to printing by offset lithography. Impregnating gives a cloth water resistance but does not change its appearance. Coating conceals the original weave of the cloth, though a pattern may be pressed into it to simulate either cloth or leather. Impregnated and coated cloths readily accept offset lithographic printing.

Pyroxylin (another name for cellulose nitrate or celluloid) has for many years been the impregnation or coating most commonly used, but vinyl and other plastic coatings are also used.

The well-known buckram is a high grade of cloth available both starch-filled and impregnated.

Purchasers of bookbinding services do

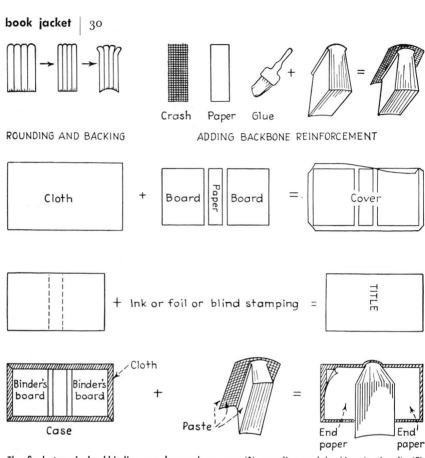

ROUNDING AND BACKING

Crash Paper Glue

ADDING BACKBONE REINFORCEMENT

Cloth + Board | Paper | Board = Cover

+ Ink or foil or blind stamping = TITLE

Binder's board | Binder's board — Cloth

Case + Paste = End paper End paper

The final steps in bookbinding, as shown above, are (1) rounding and backing (optional), (2) adding backbone reinforcement, called "lining-up," (3) making the covers or "cases," (4) stamping the cases, (5) casing-in.

not ordinarily buy the cloth separately. They let the bookbinder do that.

book jacket See JACKET.

booklets See PAMPHLETS.

book manufacturing See also BOOK-BINDING.

A bound book is really a collection of 16- or 32-page pamphlets put together with thread, glue, binder's board, and cloth. Any job printer could make a book, and any binder could bind one. However, printers who specialize in bookwork can almost invariably turn out a more professional-looking book, perhaps at considerably lower cost.

Four book manufacturers who offer both printing and binding services and who are staffed to assist in designing books are American Book-Stratford Press, Inc., 75 Varick St., New York 13; The Kingsport Press, Inc., Kingsport, Tenn. (sales offices at 555 Madison Ave., New York, and at 325 W. Huron St., Chicago); H. Wolff Book Manufacturing Co., Inc., 508 W. 26 St., New York; Quinn & Boden Co., Inc., Rahway, N.J. (sales office at 211 E. 43 St., New York).

Book publishers are not book printers. Almost no book publisher maintains his own book-manufacturing plant. Publishers who ask authors to help pay for the publication of their books (except in the case of scholarly books of very limited appeal) are known in the trade as "vanity publishers." They promise "publication," but they actually deliver very little save "printing" and usually charge too much for that.

The cost of book manufacturing (not including author's royalty) is about one-fifth to one-quarter of retail book prices. Costs tend to go down as the number of copies printed goes up. Thus, it may be possible to make 5,000 copies of a $3 book for 60 cents each ($3,000), and also 25,000 copies of the same title for sale as a $1 reprint at 30 cents each ($7,500), typesetting having been taken care of. Editions in excess of 100,000 have to be run on the lower-priced paperbound books.

An excellent primer on both book production and book design is "Bookmaking: The Illustrated Guide to Design and Production," by Marshall Lee (R. R. Bowker Co., 1965).

book paper See PAPER.

book postage rates See Appendix 3, Postal Information.

Bourges color process Eighty printer's-ink colors or color tints may be obtained in the form of thin transparent sheets from Bourges Color Corp., 80 Fifth Ave., New York 11. The sheets are useful for laying in backgrounds (where color is not wanted, it will rub cleanly off the transparent base), for altering the color values of paintings and transparencies, for determining what effect will result when one color is printed over another, for making up dummies in color, etc.

Through the use of sheets, it is easy to "retouch" without touching the original art. A model's face can be made

tanner, a blue automobile can be seen in green, duotone effects can be studied in advance of ordering the plates, backgrounds can be subdued to make desired subjects stand out.

The sheets can either be photographed as part of full-color artwork or be photographed separately to provide the engraver with ready-made color separations.

Copy may be prepared with Bourges sheets for flat-color line reproduction in two, three, four, and even five colors. Matched pencils and liquid colors also make it possible to build up the color for halftone reproduction. The reproduction of art prepared in this way saves about half the standard process cost as the colors are already separated for camera. Since Bourges sheets are matched to inks and overlap in the same way inks do, Bourges copy acts as an accurate color proof of the final printed result.

Eleven basic colors are available in five tints (10, 30, 50, 70, and 100 percent); ten designer colors in solids only; black in nine tints (5 to 100 percent); and white in five tints (5 to 100 percent). The black-and-white sheets are particularly useful for correcting photographs.

The adhesive sheets are helpful for presentations and displays and for the preparation of package designs and layouts in actual printing-ink colors.

These Bourges color sheets are of two kinds: Cutocolor and Colotone.

Cutocolor is a cutaway color film with pressure-sensitive adhesive backing and semimatte surface that does not scratch off and can be worked on with pencil, ink, watercolors, etc. (Prices: 10 by 12½, 70 cents; 12½ by 20, $1.30; 20 by 25, $2.50.)

Colotone has a removable color coating and is available with or without adhesive. The smooth color surface can be removed with a stylus or liquid color remover or can be deepened with pencil, ink, or watercolor for a variety of line or halftone effects. (Prices: 10 by 12½, $1; 12½ by 20, $2; 20 by 25, $4.)

Bourges also makes a transparent red-orange Transopaque sheet with the same removable coating. When it is used, separation copy may be prepared with an assurance of register accuracy impossible with black opaque.

The key to the Bourges system is a Color Guide composed of 3- by 5-in. swatches of all Bourges ink colors, including solids and tints. By laying these transparent swatches over your work, you can choose the exact printing color that is most appropriate. (Price: $6.)

Free literature on the preparation and printing of Bourges materials with color chart is available at leading art dealers and from Bourges Color Corp., 80 Fifth Ave., New York 11.

box, boxed

This paragraph has been boxed, i.e., put inside a box consisting of a plain ruled border. In this case a box made of 1-pt rule was specified. (See RULE.) Boxes are often used to lend emphasis to certain material or to set it off from other text matter. Material to be boxed must, of course, be set narrower than lines in the same column that are not boxed.

box printing See also CONTAINER PRINTING.

Boxes are almost always printed by the manufacturer, although sometimes labels are printed separately and then affixed to them.

break When a printed job is to run in two or more colors, the printer must be given instructions as to the "break for color." This means indicating on the proofs or the layout, or both, which items are to be printed in black and

which in what colors. A headline that is to be printed in red must be removed by the printer from the black form and put in the proper position in the red form. A printer is said to "break" a form when he removes the type and cuts from the chase, or steel frame, in which they were arranged and locked up during the presswork.

Brightype A process for making photographic negatives directly from metal type. The type, which can be combined in the same form with line or halftone engravings, is blackened, after which the printing surface is wiped clean of the blackening agent and made bright and reflective. It is then photographed in a special camera so as to produce a film positive. The film positive can be right-reading or mirror-reversed, depending on the intended use. It is sometimes possible through the use of Brightype conversion method to sharpen up worn type and get a result in offset that is superior to another letterpress run from the same type or plates.

bristolboard See also CARDBOARD.

Bristolboards, or bristols, are papers of postcard weight or heavier, made to provide a certain stiffness or rigidity.

Index bristols are made to take ink and erasing well. Wedding bristols and mill bristols are made to provide a good printing surface.

broadsides See CIRCULARS; PAMPHLETS.

brochures See PAMPHLETS.

bronze proofs In certain processes, notably rotogravure and deep-etch offset, bronze proofs of type matter are sometimes used. Bronze proofs, also called "glassines," are made with great care on transparent glassine paper and dusted with bronze powder while the ink is still wet.

The purpose of the bronzing is to make the letters even more opaque than black ink alone will make them. The proofs are then used as if they were photographic film, and it becomes unnecessary to make first a film negative from white paper proofs and then a film positive from the film negative. (Only processes that work from film positives instead of film negatives can take advantage of this shortcut.)

Some typographers use a special offset technique to print on both sides of glassine simultaneously, and the double layer of ink thus gives them the necessary opacity without bronzing.

bronzing See also BRONZE PROOFS.

Applying metallic powder to the still-wet ink of a printed page to secure the effect of bronze, gold, silver, aluminum, etc.

brush drawing See also WASH DRAWING; DRAWING TECHNIQUES.

A drawing made with a brush. Whether it is a line drawing or a wash drawing depends on the technique used. A brush dipped in india ink will usually make a solid line that can be reproduced as a line drawing. If the brush pulls the ink over the paper in a broken film, it may make a dry-brush drawing. A brush dipped in watercolor may make a wash drawing that must be reproduced by the halftone process. (See illustrations under DRAWING TECHNIQUES.)

buckram See BOOK CLOTH.

bulk See also PAPER.

"Bulk" refers to the thickness of paper. Antique paper bulks thicker than English-finish paper of the same basis weight. A 60-lb book paper may be ordered to bulk 400 pages to the inch or 600 pages to the inch, etc. The more calendering, the less bulk. (See CALENDERED PAPER.) Books are sometimes "bulked" (printed on bulked paper) to make them look like more for the money. However, bulked paper is inferior in strength and printing qualities to firmer paper. The fluff from bulked paper often "picks" and gets on the type or plates and in the ink, causing troubles in the pressroom. Weight, bulk, and finish are characteristics that can be controlled during the manufacture of paper. Any two can be specified, but never all three.

business forms The simpler kinds of business forms can be produced by the methods reviewed under CIRCULARS and LETTERS. The economical printing of complicated forms requires specialized machinery. There are companies which make a specialty of designing and producing business forms to fit any need.

Some of the printing presses used in producing business forms are marvels of versatility. It becomes quite possible to print a six-part form on six kinds of paper, in six kinds of ink; to insert five layers of one-time carbon paper (or to spot-carbonize the backs of the forms and thus dispense with the carbon paper or to use paper that produces copies without using carbons); to perforate any of the forms so that part serves as a shipping label; and to deliver completely assembled forms either as separate units or as "fanfolds" (accordion-pleated)—and to do all of this as one operation on one machine.

Wherever information is being copied, the question may well be asked as to whether the copy could not have been created at the same time the original was created. For example, one typing of an order can yield, by means of carbon copies, the invoice, a duplicate invoice, a shipping label, a packing slip, an inventory-control slip, a salesman's record, and a mailing-list record. Information about discounts, etc., can appear on some copies and not on others, if desired, by means of "blockouts," etc.

Where it proves impossible to get enough legible copies to fill the need or where duplicate copies must be made on paper or card stock which is too heavy to transmit carbon impressions, the various duplicating-equipment manufacturers step into the picture with systems for putting the original information on a "master," all additional copies being made from this master by mimeograph, Multilith, Ditto, Addressograph, Elliott, or similar methods.

These firms (see DUPLICATING) are fond of pointing out that unprinted paper never becomes obsolete. They usually recommend that simple forms be duplicated right in the office, as needed.

Mimeograph, Multilith, and Ditto also feature new techniques of duplicating business forms *in the same operation that fills in the blanks on those forms.* Mimeograph stencils, for example, are pre-impressed with the data and lines of the form. The blanks are filled in on the typewriter. Then both are duplicated together.

Some printers specializing in business forms of all types include Moore Business Forms, Inc., with offices in Niagara Falls, N.Y., Emeryville and Los Angeles, Calif., Denton, Tex., Oak Ridge, Ill., and Toronto, Ontario; Allied/Egry Business Systems and the Standard Register Co., both of Dayton, Ohio.

business reply cards and envelopes See Appendix 3, Postal Information.

butted See illustration under MITERED.

buttons See BADGES.

C|c

c Abbreviation for caps, used in c & lc (caps and lowercase), c & sc (caps and small caps), etc.

calendars It is probably safe to suppose that calendars have been produced by every known printing and binding technique. (For information on how to order calendars printed, see, therefore, PAMPHLETS or POSTERS plus the intended BINDING or PRINTING process.)

Calendars are commonly ordered from stock and merely imprinted (see IMPRINTING) with the advertiser's message. The biggest advertising-calendar firm is Brown & Bigelow, 1286 University Ave., St. Paul 4, Minn. Another well-known firm offering a complete line of styles and sizes of calendars and imprinting them to order is John Baumgarth Co., 3001 W. North Ave., Melrose Park, Ill.

calendered paper See also PAPER.

Paper is calendered to make it smooth, supercalendered to make it glossy. The process consists of passing the newly formed paper between a number of smooth cylinders under pressure. In supercalendering, which is done on a separate "stack" of rolls, some cylinders move faster than others, and a burnishing action on the paper surface results. By means of calendering and supercalendering, an antique finish of high bulk becomes a smoother antique finish of lesser bulk, then a machine finish, then an English finish, then a supercalendered or "super" finish.

The more calendering a paper is subjected to, the better it will take halftones. Halftones of 110- and 120-line screen can be printed on English-finish or supercalendered stock. Coated paper is used for finer screens. (See COATED PAPER.)

calligraphy Beautiful writing or penmanship. Type faces resembling handwriting are referred to as "calligraphic" types.

camera Large copying cameras are used in every printing process for enlarging, reducing, same-size copying, and color separation. Most of them are built to enlarge as much as twice the size of the original, or reduce to one-half or one-quarter that size, although these limits can be exceeded either by making special adjustments or by copying and then recopying. (See PHOTOGRAPHY; PHOTOSTAT; and illustration under HALFTONE.)

35

camera lucida In making layouts it is often necessary to copy an illustration or an actual object in a size larger or smaller than the original. An optical device known as the "lucy," short for "camera lucida," is a great help at such times and is procurable at most art stores.

A very simple lucy employing a half-silvered mirror sells for about $2. Similar devices employing prisms cost somewhat more. To get an image bright enough to copy, put a very strong light

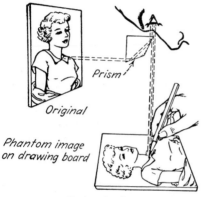

Camera lucida.

on the original while keeping your copying paper under comparatively low illumination. The desired degree of enlargement or reduction can be obtained by adjusting the relative positions of the original and the viewing device.

Much more versatile lucy's can be obtained under such names as Lacey-Luci and Camera Lucikon. These are basically copying cameras designed to throw an enlarged or reduced image of any original onto a ground glass where it can be traced. In the Lacey-Luci, the ground glass is inclined like a drawing board. In the Camera Lucikon, the ground glass is horizontal like a table. These "visualizers" can also be used for photocopying, and are even pressed into duty as process cameras and contact-printing frames in small offset shops, silk-screen shops, etc. The Lacey-Luci is

made by Lacey-Luci Products, Inc., 31 Central Ave., Newark 2, N.J. The Camera Lucikon is made by the M. P. Goodkin Company, 112–120 Arlington St., Newark 2, N.J. Prices start at about $318.

campaign planning In most advertising or information campaigns, a number of different techniques are used simultaneously. They are coordinated to supplement each other and reach the desired groups with the greatest economy.

Every member of the audience must receive information in terms he can understand from sources that he trusts. All his doubts and reservations must be answered.

Information must be presented in a way that will capture his interest (including his self-interest); otherwise his mind will be closed. The average American may be apathetic about supplying milk to the tribes of Africa, but he is interested in getting more milk at a lower price for his own family.

He must receive the new information often enough to prevent his forgetting. Most people have to be exposed to a new idea at least three times before they can clear their minds of old conflicting information.

These requirements suggest the importance of a coordinated campaign to reach every prospect through

1. His reading (books, magazines, newspapers, direct mail)
2. His listening (radio, television, lectures)
3. His seeing (theater, films, slide-films, television, and displays)
4. If possible, word of mouth via his friends, club, union, church, or children.

The specialized approach often succeeds when the general approach does not. A man not reached by information through general channels may be wide open to an approach through his special interest, be he physician, parent, farmer, or union member. For example, manufacturers of union-made cigarettes have found it advantageous to emphasize that feature in advertisements published in labor papers.

Format and design must tie in with both audience and method of distribution. Those who enjoy reading *Time* will subconsciously be favorably disposed toward something of similar format. Those who do not like *Time* may be adversely prejudiced by anything that reminds them of it.

Campaigns have been criticized both as "too slick and professional" and as "too amateurish." The amateurish approach is disarming to some, but it may also evoke the reaction "those bunglers are probably as inept in their thinking as in their publicity work. . . ."

Campaign material that looks expensive should be carefully avoided by organizations that are appealing for contributions or trying to establish a record for efficient and economical administration. A Home for Indigent Ladies of Considerable Years should not, for example, use expensive book stock for a pamphlet soliciting $60,000 to build a new wing. Instead, paper and other campaign materials must reflect economical planning to appeal to the reader.

One universal rule is to be factual, specific, and honest in any campaign. Millions of dollars are wasted annually on material that is designed to reach the emotions but fails to appeal to common sense. Americans have become increasingly skeptical of promoters who promise everything.

Many campaigns are duds because, despite a great output of words, the essential facts are not told. Before going ahead, it is a good idea to test materials on outsiders who have no knowledge of the subject matter.

A rounded campaign may include all the following activities:

1. Paid publicity: advertising via newspaper, magazine, radio, television, or outdoor display; direct mail, using letters, pamphlets, blotters, etc.

2. Free publicity: news and feature coverage in newspapers, magazines, newsreels, and on the air through releases, press conferences, press agents, etc.

The Table of Contents of this book offers a good checklist of the various kinds of promotional possibilities, each described under its own heading elsewhere in this book.

The chart on page viii lists the essential steps in launching any campaign.

Excellent material on this subject is given in the publication listed in Appendix 2, Bibliography.

cancel A 28-page pamphlet is often printed as a 32-page pamphlet, and then four blank pages are canceled, i.e., cut out and destroyed during the binding operation. These pages are called "cancels."

A book is said to have a "cancel title" if the original title page has been cut out and a new one pasted in.

c & lc Abbreviation for caps and lowercase. (See PROOFREADING.)

c & sc Abbreviation for caps and small caps. (See PROOFREADING.)

caps and small caps See also PROOFREADING.

THIS SENTENCE IS SET IN CAPS AND SMALL CAPS (C & SC). THIS SENTENCE IS SET IN EVEN SMALL CAPS. Most fonts of type include small caps in sizes up to, but not above, 14 pt. Although italic small caps have been cut for one or two faces, almost no printer can supply them.

caps, capitals See also PROOFREADING.

"Caps," abbreviation for "capitals," is frequently used to indicate uppercase letters as distinct from small or lowercase letters.

THIS SENTENCE IS SET IN CAPS. *THIS SENTENCE IS SET IN*

ITALIC CAPS. This Sentence Is Set in Caps and Lower Case. This Sentence Is Set in Caps and Small Caps.

captions A caption (legend) belongs under the picture to which it refers. To put it in some other position—above or beside the picture—is to force the reader to search for it and perhaps to lose interest.

The good caption may simply identify the illustration, or it may give a message or news story suggested by it. The latter is being used more and more with the increasing popularity of the "picture story" of the variety shown in *Life.* A good caption should complement the information given by the picture, not duplicate it.

A good way to decide upon a type face and style for captions is to look through some illustrated publications and find captions that are attractive. In this way you can select a style and size of type.

The amount of copy needed for a caption is found by determining the number of characters that the type selected will permit to the pica or inch, multiplying that by the width of the caption, and again by the number of lines that the caption is to include. Generally all lines of a caption are the same length. (A caption that is 2¼ instead of 3 lines long, for example, may look unfinished.) It may require several trials to write a caption of the desired size.

The size of a caption is frequently determined not by the extent of the ideas to be expressed, but by the space allocated to a picture next to it or in a similar position on the same or facing page. Pictures occupying adjacent or related positions are usually given identical space for captions.

Captions or legends that accompany photographs, charts, cartoons, and artwork should be written carefully with a view to their purpose and the space available.

Writing an effective caption takes more time and thought than its length would indicate. In addition to giving a message briefly, it must have some punch and be the proper length to fit the space limitations.

The caption writer is responsible for the line giving credit to the photographer or source of the chart or artwork reproduced. (See CREDIT LINES.) This credit line may appear immediately below the picture, i.e., above the caption itself, or as a final phrase in the last line of the caption. The usual form is simply such an acknowledgment as "Acme photo."

carbon copy For years it has been possible to make a few extra copies of a typed, written, or drawn item with the aid of carbon paper. More recently, office machines have been developed for making dry copies of typed and printed matter, up to 8½ by 14, in less than 15 sec and at a materials cost of about 5 cents a copy. (See DUPLICATING.) In some situations this may be cheaper and more convenient than making carbon copies.

With carbon paper, it is usually no problem to make four or five carbon copies on one run. Up to 20 carbon copies can be produced on a hard-hitting electric typewriter with the right combination of papers.

To improve the legibility of carbon copies, thin hard paper and thin carbon paper are best. A thin sheet for the original will increase the legibility of the copies. The undermost copy may be on heavy hard paper, but the use of a regular-weight letterhead for the original will reduce the legibility of the copies.

Some find that several additional legible carbon copies can be made if the message is typed *without a ribbon.* The original will then be completely illegible, but the carbons will be much sharper. In fact, an effective way to get crystal-sharp typing for offset reproduction is to type without a ribbon directly on the back of a piece of carbon paper.

Carbon paper is obtainable in red, yellow, blue, and other colors as well as in black, and in larger sizes as well as the standard 8½ by 11 in.

A layer of carbon can be applied to any paper. Business forms requiring multiple carbon copies are often simplified by eliminating separate sheets of carbon paper and putting the carbon on the underside of the forms themselves. The whole area need not be carbonized. The carbon can be applied only to selected areas, so that one carbon copy will receive only the shipping information, and another the full discount and billing information, etc. Such work is done by printers specializing in business forms. (See BUSINESS FORMS.)

A recent development produces carbon images without conventional carbon paper. A colorless chemical coating on the underside of a sheet interacts with another colorless coating on the top side of the next sheet to make the image.

Carbon paper is available in ribbon form for use in typewriters, especially electric typewriters, and yields a sharper result than cloth ribbon.

car cards See TRANSIT ADVERTISING.

cardboard See also PAPER; PAPER SIZES AND WEIGHTS.

Under "cardboard," the term most used by the layman, will be discussed those paper products that are thicker and stiffer than paper.

Cardboard is bought like paper: by the pound and in a range of prices, grades, and finishes. Therefore, much of what is said about paper is not repeated here. The basic sizes, however, are not the same.

The average user of printing is most likely to be interested in three items: (1) cover paper, for pamphlet covers, (2) bristolboard, for postcards, etc., (3) crude board for protecting the con-

tents of envelopes, for mounting posters and pictures, etc.

The table accompanying the entry on PAPER SIZES AND WEIGHTS is arranged to show the comparative weights and basic sizes of the various papers and cardboards. It shows, for example, that 94-lb postcard bristol is about equivalent to what would be 140-lb book paper if such heavy paper were made.

The terms used in the paper trade are so numerous as to be confusing, but they may be roughly organized as follows:

After the heavy-weight papers, the ledger papers, and the cover papers, come the bristolboards and then the binder's boards, boxboards, etc. There is a limit to how thick paper can be made. Heavier weights of stock are produced by combining two or more webs of paper, either without paste while still wet or with paste.

Cardboard can be obtained in the same finishes as paper. When the surface must take ink and stand erasures, index bristol is used. When a good smooth printing surface is all that is required, printing bristol, mill bristol, or wedding bristol is used. A cheaper grade is called "bogus bristol." Bristols are 0.006 in. (6 pt) thick, or more. (The bristol used in government postal cards is about 8 pt.) Basic weights for bristols are 90, 100, 120, 140, 160, 180, 200, and 240 lb for a ream of 500 sheets, 22½ by 28½ in.

It is possible to get coated bristol, coated-one-side bristol, colored bristol, and bristols designed to take lacquer, lithography, waxing, lamination, etc. Extra-tough bristols made of manila rope, jute, or kraft pulp are available for tags, etc. The so-called "tagboards" can also be very cheap. The word "manila" alone does not indicate the presence of rope fibers.

Since cardboards are usually built up out of several plies, it is quite common to use a cheap filler, together with a better grade of lining. "Lining" in paper-trade terminology means the outside layers.

Cardboards over 0.012 in. thick are often grouped under the general name "paperboards." These include binder's board (the strongest grade, 0.030 to 0.300 in. thick), chipboard (a cheaper grade), strawboard, boxboard, millboard, pulpboard, newsboard, pressboard, corrugated board, etc.

The cheapest cardboards are made from reprocessed newsprint and are not bleached white. Special cardboards are obtainable as artists' drawing board, mat board (for mounting pictures), etc. Artists' drawing board can be surfaced for watercolor, ink, etc., and is obtainable for special art techniques under such names as Ross board, scratchboard, etc. (See DRAWING TECHNIQUES.)

carding out Carding out a column of type means to insert strips of card stock, bristolboard, paper, etc., between the lines to make the column a bit deeper. This might be done, for example, in order to make 12 lines occupy the same space as 13 lines in an adjoining column. The smallest metal spacing material is the 1-pt lead, which is about 0.014 in. thick. Postcard stock is about half as thick. Carding out does not look very well, but it is about the only thing a *printer* can do when faced with uneven columns, unless authorized to do what an editor would do under the circumstances, namely, find a way to cut or add copy to get even columns.

caret See also PROOFREADING.

Proofreader's mark ($\wedge$) to indicate that an insertion is to be made.

cartoons See also ARTWORK; DRAWING TECHNIQUES.

Appropriate cartoons add to the effectiveness of almost any printed material. They help get it read and put important points across.

Sometimes good and relevant cartoons can be found in already published form. Newspapers and magazines often grant permission to reprint cartoons that have appeared in their pages, provided credit is given. For nonprofit purposes such reprint permission is often given free. However, in reproducing a two- or three-column newspaper cartoon, care should be taken not to reduce it to a size that is illegible.

Usually it is necessary to have special cartoons drawn. This has the advantage of permitting continuity of style and flexibility of layout.

To make a cartoon, two things are necessary: the idea and the artist.

Thinking up cartoon ideas is not easy, but it is a job the editor should accept and not wish on the artist. It is not easy for an artist, either, and he may have the additional handicap of knowing very little about the subject matter.

The best way to work out ideas for a cartoon is to make a list of the main points that need emphasis and then try to convert these points into visual form. Once the important points are clearly stated, the artist is much more likely to be able to help in visualizing them.

How to create cartoon ideas. Cartoons need not always be funny. Some are straightforward pictures of ordinary people taking the action that the writer desires. The artist's way of drawing people can add the necessary warmth or sympathetic appeal.

Some cartoons make their points by contrast—perhaps introducing a character who does everything wrong. Some base their humor on exaggeration—the caption giving good advice but the characters taking that advice too literally. Some take the author's figures of speech and illustrate them with disarming literalness.

Even the little gnomes who merely crawl about some pages or charts and point at things may help nurse the reader along through pages that he would otherwise skip. (For suggestions on choosing an artist, see ARTISTS.)

When a cartoon is ordered, the artist

should be told (1) the age and interests of the audience to be reached, (2) the editorial slant of the publication in which it will appear, (3) the specific idea to be put across, (4) the proportions desired, (5) the size in which the cartoon is to be printed, and (6) whether he must deliver a line drawing or may use the wash-drawing technique.

Care should be taken to use a cartoon style that the audience likes. Some groups appreciate subtle, sophisticated caricatures; others prefer their humor simple, realistic, and slapstick. A good editor uses discretion in imposing his own tastes on his readers.

For many purposes stock cuts are useful. (See STOCK CUTS.)

cartouche A flourish with pen or brush made to serve as a decorative scroll or border.

A cartouche.

case 1. Hand type is kept in compartmented trays called "cases." The capital letters used to be kept in the upper case, the small letters in the lower case. This explains the terms "uppercase" for capital letters and "lowercase" for small letters. The so-called "California job case" accommodates both, side by side.

2. The case of a book is its cover. In case bookbinding, also called "edition bookbinding," a book's cover or case is manufactured in a separate operation from the book itself. The process of gluing a book inside of its cover

A pair of typecases.

is called "casing-in." In hand bookbinding, a book's cover or binding is built around the book itself, not assembled as a separate case to be glued on later. (See illustration under BOOKBINDING.)

case in See CASE; also illustration under BOOKBINDING.

Caslon See Appendix 1, Type Faces.

cast off See also COPYFITTING.

To estimate the number of columns or pages a manuscript will make when set in type.

catalog See also PAMPHLETS; BOOK MANUFACTURING; BINDING; MECHANICAL BINDINGS.

Producing a catalog differs very little from producing a pamphlet or a book, so the information printed under those headings will not be repeated here.

Important elements to consider in planning a catalog are as follows:

1. *Size*. Is the catalog to fit in a pocket, sit on a shelf, go in a file, or lie in a desk drawer? Will it get more attention or less if it differs from the other catalogs used by the recipient? What envelope will be used?

2. *Need for durability*. Must it withstand hard wear? Or exposure to water or grease? This may determine the nature of the cover, binding, or paper to be used.

3. *Ease of reference*. A catalog needs to be well organized and indexed, so that information will be easy to find and complete.

4. *Postal regulations*. Catalogs of 24 pages or more can be mailed for a lower rate than smaller ones. The use of thin paper and compact typography will, of course, save mailing weight and expense. (See Appendix 3, Postal Information.)

5. *Typography*. (See also Appendix 1, Type Faces.)

In many catalogs a large amount of detailed technical information must be presented. The material must be compact and yet each kind of information must stand out and identify itself for ready reference.

The best way to attack this problem is to examine other catalogs whose designers faced similar problems; to pick a style that would be satisfactory; and then to encourage several printers to bid either on this style or on any simplification of it that they might suggest.

Slight changes in catalog design to fit a printer's equipment can mean big savings. However, a printer who suggests changes should be asked to set a sample page or entry in the style that he suggests.

Complicated catalogs are often set in Monotype, since in that method it is possible to mix three faces as easily as two can be mixed in Linotype and Intertype and since small price corrections, etc., in standing type are easily made.

The best printing process to use in producing a catalog is, of course, determined by the number to be run, the nature of the illustrations, and the style of typesetting desired. (See PAMPHLETS; CIRCULARS.)

In an effort to make an expensive catalog have a longer life, it is common to omit prices from the main descriptions and give them only in dated price lists.

Catalogs are often supplied in mechanical binders for ease of substituting revised pages (see MECHANICAL BINDINGS) and may be thumb-indexed. step-indexed, tab-indexed, or edge-indexed (see INDEXING).

Whenever the basic information for a catalog is on file in some reproducible form, such as punched cards or magnetic tape, it can, of course, be printed out directly from such a data base in a form suitable for offset reproduction. (See COMPUTER TYPESETTING.) Sometimes catalog information is maintained in a form suitable not only for daily reference, but also for periodic reproduction in catalog form. Some of these methods are described under COLD TYPE and include the Flexoprint, Compos-o-line, Fotolist, and Listomatic processes.

centered Placed in the exact center of an area; said of a caption, illustration, or block of type. Material that is not centered is indented, or run "flush left" or "flush right." Too great a reliance on centering makes for a disorderly page. It is better to use the flush-left or indented style when there are many elements to be organized.

center spread See also LAYOUT.

The pair of facing pages in the center of a magazine or pamphlet, so bound that they are on a single sheet of paper. This means that photographs and art-work may be spread across the two pages without difficulty.

On spreads (facing pages) other than the center spread, it is inadvisable to have headlines or photographs "bridge the gutter," i.e., run across from the left-hand page to the right-hand page, because poor alignment in the bindery may ruin the effect.

It is customary to lay out pages in pairs, however, so that on each dou-ble-page spread the left page will har-monize with the right page.

certified mail See Appendix 3, Postal Information.

chain-dot halftones See ELLIPTICAL-DOT HALFTONES.

character count The length of a piece of copy is usually expressed in terms of the number of characters (letters and spaces) that it contains. (See COPY-FITTING.)

character recognition Automatic data processing depends on getting the data into "machine-readable" form. Some-times this is done through the medium of punched cards or punched paper

tape. It can also be done by "mark sens-ing,"—a technique whereby a pencil mark in a defined area on a card can be sensed by a photocell. By refinement of this technique, entire letters or num-bers can be distinguished from other characters by their shape in a process called "character recognition." The pro-cess calls for rather sophisticated com-puter techniques, but it becomes more practical as computer efficiency rises.

One form of character recognition is used by National Cash Register to con-vert directly from cash-register tapes to computer analysis. Another form is used on bank checks (see MAGNETIC INK). In both cases, the shapes of the charac-ters have been modified slightly to make them more easily distinguishable by the machine.

Machines also exist which can "read" standard type faces. One such is the Philco General Purpose Print Reader, which can be programmed to read a considerable variety of standard type faces at speeds up to 2,000 alpha-numeric characters per second. The first applications of this machine were for conversion of large mailing lists without rekeyboarding. The machine can handle cards, manuscript pages, questionnaires, book pages, etc.

Needless to say, the character-recog-nition approach bypasses the need for such equipment as manually operated card punches or tape-perforating type-writers. More or less standard type-writers can produce machine-readable information. Existing business machines can do likewise, at least with a simple change of type wheels.

Machines also exist which can read handwriting, or at any rate some of it. Generally speaking, a machine which is unable to "make out" a word or char-acter does precisely what a human would do—sets the document aside and gets on with the job of reading what it can read.

Companies active in the field of char-acter-recognition technology include the

Philco Corporation, Farrington Electronics, National Cash Register, Addressograph-Multigraph, and the Rabinow Engineering Company.

charts A useful line of special materials for making charts, graphs, and other visual materials is offered by Chart-Pak, Inc., 1 River Rd., Leeds, Mass. This firm supplies preprinted pressure-sensitive tapes and shading films ready to stick down on charts, graphs, commercial layouts, and visual presentations. Tapes come in an opaque or transparent base and are available in 16 colors.

chase The steel frame in which pages of type are "locked up" for placing on the printing press or for making duplicate plates. (See illustration under TYPE.)

chemical pulp Paper made from wood by the sulfite, sulfate, or soda process is said to have been made from chemical pulp. It is superior in strength and permanency to paper made from groundwood pulp.

Cheshire addressing It is often convenient to prepare address labels in one place and transfer the addresses to the mailing pieces in another place. A versatile line of equipment for affixing address labels to mailing pieces is made by Cheshire, Inc., 408 Washington Blvd., Mundelein, Ill. 60060. A similar line is offered by The Sheridan Company, 21 West St., New York 6.

Cheshire machines range in price from about $8,500 to $15,000, depending on the attachments desired. Almost any type of material can be fed, and almost any type of label can be used. In general, the labels used fall into the category of the wide-roll strip or pack (2½ to 4 in. wide and one label every inch or so), the narrow-roll strip (end-to-end labels every 2¹³⁄₁₆ in.), the multiple-width strip (two to five labels wide), etc.

One of the features offered by Cheshire permits the "heat transfer" of the lettering without actually pasting on the label. Other optional features permit automatic separation of the addressed pieces by postal zone and handling dealer imprints and addressing in a single operation. Addressing speeds on this kind of labeling equipment range to about 16,000 pieces per hour.

chipboard A cheaper grade of binder's board. (See CARDBOARD.)

circulars Definitions may differ, but for the purposes of this book it is assumed that a circular is a piece of printed matter of from one to six pages, whether it is called a leaflet, a folder, a broadside, a dodger, a flier, a package insert, an envelope stuffer, or what not. Larger items are discussed under PAMPHLETS. (See also POSTERS; LETTERS.)

Circulars can effectively be run on the mimeograph, spirit duplicator, Multigraph, Multilith, or on job printing equipment. All these processes permit the use of more than one color of ink and the use of line drawings. If there are to be photographs or wash drawings, then the choice narrows to Multilith, letterpress, and offset, or perhaps photography.

One of the first decisions in planning a circular is whether or not to set type. Typesetting may cost $5, $10, or even $30 a page. It is possible to buy 1,000 completed copies of a mimeographed circular for less than the cost of setting type alone. On the other hand, type composition is generally more attractive than typewriter composition (see TYPEWRITER), although the latter can be very attractive, especially when done on the VariTyper (see VARITYPER) or on the IBM electromatic proportional-spacing typewriter.

Here are some general suggestions on printing circulars:

1. A very small, one-page job might be most economically done by a label printer. (See LABELS.)

2. If the budget allows only $10, the possibilities are probably limited to mimeographing, spirit duplicating, or Multigraphing. A well-designed mimeographed job, making use of spot drawings or diagrams and using headlines done with a lettering guide, can be very attractive. (See also COMBINATION RUN for a way of getting 500 sheets of white bond paper, 8½ by 11, printed in black ink on one side with any copy for as little as $6.) Multilithed jobs generally cost more than $10 unless the plate is prepared by hand instead of by photography.

3. If the budget allows up to $25, it may still be necessary to stick with one of the above processes in order to get the quantity required, but it also becomes possible to use the Multilith (thus opening the door to photographic reproduction of drawings, lettering, etc., with special ink, on special paper). On simple one- or two-page jobs, a $25 budget may allow type to be set for letterpress or offset reproduction. Perhaps an ad or clipping can be reproduced by offset.

4. A $50 budget for a one- to six-page circular generally makes type composition feasible and permits letterpress printing if desired.

When circulars are ordered in large quantities, it is common to print them "2-up" or "4-up." For example, a simple mimeographed receipt, size 4¼ by 5½ in., can be run 4-up on an 8½- by 11-in. piece of mimeograph paper and later cut apart.

There is a minimum charge below which letterpress and offset printing cannot go, but these processes can easily underbid even mimeographing on a per-unit basis when the quantities begin to exceed 5,000. (For illustration of different ways to fold and trim leaflets, see BINDING.)

clip book   See STOCK CUTS.

clipping bureau   A clipping bureau is a firm which watches almost all national publications and a wide selection of local ones and clips items of interest to its clients. One well-known firm is Burrelle's Press Clipping Bureau, 165 Church St., New York 7. A clipping bureau will watch for the name of a firm or individual, a product name, the treatment of a particular subject, or what you will. Such clippings can be helpful in verifying the effectiveness of a publicity campaign or in getting leads for salesmen or names for mailing lists.

A clipping bureau charges by the item, with a minimum monthly retainer (Burrelle's rates in 1966: $45 service charge for one month and 15 cents per clipping; for three months' service, $37 per month plus 15 cents per clipping.) Sometimes a new client may be startled by the thoroughness of the coverage given by a clipping bureau, as when he gets a bill for several hundred clippings of a single syndicated item.

clipsheet   See also CAMPAIGN PLANNING; COPYWRITING.

Where wide publicity is sought in a big campaign or drive, a whole packet of publicity aids may be distributed to the press in advance as a clipsheet, in a form suitable for the editor to clip out and reproduce forthwith.

A clipsheet may contain news stories, feature articles, personal interviews, editorials, fillers, cartoons, ads, photographs, "quotable quotes," in fact anything that a newspaper can carry. Pictures and cartoons are more likely to be reproduced if cuts or mats are offered free on request. (See CUTS and MAT.)

A clipsheet is usually designed like a newspaper page. It may be an 8-column or 7-column page or a 5-column tabloid page, or a series of miniature newspaper pages approximately 9 by 12 in., assembled and stapled together for convenient handling. It is printed on one side of the paper so that every item is ready to be clipped and pasted.

The editor who does not use "canned" copy can still use the clipsheet as an "idea hatcher" and send out his reporters for local news and interviews related to the drive.

cloth printing Textile printing is a field of its own and will not be discussed here. However, buyers of the printed word occasionally need to buy printed flags, pennants, armbands, insignia, cloth book covers, etc.

Cloth can be printed by the same methods as those used for paper. Pennants are often printed by silk screen since this process lends itself to putting a thick layer of pigment on the felt.

Cloth book covers are usually stamped with specially cut brass dies (specially cut because the spaces between the letters and lines must be cut away more deeply than for printing on paper). If ink is used, two "hits" are recommended to ensure coverage. Metal foil or colored foil can also be used instead of ink since it adheres to the cloth where heated brass dies have pressed down on it.

Cloth for book covers and for other purposes can also be printed by the offset and gravure processes. Even full-color photographs and artwork can be imprinted on suitable cloth by these processes.

Insignia for sweaters, flags, pennants, etc., can be embroidered or woven effectively instead of printed. Even complicated designs in several colors can be embroidered by automatic machine at comparatively reasonable rates.

To locate firms doing this kind of work, look in the Classified Telephone Directory under Labels—Fabric.

coated paper See also PAPER.

Paper is coated to make it suitable for the letterpress reproduction of fine-screen halftones. It can be "off-the-machine coated" or "machine-coated" and can be finished as dull-coated or glossy-coated.

Machine coating is sometimes called "process coating." The coating is applied at the wet end of the papermaking machine instead of afterward as a separate operation. Machine-coated paper is, therefore, cheaper and is much used for large-circulation picture magazines.

When coated paper is ordered, it is important to specify how it is to be used, whether in lithography, for varnishing, for precision register work, for gumming, or what not. Paper coated on one side only is available for labels, box coverings, etc. "Folding coated" is specified for covers and where extra durability is needed. Coated papers come in creams, india tints and colors, and also in "duplex" finishes (a different color on each side).

COD See Appendix 3, Postal Information.

coin cards These devices for facilitating the sending of coins through the mails are obtainable from die cutters generally, including (to name two sources) the Dennison Manufacturing Company, Framingham, Mass., and Freedman Cut-Outs, Inc., 34 Hubert St., New York.

cold gold See GOLDMARK.

cold type See also PHOTOCOMPOSITION.

A term coined to distinguish Vari-Typing, IBM typewriter composition, Justowriting, and ordinary typing from type composition done by the older "hot-metal" methods such as Linotype.

Properly speaking, work done on the Fotosetter, Photon, and other photo-typesetting machines is cold type, too, since hot metal is not involved. However, there is a tendency to reserve the term "cold type" for the somewhat cruder "typewriter" methods, where the images are created by having type strike through a carbon ribbon.

Cold type is used basically for just one reason: to save money. Very attractive work can be done, and the layman may not be able to distinguish it from conventional printing, but the claims made for cold type dwell on its economy and utility, not on its beauty.

Some of the advantages of cold-type composition are as follows:

1. *The machines are cheaper.* For the price of one Linotype you can get a dozen IBM Executive typewriters or perhaps four proportional-spacing Vari-Typers or two complete Justowriter installations. One publisher of a big directory turned to IBM composition because speed required the use of six keyboards simultaneously and he couldn't find a printer who could make six Linotype machines available when he had to have them.

2. *Wages are lower.* Cold-type compositors are not unionized and are paid less. This situation may change.

3. *Output is higher.* This is partly because of the simpler keyboard, partly because of the faster keyboard action, and partly because the slowdown tactics that plague union composing rooms have not yet taken hold in the cold-type field.

4. *Correction costs are lower.* More mistakes are caught as they are made instead of later because the operators can see better what they are doing.

5. *Composition that is difficult with hot type is often easy with cold type.* For example, tabular work is difficult in hot type but easy on the typewriter. Composition involving chemical formulas and mathematical equations or special symbols often shows tremendous savings when done in cold type. (Note that the white space in and around an equation is just white space in cold type, but is a mosaic of metal spaces and quads in metal type.)

6. *Editorial costs can be shaved.* Sometimes compositors can be given editorial responsibilities—and a typewriter does not mind being kept waiting while something is being looked up. One directory publisher composes directly from his source material and saves keyboarding an interim manuscript. He also puts his information into type as fast as he gets it because his "type" (being only slips of paper) can be alphabetized after being set, which would not be so easy with hard-to-read metal slugs.

7. *Type can be "kept standing" at negligible expense.*

Of course, cold type is not without its disadvantages. Lines can be justified only by typing twice, and thus the greatest savings can be expected on jobs (like directories and price lists) where justifying is not required. Work to be done on IBM typewriters or the Justowriter must avoid the use of italics or small caps. The available type faces, though fully adequate to many uses, are generally inferior in both variety and design to those available in hot metal, and are not likely to catch up. (In Linotype, a character can be designed to any width the designer wishes; in even the most expensive VariTyper, it must be fitted into one of three widths.) A really *bold* boldface simply is not available in cold type. The making of proofs of cold-type composition poses special problems: beyond perhaps one carbon copy, extras have to be made by some photocopying or whiteprint or Xerox method. And finally, comparatively few printers use cold-type methods as yet, or know anything about them, and of those who have entered the field, by no means all maintain very high standards of craftsmanship.

The techniques of cold type are still in flux and many shortcuts probably remain to be devised. Present procedures are roughly as follows:

The best combinations of carbon ribbon and paper and impression are worked out by experiment, and then great pains are taken to maintain uniformity in these things. Unless the material is very simple, it is not typed directly in pages but is typed in galleys for later pasting up in page form. Typed material may be *lightly* sprayed with some fixative like Krylon to prevent smudging during proofreading, correcting, or paste-up.

Corrections are "patched in" by placing the galley face down on a glass-topped table illuminated from underneath. The new material (also face down) is positioned over the old, then both error and correction are cut out with a *sharp* razor blade which cuts through both layers at once. The error is now discarded; the correction fits neatly into the resulting hole and is secured in place with a strip of Scotch mending tape. When this is expertly done, the patch can scarcely be detected from the face of the galley, alignment is perfect, and the work goes rapidly. Corrections for errors noticed during the typing are usually typed in the right margin, or a faulty line can be marked and then retyped correctly, the bad line being cut out during the correction process or during paste-up. Chinese white and india ink are also used as required during the correction process, also white Scotch tape. Special marks or accents which are not available on the machine can be added by pen or by some process like Artype. (See ARTYPE.)

The basic tools of the paste-up operation are, of course, the drawing board and T square or parallel rule, triangle, rubber cement, etc., often in conjunction with mounting paper on which special guidelines have been ruled. Laps are avoided unless they can all face one way because they cast shadows, though shadows that are not too close to type can easily be opaqued out on the negative. Another paste-up technique calls for the use of a light table or Camera Lucikon or Lacey-Luci. Here the guidelines are visible through the typed galleys being pasted down. Another method is to project the guidelines down from above, a procedure that is necessary when working with nontranslucent materials.

Where proofreading is done from master copy, care must be taken that editors do not mark or soil the type itself; often a tissue overlay is used to protect the type and make it possible to mark corrections more readily.

In directory work, it is possible to type each entry or even each line on a separate card and to change the sequence of the cards at will prior to "shingling" them in page form. The typing is carefully placed on the card near the upper edge. Each successive card in a column is so placed as to cover all of its predecessor except the typed line or lines. Cards can be either adhered to low-tack, double-sided Scotch tape or mechanically held by some such method as Remington's Flexoprint process. (See FLEXOPRINT.)

Display type for use with cold-type text matter is often produced on photolettering machines in which display letters can be photographically copied, one by one, from master alphabets on film. (See PHOTOLETTERING.)

A machine called the "Optype" offers a technique for justifying text type by optical methods at speeds of up to 15 lines a minute. Each line is stretched or squeezed until uniform with its fellows. During the process, type can be reduced, condensed, or slanted if desired. The machine is marketed at about $7,000 by the Consolidated International Equipment and Supply Company, 1030 W. Chicago Ave., Chicago 22.

collating Examining the gathered signatures (see SIGNATURE) of a book to see that all are included and in the proper order. (See BOOKBINDING.) Sometimes used to mean the actual gathering of such sheets or signatures or even putting together of type from different machines.

collotype See PHOTOGELATIN.

color See also COLOR PRINTING; DESIGN.

Color science is a complicated field in which artists, chemists, and physicists all claim the right to speak and do not always understand each other.

There are, however, a few general considerations that may help the layman avoid mistakes even if they do not show him how to create masterpieces. Intelligent use of color can add a great deal to the effectiveness of printed material.

To understand color, it is best to discuss it purely as a sensation and leave any technical analysis of it to the physicists and chemists. It is with color as a sensation that the artist and printer are concerned. They are more interested in its psychological impact than in its physical composition. Color can get attention. It can create a mood. It can please or irritate.

Color is used both realistically and abstractly. Realistic color, used the way the mail-order catalogs use it, can greatly increase sales effectiveness. The only products that the mail-order companies do not advertise in color are those which color does not help sufficiently to justify the cost.

Abstract (decorative) color, well handled, can also increase the pulling power of a printed message. People, like bees, are simply attracted by color, at least when it is handled so as to have pleasant associations for them.

The color combinations with the highest attention value are those with the greatest contrast—white on red, orange-red on black, yellow on black, white on black, and black on white. (However, the attention value of a sign depends not alone on the sign itself but also on its relation to its setting.)

When a job is to be run in black and one other color on white paper, red is an easy favorite for the extra color.

Note that the above-mentioned color combinations differ both in hue and in brightness. The lightness of orange-red contrasts better with black than would a darker red. Contrast is desirable when type or lettering of one color is to be run on a background of another. The degree of contrast determines the legibility.

Photographs should always be printed in black or very dark colors, never in red or blue or any other light color unless a washed-out effect is sought deliberately.

Vermilion is the best color to use in combination with photographs, as shown on the cover of *Life*. Yellow is also good with photographs.

There are times, however, when low contrast is preferred to high contrast. There must be high contrast between type and background, but there may be low contrast between the background and other elements.

Harmony in color selection is a subtle thing, but a few hints on how to achieve it may be helpful:

Colors are not attractive or unattractive in themselves; everything depends on how they are used. The person who does not like a green tie with a blue suit likes green trees against blue water or sky.

People really have no "favorite" colors. They may think they do, but they will turn against the color of their choice when it is badly handled (they may not even recognize it), and they will likewise be attracted toward any colors effectively used.

It is not possible to say that two or more colors do or do not harmonize, without knowing how they are to be arranged on the page. Certain colors may clash when equal masses are used, yet go beautifully together when a small area of one is used to accent a large area of the other. Bright colors may fight each other and give a "dazzle" effect when used side by side, yet look well when separated by an area of white, gray, or some other color.

When intense colors are combined with toned or tinted colors, it is common to use larger areas of the latter.

Any color is a mixture of white, black, and a color; or at least it can be analyzed as if it were. When white is added

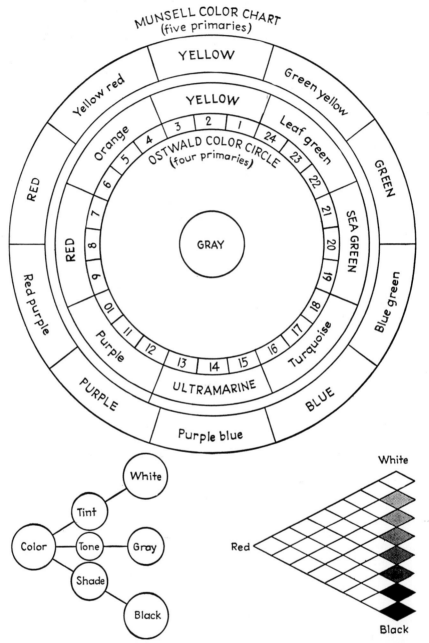

MUNSELL COLOR CHART
(five primaries)

OSTWALD COLOR CIRCLE
(four primaries)

A color can be most easily described in terms of its "hue" (red, yellow red, etc.); its "value," meaning its gray content; and its "chroma," meaning its intensity. Imagine that the above circle is really a geometric solid, the colors intense along its equator and graying toward the core, and the core ranging from white at the top to black at the bottom. At lower right is a cross section of such a solid.

to a pure color, the result is a lighter "tint" of that color. When black is added to a pure color, a darker "shade" of that color results. When both white and black are added to a pure color, that color takes on a grayer "tone."

Bright, intense colors are much harder to combine successfully than the same colors with a slight amount of gray added.

Two colors tend to harmonize better when they have the same white content or the same black content, or both. Harmony between gray and a color can be established in the same way, either by choosing a gray with the same white content as the color or by choosing one with the same black content as the color.

Gray and black and white should be handled like colors in layout work. The use of medium gray areas in a black-and-white job often adds as much as an extra color. Black type on white paper produces an effect of gray, and type masses should be regarded as blocks of gray.

Modern color theory, as developed by Munsell and Ostwald, depends on a "hue circle" of the type shown on page 50. The basis of this hue circle is that opposite colors, if pure, should form a neutral gray when mixed.

Red, orange, yellow, and brown are regarded as warm colors. They also give the effect of thrusting themselves forward. Green, blue, and gray are regarded as cool colors, giving the effect of distance.

Paper is part of the color scheme. A yellow-red that is pleasing on buff paper may be disappointing on blue-white paper.

In working with color, it is extremely helpful to have as many color samples at hand as possible. It may be worth while to keep a scrapbook of interesting color combinations. Certainly most printed jobs will be more interesting (and very little more expensive) if the printer is required to match carefully

chosen colors instead of using any red that he happens to have ready-mixed.

There are a number of books on color theory, but on the whole they are more confusing than helpful to the layman. Color samples are much more useful than color theories. The printing buyer who wants to choose and use color intelligently should equip himself with (1) sample books of colored papers from the paper merchants and paper mills, (2) some ink sample books from printing-ink firms, (3) paint-swatch books put out by paint companies and obtainable at paint stores, (4) a generous assortment of pastel chalks (available in any art supply store), and, best of all, (5) the $3.75 color-swatch book put out by the Color-aid Co., 116 E. 27 St., New York.

This last item is especially helpful since 18- by 24-in. sheets of paper of any selected color may be ordered from it by number at 30 cents a sheet. Some 210 colors and shades and tints are available—24 basic hues, each in 4 tints and 3 shades, plus 8 grays, 1 white, and 1 black. Larger "TV boards" (24 by 36 in.) are also available at 60 cents each.

These swatches are much more useful than the ink sample books since often the right color for a job is not to be found ready-mixed. It must be mixed to order, a simple enough procedure (not expensive either) if the buyer can supply a sample of the color wanted together with a specimen of the paper it is to be printed on. The Color-aid sheets are also invaluable for showing tint blocks and color areas on dummies.

For samples of printing-ink colors, write to the ink manufacturer with whom your printer deals. For samples of colored papers, inquire of the various paper merchants and paper mills.

See also BOURGES COLOR PROCESS.

Color-aid   See COLOR.

colored paper   See also PAPER.

Paper can be obtained in almost any color. The usual colors are, of course, the light ones, since dark ink is not very legible on too dark a paper. Printing with light ink on a dark paper is impractical since two impressions are usually required to get opacity. The same effect may be obtained by printing a reverse plate in dark ink on a light paper.

"Duplex" paper shows one color on one side and another color on the other side.

Colored paper costs more than plain paper, often considerably more. On very short runs, the cost of the paper is a relatively unimportant item, and colored or duplex papers can provide the effect of an extra color at little extra cost.

On longer pressruns, it is usually cheaper to run an extra color of ink on white paper than to use colored paper. The extra color of ink can be used to tint the entire surface of the paper if desired, thus giving the effect of colored paper.

color engraving See COLOR PRINTING.

Coloron Coloron sheets are transparent sheets printed in a variety of colors and tints of colors. They are used to determine in advance what the effect will be if (for example) a certain tint of blue is printed over another color—and whether type surprinted on the combination will be more legible in white, in black, or in one of the tints or solids. Each sheet shows one color (the process colors as well as the basic colors are available) in a series of panels ranging from a solid of that color through all the tints, 90 percent, 80 percent, etc., down to 10 percent. In each panel is shown type in reverse on the tint, type in reverse on the solid, type in the solid on the tint, and type in the tint on white. Coloron sheets are sold in sets by the Delta Brush Manufacturing Corp., 120 S. Columbus Ave., Mt. Vernon, N.Y., or by art stores.

color photography See also PHOTOGRAPHY.

Any photographer using any camera can take pictures in color simply by loading his camera with color film. However, color photography makes exacting demands as regards illumination and exposure, and good results require skill and experience.

The films most used commercially are Kodachrome (available only in 35mm size), Anscocolor, Anscochrome, Ektachrome, Ektacolor, and Kodacolor.

The first four yield positive transparencies that should be viewed against a diffused white light or projected on a screen.

Ektacolor, like Kodacolor, produces a *negative* transparency in which each primary color is represented by its complementary. Prints on paper can be made from Ektacolor and Kodacolor negatives and in the latter case can now be made with the simplest darkroom equipment.

Printing plates can be made direct from a transparency, either positive or negative. However, it is common practice first to make a color print on paper from the transparency, both because it is easier to retouch on paper and because photoengravers add a 50 percent surcharge for working from transparencies. If the photoengraver charges $500 to make printing plates from an oil painting, he may charge $750 to make plates of the same size from a transparency. However, the buyer may have secured a color transparency for only $100 as against $500 or more for the oil painting, so he realizes a net saving by using the transparency.

Color prints on paper can be made from any transparency. Good ones, however, are rather expensive.

Duplicates of color photographs, whether transparencies or color prints on paper, can be had at many prices and in many qualities, ranging from the under-a-dollar variety offered to amateurs in photofinishing stores, to first-quality prints for advertising or exhibition purposes worth several hundred dollars. Copy-Art Photographers, 165 W. 46 St., New York 36, offers color prints on paper at prices ranging from $4.50 for a 4 by 5 print to $25 for a 16 by 20. For 26 to 50 copies, prices are $1 each (size 4 by 5) and $8 each (16 by 20). Other companies equipped to do processing of color photographs of all kinds are Bebell and Bebell Color Laboratories, Inc., 108 W. 24 St., New York; Kurshan an'Lang Color Service, Inc., 222 E. 44 St., New York; and Authenticolor Labs, Inc., 525 Lexington Ave., New York.

For information about printing color photographs, see PROCESS COLOR.

color printing See also COLOR; FLAT COLOR; PROCESS COLOR; COLOR PHOTOGRAPHY; COLORED PAPER.

Multicolor printing can be done by sending the same paper through the press as many times as there are colors. Color means added attractiveness. It also means added cost and special care in handling in order to obtain the best effects.

In most processes it is necessary to "wash up" the ink fountain and the ink rollers, and substitute ink of the desired color. Since washups take time, even printing in a single color other than black is usually more expensive than printing in black.

The use of a second color on a printing job (black being considered the first color) requires an extra pressrun, an extra makeready, extra washing up, and an extra form of type or cuts. But this is not all. It also poses the problem of "register."

If a black-and-white impression lands on a page within $\frac{1}{8}$ in. of where it is supposed to go, no one is likely to object. If a red image that is supposed to be the rouge on a lady's cheek lands $\frac{1}{8}$ in. away on her nose, there are likely to be complaints. Two or more colors must "register." (If the design is such

that close registration of the colors is not important, the printer need not charge for the extra care that close registration implies.)

To illustrate one problem of register: a 50-in. piece of paper can stretch or shrink as much as $\frac{1}{4}$ in. during a change of humidity. If it does so between impressions, the printer is in trouble.

Flat color is the simple form of color printing in which there is usually no attempt to print one color over the other in order to get some other shade. Red is red and blue is blue. However, in many cases one flat color is printed in a transparent ink over another to give the effect of a third color.

However, full-color paintings, color photographs, and scenes from actual life do not limit themselves to any given number of colors. These can be reproduced only in process color using black and the three primary colors (red, blue, and yellow) and mixing these colors to get the full range of browns, grays, greens, purples, etc. (See PROCESS COLOR.)

All printing processes can handle flat color, i.e., nonprocess color. Process color can be done in letterpress, offset, gravure, and photogelatin. Fake process work (see FAKE PROCESS) can be done in these ways and in silk screen.

In mimeograph work, color may be added by cleaning out the black ink and substituting another color, but it is easier to buy an extra drum for each color that is to be used and just switch drums. It is also possible to fit a pad inked in color over the black-ink drum, but such a pad has to be removed and re-inked frequently. To get two colors on a single sheet, the sheet must be run twice (a different drum or a newly inked drum for each color), or the pad may be so inked that certain areas produce one color and the rest a second color.

In Multigraph work, changing the color is as easy as changing the ribbon.

In spirit duplicating, the master can be made in several different colors, and these colors will then print simultaneously.

Process-color plates are relatively expensive. Making them is basically photomechanical (see PROCESS COLOR), but skilled handwork is almost always necessary before acceptable proofs are

The illustration above is a proof of the black plate of a two-color ad.

This is a proof (in black) made from the red plate of the same two-color ad.

When the black plate is printed on paper which has previously received an impression from the red plate, the result is a two-color effect as shown here.

produced. (See FLUORESCENCE PROCESS.) There is also a process known as "fake process color," less expensive and sometimes quite satisfactory, which amounts to having a black-and-white original hand-colored by the platemaker. (See FAKE PROCESS.)

If it is decided to use a second color on the first page of a 16-page pamphlet, for example, this probably means sending all the 16 pages through the press a second time, and opens the possibility of using color on other pages besides the first one at little extra cost. The printer is able to tell which other pages can have the extra color without additional presswork. (In a 16-page pamphlet it may be pages 4, 5, 8, 9, 12, 13, 16, or it may, under certain circumstances, be all of them.)

A second color can dress up a pamphlet, circular, or a car card enormously. On short runs, an inexpensive way to get a touch of color is to use colored paper, to paste on a colored label or illustration, or even to hand-color a line illustration. Just one splotch of watercolor can spruce up a black-and-white piece.

In any job containing a process-color illustration it is possible also to use the process colors flat—the blue, the yellow, and the red. It should be noted, however, that process blue is a light shade of blue and that process red is closer to magenta than to vermilion. Process yellow is a good, solid canary, but the others do not always look well when used by themselves. Process colors are balanced with one another for process-color printing and cannot be changed to be used "flat" without completely destroying the fidelity of the reproduction.

Photographs can be run effectively in sepia as well as in black, but light colors are to be avoided for single-color photographic reproduction. Photographs printed in a flat blue or red, etc., always lack contrast and should be used only where a washed-out effect is desired.

On the other hand, photographs can

be given added depth by being run in black and a second color by the so-called "duotone" process, especially in offset. (See DUOTONE.)

In the foregoing paragraphs it has been assumed that each extra color means another pressrun. From a cost point of view, this is approximately correct. However, there are two-color presses and even presses that can print in four colors on both sides of a piece of paper in one operation. These are economical only for long pressruns.

There are some special problems involved in seeing proofs of color printing. If the work is being done in letterpress, the engraver will furnish color proofs, made on a proof press. If the work is being done in offset, gravure, or photo-gelatin, proofs usually are made on the presses that are to do the actual printing, though offset plates may also be proved on a proof press.

In either case, the proofs can be compared with the original, corrections can be made if any are necessary, and revised proofs pulled. Proofs should always be pulled on the paper to be used in the final run in order to ensure a better comparison.

However, the final result may not duplicate the proofs, and it is difficult to check on this by demanding press proofs, especially if the first color must be run and the press washed up before subsequent colors can be added.

Even if all the colors are to be printed simultaneously on a multicolor press, it is expensive to keep big presses idle while proofs are rushed back and forth by messenger. Production men who get good color results often spend a lot of time looking over the pressman's shoulder while a run is getting under way.

color proofs   See COLOR PRINTING.

color separation   See also COLOR PRINTING.

Color printing requires a separate plate for each color—red, blue, yellow, and black in process color (see PROCESS COLOR) and the selected tints for flat color (see FLAT COLOR). Color separation is the technique by which the colors of the original artwork—drawing, photograph, or oil painting—are sorted out so that all the reds appear in the red plate, the blue and the shades of blue in the blue plate, etc.

Color separation may be done by the artist or by the printer, by hand or by photomechanical processes. An artist, for example, may make a black-and-white drawing with a flag in it and ask the printer to make a plate of the flag only and run that in red, and then to make a plate of the whole thing, but without the flag, and run that in black.

An artist may also make a "key drawing" in black and white and then put a piece of translucent acetate over it and fill in, in black on the acetate, the areas that are to print in red. The printer then makes his black plate from the key drawing and his red plate from the red separation on acetate. (See BOURGES COLOR PROCESS for another overlay technique.)

Another way in which the artist can make the color separation requires work in two stages. First he makes a "key drawing" showing only the part to be printed in black. The engraver makes a cut of this and pulls a proof in very light blue ink. On this the artist then paints in india ink the part that is to be reproduced in color. Using a film that does not "see" blue, the engraver will photograph only the part in black. A cut is made from this to print in color with the first cut which prints in black.

The printer can also handle the color-separation work. Flat-color jobs present no problem, for each color goes on unmixed with any other color. Full-color originals are more difficult. Here the printer may do his separations by the fake-process method or by the process-color method. (See FAKE PROCESS; PROCESS COLOR.)

The latter is basically photomechanical, but handwork is also almost inevitable. In fact, the handwork necessary in improving a photomechanical set of plates to the point where they can give an exact reproduction of the original is often greater than the handwork needed to make freehand separations without mechanical aid. The difference is that the former offers an exact reproduction and the latter offers at best an approximation.

combination halftone and line plate
See also CUT; HALFTONE; LINECUT.

When two kinds of artwork are to be combined in one cut—one of which requires halftone treatment, and the other line treatment—the cut costs at least twice as much. An example is when lettering is surprinted over a photograph and extends beyond the picture.

combination run Some printers offer 8½- by 11-in. leaflets, printed *on one side* on 16-lb white bond and in black ink, as low as $4 per hundred. This does not include typesetting, hand-lettering, or photos, but it applies to black-and-white material that can be copied photographically (same size, reduced, or enlarged) to print on 8½- by 11-in. paper. Jobs 11 by 17 or 17 by 22 are twice or four times the price.

Such prices are possible when a printer can use a so-called "combination run." The process is as follows: The printer has a big offset press (see OFFSET), say, size 17 by 22 or 35 by 45. He waits until he has 4 or 16 different jobs, each 8½ by 11 and each for 100 copies. Then he runs all the jobs at once and later cuts them apart.

Offset printers handling work of this kind usually ask at least five working days. Extra copies ordered at the same time run about 50 cents a hundred. Strip-ins cost about $1.50 each additional. (See STRIP.) Pages cannot bleed (see BLEED) unless trimmed smaller than 8½ by 11. Work to be run on both sides cannot be estimated on quite the same combination-run basis, and work on special paper cannot be combined at all.

Sometimes Multilith prices are very little higher than combination-run prices. (See MULTILITH.)

Printing in combination run is usually done by offset lithographers who also advertise their work under Planographing. Local combination-run printers may be located under Lithography or Planography in the Classified Telephone Directory.

composing room See also TYPE.

Typesetting or type composition is done in a composing room, usually separate from the pressroom and often under another roof entirely.

composing stick See STICK.

composition The setting of type, including hand composition, machine composition, text composition, display composition, cold-type composition, etc. For further information see such headings as TYPE; LINOTYPE; COLD TYPE; PHOTOLETTERING.

compositor See also TYPE.

The person who sets type and spaces and justifies the lines.

Compos-o-line See SEQUENTIAL-CARD CAMERAS.

comprehensive In the language of the art directors, a "comprehensive" or a comprehensive drawing is a handmade, approximate facsimile of what the finished job will look like in print. As much work can go into comprehensives as into the final artwork, but ad agencies still prefer to show them to their clients instead of roughs (see ROUGH) both because beauty tends to sell itself and because two men looking at the same rough may, unknown to each other, have quite different ideas about how it is to be developed. (See illustrations under LAYOUT.)

computer typesetting Many typesetting operations are now being done by computers. Computers are relieving human compositors of such tasks as line justification and hyphenation, manual cranking from one Linotype type font to another, rekeyboarding in the event that information already keyboarded once is to be reused in a different form. Compositors who could average at best about 6,000 characters per hour when seated directly at a Linotype or Intertype or Fotosetter or Photon, etc., sometimes turn out 10,000 characters or more with less effort when working at a keyboard that itself produces only tape.

In some respects, the buyer of printing need not concern himself with the extent to which his printer has automated plant procedures. He may still submit copy in the usual way and receive a final product that looks exactly as before. Whether a Linotype is operated by hand or by tape makes no difference in the look of the output. The chief effect of the automation may have been to help the printer hold down his costs.

In other respects, the advent of computer typesetting offers new opportunities to the buyer of printing, especially if he is presenting the same fundamental information in a variety of ways, as in cumulative directories, selective reprints, etc.

The input to computer is usually by punched cards or punched paper tape. If the basic data happen to take shape in such "machine-readable" form anyway, an additional keyboarding can sometimes be completely saved. This might be the case with price lists, mathematical tables, etc.

Even if the input must be specially keyboarded—either to produce punched tape or to produce copy that will be "clean" enough for input through a

character-recognition machine (see CHARACTER RECOGNITION)—the amount of the keyboarding can sometimes be drastically reduced by taking advantage of the ability of the computer to re-sequence the elements. For example, a single entry in a book catalog may be keyboarded only once yet "set" three times—once under author, once under title, once under subject. Furthermore, a body of information can be corrected and updated by keyboarding just the new information and having the computer insert it in its proper place in the old material.

One of the most common outputs is through a so-called "impact printer," which normally prints in ALL CAPS at the rate of 10 lines a second or better. Where this kind of print-out is acceptable for reproduction, it represents fairly efficient "type composition."

It may be advantageous to print out directly on offset printing plates or, at any rate, in a form suitable for direct offset reproduction. The appearance of the final result can be considerably improved by careful attention to the choice of ribbon and paper and line spacing and indentation, etc. Print-out in caps and lowercase is also possible at extra cost. This may halve the speed of the print-out but may be specified for the sake of the gain in legibility, which approximates the legibility of an ordinary office typewriter—and has the same inability to provide italic letters or special symbols. (Some impact printers have been programmed to strike certain lines or characters *twice* to provide a sort of boldface.)

A computer which has been properly programmed can produce an output suited for use with any composing equipment—including Linotype, Intertype, Fotosetter, Photon, Monotype, Linofilm, Linoquick, Monophoto, Photon Zip, Charactron, Linotron. Furthermore, it is possible to program a computer to convert tape from one configuration to another or to generate one kind of output for an original edition and another kind for a reprint. "Programming" is, however, expensive, and it should not be assumed that what is "possible" will also be "economic."

A special-purpose, high-speed type-composing machine built by Photon went into service at the National Library of Medicine in 1964 for use in setting the *Index Medicus.* Driven by a Minneapolis-Honeywell computer, it set type at the rate of three lines a second and could mix not only caps and lowercase but also roman, bold, and italic.

In the same year, the Merganthaler Linotype Company was awarded a contract by the U.S. Government Printing Office to develop an even faster type-setter, operating on the cathode-ray principle.

The buyer of printing might take note of the possibility of keyboarding a manuscript *before* deciding on the type in which it is to be set. This makes possible far more accurate "cast-off" and can prevent the unpleasant surprise of finding that an insignificant change in the specifications would have gotten a 322-page book down to 10 even forms of 32 pages each. He might also note that he may be able to save money on "author's alterations" if he is prepared to accept as "proofs" an impact-printer version of what the computer will prepare for the composing equipment. A literal print-out of a fully encoded tape can be so encumbered with machine codes (font, indent, cap, uncap, start ital., end ital., cast, etc.) as to be almost unreadable, but programs exist that help the proofreader interpret the machine codes, as for example, by putting a special symbol under characters that will be italicized.

There will probably always be a considerable gap between what could be done by computer and what is being done. Some of the things that are demonstrably possible may be slow to yield practical economies for printers and

even slower to affect the prices quoted to printers' customers. However, such rapid strides are being made in the *speed* of computers that programs of fantastic complexity will certainly become practical once the cost of the programming can be financed—and to a certain extent each program can stand on the shoulders of its successful predecessors.

Really effective exploitation of computers waits primarily on the education of "people" to computer possibilities. For example, a very large magazine put its subscription list on a computer and wasted a fantastic number of key strokes through failure to realize that it would be unnecessary to rewrite the city after the name and street address of every subscriber. All that was necessary was an instruction like: "Until further notice add 'Chicago, Ill.' and the ZIP Code to the names and street addresses which follow."

For a long time it seemed obvious that the way to store words in a computer was character by character as they were keyboarded. Then it was observed that considerable storage space could be saved by allowing the computer to translate the words into a kind of shorthand in which a special character stood for a whole word—almost like a reversion to the Chinese! Such compressed material could, of course, be translated back into standard English on command.

In addition to setting type in columnar form (galleys), computers can also compose directly into pages. This has been done with the four-column *Index Medicus* since 1964. It has also been worked out for more complex pages involving headlines, captions, and allowance for illustrations.

See also CHARACTER RECOGNITION; LINOTYPE; PHOTON; LINOFILM; INTERTYPE; MONOTYPE.

condensed Term used to describe a type face that is narrower than the usual type of the same height.

This is 10-pt Gothic.

This is 10-pt Gothic condensed.

contact screen A halftone screen made on film, also called the "magenta screen." (See HALFTONE.)

container printing Boxes, cartons, cans, collapsible tubes, etc., are almost always printed by the manufacturer, since the problems are specialized and the printing may have to be done during manufacture. Although every known process of printing is used, offset lithography and silk screen are favorites because of the ease with which they print on uneven surfaces.

Container labeling, as distinct from container printing, can of course be done anywhere, although special adhesives may have to be used for some surfaces.

For the names of container suppliers, look in the Classified Telephone Directory under Boxes, Package Development, etc., or consult the "Modern Packaging Encyclopedia Issue" of *Modern Packaging* listed in Appendix 2, Bibliography.

Contak shading film See SHADING TINTS.

copper engraving See also HALFTONE.

Fine-screen halftone engravings are usually made on copper, while coarse-screen halftones can be made on the coarser-grained but less expensive zinc.

The term "copper engraving" also refers to the plate on which an artist has hand-engraved a picture, or to the print made from that plate.

copy See also COPYFITTING; COPY PREPARATION.

To a printer, copy means the manuscript to be set in type. The key ingredients of a printing job are copy, layout, and artwork.

copy casting Determination of the number of words or characters in a given manuscript or piece of copy. See COPYFITTING.

copy editing See also COPYWRITING; COPY PREPARATION; EDITORIAL WORK; STYLE SHEET.

In this handbook the term "copy editing" is assumed to include rewriting, revising, and polishing. These are jobs for a person of experience who can make decisions and set policy regarding a manuscript.

Once this basic, structural editing has been done, there is still a very important job—preparation of the copy for the printer. This latter process, sometimes also considered "copy editing," is more generally called "copy preparation," and is so referred to in this book. Copy preparation means putting the accepted editorial material in shape for the printer by making it accurate as to facts, grammatical, consistent as to style, and correct in spelling and punctuation, and by marking it for type. (See COPY PREPARATION and STYLE SHEET.)

The copy editor takes over after the writer has, presumably, done his best work on a manuscript. This is probably the most ticklish and exasperating stage, for the writer is usually convinced that he has done a satisfactory job. And yet, in view of the needs of the publisher and the interests of his audience, it may not be entirely appropriate. At this point the copy editor must take over, conferring with the author and working on the manuscript so that the final copy will be read and will have the desired effect on the reader.

A good writer, thoroughly familiar with the purposes and policies of a publication, will edit his own copy and thereby win the blessing of the editor. Many a writer, either through inexperience or incomplete instructions, submits a manuscript that is illogical, unclear, or uninteresting, or all three. Despite these faults, it may be a "must" for the publication because it carries the by-line of a big name, because it is technically accurate and significant though unreadable, or because it is newsworthy and unique. If this is true, the manuscript is worth the editing required to make it acceptable.

Copy editing may include complete rearrangement, revision, or rewriting. Or it may mean only slight polishing and pepping up. How far to go in copy editing will depend upon the state of the original manuscript, the policy of the publication, and the initiative and fortitude of the copy editor. If he goes too far, he may offend the holy of holies in his trade or staff; if he does not go far enough, he may be accused of passing on dull, unreadable copy. Hitting the proper balance between these two comes from long experience with reviving dead copy and close acquaintance with the policies and personnel of the publication for which it is being prepared.

"Is it logical?" is probably the first test to put to a manuscript to be copy-edited. All too often a manuscript suffers from the disorderly thinking of the writer who has omitted some step in the argument, backtracked or repeated, or wandered around without any plan or logic. A good check on this is to list the topic of each paragraph (since a paragraph should be unified around one central theme) and trace the writer's thinking—or lack of it. This will be a good guide as to what to omit, what to rearrange, what to add.

"Is it clear?" may be the next test. Are the words understandable and vivid? Are the sentences short enough to be clear? Is each paragraph unified and arranged in the best relation to the other paragraphs? When the copy editor has finished, the answer should be "Yes" to each of these.

Finally, "Is it interesting?" Obviously it must be both logical and clear to be interesting, but being interesting requires more than orderly reasoning and clear wording.

To be interesting a manuscript must have a good lead which will hold the reader's attention, and must treat the subject from the point of view of what will interest and help the reader. The lead may be that of the news reporter who often starts out with one or more of the five W's—who, what, where, when, why. Or it may be the lead of the feature writer who piques the reader's curiosity by some provocative statement or pertinent incident. It is seldom the lead of the dry historian who reviews the whole history of his topic before he gets to that topic, or even announces what it is. It is not the lead of the apologist who throws up several paragraphs of explanation and qualification, before he plunges into his subject. With manuscripts from such writers (and there are many in the professional and technical fields) the copy editor may do well to upend the whole job, putting the history at the end and the explanation or apology in a footnote if it is really needed.

The big test of a manuscript's being interesting goes beyond the lead to the words, figures of speech, and details of the whole thing. Interest is created by strong, colorful nouns and vigorous verbs which carry the action or thought forward. Specific details, actual quotes, and sharp incidents should replace the fuzzy verbiage, vague generalizations, and blurred images of the dull writer.

The importance of copy editing assumes greater proportions every day as new publications and new communication media compete for the reader's time. The day is past when an editor could complacently approve dull copy with the explanation or apology that "Our readers have to read this even though it is dull because it is authoritative in their field." That may have been true when reading material was so scarce that the reader could not be selective. Today every piece of copy has to compete for the reader's time. It must compete with films, radio, television, color photography, digest magazines, pocket-size books, comic books, 25-cent whodunits, and the general magazines. Whether it gets read or not will depend in part on the copy editing.

Perhaps the most common error of the copy editor is to suppose that he can simplify a topic he does not fully understand himself. In such cases it is imperative that he let the author see all changes. Otherwise real boners can occur, as when a copy editor "simplifies" *voltage* to *current* in a piece about electricity or *random* to *haphazard* in a piece about statistics.

copyfitting See also COPY PREPARATION.

The problem of making the copy fit the space arises in even the simplest publications and has to be solved somehow, whether by cutting copy, adding copy, or changing the kind, size, or leading of the type—or by a combination of these measures.

The easiest method of copyfitting avoids mathematics entirely and requires only the use of a typewriter. Suppose, for example, the problem is to write just enough copy to fill 10 lines of type as used in this book. Put a piece of paper in the typewriter and start to copy a few lines from the book, line for line, as shown in the illustration. It will soon become apparent about how long a line of typewriting will make one line of printer's type. It is now only necessary to write enough to fill 10 typewritten lines of the indicated length. It can be assumed that this amount of copy will also fill 10 lines when set in type, give or take a line.

The same method can be applied to caption writing. Just type up an old caption of the desired style and length, and then compose a new caption that will have the same number of typed characters. It will fit the same space as the old caption when set in type.

The trial line or lines can be taken from a back number of a magazine, from a printer's type book, or what you will. If you cannot find a sample of the right width, there is no harm in using

fractions of lines. For example, if you want the kind of type used in this book but in a 3-in. width (18 picas), copy one full column (13 picas) plus 5 picas from the adjoining column for your trial lines.

The reason why this system works is because typewriters always write the same number of characters per inch. Some have pica type and write 10 characters per inch; others have elite type and write 12 characters per inch, but whichever it is, you can count on it, and count by it.

This is pica type
1234567890
This is elite type
123456789012

Printer's types will also average a predictable number of characters per inch, the number varying with the type. It is true that the "w" and "m" are wider than the "i" and "l," but usually these differences average out. Note, however, that in printer's type the caps are wider than small letters, and this is *not* true on the ordinary typewriter. You must not inadvertently count from an all-cap model caption and then change to caps and lowercase.

Therefore, if you find that your specimen lines, when typed, average 3 in. wide on an elite typewriter, and if you type your copy to that width, you need only count your typewritten lines to determine how many lines of printer's type you are going to get.

However, if your copy is already typed to a different width, it is not necessary to retype it in order to estimate the number of lines of type it will make. Instead, rule a line vertically on your copy to show how much of each line will make one line of type, and estimate the overage. Are your manuscript lines half again as long as will fill a line of type? Then you will get half again as many lines of type as you have manuscript lines. Sometimes you can just estimate the overage, counting the full lines in each paragraph and estimating how many additional lines will be made by the excess of words to the right of your guideline. On short copy it is sometimes easy enough to mark off the length of your trial lines on the edge of a piece of paper, and use this measure to mark off the probable line breaks, as shown in the illustration.

You can do all your copyfitting by matching typed manuscript lines to typed trial lines, as outlined above, but for some work there are advantages to the so-called "character-count" method. This method is not as complicated as it is sometimes made to sound when you realize that 1 in. is 12 characters (12 letters or spaces) on an elite typewriter, 10 on a pica typewriter.

Before plunging into character counting, however, the beginner should be warned that he *must* understand printer's measurements. He must know that a pica (besides being a kind of typewriter type) is a unit of measurement. Sooner or later he must learn to use

this term in specifying column widths, etc. He must know that there are 12 points to the pica, 6 picas to the inch, 72 points to the inch. (See TYPE MEASUREMENTS.) Too many beginners try to slide by points and picas. Do not do it. There are 12 points to the pica, 6 picas to the inch, 72 points to the inch. Repeat that until you know it. Do not read on until you are sure of it.

Once you are equipped to think in points and picas, you should have no great difficulty with character counting if you will take time to work through a few examples. Remember that basically all you are doing is figuring characters per line, lines per page, etc. If you get confused, forget the tables and just count characters, taking any shortcuts that occur to you.

Suppose, for example, you have a 10-page typewritten manuscript with 25 lines on each page averaging 6 in. each. A pica typewriter has been used, so the typing is 10 characters to the inch.

```
Suppose, for example, the problem is
to write just enough copy to fill 10
lines of type as used in this book.  Put
a piece of paper in the typewriter and
start to copy a few lines from the book,
line for line, as shown in the illustra-
tion.  It will soon become apparent
about how long a line of typewriting
will make one line of printer's type.
```

```
    However, if your copy is already typed to a
different width, it is not necessary to retype
it in order to estimate the number of lines of
type it will make.  Instead, rule a line verti-
cally on your copy to show how much of each line
will make one line of type and estimate the
overage.  On short copy it is easy enough to
mark off the length of your trial lines on the
edge of a piece of paper, and use this measure
to mark off the probable line breaks, as shown
in the illustration.
```

This means 60 characters per 6-in. line. Multiplying characters per line by lines per page by number of pages (60 × 25 × 10), you get a total character count of 15,000. You are now in a position to calculate how many lines this will make in any type face you like. For example, if you choose a kind, size, and width of type that assays 50 characters to the line, your 15,000 characters will make 300 lines. If you are going to get only 40 characters per line of type, you will come out with 375 lines.

An easy way to figure out how many characters you will get per line of type is to find some specimen lines, count several, and take an average. Some think the counting goes more easily if you typewrite the lines first, after which the count can be made with the aid of a ruler.

However, there are tables from which you can learn the character count of each kind and size of type. The counts are usually given in terms of characters per pica. Suppose you are thinking of setting the above-mentioned manuscript of 15,000 characters in 9-pt Baskerville (Lino), 13 picas wide, the same type used in this book. The tables will tell you (see page 372) that this type averages 2.95 characters per pica. From this figure, the conversion table on page 374 indicates that your 13-pica line will contain 38 characters. Dividing this into 15,000 characters gives 394 lines of type.

The next question is, how many pages will be required for 394 lines of type?

Count a full column on a page of this book and you will find there are 51 lines per column, 102 lines per page. At that rate 394 lines will require just under 4 pages.

If you are working on a book like this one in which the type has been selected, and is not to be changed, that is your answer. Your manuscript will require just under 4 pages. If you must allow for heads and subheads you will have to cut a few lines. However, if you are free to change the type specifications, you can, without cutting, save more room for headings in various ways. You can put more lines per column, use less space between lines, widen the lines, or choose a more compact type face.

For example, putting 52 lines into each column would gain 2 lines per page, 8 lines on 4 pages. Or you might notice that, although this is 9-pt type, it takes up more than 9 points of space. Since there are 72 points to the inch, you ought to get 8 lines of 9-pt type to the inch, but on this page you are getting only about 7. The reason is that this is 9-pt type leaded 1 point, or 9 pt on a 10 pt body. You are actually getting close to 7.2 lines per inch, 51 per column. Change this to 9-pt solid (unleaded) and you could have 56 lines per column (8 per inch, 7 in.). That would make 112 lines per page, 448 lines in 4 pages. Or you could widen the columns by a pica, and gain about 3 characters per line, 300 characters per page, 1,200 over 4 pages. Or you could go to a more compact type face like 9-pt Granjon, which averages 3.16 characters per pica, or about 41 per 13-pica line. At 41 characters per line, 15,000 characters would require only about 366 lines, well under 4 pages.

Probably the easiest and one of the most common jobs of copyfitting is to write "to space." Here you just copy a few trial lines of material set in the specified face, count or calculate the number of lines required, and then write the needed number of lines of new copy in the indicated width. The simplest way to do this, as noted above, is to set your typewriter to the right width of line, and then write the needed number of lines.

The problem of figuring the lines of type required for a given manuscript to be set in a given face and size is also simple. Just see how many times one line's worth of characters will go into the manuscript.

The toughest problem is to select the

kind of type, size of type, and leading that will permit a given manuscript to be put into a given space. Usually this problem is solved on a trial-and-error basis. Pick the type you would *like* to use and estimate the space it requires. If your copy does not fit, at least you will know immediately whether you are close or not, and can try again. Note that a relatively small change of type size makes a surprisingly large change in the number of characters you can get into a given space. This is because a smaller size of type will give you not only more characters per line, but also more lines per column inch.

Several devices intended to speed or simplify character counting and copy-fitting are described under these headings: HABERULE VISUAL COPY-CASTER; STREAMLINED COPY FITTING METHOD; CHARACTER COUNT.

For further information on copy-fitting, see the information given in Appendix 1, Type Faces.

copying See PHOTOCOPYING.

copy preparation See also EDITORIAL PLANNING; COPY EDITING; PROOFREADING.

Before manuscript copy is sent to the printer, it should undergo a careful process known as "preparation of copy for the printer." This is the place at which a few strokes of an editor's pencil can save many dollars in type corrections later.

The essentials of copy preparation can be outlined as follows:

1. Policy O.K. The man with the deciding voice says, "Let's publish this." If he has been in on the planning from the beginning, he is likely to give the final O.K. more readily.

2. Careful scrutiny of copy to catch any inconsistencies, anachronisms, inaccuracies, etc., and to fill in any missing data.

3. Writing or rewriting headlines, by-lines, boxed material, captions, credit lines, subheads, etc., that may have been omitted.

4. Rough castoff, or character count (see COPYFITTING), to determine the space required; decision on layout and type; necessary cutting or expanding of text, headlines, captions, etc., to fit layout.

5. Scrutiny for proper paragraphing, sentence structure, grammar, spelling, and punctuation. For authoritative guidance in correct forms, the University of Chicago "Manual of Style" (see Appendix 2, Bibliography) is excellent. In addition, many editors work out their own style sheet to be used by each staff member. (See STYLE SHEET.)

6. Retyping. The printer is entitled to clean, double-spaced copy, typed on one side only of 8½- by 11-in. paper with ample margins at top and sides for his type markings. He charges extra for time wasted over illegible copy. The printer has no objections to erasures or xxxx's or partly filled pages, but he may have difficulty with handwritten corrections.

7. Marking for type (see TYPE). This may be the responsibility of a layout man, not the editor, but editors often do it whether or not they are their own layout men. Of course, the type to be used should have been determined when layout plans were made, taking into account whether the printer has the kind of type that is specified or will get it.

To prevent loss, manuscript copy ready for the printer should plainly indicate the job for which it is being set: issue of magazine, title of book or pamphlet, name of customer, etc. All pages should be numbered consecutively, and renumbered if pages are added or deleted. If it is necessary to insert pages 11A and 11B, be sure to mark plainly on page 11, "See also pages 11A and 11B." Otherwise the added pages could get lost with nobody the wiser. Do not clip or pin corrected and retyped paragraphs to the manuscript; pasting is safer.

On the last page of manuscript copy,

School Executive

Engelhardt

The Annual Report to the Public) *24 pt. Bodoni Bold*
                                 Ital cr l.c. fl. left

10/11 Bod Bold
fl. left   (By N. L. Engelhardt

8/9 Bod. Bold /Associate Superintendent of Schools
fl. left

             \New York City

10/12 Bod. Bold /With a true sense of responsibility, the superintendent makes his annual
Ital. 2 even
lines fl. left \report to the people an accounting of their children and their schools.

[Among school administrators the term "annual report"   *10/10 Oldstyle #1*

has come to mean the report prepared for public con-   *on 20 pi*

sumption. To be sure, reporting annually to the Board

of Education on all phases of school developments is

a service rendered by all good administrators. Such

reporting may snowball into considerable volume.

Each year the selection of material for the report

to the public results from the acceptance of cer-

tain criteria. These include timeliness, novelty,

emergent needs, expansion requirements, maintenance

of support, arousal of interest and frequently re-

6 pts. ld. → porting for information only.

               The Early Reports)——————— *10 pt Bodoni Bold*
4 pts. ld. →   *cr lc centered*
               Printed annual reports are as old as formalized   *on 20 pi*

public education programs in American communities.

Neale records a Boston report of 1738 and a Hart-

ford report of 1767. He states that (seventy-one)

Massachusetts communities were issuing reports by

1846. The underlying purposes differed little

The above copy has been typed to column width and marked for the printer. Note the specific directions for every line of copy or block of copy: (1) size of type to be used, (2) type face, (3) italic or not, (4) location—centered, flush left, etc.—and (5) leading or spacing between lines.

ok
H.J.T. 9/10

25—SchoolExecu

MAZEAU—NIGHT APRIL 1—MACHINE **7**
SCHOOL EXEC. 10 on 10 Oldstyle 20 PICAS
SLUG—ENGELHARDT
THE ANNUAL REPORT TO THE PUBLIC

The Annual
Report to the Public

By N. L. ENGELHARDT
Associate Superintendent of Schools
New York City

l.c. WITH a true sense of public responsibility the superintendent makes *his*
annual report to the people a accounting of their children and their school

AMONG school administrators the term annual report
has come to mean the report prepared for public con-
sumption. To be sure, reporting annually to the board
of education on all phases of school developments is a
service rendered by all good administrators. Such
reporting may snowball into considerable volume.

Each year the selection of material for the report
to the public results from the acceptance of certain
criteria. These include timeliness, novelty, emergent
needs, expansion requirements, maintenance of support, arousal of interest and frequently reporting for
information only.

The Early Reports

Printed annual reports are as old as formalized public education programs in American communities.
Neale[1] records a Boston report of 1738 and a Hartford

FOOTNOTE

School Reports by N. L. Neale. Missouri Book Co., 1921.

report of 1767. He states that 71 Massachusetts communities were issuing reports by 1846. The underlying
purposes differed little from those of today. Throughout this early school literature, certain reasons for reporting appear quite frequently. Almost invariably
the reports give the number of school children, and
comment on the quality of instruction, state the nature
of grants and appropriations, enumerate the advantages
arising from education to individuals and the public,
present a written report on the conduct and condition
of the schools.

For many years the desirability of having annual
reports has been emphasized through legislation. In
many states annual reports are required by law and
their contents prescribed. Thus for certain kinds of
reports, purposes are designated by law. They are
usually associated with budgets and financial
tions, board of educati

The same copy, now set in galley 25, has been proofread and marked for correction by the printer. (See proofreaders' marks under *proofreading*.)

mark "end." This will enable the printer to know that he has lost no pages.

These precautions are necessary because manuscripts which were once stapled are usually unstapled while being set and may indeed be divided between two or more compositors.

It is human nature to postpone any writing until just before the deadline and to complete it while the printer's messenger is waiting, if then. In such circumstances, the temptation to skimp on copy preparation is strong. Somehow the need to get copy freshly typed always presents itself most strongly just after the last typist has gone home for the day.

It should be remembered, however, that poor copy preparation is an expensive luxury and that a single correction in a galley may easily cost $1 or more.

Excellent pointers on copy preparation are given in "Words into Type," published by Appleton-Century-Crofts, Inc. (New York, 1964).

copyright The rules for copyright applications may be obtained by writing to the Copyright Office, Library of Congress, Washington, D.C. 20540.

There are procedures for protecting unpublished materials as well as published materials.

Plots, titles, slogans, ideas, and news cannot be copyrighted. (However see TRADEMARKS.)

copywriting See also COPY EDITING; COPY PREPARATION; EDITORIAL PLANNING; EDITORIAL WORK.

Copywriting is here considered to be the initial writing of a manuscript as distinguished from the rewriting, revising, and polishing discussed under copy editing. (See COPY EDITING.)

To the editor copy means any written matter—news story, poem, editorial, advertisement, photo caption. It means written matter that is to entertain, to in-struct, or to sell. Hence, the term "copywriting" could refer to any kind of writing. In printing and advertising circles it is generally used in the more workaday sense—writing in order to stimulate the reader to some definite action or new way of thinking.

Such copy is generally written to persuade the reader to a course of action. It is thus "selling" copy whether the desired action is buying certain merchandise or voting in a certain way. Only reading matter wholly paid for by the reader is likely to have amusement or instruction as its sole objective.

General slant. The copywriter must first know the product or idea that he is trying to sell. This idea may have been staked out in the earlier stage of editorial planning (see EDITORIAL PLANNING), but almost invariably he will have to do further research to determine the appeals that he is going to use to achieve the desired objective.

Experienced advertising copywriters, as well as fund raisers and organizers, have found that virtually every piece of copy of proved effectiveness appeals to the self-interest of the reader. It immediately answers his natural questions: "What's in it for me? What pleasure or profit will I derive from reading this or from doing or believing what the writer suggests?"

Copywriters are frequently cynics. Many of the most successful assume that no one does anything except for reasons of personal pleasure or profit. Apparent altruism is usually grounded in a desire to gain the good opinion of others, or at least to appease the conscience. The basic appeals used by copywriters are sometimes summarized as (1) desire for personal adequacy and social recognition, (2) desire for romance, (3) desire for long life, (4) desire to make money, (5) desire to save money, (6) desire to save time, (7) desire to save energy, (8) desire for comfort.

Equally important is knowing the age

level, economic condition, special interests, and prejudices of the audience. A reader is more likely to be moved by copy that seems to be written just for him, in the words that he might use himself, and with the tone that he has come to expect of his most trusted neighbor or business adviser.

Planning the whole. The usual construction of a piece of copy is (1) get attention so that the copy is sure to be read, (2) create interest and desire, (3) establish conviction by proving each claim or each point of the argument, (4) get action by giving an incentive, showing the means for immediate action asking directly for that action. These ingredients are as important in general advertising as in mail-order work, even if it is more difficult to check the results.

Most copywriters begin by making a checklist of points to be included in the copy. Some go further and develop a detailed outline to ensure complete coverage and strategic arrangement of the salient points. The opening sentences of a piece of copy must catch the reader's interest, or he may never read further. They must convince him that here is something that will help or amuse him. A good lead puts him in a receptive frame of mind, curious enough to read on and responsive to the story that he must already anticipate. In skillful hands the lead is an integral part of the story, setting the tone and pace of that which follows.

News reporters developed a sort of formula for their leads. At one time practically every news story began with the five W's—who, what, when, where, and why. With this formula, the first sentence gives the meat of the story, and the harried reader knows whether to read on or pass to the next news item.

Feature writers frequently put their lead in the form of a question or a believe-it-or-not attention getter. They may also play on the emotions and use some appealing detail as the lead. Thus they pique the reader's curiosity and at the same time set the tone for the whole story.

Digressive leads seem to offer a beguiling pitfall for the novice. He begins by passing the time of day with some irrelevant observation, apparently on the theory that his main point is not of itself interesting. This is a fatal state of mind in which to write copy. Either what he has to say is in some way of interest to the reader or his efforts are foredoomed to failure.

Making it readable. The importance of writing copy that will be read has led to the development of many formulas and tests for readable copy. Perhaps the best known is that developed by Rudolf Flesch and described in his book "The Art of Readable Writing" (Harper & Row, 1949, $3.95). Whether or not a writer wishes to use the Flesch yardstick, he will find it helpful to check his copy on the four main points in the Flesch test: (1) the number of words in an average sentence, (2) the number of affixes per 100 words, (3) the number of personal words, and (4) the number of personal sentences. From these data Flesch proceeds to get what he calls a "Reading Ease Score" and a "Human Interest Score."

Copy suitable for 75 percent of the adults in the United States is classed as "standard," seventh- to eighth-grade level, and typical of the digest magazines. Standard copy has 17 words in the average sentence, 37 affixes in 100 words, and at least 7 percent personal words and 15 percent personal sentences. In similar manner, Flesch describes six other degrees of readability from "very easy" (the comic-book level readable for 90 percent of the adults in the United States) to "very difficult" (the scientific level readable for only 4½ percent of the adults). He also explains how to sample and test readability.

One farm magazine experimented with the very easy and standard versions of the same material and found that the former brought far greater readership.

In his book, Flesch points out other qualities of readable copy—qualities which are less easily measured but which are frequently dependent upon the four bases of his tests and table. His thoroughly down-to-earth comments and his emphasis on the personal and human qualities make his yardstick more than a scientific test.

One editor uses the following test on the work of his copywriters:

1. Are the words familiar?
2. Are the sentences short?
3. Are they varied to relieve the monotony of the usual subject-verb-object pattern?
4. Is each paragraph short and well unified?
5. Does everything contribute to the one big object or conclusion?
6. Is the argument so simple and logical that the reader can remember the main points?

Many editors have less formal requirements but agree that simplicity is the key to readability for the average person.

Heads, subheads, and captions. Writing good titles or heads is just as important as writing good text copy, for the title must sell the article to the reader. The title or head should introduce the article in vigorous, "selling" words. Current practice favors a strong, simple verb as the keynote in a title, or a few vivid nouns.

Heads and subheads may be all that the reader sees as he scans a page. If they are well written, they will give him the story in essence. They can be so provocative that he feels compelled to read the whole story. Even if they only warn him away from stories that would not interest him, they have served a purpose.

Pictures get attention before printed words. The caption under a picture will be read before printed columns of copy. It merits good copy—clear, concise, and to the point. Instead of merely echoing the message of the picture, the caption should carry the reader on to the body of the story or to a pertinent point in the argument. Thus, the caption under three pictures on a page could drive home three significant phases of the central idea or message. (See CAPTIONS.)

Good copywriting techniques are discussed in many of the books listed with annotations in Appendix 2, Bibliography. A few key pointers on copywriting are as follows:

Before you start to write. 1. Know your product. Use it, read it, experiment with it. You cannot do justice to a book you have not read or a product you have not used. It is hard to warm over someone else's copy and improve it unless you know more than he did about the product. If you do not personally care for the product, find someone who does and talk to him. Talk to the author or editor or inventor or designer or engineer. Be sure you know every feature. And if it is a revised or improved product, learn about the changes and why they were made.

2. Know your audience. Do not take any mailing list on faith; run through some of the names and you may get some big surprises. Know all the lists you could be using. Write a different letter to each group if the arguments could be different. Study former buyers. Study the complaint file, if there is one. Work at a retail store or a convention booth for a while. Look over the orders as they come in. Be sure you know everything you possibly can about those for whom you are writing.

3. Know your marketing setup. Are your prospects used to buying by mail, or in stores, or how? Will the store they might go to have the product, or know about it? Will they think they know how to get it for less than the sum you quote? Will they send cash or expect to be billed? Will you send on approval? Be sure you know where your

audience will be buying what you offer so you can ask for the right kind of action.

When you start to write. 1. Start by asking yourself, "What's in this for the prospect?" If there are several advantages, list them all in the order of importance.

2. Now enumerate all possible objections that the prospect might raise. Be sure each objection is countered with a plus argument—and plainly so, for the prospect must not be left with any doubts unanswered. In fact, you can often answer objections without stating them and indeed can turn an objection inside out and make it seem like an advantage to the reader.

3. Prove your points. Testimonials will help, for the reader will not always take your word alone for what you claim. Use pictures if they will help. Cite statistics if you have persuasive ones, for figures make a greater impression than generalities as a rule.

4. Present the price as if it were an inexpensive alternate to some far more costly course. Guarantee satisfaction or a quick refund. Make ordering easy and quote postpaid or delivered prices.

5. Beware of the too transparent questionnaire or phony claim, e.g., that the sales letter is a Gallup poll when it is not at all.

6. Beware of claiming too much for your product or idea.

7. Emphasize sincerity above slickness. Remember that the right arguments presented to the right prospects with the ring of sincerity will get orders.

8. Strive for a conversational style. Any style you would not use in describing your item to a friend is probably wrong for a selling letter. Your purpose is not to impress the reader with your clever style, but to win him as an interested reader and a potential customer.

9. Favor the word "you." It is rarely overused. The first word of the first sentence will get more attention if it begins with that winning word, YOU.

10. Do not be too familiar. After all,

your readers will probably include all kinds of people and some may be irritated if they suspect that you are trying to backslap them into buying.

11. Do not be cocksure or patronizing or pontifical. The recipient may well know more than the writer, and it will hardly increase his confidence in you or your product if he suspects you are trying to talk down to him.

12. On the other hand, do not assume too much knowledge on the part of the reader. If you try to use trade jargon or office slang, you are likely to confuse him and annoy him a bit as well.

13. Try all copy on a few guinea pigs, paying particular attention to any points over which they seem to stumble. Often a word that can be either a noun or an adjective is read wrong at first glance and requires rereading if the passage is to be untangled. Such spots are hard for the writer to find by himself because he naturally reads the correct meaning into the equivocal word.

14. Beware of phrase worship. There comes a time in the writing of a piece of copy when it may be time-saving to put away all previous drafts and try a new version away from the highsounding phrases which seemed so deft on the first go-round. Really telling phrases from your early drafts will come to mind easily, but some that sounded so fine and meant so little will usually drop out of your way once they are out of sight. Deft phrasing is always pleasant, but it can never take the place of a good initial idea, logical order, and persuasive exposition of ideas.

15. Avoid beginning a sentence with a participial clause as a weak and often unrelated part of the whole.

16. Avoid verbal clichés, but do not be afraid to ask for the order in the straight talk that customers expect.

17. Go gently with humor. Some ad writers can get away with it, but most of us lack the gift. Besides, even the best humor passes some people by or leaves them annoyed because they miss the

point altogether or because it does not appeal to their taste.

18. Statistics are a good weapon, but a double-edged sword. You can prove anything with figures and many of your readers know it. If you distort, some will catch you and your rating will slip in their eyes.

19. Respect the prospect's time. Get to the point immediately and keep your copy brief and interesting.

coquille A drawing technique based on the use of drawing paper that has a surface consisting of raised dots. (See STIPPLE; ROSS BOARD; for an example, see DRAWING TECHNIQUES.)

costs See also SAVING MONEY; ESTIMATING COSTS.

Approximate cost figures are given in this book under several entries. (See CIRCULARS; PAMPHLETS; MIMEOGRAPH; OFFSET, etc.) All costs are based on actual prices quoted by commercial firms. It is assumed that a firm operating its own printing and duplicating equipment will find that its own costs are comparable when labor and overhead are properly accounted for. Although each figure quoted is an actual one, another buyer, in another city and at another time, may well expect to be quoted a different figure, perhaps higher, perhaps lower.

cover paper See also PAPER; CARDBOARD.

Paper suitable for the covers of pamphlets. Some weights are as light as text paper but are available in special colors and finishes. Other grades are two to four times as heavy as text paper. Cover paper comes uncoated and coated in the same variety as text paper. Basic weights for cover paper are related to the basic size, 20 by 26. (See table under PAPER SIZES AND WEIGHTS.)

Craft-Color Thin acetate sheets in 19 bright colors with adhesive backing used for making color layouts, posters, package designs, sales charts, etc., manufactured by the Craftint Manufacturing Co., 18501 Euclid Ave., Cleveland 12, Ohio.

Craftint Trade name of Craftint Manufacturing Co., 18501 Euclid Ave., Cleveland 12, Ohio, makers of Craft-Tone Singletone and Doubletone shading tints, Craf-Type, Craft-Color, etc. (See SHADING TINTS; also DRAWING TECHNIQUES.)

Craf-Type See ARTYPE.

creasing See SCORING.

credit lines Photo agencies require a credit line under a published photo, e.g., "Acme photo," under penalty of additional royalty. Publications extending the right to reprint a cartoon or other item almost invariably insist on a credit line. Both courtesy and fair play require it in any case so that the artist or photographer will have due recognition.

The credit line is usually placed flush right immediately below the photo or cartoon, or is printed in the last line of the caption.

Since credit lines are easily overlooked, editors often train themselves to make one extra page-proof check just to see whether all credit lines are in order. They know that any omission makes trouble, while free and accurate use of credit lines, even when not actually required, makes friends.

Some magazines omit credit lines under individual pictures and print them in one paragraph on one page.

crop, cropping See also SCALING; PHOTOGRAPHS.

To crop a piece of artwork or photograph means to indicate that only a portion of its area is to be reproduced, not the whole. The editor or designer will indicate by "crop marks" exactly how much is to be reproduced. The printer or engraver will follow these marks and reproduce the desired area in the desired size. (The original photograph or drawing is never physically cut, of course.)

Crop marks may be placed on the artwork itself (but not within the area to be reproduced) or on an "overlay," or on both.

Since overlays may be torn off or go askew, it is safest to put crop marks on the original, mounting the artwork or the photo on a larger board if extra margins are needed. A tissue overlay may still be used to help visualize the cropping called for or merely to protect the original.

Photos can easily be damaged in cropping and scaling. (See PHOTO-GRAPHS: CARE IN HANDLING.) A photograph should never be under any paper that is being written on. Even a soft pencil can make depressions in the glossy surface that may show in reproduction.

A grease pencil should be used to indicate the cropping of a glossy photographic print since grease marks will rub off with a cloth or tissue.

Most photos need cropping, either to eliminate unimportant background or to alter their proportions.

The editor or art director who indicates where a photograph is to be cropped must try to visualize a part of the picture with the rest cropped out. It is important to remember that while a photograph is not necessarily cropped to the same size as the finished reproduction, it must be cropped in the same proportions. For example, a 6 by 6 area on a photograph, when reduced or enlarged, will always produce a square cut. But if a 3 by 4 cut is needed in the final reproduction, the photo must be cropped in that proportion of height to width.

One good procedure is this: With white envelopes or file cards cover the portions of the picture that are not to be reproduced. Those placed horizontally will eliminate unwanted sky and foreground; those placed vertically

This picture can be improved by cropping. At present it includes several loosely connected groups and a needless amount of foreground and background. The groups on the sidelines look posed and rather uninterested in the central group—a fact that is distracting to the reader. (*Courtesy of Cincinnati Public Schools.*)

will eliminate unwanted areas at left and right. In this way an 8 by 10 print may yield an essential area of perhaps 7 by 7, or even 3 by 4 in., etc.

Suppose the essential part of your picture is square, whereas a 3 by 4 cut is needed. In that case, the covering envelopes or cards may be adjusted so that some sky or foreground is restored to give the proper proportions. Then, with a grease pencil, mark as guides the four corners of the exposed area. Remove the cards or envelopes, and using one of them as a ruler, mark in the margins the extension of the four guide points. Bring the overlay down and trace the marginal guidelines. Then, lifting it from the photo, draw in pencil the rectangle that is identical with the desired area of the photo.

Draw a diagonal of this rectangle on the tissue overlay, which can then be placed on the layout to check the space required by the photo reproduction when reduced. (See SCALING for exact method.)

Where the area allotted to the illustration is unalterable, the photo must be cropped to fit that space. Sometimes, the layout requires a vertical picture when the only one available is stubbornly horizontal in shape and cannot be cropped to a vertical shape without losing vital areas. There may be no remedy but to get a new layout or a new photo. (Good layout men try to let the photos dictate the layout plan.) Sometimes tricks are resorted to, such as having the retoucher add more sky. (See RETOUCHING.)

Cropping requires an eye for balance and composition. The photographer does the first part when he crops nature by pointing the camera. He crops again when he decides whether to use all or part of the negative in making his prints. If his pictures arrive in assorted shapes, he has already indicated the cropping he suggests. If, however, all his photos are on 8 by 10 paper, it is evident that some will need further crop-

This cropping of the larger photograph makes it much more effective. Distracting elements are eliminated. Attention is focused on the main action of the picture. (*Courtesy of Cincinnati Public Schools.*)

ping since nature does not always conform to the 8 by 10 proportion.

No matter what the shape of the print, it is worth remembering that there may be more picture on the negative than shows on the print. If a layout demands a broader or a taller shape, it may be possible to go back to the negative for a print of the desired proportions.

Cropping is an art and follows the general rules of good artistic composition and balance. For example, if in a portrait a man is shown in profile, it is customary to allow a little more space in the direction in which he is looking, less behind him. If there is space between figures, it is customary to allow equal or greater space around them.

In many instances, it is better to single out one or two appealing faces in a crowd than to reproduce the entire group. Careful cropping avoids beheading people in the photos or arbitrarily making amputees of them.

To determine just how artwork will look after cropping and reduction, a photostat can be made to scale, trimmed to the crop marks, and tried on the layout.

cursive Cursive letters are those resembling handwriting with rounded form and strokes that join or give that effect.

Lydian Italic

Lydian Cursive

cut See also LINECUT; HALFTONE.

"Cut" is a word-of-all-work commonly used to mean engraving, linecut, or halftone, or even to refer to a picture printed from these. One sends artwork to the engraver and orders "cuts" made, or checks page proofs to make sure that each "cut" has its credit line.

Practically speaking, only one printing process uses cuts, namely, letterpress (relief) printing. (See LETTERPRESS.) The other processes print from one big plate containing both type and illustrations. Therefore, cuts are not required for offset, photogravure, photogelatin, or silk screen, nor can they be used. One can, however, send the printer artwork and have him reproduce it in line or in halftone.

The simplest kind of cut explains the name. It is a woodcut with the non-printing areas cut away by an artist to leave the lines of a drawing or diagram which is to be printed. Metal, rubber, and linoleum surfaces are also used, blocked so as to be type-high. The most familiar kind of cut is perhaps the common rubber stamp, although this is more often molded than "cut." (See RUBBER STAMPS.)

Engravers formerly made cuts by copying the artist's drawing by hand on metal or wood. Nowadays a line drawing is transferred photographically to a metal surface, after which the metal unprotected by the image is eaten away (etched) with acid.

There are two important classes of cuts or engravings: (1) the linecut and (2) the halftone, sometimes called "halftone cut" or "halftone engraving." (See LINECUT; HALFTONE.)

Line drawings containing no grays as distinct from blacks or whites can be reproduced as linecuts. Photographs, wash drawings, and other artwork containing grays or middle tones, which are neither solid black nor pure white, must be reproduced as halftones.

Line drawings include drawings done in pen and ink, in brush and ink (undiluted black ink), in ink spatter technique, etc. Halftone reproduction is necessary for photographs, wash drawings, pencil sketches, etc. (See illustrations under DRAWING TECHNIQUES.)

In case of doubt, a printer or photoengraver can always explain whether a given piece of artwork should be reproduced in line or in halftone; in borderline cases, he may be able to suggest minor retouching to permit the making of a linecut from art that might otherwise have to be reproduced in halftone.

Halftones usually cost more than linecuts and must be ordered in the "screen" appropriate for the paper to be used. The two processes are more fully described under LINECUT and HALFTONE.

It is true that plates have to be made in order to produce "engraved" calling cards by the intaglio process (see INTAGLIO), but these are called "plates" or "engraved plates," not cuts. In a true engraving, the design is graven into the printing plate with a "graver," and is printed by the intaglio process. In a cut, the design is brought into "relief" by cutting away all areas that are not to print, and it is printed by the relief process. However, the word "engraving" is today used loosely as a synonym for cut. For cuts, one goes to a photoengraver; for real intaglio engravings, one goes to a steel engraver.

The cost of cuts often influences the choice of a printing process. It almost always costs less to reproduce either line or halftone artwork in offset than in letterpress. On the other hand, the offset process is sometimes inferior to letterpress on photographic work, equal on line work, superior on delicate pencil sketches.

cut-in head This paragraph has been set to include a "cut-in" subhead. This style, often found in textbooks, is particularly useful in securing extra variety and emphasis in typewritten ma-

Example of Cut-in Subhead terial. It is, however, a style that makes extra trouble for the type compositor and, therefore, costs considerably more than subheads that are centered, indented, or run flush left.

cutouts See DIE CUTTING.

cutting See also DIE CUTTING.

Almost all printers have machinery for cutting and trimming paper both before and after printing. Paper cutters can cut paper on the square, or even make a straight angular cut. Special equipment is needed for round-cornering, punching, and die cutting into special shapes. (See DIE CUTTING.)

It is necessary to let the ink dry before printed material can be cut. Otherwise, one printed sheet may "offset" onto the back of the next under the pressure of the cutter.

There are cutters that can make a cut 70 in. long. Most printers and binders have smaller equipment, perhaps not even big enough to handle a 38 by 50 or 35 by 45 ream. Therefore, it is advisable to check before ordering paper. It may be necessary to have the paper supply house cut it before delivery to the printer, or to have the printer cut it before delivery to the binder.

cutting copy See COPYFITTING; COPY PREPARATION.

cylinder presses See PRINTING PRESSES; FLATBED PRESS.

D | d

data capture This term covers any of the various methods of getting information into "machinable form," i.e., into a form suitable for direct input to typesetters, computers, or other automatic data-processing equipment. The chief methods of data capture are punched cards, punched paper tape, and the use of machine-readable alphabets. See entries under COMPUTER TYPESETTING; AUTOMATIC TYPEWRITER; CHARACTER RECOGNITION.

Davidson duplicator See FAIRCHILD-DAVIDSON OFFSET MACHINES.

Day-glo colors See LUMINESCENT PRINTING.

dead metal Areas not intended to print, including those areas on a cut or duplicate plate which are to be trimmed away or routed out. The term is sometimes used to refer to the "killed matter" thrown into the "hell box" ready for remelting.

decalcomanias In order to print the manufacturer's name and trademark on a vacuum cleaner, it is not necessary to run the machine through a printing press. Instead, a piece of paper can serve as "stand-in" for the vacuum cleaner; the desired design can be printed in full color on the paper; and the inks of the finished design can be transferred from it to the vacuum cleaner later on by a simple hand operation. This is the decalcomania process.

"Decals," after transfer, are as permanent as if they had been painted by hand on the surface. Some decals adhere through the use of varnish; some carry their own "stickative" which need only be moistened, yet which will become waterproof. (All decals have some lacquer for body and tensile strength.) In both types, the backing paper slides away when moistened, leaving only the ink film affixed to the side of the truck, the vacuum cleaner, the store window, or whatever it is.

Decals can be obtained in any size, with any type of artwork, and in any number of colors. For best results they should be used on smooth surfaces such as glass, metal, or enamel, or on surfaces that can be made smooth with a coat of varnish; special decals can be obtained for use on almost any surface. They can be affixed to surfaces that are curved in one dimension, but not to complex curves (any more than paper can be made to take the curve of a sphere).

The cost of decals is figured by the area, quantity, colors, and artwork. A simple decal, the size of a playing card, may run $12 to $20 per thousand, depending on the number of colors and quantity ordered.

Silk-screen decals tend to run a little cheaper than lithographed decals in small quantities and may be just as satisfactory unless the design is too delicate to reproduce in silk screen. Some suppliers who handle both kinds give quicker delivery on silk-screen decals. (See SILK SCREEN.)

A simple window decal is made as follows: A layer of transparent "stickative" is laid on a piece of porous paper. Many layers of opaque lacquer are then printed on top of the adhesive until a sufficiently strong film has been built up. Then the desired design is printed on this base layer, in one or more colors. Finally, another layer of adhesive finishes the decal.

If this decal is now moistened and applied to the inside of an automobile windshield so as to be readable from the outside, the wet backing paper will slide away and can be discarded. Or, the decal can be placed on the front of the windshield, and slid from the backing paper onto the glass.

Decals can also be made that are readable from both sides of the glass they adhere to.

When decals are ordered, specifications for their use should be given so that the manufacturer can get the design faced toward or away from the backing paper and can print the proper transfer instructions on the backing paper.

For the names of local decal suppliers, look under Decalcomanias in the Classified Telephone Directory. Companies handling all types of decal work include The Meyercord Company, 5323 W. Lake St., Chicago 44; and The American Decalcomania Company, 4344 W. 5th Ave., Chicago 24.

deckle edge Handmade paper comes with a feathery deckle edge on all four sides, unless trimmed. Machine-made paper has a deckle edge on two opposite sides until trimmed. The deckling runs with the grain on machine-made paper and occurs when the paper fibers at the edge of the web try to flow under the rubber dam or deckle that determines the width of the paper.

Deckle edges are usually trimmed off. They may be left for their decorative value on greeting cards, limited editions, etc.

deep-etch offset See also OFFSET.

For a single color and on short runs, offset printers can use albumin plates, which, with care, are good for up to 100,000 impressions. For critical work, including color, and for long runs where more copies must be printed, the printer may make deep-etched plates, which cost more but last much longer. On a deep-etched plate, the greasy areas that carry the ink are depressed beneath the surrounding dampened surfaces and are thus somewhat protected from wear. Deep-etched plates usually give more dependable results, since the quality of the impression is less subject to gradual deterioration during the course of a pressrun.

Even deep-etched plates wear out, however, and for very long runs (up in the hundreds of thousands) the trend is toward the use of bimetal plates. (See BIMETAL PLATES.)

Deep-etched plates should be, but are not necessarily, superior to albumin plates. The printer who is taking full advantage of recent technical advances may get longer and better runs from albumin than a less progressive competitor gets from deep-etch.

Deeptone A proprietary name used by R. R. Donnelley & Sons Company in

Chicago to describe its highest-quality offset and/or gravure work. (See OFFSET.)

delivery   See also SCHEDULING.

The delivery date often wanted on a job is "yesterday." Printers get used to hearing that every job is a rush job.

Generally speaking, the more time a printer has, the better and the more efficiently he can do his work. His dream is to have a backlog of nonrush work to draw on and keep his machines and men from standing idle between rush jobs. He may even bid lower on a job on which delivery will be accepted "any time next month."

A delivery promise, once given, is contingent on the customer's holding up his end of the bargain, as regards delivery of manuscript, correcting proofs, etc.

Extraordinary speed is possible, as witness the everyday miracle of the daily newspaper; but random jobs are not like scheduled magazine or newspaper jobs. If a printer is free to drop all other work, if his men are willing to stay overtime, if the typesetting can be divided among several compositors, if the customer can stay in the composing room and O.K. proofs as they are pulled, if the paper is on hand, if a press and folding machine are free, if the engravers and binders involved are also willing to cooperate fully, if there are no ink-drying problems, *then* perhaps one-day or two-day delivery can be achieved.

Normally, however, the following factors must be considered in working out a production schedule and arriving at a delivery date:

1. When can delivery of manuscript, artwork, engravings, and paper be expected?

2. Considering other work already scheduled, how soon can the composing room, pressroom, and bindery start on the job?

3. How long will the composition,

platemaking, pressrun, drying, binding, etc., actually take?

4. How much time will be consumed in getting the customer's O.K. on galley proofs and page proofs?

5. How will this schedule be affected by the fact that printers do not (without heavy extra pay) work holidays, Saturdays, or Sundays, and by the fact that "morning" to a printer means 8 A.M. while to the average customer it means any time before noon?

6. What is the added cost of overtime work for a rush job?

"Delivery in two weeks" (10 working days barring holidays) on average jobs is pretty good. One-week delivery on any job involving composition is excellent service. Magazines send off artwork and copy for color work from two to four months in advance of delivery dates, and often have to be content with a month's lapse between their last editorial correction and the publication date.

descender   See ASCENDER; also illustration under TYPE.

design   See also ARTWORK; DESIGNERS; ILLUSTRATIONS; MARGINS; TYPE; LAYOUT.

The simplest way for the beginner to design a pamphlet or anything else is to adapt to his own purposes the basic design of another one which is attractive or which is known to have been effective with a similar audience.

No stigma need attach to borrowing from other designs, provided the borrowing is done creatively and not slavishly. The best professional designers will freely admit that their art is that of adapting intelligently.

Finding some good models to follow may not be easy. However, someone, somewhere, has almost certainly met and solved a problem quite like yours. The local librarian can probably find helpful samples. Most libraries have a "vertical file" of pamphlets, posters, and clippings.

The Butler Typo Design Research Center (see below) publishes two volumes "101 Usable Publication Layouts" and "Ken Butler's Layout Scrapbook," each containing more than 100 layout patterns cataloged according to number of illustrations per page.

Suggestions on design. Use the words of the message as basic elements of the design. Borders, rules, and dots generally contribute nothing to the enlightenment of the reader and should be subordinated to the type or eliminated altogether.

Words should be taken singly or in natural groups and visualized as blocks to be moved around on the paper. How would they look if set big or small, bold or light, tall or wide, in caps or lowercase, in roman or italic, in long lines or short?

Do some elements need greater emphasis than others? Good ways to get it are by setting a bold black letter against a graceful script, a sans-serif against a serif type, or (sticking to one type family) large against small, italic against roman, caps or small caps against lowercase.

A few widely used display types are Bodoni (Bodoni Bold, Ultra Bodoni), Futura (also known as Spartan, Tempo, and Twentieth Century) in various weights, Memphis (also known as Beton, Karnak, and Stymie) in various weights, and Lydian (also Lydian Bold and Lydian Cursive). (See Appendix 1, Type Faces.)

A few widely used and universally liked text types are Baskerville, Caslon, Garamond, Granjon, and Times Roman.

Bold type is to be avoided in choosing a text type. The solid reading matter in books, magazines, and pamphlets is almost never set in boldface or in sans serif because people find large blocks of boldface or sans-serif type hard to read. (See BOLDFACE; SANS SERIF.)

Avoid long lines. Avoid text lines of more than 65 characters. This applies to typewriting as well as type. Small 8-pt type on a 5-in. line becomes unreadable because the reader's eye finds its way with difficulty from the end of one line to the beginning of the next.

Newspapers use 7- or 8-pt type on a 2-in. (12-pica) line and get about 33 characters per line. A 5-in. line almost requires 12- or 14-pt type with space (leading) added between the lines; if more words must go into the space than 12 or 14 pt would permit, it is better to divide the space into two narrow columns which will take smaller type as has been done in this book.

For captions and subheads, a type is often selected that offers a contrast to the text type. Sans-serif types are a popular choice. However, it should be in character with the general style.

Use color. Color usually pays for itself many times over in added effectiveness. Even full color (process color), which is expensive, may pay its way when the product itself is colorful. Look at one of the big mail-order catalogs for a lesson in which kinds of merchandise repay the use of color. (See COLOR.)

Use illustrations. It is hard to think of a printed message that cannot benefit from the use of illustrations or decorations. Cartoons get quicker reader attention than any other type of printed matter. Photographs, drawings, charts, and their captions also get read before the text does.

Whether or not a printed message is read may depend on whether it looks interesting or looks dull on the first glance.

Many people say a picture is worth ten thousand words, but too few of them act on it when preparing printed matter. Perhaps this is because editors are more often writers than artists. Admittedly, good pictures are hard to find (see ILLUSTRATIONS) and may seem unessential, but even purely decorative ones have an informative effect—they help attract the reader's attention and keep him reading.

Editors often make it a rule to get some sort of break from unrelieved text on every spread with a cartoon, chart, box, photograph, or at least a display heading.

What is design? It is really the art of drawing the straightest line between two points: between writer and reader, between idea and action. A designer should be told "Help us achieve this objective," not merely "Make this pamphlet pretty."

Of course, many designers take a very limited view of their job, and would not know what to do with any except the most literal instructions. These are draftsmen, however, not designers.

A good designer deserves to be taken in on the whole thinking behind the operation. Then if he knows his stuff, he may easily see a way to get twice the results at half the expected cost.

For instance, a designer was asked to plan a mailing piece. The budget was $200 for 10,000 copies. He suggested, "Let's cut the budget to $50. You're advertising these books as cut-price bargains. People will believe you more quickly if the mailing piece looks as though you had been forced to pinch pennies to get it printed." He proved to be right. The deliberately cheap-looking mailing piece outpulled an expensive-looking predecessor.

Good design is design suited to its purpose. This may mean either following tradition to gain easy recognition and acceptability, or breaking with tradition to gain attention.

A grocery ad can best concentrate the reader's attention on price if it uses familiar grocery-ad typography. On the other hand, if its purpose is to say "This is the most exclusive food store in town," effectiveness may be served if the design looks like something Benjamin Franklin might have set or is otherwise unusual.

The important thing is that the design help get the message across, and not claim for itself attention that should be focused on the message.

Much good design is unobtrusive design, deliberately preferring the familiar to the bizarre, and purposely clothing the message in the familiar, the welcome, and the acceptable.

Even design intended to startle must not mislead, lest it turn away those very people who would actually be interested in the message.

The most effective advertisement is not that which makes people say "That's a good ad," but rather the one which makes readers exclaim "That's a good buy," or "That's a smart company." (See also the checklist of layout pointers given under LAYOUT.)

A design service for magazine editors is offered by the Butler Typo Design Research Center, Mendota, Ill., where for a fee a magazine's design will be evaluated. The Center, also known as the "Butler Clinic," likewise offers a format and cover-design service.

designers See also DESIGN.

Wherever possible, if the budget permits or can be stretched, hire a good designer. He will not only produce a better-looking job but may actually get it done for less money.

Top-notch free-lance artists experienced in designing pamphlets, books, packages, etc., are listed in "The Literary Market Place." (See Appendix 2, Bibliography.) Their fees are likely to be at least $100 for the simplest jobs, but they can often save more than the cost of their services by the effectiveness of their work.

Printers sometimes offer good designing service. Ad agencies may also have designers on their staff. Not all designers can do just anything, however. A "type" man or a magazine illustrator may be no good at all on posters. One designer may have a formal, classic style; another may have a modern, asymmetrical style; a third may have a friendly, free-and-easy style.

Amateurs who "know what they like" sometimes turn out to be excellent designers, once they realize how rare good taste is and acquire the courage to hold out for what they want.

The best way to explain to a printer or designer what is wanted is to show actual samples of the kind of design the purchaser has in mind.

diazo copying See WHITEPRINT.

Dick strip Machine addressing is often done on rolls of paper 2 to 3 in. wide. The rolls of addresses are then inserted in a Dick Mailer, a machine for cutting off the addresses one at a time and sticking each onto a magazine or other material to be mailed. This machine looks a little bit like a carpenter's plane. The roll, or "Dick strip," is advanced from one address to the next by a simple thumb motion. Every time the machine is pressed down, another address is gummed, cut off, and affixed.

For information about the Dick Mailer, write to The Dick Mailer Co., 137 W. Tupper St., Buffalo, N.Y.

Automatic equipment for affixing such labels to mailing pieces is described under CHESHIRE ADDRESSING; ADDRESSING.

die cutting The cutting of special shapes (cutouts) in paper, cardboard, cloth, etc., is done by die-cutting firms. Die cutters have some shapes of dies in stock. If one of these will do, the expense of having a special one made can be avoided.

There are two types of dies: high dies and steel-rule dies.

High dies look like heavy-duty cookie cutters. They cost from $25 (for small, simple shapes) on up. They are used in special stamping presses and can cut through many layers of material at once. Once the die is paid for, the cost of cutting is low.

Steel-rule dies are made by tracing the lines of the pattern on ¾-in. plywood, by cutting along the lines of the pattern with a jigsaw, and by fitting a steel cutting rule into the slots. The piece of plywood with the sharp edges

of the steel rule projecting in the shape of the desired pattern is placed in a heavy-duty printing press. One sheet of material at a time is then fed into the press and cut. A steel-rule die costs from $6 up for simple shapes, to $100 or more for complicated multiple shapes such as Christmas package seals.

High-die cutting, once the die is paid for, costs from 75 cents per thousand up. Steel-rule-die cutting costs from $3 per thousand up—about as much as printing the job in an additional color.

die stamping The process of printing on cloth book covers is usually called "die stamping." It can be done with ordinary type but is more commonly done with brass binders' dies since type metal wears or deforms rapidly when printed on cloth or other comparatively uneven surfaces. Brass is also favored because it does not soften under heat, and heat is sometimes used in the die-stamping process.

Die stamping can be done with ordinary printer's ink. However, two "hits" of ink are often necessary to get good coverage, and even this may not give a satisfactory result on some kinds of cloth or where a light color is to be printed over a darker cloth. In such cases, foil is used. Foil resembles carbon paper except that it comes in colors and in gold and silver as well as in black and also uses a plastic rather than a paper backing. The brass dies used in foil stamping are usually heated to ensure a good transfer of pigment to cloth. Where foil is to be used, useful economies can be made by grouping the design elements so as to use a minimum of foil.

Brass binders' dies are fairly expensive—much more so than zinc or copper linecuts—since they require deeper and more careful routing. On comparatively short runs, type can be used instead, or so-called "binders' electros" made from type, or even plates molded from type in rubber or plastic, but none of these can be used where heat is required.

Cloth book covers are also sometimes printed by offset.

diffusion transfer A photocopying process which considerably simplifies and expedites the traditional photographic steps of exposing a negative, developing it, fixing it, drying it, using it to expose a positive, developing the positive, fixing it, and drying it.

In a typical diffusion-transfer copier, for example, a piece of photographic paper is placed face up on a glass-topped box and the original to be copied is placed on it face down. Both are held down while a timed exposure is made by turning on a bank of lights under the glass. The photo paper is then immersed in a developing solution which hardens the areas which were against the white areas of the original, leaving the others soft. The photo paper is now placed in contact with the final copy paper, and both are drawn between rollers, which squeegee them together. Finally, they are peeled apart, the copy paper having acquired a permanent black image duplicating the original. The whole process takes only a minute or so.

Now most of the companies which make diffusion-transfer copiers are also offering electrostatic copiers to meet the Xerox competition. However, the diffusion-transfer copiers are basically less expensive to operate (despite the higher cost of materials) when the volume of copying work is comparatively small. Kodak's Verifax copiers employ a principle very similar to diffusion transfer but involving a slightly different chemistry.

Some copiers are better than others at making extra copies from the same intermediate. However, take note that the claim "extra copies at 1 cent each" is misleading unless you know that you have to make an initial copy at perhaps 10 cents before you can begin to get second, third, etc., "extras" at a cent.

Among the companies selling diffusion-transfer machines are American Photocopy Equipment Co. (Apeco); Speed-O-Print Business Machines Corp.; Anken Chemical & Film Corp., A. B. Dick Co.; SCM Corp.; and General Aniline and Film.

direct mail advertising See also MAIL ORDER; MAILING LISTS; LETTERS; COPY-WRITING; Appendix 3, Postal Information.

Whenever anybody mails a sales message to anybody else, he is using direct mail advertising as distinguished from space, radio, or television advertising. The magazines themselves are heavy users of direct mail advertising to subscribers and advertisers. Sears, Roebuck, the Book-of-the-Month Club, the National Association of Manufacturers, etc., constantly use direct mail.

The term "direct mail" includes "mail order," but the latter term is more restricted and indicates that the reader sends in his order and payment by mail. (See MAIL ORDER for a discussion of this important phase of direct mail work.)

Most of this book is really about direct mail advertising, since there are separate entries about each of the tools of direct mail. (See LETTERS; HOUSE ORGANS; CIRCULARS; ENVELOPES; BLOTTERS; CALENDARS; POSTCARDS; NOVELTY PRINTING; etc.) There are many additional entries on the techniques for producing and using such direct mail materials. (See MAIL ORDER; MAILING LISTS; COPYWRITING; DUPLICATING; ADDRESSING; Appendix 3, Postal Information; etc.)

A few of the many jobs that direct mail advertising can do are as follows:

Get consumer orders direct by mail
Get dealer orders direct by mail
Get inquiries for salesmen to follow up
Pave the way for salesmen
Presell the prospect
Keep customers sold between salesmen's visits
Maintain member interest in an organization
Boost the morale and know-how of employees

Direct the activities of a member or sales organization
Bring customers into a store
Reactivate old customers
Collect accounts
Secure names of additional prospects for the mailing list

As compared with space advertising, direct mail costs a little more per reader impression. However, with targeted direct mail aimed at well-chosen lists, there need be no waste circulation and there is an opportunity to tell the whole sales story, without competition, not just a part of it.

Success in a direct mail campaign requires clearly conceived objectives, careful planning, and skillful use of the tools and techniques of the trade. Four important ingredients of a good campaign are:

1. A good mailing list, consisting of genuine prospects, and nothing but genuine prospects.

2. A message presented in such a way as to be of genuine interest to the recipient.

3. Arrangements to make it as easy as possible for the prospect to take the desired action before he forgets or loses interest.

4. Economy and effectiveness in the use of printing, paper, envelopes, artwork, postal regulations, etc.

The lessons of mail-order experience are worth studying (see MAIL ORDER) even if the campaign is not intended to bring in orders by mail.

Anyone who expects to engage in much direct mail work would do well to join the Direct Mail Advertising Association Inc., 230 Park Ave., New York 17. Annual dues are on a sliding scale, depending upon the number of direct mail pieces sent out by the member, with a minimum of $100. There is a special $20 rate for teachers of advertising and related subjects. Members of DMAA receive a subscription to the *Reporter of Direct Mail Advertising*, an independent trade journal.

There are many good books on direct mail advertising. Some of the best are listed and described in Appendix 2, Bibliography.

displays See also POSTERS; SILK SCREEN; DIE CUTTING; MOUNTING AND FINISHING; SIGNS; TRANSIT ADVERTISING.

A printed display is basically a printed poster (printed by any method) plus additional processing, including mounting, easeling, creasing, die cutting, animating, etc. There are a number of firms that specialize in creating and producing displays of all kinds. A good way to get the name of one, apart from looking in the Classified Telephone Directory, is to keep an eye peeled for displays similar to your needs, and ask who made them. This applies whether you are looking at mass-produced cardboard displays, or at convention or window displays.

Animation is being used more and more in cardboard displays, and there are now motion devices costing (in quantity) under a dollar that will operate for a month on a single flashlight-battery cell. Two sources for motion devices are Hankscraft Co., 369 Lexington Ave., New York 17; and Haft and Sons, Inc., 950 Kent Ave., Brooklyn, N.Y.

display type See "Display Faces" beginning on page 361 in Appendix 1, Type Faces.

distribution See "How to Use This Book," pp. v to viii. CAMPAIGN PLANNING; LETTERS; ADDRESSING; DIRECT MAIL ADVERTISING; MAIL ORDER; SHIPPING INFORMATION; Appendix 3, Postal Information.

Each copy of a printed or duplicated piece of literature must be in the hands of a likely reader before those responsible can regard their work as completed.

No matter how well the editor, writer, designer, and printer do their jobs, their work goes for naught if the intended readers never see it.

Distribution should never be an afterthought. It must be part of the original planning. The basic design of the material and the editorial approach must take into account the people who are to read the message and the conditions under which it will pass into their hands.

Furthermore, because effective distribution is very likely to cost more than the material itself, this must be allowed for in the budget.

How will the reader receive the material? Will the postman slip it under his door or lay it on his desk? Will he find it on his chair at a meeting? If so, will he sit on it or put it in his pocket? Will it be handed to him on a street corner? Will he pick it up on a store counter or newsstand?

Unless distribution is planned and supervised from the point of origin, there is an excellent chance that any bulk shipment leaving the office will never be unwrapped and distributed to individual readers by even the best-intentioned recipients. Distribution involves a lot of work. It costs at least the postage and addressing if carried by the postman, and usually at least a cent per item if done by boy from door to door. It can easily be slighted or overlooked by people whose major concern is something else.

Organizations may be both the best and the worst agents for the distribution of materials. They are the best because people tend to trust material received through a trusted organization. They may be the worst because, unless they distribute a lot of material, they may promise to distribute and then fall down on the job for lack of experience.

It is often assumed that wide distribution of an item can be better achieved by setting a low price. This is not necessarily true. A low price may merely mean that there is no money available for promotion adequate to bring the item to the attention of those who might be interested.

The fact is that it costs a good deal to "sell" even free material—if it is kept in mind that the objective is to get the material read, not just shipped out of a central office. Even if the intermediaries in the distribution process or the ultimate readers do not have to be "sold" on paying for it or writing for it, they do have to be sold on redistributing it or reading it. The only real alternative to adequate promotion of even free material is the waste involved in undistributed or unread copies.

It is fair to assume that a person is more likely to read something that he paid to get than something handed him free. For this reason, it is sometimes better to make a small charge for material than to give it away. Certainly, dealers and organizations are far less likely to waste bulk shipments that they have paid for than material that cost them nothing.

Another way to attack the same problem is to give the item a list price, even though it is largely given away free, so as to increase its value in the eyes of recipients.

Making a charge for materials will, of course, cut down the number distributed and may be undesirable for this reason. When a man writes in for something, he proves by this fact alone that he is interested.

Selling printed material is sometimes harder than it looks. However, it can be done, and the usual channels can be analyzed in terms of pamphlets, newsstand one-shots, bookstore items, mail-order items, and periodicals.

Pamphlets. Very few pamphlet series are self-supporting. Usually it costs far more to get an order for a pamphlet than can be charged for it. Pamphlets must really be sold in bulk if they are to pay for themselves—perhaps to an organization which in effect will do the retail "selling" without charge or perhaps to an individual who is buying in quantity to give them out himself or who is buying assorted titles or subscribing to a series.

One-shots. Pamphlets or booklets that

find their way to the newsstands are known in the trade as "one-shots." They are handled as if they were the first issue of a magazine, even though no second issue is planned. If a one-shot promises to be a really fast-selling piece of merchandise, it may be taken on by the same distributors who handle magazines and paperbacks. Every city and trading area has such a distributor, and there are a dozen or so national organizations engaged in supplying these local distributors with national publications.

Their proposition may be somewhat as follows: "Give us, say, 250,000 copies of your pamphlet. We will place them with our wholesalers in the most promising cities and areas throughout the country. They will place them on their newsstands. We will pay you half the retail price for those which sell. Any we cannot sell we will return to you, billing you for the transportation charges, or we will instruct the dealers to destroy unsold copies and return only the cover."

One-shots are great risks for a publisher. It is almost essential that he be able to make ends meet even if half are returned unsold. A one-shot is in competition for the reader's money with the best-known magazines in the world. It must sell itself on sight or lose out. A title as self-explanatory as "Your Income Tax—How to Keep It Down" is almost essential.

Bookstore items. There are only a few hundred real bookstores in the United States. On the whole, they do not like to bother with low-priced items. They get a minimum discount of 40 percent from list price and prefer to buy speculative items on a consignment basis (to be paid for when and if sold). It is difficult to get them to stock any item without sending a salesman to show it to them and take their order. In the case of an item that bookstores and libraries will want to order from time to time, it may be desirable to offer to send a supply on consignment to the major book wholesalers. A list of book whole-salers, with their specialties, is to be found in "The Literary Market Place," published annually by the R. R. Bowker Company, 1180 Ave. of the Americas, New York.

In general, the way to reach the bookstore market is to arrange for publication of the material through one of the regular book publishers. This is possible even if, or perhaps especially if, the authors or sponsors of the material want to order a sizable number for their own use.

Mail-order items. See MAIL ORDER.

Periodicals. The special advantage of issuing material in periodical form is that the publisher is selling a $5 or a $10 unit, not just a 25-cent item, and he is getting paid in advance of delivery. He can thus afford to pay the relatively high cost of persuading a prospect to subscribe. A secondary advantage is the fact that periodicals may qualify for the very cheap second-class mailing privileges. (See Appendix 3, Postal Information.) Where the publisher of a 25-cent pamphlet can spend at most 12½ cents to get one reader, the publisher of a 25-cent magazine may be able to spend up to $10 or more to get one subscriber. The economics of the operation can be illustrated by the following figures:

	Revenue	Expense
Subscription	$ 5.00	
Advertising	12.50	
Printing and mailing	......	$ 5.00
Editorial and overhead	......	5.00
Total	$17.50	$10.00

This allows up to $7.50 to get the subscription, but this is not the whole picture. The average new subscriber may keep his subscription three years and thus be worth three times $7.50.

Newsstand sales can also be profitable. Dealers get a discount of 20 percent from wholesalers, who, of course, get more. However, since newsstand sales vary from month to month and the publisher must accept a loss on any unsold copies, publishers prefer to sell to subscribers rather than on the stands.

distribution of type Type that has been set by hand has to be distributed after use if it is to be used again; i.e., the pieces of type are put back in the compartmented case from which they came.

Ditto See SPIRIT DUPLICATOR.

dodgers See CIRCULARS.

Doubletone paper See SHADING TINTS.

drawing techniques In planning artwork for publication, the editor and artist must decide on the drawing technique to be used. They may be influenced by such different factors as (1) the subject to be treated, (2) the editorial effect to be obtained, (3) the method of reproduction to be used, (4) the requirements of the layout, e.g., heavy lines and blacks for a bold effect or delicate lines and faint shadows for a light effect, (5) the special talents of the available artists, and (6) the artwork already at hand.

For purposes of comparison, 10 of the major drawing techniques are illustrated (pages 88 and 89) along with a photograph, which is probably the most widely used of all illustration techniques.

The steps in reproducing artwork vary with the drawing technique used and the printing process.

In letterpress printing, a plate must be made for any photograph or drawing. (See LETTERPRESS.) The five illustrated on page 88—pen and ink, brush drawing, lithographic crayon on Ross board, scratchboard, and line drawing with added shading—may be reproduced by means of a linecut (see LINECUT) since every element is either black or white with no grays. (Areas that seem gray are really made up of fine black dots or lines.)

The six on page 89—line and wash, wash, poster technique, airbrush, and photograph—require halftone reproduction, which can render grays by mechanically converting them into black dots. Linecuts are often cheaper than halftones but not always.

In mimeograph, only the first five drawing techniques can be used and then only by means of tracing with a stylus on a regular stencil or by a photochemical stencil. (See MIMEOGRAPH; STENAFAX.)

All can be reproduced by photooffset, gravure, photogelatin, or even silk screen. (See OFFSET; GRAVURE; PHOTOGELATIN; SILK SCREEN.) Usually the extra cost of reproducing an illustration in these other processes is less than the cost in letterpress, since a plate must be made in any case and it is very little more trouble to put an illustration on the plate than to put type on it.

Sometimes the nature of the artwork determines the printing process to be used. Sometimes the printing process determines the nature of the artwork.

Line drawings print well in any process on any kind of paper, except that unusually fine lines print best on a relatively smooth paper. It is desirable to match drawings and type as regards weight of line. Bold drawings do not always look well next to delicate type, and vice versa.

Photographs reproduce best in letterpress (but coated or calendered paper must be used), gravure, or photogelatin. Offset reproduction of photographs tends to be of lower quality, although the best offset work can be very good. (See LETTERPRESS; OFFSET; GRAVURE.)

Offset is perhaps the best process for reproducing wash drawings and pencil, crayon, or charcoal sketches.

Glossy paper can be used in any process, but is essential only in letterpress and then only for the reproduction of fine-screen halftones. If shiny paper is considered undesirable, then the other processes have a double advantage over letterpress: (1) they can use a dull paper for the finest halftones and (2) this paper can cost less. (Fine-quality halftone work can also be done on a rather expensive *dull*-coated paper.)

The drawing techniques themselves require special materials in order to achieve their distinctive features.

A pen-and-ink line drawing is done on smooth white paper with a pen and india ink. Every line is either white or black. There are no grays.

A brush-and-ink-line drawing is done on smooth paper with a brush saturated in india ink. Again there are no grays. *A dry-brush drawing* is done with a brush dipped in india ink but used on the drawing only after there is so little ink left in the brush that it has to be rubbed onto the paper rather than flowed on. Because the ink adheres only to the high spots of rough paper, effects of gray can be achieved.

The stipple-board (or coquille-board) drawing—litho crayon on Ross board —is done with crayon or ink on special stipple board which has hundreds of tiny raised dots. A light touch coats only the peaks of these dots with pigment, giving a halftone effect. One well-known stipple board is made by the Charles J. Ross Company of Philadelphia. Ross boards may combine the stipple and the scratchboard features (see below) but always have the latter.

The scratchboard drawing is done with india ink on a special drawing board that has a thick surface coat of white clay. The artist need not draw laboriously around white highlights. He boldly covers an entire area with india ink and later restores certain areas to whiteness by scratching off the ink and the top layer of clay coating. (See SCRATCHBOARD.) Stippled scratchboard drawings can be made on board that combines the features of both stipple board and scratchboard.

A woodcut style is sometimes carried out in wood or linoleum (see BLOCK PRINTING), but is often imitated in india ink on paper.

The line drawing with added shading may be the work of the artist alone or it may be a collaboration between artist and engraver. If instructed to do so, the engraver may "lay a benday" (see SHADING TINTS) on the plate when he makes a linecut of a line drawing, meaning that he will add any desired kind of shading to those areas which are entirely white on the original drawing but which the artist indicates should be shaded in the printed version.

There is an increasing tendency among artists to lay their own shading tints right on the artwork, thus avoiding engravers' charges for tint laying and seeing in advance what the finished product will look like. This may be done by applying an adhesive shading film to parts of the artwork that are to have the effect of gray. A similar effect is obtained by making the drawing on special Craftint paper printed with a pattern which is invisible until the artist "develops" it by applying a colorless liquid developer to the areas to be shaded. (See SHADING TINTS.)

Note that stipple board and scratchboard may give an effect similar to that of shading films and are sometimes listed with the shading tints.

A pencil or crayon drawing on smooth paper (not shown) is a drawing made up of gray lines, not the black lines of india ink or the black and white of soft black pencil on rough stipple board. Hence, a pencil drawing must be handled as halftone work, not as line work.

A wash drawing is done with a brush and watercolor paint, "washing" on the various grays between solid black and pure white.

In the so-called "poster technique," opaque tempera (show card color) is used. When the drawing is to be reproduced in black and white, the artist usu-

DRAWING TECHNIQUES

The most used drawing techniques are here shown applied to a single object, a Ronson table-model cigarette lighter. All the examples were prepared by I. N. Steinberg's staff, York Studios, 57 W. 69 St., N.Y. 23. The choice of technique is determined by the effect desired, the method of printing, and the kind of paper to be used. The drawings on this page can be reproduced as line cuts. Those opposite must be reproduced by the halftone process. The method of reproduction used here does not do full justice to the halftone renderings, which would show to better advantage in a finer screen on coated paper, or in gravure, photogelatin, etc. Wash drawings do especially well in offset.

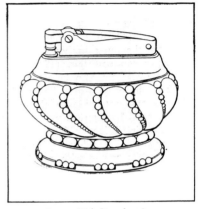

Pen-and-ink line drawing.

Brush drawing.

Lithographic crayon on Ross board.

Scratchboard drawing.

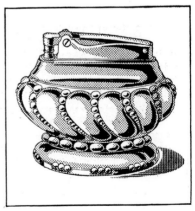

Line drawing with added shading.

Line and wash drawing.

Wash drawing.

Poster technique.

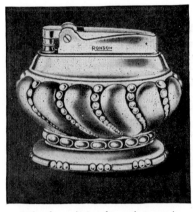

Airbrush rendering from photograph.

Unretouched photograph.

Retouched photograph.

ally works with a series of graded, ready-mixed grays ranging in tone from white to black. Being opaque, the shades usually remain distinct from each other, though an effect of blending can be achieved by means of fine brushwork.

Airbrush drawings are made with an airbrush, with which very delicate, soft effects can be achieved. (See AIRBRUSH.)

Photographs really have no lines, no solid blacks and whites; everything is a blend of tones. They must be reproduced by the halftone process.

Other illustration techniques are described under BOURGES COLOR PROCESS; TONE-LINE PROCESS.

drop folio   See FOLIO.

dropout halftone   See HIGHLIGHT HALFTONE.

dry brush   See DRAWING TECHNIQUES.

dry mounting   See also MOUNTING AND FINISHING.

The preferred method of mounting photographs. By this method, photographs can be affixed to a cardboard backing quickly, permanently, and without wrinkles, bubbles, or stains. Dry mounting is somewhat more expensive than paste mounting. Given the right equipment, it is easier, cleaner, and quicker.

In the dry-mounting process, a piece of specially processed dry-mounting tissue paper is cut to the size of the photograph and placed between the photograph and the backing. The photograph is then pressed down with a medium-hot electric iron or a special heated mounting press. The coating on the mounting tissue melts slightly and binds the photo to the backing.

dry offset   See LETTERSET.

dummy   See also LAYOUT; PASTE-UP DUMMY; DESIGN.

A page-by-page layout for a pamphlet, magazine, or book. Sometimes a dummy is sent to the printer along with the manuscript. On other work, especially magazine work, the printer may not receive a dummy until after he has supplied galley proofs of the text. A dummy that has been made up from galley proofs is called a "paste-up dummy" or a "paste-up." (See PASTE-UP DUMMY.)

To a book salesman, a dummy is a prepublication imitation of a book, showing jacket, binding, table of contents, and perhaps a sample chapter.

Printers, paper merchants, and binders are usually glad to make up blank, bound dummies for the use of the layout man. However, a bound dummy is not so easy to work with as separate pages, and the actual paper to be used may be unsuitable for the erasing that layout paper must survive.

Magazine printers often supply layout and dummy paper already ruled with the margins and columns used by that magazine.

To make a dummy, get a pad of layout paper (ordinary white paper, but tough enough to take two erasures). It should be as large as two facing pages of the publication. For a publication 8½ by 11, the layout paper should be big enough to hold the double-spread area, 17 by 11.

Mark off the page sizes, the margin sizes, the column sizes, etc., for, say, pages 2 and 3. If these same proportions apply to other spreads as well, transfer these markings to as many other sheets of layout paper as necessary. Pinpricks through the line intersections of pages 2 and 3 to the sheets intended for pages 4 and 5, 6 and 7, etc., will give a good guide for drawing the lines on those pages.

Use one side of the paper only. Nothing is more maddening than to decide to swap page 4 for page 12 only to discover that page 4 is on the back of page 3 and must be redone in the new location. When facing pages of a dummy have been prepared on one side of the layout paper, it is a simple matter to cut them apart when it is necessary to join them to new partners.

Before a dummy is sent to the printer, certain information must be added about margin widths, folio numbers, etc. It is not necessary to repeat this information from page to page. If the margins, subheads, captions, etc., are to be the same throughout, it is enough to tell the printer how to handle them on the first text page, or the first time they occur.

duograph See DUOTONE.

duotone Black-and-white photographs are sometimes reproduced in two colors for added depth and beauty. This is called the "duotone" or "duograph" process. Two halftone cuts with different screen angles are made from the same original. One is run in blue, green, tan, or some other color. The other is printed in black right over the first. The result is to extend the range of the photograph to include not merely all the grays, but also all the tints, tones, and shades of the added color.

Somewhat the same effect may also be achieved with only one impression through the use of duotone ink. This is a special ink designed to bleed into the paper (the way a pen stroke on a blotter has fuzzy edges). The ink is and remains dark where laid on the paper; but as it bleeds away from these areas, it turns much lighter and exhibits an undertone of a different color. Photographs reproduce well in duotone ink. However, duotone ink is not so satisfactory for printing a page combining both photographs and type since the tendency of the ink to bleed or fade off has an undesirable blurred effect on the type.

duplex paper See COLORED PAPER.

duplicate plates It is often desirable to make duplicate printing plates of pages of type and/or cuts. The usual reasons are as follows:

1. Duplicate plates provide an inexpensive method of exact duplication when the job is to be run 2-up, 3-up, etc., i.e., two or three copies side by side on one sheet.

2. They will ensure sharpness and clarity in a long run where type would wear excessively.

3. They insure against the costly delays that result when the original type and cuts are damaged during the pressrun.

4. They are more conveniently stored and usually require less space than type forms.

5. They permit exact duplication of the same advertisement in several different publications simultaneously.

The cheapest duplicate plates are stereotypes. The finest duplicate plates are electros. (See STEREOTYPE; ELECTRO.) New kinds of duplicate plates are coming into use, including plastic plates and rubber plates. (See PLASTIC PLATES; RUBBER PLATES.) They are made on the stereo principle but wear longer and are less subject to stretching or shrinking in the making. One of their advantages is low mailing weight.

Magnesium and Dycril plates are not strictly duplicate plates since they are not molded; each is an original plate made in much the same way that zinc and copper cuts are made. However, both magnesium and Dycril plates are often used where duplicate plates might otherwise be used and are becoming increasingly important. (See MAGNESIUM; DYCRIL.)

duplicating See also PHOTOCOPYING.

The work of duplicating form letters, price lists, etc., is usually called "duplicating" rather than "printing," although in some cases the same processes are used. There is also a distinction to be made between *duplicating* on the one hand and *photocopying* on the other. Processes like mimeograph, offset duplicating, spirit duplicating, and hectograph, where the economies usually begin at quantities of 25 and up, are called *duplicating;* processes like Xerox, Verifax, Thermo-Fax, etc., where even single copies can be made economically, are called *photocopying.* In general, duplicating starts with the making of a "master" of some sort, after which the making of copies is fast and inexpensive, whereas the photocopying methods either work without a master or make a very inexpensive one from which only one or a few copies can be made. In general, duplicating costs very little after the master is made; photocopies cost from 4 to 10 cents each, with little reduction for quantity. The Xerox Model 2400 (which carries a minimum monthly charge of $350) bridges both areas, providing single copies at 4 cents each and quantities over 25 at ½ cent each.

For further information about any of the above-mentioned processes, look under that process. (See also LETTERS and the chart "How to Choose the Right Printing Process" inside the covers of this book.)

Stencil duplicators, such as the mimeograph, have traditionally been the workhorses of office duplicating. Models are available at a great variety of price ranges. They can produce from 25 to 2,500 copies cheaply, quickly, and, in the hands of a good operator, with excellent appearance and legibility. They can be left unused for weeks at a time and still be ready to produce on a moment's notice.

Spirit duplicators, such as those made by Ditto, have their own advantages—and some limitations. (See SPIRIT DUPLICATORS.)

Offset duplicators, such as the Multilith, offer a considerable range of capacity, being competitive with the lowest-priced methods when the volume of work is adequate and competitive with

standard commercial printing where skilled operators are given quality equipment. Offset masters can be made by many methods, some quite inexpensive. (See OFFSET DUPLICATORS.)

Computer installations incorporate yet another kind of equipment that can be effectively used for duplicating purposes under certain circumstances, namely, the impact printer, such as the Analex or IBM 1403. Many of these machines can write 1,000 lines a minute, up to 132 characters wide, on any kind of paper, including carbon-interleaved forms. While they are usually used for writing out the results of computer data processing, they can perfectly well be pressed into service to do repetitive writing. Such a printer might, for example, print out some 2,400 pages of double-spaced typing per hour—not so attractively as an offset duplicator to be sure, but worth keeping in mind where computer time is available and duplicator time is not.

There is little doubt but that the offset duplicator is the most versatile of all duplicators. Masters for it can be prepared by almost any photocopying or photographic process as well as by typing, drawing, printing, etc.—in fact, masters can be made from masters. Where masters are to be made by photocopying techniques, the preparation of the original is made easier by the fact that errors can be corrected by opaquing, cutting out, pasting—any method. With the most inexpensive masters, it can be economic to make runs as low as 25 copies—even 10 copies where the duplicator is designed for quick changing of masters. With high-quality masters and duplicators that have adequate inking capacity, halftones can be reproduced and long runs can be undertaken. Many accessories are available, including devices for collating lengthy documents as they emerge from the press.

It should be noted, however, that the less-expensive offset duplicators will not produce *quality* halftones or heavy reverse panels. Any color of ink can be used, but the washups involved in changing colors can be tedious. Offset duplicators cannot imprint carbon-interleaved forms, and they are not so adaptable as other kinds of presses for work such as on-press numbering and perforating. Some of them need not be washed up every day—but operators who take pride in producing quality work tend to wash up daily anyway.

Many diffusion-transfer copiers are priced in the $100 to $200 range, although the prices can run to the $600 range for larger or more automatic models. Thermo-Fax and stabilization copiers start at about $200. Diazo copiers begin at about $300. Electrostatic copiers start at about $1,000—or are leased.

Dura The Dura Mach 10 automated typewriter is built around the IBM Selectric typing head. (See also AUTOMATIC TYPEWRITER.) Like the Friden Flexowriter with which it competes, the Dura is available with a variety of capabilities—with reader only, with reader and punch, with punch only, with neither (as an input-output adjunct to other equipment), etc. Advantages include high speed (15.4 characters per second), quiet operation, and automatic insertion of the "downshift" symbol when the shift key is released. Optional features include a dual reader (useful where the addresses are on one tape and the form letter is on another), a machine-language converter for translating other machine-language codes into Mach 10 codes, an automatic envelope feeder, coded ribbon control, partial carrier return, and parity checking. Proportional spacing is not available.

Dycril A photosensitive plastic which can be used for making linecuts and halftones. It can be exposed and etched in much the same way as zinc or copper or magnesium. (See CUT.) However, the portions exposed to light are hardened not only at the surface but also in depth, so that undercutting is eliminated during the process of washing out the unexposed areas. Dycril plates are flexible and can be used either flat or curved. They cost more than offset plates or molded-plastic plates.

dye transfer See VERIFAX.

E | e

easeling The work of attaching easels to the backs of posters and displays is done by firms specializing in mounting and finishing. (See MOUNTING AND FINISHING.)

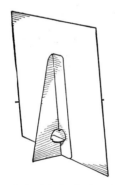

Easel glued to back of poster.

edge index For a discussion of thumb-indexing, step indexing, and tabbing, see INDEXING. Edge indexing is an inexpensive alternate to the above. It also has the merit of allowing use of an unlimited number of headings (other forms permit only 12 to 25), and of adding nothing to the overall time required for a binding job. To use a typical edge-indexed directory, bend the

94

pages until they fan out and look for tiny black marks resulting from printed rules that run right to the edge of the paper. If you want the section on, say, "Transportation," look down the right edge of the first right-hand page for this heading and look for a black mark just opposite this heading. Open at that place.

Edison Margin Justifier See MARGINATOR.

editing See EDITORIAL WORK; EDITORIAL PLANNING; COPYWRITING; COPY EDITING; COPY PREPARATION.

edition Some books are published in several editions, e.g., a deluxe edition, a regular edition, a book-club edition, a paper-covered edition, a cheap reprint edition, etc.

In a slightly different sense, a book may have a first edition, a second (revised) edition, etc.

Books are advertised as having reached their "third impression," "7th large printing," etc., when they have merely been reprinted the stated number of times without change. They are advertised as having come out in a new edition when revisions have been made, new matter has been added, or format or price has been changed.

editorial planning See also EDITORIAL WORK; COPYWRITING; COPY PREPARATION.

Before any publication goes to the printer—in fact, before it is written—there should be time for editorial planning. This means working out the details of the publication itself; it also means planning the publication as an integral part of the overall program or campaign. Without such planning, any publication, whether it is a circular, a periodical, or merely a covering letter, may misfire or fall short of its potential.

Who participates in this planning will depend upon the nature of the organization and the publication. Major projects, such as a special brochure or series of leaflets, will probably require an official O.K. from on high—the boss, the board of directors, the policy committee, or whoever holds the purse strings. The best assurance of quick approval at the finish is to have these people in on the planning from the start. Besides, they should have constructive suggestions and ideas worth the asking.

The first questions are: "Who are the people we are trying to reach?" "How are we going to reach them?" and "What do we want to get across?" Once these questions are settled, the following checklist may serve as a reminder of additional points that require decision.

1. *Space allocation.* Shall it be a four- or six-page leaflet? A 20-page pamphlet or a 24-page one, which mails for a lower postal rate? (See Appendix 3, Postal Information.) Shall it be a one-page letter with reply questionnaire on the bottom or a letter with separate questionnaire enclosed? Shall it be a one-page magazine article without pictures or a two-page article with pictures?

2. *Kind of illustration, if any.* Will illustrations bear the burden of the story? Or will they be attention getters for the copy? What kind of illustration should be used—photograph, cartoon, pictograph, or line drawing?

3. *Use of color, if any.* How can color be used to improve the publication? What is the added cost for each added color? Is there a cheaper way to dress up a publication? (See COLOR for suggestions.) What can be done with black-and-white printing to give variety to a publication? (See SHADING TINTS; DESIGN; LAYOUT.)

4. *Printing process.* What printing processes are within budgetary limits? Which is the best for this particular job? Consider cost, possibility of illustration and color, number of copies to be run, etc. (See also the charts inside the covers of this book.)

5. *The copywriter.* Shall he be a member of the staff? Or shall the publication be written by, or ghostwritten for, a "big name" from outside, whose authority will carry weight? If an outsider, what indoctrination should he have as to general policy and to this particular publication in relation to the overall program? How much can he be paid?

6. *The artist.* What style of artwork is most appropriate to the subject and the audience? (Most people prefer realistic cartoons to stylized ones.) How many pieces of artwork will be needed? Of what size and shape? What should each drawing show? What reference material should the artist have in order to draw the picture accurately? (See ARTWORK.) How much will the budget allow for each piece of artwork? What artist should do the job? (See ARTISTS.)

7. *The photographs.* Are the pictures to be used chiefly as attention getters? Or must they be on-the-spot news pictures? What good photographs are on hand? What others are available? (See PHOTO AGENCIES.) What photographs will have to be taken? Should they be horizontal or vertical? Who and what should be in the picture? (In specially staged pictures every detail should be

worked out as to background and properties, grouping of people, etc.) Are pictures planned to supplement the copy instead of duplicating it?

8. *Distribution.* Where is the publication to go? To what kind of reader audience? Could the same piece be used effectively for other mailing lists too? How is it to be shipped—as a self-mailer, as an enclosure, or as a separate piece in envelope or wrapper? What are the comparative costs of these? (See DISTRIBUTION.)

Testing of copy is very desirable at some stage of the development of a publication. The director of one of the most scientific of the nationwide public-opinion polls reports that he tries out the first draft of his questions on a sample group. Then, when the interviews are studied, some causes for misunderstandings always come to light and suggest that certain questions be rewritten and others added.

The same technique will help almost any piece of copy. Try it out on other staff members. Send it out to a selected list. (See MAIL ORDER.) Better still, talk it over with people who are typical of those whom the publication is to reach.

Almost any publication brings bigger dividends if it is planned in relation to other publications and as part of an overall campaign or long-range program. (For suggestions see CAMPAIGN PLANNING.)

Good pointers for the editorial planning of a magazine are given in the books listed in Appendix 2, Bibliography.

editorial work This general term includes a multitude of activities, which are dealt with in this book under the following headings:

Editorial planning: laying down general policy; passing upon manuscripts; budgeting money, space, and staff effort; planning illustrations; etc.

Copywriting: writing copy, headlines, captions.

Copy editing: rewriting, revising, and polishing.

Copy preparation: putting accepted editorial material in shape for the printer by making it accurate as to facts, grammatical, consistent as to style, and correct in spelling and punctuation, and by marking it for type.

Proofreading: checking and correcting proofs.

Dummying: indicating which material is to go on which pages and in what arrangement.

Illustration: how to select, procure, and use them.

In a large publishing operation, the staff may include specialists in each type of editorial activity. In a small operation, the person in charge can (1) be a jack-of-all-editorial-trades; (2) deal with a printer equipped to offer editorial services (whose prices, at least in the long run, will reflect the extra service rendered); or (3) hire free-lance editorial assistance. In "The Literary Market Place" (see Appendix 2, Bibliography) a number of free-lance editors are listed with addresses, telephone numbers, and areas of specialization.

An authoritative reference book invaluable in editorial work is the University of Chicago "Manual of Style" listed in Appendix 2.

EF Abbreviation for English finish.

eggshell See ANTIQUE.

Egyptian A family of type styles more frequently called "square serif." For examples, see Appendix 1, Type Faces.

Ektalith Ektalith is a Kodak photocopying method similar in its chemistry to Verifax except that exposures are made through a lens instead of by reflex contact exposure; it is thus able to enlarge and reduce. Its primary use is for making offset masters by photocopying technology, but it can also be used in the same way as the Verifax and (using special materials) can make projection transparencies and intermediates for diazo copying. It can make a press-ready offset master within a minute or a high-quality intermediate negative ready for printing down on presensitized master plates within 5 min. Halftone work can be done. A darkroom is not required. As compared with a Xerox 2400 installation, an Ektalith department offers greater flexibility, better quality (especially on solids), and greater speed and economy on long runs. The Ektalith costs are higher both in time and materials on one to three copies, a special operator to handle the work is almost inevitable, and the initial investment is higher.

electro, electrotype See also CUT; STEREOTYPE; DUPLICATE PLATES.

An electrotype, usually abbreviated to "electro," is a metal duplicate of a page of type and/or cuts. It is possible to print from it exactly as if the original type and cuts were being used.

Electros are used on long runs because they wear longer than type. Their use also protects expensive cuts. If an electro is damaged on the press, another can easily be made. If an original cut is damaged, replacing it requires going back to the artwork, takes longer, and costs more.

Electros are also used where an ad must be supplied to several magazines at the same time, or where a job is to be printed 2-up, 3-up, etc., to obviate the need for duplicating the typesetting and engraving.

For exceptionally long runs, electros can be nickel-faced at extra cost.

A comparison of the various methods of making duplicate printing plates is given under DUPLICATE PLATES.

The method of making an electro is as follows.

The type and/or cuts to be duplicated are locked up "for foundry." This means that they are locked in a chase as if for printing, but with one major difference: they are made up with higher spacing material and surrounded with type-high "bearers" to prevent damage to the edges of the form. (See FOUNDRY PROOFS.) The compositor or printer does this and then ships the form to the electrotyper.

The electrotyper cleans the type, levels it, dusts it with graphite, lays a sheet of molding material over it, and forces the two surfaces together in a hydraulic press. The mold thus takes the shape of the type and cuts. Copper is then deposited electrolytically on this molten mold. The resultant copper "shell" is then carefully separated from the mold and backed with molten lead. If an electro is then to be used alongside type, it is mounted type-high. For some uses, however, it is left unmounted.

Color-separation electros from a single original form can be made, as for example, when the border and several lines of type are to print in red and the rest in black. Curved electros can be made for use on rotary presses.

Electrofax A process of electrostatic photocopying similar in principle to Xerox but with the difference that the image is formed directly on the copy paper, instead of being formed first on a metal surface for subsequent transfer to the copy paper. A special coated paper must be used, but it is not expensive, being coated with one of the more common white pigments, namely, zinc oxide.

There are two basic applications of the Electrofax process, both of which start by applying a uniform electric charge to the entire surface of the copying paper. The brightly illuminated original is then exposed through a lens so as to cast its image on the electrified copy paper. This copy paper loses its charge where the light strikes and retains it where the light was absorbed by black type or lines on the original. The remaining charge on the copy

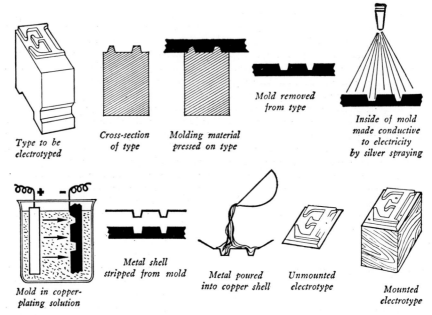

Type to be
electrotyped

Cross-section
of type

Molding material
pressed on type

Mold removed
from type

Inside of mold
made conductive
to electricity
by silver spraying

Mold in copper-
plating solution

Metal shell
stripped from mold

Metal poured
into copper shell

Unmounted
electrotype

Mounted
electrotype

How electrotypes are made. (Drawings courtesy of International Association of Electrotypers and Stereotypers.)

paper is now allowed to attract ink pigment.

In the dry process, ink powder is applied with a magnetic brush, then fused to the paper by heat. In the wet process, ink particles suspended in an electrolytic solution attach themselves to the charged areas of the copy paper, which is then squeezed dry. No fusing is necessary.

A number of companies have taken out licenses to market copying equipment employing the Electrofax principle; among them are American Photocopy Equipment Co. (Apeco), SCM Corp., Charles Bruning Co. (a division of Addressograph-Multigraph Corp.), and Dennison Mfg. Co.

elite See also TYPEWRITER.

Elite type is the smaller of the two common styles of typewriter type. It measures 12 letters and spaces to the inch instead of 10 as in pica style. (See PICA and sample under COPYFITTING.)

Elliott addressing See also ADDRESSING.

Elliott addressing machines operate on the stencil principle. A fiber frame, usually about 2 by 4½ in. holds a piece of stencil tissue which prints like a miniature mimeograph stencil.

These stencil address cards are guaranteed by the manufacturers for 10,000 impressions. In the 2- by 4½-in. size, they cost about $20 a thousand. Although the cutting of the address cards can be done on any office typewriter, specially equipped typewriters are recommended. The manufacturers will put a three-line address, plus a one-line index, on their stencils for about $24 per thousand plus the cost of the stencils. Extra lines cost $3 per thousand.

Small organizations expecting to need no more than 500 address cards may obtain complete Elliott addressing equipment for $139.

A hand-fed office machine costs $295; an electrically operated desk-top model with semiautomatic feed costs $495;

Elliott addressing machine, desk-top model.

completely automatic feed costs $895 and will address envelopes as large as 9 by 12 in.

Electrically operated console models cost between $1,300 and $6,000. Speeds of these models range up to 8,200 impressions per hour. Machines can be custom-built for such special jobs as billing, making up payrolls, dating, and numbering. Some firms, including the Literary Guild and Montgomery Ward, maintain billing information right on Elliott address cards.

Elliott address cards can be "keyed" by punching small holes in the frame. Thus an Elliott machine with automatic address-selector attachment can be set to print only address cards with holes in certain positions, or to print all except cards with holes in certain positions. Some address cards have provisions for punching in 240 different positions.

For information, write Elliott Business Machines, Inc., in your city or in Randolph, Mass. 02368.

A tray of Elliott addressing stencils, showing how an inverted card becomes an index card. The stencils also come in different colors for visual keying.

Elliott address stencils can be cut on any typewriter and can be keyed by means of punch marks on the frame.

Advantages claimed for the Elliott addressing method include lower initial costs, the fact that address cards can be prepared on the typewriter, lower cost of address cards, less filing space required, lighter file drawers (one-twelfth as much as for the same number of metal plates), perfect addressing even on stuffed envelopes of varying thickness because the address card is flexible, visible addressing (envelopes put in face up, not face down), less noise both in cutting address cards and in running them, faster addressing, more durable address cards, easier indexing since the indexing line can read DOE, J. R., although the plate reads Mr. J. R. Doe. (See ADDRESSOGRAPH for the special advantages of that process.)

In general, it can be said that users of both Elliott and Addressograph machines report highly satisfactory service. Both processes can produce work of excellent appearance. Both types of plate can give more service than they are usually called upon to give.

elliptical-dot halftones This improvement on the conventional square-dot halftone screen tends to minimize the "jump" in tone value between the darkest middle gray that consists of completely separate dots and the next darker gray that consists of dots all joined at their corners. Elliptical dots are slightly diamond-shaped and coalesce first through one opposite pair of corners, then through the other. Also called "chain-dot" halftones, elliptical-dot halftones can be used in either letterpress or offset work.

Elrod A machine that extrudes melted type metal in the form of leads and rules any desired width and of indefinite length.

em See TYPE MEASUREMENTS.

Embosograf A machine and a process for manufacturing neatly lettered and brightly colored signs in small quantities.

Special type with sharp edges is used. The type is assembled and arranged as desired on a ruled setup chart. A piece of (say) blue "top paper" is placed color side down on the type. A piece of (say) yellow cardboard is placed face down over the top paper and type.

The whole assembly is now pushed under a pressure plate, which comes down and crushes the cardboard against the top paper and the type. The type assembly is now removed from under the pressure plate, and the cardboard is lifted off. Surplus blue top paper is peeled away, leaving neat blue letters against a yellow background. The letters have an embossed effect. Printing can also be done on plastic or aluminum.

Any colors can be used. After the first impression, the type adheres to the setup chart, which has a waxed surface and can be used for as many more impressions of the same sign as desired. It is as easy to make every sign in a different color as to use the same color scheme consistently.

Embosografed signs are used in retail stores, on office-building directories, on college campuses, etc. Complete equipment, including press and a selection of type, costs from $650 to $900. The equipment is made by the Embosograf Corporation of America, 38 W. 21 St., New York 10.

embossing Producing raised letters or designs on paper or other material. The work is done with matched dies, a relief die striking from beneath the paper into an intaglio or hollow die above the paper. (See RELIEF and INTAGLIO.)

One common example of embossing is the work done with a corporation seal; another, the stamp on a post-office envelope.

The expense of embossing lies primarily in the making of the dies, and in the careful press makeready that is required. After that, the material to be embossed is run through the printing press in the same way as for ordinary printing. Prices depend upon the quality of the work as well as the quantity ordered.

Any colors to be used are put on first, in ink, by regular printing methods. Because of the accuracy and precision required in this type of work, it is recommended that those having had no previous experience with embossing contact the embosser for advice on layout, gripper, and other requirements before printing.

Two firms doing embossing work are Consolidated Decorating Co., 230 Third St., Brooklyn, N.Y.; and Freedman Die Cutters, Inc., 285 Lafayette St., New York.

en See TYPE MEASUREMENTS.

endpaper The paper pasted to the inside of the cover of a book. It is part of the same piece that forms the first leaf of the book. (See illustration under BOOKBINDING.) It is usually of a somewhat stronger material than the text pages. It may be white or colored, printed or unprinted. (The endpapers in this book carry a printed chart.) Endpapers are sometimes called "endsheets," "lining papers," or "pastedowns."

Printed endpapers add attractiveness to a book. It is sometimes possible to "gang" them up on the same offset plate with the book jacket and thus get them printed in the jacket colors at little additional expense over the printing costs of the jacket.

endsheet See ENDPAPER.

English finish See also PAPER.

Paper that has been calendered to a smooth finish, but not to a shiny finish. English-finish paper will take 110-screen halftones satisfactorily. It is not coated. English finish is abbreviated EF.

engraver's proofs After an engraver has made a linecut or halftone, he delivers it together with an engraver's proof of it. From this proof the customer determines whether the cut is acceptable. An engraver's proof says in effect, "Results of this quality can be obtained from this cut. If your printer comes up with poorer results, it is not the fault of the cut."

Unfortunately for the printer, engraver's proofs are usually pulled on the finest coated paper. If possible, the buyer of a cut should request that the engraver pull his proofs on the paper on which the job is actually to be printed.

It is always desirable to send engraver's proofs to the printer along with the cuts, so that the pressman may know what kind of results the cuts are expected to yield. This is essential as regards process-color engravings, in which case not only the finished proof is sent but also "progressive proofs" showing the pressman how the job should look after each color has been added.

Engravers usually supply two proofs and charge extra if more are requested.

engraving See also CUT (in the sense that one orders "engravings" or "cuts" from a photoengraver).

To the layman, the word "engraving" may immediately call to mind the engraved calling card. This is a specialized example of the process of intaglio printing. (See INTAGLIO.)

Orders for engraved calling cards, wedding announcements, social stationery, etc., can be placed with most department stores and some jewelers. This method of printing is expensive compared with ordinary printing because a subsurface-engraved plate must be made first and because the printing process itself is inherently slow. The resulting dull-black raised lettering can be very crisp and attractive.

There are two cheaper processes which have some of the characteristics of engraving. In the process called "thermography" a calling card is printed from type in the ordinary way and then, while still wet, is sprinkled with a resinous powder and heated. (See THERMOGRAPHY.) The result is raised lettering. Embossing is another method of producing raised lettering. In this case the paper is indented from its underside as much as it is raised on the upper side. (See EMBOSSING.)

For genuine engraving, look in the Classified Telephone Directory under Engravers—Steel and Copper Plate, or try John B. Wiggins Co., 638 S. Federal St., Chicago; Ross-Cook Engraving Company, Inc., 307 W. 38 St., New York. For thermography, try Ahrendt, Inc., 333 Ave. of the Americas, New York 14.

engrossing The hand-lettering done on diplomas and citations. It is done by artists who specialize in decorative lettering and illuminating. The words "calligrapher" and "engrosser" both mean someone skilled in penmanship. The word "engrossing" applies to the lettering; the word "illuminating" applies to any added decoration.

A good engrosser can turn out from 10 to 30 high-school diplomas an hour, in any desired style of lettering. The letters flow from his pen with amazing speed. Rates vary with the amount to be engrossed, the area to be covered, the style of letter desired, and the degree of perfection required.

Perhaps the best way to locate a nearby engrosser is to ask a local high school or college for the name of the man who does their diploma work. A few engrossers and illuminators are J. R. Rosen Studio, 80 Boylston St., Boston; Ames & Rollinson, 50 Church St., New York 7; Harris Studio, 53 W. Jackson Blvd., Chicago.

enlarging Three methods of enlarging are by camera lucida, pantograph, and photography. The first two are mechanical. (See CAMERA LUCIDA; PANTOGRAPH; PHOTOGRAPHY.)

A much-used application of the photographic principle for enlarging is, of course, the photostat. (See PHOTOSTAT.)

The invention of photography has made possible and simple the faithful copying of any illustrative material in enlarged or reduced size. Everyone who has used a Brownie box camera is familiar with the process of making a reduced-size copy. To enlarge requires only a very big camera, or its equivalent, moved very close to the object to be copied.

The object to be copied can be illuminated from in front; or, if it is transparent like a photographic negative or a Kodachrome transparency, it can be illuminated from behind.

Photographic enlargements can be made in any size. The process is the same as if a lantern slide were to be projected upon a big piece of sensitized paper instead of the usual screen, with the paper then being developed and fixed.

Standard sizes for photographic paper are 4 by 5, 5 by 7, 8 by 10, 11 by 14, 14 by 20 in.

To make a very rough enlargement or reduction, artists frequently use a camera lucida.

envelopes It pays to buy standard-size envelopes and to order them well ahead of the need for them from an envelope mill or envelope jobber. Envelopes can be imprinted at very low rates by companies specializing in this work. Regular printers can supply and imprint envelopes but may have to charge for the use of presses, which are more costly than those necessary for envelope printing. Printers are also justified in charging more than minimum prices for rush work or work of unusually high quality.

It is particularly important to plan for and order envelopes at least as soon as the material to be mailed in them is planned. Many an otherwise well-planned mailing has been held up, either because standard envelopes were not ordered in time or because the job required a nonstandard envelope which took longer to make than expected. Low prices and overnight delivery do not go together on envelopes any more than on anything else.

Careful planning and stock control are necessary to keep envelopes on hand. A single exceptional mailing may clean out a supply intended to last for several months.

The No. 10 (4⅛ by 9½) and the No. 6¾ (3⅝ by 6½) envelopes are the most commonly used for letters. Those who use less common sizes usually do so expressly to make their communication stand out as distinctive in the addressee's pile of mail. (See illustration for other standard sizes.)

Post-office regulations prohibit envelopes which are not rectangular or which are smaller than 3 by 4¼ in. There is no mandatory maximum size. Not recommended, but acceptable: envelopes larger than 9 in. wide or 12 in. long; envelopes having a ratio of width to length of less than 1:1.414; envelopes not sealed or secured so that they may be handled by machine.

Large envelopes are sometimes purchased without printing, since an imprinted label can be affixed to them to carry an address. This makes for flexibility since the envelopes can never become obsolete and can be ordered well ahead. (Labels are more quickly procured and less costly to scrap. For styles and prices, see LABELS.)

There are many specialized kinds of envelopes. Window envelopes have the advantage of making it unnecessary to fill in the recipient's name on the envelope as well as on the enclosure. Bills sent out in window envelopes cannot be inserted in the wrong envelope by mistake.

Business reply envelopes (see Appendix 3, Postal Information) have come to be a necessary enclosure in mail-order work.

Pennysaver envelopes, frequently called "postage savers," seal like ordinary envelopes but have one unsealed flap. Spot-of-gum postage-saver envelopes facilitate automatic inserting and are therefore popular with large mailers of third-class matter. Catalog envelopes made on the penny-saver principle are called "booklet" envelopes. All can be used in third-class mailings. Of course, fully sealed envelopes can be used for third-class mailings, too, provided the words "Third Class" are imprinted on the face or back of the envelope but not in the permit imprint or meter stamp. (See Appendix 3, Postal Information.)

Through the use of a special double envelope, a letter stamped with first-class postage can go out along with heavy enclosures on which only third-class postage is paid. It is also permissible to stamp "First-class Message Enclosed" on such a package and put the extra postage on the outside.

Many specialty envelopes are obtainable, some of which combine into a single piece a sales letter, an envelope, an order form with coin pocket, and a prepaid reply envelope. One firm that specializes in such mailing devices and will send a useful catalog on request is the Direct Mail Envelope Co., Inc., 448 W. 16 St., New York 11. Many letter-shops offer one or more such specialties.

The U.S. Post Office sells envelopes at very low rates and will imprint them with return name and address. (See Appendix 3.) However, post-office envelopes require a considerable investment in postage (unstamped envelopes are not supplied); names are imprinted in only one standard style; and delivery of printed envelopes may take four to five weeks.

Note that envelopes are not actually required for all mailings. The Post

ENVELOPES – THE MOST COMMON SIZES

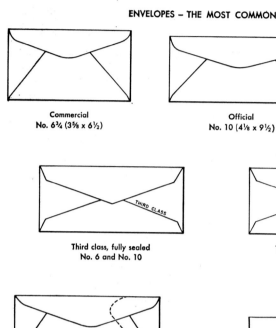

Commercial
No. 6¾ (3⅝ x 6½)

Official
No. 10 (4⅛ x 9½)

Baronial
No. 5½ (4⅜ x 5⅝)

Third class, fully sealed
No. 6 and No. 10

Third class, postage saver
(spot-of-gum)
No. 6 and No. 10

Third class, postage saver
(loose flap)
No. 6 and No. 10

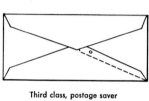
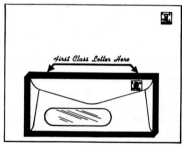

First Class Letter Here

Two compartment
7½ x 10½ to 11½ x 14¼

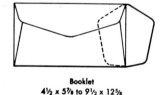

Booklet
4½ x 5⅞ to 9½ x 12⅝

Office permits almost anything that will not fall apart in transit to be sent as a self-mailer without envelope. (See SELF-MAILER.) Where self-mailers can be used, the saving on envelopes, handling, and perhaps postage may be considerable. Periodicals are frequently handled as self-mailers.

The classic example of the self-mailer is the postal card. This is one of the bargains of the postal service. It is first-class mail, it costs only 4 cents, and Uncle Sam throws in the paper stock, free. Where large quantities are to be imprinted, the Post Office will supply them in large sheets of various sizes so that they can be imprinted in one impression and cut apart later. (See Appendix 3.)

In designing the form in which a return address is to be imprinted on an envelope, it should be remembered that

With the window style of this Combine-velope, the subscriber's name and address can be imprinted from a plate or stencil right on the order form, or it can be typed or written in.

When the reader tears off the right half of the Combine-velope (see below, left), he has this business reply envelope in which to return his subscription and remittance promptly.

When opened up, the Combine-velope shows the new or renewal subscription message on the left. On the right are the handy order form and the pocket side of the reply envelope. These features make it easy to subscribe and send remittance.

An order form or questionnaire form can be made to do double duty as a reply envelope, as shown above. No pocket is used in this case, since no remittance is expected. Instructions on how to fold and seal should be given the recipient.

many envelope-imprinting machines do not carry enough ink to permit the use of reverse blocks; and some do not give sufficiently accurate results to permit halftones.

For the names of envelope supply houses, consult any city Classified Telephone Directory, under Envelopes. For a useful "Envelope Selector Chart," write to the United States Envelope Company, 21 Cypress St., Springfield 2, Mass.

estimating costs See also SAVING MONEY.

A certain amount of price information is given throughout this book as part of the discussion of methods. It should be remembered, however, that an estimate on one job can never with certainty be applied to another job, no matter how similar. The authors do not present this price information to suggest that the reader need not pay more. He may have to pay more for entirely legitimate reasons. They feel, however, that he will want to know that rotogravure jobs usually start at $2,000 or so and that there is no use asking for bids in "roto" on a $100 job.

A printer's estimates vary according to (1) his equipment and its suitability to the job, (2) his desire to get the job, and (3) his standards of work and service.

All printing costs should be seen as the sum of two costs: fixed costs and running costs. The fixed costs—design, typesetting, artwork, engravings, plates, press makeready, and bindery makeready—must be a part of the price whether the edition is to be 1,000 or 1,000,000 copies. Thus, 1,000 copies of a job may cost $100 and 2,000 copies cost only $110. Fixed costs loom large on small runs but become a negligible factor in the unit costs of very long runs.

The cost of a great many jobs (neither very large nor very small) comes to about three to four times the cost of the paper. On long runs, this can be reduced to twice the cost of the paper. This rule of thumb will turn a printer's hair gray. He will at once begin to point out that everything depends on the number of colors, the length of the pressrun, the number of illustrations, the type of binding, etc.

Nevertheless, any job that seems likely to cost ten to twenty times the cost of the paper may well be studied to see whether the extra expense is really justified. It may or may not be.

A printer's estimate may be entirely justified, and the only way to reduce the ratio may be to redesign the job for another process, perhaps silk screen as against lithography, or mimeographing as against letterpress work.

A rough (very rough) way to predict the cost of a letterpress or offset job follows. (See also DUPLICATING.)

This method of rough estimating is not recommended to any printer. However, it may be helpful to customers whose plans are only in the formative stages. On 9 jobs out of 10, it will prove to be right within 33 percent, one way or the other. There is often that much variation between printers' bids.

1. Estimate the number of words and multiply by 2 cents.

2. Estimate the weight of the paper that will be used and multiply by 60 cents to cover paper, presswork, and binding.

While this shortcut will startle printers, it proved accurate within 20 percent when tested in three large publishing houses! Only in the case of very lavishly illustrated or very short-run jobs does it become seriously inapplicable.

To figure the paper requirements of a job, get some paper of the approximate weight desired and make up a dummy in the proposed size and number of pages. Weigh it. Then multiply by the number of copies to be printed and add 10 percent for waste and another 10 percent for trim (if any). This will give the approximate number of pounds of paper that should be ordered.

In general, the rates for printing a periodical are lower than for commercial work because the periodical with standardized format can be set up more easily after a few issues.

To figure cost more closely, the following estimates may be useful:

Cold-type composition costs ranged in one survey from ¾ to 1½ cents a word. Linotype text composition ranged from 1.2 to 3.3 cents. Book paper ranged from 15 to 20 cents a pound (in quantity). Offset plates ranged from $1.50 to $3 per 8½ by 11 page, i.e., $6 to $12 per 17 by 22 plate. Display composition cost 50 cents to $1 a line. Pressready and washup each cost about the same as offset plates. Folding cost about $2.50 per 1,000 signatures. Pamphlet binding cost $5 per 1,000 signatures. Duplicate plates cost about 20 cents a square inch for electrons, 7 cents for rubber or plastic plates.

etching   To etch means to eat with acid, as when an artist scratches a picture on a paraffin-coated copperplate and then uses acid to etch or eat away the copper where his strokes have gone through the protecting paraffin. Proofs taken from such an etched plate (see

NAME OF CUSTOMER_____

ADDRESS_____

TITLE AND DESCRIPTION OF JOB_____

_____

_____

_____

_____

_____

*Date*_____

SPECIFICATIONS

No. of Copies_____

No. of Pages_____

Trimmed Page Size_____ x _____

Untrimmed Page Size_____ x _____

Printing Sheet Size_____

STOCK—TEXT _____

_____Sheets_____lbs._____lbs. at_____per lb.

STOCK–COVER _____

_____Sheets_____lbs._____lbs. at_____per lb.

Add _____% for Profit.

CUTTING_____

COMPOSITION

Linotype _____

Monotype _____

Add_____% for Profit.

Hand _____

Make-up _____

Break for Color _____

Foundry Lock-up _____

Press Lock-up _____

ENGRAVINGS_____

Add _____% for Profit.

ELECTROTYPES

_____ Size _____x_____ inches _____

Routing for Color _____ Fixing _____

Add_____% for Profit.

MAKE READY

_____ Forms _____ hours each _____ hours at _____ per hour ____

RUNNING

_____ Forms _____ pp. _____ Imp. Each _____ hrs. at _____ per hour

INK (Allow for Overrun)

Color _____ Amount _____ lbs. _____

Add_____% for Profit.

BINDING See Details "Over"_____ M at _____ per M.

Add_____% for Profit.

CARTAGE _____ lbs. _____ Pkgs. at _____ per Pkg.

TOTAL

DISCOUNT

PER M FOR ADDITIONAL COPIES

One printer makes all estimates on the above form to make sure he allows for every important cost factor. The columns allow him to figure a job several ways.

INTAGLIO) are also called "etchings." Had the artist removed the metal with gravers and other tools instead of exposing it for the acid to eat away, he would have been making an "engraving."

Etching is also done by photoengravers, who prepare their plates photographically instead of by hand. (See LINECUT.)

Executive typewriter See IBM EXECUTIVE TYPEWRITER.

expanded Type that has been designed to make the letters wider than usual (as compared with their height) is said to

be expanded or "extended." Exceptionally narrow type is called "condensed" type. This sentence is set in 9-pt Century Expanded.

express See REA EXPRESS.

extended See EXPANDED.

eyeleting The process of reinforcing a punched hole. Often calendars are fitted with a metal-reinforced eyelet so they can be hung on a nail. The work is done by firms specializing in mounting and finishing. (See MOUNTING AND FINISHING.)

F|f

facsimile As generally understood, an exact copy. Old books and documents are sometimes reprinted in facsimile editions which reproduce not only the exact type arrangement but also discoloration of the paper, any marginal notes, etc.

Any halftone printing process will do this type of facsimile work, but the best method is probably photogelatin (because screenless), with gravure as next choice. (See PHOTOGELATIN; GRAVURE.)

A photographic copy is a facsimile. In certain legal work, a photographic copy or a photostat of a document is acceptable where other types of copies would not be.

The word "facsimile" is also used to describe methods of sending pictures, drawings, or written material by wire or radio, to be reproduced at the receiving end.

Fairchild-Davidson offset machines A line of small offset presses, similar to the Multilith (see OFFSET DUPLICATORS), made by Fairchild-Davidson, a division of Fairchild Camera and Instrument Corp., 5001 E. Jericho Turnpike, Commack, N.Y.

The Fairchild-Davidson Dualith prints by both offset and letterpress, the conversion to letterpress taking about 10 minutes and permitting printing on the Multigraph principle from type, rubber plates, or curved electros. Special attachments permit perforating, numbering, and imprinting from linotype slugs.

Fairchild engraver See SCAN-A-GRAVER; SCAN-A-SIZER.

fake process See also PROCESS COLOR; COLOR PRINTING.

Full-color reproduction by the process-color technique is potentially exact but expensive. If approximate results will do, considerable saving can be made by using the fake-process technique.

Regular process-color printing begins with some high-precision photographic "color-separation" work. In fake process work this stage is much abbreviated, and the platemaker (who must also be something of an artist) makes the separations by hand.

By the fake-process method, a black-and-white original can be converted into a colored picture; or a full-color original can be copied though not reproduced.

109

Fake process work is recommended only where slight changes in color values are not objectionable. It may do complete justice to the picture of a package or a sunset, while failing utterly to give satisfactory reproduction of the closeup portrait of a steaming beef stew. Any attempt to achieve too much in fake process would boost the cost up above the cost of genuine process color.

Both genuine process-color methods and fake process-color methods are used in offset, gravure, and photogelatin as well as in letterpress. Printers can advise on when to use which.

fill-in See also LETTERS.

When name, address, and salutation are typed in at the top of a form letter, this is referred to as a "fill-in." Fill-ins can also occur within the body of the text, especially when the work is done on an automatic electric typewriter. (See AUTOMATIC TYPEWRITER.)

Fill-in work is also known as "personalizing."

film See also MOTION PICTURES; FILMSTRIPS.

The word "film" is generally applied to transparent sheeting such as the cellulose acetate on which photographic film is based, cellulose nitrate (celluloid), cellophane, polyvinyl acetate (vinylite), polyethylene (Pliofilm). Sometimes the word "foil" is given the same meaning.

Transparent film can be obtained in various thicknesses at most art supply stores. Sometimes it is given a slight grain (making it frosty in appearance) so that it will accept pencil and ink markings.

It is possible to draw on smooth film by using special inks, by mixing some soap with watercolors, or by using paints with a turpentine base.

Filmotype A photolettering machine in which characters are manually selected from a master film and printed down on 35-mm photographic paper in the form of headlines, borders, etc. Fonts are available in a wide variety of styles. Changes in type size are made either by purchasing additional fonts in the desired size or by subsequent enlargement or reduction of the product. Equipment is available for the automatic development of the exposed lines. For information write the Filmotype Corporation, 7500 McCormick Blvd., Skokie, Ill. See also PHOTOLETTERING.

Filmotype.

filmstrips See also MOTION PICTURES.

The term "filmstrip" is generally used synonymously with "slidefilm" to describe a continuous strip of 35mm film containing 20 to 100 frames of still photographs, diagrams, or charts. These pictures are projected upon a screen, one at a time.

Filmstrips may be in color or in black and white. Some contain printed captions right on the pictures, some are intended to illustrate or be accompanied by a talk, and some are made to be used with narration and sound effects recorded on a 7- or 12-in. phonograph record or on tape. 12-in. discs are by far the more prevalent kind.

The term "slidefilm" is sometimes also applied to a set of individual slides, usually 2 by 2 in., in glass or cardboard mounts.

Some machines will handle both 2 by 2 in. slides and a filmstrip; most machines handle only one or the other.

Filmstrips are much cheaper to make than movies. For some purposes, they are as good or better. They are particularly valuable for educating people in the details of a subject, since the pictures can be left on the screen as long as the instructor desires and he can adjust the pace to meet the needs of his audience. Movies are better when the objectives are to show motion or to get an emotional response.

The problem of making a filmstrip is basically that of creating or assembling the pictures in the right order. Most filmstrips consist of about 40 to 120 still pictures.

It is customary to make the artwork of one uniform size, namely, 6¼ in. high by 8¼ in. wide, so that all pictures can be photographed in the same focus. This *proportion* must be adhered to, although the size may vary if necessary. (See SCALING.)

Photographs are usually carefully retouched (see RETOUCHING) both to emphasize important detail and to correct flaws. Even minor flaws become prominent when a picture is enlarged upon the screen.

Drawings may be used. However, if drawings in black ink on white paper are used, the result may be to throw a blinding amount of white light on the screen, and it may be better to reverse these, black for white, or to make the drawings in black on gray with white highlights.

Photographs for filmstrip use should be low in contrast, since they will gain in contrast when copied onto the master negative and again onto the positive projection print. However, there is available today an internegative film which greatly reduces the buildup in contrast.

Making the master negative from finished artwork will cost approximately $2 or $2.50 per frame.

The artwork, however, will run up the cost, perhaps to $25 to $60 per frame, i.e., per picture.

Silent filmstrips may be distributed with a printed or mimeographed narrator's text. Most silent filmstrips are prepared with short captions printed below, above, or directly on each picture. A good technique for putting captions on photographs is to draw or print white letters on transparent film (cellulose acetate) and then airbrush in black behind the letters on the underside of the film so that the letters will stand away even from white parts of the photo. Many printing companies using the "hot press" technique are equipped to print such captions. The transparent titles are laid over the illustration and both are copied together.

Sound filmstrips employ a 12- or 16-in. record or a script to carry the narration and musical accompaniment. Usually a bell sounds to tell the operator of the filmstrip projector when it is time to turn to the next picture. Most new sound filmstrips are recorded with inaudible impulses that will automatically advance the film from one frame to the next. Sound filmstrip equipment must have special provision for an automatic filmstrip advance.

The use of sound increases the effectiveness of a filmstrip and also its cost. The narrator, the music, the studio, and the sound crew all cost money.

The preparatory work on a set of separate glass or paperbound film slides is the same as for film. A set of slides costs a little more and has the advantage that the pictures can be rearranged at will; the disadvantage that they can accidentally get into the wrong order or get turned upside down. If there is time, it is very easy also to make changes in a filmstrip, simply by rearranging the original artwork and then shooting a new negative and positive.

Filmstrips or slidefilms can be made in color. A simple way is to shoot the artwork with an ordinary roll of 35mm color film, as many times as there are sets to be made, and have these films finished in 2 by 2 in. slides. A 35mm camera requires a special stand for shooting filmstrip successfully.

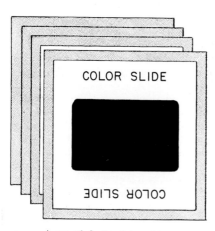

A set of 2- by 2-in. slides.

Most color filmstrips are prepared from original drawings in color or from color transparencies. The preparation of artwork for color filmstrips is similar to that for black-and-white filmstrips. The use of transparencies poses a different problem, for transparencies cannot be retouched easily and therefore should be of excellent quality if they are to be used for filmstrips.

Several firms equipped to make color filmstrips to order are: Allied Film Laboratory, 9930 Greenfield Rd., Detroit, Mich.; Cinéque Colorfilm Laboratory, 424 E. 89 St., New York; Manhattan Color Laboratory, 210 W. 65 St., New York; and Slide-O-Chrome Corp., 155 E. 24 St., New York.

Charges run approximately $2 or $3 per frame for preparing a master negative and a test print from color artwork or transparencies. After that the reproduction charge ranges from 20 cents a foot for less than 100 feet to 15 cents a foot for 1,000 to 2,000 feet, and 10 cents a foot for 5,000 to 10,000 feet.

There are estimated to be close to 1,000,000 filmstrip projectors in U.S. schools alone, a much smaller number having a sound attachment. Projectors may also be rented, with or without operator, from many local film-projection services listed in the Classified Telephone Directory.

Firms that are organized not only to make filmstrips to order but also to undertake the distribution of them include The Jam Handy Organization, 2821 E. Grand Blvd., Detroit, Mich., 48211, which also has offices in New York, Chicago, and Hollywood; William P. Gottlieb Co. (University Films, Inc.), 36 W. 60 St., New York; and The Chartmakers, Inc., 25 W. 45 St., New York.

Those who plan to buy or use films or filmstrips will get valuable suggestions from the books on films listed in Appendix 2, Bibliography.

finishing See MOUNTING AND FINISHING.

first-class mail See Appendix 3, Postal Information.

flat In order to make an offset plate, film negatives or positives are first stripped into place in "windows" cut into a large sheet of goldenrod-colored paper, which holds them in the proper arrangement. This assemblage of film and paper is called a "flat." It is somewhat easier to store flats against the possibility that a rerun may be called for than to store plates, although both may be done.

flatbed press A press in which the type or plates lie flat, as distinct from the *rotary press,* in which they are curved around a cylinder. To the confusion of the layman, the term "flatbed press" is often used interchangeably with the term "cylinder press," both having a "flat bed" for the type forms. The cylinder from which the cylinder press gets its name serves to carry the paper, not the type or plates. Presses which have *two* cylinders—one to carry the curved printing plates and the other to press the paper against them—are called "rotary presses." See PRINTING PRESSES.

flat color See also COLOR PRINTING.
Color printing is either flat-color work or process-color work. Flat color is cheaper because simpler. (See PROCESS COLOR.)
In flat-color work red is red, blue is blue, and yellow is yellow; and the three are not blended on the page to give effects of purple, violet and magenta, green, orange, etc.
A pamphlet having red headlines and black text is a flat-color job. It remains so if blue borders and yellow tint blocks are added. If a green panel is needed, it is possible to get the effect of green by running a transparent blue over yellow, and the job is still classified as flat color.
If, however, it is necessary to reproduce a full-color photograph or painting, with all its shades and tones, then the job falls into the process-color category.
Cuts and plates for flat-color work are purchasable singly at ordinary rates, just as if they were all to print in black.

Cuts and plates for process-color work are made only in matched sets and cost considerably more.
Flat color does not necessarily mean full-strength color—the color can be made to appear much lighter than full strength by printing it in a dot or line pattern. (See SHADING TINTS.)
Silk-screen work is usually done in flat colors, as are many posters and illustrations for children's books. (See TINT BLOCKS.)

flexographic printing What used to be called "aniline printing" is now referred to as "flexographic printing" since the former term had come to be somewhat of a misnomer. The flexographic printing industry specializes in printing paper bags, envelopes, food wrappers etc. It has learned to print on such normally difficult surfaces as cellophane, wax paper, polyethylene (Pliofilm), etc. Originally aniline dyes were incorporated into the quick-drying alcohol-base liquid inks that gave the process its former name. Now many kinds of ink are used, but the presses are all web-fed rotaries printing in fast-drying inks from rubber plates. The process is comparatively low in cost, and although once low in quality, new methods have greatly improved it.
The process is of no great interest to most buyers, since ordinarily they will be buying not flexographic printing, but imprinted paper bags, etc.; they can let the paper-bag manufacturer take the responsibility for getting the printing done. However, if you want to avoid unpleasant surprises, you have to design with the limitations of the process in mind. Insist on seeing samples comparable to what you are ordering, and do not expect better quality than you are shown.

Flexoprint A method of setting up price lists, directories, etc., in visible file panels in such a way as to permit overlapping typed entries to be photographed direct from the panels for the

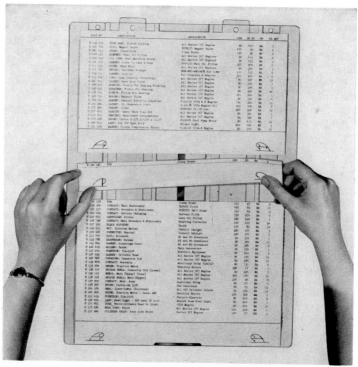

Acme Photo Panel #SVPP 1217-1, showing method of attaching and removing Photo Panel cards. Photo Panels are also available in multicolumn arrangements of two, three, four, or more columns and in special, customized sizes.

purpose of making offset printing plates and running off copies. Each card is slotted to ride on rails in the visible file panels and to space itself from the cards that precede and follow. Insertions and deletions are made simply and rapidly. Means are provided for sliding cards from one column or tray to the next. The equipment is made by Remington Rand Office Systems, 122 E. 42 St., New York 17. Somewhat similar equipment is also made by Acme Visible Records, Crozet, Va.

fliers See CIRCULARS.

flock printing Also called "frost printing," "flock application," and "glitter application"; often used to apply special velvet or frosted finishes to Christmas cards, boxes, etc. Instead of printing ink, sticky glue or varnish is applied to the paper and then sprinkled with rayon fibers, cotton lint, metallic powders, frosting powders, etc. The flocking material adheres only where the glue or varnish has been left by the type or cuts.

The glue sizing or adhesive is printed by either letterpress or silk-screen process. The latter is often preferred, since by this process a heavier layer can be deposited on the paper. One firm that specializes in flock printing is Screen-Flock Industries, Inc., 4257 W. Drummond Pl., Chicago 39.

flop A picture can be flopped, left for right, during the process of reproduction, if the engraver or printer is so instructed. This is often desirable when a person faces out of the layout and should face in. (See discussion and illustration under NEGATIVE.)

fluid duplicator See SPIRIT DUPLICATOR.

fluorescent printing See LUMINESCENT PRINTING.

flush As used in printing, this means "even with." Headings are often run flush left, i.e., flush with the left margin. Headings that are not run flush left or flush right are indented, centered, or run "full measure" (flush with both margins).

The word "flush" when used alone means flush left, unless a mark on the layout or proof shows that it should be interpreted as meaning flush right.

A "flush-mounted" cut means one on which the printing areas run right to the edge of the block, no room being left around the edges for nailing. Flush-mounted cuts are either nailed through nonprinting areas within the design or fastened down with adhesive or by "sweating." (See ANCHORING.)

folding See also BINDING.

A single leaf of paper has two sides, hence two pages. Folded once, it makes a four-page leaflet. Folded again it makes an eight-page leaflet, etc.

Thus, 4, 8, 16, and 32 pages are standard units for booklet work; larger books are made in multiples of 16 or 32 pages. 6-, 12-, 20-, and 24-page units can also be handled on some folding machines.

Note that an 8-page unit must be trimmed before pages 2, 3, 6, 7 can be read. Before trimming this is called a French-fold leaflet. (See illustrations under BINDING.)

Trick folding and folding other than that outlined above may have to be fed through a folding machine a separate time for each fold, or even involve handwork, so it may cost more.

Many small printers have no folding machines but send out all folding and binding operations to a binder. Many have folding equipment, however, either integral with certain presses or separate.

Some folding machines put a thin line of paste down the fold of an 8- or 12-page leaflet, thus making separate stitching unnecessary.

Machine folding can be obtained for as little as $2.50 per thousand pieces, whether one, two, three, or even four folds are called for. (See ESTIMATING COSTS.)

folio (1) A page number. (2) A sheet of paper that has been folded once. (3) A large book, about 12 by 15 in.

A drop folio is a page number placed at the bottom of the page.

font Complete assortment of types of one face and size, including capitals, small capitals, small letters, numbers, punctuation marks, etc. Most Linotype, Intertype, or Monotype fonts contain also matching italic *or* bold letters.

Occasionally a proofreader will find that one letter has slipped in from a different font—a different type face or different size, for example. He must watch for this "wrong font" and mark it (wf) for the printer to correct.

footnote In a manuscript, footnotes may be typed either at the bottom of the page or immediately following the reference. They are often separated from the rest of the typed page by a line.

The word in the text requiring a footnote should be followed by a superior number with a corresponding one preceding the footnote. Using an asterisk or dagger in place of a superior number is not recommended except in scientific or algebraic matter where superior numbers might be mistaken for part of a mathematical expression. In tables, however, symbols are commonly used to avoid confusion with exponents. If the number of footnote references is large and superior numbers are not desirable, superior letters may be substituted for the asterisk and dagger series.

Footnotes throughout a single article, chapter, or section are usually numbered consecutively in manuscript. This is done both because many publishers prefer to follow this method in the printed book and because in any case there is small likelihood that each typed page will make up into one printed page.

foreign-language printing Setting type in a foreign language is a highly specialized business, not only because of the different accents and special type faces required, but because of the many proofreading pitfalls that await the unwary.

Many feel it is not enough merely to have proofs read by someone who "knows" the language in question. That someone must (1) know the language, (2) know it on a highly educated level and have a journalist's competence in using it, and (3) be an experienced proofreader.

Almost any good printer who knows where to find a proofreader with these qualifications can set material in those languages which use the roman alphabet, at least in French, Spanish, German, Italian, etc.

Others have found that it is satisfactory to proofread a foreign language by comparison, depending on the original to be correct and having experienced proofreaders who know simply the alphabet and the accents of the language.

In any case, the safest policy is to give foreign-language work of any kind to a printer who specializes in foreign-language printing. He will have the type and the accents. He will know how important it is to get a qualified proofreader and will have one of proved competence on the staff or on call.

One of the most versatile of the foreign-language printers is King Typographic Service Corp., 550 W. 43 St., New York 36, which gives typesetting, proofreading, and printing service in virtually any language, including Chinese, Russian, Hebrew, and Arabic.

form See also BUSINESS FORMS.

To a printer a form is the assemblage of type pages or cuts that are to be printed on one side of one sheet of paper. A 96-page job may consist of three forms of 32 pages each. (For illustration, see TYPE.)

format The shape, size, and style of a book, pamphlet, magazine, or other publication. For example, a book may be published in a clothbound, 5 by 8 format for sale at $5 and later in a paperbound, 4 by 6 format for sale at 50 cents. The format must be determined before layout and dummy can be made. (See also LAYOUT; DUMMY.)

forwarding of mail See Appendix 3, Postal Information.

Fotolist See SEQUENTIAL-CARD CAMERAS.

Fotosetter See INTERTYPE.

Fotorite See STABILIZATION PROCESS.

Fotosetter See INTERTYPE.

Fototronic See INTERTYPE.

Fototype The Fototype method of setting type utilizes letters that are printed on separate slips of white index-card stock. These letters can be assembled to form headlines, using a special composing stick. Once a headline is set, it is backed with double-coated tape and is ready to be photographed.

Fototype is most often used in combination with typewritten or VariTyped text for offset reproduction. (See VARITYPER.) A line of Fototype can be pasted down alongside other material, or it can be enlarged or reduced photographically and "stripped in" alongside other material in its enlarged or reduced size.

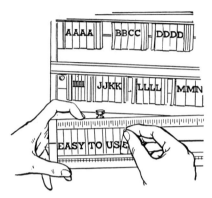

Setting Fototype.

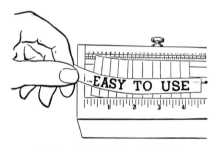

How Fototype is backed with Scotch tape. The letters that will be photographed are on the underside and duplicate those seen here.

Fototype comes in approximately 300 sizes and styles. It is sold in kits consisting of 100 of the most frequently used characters and 50 each of the others. The average kit costs about $11.25 for a set of capital letters and $18.75 for capitals and small letters. Refill pads of any letter cost 45 cents each.

"Reverse" alphabets (white letters against black) are available, but the ordinary alphabets can, of course, be re-versed by getting a negative photostat.

For full information write the Foto-type Co., 1414 W. Roscoe St., Chicago 160657.

The following lines were set in Fototype:

ANYONE CAN SET FOTOTYPE

for Emphasis

EASY TO USE

COMPLETE KITS

Also available is transparent Fototype, which is designed for use with positive-working offset plates. Transparent Fototype is used in the various diazo copying and blueprinting processes now on the market as well as for visual aids.

foundry proofs See PROOFS.

Foundry proofs are easily recognized by the broad black bands like bands of mourning around each page of type. These bands are from the "bearers" (sometimes called "guards") that lend support to the type page when the foundry makes stereotypes or electro-types. (See illustration; also STEREOTYPE; ELECTRO.)

The editor or purchaser of printed matter will receive proofs in the following order: galley proofs, revised galley proofs, page proofs, revised page proofs, and (if duplicate plates are to be made) foundry proofs and plate proofs.

Foundry proofs are supplied, not for corrections, which should have been completed in the page-proof stage, but to show that the corrections indicated on the final page proofs have been made. In the absence of instructions to the contrary, the printer may order duplicate plates without waiting for O.K.'d foundry proofs to be returned by the customer.

Even though you may have to wait a little longer, you'll be glad you ordered Wayne Rolling Gymstands. Their specification saves many square feet of usable floor space by folding out of the way when not in use. They provide comfort and maximum visibility through scientifically correct design. They insure safety and simplicity of movement because of ingenious construction features.

You can get more income from your athletic events by installing a Wayne Gymstand. Remember, Wayne's more than 28 years of specialized experience in designing, building and erecting every type of steel grandstand may save you time, money and "head-aches." Send us the measurements of your present or proposed gymnasium for our engineer's recommendations and estimate.

✦ROGRESSIVE COMPOSITICN COMP4

A foundry proof.

foundry type See also TYPE.

Foundry type is hand-set type, cast in individual characters and kept in a "typecase" (see CASE), each character in its own compartment.

four-color printing See PROCESS COLOR.

fourth-class mail See Appendix 3, Postal Information.

freight See also SHIPPING INFORMATION.

For years "shipping by freight" meant "railway freight." The rate was low and delivery slow, but for shipments too large for fourth-class mail (parcel post), railway shipping was it. For a time the Railway Express Agency, owned by the railroads since 1929, had a virtual monopoly on small shipments—those too heavy or too bulky for parcel post and less than car lots (LCL) for railway freight.

Since World War II, trucks and planes have shattered the old pattern. Motor freight lines have spread a vast shipping network into every metropolis and into sparsely populated areas where there is no railroad service. They offer pick-up and delivery service as fast as a truck can get there and at competitive rates. Air freight service is now offered by almost every passenger airline and cargo flight.

Each freight service—rail, truck, plane, and boat—has a complex rate schedule based on the commodity to be shipped and its weight and bulk. For example, books take one rate, magazines and newspapers another, and miscellaneous printed matter still another. For air freight, rates vary from one airline to the next. If two airlines must handle one shipment in order to get it to a certain destination, there may be two rates.

Freight forwarders or carriers are companies whose business it is to cope with these complexities. They use truck, railway, plane, boat or a combination of these to get a shipment from one major city to another quickly and economically. The freight forwarder quotes one rate to the shipper although he may use several different carriers— for example, motor freight to a railway center, then rail freight, and finally a second motor freight carrier at the other end. A shipment of printed matter (other than books, magazines, and newspapers) from New York to the West Coast can be delivered by freight forwarder in six to seven days at a cost of $9.43 per 100 lb. There are also package rates on shipments of less than 100 lb.

Some freight forwarders specialize in particular runs such as "daily service from New York to Detroit and Milwaukee" or "daily service from New York to the West Coast." Some handle chiefly international freight.

Four well-known freight forwarding companies are Acme Fast Freight, Inc.; National Carloading Corp.; Universal Carloading and Distributing Co., Inc.; and Western Carloading Co., Inc. For additional companies serving your area, turn to "Freight Forwarding" in the Classified Section of the Telephone Directory.

REA Express, the name taken by the Railway Express Agency in 1960, has become an all-modal carrier using railroads, airlines, steamship companies, and motor freight carriers in this country and overseas. In a sense, REA is a freight forwarder since it uses all kinds of freight services, specializes in small shipments (LCL and LTL), and handles the same-destination packages of many shippers as though they were one unit (what they call "unitized" shipping). (See REA EXPRESS.)

Certain features of each mode of freight carrier service should be kept in mind.

Rail freight, although slower than motor freight, is often the cheapest way to ship material of large weight and bulk to points reached by railroad. There is no maximum as to weight or volume that can be shipped by rail freight. Most railroads east of the Mississippi accept no shipments of less than 5,000 lb; some have a minimum of 8,000 lb. West of the Mississippi, weight limits vary from one line to the next.

Rail-freight rates per 100 lb vary according to the kind of material being shipped, the distance to be covered, and the region through which it will travel. Printed matter takes a freight rate which is cheaper than that for breakable articles such as furniture and household goods. The rate for shipping bulk paper depends upon the kind of paper as well. Full insurance is included in the regular rate.

For further information about rail freight rates, consult *Leonard's Guide and Service* (described in detail under SHIPPING INFORMATION) or call the local freight agent of any railroad.

Motor freight, also called motor carrier and truck, may be faster and easier than shipping by railroad since it means door-to-door delivery between points that a truck can reach. In general, motor-freight rates are higher than those for rail freight. Package rates (for parcels of under 10 lb) make motor freight competitive with fourth-class mail. (See Appendix 3, Postal Information) REA Express (q.v.), United Parcel Service (q.v.) and Greyhound Package Service. (See SHIPPING INFORMATION.)

Most trucking lines operate within a certain limited area, as between New York, Pittsburgh, and Richmond, Va. However, a company may contract for shipments beyond its limits by subcontracting to another line. For companies in a certain area see Express and Transfer in the Classified Telephone Directory.

Invaluable help in locating motor-freight rates and routings can be found through the use of *Leonard's Guide and Service* and the six motor-freight directories (New York, Philadelphia, Chicago, Boston, New England, and Los Angeles–San Francisco) published by the same firm and described in detail under SHIPPING INFORMATION.

Air freight is handled by almost all of the passenger airlines as well as the cargo flights, with rates varying from one airline to the other. Air freight is faster than railway, truck, or boat. Usually shipments must be delivered to the airport by the shipper and picked up at the final destination by the consignee, except as a freight forwarder provides pickup and delivery service.

In general, air-freight rates are higher than those for rail and motor freight, but this, too, can vary according to the size and bulk of the shipment and the destination. For one overseas shipment the rate for air freight was actually cheaper than the rate for freight by boat.

There is no one source for air-freight rates which is comparable to *Leonard's Guide* for rail freight and REA Express rates or to the motor freight directories published by the same firm. (For details about *Leonard's Guide* and directories, turn to SHIPPING INFORMATION.) Rates

must be obtained from the various airlines or freight forwarders.

For small packages, the shipper should also consider air parcel post (see Appendix 3, Postal Information) and air express (see REA EXPRESS). At 1966 rates, air parcel post is less expensive than air express and air freight for a 5-pound package. For a package of 25 pounds, air freight is the cheapest on the long hauls. See also SHIPPING INFORMATION and its table of air rates.

freight forwarders See FREIGHT.

French fold See FOLDING; BINDING.

When a piece of paper is folded twice, the second fold at right angles to the first, an uncut eight-page folder is formed. The result is a French-fold leaflet, which handles like a four-page leaflet although actually printed on only one side of the paper.

frisket See MASK.

frost printing See FLOCK PRINTING.

full measure To set a line of type "full measure" means to make it the full width of the column, flush with both margins. The instruction is not needed unless the printer might otherwise assume that some kind of indention or centering was intended.

furniture Printer's term for the wooden or metal spacing material used to separate type pages from each other or to fill the space between the type and the metal chase in which it is locked up for press.

Leads, slugs, and furniture are all used for spacing. Leads are 1, 2, or 3 pt thick, slugs are 6 or 12 pt thick. Furniture is the thickest of all. (For illustration of furniture in use, see TYPE.)

Futura See the two charts entitled "The Futura Family" in Appendix 1, Type Faces.

G | g

galley, galley proof A galley is the shallow metal drawer or tray in which type is kept after it has been set. Each galley normally holds enough type to make two or three pages (book size) although at first the type is not divided into pages. (See illustration under TYPE.)

Proofs that are pulled before the type is divided into pages are called "galley proofs." They are usually about 6 to 8 in. wide by 24 in. long. Each one shows whatever lines happened to fit on that particular galley. Each is marked at the top with a galley number, so the printer can identify that particular tray of type.

Galley proofs should show only one column of type and are made with wide margins to provide room for proofreader's marks.

Printers normally supply three sets of galley proofs, one marked "Return this set with corrections," another to be used in the paste-up dummy (see PASTE-UP DUMMY), the third to be kept by the customer. If extra sets of galley proofs are needed, perhaps for the author, they should be ordered in advance and will be charged for at the rate of 5 to 7 cents for each proof of a single galley.

Some editors order one set of galley proofs pulled on colored paper to distinguish it from the master set, and use this one for paste-up purposes. (These are occasionally called "pink proofs" or "pinks.") Others prefer to paste up with a white set of proofs, since it is then easier to see from the dummy how the finished page will look. If revised galleys are necessary, they are usually pulled on colored paper to avoid confusing the two sets.

In some instances the printer can be instructed to skip galley proofs and go directly into page proofs. This is practical only when each page is selfcontained with no carry-overs and when the copy has been written to fit the page. The danger in skipping galley proofs is that corrections on one page may affect succeeding pages and thus greatly increase the cost in both time and money.

Reader's galleys (master galleys) are sacred. They must not be cut up or marked except with necessary corrections for the printer.

It is very important that all the original copy be kept with the master proofs when these are sent from printer to customer or from customer to printer. Such material (manuscript, artwork, layout) is almost sure to be needed for reference when working with proofs.

Garamond, Garamont See Appendix 1, Type Faces.

gatefold When an illustration bigger than the printed page is to be inserted in a book, magazine, or pamphlet, this can be done by means of a gatefold insert as illustrated.

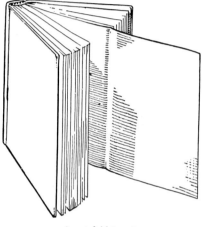

A gatefold insert.

In a slim pamphlet or magazine, it is better to run such an illustration across the center spread; if a center spread is not available, or if, as in the case of a bound book, the nature of the binding conceals the center fold, then the gatefold insert may be necessary. If a gatefold insert is added before trimming (see BINDING), it must be narrow enough so that the outer fold escapes the trimming knife.

gathering When a book or booklet consists of several units or signatures, these have to be gathered into the right sequence as part of the binding process. (See illustration under BOOKBINDING.)

gelatin printing There are two important gelatin printing processes: hecto-

graph and photogelatin. (See HECTO-GRAPH; PHOTOGELATIN.)

The hectograph process is used for duplicating office forms and communications when the quantities needed are between 10 and 50.

The photogelatin process, also called "collotype," is used for reproducing paintings, large photographic illustrations, facsimiles of old documents, etc., in quantities up to several thousand. It has the special advantage of reproducing halftone subjects without the use of the halftone screen required in other processes.

gelatin transfer See VERIFAX.

glassines See BRONZE PROOFS.

glossy A photographic print on glossy paper. Photographic prints intended for reproduction are usually made on 8 by 10 glossy paper.

Glossies are not easily scratched or soiled in handling. A glossy print has a greater range of tonal values; the blacks are blacker, and the whites are whiter than in dull prints. However, it is perfectly possible for a printer to reproduce from a photographic print made on dull or mat (sometimes spelled "matte") paper.

Goldmark Gold leaf prepared in a form which permits gold writing or decorating to be done without the heat usually required. If you lay a piece of Goldmark (also called "cold gold") on a leather, plastic, paper, wood, or metal surface and write your name on it with a ball-point pen, or a pencil, a genuine 23 K gold facsimile of your signature will be transferred to the article. Goldmark is made by Hastings & Co., Inc., 2314 Market St., Philadelphia 19101.

Gothic See Appendix 1, Type Faces.

government printing The U.S. Government Printing Office is the largest printing plant in the world. As far as the Federal government departments are concerned, it is the only source from which they may order their printing, for Congress has given it a monopoly over public printing and binding, except for certain requirements outside Washington. In the fiscal year ending June 30, 1963, it handled $130,837,702 worth of government printing.

To those who have the privilege of dealing with the Government Printing Office, generally known throughout the Federal establishment as the "GPO," and those who are interested in its operations, the following paragraphs are addressed.

The GPO is equipped to do almost every type of printing and binding, including forms, pamphlets, books, periodicals, posters, and other color work. It grants waivers for direct procurement of some stock-item specialties, and it contracts on open bid for other printing that it cannot produce economically.

The major divisions of the GPO that serve the various Federal departments and agencies, including, of course, the Congress itself, are as follows.

Planning Divisions. These are headed by a planning-production manager. The Division of Planning Service receives all requisitions and copy, provides production and delivery schedules, answers inquiries on progress of work, acts as liaison for other office departments, follows up the back-and-forth transmission of proofs, issues waivers for direct procurement of printing, writes specifications for work to be procured from commercial sources, and in general is the equivalent of the sales staff or the public-relations office in a commercial plant.

Division of Plant Planning. This sets up the specifications or production plan, makes the estimates, and fills orders for blank paper and supplies.

Division of Typography and Design. This furnishes layout service, advice on typography and standards, casual art-

work, retouching, and photographic service. (The National Archives Photographic Department can also serve other government agencies on a reimbursable basis, and does good color work.) This division is also charged with the maintenance and supervision of quality standards.

Composing Division. There are several composing rooms in the GPO which make up the Composing Division. These are the Linotype section, the Monotype section, the job section, the patents section, and the hand section. The division has 81 Monotype keyboards, 114 casters, 168 slug machines, 5 strip casters, and 2 Ludlows, with a sufficient variety of type faces to afford good typographical effects for selected jobs. Naturally, since the purpose of government publications is utilitarian, it is best equipped in a few standard text faces. Some of the Monotype faces available at GPO in a wide range of sizes include Alternate Gothic; Baskerville; Bodoni; Bodoni Bold; Bodoni Ultra; Bookman; Caslon OS 336; Caslon 37; Caslon Bold; Garamond; Garamond Bold; Franklin Gothic; Kennerley; Kennerley Bold; Sans Serif Medium, Bold, and Extra Bold; and Stymie Light, Medium, Bold, and Extra Bold.

Some of the Linotype and Intertype faces available at GPO in a wide range of sizes include Baskerville, the Bodonis, Century Expanded, Futura Demibold with italic, Garamond, Garamond Bold, Granjon, Ionic, Memphis Medium and Bold, Vogue Bold and Oblique, Vogue Extra Bold and Oblique.

Platemaking Division. The GPO probably has more extensive platemaking facilities than almost any other printing plant. It is equipped to produce every kind of printing plate. This division has long been in the foreground of research and experiment on plastic plates and plastic electrotype molding.

Letterpress Division. The GPO has every type of letterpress equipment from platens to web-fed rotaries. Some of its rotaries will print, perforate, fold, and paste or staple up to 64-page units at speeds up to 12,000 per hour. Its postcard presses produce 2½ billion postcards annually. Its three specially built *Congressional Record* presses run at a speed of 20,000 impressions per hour. Between congressional sessions these presses usually run the tremendous income-tax printing program.

Offset Division. This is responsible for the processing of all jobs or publications produced by offset lithography. It includes the offset copy preparation, offset negative, offset platemaking, and offset press sections.

Binding Division. This well-equipped bindery handles congressional work and processes nearly all forms, pamphlets, and books produced for the Federal government. In addition, it is capable of producing case-bound volumes in fine leather bindings. Recent years have seen many formerly hand-performed operations being taken over by high-speed machinery either fully or partially automated.

Division of Tests and Technical Control. This is responsible not only for testing and research on all materials used by the GPO but also for manufacturing printing and writing inks, press rollers, and adhesives. It provides technical and scientific counsel to the production divisions as well as to other government departments that require it. This division has worked closely with the Bureau of Standards and with commercial printing and printing-supply research organizations.

Documents Division. This distributes and mails Federal publications for the originating Federal departments, and maintains a sales organization for documents that have general public interest. This division generally uses mailing lists furnished by the Federal department, but it has also built up many accurate lists of its own for the purpose of promoting sales. Certain departments have specially classified lists which are often made availabe to other agencies.

Any government purblication that is of sufficient interest to create a public-sale demand is printed, stocked, and sold by the GPO Superintendent of Documents. The originating department pays all preparatory costs and the Superintendent of Documents is charged only the additional rate for paper and material, presswork, and binding.

To this cost he adds 50 percent, as required by law, to establish a sale price, this margin allowing for overhead and expenses. He makes a discount of 25 percent for quantity orders, and any profit that he accumulates is turned back to the general funds of the Treasury. Under this arrangement, the public can buy, at low cost, either by mail order or at the bookstore maintained in the GPO Documents Division, valuable government reports covering a wide range of subjects. The advantage to the departments is that this method of distribution gives cost-free circulation to their publications.

The GPO, of course, maintains all the other divisions and sections necessary to any well-organized production plant. It also operates five duplicating plants formerly under the jurisdiction of the Treasury Department's Procurement Division. These plants, including a shop in Washington, D.C., have a fine record of quick service on Multigraphing, mimeographing, and Multilith jobs considered too small for GPO's big presses. Many government agencies also have their own equipment for such work.

Every user of the GPO should purchase from the Superintendent of Documents a copy of the GPO "Style Manual" and also a copy of the GPO "Type Book." The "Style Manual" is a mine of information on how to prepare copy for the printer.

Editors who do not feel competent to design their own publications can ask the GPO Division of Typography and Design to assist in designing their publications.

One way in which nongovernment groups can enjoy the privilege of having their material printed by the GPO is to have a congressman read that material into the *Congressional Record* and then order reprints. Such reprints are available at very low rates. Sometimes a congressman is willing to go still further and send material out under frank.

grain In all machine-made paper, the fibers tend to align themselves in the direction in which the pulp flows, despite mechanical shaking intended to minimize this. (Handmade papers have no grain.) It is harder to tear or fold paper across the grain. The pages of a book turn more easily when the grain runs parallel to the binding edge.

Paper for a 6 by 9 book to be printed on 25 by 38 stock would therefore be ordered with grain long, i.e., the 38-in. way. This is sometimes abbreviated as 25 by 38, the underlining indicating the way the grain is to go.

graphotype See also ADDRESSOGRAPH; ADDRESSING.

The graphotype is a machine for embossing letters in the thin sheet metal used in Addressograph plates.

gravure Photogravure or gravure printing is the most important commercial application of the intaglio (pronounced "in-tal′-yo") principle. (See INTAGLIO.)

Printing is done from large copper plates or copper-covered cylinders. These plates are relatively expensive, but once they are made, the cost of running them is comparatively low. The process lends itself to high-quality reproduction of photographs and other tonal illustrations, even on the most inexpensive paper. Its reproduction of type is not quite so good. The letters have slightly fuzzy edges, because all reproduction by this process necessitates the use of a crossline screen. Type reproduced in gravure is entirely legible, but it is best not to use small sizes, certainly not below 8 pt, nor to use a text type with very thin serifs, like Bodoni.

The two important divisions of the gravure industry are sheet-fed gravure and rotogravure.

Small runs, from 10,000 to about 100,000, are best handled on a sheet-fed gravure press. Larger runs of 100,000 and up (monotone) and 250,000 up (four-color) may be handled economically on a web-fed rotogravure press, although it should be noted that many rotogravure presses handle the equivalent of 20,000 sheets per hour, each as big as 44 by 70 or more—sometimes in four colors, on both sides—so that a job has to be pretty big to warrant the use of these giant presses. In general, very few monotone jobs are done in rotogravure for sums less than $1,000 to $3,000. Large color jobs range higher, but in long runs unit costs are very low. (See the chart "How to Choose the Right Printing Process" inside the covers of this book.)

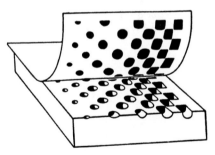

In the News-Dultgen gravure process, used for long-run color work, the ink cups vary *both* in depth and in area, not just in depth. (*Drawing courtesy of Interchemical Corporation.*)

The minimum cost of making a plate in sheet-fed gravure is about $250 for an area 25 by 38. Once made, the sheet-fed gravure plate can be kept for a rerun; i.e., gravure plates can be run again for gravure printing but cannot be used in any other printing process.

The approximate cost of making a cylinder for rotogravure is $300 to $500. A rotogravure cylinder may also be kept for a rerun for a reasonable length of time.

Rotogravure is a high-quality process

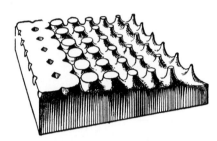

Relief halftone (enlarged).

Gravure plate (enlarged).

Rolling ink onto the surface areas of a relief halftone plate.

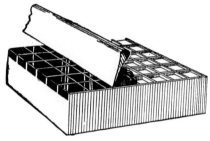

Flooding ink into the depressed gravure cups, then scraping surface areas clean.

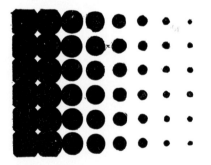

The relief engraving prints only from ink on raised areas; the gravure plate prints only from ink in its depressed areas. The relief dots vary in size; the gravure "ink cups" are of uniform size, but of varying depth. The shallowest carry barely enough ink to soil the topmost fibers of the paper, or none at all. The deepest carry enough ink to soak the paper to the point where the squares run together.

for reproducing black-and-white photographs and is beautiful as a color process.

One adaptation of the gravure process used in large-run color work is known as the "News-Dultgen process." (See illustration.)

The gravure principle has been widely adapted for such special purposes as printing paper bags, cartons, labels, etc. Presses for these purposes often take a web of paper only a few inches wide.

Firms doing sheet-fed gravure work include Beck Engraving Co., Philadelphia; R. R. Donnelley & Sons Co., 2223 S. Parkway, Chicago 16; Photogravure & Color Co., 207 W. 25 St., New York 1.

Firms doing rotogravure work include Alco Gravure Co., Hoboken, N.J. (plants also in Baltimore, Chicago, and Memphis); Art Color Printing Co., Dunellen, N.J.; Chicago Rotoprint Co., 4601 W. Belmont Ave., Chicago; Cuneo Press, Inc., 2242 S. Grove St., Chicago (affiliates are the Neo Gravure Co., Weehawken, N.J., and the Pacific Neo Gravure Co., 325 Minna St., San Francisco); R. R. Donnelley & Sons Co., 2223 S. Parkway, Chicago; and Standard Gravure Corp., 643 S. 6 St., Louisville, Ky.

Special gravure service to advertisers is provided by Intaglio Service Corp. of Chicago and New York, and by International Color Gravure, Inc., 39 W. 60 St., New York. Both will make film positives from artwork or photographs, make trial plates and pull proofs, do any necessary correcting of the positives, and then make duplicate positives to send to as many magazines as are to run the advertisement. The magazines make their rotogravure cylinders from these sets of positives.

green copy One of the first copies to come off a printing press. An editor who catches a serious error in a green copy may still have time to stop the presses before a whole edition has been run off. Green copies often contain defects of inking and makeready, since they are printed while the pressman is still making final adjustments.

greeting cards Greeting cards are widely used for semicommercial and business purposes as well as for personal mailing. In fact, they have become a specialized form of direct mail advertising. Christmas cards, birthday cards, etc., are obtainable in considerable variety from most department stores, stationers, printers, and photographic stores, either plain or imprinted with the buyer's name and message.

Most of the imprinting of customers' names on stock cards is done by the ordinary letterpress method. The little job printer around the corner can do it as well as anybody else. Most cards are imprinted at the point of sale, by the printer or the stationer.

Those who wish to have their own custom-made greeting cards can furnish their own artwork and design and have the cards printed to special order. (See DESIGNERS; ARTISTS; ILLUSTRATIONS.) The soft illustrations so often used are best reproduced by the offset process. (See OFFSET; see also CIRCULARS for information on how to choose the right process for small work such as greeting cards.)

Photographs are best reproduced as actual photographic prints on photographic paper. If the quantity does not exceed 100 or 200, the cost of doing them this way will be less than the cost of making halftones and printing them. Type or lettering can be made a part of the photographic print by techniques with which every photographer is familiar.

Special blank cards and envelopes are available from most shops dealing in paper supplies and photographic stores.

gripper edge It is usually impossible to print anything within ⅜ to ⅝ in. or so of the gripper edge of a sheet of paper. This amount of room must be allowed for the metal fingers, called "grippers," that draw the paper into the printing press. The requirements vary between printing presses, but the factor must be considered in laying out a printing job, especially if it is to bleed on all sides.

groundwood pulp See also PAPER.

Newsprint is made largely from groundwood pulp, sometimes known as "mechanical pulp" to distinguish it from the "chemical pulp" used for better-quality papers.

Groundwood pulp is made quickly and cheaply and produces a sheet of good printability and opacity. It is used for regular newsprint, supercalendered rotogravure paper, the cheaper book papers and coated papers, and the cheaper kinds of bristols and boards.

Paper made from groundwood pulp yellows on long exposure to light because the deteriorating agents in the wood are not removed during manufacture. It lacks strength, owing to its short fibers. Because of these factors, it is not used where permanence is important. Paper free of groundwood content is called a "free sheet."

gummed paper Paper can be purchased already gummed, or it can be gummed to order. (For gummed labels, see LABELS.)

gutter See also MARGINS.

The gutter of a book, magazine, or pamphlet is the inside margin where facing pages join.

H|h

Haberule Visual Copy-caster A desk book that combines all the following in one unit: one-line showings and alphabets of all the most-used type faces; character counts for these and for virtually all other type faces in all available sizes from 4 to 48 pt; tables for figuring characters per line without arithmetic; and a special yellow plastic rule for determining (again without math) how many lines of which sizes and leadings will fit in a given space or how much space will be required for a given number of lines. It is priced at $12.50 and is available from art stores or from the Haberule Company, Stuart, Fla. 33494.

Hadego An ATF machine of Dutch origin for setting display type. In function it resembles the Ludlow, except that the letters are photographically printed on paper instead of being cast in metal.

hairline This is a hairline rule:

A 1-pt rule (1/72 in.) is wider than a hairline. (See RULE for comparison of different kinds.)

halftone See also CUT.

There are two kinds of cuts (engravings): the linecut and the halftone. (See LINECUT.) Halftone cuts, also called halftone "engravings," must be used to reproduce photographs and drawings that contain grays (middle tones or halftones) which are neither jet black nor pure white. (See DRAWING TECHNIQUES for an explanation of when to use a halftone.)

A special technique had to be developed to reproduce grays because of the fact that printing ink is black, not gray. If ink is rolled onto type or a cut and then impressed into the paper, the paper either becomes black or stays white, with no halfway measures.

Early engravers overcame this problem by engraving by hand closely spaced fine black lines to get the effect of gray. For a light gray, the lines were lighter and farther apart, so that the paper would be only 10 to 20 percent covered with ink. For a dark gray, the lines were heavier and closer together, so that the paper would be perhaps 50, 70, or even 90 percent covered with ink.

The same results can be achieved with dots. The ink-spatter technique (see SPATTER) can produce grays of

129

varying tonal values, depending on the size and number of the dots produced by the spattering.

By the halftone technique, any desired gray tone can be manufactured out of tiny black dots with white space between them. (See illustration.)

Halftone cuts are produced commercially by photomechanical methods, without handwork, as follows:

Artwork is put before a photoengraver's camera. A special screen is put into the camera just in front of the negative-film and a fraction of an inch away from the film. The screen is like a window screen, except that it is much finer, having from 50 to 200 lines to the inch in each direction, and except that the lines instead of being wire are blackened scratches in plate glass.

The film is now exposed and developed, and becomes a negative of the original photograph or drawing, except that the outline of the screen appears on the film in the form of white (unexposed) lines, and thus breaks up the image into dots.

The action of the screen is such as to produce large dots where the light was strong and small dots where it was weak.

A zinc or copper plate is now sensi-tized, placed in a vacuum frame in direct contact with the screened negative, and exposed to strong light. The surface hardens where light gets through the negative. The unhardened surface is washed away, exposing the bare metal. The bare metal is etched (eaten away) with acid. Where much light fell on the original negative, all of the surface is eaten away, save very tiny dots. Where only dim light fell on the original negative, very little of the surface is eaten away. This surface will carry lots of ink and print as dark as the original artwork was in that place.

The development of "powderless etching" eliminates much handwork. One large engraver serving many small accounts by mail has now shifted entirely to powderless etching and offers halftones of up to 133 screen at rates below the usual for 100-screen zincs. For example, he offers a flush-mounted, type-high halftone in 100, 110, 120, or 133 screen at $1.75 for 4 sq in., at $4.47 for 20 sq in., and at about 11 to 12 cents a square inch beyond that. His name is Basil L. Smith, P.O. Box 8169, Philadelphia 1.

With conventional glass screens it is difficult, short of additional manipulation, to get a complete "dropout" of the

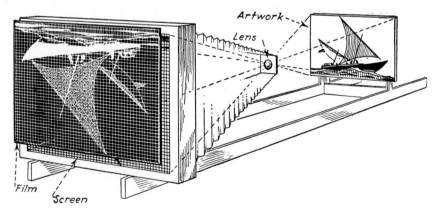

Diagram of copying camera showing artwork, lens, halftone screen, and film negative. The coarseness of the screen is greatly exaggerated. The image on the film negative is shown as it will appear after development.

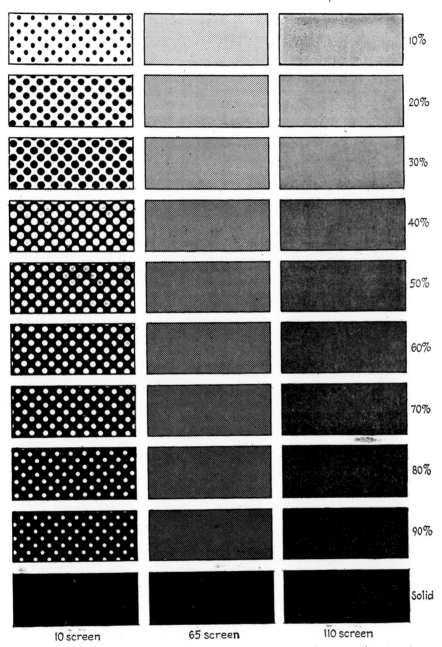

10 screen   65 screen   110 screen

How the halftone process mixes black dots with white paper in varying proportions to get any desired gray. Colored inks can be thinned with white in the same way. The so-called "10 screen" shown here is not actually used in printing—it is a fivefold enlargement from a 50 screen. The halftones on page 5 are 100 screen and on page 12 the halftone is 120 screen.

dots in the area which should be pure white, but this is easy through use of a "magenta contact" screen. This Eastman Kodak product has dyed lines, not black lines, and its opacity can thus be manipulated with the aid of filters.

Other methods for dropping out the halftone dots in the highlights require that an artist use special paints to distinguish between areas to be held and areas to be dropped. (See HIGHLIGHT HALFTONE.)

Halftone cuts of 50 to 100 dots to the linear inch (50 to 100 screen) are called "coarse-screen" halftones and are usually made on zinc. Halftones of 110, 120, 133, 150, 175, and 200 screen are called "fine-screen" halftones and are usually made on copper.

Coarse-screen halftones are used for printing on rough papers like newsprint. The finer-screen halftones must be printed on smooth paper. 100- and 110-screen halftones can be printed on English-finish, machine-finish, or super-calendered paper. Screens finer than 110 really demand coated paper.

Coarse-screen halftones can be printed on smooth paper, but fine-screen halftones will not reproduce well on rough paper.

It is not good practice to make a halftone from the proof of another halftone. The result is likely to be a *moiré* effect somewhat like watered silk or herringbone patterns. This is caused by one screen pattern crisscrossing the other. (See illustration under MOIRÉ.) A good halftone must be made from the best possible original copy.

Photographs and drawings are often printed so as to "bleed." (See BLEED.) Halftones that are to bleed must be ordered wider or deeper (by at least ⅛ in. for each edge that is to bleed) than they will be after trim.

Halftones that are cut square, with no special vignetting, surprinting, or other handwork, are least expensive. As it happens, the ordinary, simple, square halftone is probably the least confusing to the reader. It pays on both counts to avoid special trick layouts with photographs.

The halftone process is used for the reproduction of middle tones in almost all printing processes, not merely in letterpress (relief) printing as discussed above.

The steps in making ready a halftone for offset reproduction are substantially identical to those outlined above, except that the type is transferred to the printing plate at the same time the halftones are.

See SCAN-A-GRAVER for a description of an electronic process for making newspaper halftones.

See GRAVURE for a description of the different way in which the halftone technique is adapted to gravure printing.

See PHOTOGELATIN for a description of a screenless method of reproducing halftones. (It is not really screenless, but the screen occurs naturally like a grain in specially treated gelatin.

For help in choosing the right printing process where there are photographs or other halftones, consult the charts inside the covers of this book.

An ingenious "Halftone Screen Determiner" is made by Arthur H. Gaebel, Inc., 4 Chatsworth Ave., Larchmont, N.Y., price $1.50. It is simply a piece of heavy transparent acetate sheet imprinted with a graded pattern of fine lines. When laid over a halftone, the fine lines interact with the lines of the halftone to form a *moiré* pattern in the form of converging lines pointing to the number of the screen being measured.

hand addressing See ADDRESSING.

handbills See CIRCULARS.

hand-lettering See LETTERING.

hanging indention See INDENTION.

head See HEADINGS, HEADS.

headband The decorative tape at the top and bottom of the spine of a book, just inside the cloth of the binding itself. Headbands serve no structural pur-

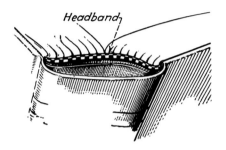

Headband

pose—they are merely glued on to give the book a more finished appearance. Most of the books manufactured today have no headbands.

headings, heads See also DESIGN.

Skillful use of headings and subheads can increase the legibility and attractiveness of any piece of printing and its editorial effectiveness.

Because readers frequently scan a page quickly, heads and subheads assume tremendous editorial importance. They should give the basic essentials of the story so that the 6-second scanner will get the main points even though he may never read the body of the article. Having these basic facts, he knows what the article is about and is more likely to go back and read the whole carefully. With subheads that are simply teasers, he may not get enough meat to interest him or to remember.

The simplest way to get good attention value for a heading is to use type as large as possible. If the heading is too long to be set in large type, then the key word alone can often be set large.

Hand-lettered headings may be attractive but are hardly essential, considering the great variety of type styles and sizes available. (See Appendix 1, Type Faces.)

Variety in headings can be achieved by using italic or sans-serif type for contrast with roman, caps in contrast with lowercase, light with bold, etc. Headings can be run across one or many columns and set flush left or right, or centered in a black or white space, or boxed, etc.

Flush-left Subhead

The flush-left subhead is one of the most useful and economical. The line of the text that follows it is usually indented.

Centered Subhead

The centered subhead is also popular, although not so easy for the eye to find. A wide centered heading sometimes looks as though an inaccurate attempt had been made to indent it or set it flush left.

Run-in Subhead. One of the best headings for saving space is the heading that is run in. It is economical if set in the italic or small caps of the text type, or in some other face that the compositor can mix with the text face without undue trouble.

> *Boxed Heading*

The boxed heading has a certain display value, but it adds to the expense because cutting and mitering rules is more expensive than setting type. The cut-in heading (also called a "cut-in sidenote") has good atten-

The Cut-in Heading tion value and is often used in textbooks; it also adds to the expense of

the typesetting. Marginal headings, often called "sidenotes," also have their virtues, but cause a lot of extra work for the printer and are wasteful of space.

The term "sidehead" is used to mean either a cut-in heading or a marginal heading.

Headings are often set in the *italic* or *ITALIC CAPS* or the CAPS AND SMALL CAPS of the text type, and in the same size. Alternately they may be set in **boldface** or in **Bold Sans Serif**, or perhaps in LIGHT SANS SERIF CAPS. Caps are regarded as slightly less legible than small letters and are, therefore, not used quite so much.

Many editors make it a rule to break every column with at least one subhead. Some like to use a subhead every 3 column in. or so, feeling that solid text looks less readable than text broken by frequent subheads.

headlines See HEADINGS, HEADS.

head to come Meaning that the headline or title will be supplied later, after the printer has set the text matter in type.

hectograph See also SPIRIT DUPLICATOR; DUPLICATING.

A hectograph is an office duplicating machine which can produce from 10 to 50 (under some circumstances, up to 100) copies of typed, written, or drawn material at very low cost. Beyond 50 copies on the hectograph, the copies grow faint and progressively harder to read. To get more, it is necessary to prepare a new master. (See SPIRIT DUPLICATOR for a similar process that will yield up to 300 copies.) Hectograph machines are made in both flatbed and rotary forms. Their printing characteristics are the same.

Up to four colors can be reproduced simultaneously from the same master. Black, however, is not used. A purple carbon aniline dye gives the maximum number of copies. The best results are attained when special hectograph paper is used.

The hectograph (gelatin) process works as follows: The item to be reproduced is typed, written, or drawn on a hard-surfaced paper master. Special hectograph imaging materials containing an aniline dye are used. This is obtainable in the form of writing ink, printing ink, pencil, ribbon, or carbon paper, and in four colors. This master is now laid face down on the gelatin surface. The dye is dissolved and transferred to the gelatin within a few seconds. The gelatin will now release some of the dye, when blank paper is pressed against it, thus duplicating the message. Within 24 hr, the same gelatin can be used again since by that time the dye will have sunk into the gelatin and will no longer print.

Flatbed hectographs with very large beds are used to copy mechanical drawings, maps, operating reports, statistical charts, etc.

Machines operating on the gelatin hectograph principle are marketed by Heyer, Sears, and others, at prices as low as $3 to $4.

Heyer Addresser A low-cost portable addressing machine operating on the spirit-duplicator principle. In operation it is held in one hand and rolled across the item to be addressed with a rocking motion that first moistens the surface with quick-drying alcohol, then rolls on an address. For more details of the process, see MASTER ADDRESSER. The price, including enough materials for a list of 250 names, is $10.95. For information, write to Heyer, Inc., 1855 S. Kostner Ave., Chicago.

highlight halftone See also HALFTONE.

A highlight halftone is one in which the white areas are really white instead of being slightly grayed by tiny dots as in an ordinary halftone. Highlighting is required to get the best reproduction of most pencil and crayon sketches and wash drawings. Some, but by no means all, photographs benefit by it.

A highlight-halftone engraving for letterpress printing costs three times as much as an ordinary halftone. One method of getting highlight-halftone effects at less than highlight-halftone prices is described under VELOX.

Highlighting is done by painting out the highlight areas on the film negative with opaquing fluid, or by etching faint dots until they disappear. Similarly, near blacks can be made solid black by painting over these blacks on the metal after exposure but before etching. This must be requested specially if wanted and is charged for at time rates.

A "dropout" halftone is the same thing as a highlight halftone. The highlight dots are dropped out. This can be done in the camera as well as afterward as described above.

Highlight effects can also be obtained in offset and other processes. The extra cost varies but is usually competitive with letterpress.

Hooven letters See AUTOMATIC TYPEWRITER.

hot type Type which is set with hot metal, as in Linotype and Monotype composition. See also COLD TYPE.

house organs See also PERIODICALS.

Many companies issue house organs, or magazines, for the benefit of their employees or customers. Thousands of such publications are issued every month. Companies not wishing to handle the editorial and production work within the staff sometimes have their publications edited outside, perhaps by their advertising agency or by a firm specializing in the editing and production of house organs. One such firm is The Gebbie Press, P.O. Box 1000, New Paltz, N.Y., which also publishes a directory of house magazines.

One source for a monthly art clipbook is Multi-Ad Services, Inc., 142 Walnut St., Peoria, Ill.

I i

IBM Executive typewriter The IBM Executive electric typewriter made by the International Business Machines Corporation writes in type styles that can hardly be distinguished from type. Such styles can be used because this typewriter gives wide characters more room than narrow ones. For example, there are 10 characters in each of the following lines, but the "i" is taking two units of space, the "a" three units, the "A" four units, and the "M" five units. Such "proportional spacing" is automatic.

By reason of its attractive type styles, the IBM Executive machine, priced at

IBM BOLD FACE NO. 1

iiiiiiiii
aaaaaaaaaa
AAAAAAAAAA
MMMMMMMMMM

Normal & expanded

SHADOWED

IBM Executive typewriter.

136

around $700, is widely favored over ordinary typing for preparation of price lists, bulletins, directories, etc. (See COLD TYPE.)

More than 17 styles of type are available on the IBM Executive, but the face specified at time of purchase cannot later be changed. In this respect, the machine is less versatile than the VariTyper. (See VARITYPER.) However, it is possible to specify when ordering a machine that certain of the typebars be demountable, permitting a shift in seconds from, say, a dollar sign to a pound-sterling sign and from certain little-used mathematical signs to certain others, and to special symbols that can be made up to order. (See also TYPIT.)

The standard IBM Executive has a 13-in. carriage and can write a 12-in. line. Also available are 16- and 19-in. carriages. Special card-holding platens are also available, including one which holds a Flexoprint card flat and permits writing at the very top edge.

Carbon ribbons are most used for reproduction and come in various weights and hardnesses. For consistent work, it is important to get the right combination of ribbon, platen, and paper and to stick with it—even to watch the *age* of the ribbons since fresh ones often write blacker than those that have been kept for a time.

The IBM Executive typewriter, though less versatile than the VariTyper, is considerably faster and cheaper and is thus much used where variety of type styles is not essential. Even where a certain amount of variety is important, it is possible to buy three Executives, each with its own type style, for less than the price of a VariTyper. Variety can also be achieved through the use of CAPS, letterspaced CAPS, underscoring, indention, shadowing (see illustration), etc.

Lines can be justified on the IBM Executive by means of a second keyboarding, but greatest economies occur on work such as directories, where justification is not required. See also JUSTO-WRITER for equipment permitting fully automatic justification of the work of the Executive.

illustrations See also ARTISTS; ARTWORK; CARTOONS; CUT; DRAWING TECHNIQUES; PHOTO AGENCIES; PHOTOGRAPHERS; PHOTOGRAPHS: HOW TO SELECT; PHOTOGRAPHY.

Illustrations can be reproduced in every printing process but in some better than in others. Sometimes the kind of illustrations to be used determines the printing process. Sometimes the printing process to be used determines the kind of illustration.

Illustrations are of two kinds: line and halftone. (The distinction is made clear under CUT and under DRAWING TECHNIQUES, and is further described under HALFTONE.)

Line drawings can be reproduced by any process. Halftone illustrations have been reproduced by every printing process, but it is uncommon and undesirable to attempt to reproduce them in the hectograph, mimeograph, Multigraph, or silk-screen processes. Some small offset duplicators lack the ink capacity to print large halftones.

The most versatile method of repro-ducing halftone illustrations is offset. It can be quite expensive or very cheap. Excellent work is obtainable; abominable work is not uncommon. Every offset printer has boundless faith in his own ability to do high-quality work—faith which is often misplaced. Letterpress is somewhat less of a lottery than offset because the process permits the showing of more meaningful proofs and because there is less chance of getting variations in quality during a pressrun. Letterpress, however, leaves something to be desired in the reproduction of wash drawings and pencil sketches and wherever halftones are to be silhouetted; offset does these better.

Rotogravure is a high-quality, low-cost method of reproducing halftone illustrations of all kinds where quantities are large; photogravure warrants consideration on runs of intermediate size. Photogelatin competes successfully with gravure on short runs.

In letterpress and most offset, the halftone screen is usually perceptible, if not obtrusive. In some offset and in gravure, the screen becomes nearly invisible. In photogelatin, there is no mechanical screen.

Offset is also the most versatile method of reproducing line work, although line work can usually be handled without difficulty in any process.

For further information see OFFSET; LETTERPRESS; GRAVURE; PHOTOGELATIN; etc.

Artists should always be told how their illustrations will be reproduced, so that they may prepare their illustrations in the right way. On all but the simplest jobs, it is a good idea to have the artist talk to the printer or engraver since artists and printers are prone to pass the buck back and forth when things go wrong.

It is common practice to prepare artwork the same size as it will appear in print, or 50 percent larger, or perhaps twice as large. The artist must know the final size since he must prepare his work so that its details and the thickness of its lines will look right after reduction.

Line drawings can be reproduced from clippings without difficulty if the clipping has clean, crisp lines.

It is not good practice to reproduce halftones from a newspaper or magazine clipping, because they have already been "screened," i.e., broken up into tiny dots, and any attempt to rescreen such a clipping may produce a final result with a *moiré,* or watered-silk, pattern across it. However, if the original photograph is unobtainable and the clipping must be used, the *moiré* effect can be minimized (see MOIRÉ). Offset printers are sometimes willing to reproduce "in line" from a halftone clipping without rescreening. They attempt to reproduce each dot in the halftone as if it were a line drawing, and some succeed very well.

It has been proved that a well-illustrated piece of printed material will be read more thoroughly and by more people than the same material in unillustrated form. This is true whether the illustrations are informative or merely decorative. In that critical moment when a reader has glanced at a piece of printed material and is deciding whether to read it or put it down, the material that is attractive to the eye gets read most often.

Many editors, therefore, make it a rule to get some kind of illustrative material on every page or on every pair of facing pages. They may use photographs, cartoons, spot drawings, graphs, charts, or maps. If appropriate material is not available, they may insert an unrelated cartoon or an illustrated news item. In a pinch, they fall back on typographic display, featuring headlines, boxed material, etc. These are often given extra attention value by printing them on gray or colored tint blocks.

A technique for making do-it-yourself spot drawings is offered by Artype, Inc. (see ARTYPE) under the name "Modul-Art." The product consists of cartoon elements—heads, bodies, arms and legs, clothing, scenery, facial expressions—ready to cut out and assemble much as Artype letters can be assembled into words. The technique is recommended for use in making filmstrips, illustrating instruction manuals, etc.

Imagic A photocopying process based on creating a slightly oily image to which ink can be adhered. The original is given an almost invisible overall coating of a special oil, then brought into contact with the copy paper and exposed to infrared radiation. The black areas absorb the heat most rapidly, with the result that the oil vaporizes and migrates to the copy paper. Ink powder is now brought in contact with the copy paper and adheres to the oily areas.

imposition The operation of bringing together and arranging the type or plates for all the pages that are to be printed on one side of a sheet of paper. These must be so spaced and arranged that they will come in the right order and have the right margins after the sheet is folded to page size. The imposition for any job will vary according to the folding machine that the binder proposes to use. (See illustration.)

impression (1) A printing press is said to be capable of delivering 3,000 impressions an hour when it can impress inked type against paper at that rate. (2) A book is said to be in its "3rd impression" when the publisher has had to order three successive printings of it to keep up with the demand. (See also EDITION.) (3) A pressman must carefully control the depth of impression of his press; the type must not hit the paper too heavily and punch through, nor must the impression be too light to fully transfer ink to paper.

Imposition for one 8-page form of a 16-page 6 x 9 pamphlet.

imprinting Printed catalogs are often imprinted with the name of the dealer who is to distribute them. Christmas cards can be imprinted with the sender's name.

Imprinting can be handled by any letterpress printer by stopping the presses every so often during the original run, to change the imprints. However, on high-quality, close-register work on expensive presses, this can be more work than it is worth.

Imprinting during the original press-run is still more difficult for the offset, gravure, or photogelatin printer, although some presses are equipped for it.

Imprinting is most easily and cheaply done on small presses especially designed to facilitate quick changes of imprints. Some imprinting presses do not pretend to do high-quality work and usually cannot handle halftones or reverse plates satisfactorily. They are, however, quite adequate for their job of striking in a name and address.

Frequently, the printer who did the original run will subcontract the imprinting to a firm specializing in this sort of work. In the larger cities, such firms will be found listed in the Classified Telephone Directory under Imprinting.

indention See also PROOFREADING.

The first line of a paragraph is usually indented 1, 2, or possibly 3 ems. This paragraph is indented 1 em.

Purpose of Indention

THE PURPOSE OF INDENTION is to help the reader's eye catch the beginning of each new paragraph. Therefore, the first paragraph in an article or chapter is often not indented, at least if it follows a centered or indented heading. If it follows a flush-left heading, it is better indented. This paragraph has not been indented, and the first phrase has been set in small caps to provide a sort of squared-off beginning following the centered heading.

Every line of the following quotation from "The Bookman's Glossary" is indented 2 ems:

> *"Indention*—The setting of lines of type to a measure that is narrower than the full width of the type page or column. Quoted matter is often thus set."

The following further quotation from the same source has the first line flush left and the rest indented 2 ems:

> *"Hanging indention*—A form of typesetting having the first line set to the full width of the measure, while the succeeding lines are set one or more ems from the left edge. This paragraph shows the hanging indention."

Directions for indention should be specified on the original manuscript when it is marked for the printer.

index See INDEXING; EDGE INDEX; THUMB INDEX.

indexing Indexing and tabbing are binding and die-cutting processes and include the making of the dictionary type of thumb indexes, index cards, loose-leaf pages, address books, etc. (See BINDING; MOUNTING AND FINISHING; also EDGE INDEX; THUMB INDEX.)

Indexing is also, of course, an editorial operation. (See EDITORIAL WORK.) Any book that will be used for reference should have an index.

The task of indexing is usually more tedious than difficult. It requires a definite plan in advance, consultation with the publisher to avoid typographical difficulties, and painstaking attention to details. The steps in indexing are usually as follows:

1. Go through duplicate page proofs, underlining all words that should go in the index *as words;* and write in the margin all subjects (not merely words) that should be indexed.

2. Enter each of these words and subjects with the page number on a 3 by 5 card, being consistent in form and style of entry (only one entry to a card).

3. Alphabetize the entire group of cards.

4. Combine all references to the same entry in the proper order on one card.

5. Number the cards in sequence so that none will be lost by the typist or the printer.

6. Read all entries to be sure that the wording is correct and in uniform style.

7. Use these cards for printer's copy, or type from them to sheets of typewriter paper.

For good suggestions on indexing see the books listed in Appendix 2, Bibliography.

Authors usually hate to make indexes and, through lack of skill, often make very poor ones. It is possible to get indexing work done by professional indexers on a free-lance basis. (See EDITORIAL WORK.) To locate free-lance editorial assistants who specialize in indexing, consult "The Literary Market Place," listed in Appendix 2.

inferior characters Scientists have a virtual monopoly on inferior characters (often called "subscripts") for such notations as H_2SO_4 and X_a. See PROOFREADING for a chart showing how to indicate to a printer that inferior characters are to be used.

initials

DECORATIVE initial letters are often used at the beginning of an article or chapter. Such initials which stand above those that follow are called "standing" initials. Sometimes they lend a note of interest to an otherwise plain page. Alternately, they may be the one thing too many on a cluttered page.

THE ALIGNMENT of initial letters must be watched carefully if they are to look well. The base of the initial letter should align accurately with the base of one of the lines of text. If the initial is handled as in this paragraph, it should also align at top if possible. If exact alignment is not possible, then it should project above the top line, never sink below it. The first word or phrase of a paragraph following an initial is often set in even small caps, as in the first two words above, to give a squared-off start to the block of type.

The "T" above projects into the margin because this departure from mechanical alignment makes for better optical alignment.

Many initial letters are too heavy for the type they accompany. This can be remedied by using outline letters, or by printing them in red or blue or some other color.

Note that a 36-pt initial cannot be assumed to equal three lines of 12-pt type, as the accompanying illustration will show. Careful measurement is necessary in specifying sizes for initials.

The standing initial shown in the word "Decorative" is easier to use and more legible than the set-in style. In the latter, the reader is sometimes confused by trying to read the initial letter with the second and third lines as well as with the first line, even when these lines are slightly indented to minimize this danger.

inks In addition to regular inks in black and all colors, specialized inks are available—gloss inks, safety (bank note) inks, perfumed inks, invisible inks, carbonizing inks, metallic inks, cold inks, heat-set inks, and moisture-set inks. Printers can obtain all of these through their regular suppliers or, to name one source, from Interchemical Corporation, Printing Ink Division, 67 W. 44 St., New York 36.

Printing ink can be prepared for any kind of surface, and one ink will by no means suffice for all kinds of work. The inkmaker should be told by the printer, who must in turn be told by the customer, whether there are any unusual problems involved.

For instance, is the printed product to be enclosed with any product such as food which it could affect or which could affect it? Is it to be varnished or pasted, or exposed to strong fumes, strong sun, or rain? If so, a modification in the ink may be indicated.

Inks can be made to print successfully by any process on cedarized bags, soap wrappers, cellophane, moisture-proof cellophane, cotton, nylon, burlap, book cloth, plastics, rubber, tin, aluminum glassine, jute, newsprint, and on manila, kraft, machine-finished, coated, and bond paper, but the inkmaker must be given full particulars.

Note that there are several kinds of mimeograph and hectograph inks for those duplicating processes.

All ink manufacturers issue catalogs showing samples of some of the colored inks that they can supply. Some of the catalogs show not only how each color

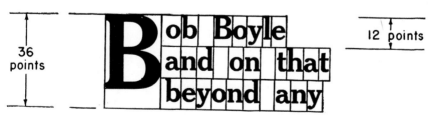

A 36-pt initial cannot be assumed to be as tall as three lines of 12-pt type.

will look when printed solid, but also how it will look in a 25 percent tint, a 50 percent tint, etc. (See SHADING TINTS; TINT BLOCKS; COLORON.)

In selecting colors, there is no real need to limit the choice to those shown in the sample book. Some of the catalog colors are not kept ready-mixed anyway. A color mixed to order may even be less expensive than one picked from a catalog, if the pigments involved prove to be less expensive than those which make up the catalog shade. Note that some colors are much more expensive than others, and some are inclined to fade.

Ink colors may be ordered by submitting a swatch to be matched (as big as possible—1 sq in. is not enough) or by giving a Color-aid number. (See COLOR.)

inserts See also BINDING. (Inserts in the sense of envelope stuffers are dis-

cussed under CIRCULARS and PAMPH-LETS.)

Most pamphlets and books are put together in even units of 16 or 32 pages. Each unit or signature is folded out of one sheet of paper. If the signature as a whole is printed in black ink on antique paper, each page in it will be in black ink on antique paper.

It is often necessary to add an insert, perhaps a halftone on coated paper, perhaps a colored illustration. Inserts can be added anywhere, but money may be saved if their placement is decided with the binding problems in mind.

Inserts can be added as tip-ins or wraps. Tip-ins are simply given a narrow coating of paste along the inside edge and placed between two other pages. A wrap is wrapped around one of the signatures before binding, so that it is sewed into the binding as securely as any other page. (See illustration below.)

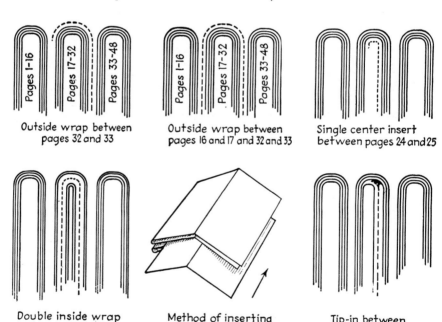

Outside wrap between
pages 32 and 33

Outside wrap between
pages 16 and 17 and 32 and 33

Single center insert
between pages 24 and 25

Double inside wrap
between pages 20
and 21, 28 and 29

Method of inserting
inside wrap within
16-page signature

Tip-in between
pages 26 and 27

Methods of fastening inserts into books and pamphlets.

Instant lettering This is the trade name for transfer sheets of letters, numbers, symbols, etc., manufactured by Arthur Brown and Bro., Inc., 2 W. 46 St., New York 36. Instant lettering can be applied to any smooth surface, such as paper, film, glass, or metal. It is quick and simple to use, as indicated by these steps: Peel off the protective backing sheet; place the type sheet in position with the aid of imprinted guidelines; rub down the letter with a soft pencil or ball-point pen; lift away the type sheet and the letter is transferred; repeat until all letters or numbers are in place. A 10- by 15-in. standard sheet includes capitals and small letters of one font, with extra letters most frequently used. The price is $1.50 per sheet, two sheets for $2. All styles of lettering come in black and white. Some come in red, blue, yellow, and gold.

Special sheets can be imprinted with trade names, logotypes, and artwork. For these there is a preparation charge of $24 per sheet, with a minimum order of 50 sheets at $2 per sheet.

insured mail See Appendix 3, Postal Information.

intaglio One of the five basic methods of printing. (See PRINTING.) The major commercial applications of intaglio printing are gravure, rotogravure, and engraving, e.g., engraved stationery. (See GRAVURE; ENGRAVING.) An etching is also an example of intaglio printing.

The word "intaglio" (pronounced "in-tal'-yo") is from the Italian word for "engrave," "cut," or "carve." Intaglio printing is done from depressed areas. In an engraving, the lines that are to print are cut below the surface of the plate. The whole plate is flooded with ink and then wiped clean again. Although the surface is clean, ink remains in the engraved lines and will print when paper is pressed against the plate.

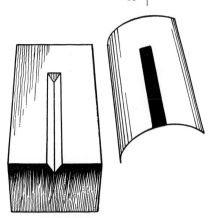

Intaglio printing is done from the ink caught in depressed areas.

interleaving Inserting unprinted sheets between printed sheets. This can be done in such a way as to produce a book in which every other leaf is blank, to provide space for corrections and additions. (See also SLIP-SHEETING.)

Intertype The Intertype is a keyboard composing machine substantially identical (from the print user's point of view) to the Linotype. (See LINOTYPE.) There are, however, differences between the Intertype version of certain type faces (Garamond, for example) and the Linotype interpretation of the same basic designs. (See Appendix 1, Type Faces.)

The Intertype *Fotosetter,* which was the first phototypesetter to gain wide acceptance, turns out type on film or photographic paper instead of on metal slugs. The film can be used directly for the making of offset or gravure plates, thus eliminating the whole process of making reproduction proofs from metal type and photographing these proofs to get film.

Regular Intertype faces are being made available on this machine. The work produced is of the highest quality. Since the process is photographic, a single set of matrices can be used to set type in a variety of sizes. Procedures

Fotosetter matrix showing photographic image of letter to be duplicated on film.

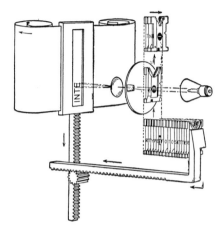

Matrices are exposed one by one in a sort of camera.

Close-up of Intertype Fotosetter.

have been developed that make it easy to make corrections in the film.

The matrices resemble standard matrices but have a photographic image of the letter embedded in their side. After a line has been set and justified, the matrices are automatically exposed one by one in a sort of camera, and sensitized film receives the image.

Full kerning of characters is possible on the Fotosetter. Line widths up to 51 picas can be handled, justified. The range of available type sizes is from 4 to 72 pt, with the possibility of getting still larger sizes by enlargement.

The Intertype *Fotomatic* is an adaptation of the Fotosetter designed especially for operation from punched paper tape. It can set up to eight newspaper lines a minute. (Intertype's tape-pro-

grammed Monarch linecaster can cast up to 14 lines a minute.)

The Intertype *Fototronic* works on an entirely different principle from the Fotosetter and Fotomatic; its master alphabets take the form of disks (as in the Photon) instead of magazines of brass matrices. The Fototronic retains all the versatility of the Fotosetter, with added speed. Its keyboard is that of a standard electric typewriter. When tape-actuated, it can set up to 20 characters per second from a range of 480 characters on two disks. Additional disks can be substituted in 45 sec.

Special Intertype *computers* are available for relieving keyboard operators from so-called "end-of-line" decisions and from other predictable routines such as switching to boldface for

Intertype Fotomatic.

Intertype Fototronic system (keyboard console in foreground, photo unit in background).

the first word of a dictionary entry or indenting paragraphs.

An Intertype computer, acting as a sort of typographic intelligence-processing center can accept "raw" (unjustified, unhyphenated) data from up to 12 input keyboards and deliver finished tape through up to 12 reperforators serving any desired combination of metal linecasters or phototypesetters.

Intertype computers vary in their cost and sophistication according to the needs of the customer. The Series 300 can hyphenate 50,000 English words perfectly, including 10,000 "exceptions" which it carries in memory. The Series 200 is accurate in about 97 percent of its hyphenation decisions; its errors are handled like author's alterations. The Series 100 is monitored by a human op-

erator who watches the hyphenation decisions.

Intertype computers are designed to permit operation with punched paper tape of any configuration—5-, 6-, 7- or 8-level, with advanced or in-line sprocket holes.

Some of the other advantages of introducing a computer into the typesetting operation are higher production at the keyboard, thanks to the inherently faster (typewriter) keyboard; capacity to insert author's alterations without regard to consequent changes in line breaks; capacity to keyboard first and decide later on style and size of type or leading; no lost time on the linecasters or phototypesetters from passing "erased" lines; reduced time for training of keyboard operators.

The Intertype computers will also accept as "input" data derived directly from the optical scanning of typewritten manuscript—for example, data converted from manuscript to magnetic tape in the Farrington optical scanner. (See CHARACTER RECOGNITION.) Since ordinary typewriters are cheaper than tape-perforating typewriters, there is a point in any large-scale keyboarding operation where optical scanning becomes cheaper than tape perforating.

ital Abbreviation for italics. (See ITALIC; PROOFREADING.)

italic See also Appendix 1, Type Faces.
This sentence is set in italic type.
This sentence is set in roman type.

Words underlined in manuscript copy will be set in italic unless the printer is instructed otherwise.

Italic is regarded as slightly less legible than roman and is, therefore, used for occasional emphasis rather than for entire texts.

In many type faces, there is no italic larger than 36 or 48 pt, even though the type faces are available in roman up to 72 pt or larger.

J|i

jacket The decorative and protective paper wrapper for a book. Fees for jacket designs start at about $100. Artists who have made a reputation as jacket designers are listed in "The Literary Market Place," available from the R. R. Bowker Co., 1180 Ave. of the Americas, New York 36, and the Directory issue of *Art Direction*, 19 W. 44 St., New York 36.

justify, justification See also LETTER-SPACING.

The lines of this paragraph have been deliberately left unjustified. Note how the lines are of varying widths, presenting a ragged appearance at the right-hand edge. To justify a line of type means to make it of predetermined width, matching the rest of the column. Type lines are justified by

Justowriter.

putting more or less space between the words.

The lines of this paragraph, like the others in the book, have been justified. Short lines of less than 30 characters are difficult to justify. They sometimes make it necessary to choose between having an undesirable amount of space between words and letterspacing a word or two, i.e., spacing between letters as well as between words. Letterspacing is to be avoided.

Justowriter A composing typewriter made by Friden offers the same proportional-spacing feature as the IBM Executive typewriter, plus provision for automatic justification of the lines. A Justowriter installation consists of a pair of automatic typewriters and costs about $5,700. Text copy is keyboarded on the recorder unit without justification, and a punched tape is produced as an automatic by-product of this keyboarding. When this punched tape is run through the reproducer unit, the result is proportionally spaced and justified composition suitable for reproduction. Like the IBM Executive itself, the reproducer unit offers only the type style that was specified when it was ordered, and it cannot intermix roman and italic. The reproducer unit operates at the rate of 100 words per minute.

K | k

Kalvar The Kalvar photographic process differs radically in its chemistry from older photographic processes. When Kalvar light-sensitive materials are exposed to ultraviolet light, tiny amounts of gas are formed within a plastic coating. A heat treatment then utilizes the gas to form hardened microscopic plastic bubbles. The result is a virtually grainless film whose opacity is proportional to the density of the bubble formation, which in turn is proportional to the exposure.

The Kalvar process has been adapted to aerial photography, microfilm, and various graphic-arts applications. One product, called "Converkal," can be used to make negatives directly from heated typeforms, without ink, without special lighting, and without darkroom processing or opaquing. By means of another product, called "Kalvorlith," negative-to-positive contact printing can be done.

kerned letter A type letter that extends beyond the body on which it is cast, so as to overhang the body of the next letter. Italic and script types have a larger number of kerned characters than the
150

ordinary roman types. Kerned letters must be handled carefully to avoid breaking.

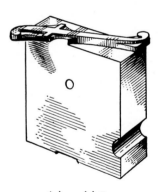

A kerned letter.

kill Direction to the printer to discard type matter that has been set but is not to be used.

Klischograph See SCAN-A-GRAVER.

kraft paper See SULFATE PAPER.

Krylon See SPRAY.

L|l

labels See also DECALCOMANIAS.

Labels, tags, seals, etc., can be printed most economically on special machinery developed for that purpose. For example, the Ever Ready Label Corp., 357 Cortlandt St., Belleville, N.J. 07109, offers standard 3- by 5-in. gummed shipping labels at $4 per 1,000, minimum order 6,000. Gummed labels, 1¼ by 2 in., printed with any message in blue or red, are $3 per 1,000, minimum order 12,000. The price includes typesetting. Any printer not specializing in labels would be justified in charging double that price or more. The Ever Ready catalog, available on request, gives prices on specially printed labels of all sizes and shows a wide variety of stock labels, as well as pressure-sensitive labels and decalcomanias.

Pressure-sensitive labels, either removable or permanent, have become increasingly popular in merchandising. As an example of cost, Ever Ready offers a standard pressure-sensitive label, 1 by 1½ in., printed in red or blue, at $5 per 1,000, minimum order 12,000. Two other sources for pressure-sensitive labels of all types are the Transparent Products Co., 324 E. 24 St., New York 10; and the May Tag and Label Corp., 119 W. 19 St., New York 11.

For permanent identification, decalcomanias are generally more satisfactory. (See DECALCOMANIAS.)

For the names of companies specializing in labels, tags, seals, etc., in your area, look under Labels in the Classified Telephone Directory.

lacquering See VARNISHING.

laid paper Paper which, when held up to the light, shows finely spaced parallel lines and more widely spaced crosslines. The pattern arose naturally out of the screen in the frames used in making paper by hand. In machine-made paper, the pattern is added like a watermark for decorative purposes. Paper lacking the laid pattern is said to have a "wove" finish. Laid paper has no advantage over wove paper except its unique appearance.

laminating In the graphic-arts industry, "laminating" means bonding a thin plastic sheet to printed paper. (See also VARNISHING.) Various kinds of plastics can be used—cellulose acetate, poly-

151

ethelene, vinyl, polyester, etc.—depending on whether the goal is high gloss, low cost, resistance to soiling, tear strength, etc.

Usually, laminating is done by applying an adhesive to the plastic film as it unwinds from a roll, after which the web is brought in contact with the printed material. The adhesive can also be applied to the printed material instead of the plastic to permit window lamination. In this latter case, the die cutting must be done first; otherwise this and other finishing operations are normally done after the lamination process.

Lamination ordinarily offers more and costs more than varnishing. It is often used on menus, juvenile-book covers, catalog covers, etc. Successful lamination requires close attention to detail. Best results are obtained on smooth, coated paper, though the paper need not be of premium quality. Trouble sometimes arises where anti-offset sprays have been used or where inks have left a waxy, oily, or greasy residue. It is difficult to do later imprinting or embossing on some laminates, so such problems should be discussed and faced in advance.

layout See also DESIGN; DUMMY; PASTE-UP DUMMY.

The layout is the designer's blueprint for the printer to follow. It is a drawing of the job to be printed, page by page, showing margins, blocks or columns of type, illustrations, headings, photo captions, etc., drawn to exact size. Every item is carefully identified and marked for size, down to the page numbers and credit lines.

A multipaged layout, having the same number of pages as the finished job, is also called a "dummy." This becomes a paste-up dummy when proofs of the type and illustrations have been pasted into place for the printer's guidance. (See DUMMY; PASTE-UP DUMMY.)

A comprehensive layout or just a "comprehensive" is a layout made with great care to show exactly how the finished job will look. Headlines are lettered in with a pencil in the exact style of type to be used. Lines of text type are ruled in. Some comprehensives are even more beautiful than the finished job.

A rough layout or "rough" is a layout designed for utility and not beauty. It can tell the printer everything he needs to know, but it would not be a good kind of layout for an advertising agency to show to a client's board of directors.

Although the layout is intended primarily as a guide for the printer, it also becomes a working plan which may be torn to shreds and revised before the opus goes to the printer. In this respect the layout serves as a preview of what is to come later from the printer in the form of proofs.

The layout must be planned, at least in broad outline, before any typesetting is done, since it controls or is controlled by the manuscript, the type selection, and the illustration. Whether layout should come before text, however, is a question as controversial as the one about the hen and the egg.

The layout for a book is almost always made after the manuscript is written. The publisher and his designer make it their business to adapt the design of the book and the illustrations, if any, to the manuscript.

In a heavily illustrated book, it may prove easier to subordinate the text to the illustrations and design, and rewrite when necessary.

The layout for an ad or handbill may come before the text. To begin with, the copywriter and the layout man have to know what space is available. The sequence then is as follows: decide what idea is to be put across; determine the approach as regards headline and illustration; decide the other required elements such as trademarks, coupon, etc.; plan the arrangement or layout; decide on the number of words of text. Copywriting and layout must proceed hand in hand, so as to assist each other, not straitjacket each other.

In a magazine or pamphlet there are at least three different ways to answer the question, "Which comes first—layout or writing?"

1. Write the copy. Then make a layout to fit the copy.

2. Make the layout. In an eight-page pamphlet, for example, allot a single page to each of eight phases of the subject. Then write the copy to fit the mold that has been prepared.

3. Conceive the copy visually. In writing each heading, caption, and paragraph, visualize its position and weight on the printed page. Then prepare a rough layout and write the final copy to fit. This means that copy and layout are being designed as an integrated job. It means that editor and designer must be the same person or else they must work and think as a team.

To make a layout, it is necessary first to study carefully the raw material—copy, artwork, and illustrations, if those are at hand. Then it is well to evaluate their relative importance in achieving the object desired.

The next step is to try a few rough thumbnail sketches, arranging and rearranging pictures and copy to get the most pleasing design and the one that will present the message most effectively. (See DESIGN.) Whenever a job consists of more than one page, page layouts should be made in pairs so that the two-page spread is used as a single design unit.

Experience shows that it is safer to use only one side of the paper in making a layout. If page 4 is laid out on the back of page 3 and it is later decided to move one of the two pages to some other position in the book, one of the page layouts may have to be duplicated.

When a layout is being made, the margins are drawn in and the page numbers noted first. If a page is to be divided into columns, these must be drawn in as well.

Headlines and illustrations are the controlling elements in a layout and should be added next. However, the space requirement for the text may be calculated first, and the remaining space allotted to headings and illustrations.

Since text has a way of crowding the illustrations out of the book, the illustrations are sometimes handled as a "must" and cutting, if any, is done in the text. Some editors require one illustration per page to keep the pages looking interesting, whether or not a particularly relevant one can be found.

Illustrations must be cropped (see CROP) and scaled to size (see SCALING) so that the layout may show the exact space that they will occupy after reduction or enlargement. It is sufficient to draw a box on the layout and write in it "photo A," marking the appropriate photo with the same letter.

Captions for the photographs should be indicated as well, so that the printer may know exactly the size and space to be allotted to each one. (See CAPTIONS.)

Headlines may be "roughed" in or sketched in, letter by letter, in the kind and size of type desired so that the designer, editor, and author may have a more complete picture of the page as a whole.

Marginal notes on the layout give the printer exact type and spacing information or refer him to the manuscript for more complete directions.

Type specifications are also given on the typewritten manuscript which carries reference to page numbers on the layout.

Excellent suggestions for layout and the basic principles of design are given in publications listed in Appendix 2, Bibliography.

Additional basic layout pointers for beginners are as follows:

1. First of all, learn all you can about time limits and mechanical requirements such as printing process, color limitations, etc., on this job.

2. Use the tools of the trade—a layout tracing pad for ease of rearranging trial layouts by tracing, a variety of pencils for ease in getting desired weights quickly, a drawing board, and T square.

3. Check off elements to be included, both the "musts" and the "maybes." This will include head or heads, subheads, copy blocks, illustrations, logotypes, testimonials, order forms, etc. Be sure you know enough about each—see the photo or illustration if there is to be one, know the length of the copy, know the exact wording of the heads.

4. Evaluate the various elements. If necessary reduce them to a manageable number or expand them by pulling heads or subheads or lists out of the text.

5. Avoid nonselling heads. Kill them and try starting with the first really hard-hitting sentence of the copy. Or, if you are not allowed this liberty, play down the poor head and play up the meat of the message. (For example, the top of the page or the position *above* an illustration has far less attention value than the optical center or space below the illustration, although it may seem important to the layman, and is a good place to bury a necessary evil.)

6. Strive for at least one major design theme or highlight in any layout—headline treatment or picture of product or use of product. Smack it across the optical center and then build around it. You can find something to emphasize in the most monotonous message.

7. Show intended margins. Ignoring margins is a very common error on the part of beginners.

8. Try to indicate various weights of type in your layout by changing pencils or by going from straight to wavy lines, etc. Do not just draw a box to indicate a photo—get a photostat to size or clip magazine photos to show tone values on the page. But do not get too meticulous too early or you will be reluctant to try other arrangements.

9. Try various reductions of photos, illustrations, and logotypes. Do not get hypnotized by the happenstance of the size the art happens to come in.

10. Crop freely. Most photos need it. Never butt photos, avoid montages, keep adjoining photos in scale. Be sure to see the photos you are working with.

11. Never print black-and-white photos in a color, unless you deliberately want a washed-out effect.

12. Never run type across photos, for it is more often done badly than well. Certainly never run small type. Likewise, never run type across any distracting drawing or pattern or device.

13. Favor tint blocks over boxes. These may be solid blocks, if the color is not too heavy, or screened blocks. It is often perfectly satisfactory to run type through the edge of a block as this may help to unify a layout, but there are problems. Remember that black type on a dark block will lose legibility. White reverse type on a light block loses legibility. Never run a photo into a color block unless the color is removed from under the photo.

14. Never divide a layout into unrelated sections—provide bridges to carry the eye from one part to another.

15. Keep captions under the illustrations. That is where people are used to looking for them.

16. If you cannot use color, remember that you can get some of the values of a two-color job with black and white and gray. Remember that plain white paper, unprinted and unillustrated, may add a valuable accent of white. Gray may be attained by screening the black, or a gray area may be attained by the use of a block of smaller type. A touch of black used massively will add contrast.

17. Avoid running type in color. If you do use color, go to a bolder weight than you would use in black. A far better

The above trial sketches developed into the layout opposite and then into the finished ad which is shown below.

way to emphasize type with color is to print in black on blocks of color, something the beginner often forgets to try. Think a long time before running all your type in a color other than black. If there is to be color in your job, use the same color in your layout to insure against surprises in the finished job.

18. Avoid tempting Providence by asking for deviations from the norm —eccentric borders, critical bleeds, hairlines in reverse, critical register problems, etc.

19. Get contrast into your type—black vs. light, large vs. small, italic vs. caps.

20. Never combine two similar type faces or two scripts. Rather contrast heavy with light, sans serif with old style, etc. Avoid needless changes in text sizes.

21. Unjustified lines (lines of uneven length) are entirely readable, but go easy on flushing them right. This may be effective for occasional lines, but it makes hard reading when it is applied

Relativity
by ALBERT EINSTEIN

*A*lbert Einstein wrote this book for the layman.

Its title is RELATIVITY: The Special and General Theory. Its purpose: to explain Einstein's theory so that anyone with the equivalent of a high school education can understand it. The book has had a curious history. Einstein was not yet the Nobel prize winner when he wrote the book in 1920. Only THE LONDON TIMES, in England and THE NEW YORK POST in the U.S.A. carried reviews. Because of the lack of reviewers' comments, and because at the time the real significance of the theory was not appreciated, the book soon went out of print. So for about twenty years this important work — one of the bases for the understanding of atomic energy — was unavailable to the general

public except through libraries. Now Hartsdale House re-publishes this great lost book in a more attractive form in a regular trade edition. June 2. **$2.50**

That Einstein did not overestimate the simplicity of his presentation may be seen from the reviews received; the only two the book received.

"The book is intended to give an exact insight into the theory for those who are not conversant with the mathematical apparatus of theoretical physics. In the opinion of this reviewer, in this attempt he has been eminently successful."
—*London Times*

"Written in an unpretentious, straight-forward style. The trend of his exposition can be followed in the main by any attentive reader." —*New York Post*

HARTSDALE HOUSE INC.
220 WEST 42nd STREET, NEW YORK, N.Y.

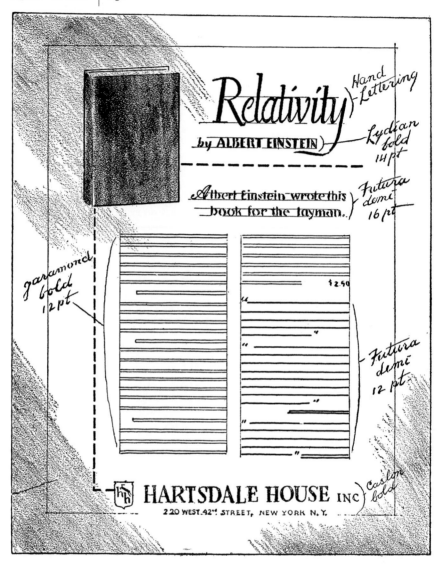

to a whole paragraph. The same objection does not hold for flushing uneven lines left.

22. Letterspace caps, if you like, but do not use varying amounts of letterspacing in the same layout. Never letterspace lowercase.

23. Never capitalize entire words within blocks of text. Use small caps instead.

24. Do not use decorative initial letters. They are definitely old hat today.

25. Indent paragraphs. Without indention you need at least a line of space to separate paragraphs, and usually you do not want to break up the unity of your text block in this way.

26. Take time to do careful copyfitting. Anticipate problems of word break and line break. By altering words

now you may solve a problem which would be insoluble for the compositor.

27. Specify every detail. Never leave it to be guessed whether you want roman or italic, caps or lowercase, indented or flushed lines. Specify lengths of lines, amount of leading, etc. Be sure that your layout and copy agree. All instructions must be in writing.

28. Never use a line longer than 65 characters or shorter than 35. Select your sizes of type and lengths of line so as to stay within these limits. If you run shorter than 35 characters per line (about six words), you get bad word breaks and word spacing. If you run longer than 65 characters, the eye will have difficulty finding its way back to the start of the next line, although this difficulty can be lessened by increased leading.

layout paper See also LAYOUT.

An opaque paper on which a layout may be drawn to size. Stationers and art suppliers can furnish suitable paper, strong enough to take erasures, in large pads, 9 by 12, 13¾ by 16¾, 18½ by 23½, etc.

Layout tissue is thin translucent paper suitable for tracing and often used for making layouts. Sometimes layouts are drawn or traced on tissue, which is then pasted down on opaque layout paper.

Magazine editors needing many layouts of the same size usually have their own layout paper printed with faint blue guidelines for margins and columns. One particularly good plan is to have actual columns of type printed in this light blue just as the lines and columns appear on a typical pair of facing pages. This facilitates the counting of lines and measuring of columns. Occasionally layout paper is also printed with an allover pattern of graph squares in very light blue to facilitate placement of engraver's proofs, photostats of artwork, headings, and special boxes.

lc Abbreviation for lowercase. (See PROOFREADING.)

ld Abbreviation for lead. (See LEADING; PROOFREADING.)

lead See LEADING.

leaders See also RULE.

A leader (rhymes with "feeder") is a row of dots or dashes used in tabular work to lead the eye across a space, as shown in the accompanying table.

Type of leader	Dots per inch	
	8 pt (shown)	12 pt
2 dots per em..............	18	12
4 dots per em........................	36	24
6 dots per em	*	36
2 strokes per em_____	18	12
4 strokes per em.....................	36	24

* Not furnished below 10 pt.

Leaders are also used instead of rules to provide dotted lines where people are expected to sign and fill in.

Leaders serve no essential purpose in index work. Many prefer the first style shown below to the second.

Leaders, 901–904
Universal dot leaders, 902

Leaders........................ 901–904
  Universal dot leaders........ 902

leading Leading (rhymes with "wedding") is a term referring to the spacing between type lines and paragraphs. When type lines are too close together on the page and seem to need air, they probably need leading. This means the insertion of thin strips of lead between them. Like the bulk of this book, this paragraph is set in 9-pt type and is leaded 1 pt.

A lead is a thin strip of sheet metal 1, 2, or 3 pt thick. Unless otherwise specified, the word "lead" refers to a 2-pt strip. This paragraph is set in 9-pt type and is unleaded, i.e., set solid.

This paragraph is leaded 2 pt. In Linotype, Intertype, or Monotype composition, the effect of leading can be most easily achieved by adjusting the machines to cast, say, 9-pt type on an 11-pt body. Hence, instructions to the printer can be written on the manuscript as follows: "Set in 9 pt (name of type face) leaded 2 pt," or "Set 9 on 11," or simply "9/11 pt." (See illustration under TYPE.)

leaf A single sheet of paper, each side of which is a page. Thus, a leaf consists of two pages.

leaflets See CIRCULARS.

legend See CAPTIONS.

Leroy A mechanical device used by draftsmen to assist them in keeping their lettering neat and even. It is of value chiefly to those who are not skilled in lettering. A professional showcard writer could work better and faster without it.

Using a Leroy lettering set.

A Leroy lettering set (see illustration) consists of a template on which the selected letters or symbols are incised, a pen, and a scriber to hold the pen and trace the guide letters on the template. Leroy templates are priced from $5.25, pens from 85 cents, and scribers from $4.75. A less expensive line, the Doric Lettering Set, offers three templates,

two pens, a straightedge, and a scriber for $15. For catalog, write Keuffel & Esser Co., Adams and Third Sts., Hoboken, N.J.

Similar work can be done through the use of Wrico and Wricoprint lettering guides, made by the Wood-Regan Instrument Co., Nutley, N.J.

lettering See also PHOTOLETTERING; Appendix 1, Type Faces.

Often there are times when hand-lettering is required despite the number of type styles and sizes in existence. However, type is always preferable to poor or mediocre hand-lettering, even if it is necessary to set type in one size and then enlarge it by photostat, retouch it, etc. (For a comparison of the basic methods of lettering and type composition, see the chart under TYPE.)

Few artists are expert at lettering. Some will attempt it. Others prefer merely to rough in any lettering that must be part of their work and leave the finished lettering to be done by a specialist or to be set in type and "stripped in" by the printer. (See STRIP, STRIP-IN.)

Hand-lettering can be done in two ways—fast or slow. A really good calligrapher or sign painter can make letters flow out of his pen or brush almost as fast as the layman can write—not finished letters, but attractive ones.

The slow way is laboriously to sketch the outline of each letter and fill it in, trying to get every curve and hairline "just so." Lettering of this sort is likely to cost at least $1 a letter.

A substitute for hand-lettering is photolettering, a technique that might be described as mechanized hand-lettering. (See PHOTOLETTERING.)

There are several mechanical lettering aids for special jobs, as follows:

For putting display lettering on mimeograph stencils, excellent cutout lettering guides are available. (See MIMEOGRAPH.)

For simple sans-serif lettering with

either pencil or pen, a Leroy or Wrico lettering set permits work that is neat, rapid, and nearly foolproof, if not inspired. (See LEROY.)

For maps and charts, one can buy individual letters or words printed on self-adhering transparent adhesive acetate. These can be adhered where needed, and cut apart and shaped to the required curve or line. (See MAPS; also FOTOTYPE and ARTYPE for methods of "setting type" in the office or art department.)

Hundreds of samples of hand-lettering are shown in the books on lettering listed in Appendix 2, Bibliography.

Three-dimensional cutout letters which can be pasted to any background or held in slots in molding are available. (See MITTEN'S LETTERS.)

Letteriter An automatic typewriter built around the mechanism of the IBM Selectric typewriter. It can both punch and read 8-channel paper tape and is similar in its capabilities to the Flexowriter and the Dura automatic typewriters. It is produced by Greene Datatape, Inc., 300 Hoyt St., Kearney, N.J. (See also AUTOMATIC TYPEWRITER.)

letterpress The most common form of printing as differentiated from offset or gravure printing, etc. It is the oldest printing process and is used for practically all newspapers and a great many magazines and books (including this book). Letterpress printing is done on the relief principle whereby raised surfaces are inked and then pressed against the paper. (See RELIEF.)

There are two steps in letterpress printing: (1) setting the type and/or making the cuts for illustrations and (2) printing from them. (Sometimes electrotypes or stereotypes are made, too.)

For setting of type see TYPE and Appendix 1, Type Faces. (Setting type and taking a proof from it by the letterpress method are usually the first steps in other printing processes, too.) Making cuts is discussed under CUT. Printing from type and cuts will be discussed in this section.

The letterpress printing process is capable of producing both very fine and very cheap results on either very short or very long runs. It is used for printing the highest quality of photographic books as well as for the daily newspaper.

This process offers a printer more control over his presswork than the other printing processes do. On the other hand, extra control implies extra work.

Cheap letterpress printing is done with a minimum of makeready. (See MAKEREADY.) A printer sometimes cuts corners and does not use his opportunities to control the process. High-quality letterpress printing is done with very careful makeready, high-quality inks, and good paper, and the pressman may spend hours adjusting and watching the press to get the most out of both type and cuts. Even magazines whose inside pages are printed by rotogravure or offset sometimes do their covers by letterpress because of its dependable quality.

Letterpress printing may be regarded as the norm against which to compare other processes. It is the one to use unless there are reasons for preferring some other process.

The letterpress process gives sharper, cleaner reproduction of type than any other process. (Practically all books are done in letterpress unless the illustrations are such as to require another process.)

Letterpress is almost always to be preferred when printing is done on glossy paper—and only glossy paper takes varnish well.

Some common reasons for using other processes are as follows:

1. On the cheapest jobs, it may be advisable to reproduce from typewritten material, instead of from type, in which

case mimeograph, spirit duplicating, Multigraph, Multilith, or offset may prove cheaper.

2. When there are many line illustrations, offset may be cheaper. Photographic illustrations, however, cost very little less in offset unless quality is sacrificed.

3. When photographs must be reproduced and the quantity is very small, making the requisite number of copies by photography may be cheaper than making cuts for letterpress. (See PHOTOGRAPHY: AS A PRINTING PROCESS.)

4. Reprints are often cheaper in offset, if the type has not been kept standing. The letterpress printer will have to reset the type, while the offset printer can simply photograph the first edition.

5. Posters are usually cheaper in offset or silk screen unless they are unillustrated, plain type jobs, using type that the printer has on hand. This is because very large cuts for letterpress, whether linecuts or halftones, are considerably more expensive than offset plates or silk-screen frames.

6. In order to print halftones of higher than 120 screen, the letterpress process must use expensive coated paper. Other processes can use less expensive paper with no gloss. Offset, gravure, and photogelatin surpass letterpress in their reproduction of soft pencil work, fine line work, soft color effects, etc.

7. It is necessary in letterpress printing to use a screen for halftone illustrations. If this is objectionable, as it may be in facsimile work, then the choice may fall on the photogelatin process, which has no screen, or on the gravure process, in which the screen is practically invisible. Very fine screens can also be used in offset.

8. Buyers of printing often have to use the available press capacity instead of that which would be ideal, a fact that has dictated many a choice of printing process.

A comparison of letterpress and other printing processes is given on the charts inside the covers of this book.

For an analysis of the cost of letterpress printing, see ESTIMATING COSTS. For a discussion of the importance of matching the printing press to the job, or vice versa, see PRINTING PRESSES. For a discussion of how type and cuts can be duplicated for longer letterpress runs, see DUPLICATE PLATES. For a description of a specialized application of the letterpress principle, see MULTIGRAPH.

letters   See AUTOMATIC TYPEWRITER; PROCESS LETTERS; DIRECT MAIL ADVERTISING; MAIL ORDER.

Form letters are often much more effective than printed leaflets and pamphlets, whether they can be mistaken for personally typed letters or not.

For perfectly "personalized" form letters, indistinguishable from a hand-typed letter, see AUTOMATIC TYPEWRITER. For personalized form letters that will fool experts but that are not typed out word by word, see PROCESS LETTERS.

The Multigraph is perhaps the most widely used method of imitating typewritten letters, though a practiced eye may notice that its work is too even to be genuine typewriting. (See MULTIGRAPH.)

All these methods permit typing in name, address, salutation, and perhaps additional personalizing data.

The mimeograph duplicates form letters neatly and efficiently without, however, attempting to imitate the distinguishing imperfection of typewriting, namely, the faint, fuzzy edge on each character left by the typewriter ribbon. (See MIMEOGRAPH.)

The Multilith can do any letter work that the mimeograph can do; in addition it can duplicate both letterhead and typewriting at the same time and handle small photographs, diagrams, etc. (See OFFSET DUPLICATORS.)

Form letters can also be duplicated by regular printing processes as, for ex-

Comparative Cost of Duplicated Letters[a]

	Person-alized	Cost of letters without signature				Kind of signature[b]	Cost of signature
		25 copies	100 copies	1,000 copies	5,000 copies		
Mimeograph	No	$3.50	$3.50	$6.00	$17.50	Same ink as letter	No additional cost
Multilith	No	7.50	7.50	9.00	21.50	Same ink as letter	No additional cost
Multilith (printer supplying paper)[c]	No	7.75	7.75	12.50	39.00	Same ink as letter	No additional cost
Multigraph	No	12.50	12.50	14.00	26.50	Blue-ink signature from plate	$6 for new signature plate; $1 per 1,000 for running it[d]
Multigraph with one-line fill-in[e]	Yes	15.00	16.00	34.00	6.50	As above	As above
Multigraph with full fill-in[f]	Yes	17.00	18.50	65.00	260.00	As above	As above
Process with one-line fill-in[e]	Yes	22.00	23.00	42.50	140.00	Blue-ink signature from plate or hand-signed	$1 per 1,000 for signature from plate; $25 per 1,000 for tracing signature; $15 per 1,000 for hand-signed signature not traced
Process with full fill-in[f]	Yes	25.00	27.50	72.50	365.00	As above	As above
Automatic typewriter	Yes	25.00	25.00	200.00	875.00	Hand-signed	$25 per 1,000 for tracing signature; $15 per 1,000 for hand-signed signature not traced

[a] These estimates for a letter of about 150 words do not include cost of stationery (except as indicated), folding and stuffing, or stamping, sealing, and addressing envelopes. Lettershop prices vary, widely. These are 1965 estimates from the Letter Service of Lincoln Graphic Arts, Inc., 35 9th Ave. New York.

[b] Hand signing is possible in all processes, of course.

[c] Note that in Multilithing, the letterhead can be photographed and reproduced when the body of the letter is reproduced so that no printed letterhead paper need be supplied. (See also COMBINATION RUN.)

[d] This price is for a Multilithed signature, which some consider neater and less like a rubber stamp than a Multigraphed signature. For a Multigraphed signature, the quoted price for running the plate is $1 per 1,000.

[e] "One-line fill-in" refers to the salutation only.

[f] "Full fill-in" refers to name, address, and salutation.

ample, when reproduced on the first page of a circular.

In all large cities there are lettershops and mailing services equipped to produce letters by one or several of the above methods.

Price estimates on the same 30-line, 1-page letter are given in the accompanying table. The cost of addressing envelopes is not included in these estimates. It is desirable, however, to have them addressed by the same people who do the fill-in work on personalized letters, so that styles will match. It is a waste of money to put an expensively personalized letter into an obviously machine-addressed envelope, especially if the letter is going to a home address where the recipient himself will open the envelope.

A specialty letter, often used to get inquiries, is made by the Reply-O-Letter Co., 1860 Broadway, New York. On the letter itself there is a window where the address ought to be, and the address which is seen through this window is on a prepaid reply card, held in place in a special pocket. All the recipient needs to do is pull out this reply card, initial it (his name is already on it), and drop it in the mail. (See also ENVELOPES for information about other specialties combining letter, envelope, order form, and reply envelope in a single piece.)

letterset The offset principle has had its greatest development in the field of offset lithography. However, *offset letterpress,* also called "dry offset," has equal claim to the word "offset." In recognition, however, of the extent to which usage has made the word "offset" synonymous with lithography, the word "letterset" has been proposed and widely accepted to denote offset letterpress.

Letterset printing offers many of the advantages of offset lithography without the latter's chief disadvantage—water. Much work has been done toward the development of quality letterset printing

plates which will also be competitive in cost with offset lithographic plates.

lettershop See DUPLICATING; ADDRESSING; LETTERS.

In all large cities there are lettershops equipped to handle mimeographing, Multilithing, Hoovenized letters, addressing, folding, stuffing, and mailing work. They may be found under Letter Service and Addressing in the Classified Telephone Directory.

Some have little more equipment than a mimeograph machine and a few typewriters. Others have a wide variety of the latest automatic duplicating, addressing, and mailing machinery.

The duplicating and mailing costs mentioned in this book are typical lettershop charges which, of course, include labor and overhead.

Firms doing much mailing work sometimes save time, if not money, by buying and operating their own lettershop equipment.

letterspacing The compositor has letterspaced the last word in this s e n - t e n c e . He has put a thin space after each letter. Small (lowercase) letters are not often letterspaced except when there is no other way to justify a very short line. (See JUSTIFY.) German printers letterspace words that they wish to emphasize instead of using italics.

Headings set in capitals are often letterspaced slightly to make them more legible; thus, C A P I T A L S. A thin space has been added between each two letters except between "T" and "A," where there was already enough space because of the design of the letters.

To instruct a printer to add letter spacing, put a diagonal stroke [/] where the spacing is to go and write "letter space," "letter #," or "insert thin spaces," etc. Note the various amounts of letterspacing which can be indicated:

LETTERSPACING
(Set tight)

LETTERSPACING
(1 pt spaced)

LETTERSPACING
(2 pt spaced)

LETTERSPACING
(3 pt spaced)

ligature Two or more letters cast as one piece as "fi" and "fl."

lightface See also Appendix 1, Type Faces.

This sentence is set in lightface type, which is used for the body of text of a printed job. **This is set in boldface type, which is used generally for emphasis.**

Linasec A special-purpose computer offered by the Merganthaler Linotype Co. which accepts unjustified composition in the form of punched paper tape and determines line breaks, hyphenation, and justification.

linecut See also CUT.

Cuts (the word is used synonymously with engravings and includes photoengravings) are of two kinds: linecuts and halftones. (See HALFTONE.) Linecuts may also be referred to as zinc etchings, line etchings, line engravings, line blocks, and line plates.

Pen-and-ink drawings are typical of the kind of artwork that may be reproduced by linecuts; photographs are typical of the kind that must be reproduced by halftones. (For an understanding of the distinction between art that can be reproduced in line and art that must be reproduced as a halftone, see HALFTONE; DRAWING TECHNIQUES.)

Linecuts are required only for letterpress (relief) printing, not for offset or other processes. These other processes have their own ways of reproducing line drawings, sometimes at no extra cost.

The familiar rubber stamp is a kind of linecut. Woodcuts and linoleum blocks are handmade linecuts. (See BLOCK PRINTING.)

Linecuts for commercial printing are made by photoengravers by a photomechanical process. The design is transferred photographically to a zinc or copper plate. Then acid is used to etch (eat away) the metal surface that is not protected by the design. The metal is then mounted on a wooden block so as to be type-high.

When lines of type are to be run within a line drawing, the cut can be mortised (see MORTISE) to leave a notch, slot, or hole for receiving the type. However, it is difficult to wedge type into a mortise (particularly an inside mortise) securely enough to safeguard against work-ups in printing. It is safer to have an electro made from the combined cut and type, then print from the electro. Of course, it is possible to take type proofs (or photostats of them to same scale as artwork) and paste them down as part of the artwork, and make a complete linecut of both; this is probably the easiest procedure by far, and the one most commonly used. The electro method, however, will give better reproduction of the type; type always loses some crispness when reproduced by linecut.

If the type or lettering must run across and through the lines of the drawing, then the photoengraver can be instructed to surprint the lettering on the drawing (at extra cost). Just give him both and put an overlay on the artwork to show placement of the type. Alternately, have the type proofed on transparent acetate and lay it over the artwork, so the engraver can photograph type and drawing at once.

Linecuts are usually made on zinc or magnesium; they may be made on copper (at double the cost) for fine work.

A special rate is charged for benday linecuts and applies to any cut containing fine shading, whether this shading has been added by the engraver on the benday principle or has been added on the artwork by an artist's shading tints. (See SHADING TINTS.) If added by the engraver, there is also an additional time charge.

An additional 33 percent is charged for a reverse plate, where the black lines on white of the original artwork are reversed to white lines on black. This charge may be avoided by supplying a negative photostat to the engraver instead of the original art.

A mounted linecut held with nails driven through the nonprinting areas, which have been routed out.

A linecut is fastened to the mounting block with nails or (increasingly) by adhesive. If it is to be nailed, ordinarily a shoulder about ⅛ in. wide is left. However, when the cut is to run closer than ⅛ in. to other material, this shoulder must be omitted and the cut may be "blocked flush" on any or all four sides. The nails are then driven through any white space that may be left within the design. If there is no such space and if it is necessary to block flush on three or four sides, then the cut can be "anchored," or fastened with solder to metal anchors, in the wood mount. Cuts that are full column width are often ordered blocked flush on the sides to aid

the printer in making up his pages. (See ANCHORING.)

Line drawings, like other artwork, can be reversed left to right by the engraver so that objects that were facing left, face right. This, of course, turns lettering into looking-glass lettering and makes cars drive on the wrong side of the street.

To reverse a drawing left to right, but not black for white, the engraver is asked to flop his negative. (See FLOP.)

The prices of cuts are ordinarily figured by a standard scale supplied by photoengravers from which the "unit" value of any cut may easily be figured. Thus a minimum-sized zinc linecut has a unit value of 73 on the scale. The cost per unit is a matter for negotiation between engraver and customer, and depends on volume, quality demand, etc. At 7 cents a unit, the above-mentioned cut would cost $5.11.

There are some mail-order engravers specializing in magnesium cuts (a metal which may yet displace zinc as the preferred metal for linecuts) who price their cuts by the square inch instead of the unit. One is Basil Smith Photoengraving Corp., 1211 Arch St., Philadelphia, charging about 12 cents a square inch for *mounted* linecuts, with a minimum of $2. (Write for detailed scale.)

line drawing See DRAWING TECHNIQUES.

linen finish See PEBBLING.

line plate See LINECUT; CUT.

lining (1) In the paper trade, the lining of a piece of cardboard is the outside ply, not the inside as one might expect. It is often of a better grade than the "middles." (2) In bookbinding, the lining is the material that is glued to the back of a book, after sewing and backing, to add strength to the binding. (3) In typesetting, figures that have no descenders, i.e., that do not extend below the printed line, are called "lining" figures: 1, 2, 3, 4, 5, 6, 7, 8, 9, 0. (Old-style figures: 1, 2, 3, 4, 5, 6, 7, 8, 9, 0.)

Linofilm The Linofilm system, developed by the Merganthaler Linotype Company, consists basically of a keyboard unit which produces 15-channel punched paper tape and a photo unit which converts the information on the paper tape into characters on film or paper. A third (optional) unit makes possible photographic resizing and rearrangement of the output of the photo unit, thus permitting page makeup without patching or paste-up. The photo unit can handle the output of two to four keyboards.

Basically, the Linofilm can do any-thing that the Linotype can do (except produce metal type) and with greater speed and more versatility. It is faster because the keyboard is faster, being essentially an electric typewriter. Up to 18 different fonts can be selected at the push of a button, and they can be set in sizes from 6 to 54 pt at the twist of a dial. Display sizes can thus be keyboarded at the same speed as text matter, and compatible type faces (roman, italic, and boldface, for example) can be freely mixed in the same line. One of the 18 fonts can be a matrix of special accents to be used in combination with one of the other fonts. There is push-button control of justification, quadding, centering, and erasing.

The Linofilm keyboard produces not

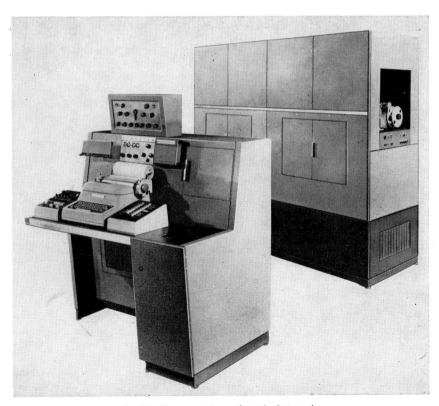

The Linofilm composing unit and photo unit.

only a punched tape but also a "hard copy" typescript for instant verification of what has been set.

Composition of considerable complexity is possible right at the keyboard, including headlines, subheads, space for illustrations, captions, tabular work, formulas, etc. More complex problems of makeup, including the makeup of newspaper pages and ads, can be done either by paste-up or with the aid of the Linofilm composing unit. This unit has an illuminated ground glass on which a translucent layout can be positioned and on which lines or blocks of type can be projected, moved about at will, and even enlarged or reduced as required.

The Linofilm revolving turret houses 18 grids or fonts. This is the equivalent of more than 72 magazines of hot metal matrixes.

Thus, every line of a complicated advertisement can be set in galley form at keyboard speed in a limited number of sizes, and then the several elements can be repositioned (and resized if necessary) to match the final layout. If corrections are later required, they can be made either by patching or by recomposing, whichever is more convenient. The output of the Linofilm composing unit is identical with that of the photo unit, except that the elements have been rearranged and resized and copied onto a new piece of photographic film or paper.

When a correction necessitates reset-

ting an entire paragraph of text matter, it may not be necessary to rekeyboard the whole paragraph. Instead, the corrections can be made semiautomatically in the punched tape by means of the Linofilm "tape combiner." With this device, the original tape is made to drive an electric typewriter and simultaneously to create a duplicate punched tape. An operator stops this automatic action only in an error zone, at which point he can manually substitute the correct information and can monitor any consequent line-break problems.

Although the Linofilm photo unit accepts only special 15-channel punched tape, an accessory is available for driving the keyboard unit from 6-level punched tape. Since the manual operation of the keyboard is unaffected, this permits newspapers to set text matter from over-the-wire information while monitoring the hard copy to see when headlines should be inserted.

Another attachment for the Linofilm keyboard unit, called the "Linomix," makes it possible to intermix up to three different type faces, sizes, line lengths, and leadings, with a single motion.

See also LINOFILM QUICK.

Linofilm Quick This is a simplified version of the Linofilm photo unit, using a 6-level punched-paper-tape input and delivering about 20 newspaper lines a minute in sizes 5 to 18 pt and in line widths up to 45 picas. It can intermix faces (with base alignment) from either two or four matrices, each matrix offering the equivalent of roman with italic, in a single size.

linoleum block See BLOCK PRINTING.

Linotype The Linotype and its substantially identical competitor, the Intertype, are type-composing machines that cast each line as a solid metal "line of type." They are used almost universally for newspapers and share the periodical, book, and job printing field with the Monotype. (See MONOTYPE.)

There are just these three methods of machine composition of metal type—Linotype, Intertype, and Monotype. The first two are, for practical purposes, the same.

The Linofilm Quick.

Setting type by machine is far cheaper than doing it by hand if there is much of it. For this reason the smaller sizes of type (4, 5, 6, 7, 8, 9, 10, 11, 12, and 14 pt) are almost always set by machine. However, a hand compositor can set half a dozen lines in the time it would take a Linotype operator to adjust his machine to a new size and kind of type and length of line. (A printer may have to charge $2 or more merely to set one line on the Linotype, in order to cover the cost of setting up the machine.) Linotype machines will handle sizes as large as 18, 24, 30, 36

pt, and even larger, but, because it is uncommon for printers to have these sizes on the machine, they are frequently set by hand. (See LUDLOW.)

The operator of a Linotype machine sits at a keyboard somewhat like that of a typewriter. Above the keyboard are "magazines" with narrow channels, each containing a number of matrices for each letter or character. When he touches, say, the letter "L," a matrix (mold) for that letter drops into place. When the line of matrices is complete, molten type metal is forced against the matrices, and the result is a Linotype slug, ready for printing.

Two great problems had to be solved before the Linotype could displace the setting of type by hand. First, there was the problem of spacing between words so as to "justify" (fill) each line. (See JUSTIFY.) Second, there was the problem of automatically putting each used matrix back in its own channel in the magazine, ready for reuse.

The invention of the spaceband solved the first problem. When a Linotype operator pushes the space bar, a spaceband drops alongside the last matrix of the word just set. The spaceband is simply a pair of two opposed wedges. When these wedges are pushed together, the spaceband gets wider. When a line is nearly full, the spacebands are expanded until it is exactly full.

The problem of getting the used matrices back in the magazine ready for reuse was solved on the latchkey principle. Each matrix has a built-in key, like the key to a Yale lock, which will unlock the door to its own channel and no other. The used matrices are automatically pushed, one by one, past each channel in the magazine, but each can drop off the distributor bar only when over its own proper channel.

Most Linotype matrices are two-letter matrices, like those shown and carry an italic as well as a roman version of the same letter, or perhaps a bold (instead of italic) with roman. If the matrices for any word are raised a notch, the line will be cast with that word in italic (or bold).

In order to change from one kind or size of type face to another, the Linotype operator must change magazines. For example, the 9-pt Baskerville matrices with which this book was set are kept in one magazine. The 9-pt Futura Demibold matrices used for the head-

A Linotype slug.

Thus, a Linotype operator who is using two-letter roman-with-italic matrices can set italic as easily as roman. If he is using roman-with-bold matrices, he can set bold as easily as roman. He is not able to set all three without extra trouble and extra cost, unless the machine he is using is a "mixer" designed for such special work.

Extra trouble and extra expense are also involved in setting SMALL CAPS. Since there is no special section on the Linotype keyboard for small-cap keys, they are scattered about under characters that have no italic (figures, punctuation, etc.).

ings are kept in another. It is possible to put as many as four main and four auxiliary magazines on some Linotype machines at the same time, but the operator must shift from one magazine to the other as his copy may require.

If typesetting on the Linotype or Intertype is desired, the following points should be kept in mind:

1. In consultation with the printer try to choose a font of type that is available, i.e., one that is not tied up all the

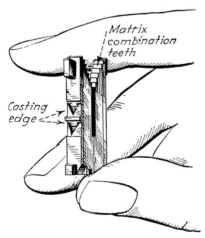

Matrix: Linotype and Intertype.

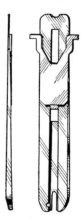

Spaceband: Linotype and Intertype.

time on another job. Note, however, that the busy fonts are usually the most desirable ones. Printers will buy fonts specially for important customers who plan to use them a lot.

2. If the selected font combines roman and italic, avoid the use of bold-face; if it combines roman and bold, avoid the use of italic.

3. Most Linotypes will not set a line

A phantom illustration of a Linotype machine. A touch of a key at the keyboard (1) releases one of the matrices stored in the magazines at (2). It falls (3) and joins other matrices and spacebands at (4). The completed line of matrices is moved to (5) where molten type metal is forced against it, and a line is cast. The used matrices then move to (6), are slid on to the elevator bar (7), are lifted to (8), and travel along the distributor bar (9), until each returns (10) to its proper channel in the magazine. (Photo courtesy of Mergenthaler Linotype Co.)

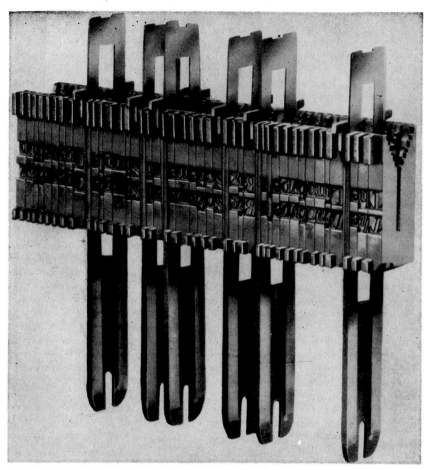

A line of Linotype matrices and spacebands. The upper of the two rows of characters casts unless some or all the matrices are lifted a notch so that the lower (italic) characters cast. The spacebands are wedge-shaped. Pushing them up increases the space between the words until the line is full. *(Photo courtesy of Mergenthaler Linotype Co.)*

longer than 30 picas without consider-able extra expense for setting each line in two parts. Some Linotypes will han-dle a 42-pica line.

4. In checking corrections make sure that the changed line has replaced the faulty one, and not some other line. Read two or three lines before and after the change.

5. Where possible, make corrections of such a length that only one line need be reset, and not an entire paragraph.

See also LINOFILM.

liquid duplicator See SPIRIT DUPLI-CATOR.

list broker See MAILING LISTS.

Listomatic See SEQUENTIAL-CARD CAM-ERAS.

litho Abbreviation for lithography. Litho coated paper means coated paper suitable for use in offset lithography. (See OFFSET; OFFSET PAPER.)

lithography See OFFSET for a discussion of how and when to use lithography commercially; see PLANOGRAPHY for an explanation of the principle employed in this type of printing.

"Photo-offset lithography" is the full name of the modern commercial application of lithography, which may be referred to as "offset" or "photo-offset" or "offset lithography."

Lithography (literally, stone writing) is an example of the planographic process. Some fine artists still work on stones, but in commercial work, stone has given way to metal as a material for making printing plates.

The word "lithography" is sometimes used in connection with fine color reproduction work as though the process were somehow superior to mere offset. The ten-dollar word has a loftier ring but it means the same.

Lithure See BIMETAL PLATES.

lock up To lock up pages of type or cuts means to clamp them into a steel frame, called a "chase," ready for putting on the printing press. (See TYPE.)

logotype A piece of type that carries, not just a letter, but one or more words,

Logotype and adcuts.

such as the name of a firm or a product.

Many firms adopt a special style for their name and have logotypes made so that this style can be followed whether or not the printers they deal with have this style of type.

Logotypes that are made from hand-lettering or a drawing instead of from a standard type style are sometimes called "adcuts."

Logotypes and adcuts are made to order by American Type Founders, 200 Elmora Ave., Elizabeth, N.J.

The words "ligature" and "logotype" are sometimes confused. The former refers only to a combination of two or three letters that have been designed to overlap each other, as "fi," "ffl."

loose-leaf binding See MECHANICAL BINDINGS.

lowercase See also PROOFREADING.

Lowercase, designated "lc," is the printer's term for small, as opposed to capital, letters. Hand type for small letters used to be kept in the lower case, that for capital letters in the upper case. (See illustration under CASE.) Hence, "u and lc" (upper and lowercase) has the same meaning as "c and lc" (caps and lowercase).

Ludlow See also TYPE; Appendix 1, Type Faces.

The Ludlow Typograph, or Ludlow, is a machine for casting lines of type in a range of sizes from 4 to 96 pt and up to 240 pt for special advertising figures. It and a similar machine called the "All-Purpose Linotype" (APL) are used primarily to handle type sizes from 18 pt up; sometimes also lines of smaller type too few in number to be worth setting on the big-keyboard Linotype and Intertype machines.

Ludlow composition is really hand composition, except that the compositor sets matrices (molds) instead of actual type and casts a line of new type from these matrices. (See illustrations below.)

Ludlow matrices.

The choice between using foundry type and using Ludlow or APL types depends in the first instance, of course, on the type styles available. Some types are available only in the form of foundry type.

Where the customer is willing to use either a foundry-type style or something similar that is "on the machine," printers usually favor the latter. This is because Ludlow and APL faces are cast up new for each use, whereas foundry type wears out with use.

Sometimes foundry type is used and then melted down to prevent mixing the worn letters with unused type. Foundry typefonts that have been thinned out in this way can be replenished, but this is a more costly procedure than to use Ludlow or APL slugs. (See FOUNDRY TYPE.) There is, of course, no disadvantage to melting down hand type that has been used only once if the printer has Monotype equipment with which he can cast more hand type. (See MONOTYPE.)

A special advantage of using Ludlow or APL composition occurs when the same line must be set many times. This is the case, for example, with the running heads in books. In such cases, the line need be "set" only once; as many lines as needed can then be cast from the one line of matrices.

Ludlow slugs have a distinctive T shape, the body being the same thickness for virtually all sizes, and the type being cast in a "shoulder" which extends beyond the body. The overhang

is supported by blank slugs assembled by the compositor.

What interests the buyer of composition is the fact that a printer who has certain Ludlow faces usually does not have similar faces offered by other typefounders.

Some popular Ludlow faces and some similar faces offered by other typefounders are as follows:

Ludlow	Corresponding Face by Other Typefounder
Eden	Corvinus
Radiant	Lydian
Coronet	Trafton
Mayfair	Liberty
UMBRA	SHADOW

luminescent printing Luminescent, phosphorescent, and fluorescent qualities can be obtained by dusting wet ink with special powders, by using special paper, or by using special ink.

Autoluminescence, i.e., the property of giving off visible light indefinitely, depends on the use of radium or some other radioactivated element mixed with a fluorescent salt which will glow under the radiation from the radioactive material. Watch dials are an example.

Phosphorescence is the property of giving off visible light for a limited period after excitation by exposure to an external light source. The period can be

Ludlow slugs.

A Ludlow slug, a proof taken from **that slug,** and the line of Ludlow matrices from which the slug was cast.

from a few minutes to 12 hr, depending on the chemical used.

Fluorescence is the property of giving off visible light under excitation by external radiation of a different wave-length. A number of chemicals give off visible radiation while exposed to invisible ultraviolet radiation.

Luminescent printing was developed for several war uses, notably to make airplane instruments and maps visible under "black light" (ultraviolet radiation) invisible to the enemy.

In general three methods are used to obtain a luminescent effect: (1) The printing is done with tacky varnish, and luminescent powder is dusted over the surface and adheres to the varnish. (2) Luminescent paper is used, and printed lines show against this glow. (3) A luminescent chemical is mixed with the ink. When a substantial thickness of ink must be applied, the silkscreen process is often used. (See SILK SCREEN.)

Day-Glo fluorescent pigments are made by Switzer Brothers, Inc., of 4732 St. Clair Ave., Cleveland, Ohio. This Cleveland firm and other manufacturers licensed under Switzer patents use these pigments to make inks and other daylight fluorescent color materials. These "brighter-than-bright" colors are finding considerable use on 24-sheet posters, car cards, point-of-sale materials, and other promotional pieces. The Day-Glo fluorescent colors are available in silkscreen-process printing paints, letterpress and gravure inks, paints for brushing and spraying, solidly coated papers and paper products, banner satin, flock, and bronzing powders.

Generally, the fluorescent colors have only a limited life when exposed to sunlight—60 days for screen-process printing paints and 120 days for bulletin paints. A thick color film of approximately 1½ mils is recommended for outdoor exposure. Very effective results can be obtained by letterpress and offset printing in reverse with conventional inks on Day-Glo coated paper stock. Unusual light and color effects are obtainable at night by using the combination of "black light" (ultraviolet) lamps with incandescent lights that flash off and on. When the conventional lights are on, the Day-Glo elements are quite colorful, and when the incandescent lights are off the Day-Glo colors glow with exceptional brilliance against the background of darkness.

Companies specializing in the manufacture of Day-Glo fluorescent materials under Switzer license include: American Crayon Co.; National Card, Mat & Board Co.; Crocker Hamilton Papers, Inc.; Dane & Co., Ltd.

luminous printing   See LUMINESCENT PRINTING.

Lumitype   See PHOTON.

M | m

machine-coated paper An inexpensive grade of coated paper. It is so called because the coating mixture is applied on the paper-making machine itself, not as a separate operation. It should not be confused with machine-finish (MF) paper, which is not coated. (See PAPER.) Also called process-coated paper.

machine-finish paper See also PAPER. A machine-finish paper (abbreviation MF) is an uncoated paper that has been calendered until it is smoother than an antique, not so glossy as a supercalendered paper, and not quite so smooth as an English-finish paper. It will take 85- to 100-screen halftones.

magazine To Linotype and Intertype operators the word "magazine" means the heavy metal container in which the matrices are kept. A magazine contains a complete font of matrices for one size of one type face. (See LINOTYPE.)

magazines See PERIODICALS.

magenta screen See HALFTONE.

magnesium plates Linecuts and halftone engravings are now being made on magnesium as well as on zinc and copper. Magnesium is a metal that is lighter than aluminum, fine-grained, easily etched, and very long-wearing. Magnesium engravings can be made on automatic etching machines by methods which eliminate the need for the repeated powdering and burning-in required by traditional methods of etching zinc and copper. Magnesium plates made in quantity by automatic methods are said to compare favorably in cost with offset plates, a fact of great interest to newspapers and letterpress printers who had feared that they might be unable to use their existing press and platemaking equipment for work composed on the Fotosetter, VariTyper, Photon, etc. In some applications, magnesium engravings are being used in place of electros, both on a cost-comparison basis and because magnesium plates are of more dependable thickness and do not deform under pounding as lead-backed electros may do. Magnesium is also being used for binding dies. (See DIE STAMPING.) A drawback to magnesium is a tendency toward pitting while in storage.

magnetic ink Bank checks are now mechanically sorted and routed by machines which "read" numbers printed or typed in magnetic ink. The process is called "magnetic-ink character recognition" (MICR). Special typefonts are required, but the printing can be done by conventional methods, and the ink used must contain iron oxide similar to that used in coating magnetic tapes. The sorting machines first magnetize this ink, then "read" it. This can be done even on checks which have become too dirty to be read visually.

Details of the MICR techniques for mechanized check handling may be obtained from the American Bankers Association, 90 Park Ave., New York 16.

The technique also holds potential for making possible machine sorting and analysis of unpunched forms of all kinds—coupons, utility bills, installment collections, etc.

magnetic recording See RECORDINGS.

mailing information See Appendix 3, Postal Information.

mailing-list corrections See MAILING LISTS; also Appendix 3, Postal Information.

mailing lists Mailing lists of every conceivable description can be obtained through professional list brokers, or list compilers, or direct from list owners at rentals ranging from $10 to $35 per thousand names. Currently available lists include such specialized groups as the former subscribers to magazines and book clubs, buyers of merchandise by mail, expectant mothers, doctors, licensed pilots, etc. Usually such lists are rented for one-time use, addressed on envelopes supplied by the renter and returned to him for mailing, with the understanding that the names will not be copied.

Procuring mailing lists. Some mailing lists exist in published form and can be obtained from trade directories and other reference books. However, many lists—particularly lists of those who have bought something by mail—have not been published and exist only on cards or address plates in the hands of the firm that compiled and maintains them. They are generally procurable direct or through list brokers, on a rental or exchange basis. List buyers generally ask the right to test an alphabetical or geographical cross section of the names on a large list before renting the whole. (See MAIL ORDER.)

A firm's most valuable mailing lists are usually its own lists. Lists of customers, prospects, publicity outlets, etc., can become invaluable tools for supplementing the work of salesmen and spreading information.

Building and maintaining mailing lists. Good lists are built with care. Each addition is checked, each card is dated, every address plate is proofread when it is cut, all lists are checked against orders received or are reviewed at intervals by salesmen and field representatives. Good lists are also "cleaned" regularly to correct changes of address, to remove the deceased, and to substitute current officeholders and business executives for any who have left. (See Appendix 3, Postal Information, for methods of enlisting post-office aid in cleaning lists.)

It is easy to forget that a mailing list is nothing but a list of living, breathing individuals; however, it must be maintained as such. List maintenance cannot safely be left in the care of unskilled help. At least once a year and preferably oftener, every list should be reviewed by some responsible executive. Salesmen should be encouraged to review regularly the mailing lists of their customers. They will seldom fail to catch errors or omissions.

Some firms rent out seldom-used lists for the primary purpose of keeping them up to date. Changes can run as high as 50 percent a year, rarely less than 20 percent.

One firm, dealing with schools, formerly addressed each principal by name. It now uses the title "Principal" instead of the name, after finding it impossible to keep up with name changes.

Lists that will be used from 8 to 12 times in two years are usually put on address plates. (See ADDRESSING.) Often the cards or address plates are tabbed or keyed, so that it is possible to address only certain groups within the list. Tabbing has one disadvantage: It may be necessary to run 10,000 address plates through the machine to address 2,500 of them. One answer is to keep proof cards, made from the address plates, in one master file, but to maintain the address plates as several separate lists. Since postal regulations require that third-class bulk mailings be sorted and tied geographically, there is also an argument for keeping the address plates in one geographically arranged list. With certain systems of machine addressing (see ADDRESSING), it becomes possible to select at high speed the desired names out of a large list before doing the actual addressing.

There are many concerns that compile local or national lists; some that specialize in lists of doctors, dentists, nurses, etc.; others that handle only lists of teachers or lawyers or automobile owners. Most, if not all, of them are thoroughly reliable and can be depended on to furnish the best list within the limits of available information to suit your own particular specifications.

Practically every trade or industry has a directory published once a year or even more often. These directories contain full information about every organization in the industry and, in most cases, include a list of the top personnel of each company.

Many cities issue annual or semiannual lists of all residents and business organizations. In some cases, the information goes so far as to list the occupation and employer of the individual, making it possible to complete company employee lists.

Dun & Bradstreet has lists of practically the entire business community of the country. Most of the credit-rating books do not list local addresses, but they can be checked against telephone directories for this information.

Practically every telephone book (complete with classified section) published in the entire country is available for a small fee through your own local telephone company.

Fraternities, sororities, chambers of commerce, Rotary, Kiwanis, Lions, professional and technical societies, religious, labor, and political organizations, trade associations, social and golf clubs—all have membership lists; some of them are for sale, and some may be procured free of charge.

Although many lists are available for the asking, many others are carefully guarded. Lists are private property, and you had better check before you buy to be certain you are not paying for a piece of stolen property.

State, city, county, and village clerks or other officials frequently have lists or will compile them for you from voting, tax, license, permit, or even real-estate or building records.

The names of advertisers in various magazines may serve your needs as an industry or general list.

A good news-clipping bureau can give you, particularly from small city or suburban newspapers, lists of engagements, marriages, births, deaths, new businesses or organization changes, fire damages, building permits, moving notices, etc.

The United States government publishes more directories than any other known source. A list of these directories will be mailed to you free of charge by the Superintendent of Documents, Government Printing Office, Washington 25, D.C.

Many publishers, particularly in trade lines, rent or sell all or part of their lists. Some of them allow their lists to be used only by advertisers in their own publications.

Ledger records, sales slips, and COD orders of your own company are profitable mailing list sources. Remember, your customers, past and present, are your competitors' best prospects. Your own salesmen and service representatives can, if properly trained in the job, add the best possible prospects to your list.

Many a good prospect has been added to a list by leaving space on order blanks, etc., for your customers to list the names of friends or business associates.

Among the firms that act as brokers for mailing lists are George Bryant & Staff, 71 Grand Ave., Englewood, N.J.; Walter Drey, Inc., 257 Park Ave. S., New York; Guild Co., 160 Engle St., Englewood, N.J.; Lewis Kleid, Inc., 230 Park Ave., New York; Willa Maddern, Inc., 215 Park Ave. S., New York; Mosely Mail Order List Service, 38 Newbury St., Boston; Names Unlimited, Inc., 352 Park Ave. S., New York.

The major list compilers, who will supply useful "lists of lists" on request, include W. S. Ponton, Inc., 44 Honeck St., Englewood, N.J., and R. L. Polk & Co., 60 E. 56 St., New York (also Detroit). A more comprehensive listing of list sources is given in "The Literary Market Place." (See Appendix 2, Bibliography.)

List compilers specialize. School lists, for example, can be obtained from the Educational Lists Co., Inc., 17 E. 22 St., New York. A good source of information on where to find specialized lists is the office of the trade paper of that field.

A national directory of mailing-list sources is published by B. Klein and Company, 104 Fifth Ave., New York.

For further information on mail-order techniques and mailing lists, see the books listed in Appendix 2, Bibliography.

mailings See DISTRIBUTION; ADDRESS- ING; DIRECT MAIL ADVERTISING; LETTERS;

MAIL ORDER; Appendix 3, Postal Information.

mailing tubes See also SHIPPING INFORMATION.

Mailing tubes are expensive compared with envelopes, but there is no cheaper way of shipping maps and other items that must not be folded. Even when many copies of an item are to go to one address, it is sometimes desirable to ship each copy in its own mailing tube, for the recipient may need the tubes for his own single-copy distribution.

When inquiring about mailing tubes, give specifications as to length and diameter desired, and whether paper cuffs are needed for tucking in to keep contents in place.

For suppliers: look under Mailing Devices in the Classified Telephone Directory, or write to Hudson Paper Tube Co., 372 Broom St., New York; The Cleveland Container Co., 4925 S. Halsted St., Chicago, and 4900 Valley Blvd., Los Angeles.

For a 27-in. mailing tube with 2-in. diameter and paper cuffs, the following prices are typical: 7.5 cents each for 100, 6.5 cents each for 500, 5.8 cents each for 1,000, plus shipping charges.

mail order See also DIRECT MAIL ADVERTISING; MAILING LISTS.

The mail-order industry is a specialized one, existing on sales made entirely through the mails. The giants in the field are of course Sears, Roebuck and Montgomery Ward. Their catalogs offer an object lesson in how to prepare persuasive, explicit advertising copy and illustrations. Their operations are not typical of the mail-order field, however, since they can keep costs lower than is possible in most mail-order operations.

Selling by mail is not quite so simple as the novice sometimes assumes. Under certain circumstances it can be extremely effective, but only in the hands of someone who has studied the accumulated know-how of the business. There are no "tricks of the trade" in the shady sense. Actually, the mail-order business is operated almost invariably on the money-back-if-not-satisfied basis. There are, however, many tricks of simple salesmanship.

Before venturing into this field, outsiders should ponder these principles, considered basic by mail-order men:

1. The product or service being offered should be something that is, or can be made to seem, unique—unobtainable elsewhere.

2. Success depends on a good mailing list. (See MAILING LISTS.)

3. The best prospects are people known to be in the habit of buying by mail.

4. If possible, a large mailing list should be tested before the whole of it is used.

5. It is hard to make ends meet on units of sale of less than $5 unless repeat business is expected.

6. Many mail-order men count a mailing successful if it brings back twice its cost; if, for example, a mailing that costs $100 per 1,000 brings back orders totaling $200. This would mean 20 orders for a $10 item, and there would be no profit unless the item could be produced and mailed (including allowance for bad debts) for under $5 each.

Some magazines are content if subscription receipts equal the cost of the subscription campaign!

7. Since the difference between a 2 and a 3 percent return may make all the difference between loss and profit, little things should be watched. The prospect should be asked to order, ordering should be made easy for him, and inducements should be offered for prompt action.

It would be difficult to overstress the importance of a good mailing list. Practically nothing can be sold profitably to a list of names taken uncritically from a telephone book. Good returns are difficult to get from any list of people not known to have the habit of buying by mail. (See MAILING LISTS.)

It is customary to test every large list before using the whole of it. If, for example, a list of 25,000 names seems promising, 2,000 names can be taken from it and tested. These people should receive the exact material that is proposed for the whole 25,000. If 2 percent of the 2,000 respond, it may be assumed that approximately the same percentage of the remaining 23,000 will respond when the same mailing is sent them under similar conditions.

Considerable reliance can be placed on such a test if certain rules are followed. The statisticians can prove that, in the above instance, there are 95 chances in 100 that the results for the remaining 23,000 will fall between 1.37 and 2.63 percent and that there are 997 chances out of 1,000 that the results for the 23,000 will fall between 1.06 and 2.94 percent.

The rules for planning and evaluating tests are as follows:

1. The names being tested must be a true random sample of the whole list. They must not be weighted geographically or as to age, income, or any other factor. The best way to get a true random sample is to take every tenth, twentieth, etc., name. Another way (if the list is arranged alphabetically by name) is to take all those whose names begin with "L" and "R," for example. In actual practice, of course, it may be impractical to take every tenth name, because there would be no way to skip the test names in a subsequent mailing. A common compromise, where lists are arranged geographically, is to take one or more states assumed to be typical.

2. The material mailed in the test must be identical in every way with the material to be mailed to the whole list—identical in method of addressing, envelope, enclosures, paper, method of printing, etc. By rights, the date of mailing should be identical, too. This is of course impossible, but it is possible and

Law of Probability as Applied to Evaluation of the Results of Test Mailings

Size of test mailing	If the return on the test mailing is:						
	1%	2%	3%	4%	5%	10%	20%
	then 95 chances out of 100, the return on the identical mailing to the whole list will be (in percent) between						
100	0–2.99	0–4.80	0–6.41	0.08–7.92	0.64–9.36	4.00–16.00	12.00–28.00
250	0–2.26	0.23–3.77	0.84–5.16	1.52–6.48	2.24–7.76	6.20–13.80	14.94–25.00
500	0.11–1.89	0.75–3.25	1.48–4.52	2.25–5.75	3.05–6.95	7.32–12.68	16.42–23.58
1,000	0.37–1.63	1.12–2.88	1.92–4.08	2.76–5.24	3.62–6.38	8.10–11.90	17.48–22.52
2,000	0.55–1.45	1.37–2.63	2.24–3.76	3.12–4.88	4.03–5.97	8.66–11.34	18.21–21.79
5,000	0.72–1.28	1.60–2.40	2.52–3.48	3.45–4.55	4.38–5.62	9.15–10.85	18.87–21.13
10,000	0.80–1.20	1.72–2.28	2.66–3.34	3.61–4.39	4.56–5.44	9.40–10.60	19.20–20.80
100,000	0.94–1.06	1.91–2.09	2.89–3.11	3.88–4.12	4.86–5.14	9.81–10.19	19.75–20.25

Note: The size of the test mailing, not the size of the list being tested, governs the reliability of the test results. The ranges given above are for twice the probable error. To get a range with a "997 chances out of 1,000" reliability, take three probable errors; i.e., increase the range by one-half the given amount both above and below the test result.

desirable to mail on the same day of the week and to reckon with such factors as the season, weather, current news, and holidays.

3. The test mailing must be large enough to give results of the desired accuracy. Surprisingly enough, a larger list does not require a larger test sample. A sampling of 2,000 names will give just as reliable information about a list of 1,000,000 names as about a list of 10,000 names. On the other hand, a sampling of 100 names will tell little about a list of any size.

4. The mathematical laws of probability make it possible to predict with assurance the "probable error" in the results of any test mailing. The accompanying table shows how much reliance can be placed on a given return from a sample of a given size.

The unit of sale is very important in mail-order work. If the cost of addressing, printing, postage, materials, and labor on each letter mailed is 10 cents, or $10 per hundred, then each 100 letters mailed must bring in at least this $10 plus adequate payment for the mer-

chandise, usually at least a total of $20. On a $1 item this would necessitate a 20 percent return (which is unusually high); on a $2 item, a 10 percent return would suffice; on a $5 item, a 4 percent return might be acceptable.

Anyone who is contemplating mail-order work should by all means read some of the very excellent books on the subject. These are listed and described in Appendix 2, Bibliography.

Mathematics of the law of probability. The table is a guide to the reliability of test mailings of various sizes. The mathematics underlying it need not concern the layman, but for those interested in working out the problem themselves, the formula is

$$\text{Probable error} = \pm \sqrt{\frac{PQ}{N}}$$

where P is the number of positive responses, Q is the number of negative responses, and N is the number in the test mailing $(P + Q)$. A 2 percent return on a 2,000 test mailing may be evaluated as follows:

$$\text{Probable error} = \pm \sqrt{\frac{40 \times 1,960}{2,000}}$$
$$= \pm 6.3$$

This means that there is a fifty-fifty chance that returns on the whole list will equal the test results plus or minus 6.3; i.e., they will fall between 33.7 and 46.3 for each 2,000 mailed, or between 16.8 and 23.1 per thousand, or between 1.68 and 2.31 percent.

Most direct mail operators, however, want more than a fifty-fifty assurance of the reliability of their tests. The law of probability provides this kind of assurance, too.

For example, there are only 50 chances out of 100 that the results of the full mailing will equal the test results plus or minus the probable error. But there are 95 chances out of 100 that the results of the full mailing will equal the test results plus or minus twice the probable error. And there are 997 chances out of 1,000 that the results of the full mailing will equal the test results plus or minus three times the probable error.

Good books on mail-order techniques, direct mail advertising, and mailing lists can be found in Appendix 2, Bibliography.

makeready The process of adjusting the type on a printing press to give a perfect impression. The type and cuts must be set so as to print evenly and with exactly the right pressure on the paper. "Press-ready" means adjusting the press itself to the requirements of a new job. The paper guides may have to be reset. The color or kind of ink may have to be changed. Feeding and binding attachments, if any, must be adjusted. Makeready is at best a time-consuming operation. It can take hours.

The first proof may show many flaws. The impression may be too heavy or too light. The ink coverage may be too dark, too faint, or too uneven.

After these faults are corrected, proofs will still show light or dark areas in all probability. This is because of unevenness within the type form itself. All cuts and type are supposed to stand type-high, i.e., exactly 0.918 in. high. Unfortunately, absolute precision is only a goal, not an accomplishment.

To correct the unevenness of the type as shown by the light and dark areas of the proof, the pressman must build up the low spots and take down the high spots. He will add a piece of tissue paper, or cut away some packing to achieve an even effect. Sometimes this is done under the tympan sheet, which covers the entire impression surface and supports the paper while it is being printed. Sometimes it is done behind the type.

Careful makeready is essential to fine presswork. It cannot be hurried. Time must be allowed for it in every printing process, especially in color work. It is a particularly important and demanding operation when halftones are to be printed.

Makeready is a larger factor in letterpress printing than in offset or other processes that do not print from type. This is both an advantage and a disadvantage. It gives the letterpress pressman greater control over his process, but at the same time it gives him more work.

The offset pressman has less makeready work. On the other hand he has fewer tricks up his sleeve when proofs are not good. Part of the work that the letterpress man calls "makeready" is the responsibility of the platemaking department in offset, gravure, and photogelatin printing.

makeup To make up a page is to assemble and arrange the headings, illustrations, captions, and text.

In most cases this is a joint task of the author or editor and the printer's makeup man. The former is responsible for editorial decisions as to what will go on which page; the latter is responsible for the mechanical assembly of the type and cuts in the space designated.

With a magazine, pamphlet, or broadside, the editor indicates the makeup by his paste-up dummy (see PASTE-UP DUMMY), which shows the exact spacing, allocation of copy to columns and pages, and the placing of illustrations and captions.

Some printers permit the editor or his representative to work in the composing room with the makeup man to show him where to shove the blocks of copy, cuts, heads, etc. (By union rules editors do not actually handle the type.) This procedure is followed chiefly on newspaper and rush jobs and where the editor and the printer have had long experience with makeup and with working together. This is not recommended for the hesitant beginner.

Both men, whether working separately or together, should check on the accuracy of page numbers, datelines, and page references, continuations of articles, positions of ads, agreement of cuts and captions, cover and masthead data, table of contents against the location of articles listed, and finally the headings and by-lines in relation to the articles with which they appear.

manila See also PAPER.

Manila has come to mean simply yellowish paper or bristol. Rope manila is the designation for the very strong stock made from manila hemp. The addition of hemp or jute fibers gives extra strength to paper.

manuscript See COPY; COPY PREPARATION.

maps Map printing is a specialized department of the graphic arts; at least, the preparation of the artwork and plates is specialized. Once prepared, maps can be reproduced by lithography, letterpress, or other processes.

Simple maps can be made by an artist or draftsman, but professional map makers use many techniques and skills especially developed for their work. A map draftsman can get more information across, more legibly, than can a lay artist, simply because he knows the conventions and the best ways of handling the lettering.

Many maps are prepared like simple line drawings or wash drawings and are reproduced as such. Areas or parts to be reproduced in color are indicated on one or more overlays.

By far the easiest way to get a map is to go to one of the companies which specialize in maps, such as George F. Cram Co., Inc., 730 E. Washington St., Indianapolis 7; C. S. Hammond & Co., Maplewood, N.J.; Rand McNally & Co., P.O. Box 7600, Chicago 80.

An artist with a map assignment and no recent knowledge of the many shortcuts which are in use in map-making establishments would do well to write to Artype, Inc., 127 S. North West Highway, Barrington, Ill., and Keuffel & Esser Co., Adams and Third Sts., Hoboken, N.J., for information about their map-making aids. Artype can, for example, supply lettering symbols, etc., preprinted on transparent self-adhering plastic sheets, and K & E offers a line of special plastic sheeting through the use of which the artist's work can become the lithographer's negative without any intermediate steps.

The process of mapmaking is described by Rand McNally as follows:

"The first step in cartographic production is called 'scribing.' Scribe sheets are clear plastic sheets coated with a special paint. The surface is light-sensitized so that by placing the compilation in contact with the scribe sheet and exposing to strong light, the image of the compilation is transferred to the scribe sheet. Next, by pulling a pointed stylus across the scribe sheet, using the image as a guide, the painted surface is scraped away, leaving transparent lines.

A separate sheet is scribed for each color that will appear on the finished map.

"Step No. 2 is to arrange the place names as they will appear on the final map. First, a composite image of all the lines from the several scribe sheets is printed on a piece of clear plastic. This becomes a guide for positioning the type. The type is printed on lightweight, transparent film with an adhesive backing. Each place name or item of type is cut out by hand and placed in proper position on a separate sheet of transparent plastic laid over the line work guide. The completed type assembly is then photographed to get a negative. Finally, this type negative will be exposed in combination with the scribed lines to secure a composite type-and-line positive which is used to prepare a printing plate for the press. The task of preparing the type stickup is one of the most painstaking processes in map making, consuming several hundred man-hours for a 9¾ x 11⅜ map.

"Shaded relief, showing mountains and land formations, is prepared as airbrush art by personnel skilled in art, cartography, and geography. The operator's reference material is a study of contours and relief shown either on previously prepared authoritative maps (usually government charts) or aerial photographs. The airbrush print is then photographed to produce a film negative.

"How do you get the various colors and hues on a map? Through a process called 'Dy-Stripping.' The lines from each of the scribe sheets are produced by a photographic process on a material similar to scribe sheets. In this process, the lines appear as clear tracings through a special paint coating over a clear plastic base. The draftsman, guided by an outline map hand-colored with crayons, then peels off portions of the coating within these lines to create 'windows.' A Dy-Strip is created for each color tint that will appear on the finished map. Once the windows are peeled open, the excess lines are blocked out. Through a photographic process, a film positive of appropriate density for the particular color tint is created from the Dy-Strip in combination with what lithographers call a 'screen,' a device which controls the pattern of light passing through the Dy-Strip windows. All the lines from the blue scribe sheet (grid, rivers, lakes, streams), the blue type, and the several blue Dy-Strips are projected onto the same film positive, from which the final printing plate for the blue areas will be made. In the same way, film positives and printing plates are made for each of the other main colors on the map."

It is not permissible to trace or copy a copyrighted map in whole or in part, for either personal or business use, without permission from the copyright owner and perhaps payment of royalty. This does not apply to most United States government maps, which are public property. Useful information on where to find both noncopyright and coypright base maps is available in the book "Scientific Illustration," by John L. Ridgway, listed in Appendix 2, Bibliography.

marbling Books, especially large dictionaries, sometimes have marbled endpapers or edges decorated with a variety of colors in an irregular pattern resembling the veins of marble.

The pigments are floated on a liquid surface, stirred into the desired pattern, and then the area to be marbled is allowed to touch the surface so that the colors adhere to it. The surface is then cleansed of color, and the whole process is repeated for the next impression.

marginal head See HEADINGS.

Marginator A typewriter attachment that permits typewritten material to be retyped in such a way that all lines are of equal length and align with each other at the right as well as at the left margins. It was formerly called the "Edison Margin Justifier." (See TYPEWRITER.) It is available from the Marginator Co., 299 S. Lake St., Burbank, Calif.

margins See also DESIGN.

In conventional book and pamphlet work, the bottom margins are larger than the top margins in such ratios as 2:1, 5:3, 8:5, or 3:2. Outside margins are larger than inside margins in the same proportion.

On a 6 by 9 page, deluxe margin allowance might be divided as follows: 4½ picas inside, 6 picas top (head), 8½ picas outside, 12 picas bottom (tail).

On a 6 by 9 page, moderate margin allowance might be 4½ inside, 6 top, 7½ outside, 10 bottom.

Common margins on a 5½ by 8½ page are 3 picas inside, 3½ top, 4½ outside, 6 bottom.

Where space must be saved, 3 picas all around, or even 2 picas, will suffice, always with an attempt to make the bottom margin a little larger than the others.

The real limit to the smallness of margins is the danger of variation in the binding. Margins within the same book may average 3 picas, while varying from 2 or 2½ to 3½ or 4 picas. A ⅛-in. margin might disappear entirely, taking some of the type with it.

Whether or not generous margins add to readability is a matter of opinion. There are no margins around newspaper columns, yet few complain of poor readability.

In figuring margins, it is usual to count running heads (unless very short) as part of the type page; page numbers, if on a line by themselves, are counted as part of the margins.

Margins cannot be determined without reference to the type to be used. Half-inch margins around a 6 by 9 page would yield a 5-in. type line, which is too long to be readable unless set in large type, generously leaded. Space saved on small margins would be lost on big type. Where the maximum number of words must be printed on a page that is readable, it is often advisable to go to two columns, as in this book.

Marline rate See ADVERTISING.

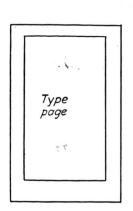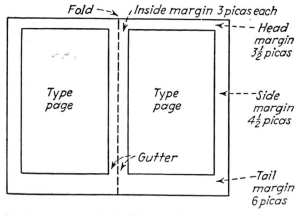

On a single page, top and side margins may be about equal, the bottom margin larger.

Two facing pages (5½ by 8½ in.) with typical margins, larger at bottom than at top, and larger outside than inside. Page numbers and short running heads may be considered part of the margins.

mask In the printshop or art studio, a piece of paper so cut as to prevent ink or paint from touching areas protected by it.

A retoucher who wishes to use the airbursh to lighten the background in a photograph will first mask out those areas which are not to be retouched. He may use a paper mask, adhering it with rubber cement, or he may simply use a coating of rubber cement, which he will peel off later.

The words "mask" and "frisket" are used interchangeably in the above sense, with printers favoring the latter term. With a frisket it is possible to take a proof of only certain sections of an inked form.

Master Addresser A low-cost addressing machine operating on the spirit-duplicator principle. There is a model at about $31 complete with supplies for a 500-name list, another with automatic tape advance at about $60. Materials for 500 additional addresses cost about $3.

The addresses are typed on a roll of paper on any typewriter, special matching carbon-paper rolls being used face up under the paper to create a carbon image of the address on the underside. From this master roll up to 200 impressions of each address can be taken, at a rate of about 20 per minute. On the $31 machine unwanted addresses can be skipped. Addressing can be done on any kind of material—envelopes, postcards, forms, etc. The machine automatically moistens the area to receive the imprint as the envelopes are fed in. About a pint of moistening fluid (alcohol) is used per 500 addresses, price 75 cents. (The moistening is almost imperceptible—just enough to dissolve off an impression from the aniline dye in the carbon image.)

Addresses can also be kept on cards or forms instead of on rolls—including punched cards, one card being fed into the machine along with each item to be addressed. The addresses can be placed on the cards by direct typing or by special self-adhering typed labels.

The combination of a Master Addresser unit with marginal punched cards such as McBee cards yields great addressing versatility. One large retailer codes a customer list of 20,000 under 160 headings and finds it practicable to select as few as 50 names from the 20,000 for special sales promotion based on their known interests.

For further information and the name of a nearby source of supply (the equipment is sold in many stationery stores) write to the Master Addresser Co., 6500 W. Lake St., Minneapolis 16, Minn.

masthead The block of information in a newspaper or periodical that gives the title, publisher, names of editors, advertising manager, business manager, etc., address, date, volume and issue number, subscription rates, notice of entry as second-class mail, etc.

The masthead of a newspaper usually appears on the editorial page; of a magazine, alongside the table of contents.

mat See STEREOTYPE; MATRIX.

matches Slightly more than 10 billion imprinted books of matches, many of them in product-replica packages, are used annually in the United States for advertising purposes. Prices can be obtained from the Diamond Match Co., 600 S. Delaware Ave., Philadelphia; Lion Match Co., Inc., 2 W. 45 St., New York; or Continental Match Co., Inc., 2 W. 45 St., New York (for imported Italian matches).

For advertising purposes, two general methods are followed: (1) The matches are sold to the advertiser, who distributes them to customers, as in hotels and restaurants. (2) The advertiser merely buys the space on the covers, distribution being handled by the match company in geographic areas specified by the space buyer. The advertiser designates the number of matches to be distributed in each area and the dates of distribution.

In planning mail promotions involving matches, advertisers should note that only safety matches are mailable under United States postal regulations, and these must be packed in foil-lined asbestos or metal containers.

matrix A matrix (rhymes with "cat tricks" or "play tricks") is a mold. The kind of matrix used in casting Linotype, Monotype, or Ludlow types is described under those headings. The matrix or "mat" used in the stereotype process is described under that heading.

mat services See also STOCK CUTS.

Most newspapers, both large and small, subscribe to a mat service in order to provide their advertisers with pictures of merchandise, decorative spot drawings, borders, etc.

Printers of one or more periodicals may subscribe to a mat service in their own name and thus be able to offer the service to all their clients. Some department stores have their own subscriptions; specialty stores may subscribe to specialized mat services or buy a single catalog of a certain kind of material.

The subscriber to the mat service receives both an assortment of mats, from which stereos can be cast (see STEREOTYPE) and a catalog of proofs of the illustrations contained in the mats. Every month or so (for the specialized services, perhaps every season or every year), he receives new and timely pictorial material, copy ideas, and suggestions for campaigns built around this material.

If an advertiser needs a picture of, say, some lace curtains, he can look up such a picture in the catalog, note its key number, and then locate the corresponding mat. In the same way he can find a picture of a pretty girl, a man painting, some Christmas holly, a roast of beef, etc.

Two mat services are Metro Associated Services, Inc., 80 Madison Ave., New York; and East Texas Engraving Co., P.O. Box 2038, Tyler, Tex. A directory of mat services is contained in the *Editor and Publisher* annual.

mat surface A mat-surface photographic print has a dull, nonreflecting finish, as opposed to a glossy print, which has a shiny surface. Mat prints can be used for reproduction, but "glossies" are usually preferred because they are less subject to soiling and offer a somewhat greater range of tonal values. Mat prints are generally used for exhibition and framing purposes.

The word "matte" has the same meaning and pronunciation as "mat."

matte See MAT SURFACE.

measurements See TYPE MEASUREMENTS.

mechanical A mechanical is a layout prepared for the engraver or printer, which contains the actual copy to be reproduced (or instructions for stripping in copy) and all information necessary for handling it. Reproduction proofs are pasted down clean and square, rules or reverses are drawn or pasted in, guidelines show the positioning of any artwork which must be stripped in, the break for color is indicated, etc. Because the "mechanical" is usually executed in black and white even though the job is to run in color and because it is intended to be photographed, not looked at, its appearance is markedly different from that of the "comprehensive" layout (see COMPREHENSIVE) which may have preceded it.

mechanical bindings A great variety of plastic and metal mechanical bindings are available. They offer the following advantages:

1. They are colorful and attractive.
2. Pages open flat.

3. Pages may be arranged in any order, may be of varying weights and sizes, and are usually trimmed on four sides. There is no need to bind in even forms, as of 8, 16, or 32 pages.

4. Service is quick. There is no need to put books under pressure as a guard against warping, as there is with a glued cloth cover.

Some of the disadvantages of mechanical bindings are:

1. They cost more than those simply wire-stitched, sometimes substantially more.

2. In some of the spiral types, the left-hand page is higher or lower than the page opposite, by half the distance between holes, when the book is open.

3. Mechanically bound books are a little bulkier to pack and ship.

Closed style   Loose-leaf style

Two ways of punching paper for use in mechanical bindings.

4. Mechanical bindings do not provide the support and protection often desired in permanent bindings. They may not last as long as case bindings.

5. Pages may be torn out or stolen more easily.

Any mechanical binder having broad rings can be made to serve as a loose-leaf binder if the pages are punched as shown in the illustration.

Most firms of binders offer one or more styles of mechanical bindings. The costs depend on style, length of binding edge, thickness, nature of cover, the work involved in gathering the pages into the proper sequence, and the number ordered at one time.

It is possible to put a good mechanical binding on an 8½ by 11 book, ¼ in. thick, from about $70 per thousand. A book twice as thick would cost about half again as much. This covers only punching the holes and applying the binding. It does not include the cost of any printing or the cover paper.

Mechanical bindings are frequently used on calendars, diaries, price books, memo books, catalogs, and stenographic notebooks.

mechanical wood pulp See GROUND-WOOD PULP.

metered postage See Appendix 3, Postal Information.

MF Abbreviation for machine finish. (See MACHINE-FINISH PAPER.)

Microcard See MICROFILM.

Microfiche See MICROFILM.

microfilming A photographic method of making one or more low-cost, space-saving copies of literary or visual material. A researcher can gain access to a rare book located in a distant library by having that library make and send him a microfilm copy of it. The cost is about 4 or 5 cents per page, depending upon the copy. A manuscript can be microfilmed as a precaution against loss. If the original is lost, a replacement copy can be made from the microfilm. Banks commonly make microfilm copies of checks. The cost of storing bulky and seldom-used records can be reduced by microfilming them and discarding the originals.

In the microfilming process, original

material is photographed on 16mm or 35mm film at about one-tenth to one-thirtieth of its original size. The first film copy is of course in negative form, with white letters on black background. Positive prints can be made from this original negative, if desired, though the original negative is entirely satisfactory for reading purposes.

Microfilm is read in special machines that enlarge the material to approximately its original size and project it on translucent glass or opaque screen. To "turn the page" a lever is pressed; to turn many pages, a crank is revolved.

Engineering drawings can be filmed and negatives mounted in aperture cards and punched for ready reference. New machines permit immediate copies or enlargements.

Information is obtainable, free on request, from the following makers of microfilming equipment: Recordak Corporation, a subsidiary of Eastman Kodak, 770 Broadway, New York 3; Remington Rand Office Systems, div. of Sperry Rand Corp., 122 E. 42 St., New York 17; Bell and Howell Equipment Co., Chicago; Griscombe Products, Inc., 133 W. 21 St., New York 11. The larger public and university libraries have microfilm equipment and are good sources of advice on its use. They can also supply the name of the nearest commercial firm doing this type of work. One such firm in New York City is the Microfilm Corp., 13 E. 37 St.; another is Graphic Microfilm Corp., 115 Liberty St., New York 6.

Prices for 35mm copying run from about 3 cents per exposure, with certain minimum charges. Often two pages or more can be copied at one exposure.

Prices for 16mm copying on automatic machines run about $7.50 to $15 per thousand exposures, depending on the size of the copy. Material to be copied in such machines must be furnished in separate sheets; bound volumes must be handled on nonautomatic 16mm or 35mm machines.

35mm microfilm is preferred if the material is referred to often or if photo enlargements are likely to be required. 16mm may be satisfactory if the copying is done for record purposes only and will be consulted only in an emergency.

Enlargements can be made from microfilm at a cost of 10 to 25 cents per 8½ by 11 enlargement, depending on the quantity ordered. Sometimes two or more pages can be reproduced on each enlargement.

Occasionally material is copied on 70 mm film or sensitized paper. If the reduction is not too great, such microfilm can be read without the aid of a special machine. Such copying service costs about 25 cents per negative exposure on paper and about 60 cents on film.

An outgrowth of microfilming is the development of unitized microforms: the Microcard (an opaque card which has a positive image) and the Microfiche (a transparent sheet of film with a positive or negative image). With these, about 40 book pages can be photographically reduced and printed on one side of a 3 by 5 index card, either paper or film. A book of 100 pages can be reproduced on three such cards.

When a Microcard or Microfiche is inserted in a special reading machine, each page is enlarged to its original size on a ground-glass viewing screen. One portable model, weighing 6 lb, can carry 8,000 pages of material in Microcard form.

The first use of unitized microforms was to make available out-of-print material that libraries were seeking, but thousands of these are now being issued daily by governmental and other research bodies for hitherto unpublished research materials. These separate cards and film sheets facilitate the filming of new material and the location of specific entries.

Information on unitized microforms is obtainable from Microcard Corporation, West Salem, Wis.

The Microtext Publishing Corp., 114

Liberty St., New York, can handle material through a process essentially the same as the Microcard.

The Microlex Company, Rochester, N.Y., prepares photographic prints of microtext on 6½ x 8½ cards which will accommodate 200 pages of text on each side. This firm handles legal material exclusively.

Microprint is a printing-press micro-reproduction publishing process developed by the Readex Microprint Corp., 5 Union Sq., New York. By this process 100 pages, arranged in 10 rows of 10 pages each, can be reproduced on a 6 by 9 card.

milline rate See ADVERTISING.

mimeograph See also DUPLICATING.

Mimeograph was originally the trade name of A. B. Dick Company of Chicago, used to identify its equipment, supplies, and accessories for stencil duplicating. The word has become a part of the language, however, and is used freely to refer to the process, not the firm, even where another make of machine is being used.

Stencil duplicating is one of the most widely used of all office duplicating methods. With a mimeograph stencil sheet, which costs 12 to 20 cents, and a mimeograph duplicator, a few or a few thousand copies of typing, handwriting, line drawings, halftones, pictures, solids, or ruled forms, on card stock or paper from 3 by 5 in. to 10⅛ by 15 in. in size, can be made in a short time.

Many schools use mimeographs and teach their operation in commercial classes. Many typists are taught to prepare duplicating stencils when they learn to type.

Mimeographs can be used continuously or can stand idle days or weeks at a time and still be ready to turn out a rush job within a matter of minutes.

Mimeograph stencil sheets are made of a porous tissue covered with a coating that is impervious to ink. Typing or drawing upon them with a sharp instrument pushes the coating aside and exposes the porous tissue. The stencil is then attached to a cylinder which contains ink. As the cylinder rotates, each sheet of paper passing beneath it is pressed against it by an impression roller. Ink is forced through the porous openings of the stencil onto the paper, thus duplicating the message originally typed or drawn.

Effective mimeographed work requires (1) a good stencil, properly prepared, (2) even ink distribution, (3) a duplicating machine in good mechanical condition, and (4) the right kind of paper.

Some mimeograph inks dry by absorption while others dry by oxidation. Most commonly used inks today dry by both methods. A paper of medium absorbency is preferable for duplicating work. Recent developments in paper manufacturing and modern inks do allow mimeographing on harder, smoother papers than could be used a few years ago. When paper with too hard a finish is used, a small amount of the ink might stay on the surface of the paper and rub off on the next sheet of paper that comes into the receiving tray of the duplicator. This can be prevented, when using oil-base inks, by slip-sheeting, or putting a blank sheet of paper or card stock over each copy as it comes into the receiving tray. These slip sheets are removed later when the ink is dry. (See SLIP-SHEETING.)

The trend is away from oil-base inks toward quick-drying, water-soluble inks, such as A. B. Dick's patented Contac-Dri, toward emulsion inks, such as A. B. Dick's 6000 S.E., or toward the modern paste-type inks, which are very popular now because of their ease of use.

Mimeograph duplicating also may be done with colored inks. A clean ink pad is placed over a protective cover or sheet of typing film, which is placed over the regular ink pad. Colored ink can be applied to the clean pad externally with a brush or applicator. About 150 copies can be run this way before reinking is necessary. When there is an inch or more of space between the stenciled areas, two or more colors can be used at the same time. Colored copies are also run by the use of extra cylinders, which are kept for the particular colors used.

To keep a mimeograph in good working condition, the correct ink must be used, the ink pad must be cared for properly and changed regularly, and the rubber feeding parts must be cleaned regularly and replaced when worn. The duplicator should be covered when not in use to keep it free from dust, and the machine should be oiled regularly according to directions.

If the paper is to feed properly, it must be uniform in size, properly centered in the machine, firmly gripped between the sponge-rubber grippers, and "combed." (To comb a ream of paper means to bend it back and forth and fan the edges slightly, to be sure that no sheet is sticking to its neighbor.) After combing, the paper is squared up again before being inserted in the machine. The last 20 sheets or so are usually not fed through the machine, since they are likely to feed improperly.

Any standard typewriter in good condition may be used to type a stencil. The type keys should be cleaned thoroughly with a stiff-bristle brush before beginning this work. The ribbon of the typewriter is then shifted from the printing position so that the type keys strike the stencil itself. A cushion sheet (supplied with each package of stencils) is inserted between the stencil sheet and the backing, and the assembly is placed in the typewriter. The type keys should be hit with a firm, staccato touch. Characters with a large printing surface (W, #, S, M) should have a little extra pressure; small characters and the punctuation marks, less pressure. (For a variety in type styles, see VARITYPER.) A medium setting on electric typewriters should work nicely.

A carbon copy can be made when the stencil is cut by inserting a sheet of carbon paper and one of onionskin between the cushion sheet and the backing sheet.

Super Mimeotype (blue) stencil sheets are recommended by A. B. Dick Company if typing is to be combined with illustrations, lettering, or ruled forms or if a maximum number of copies (5,000 or more) will be run. Yellow, white, or orange stencil sheets are recommended for straight typing jobs. (The contrast of the blue stencil sheet when placed on the illuminated drawing board for tracing or lettering is better than that of the light-colored stencil sheets.) For typing, a black cushion sheet is inserted with the light-colored stencil sheets. The visibility while typing is high, and a proof copy is produced on the backing sheet. Standard-run blue, dark green, transparent green, white, orange, or yellow stencils are also available.

Signatures may be reproduced as part of a mimeographed letter. When a blue stencil is to be signed, the cushion sheet is removed and a flexible writing plate (signature plate) is placed under the stencil. A ball-point stylus is used for writing. Writing should be done with a firm, uniform pressure. When a yellow stencil is to be signed, the cushion sheet should be inserted between the stencil and the backing and the assembly placed on a hard, smooth surface such as a glass desk top. Do not use a wooden desk top because the stylus will have a tendency to follow the grain of the wood.

An illuminated drawing board, called a "Mimeoscope," is used when tracing, lettering, drawing, handwriting, and ruling forms. It has a translucent glass top under which an ordinary 60-watt bulb or a fluorescent lamp gives excellent illumination with no glare. Artwork to be traced is laid on the glass and covered with a protective sheet of transparent plastic with a special textured finish. A stencil sheet is placed over this.

Writing, lettering, ruling, and drawing are done with styli (penlike tools), which may be obtained with various kinds of points. There are wire-loop and ball-point styli for solid lines, tracing, and drawing; serrated wheels for dotted lines; blunt loops for shading; and points bent at angles for lettering. Areas may be shaded by first outlining the area to be shaded and then placing a "screen plate" (a plastic rectangular plate impressed with a pattern) under the stencil and rubbing over the plate until the pattern is reproduced in the stencil.

Lettering guides are used to make attractive lettering on stencils. They are oblong pieces of plastic pierced with letter outlines available in various styles and sizes. The lettering styli fit these openings and are drawn through them to make corresponding outlines upon the stencil.

Material too intricate to be traced upon a regular mimeograph stencil, plus solid black areas and halftones, may be reproduced electronically on special mimeograph stencils. The stencil is prepared from an original, which may be a paste-up or existing material. The work can be done in offices with special electronic stencil-printing equipment or by a distributor or office of A. B. Dick Company from copy submitted. (See also STENAFAX.)

The mimeograph can now duplicate all types of copy, including photographs, solids, and bold copy (headline type), with the use of electronic stencils. The Mimeofax is used by A. B. Dick Company distributors in order to offer this electronic stencil service to their customers. The Mimeofax consists of two drums, a sending unit, and a receiving device. An original, which can consist of paste-ups of drawings, photographs, bold type, or complicated drawings, is put onto one drum, and a blank, plasticlike stencil is attached to the other drum. As the drums rotate at equal speeds, an electric eye scans the original, and when it picks up an image, an electric charge is sent to a burning needle which is attached to the other drum. An electric arc passes from the needle to the surface of the stencil, burning away a very small portion of the material. The burned lines or images are so close together, up to 500 per inch, that they are hardly visible to the human eye. When the stencil is put on a mimeograph, ink will pass through these burned-away areas, and where solids are to be duplicated, the ink will spread enough between the lines to produce a solid image.

Typewritten copy cannot be added to electronic stencils, but the two types of stencils can be used together by "patching" electronically prepared material into a Mimeotype stencil. Pages of illustrations prepared and ready to be traced in on Mimeotype stencils are available from A. B. Dick Company at a reasonable price.

Special services of A. B. Dick Company and others in the stencil-duplicating field include die impressing and form topping of stencils. Die impressing is a method of cutting standard forms, headings, typing, or designs into the stencil sheet so that the typist needs to add only the variable information. The form and the newly typed information are duplicated at the same time.

Form-topping is used when duplicated copy is run on a printed form. A facsimile of the form is printed on the surface of the stencil sheet. It guides the typist in positioning the fill-in copy, but the printing does not reproduce. Die-impressed and form-topped stencils are extensively used in business control systems, where a single writing on a prepared stencil is all that is necessary to duplicate basic information on the forms needed for various functions. Part of the information on the stencil may then be blocked off when it is not

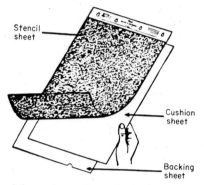

Stencil sheet

Cushion sheet

Backing sheet

Before a mimeograph stencil is put in a typewriter, a cushion sheet is inserted between the stencil sheet and the backing sheet.

A stencil being cut in a typewriter.

To Make Corrections on Stencils

waa

wa▉

1. Cover error with a thin coat of correction fluid using a vertical stroke through each letter.

2. Wait 30 or more seconds for correction fluid to dry.

was

3. Retype - using normal or slightly lighter touch.

Three steps in correcting a typographical error on a mimeograph stencil. At right, a mimeograph stencil being wrapped around the inked cylinder.

Cross-section of typed stencil sheet.

A mimeograph duplicator.

A typical lettering guide for use on a mimeograph stencil with a stylus.

STYLI

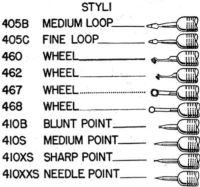

405B	MEDIUM LOOP	
405C	FINE LOOP	
460	WHEEL	
462	WHEEL	
467	WHEEL	
468	WHEEL	
410B	BLUNT POINT	
410S	MEDIUM POINT	
410XS	SHARP POINT	
410XXS	NEEDLE POINT	

Special styli are used to write, letter, rule, or draw on stencils.

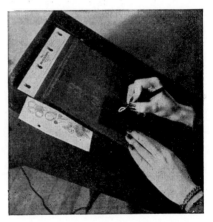

To shade part of a drawing a "screen-plate" having a raised pattern of dots or lines is put under the stencil. Rubbing transfers the pattern.

Shown two-thirds actual size

Sample alphabets available on the A. B. Dick Co.'s mimeograph lettering guides.

Tracing, lettering, and drawing on a stencil can be done more easily over an illuminated drawing board (right) called a Mimeoscope.

needed for some of the forms. These stencils are prepared to order.

Also available are dual stencil sheets —two stencil sheets attached to one backing. Two stencils are typed at once, thus eliminating the retyping of material that is needed for duplication at two points.

Used stencils may be filed in special file folders and rerun later.

Practically all lettershops handle mimeograph work. They usually charge from $1.50 per stencil cut and from 30 cents per 100 for running copies.

Mimeograph machines range in price from under $100 to over $1,000, with postcard-size printers available as low as $10. A. B. Dick machines are of top quality and are priced accordingly, as are the Gestetner machines, imported from England. For prices, write A. B. Dick, 5700 W. Touhy Ave., Chicago 60648; and Gestetner Duplicator Corp., 50 McLean Ave., Yonkers 5, N.Y. Some of the lower-priced machines can be seen in stationery stores or in the Sears, Roebuck and Montgomery Ward catalogs.

Mimeoscope   See MIMEOGRAPH.

mitered   See illustrations below.

Mitten's Letters   A line of three-dimensional, white, molded display letters which can be pinned or glued to any background or mounted in tracks to make signs and displays. They come in many styles and in sizes from ¾ to 9 in. in height.

Mitten's Letters are sold at per-letter prices or in prepackaged fonts. Single-letter prices range from 12 cents for ⅜-in. to $2.44 for 9-in., and fonts from $13.10 for 182 ⅜-in. letters to $210.82 for 108 9-in. letters.

moiré   When one screen pattern (see SHADING TINTS) is laid over another, the result is a *moiré* (pronounced "mwa-ray") effect. This may happen when a halftone cut is made from a picture that has been printed by the halftone process and thus already contains a screen pattern. The resulting *moiré* effect can be highly objectionable.

If a screened clipping is all that is available, it can be reproduced with very little *moiré* effect if the engraver will experiment to find the right matching screen and will try turning this screen at various angles to the screen in the clipping until the angle of minimum *moiré* is found. (See illustration.)

Monophoto   See MONOTYPE.

Panel made with mitered corners.

Panel made with butted corners.

The fabric-like texture in this photograph is a so-called "*moiré* effect," resulting from the fact that this halftone was made from a clipping that had already been screened once.

Monotype One of the two basic machines for composing type. Like the Linotype (see LINOTYPE), it can set type for books, magazines, pamphlets, advertisements, etc., much faster than the work can be done by hand. Like the Linotype, it produces, for each job, fresh new type, never before used. The used type is melted down and does not have to be distributed into typecases.

Unlike the Linotype, the Monotype produces single type characters, not solid lines of type. Corrections can thus be made by hand, without the need of setting a whole new line.

Monotype composition tends to be a little more expensive than Linotype on simple material; perhaps a little less expensive on more complicated work, tabular work, etc. The Monotype can handle roman, italic, and bold as easily

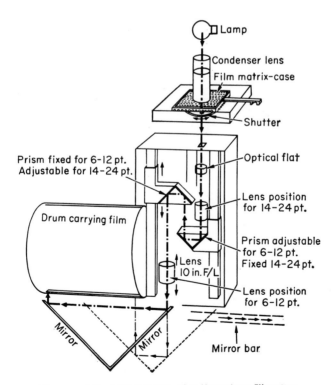

Diagram of the optical system of a Monophoto Filmsetter.

as the Linotype handles only two of them; and it can mix entirely unrelated fonts of type more readily. Furthermore, it can easily set lines up to 60 picas long, while most Linotypes have to cast lines over 30 picas in two slugs.

The type faces available on the Monotype are substantially the same as those available on the Linotype, with only subtle differences. (See Appendix 1, Type Faces.) Printers who have Monotype equipment are less likely to have Linotype, Intertype, or Ludlow equipment; and vice versa.

The Monotype consists of two parts: a keyboard and a composing or casting machine. A manuscript is first "keyboarded" as if the operator of the keyboard were making a typewritten copy. However, instead of a typed copy, the keyboard produces a perforated paper tape. This tape is then put on the composing (casting) machine, which automatically casts each letter singly and pushes the completed lines into a waiting galley.

A device on the keyboard machine tells the operator when each line is nearly full and how much it lacks of being full. He then pushes two special keys, which in effect says to the composing machine, "This line is so many ems too short. Please cast each of the spaces between words just enough wider than the minimum to take up the extra space." The composing machine is able to obey this instruction because it casts all the lines *backward* and thus gets the instructions about spacing before working its way through the line, beginning with the last letter of the last word.

It is possible to use harder type metal in Monotype casters than in Linotype or Intertype machines. If a harder metal is actually used (some shops use one standardized metal in all machines), Monotype composition will wear longer. In England it is quite common to print the original edition (or even several editions) of a book from the type and then to make electrotypes from the type if

still larger editions must be run. This is rarely done in the case of slug-cast composition, since even relatively small runs wear the softer metal so much that the making of duplicate plates from this worn type is undesirable.

The original Monotype system was built around a wide, 31-level, punched tape. Equipment is now available to permit punching narrow (6-, 7-, or 8-level) tape on Monotype keyboards, to utilize such narrow tape in actuating the Monotype caster, and to convert from one kind of tape to the other, so that Monotype equipment is compatible with the various techniques described under COMPUTER TYPESETTING.

The Monophoto is an adaptation of the Monotype caster which produces justified lines of type on film or photographic paper instead of in cast metal.

montage When several pictures or portions of pictures are combined into one to tell a story that they might not tell singly, the result is a montage.

A good montage gets its basic message across at first glance even when its elements, taken individually, repay longer inspection. It is more than just a trick way of grouping separate pictures on a page.

A montage is first sketched, often with the aid of a camera lucida. (See CAMERA LUCIDA.) Then if the negatives of each element are available, they may be properly masked and projected, one by one, in an enlarger onto the same piece of photographic paper. Some retouching with an airbrush is usually necessary. Alternately, each photo can be "blown" to size, cut out, and assembled with the others like a jigsaw puzzle.

Montage making demands considerable skill and know-how. For best results, enlargements should be made to the desired size *from the original negatives,* and these prints should be butt-joined in mounting, not lapped. Lapped edges will create shadow lines that can-

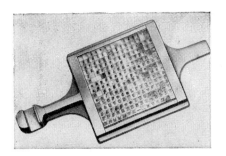

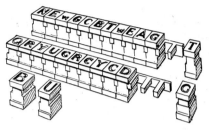

255 Monotype matrices like those above can be held in the matrix case shown at upper left—enough for roman, italic, and bold. From these matrices, the Monotype automatically casts lines of single pieces of type like those below.

The Monotype keyboard, below at left, is used like a typewriter, but it produces the perforated ribbon shown at the left. This paper ribbon, which resembles the rolls used in player pianos, guides the automatic composing machine (caster), shown below at right. It says to the caster, in effect, "Move the matrix case to the seventh row across, the fourth row down, and cast a piece of type from the letter that you find there." (*Photos courtesy of the Monotype Corp.*)

not be retouched away short of making a new copy negative or a new print, and then retouching that. Lapped edges are all right if they can follow a natural line in the picture.

Something is lost every time a photograph is copied. A great deal can be lost if the procedure is from original print to copy negative, to print, to lap-joined montage, to copy negative, to final print.

Morisawa Photo Typesetter A machine for producing display-type composition on film or photographic paper at speeds of about 30 characters per minute. It is possible to place lettering anywhere within an 8½ by 11-in. area, with a visual record of the location of lines previously composed, so that simple advertisements can be composed in their entirety without the need for subsequent paste-up. From a single font slide costing $45, it is possible to set type in almost any size (up to 60-pt) and also to letterspace it, expand it, condense it, incline it, and backslant it. Word spacing and letter fitting are automatic; lines can be readily set flush left and in tabular formation and (with practice) can be centered or set flush right. The Morisawa is made by the Minolta Camera Company of Japan and is distributed within the United States by the Fairchild Graphic Equipment Division of the Fairchild Camera and Instrument Corporation, 221 Fairchild Ave., Plainview, N.Y. 11803. It sells for $2,550.

mortise A printing plate or cut is said to have been mortised when a hole or

The Morisawa Photo Typesetter.

notch has been made in it to accommodate type. Wherever possible, it is better to paste the lettering or a proof of the type on the original artwork and thus make it a part of the plate or cut, since type inserted in a mortise sometimes falls out on the press.

Letters are sometimes mortised for better fit in headlines. (See illustrations below and on page 337.)

A mortised cut. This is a notched mortise, open on one side. Type can be held in place more securely in such a mortise than in an inside mortise.

motion pictures   See also FILMSTRIP.

Motion pictures and filmstrips offer a medium of communication that has tremendous and proved effectiveness. They deserve to be considered along with radio, television, and the printed word in all campaign planning.

A good, one-reel 16mm motion picture with sound usually costs $9,500 to $25,000, or more, but it may still be the cheapest device for claiming a few minutes of the undivided attention of 1 or 20 million people. No other medium is so effective in bringing people to a new viewpoint.

A good filmstrip, consisting of approximately 50 still photographs or charts, with a 15-min sound recording (see RECORDINGS) will cost from $1,500 up, but may be the most effective way of presenting and explaining certain factual information to selected audiences.

Motion-picture film comes in three widths:

8mm—for amateur use and, in recent years, increasing use in education and business communications of all kinds

16mm—for all nontheatrical uses

35mm—for theater use

All 8mm and 16mm films use a safety (cellulose acetate) noninflammable base and may be shown with portable projectors. In recent years 35 mm film has also become available for general use in cellulose acetate or safety film. However, prints around from the previous period (circa 1950) have an inflammable, cellulose nitrate base. For this reason, *all* 35mm film must by law be projected only from specially constructed fireproof booths.

Therefore, the 16mm size is generally used for films to be shown in schools, offices, meeting halls, etc. However, films are frequently shot in 35 mm and then printed (by reduction) in 16mm.

Although films may be either silent or with sound, few silent films are produced. Most projectors in frequent use are sound projectors.

Sound film production costs 33 to 100 percent more than silent, but the prints cost no more; silent pictures must be about one-third longer to allow for the titles.

Color films can be handled exactly as if they were black-and-white films. It is often not much more expensive to shoot a film in color than to shoot it in black and white, since the cost of the film is not the major part of the expense. However, making color prints is about three times as expensive as making black-and-white prints, perhaps $30 per reel for color as against $10 for black and white.

There is no getting away from the

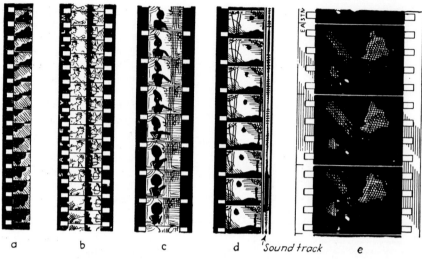

a   b   c   d   *Sound track*   e

Types of motion-picture film (actual size): (a) 8mm silent film, (b) 8mm films before slitting, (c) 16mm silent film, (d) 16mm sound film (showing sound track). (e) 35mm silent film, or filmstrip.

fact that good movies cost a lot of money, usually from $1,000 per minute of running time for simple subject matter up to $5,000 or more per minute for animation in color.

However, audiences naturally judge movies by Hollywood standards and may react adversely to any that are too obviously amateurish. Somehow, those produced at less than $750 a minute generally look amateurish as do some costing much more, of course.

Some of the factors involved are as follows:

1. A movie of a man talking is usually deadly dull, even if care has been taken to change the angle of the camera frequently.

2. Live sound or "lip synch," as it is called, is more costly than the kind of unsynchronized narration that is added afterward and merely comments on the action.

3. Professional actors and narrators are usually cheaper in the long run than amateurs, because fewer retakes are necessary.

4. Although the building of special studio sets is expensive, it may be no more so than shooting on location, since the latter poses special problems of lighting and acoustics, not to mention travel and weather.

Motion pictures can in part be pieced together out of existing footage ("stock shots") obtained at $1.50 to $3.50 per foot from a stock-shot film library. Three well-known stock-shot libraries are: Sherman Grinberg Library, 630 9th Ave., New York; Stock Shots, 333 W. 52 St., New York; and Fotosonic, Inc., 15 W. 46 St., New York. Other sources of stock footage (usually old newsreel footage) are 20th Century Fox-Movietone News, NBC, David Wolper Productions, and others. A number of government agencies also make stock footage available at cost, notably the U.S. Department of Agriculture.

The best material is held by Hollywood and the newsreel companies, which sometimes are, and sometimes are not, willing to release it. Furthermore, available material is sometimes of low photographic quality, being made from second or third duplicate negatives.

It is difficult to use silent footage

in modern pictures, since today's films run at 24 frames per second, whereas the old silent films ran at 16 frames per second.

Music costs include not only a copyright fee (or composer's fee), plus sound crew and studio, but also a narrator's fee and union rates for musicians. Music can also be purchased from a stock music library for a nominal fee.

For all these reasons it is impossible for a motion-picture producer to give a reliable estimate of cost in advance of completing a script. Negotiations for making a film usually are about as follows:

Producer and sponsor discuss the ground to be covered and the budget. Perhaps they screen a few films and agree that "a one-reeler like that one, which cost $15,000" is the sort of thing wanted. The producer then submits a "treatment" or general outline. If this is approved and if the sponsor authorizes the producer to have his scriptwriter go ahead on a final "shooting script," it is usually understood *that the sponsor is obliged to pay for the shooting script, even if he decides not to use it.* Often the sponsor is asked to pay for the treatment since much research and work can go into an apparently simple treatment.

The scriptwriter then hammers out a script. Usually this takes at least a month, perhaps considerably longer.

With a detailed and approved script in hand, the producer can now give a fairly accurate estimate of the cost of making the film, though he may suggest making the picture on the basis of charging audited cost plus overhead, rather than a flat fee.

Payment for the script and perhaps for a part of production cost is now due. Another payment will be due when the shooting has been completed, with a third and final payment due on delivery of the final print or prints.

The buyer of a motion picture cannot see before he buys. He must buy on the basis of the seller's reputation and previous record for doing quality work, economically, on time, and at fair rates. A producer's references should be checked with care.

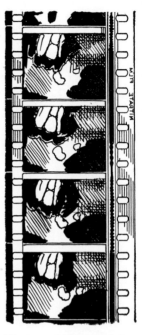

35mm sound film, actual size.

Reputable producers of commercial and/or educational films include: A.C.I. Productions, 16 W. 46 St., New York; Affiliated Film Production, 164 E. 38 St., New York; Audio Productions, Inc., 630 Ninth Ave., New York; Dynamic Films, 405 Park Ave., New York; Elektra Film Productions, 33 W. 46 St., New York; Elliot, Unger & Elliot, 711 Fifth Ave., New York; MPO, 222 E. 44 St., New York; Fred A. Niles Communication Centers, Inc., 108 West End Ave., New York; Pelican Films, Inc., 292 Madison Ave., New York; Henry Strauss Productions, Inc., 31 W. 52 Street, New York; Sturgis-Grant, Inc., 328 44 St., New York; Telemated, 8 W. 40 St., New York; U.S. Productions, Inc., 5 E. 57 St., New York; Vision Associates, 680 5th Ave., New York; Wilding, Inc., 405 Park Ave., New

York; John Campbell, P.O. Box 3443, Greenwich, Conn.; Reid H. Ray Film Industries, 1750 Pennsylvania Ave., Washington, D.C.; Agra Films, Inc., Jefferson Rd., Atlanta, Georgia; The Jam Handy Organization, 230 N. Michigan Blvd., Chicago; Centron Corp., W. 9th at Avalon, Lawrence, Kansas; Milner-Fenwick, 3800 Liberty Heights, Baltimore; Calvin Productions, 1105 Truman Rd., Kansas City, Mo.; Charles Guggenheim, 14 N. Newstead St., St. Louis, Mo.; On Film, Inc., Princeton, N.J.; Calvin-De Frenes, 1909 Buttonwood St., Philadelphia; Walter G. O'Connor, 100 N. Cameron St., Harrisburg, Pa.; Crawley Films, Ltd., 1 Place Ville Marie, Montreal, Canada.

The distribution of film prints can be handled in several ways.

There are over 2,000 commercial and educational film libraries in the United States which lend or rent 16mm films to owners of projectors in their area. There are estimated to be over 840,000 projectors in active use. A list of some of the commercial film libraries is obtainable from the National Audio-Visual Association, Fairfax, Virginia. Another list of film libraries is available from the Superintendent of Documents, U.S. Government Printing Office, Washington, D.C.

These film libraries, which include state universities, big city school systems, etc., buy some films at $25, $35, or $50 a reel and rent for about $4 per black-and-white reel per showing (projector and operator supplied at extra cost if requested). They also accept gifts of government and other nonprofit films of general interest and circulate them and may undertake for a fee to circulate commercial films of sound audience appeal.

A good film free of commercial or one-sided propaganda may, with proper promotion, have as many as 1,000 prints in free-loan distribution. There are specialists who distribute sponsored business and public relations films. The leading free-loan distributors of sponsored films include: Associated Films, 347 Madison Ave., New York; Modern Talking Picture Service, Inc., 3 E. 54 St., New York; Sterling Movies, U.S.A., Inc., 375 Park Ave., New York; Ideal Pictures, Inc., 58 S. Water St., Chicago 1, Illinois.

If distribution of this sort is contemplated, it is well to consult the intended distributor before the film is made, both to ensure that he will be willing to take it, and to get his help on giving audience appeal to the film.

Of course, television is the major user of nontheatrical films today (see TELEVISION) and, for sustaining programs, many stations depend heavily on free or cheap films that aren't too heavy on the sponsor plugs. This opens up a large field for the sponsored film.

Schools and community organizations represent approximately 90 percent of the free-film utilization today. Free films used by television reach the largest audience—an estimated 35,000 persons per telecast as compared to 100 persons per booking in school and community groups.

An interesting study of the sponsored business film was completed in 1965 by the Association of National Advertisers, 155 E. 44 St., New York 17. It covered 209 business film case examples.

Nearly one-third of these films were shown on television with a median TV audience of 1,500,000 per year of film life. (Of these audiences four-fifths were predominantly children and young people.) The median non-TV audience was 47,256 per year of film life. (About two-thirds of these were predominantly adult.) Production costs per minute of viewing time ranged from $342 to $1,360. The average distribution cost per booking was $2.50 to $3.00 for a non-TV audience.

motor freight   See FREIGHT.

mounting and finishing   See also DISPLAYS; DIE CUTTING.

Mounting is a fairly simple operation

in which the mounting cardboard may be the major item in the total cost. Special mounting machines apply glue to the paper poster or the cardboard backing and then squeeze both together in a sort of wringer. Sometimes a piece of blank paper identical to that used for the poster is glued to the underside of the backing to equalize the strains that might otherwise cause curling.

Firms specializing in mounting and finishing are generally equipped to do not only mounting, but also one or more of the following "finishing" operations: die cutting, creasing (scoring), varnishing, laminating, easeling, labeling, hinging, stringing, round-cornering, tin-edging, eyeleting, gumming, pebbling, paraffining. (See DIE CUTTING; SCORING; VARNISHING; EASELING; EYELETING; PEBBLING.)

There is no clean-cut distinction between "binders" and "mounters and finishers." Some binders do only book and pamphlet work; others cover also the more specialized operations.

Some printers have all the operations under one roof: printing, binding, finishing, and imprinting. Most, however, let out their binding, mounting, finishing, and imprinting (see IMPRINTING) to firms specializing in these operations. Small buyers are well advised to place the responsibility for all operations on the printer; large buyers may save by dealing directly with the firms that actually handle the separate operations.

For mounting and finishing firms, see the Classified Telephone Directory.

movies See MOTION PICTURES.

MS, Ms, ms Abbreviations for manuscript. In the plural, it is MSS, Mss, or mss.

Multigraph See also DUPLICATING.
The Addressograph-Multigraph Corp. makes two basically different kinds of duplicators, the one that operates on the offset principle and is called a "Multilith," and the older one which prints

A piece of Multigraph type, much enlarged. (Courtesy of Addressograph-Multigraph Corp.)

from raised surfaces on the letterpress (relief) principle, as described below.

In appearance, a Multigraph machine resembles a mimeograph machine. The printing is done from a large drum, which, however, is of very different construction. It is equipped with slots running the long way of the drum, into which special metal type can be inserted. Many styles and faces of type can be used, also curved electrotypes, rubber plates, zinc etchings, stereotypes, etc. In fact, any medium with a raised surface that is used to make an impression on paper can be prepared for use on a Multigraph.

When the type on a Multigraph drum is covered with a wide inked ribbon and printed through this, form letters and other materials can be produced which closely resemble actual typing.

When the Multigraph duplicator is equipped with a printing-ink attachment, the type is inked from rubber rollers; the machine then becomes simply a small, office-size printing machine and will print menus, postcards, tickets, forms, letterheads, price lists, etc. It is frequently used to imprint dealers' names and addresses on advertising pieces.

Composition on the Multigraph takes a little more time than by other dupli-

A Multigraph flexible drum, showing how type and cuts are fastened into its slots. Nonflexible drums are also used, and work the same way, except that the whole drum is changed, not just the surface layer.

A hand-driven Multigraph machine, showing how inked ribbon is fastened over drum.

cating processes. Running is a little more expensive, since ribbons cost more than duplicating ink; however, the ribbon can be reinked and used a number of times. Multigraph work tends to be a little neater than average mimeographing or spirit duplicating and does not require an absorbent type of paper; rather, any type of paper or card stock can be used and the finished result has the special qualification of more closely resembling actual typing.

The Multigraph principle is especially valuable on duplicating jobs that require frequent partial changes of information, such as price lists and menus.

Work can be done in colors other than black by changing to another ribbon, or by changing the color of ink in the ink fountain.

Movable type is made for use in the Multigraph in practically all sizes and styles. The channels of the Multigraph will also accommodate processed Linotype, Intertype, and Monotype composition, ruling lines, etc.

With extra attachments, the Multigraph can strike in a blue signature at the foot of a letter, and do numbering, slitting, and perforating.

Sixteen cents a line is a common base charge made by lettershops for doing Multigraph work, with running charges of $3.50 to $5 per thousand impressions.

A hand-fed, hand-operated Multigraph is available at about $350, with $100 or more added for type. An automatic Multigraph is available at about $2,000, type extra.

Multigraph duplicators are manufactured by Addressograph-Multigraph Corporation, Cleveland 17, Ohio. See also FAIRCHILD-DAVIDSON OFFSET MACHINES.

See also the chart "How to Choose the Right Printing Process" inside the covers of this book.

Multilith See OFFSET DUPLICATORS.

music printing Music can be reproduced photographically from a hand-written manuscript; it can be set up with a special music type; it can be engraved; or the master copy can be printed from a music typewriter. (See also ARTYPE.)

Engraving is the most satisfactory. Notes and symbols are punched, one at a time, into a soft metal plate, using special punches. Lettering is added in the same way. The plate is inked, the surface ink is wiped away, and a proof is taken by the intaglio process (see INTAGLIO) from the ink remaining in the depressed areas. The proof can then be reproduced in offset or any other process.

This engraving (intaglio) process gives a much cleaner result than hand notation and gives much more flexibility than music type. However, it requires special skill and is relatively expensive. For this reason many music publishers are turning to other processes listed above or to foreign engravers. Music engravers in this country include G. Schirmer, Inc., 48-02 48 Ave., Woodside 77, New York; Rayner Dalheim and Co., 2801 W. 47 St., Chicago 32, Illinois; Louis J. Pennino, 4300 Bergenline Ave., Union City, New Jersey 07087.

Music typewriter production is becoming more widely used because it is relatively inexpensive. It cannot be used readily with all kinds of layout, but certain types of format are easily adapted to this process. One firm offering music typewriter production is Music Art, 147 W. 46 St., New York, New York.

In ordering music engraved, autographed, or set in type, it is advisable to have the composition or lettering of the song words, if any, done at the same time by the same firm, even though it may seem that this could be done by the printer who is to do the final printing. The reason is that it may prove impossible to make the words fit unless the music compositor is responsible for seeing that they do.

N | n

negative The negative of a picture is a photographically transformed copy in which the white areas are shown in black, the black areas are shown in white, the light grays have become dark grays, the dark grays have become light grays, etc. (See illustration on next page.)

Photographic negatives are generally made on transparent film. Photostat negatives are made on paper and are not transparent. (See PHOTOGRAPHY; PHOTOSTAT.)

An ordinary paper negative reverses the image two ways: it turns black into white, and vice versa, and turns the image left for right, just as a mirror reverses things left for right and makes lettering read backward.

A photostat negative, "positive negative," or "readable negative" reverses the image just one way: black for white. Lettering remains readable.

A film negative, being transparent, can be looked at from either the "positive-negative" side, or the "negative-negative" (emulsion) side.

The word "negative" is generally applied to something that exists only in order that a positive may be made from it. A negative that is meant to remain

206

that way is called a "reverse." Any line drawing can be converted by the engraver into a reverse plate. (See REVERSE PLATE.)

Photographs or drawings which, from the layout point of view, face the wrong way, can be flopped (see FLOP) and made to face the other way. However, any lettering contained in them will then read backward, cars will run to the left, military decorations will appear on the wearer's wrong side, etc.

newspapers See also COPYWRITING; PERIODICALS; PUBLICITY RELEASE; ADVERTISING.

Newspaper work differs in many ways from other printing. Almost every newspaper owns its own printing plant and has it under the same roof as the editorial offices; relatively few other print users do so. The need for speed requires standardization of typography and continuity in editorial style.

In other lines, an editorial worker can get by without knowing anything of the mechanics of printing. On a newspaper, efficiency demands that every staff member know at least the elements of the paper's mechanical requirements. This fact sometimes leads newspaper

Photographic negative.

Positive print.

"Positive" original.

"Flopped" positive.

Photostat negative, reverse, "positive negative," or "readable negative."

Ordinary or "negative negative."

Photographic positive. (*Photo by Louise Rosskam.*)

Flopped photographic positive.

A curved stereotype plate. (*Courtesy of The New York Times.*)

people to think they know all about printing, when in reality they know only one very specialized corner of letterpress printing.

Large newspapers are almost always printed by the letterpress process on rotary web presses. (See LETTERPRESS.) Type is set on the Linotype or Intertype, assembled with any illustrations or advertising plates, and then duplicated by the stereotype process. (See STEREOTYPE.) Curved stereotypes, not flat ones, are made to fit the cylinders of the rotary presses. The paper is fed from a roll into the rotary presses, which print it and then fold and cut it into finished newspaper sections.

Smaller newspapers may be composed by Linotype and printed on flat-bed presses, but they are also increasingly composed by cold-type methods and printed by offset. (See COLD TYPE.)

For sources of information on the editorial end of newspaper work and the mechanics of newspaper printing, see Appendix 2, Bibliography.

There are two ways for outsiders to use newspapers as channels of communication: (1) through free publicity and (2) through paid advertisements.

Newspapers are glad to run any legitimate news item free of charge and welcome publicity releases written with the reader's interest in mind, not just with the publicity man's ulterior motive in mind. (See PUBLICITY RELEASE.)

In preparing advertisements for newspaper publication, the following points are worth keeping in mind. (See also ADVERTISING.)

Newspaper space is sold at so much per *agate line*. Since there are 14 agate lines to the inch, a 2-in. ad, two columns wide, will occupy 56 agate lines.

Agate-line rates vary in the same newspaper between national advertisers and local advertisers, between amusements and food, etc. Certain preferred positions cost extra. Many advertisers buy two-thirds of a page, or a full page lacking one column, in preference to a full page, feeling that they get the same attention at a lower cost, plus the advantage of being next to reading matter.

Newspaper ad rates include the setting of the type, but many advertisers have their material made up by independent typographers and supplied to the newspapers as complete plates because they find it easier to get exactly what they want in this way. Many newspapers subscribe to a mat service in order to be able to provide their advertisers with pictures of merchandise, spot drawings, etc. (See MAT SERVICES.)

Halftones finer than 65 screen cannot be used in most newspapers, nor can plates containing extra-fine shading. Solid black areas, including giant type, must be broken up by the use of a shading tint. (See SHADING TINTS.)

Borders are used in newspaper ads more often than elsewhere since the problem of keeping an ad distinct from its neighbors is more acute.

Some good sources for information on the preparation of advertisements for newspaper publication are listed in Appendix 2, Bibliography.

newsprint See GROUNDWOOD PULP; PAPER.

news release See PUBLICITY RELEASE.

nickel-faced plates Both electrotypes and stereotypes can be faced with nickel for extra wear. (See ELECTRO; STEREOTYPE.) In the case of stereos, the nickel is deposited on the plate only after the plate is made. There is thus a slight loss of detail. Nickel (or chromium) facing costs extra. So-called "steel-faced" plates are really faced with nickel.

nixie A piece of mail which cannot be delivered because of incorrect or obsolete address.

novelty printing See also BADGES; BALLOONS; BLOTTERS; CALENDARS; MATCHES.

Many printed messages can be distributed advantageously in novelty form on pencils, balloons, blotters, calendars, badges, matches, pennants, caps, buttons, fans, mirrors, tape, beer coasters, cigarettes, etc.

Printing can be done in invisible ink, in perfumed ink (any scent), in ink that is later given a "velvet" or "frosted" finish (see FLOCK PRINTING), and on any surface, including sandpaper, cellophane, metal, foil, cloth, wax, and luminous paper. Anyone can do his own printing on almost anything through the use of decalcomanias. (See DECALCOMANIAS.)

In general, the firm selling the novelty will know about printing messages on it. When a sample of interest is encountered, the manufacturer can often be located through the firm that issued the sample.

Many sources for printed novelties can be found in the Classified Telephone Directory. For example, the Manhattan "Yellow Pages" have listings under: Badges, Bags, Calendars, Pencils, Thermometers, Playing Cards, Pens, Balloons, Matches, Tape, Rulers, Flags and Banners. Most of these and many additional imprinted items such as aprons, fans, ball pens, calendars, diaries, caps, scorepads, pot holders, yardsticks, key cases, bumper signs, phone indexes, mending kits, neckties, coin holders, cocktail stirrers, letter openers, pocket protectors, shoehorns, shopping bags, noisemakers, place mats, etc., are offered by one or another of the firms listed under Advertising Specialties, such as the Economy Novelty and Printing Company, 244 W. 39 St., New York; and Alert Advertising Specialties, 861 Manheim Ave., Brooklyn, N.Y.

numbering Numbering of tickets, membership cards, books, etc., can be done in letterpress during the regular pressrun at virtually no additional expense. Special numbering devices are available which can be locked up with the rest of the form. The pressure of the paper against the device causes the number to advance after each impression.

In offset and other processes, numbering requires an extra attachment or extra operation. (See also TICKETS.)

O | o

oblique *This sentence is set in Futura Oblique.* In the sans-serif type faces the term "oblique" is often preferred to "italic" in describing inclined letters, since true "italic" type has serifs.

office copying See PHOTOCOPYING.

offset Photo-offset lithography is commonly called "offset" or "photo-offset." It is the important commercial application of lithography (a "planographic" process). (See also LITHOGRAPHY; PLANOGRAPHY; LETTERSET.)

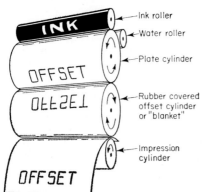

Diagram of an offset **plate.**

210

The Multilith is a small-size offset printing press.

Firms that advertise planographing and emphasize "no plates required" do the work on an offset press. Of course, when they say "no plates," they mean "no cuts." Offset lithographers make their own special kind of plates.

Offset tends to be cheaper than any other process:

1. Whenever many line drawings are to be reproduced.

2. Whenever type need not be set, as when it is done on the typewriter or when, in a reprint, an earlier edition can be photographically copied.

3. Whenever large illustrations (larger than book or magazine size) are to be used. (See SILK SCREEN and PHOTOGELATIN, which also compete here on the small runs.)

4. On process-color work or fake-process work. (Photogelatin may be cheaper on small quantities.)

Offset has the following advantages over letterpress:

1. It can use either coated or uncoated paper, but the paper must be "sized for offset." It does not require glossy paper for halftones.

2. It is cheaper when many illustrations are involved.

Offset has these disadvantages:

1. Its reproduction of photographs is sometimes inferior in quality to letterpress, gravure, or photogelatin.

2. The cheaper grades of offset work often have a gray look that is worse than the worst letterpress.

Offset is not really a plateless process. On the contrary, the whole job is put on a plate—type, illustrations, and all. But since the plate has to be made anyway, it costs no more to put line drawings on it than to put type on it, provided the line drawings are in the same scale as the type copy and mounted with it. It does cost about 10 cents per square inch extra (with a $3 minimum) to put each halftone on it; more if the highest quality of halftone reproduction is demanded.

To make an offset plate, the printer sets up his "copy" in front of a big camera and photographs it on film. He reduces or enlarges it so that the *film* image will be of the exact size the final result is to be. He may photograph the type "repro" proof (see REPRODUCTION PROOFS) "same size," and an illustration in reduced size. If so, he must then take these two separate negatives and "strip" them together in the proper position. (See STRIP.) He will make an additional charge for each strip-in to cover the cost of the extra negative and the stripping time.

The film can now be retouched to remove paste marks and other imperfections, although smudgy type can never be fixed by retouching.

The film is then placed over a sensitized plate, and both are exposed to strong light. The image is transferred to the plate by photochemical action. The end result is a plate that is receptive to greasy ink wherever it is supposed to print, and receptive only to water where it is not supposed to print.

The word "offset" comes from the fact that the inked surface does not print directly on the paper—instead it prints on a rubber-covered cylinder, and from the rubber the image is offset onto the paper.

The rubber blanket presses the ink firmly onto the paper; hence it is possible to print halftones on rough-surfaced papers.

Offset can be of very high or very low quality. Quality work demands not only good equipment but (even more important) highly skilled personnel. Routine office duplicating, on the other hand, can be done on small offset duplicators priced in the $1,000 to $2,000 range, with comparatively unskilled personnel. Offset is a process, however, where even minimum standards of quality require that the operator take enough pride in his work to find out what to do when printing is more gray than black, when a plate rated for 1,000 impressions starts to fail after 100, when white specks appear in the blacks or black specks in the white areas, when a job is too dark at one end and too light at the other, etc. He should know (or else he will learn the hard way) that it is not practical to attempt photographs or solid reverse panels on an offset duplicator that has an ink-distribution system barely adequate for straight type jobs.

For many years, offset plates were chiefly of two kinds: those prepared right in the typewriter like mimeograph stencils and those prepared by pasting up artwork, making a photographic negative, and printing down the negative on a plate. In office duplicating work, the first kind of plate might be made in the office, but when type or illustrations were to be reproduced, the job was sent outside to have the plate made, often for about $2 or $3 for the common 8½ by 14 size. In large lithographic plants, the photographic process was, of course, employed almost exclusively.

Then a series of rapid improvements and simplifications were made, affecting almost every aspect of offset platemaking. It is now possible to make very inexpensive offset duplicating masters on any of a number of office photocopying machines, so that an offset duplicator teamed with an appropriate photocopier can handle runs of almost any length. For example, runs up to 10 might be handled on the photocopier, runs from 11 up on the offset duplicator. Because of the need to wash up the rubber blanket between jobs, standard offset duplicators are not often used for runs as low as 11 copies. If such runs are frequent, a duplicator can be obtained which runs the required number, kicks out the old master, washes up its own rubber blanket, and opens its mouth ready to receive the next master. An office-duplicator offset master can be made on some photocopiers at a cost

as low as 5 cents, though a cost of 15 to 25 cents would be more common. It is also possible to prepare an offset-duplicator master *from* an office-duplicator master, simply by printing.

It should be noted that although many photocopiers can make offset masters, not all of them can enlarge or reduce, and they are not all of equal quality. For example, unless the Xerox 914 is reserved solely for high-volume production of offset masters, the work done on it may be of rather marginal quality, and it will not handle halftones at all.

Where the volume of work justifies it, there are machines especially adapted for the volume production of low-cost masters for offset duplicators. One is the Xerox platemaker. Another is the Kodak Ektalith plate processor.

Itek plate master.

(See EKTALITH.) Two more fully automated platemakers (in the $6,000 to $10,000 class) are also available, one made by Itek and the other by Addressograph-Multigraph. Both will produce finished plates ready for immediate use at rates up to two a minute and at materials costs of about 25 cents for the 8½ by 13 size. The chief difference between the two is that the Itek has an open camera, able to photograph three-dimensional objects such as open books, while the A-M machine can accept only originals that can be fed through a slot.

Plates for office-size offset duplicators are usually made of paper, though metal may be used for quality work and extra-long runs. The paper plates vary in cost and durability; money can be saved by using short-run plates for short-run jobs.

Plates for the larger presses used in commercial offset lithography are usually of metal. On the shorter runs (in the lower tens of thousands), the so-called "albumin" or "presensitized" plates are used. For long runs, and especially color work, the more durable "deep-etched" or "bimetal" plates may be used.

The first steps in printing a job by offset may closely resemble comparable steps in letterpress. Metal type may be set in galleys and proofed and corrected and made up into pages and proofed again. Artwork may be photographed almost as if in preparation for the making of engravings. But here the resemblance ends. Once a perfect proof has been pulled from the type, the type can be discarded, since the offset printer needs nothing more than a proof.

If possible, type proofs and artwork—or possibly photostatic copies of artwork—are pasted up together. If necessary, space is left for photographs that require a different reduction and must therefore be photographed separately.

The offset printer then photographs everything that will be part of the finished job, always making each negative the exact size it is to print. He then combines all elements that are to go on one plate into a "flat"—a piece of orange or red opaque paper in which windows are cut to accept the several pieces of film negative. Finally he places this "flat" on a sensitized plate, squeezes them tightly together in a vacuum frame, and exposes them to arc lights. This is called "burning in" a plate. In effect, the arc lights harden the surface of the plate where the light is not held back by the black portions of the negatives or by the orange paper. The plate is then rolled up (inked) and washed up—really scrubbed—and the unhardened portions of the coating are removed, exposing the metal beneath. The metal is wettable and thus ink-repelling since the remaining emulsion still carries the grease-receptive ink. The plate is ready for press. A separate plate must be made for each color.

The procedures for making deep-etched and bimetal plates each differ somewhat from the steps described above, but both lead to essentially the same kind of ink-repelling or ink-receptive end product.

For a discussion of when to use offset and when to use letterpress, see LETTERPRESS. (See also LETTERSET.) For a discussion of costs, see ESTIMATING COSTS. (A comparison of all printing processes is given on the charts reproduced inside the covers of this book.)

For a discussion of some of the many methods of type composition that bypass the "hot-metal" stage and produce paper or film proofs directly, see PHOTOTYPESETTING.

offset duplicators See also OFFSET. Offset duplicators range in size from small office duplicators handling paper 3 by 5 in. up to 9¾ by 14 in.—to large machines using sheet sizes up to 20 by 24 in. One of the best known is the Multilith, manufactured by the Addressograph-Multigraph Corp. It will do anything that a mimeograph will do, and more besides. However, it costs a little more to begin with and is a little more demanding on its operator.

An offset duplicator will reproduce anything that can be written, lettered, typed, drawn, traced, stamped, ruled, or printed on the paper masters from which the machine duplicates. Masters can also be prepared by PHOTOGRAPHY and XEROX (q.v.), thus permitting reproduction of type, illustrations, photos (i.e., halftones), etc. (See also EKTALITH.)

However, large photographs or large solid areas of ink are to be avoided on the smallest unit, since the inking mechanism cannot handle a large flow of ink. Furthermore, it takes more skill than many operators possess to get top-notch reproduction of photographs on the Multilith in any size.

One of the special advantages of the Multilith process is its ability to duplicate simultaneously both the letter and the letterhead, both the variable information on a form and the form itself. Paper masters can be obtained on which basic forms or letterheads are already prepared in reproducing ink. Any new information can be added by any composing method and the whole then duplicated.

Color work can be handled by cleaning up the ink rollers (a simple operation with a blotter-type cleaner sheet) and by using new ink of a desired color.

Actually, there are two "versions" of the Multilith process; the original and so-called "conventional" process, and a simplified version in which both the ink and moistening solution are applied to the master from a single set of rollers.

The latter method makes daily clean-up unnecessary. Even after periods of inactivity, any type of Multilith master can be put on a Simflo Control duplicator and copies duplicated within a matter of seconds.

Multilith models are available from about $1,000 with automatic friction feed. All models are electrically driven. A heavy-duty model, capable of doing more work, is priced at just over $3,000, including automatic, electrically con-

Most widely used Multilith offset.

trolled suction feed and other extras. With extra attachments, this model can strike in a signature and do numbering, slitting, and perforating. A larger model, 18 by 15 in., is available at about $5,500.

Multilith offset duplicators are manufactured by the Addressograph-Multigraph Corporation, Cleveland 17, Ohio. (See also MULTIGRAPH.)

Other office machines operating on the offset principle are made by Fairchild-Davidson, a division of Fairchild Camera and Instrument Corp., 5001 E. Jericho Turnpike, Commack, N.Y. (see FAIRCHILD-DAVIDSON OFFSET MACHINES) and by the A. B. Dick Company, 5700 Touhy Ave., Chicago.

In determining whether to use an offset duplicator, consult the charts inside the covers of this book.

offset paper Any finish of paper can be printed by the offset lithography process, including antique, machine-finish, English-finish, super, and coated. However, because moisture is used in offset printing, it is necessary that the finish used does not give trouble, whether by picking, by refusing ink, or by unreasonable expansion or contraction on close-register jobs.

Paper merchants can supply paper that has been "sized for offset," or otherwise treated to give good results in offset, if asked for offset book paper, offset or litho-coated, litho-English-finish, etc.

Note that LETTERSET (q.v.), since it does not involve the use of water, does not require paper sized for offset.

one-shot In magazine-distributing parlance, a magazine of which there is only one issue; in other words, a book or pamphlet as opposed to a periodical. (See also DISTRIBUTION.)

onionskin A light, thin bond paper.

opacity Opacity in printing papers is expressed in percentages. A lightweight bond paper may have an opacity of 79 percent, meaning that 21 percent of the light that falls on it goes through. A 24-lb bond paper of high opacity (the cheaper sulfite bonds are of higher opacity than pure rag-content bonds) may have an opacity of 93 percent.

Opacity, important in lightweight printing paper, is sometimes achieved by the addition of such fillers as titanium dioxide.

Optype A machine for optical justification of text type. See COLD TYPE.

outdoor advertising See also SIGNS; POSTERS; TRANSIT ADVERTISING.

Billboards offer a means of putting a short message where people living and working in any selected area will see it repeatedly and where travelers will see it as they pass through. Outdoor advertising is widely used on a national basis for such products as food, soft drinks, automobiles, gasoline and oil, accessories, beer, movies, and cigarettes. It is used locally for political campaigns, hotels, restaurants, banks, food products, community drives, etc.

In the trade, outdoor displays are classified as posters, painted displays, and "electrical spectaculars." The standard billboard takes a so-called "24-sheet poster," on which the message area is 8 ft 8 in. high by 19 ft 6 in. long. Less common is the so-called "3-sheet poster," which is 8 ft 7 in. high by 4 ft 10 in. wide.

The best way to arrange for a local poster campaign is to get in touch with the outdoor advertising company whose name appears in small letters beneath local poster panels.

Most outdoor advertising space (apart from signs on an advertiser's own property) is controlled by firms that specialize in maintaining this space for use by national and local advertisers. Most such firms are members of the Outdoor Advertising Association of America and have accepted the standards of size, construction, public safety, and convenience worked out by that group.

The space cost of outdoor advertising depends largely on the number of people who pass that space. The better the location and the larger the community, the more valuable the space. In cities of over 50,000 population, space big enough for a 24-sheet poster costs about $50 a month. The national average cost is $42.71 a month. Poster advertising space, however, is sold in units called "showings." A showing consists of a sufficient number of panels to provide coverage of the entire market.

Outdoor advertising companies can handle the design and painting or printing of outdoor displays for local use, or they can advise regarding it. Outdoor Advertising Incorporated, the national sales representative for the industry, with head office at 360 Lexington Ave., New York, helps national advertisers and agencies in preparing campaign plans and in seeing that the advertising is most productive.

On quantities up to about 500, the silk-screen process of reproduction is most often used. (See SILK SCREEN.) Larger quantities are usually done by offset lithography. (See OFFSET.)

There are about 25 offset lithographers in the United States who specialize in 24-sheet posters, and many more printers (offset, silk screen, letterpress) who handle 3-sheet posters.

Artwork for posters is usually done by artists who specialize in such work, and their sketches vary in cost from $100 all the way to $1,000 each.

Typical prices for lithographed 24-sheet posters are given in the accompanying table. A so-called "24-sheet"

Prices of 24-sheet Lithographed Posters

Quantity	30 printings (price per poster)	50 printings (price per poster)
500	$6.44	$8.80
1,000	3.90	5.49
2,000	2.80	3.79
10,000	1.65	2.00

poster is actually printed as 10 sheets. To put an average of three colors on each of these 10 sheets requires a total of 30 printings. Usually there is no need to print every sheet in every color; some sheets require more printings than others. Prices are per complete poster.

Fluorescent (Day-Glo) ink is often used on outdoor posters because it is much brighter than ordinary ink colors and makes a poster glow in the daytime as though illuminated. Day-Glo ink is applied by silk-screen process. The cost is estimated as an additional printing for each color covered, plus 10 cents per poster for each square foot of Day-Glo coverage.

For excellent information on how to plan, design, and buy outdoor advertising, consult the books included in Appendix 2, Bibliography.

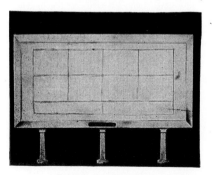 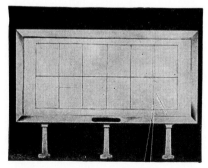

Typical "24-sheet" posters showing how sheets are actually positioned.

overlay Editors and artists use overlays of paper, tissue, acetate, etc., to protect artwork and photographs. Sometimes markings are placed on the overlays to show how the art is to be cropped, or

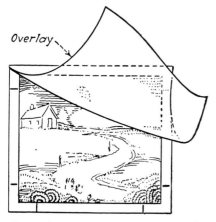

Photo with crop marks and protective **overlay.**

to show the break for color, i.e., which areas are to print in which colors. The art for different colors is often executed on or pasted onto separate plastic overlays. (See COLOR SEPARATION.)

Printers also use the terms "overlay" and "underlay" with reference to the thin sheets of tissue placed under the impression surface or under the type during the makeready process. In this way they control the amount of pressure with which the ink is pressed into the paper.

overmatter See OVERSET.

overprinting The overprinting of circulars and posters to show a local advertiser's name is called "imprinting." (See IMPRINTING.)

Firms that do imprinting are also well equipped to block out wrong prices, etc., and overprint them with the new information. It is difficult to block out printed characters so that they positively will not show through, but the use of metallic inks sometimes helps, as does the use of the silk-screen process.

overrun Printing-trade customs permit a printer to deliver a slight overrun or underrun and to modify his contractual price accordingly. (See PRINTING-TRADE CUSTOMS.) Thus, a printer who has contracted to print 10,000 copies of something for $100 may deliver 10,500 copies and charge a bit more, or 9,500 copies and charge a bit less. The same custom prevails when paper is made to order.

Overruns or underruns are unavoidable since it is impossible to predict in advance exactly how much to allow for spoilage during makeready, handling, and binding. A printer must always start with a little more paper than the finished job requires, to allow for spoilage.

overset Material that has been set in type ready for use and then not used is referred to as "overset matter" or "overmatter." When a magazine is finally closed for the press, there are generally some items that have been crowded out, and these may be kept as overset for possible use in the next issue. If they are never used, the printer will eventually bill for them as "killed matter."

Page proofs of circulars, ads, etc., may carry a paragraph or two of overset wordage in the lower margin if there was too much type for the allotted space. It is up to the editor to decide how to make room for the overset material, or to authorize "killing" it.

Ozalid See WHITEPRINT.

Ozalith Positive-working sensitized paper and aluminum offset plates, manufactured by Ozalid Repro Products of General Aniline and Film Corporation, Binghamton, N.Y. 13902. They can be made from any translucent original in the same way as a whiteprint (see WHITEPRINT) plus additional fixing, and permit the making of plates for small offset presses in less than two minutes.

P | p

package and parcel shipping See SHIPPING INFORMATION; UNITED PARCEL SERVICE.

packages See CONTAINER PRINTING; WRAPPING AND PACKING.

padding A very simple and inexpensive binding operation. To convert plain paper into pads of paper, the paper is trimmed to the desired size, padding cement is brushed across one edge, and cloth may be applied. If the pads are to be backed with cardboard, the board is interleaved with the paper at the desired intervals before trimming. It is customary to back at least 10 pads at once and cut them apart after drying.

Any printer or binder can do padding. It is not only a way of making printed forms easy to handle but a good way to convert wastepaper into useful scratch pads.

page One side of a sheet of paper. Page numbers, also called "folios," in a booklet or pamphlet always begin on the right. This means that the right-hand page always has an odd number, the left an even number.

A booklet or pamphlet is made from folded sheets of paper, each sheet making a unit of two leaves or four pages. Hence the pages of any pamphlet, booklet, or broadside should be planned as a multiple of four, i.e., 4, 8, 12, 16, etc.; preferably in units of 16 or 32. (See BINDING.)

page proof See PROOFS.

pamphlet binding See BINDING.

pamphlets See also CIRCULARS; DESIGN.

For the purposes of this book, a pamphlet is assumed to have eight pages or more. Smaller printed items are discussed under circulars, posters, and letters. (See CIRCULARS; POSTERS; LETTERS.)

In planning a pamphlet, the points outlined in the Introduction should be checked. Only after that should decisions be made regarding (1) budget, (2) format (see DESIGN), (3) method of type composition, (4) printing process, (5) illustrations, and (6) paper.

For a pamphlet, type is usually set, although the text may be done on a typewriter (see COLD TYPE). Setting type (see TYPE) costs anywhere from $3 to $10 per page and more. The illustrations, if any, may be another cost.

A neighborhood job printer may be as well equipped to handle pamphlet work as anyone.

These factors are worth remembering:

1. One hundred copies are likely to cost practically as much as 1,000 copies. This is because printing even one copy involves a charge for type composition, artwork, plates, if any, and making the printing press ready. If a color other than black is used, there may be a further charge for cleaning one kind of ink off the press and substituting another color.

2. Economies can be effected by choosing a size that can be cut and folded from the paper without waste. (See PAPER; PAPER SIZES AND WEIGHTS.)

3. The pages of a pamphlet should be planned as a multiple of four, i.e., 4, 8, 12, 16, 24, 32 pages, etc. A 10-page pamphlet would have a loose sheet of 2 pages in the middle, and a 20-page pamphlet would usually be either a 16 plus a 4, or a 24 with 4 pages "canceled" (wasted).

4. A 12-page self-cover pamphlet is cheaper than one that consists of 8 pages of text plus a cover on heavier paper. The effect of a separate cover is sometimes attained by using a reverse plate. (See REVERSE PLATE.)

5. Sometimes an extra color of ink is more effective and cheaper than an expensive paper. On very small runs, the reverse is likely to be true.

6. A printer should be selected who customarily turns out work of the desired quality.

Very small printed items can often be handled with great economy by a label printer. (See LABELS.) On large runs, a printer with an automatic-feed multicolor press (perhaps with a folding attachment) may be able to underbid a smaller printer. (See also IMPRINTING; PAPER; COSTS; TYPE; CUT.)

Where the flat size of an unfolded pamphlet is less than 8½ by 11 in., or even 11 by 17, the owner of an office-size Multilith offset press can often underbid a printer whose presses are larger and more expensive to operate.

Both the offset and letterpress processes are suitable for a wide variety of pamphlet work; letterpress is sometimes thought to give more consistently satisfactory reproductions of photographs.

Rotogravure becomes economical only with quantities reaching well up into the hundreds of thousands. (See GRAVURE; also the inside front cover of this book.)

pantograph A tool used by draftsmen and artists to make enlarged or reduced copies of maps, charts, drawings, lettering, etc. A pantograph consists of a fixed pivot, a tracing point, and a copying (pencil) point, the three held in mathematical relation to each other by a parallelogram of four bars. The device can be adjusted to enlarge or reduce by any desired proportion.

High-precision pantographs are used in making patterns for type matrices from large-scale original drawings and in some steel-engraving work. Much drafting work that used to be done by pantograph is now done through the use of photostatic copies or a camera lucida. (See PHOTOSTAT; CAMERA LUCIDA.)

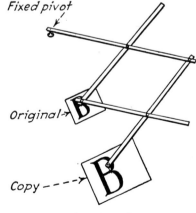

A pantograph.

paper See also PAPER SIZES AND WEIGHTS; CARDBOARD.

The easiest way to buy paper is to let the printer do it. For use on office duplicating machinery, it is safest to buy the paper recommended by the manufacture's service agency.

However, print users can profit by knowing something about paper even if they never expect to buy any themselves. Some knowledge of paper is indispensible to the wise and economic planning of printed matter. Printing planned with standard paper sizes in mind can be cheaper all along the line—in paper, press, binding, and mailing costs.

Paper is sold by the pound, and the prices range from about 8 cents per pound for contract newsprint to 15 to 30 cents per pound for book papers. Special papers, particularly when ordered in small lots, cost 40 to 50 cents per pound and up.

Almost all paper is made of wood. Some is made of rags (cotton or linen) or has a rag content. (See RAG CONTENT.) An excellent quality of paper can be made without any rag content.

Groundwood paper, which contains a high percentage of mechanical or groundwood pulp, is cheapest and is used for newspapers, rotogravure sections, some magazines, and some books. It has excellent opacity and printability, but turns yellow and brittle after prolonged exposure to air and light.

Sulfite, sulfate, and soda-pulp papers are made more slowly by chemically separating the wood fibers from the substances that make groundwood paper perishable. These papers tend to be stronger, whiter, free of blemishes, and durable. A sheet of paper made from pulp free of groundwood is called a "free sheet." The cost is at least twice as high as for groundwood paper.

Paper begins as a milky pulp of fibers and water, which flows onto a moving wire screen. The water is sucked out through the screen, and the limp, moist web of fibers is separated from the screen and passed around steam-heated drying drums and then between heavy rollers. The smoothing action of the rollers is called "calendering."

If subjected to light calendering, the paper comes out as "antique" paper, like that used in newspapers or most books. If calendered longer and harder, it becomes smoother. The steps are as follows:

Process	Description of Paper
Minimum calendering	Antique finish, high bulking (rough, fluffy finish)
Light calendering	Antique finish, nonbulking (smoother finish)
More calendering	Machine finish (MF); English finish (EF)
Separate calendering	Supercalendered (super)

A Sunday newspaper contains two kinds of paper. Probably the rough-surfaced news section and the smooth-surfaced rotogravure section had the same start in life, but one was rolled out smoother (i.e., calendered more) than the other.

The shinier papers take pictures better but are considered harder on the reader's eyes. The cost is usually about the same.

Coated papers, however, are quite different. (See COATED PAPER.) When the halftone was first invented, there were no papers smooth enough to do it justice; so coated papers were developed. Ordinary machine-finish paper was brushed or rolled over with a coating of clay, casein, etc., which made it heavier without increasing its strength.

Because coated paper was expensive, the big picture magazines wanted something cheaper. Papermakers then found a way to add the coating *during* the primary process of manufacture instead of afterward. The result was machine-coated paper, also called "process-coated" paper. This takes halftones better than uncoated paper, though the highest qualities of coated paper are still made by the brush-coated or roller-coated methods.

Letting the printer select and buy the paper is the safest plan, since it centers responsibility. Poor printing cannot so easily be blamed on the customer's selection of poor paper. Where quantities are small, it is certainly the best plan. Printers charge a commission on buying paper for a client. This can be saved by dealing directly with the paper merchant and having him deliver to the printer.

Printers also are quite naturally inclined to use what paper they have on hand, which may not be quite so appropriate to the job (in size, weight, finish, or quality) as paper that might be obtained from a paper merchant.

In ordering paper eight qualities must be taken into account:

1. *Surface.* Antique, eggshell machine-finish, English-finish, supercalendered, glossy-coated, dull-coated, coated-one-side, etc.

2. *Finish.* Wove, laid, pebbled, etc.

3. *Proposed use.* For example, paper to be printed by offset lithography is usually ordered as offset book paper, litho-coated, etc. Mimeograph paper, hectograph paper, etc., are so designated. The paper supplier should be informed if the paper is to be used with adhesives or special inks; if it must be of a quality to accept writing ink, erasures, carbonizing, gumming, lacquer or varnish, lamination, waxing, precision register printing; if it must be weather-resistant, warp-resistant, water-repellent, colorfast, nonalterable, rigid, able to withstand repeated foldings, etc.

4. *Quality.* It is easy to buy too much quality, or too little. The important thing is to buy enough of the essential qualities, without paying for excess or nonessential quality. Good receptivity to the kind of printing process that is to be used is of first importance. Other important qualities are permanence, durability, strength, foldability, opacity. Groundwood paper offers economy, opacity, and printability. Rag, jute, hemp, and sulfate, or kraft content contribute to bursting strength and folding endurance. Kraft paper excels in folding endurance. Rag paper was traditionally imagined to have greatest permanence, but it is now known that the permanence of the early handmade papers was due more to their freedom from acid than to the use of rags. Long-life, acid-free papers are now available at little or no extra cost in wood fibers as well as rag fibers. Strength sometimes has to be sacrificed to get opacity, and vice versa.

5. *Weight.* This book is printed on 70-lb paper. (See PAPER SIZES AND WEIGHTS.)

6. *Size.* Paper can be purchased from stock in a wide variety of sizes, and it can be made to order in any size if the quantity required is large enough (at least 5,000 to 10,000 lb, often more). (See PAPER SIZES AND WEIGHTS.)

7. *Grain.* All machine-made paper has a grain, which makes tearing and folding in one direction easier than in the other. Paper can usually be ordered with the grain in either direction. (See GRAIN.)

8. *Color.* "White" paper comes in a wide variety of shades. Creams, buffs, india tints, etc., are available as well as all colors. Colored paper costs more than white except in the case of such unbleached papers as kraft paper and the so-called "manilas." (Manila as applied to paper means a shade, not a fiber, unless identified as having hemp content.) Paper is usually made in light colors, since it is easier to print with dark ink on a light surface than the other way around.

Extra-heavy paper is sold as cover paper or ledger paper. (See also CARDBOARD.)

Paper buyers will find detailed and authoritative information on paper in the books listed in Appendix 2, Bibliography.

paper sizes and weights See also PAPER; CARDBOARD.

Paper can be made to order in almost any desired weight, bulk, finish, and color, but such special orders are uneconomical unless 5,000 to 10,000 lb or more are to be ordered at one time.

For small jobs and for rush jobs, standard sizes and weights are used. It pays to design a piece of printing so that it can be cut economically out of a stock size.

Suppose, for example, a circular is planned in size 9 by 12 in. (before folding), and the only paper available is 17 by 22. This paper will yield two circulars to the sheet, wasting one strip 4 by 17 and another 5 by 18. (See illustrations.)

Simply by changing the specifications to 8½ by 11, each sheet will yield four circulars. Half the paper will do the job. (The example cited is a very common one, although 9 by 12 is also a standard size. Many offset printers cannot print, and do not handle, any paper larger than 17 by 22 or 17½ by 22½.)

The standard paper sizes are what they are because standard-sized printing jobs can be cut or folded out of them without waste. (See the accompanying

Standard Paper Sizes Worth Remembering

Use	Size	Cuts out of
Business letterhead	8½ x 11	17 x 22
Books and pamphlets	8½ x 11	35 x 45
Books and pamphlets	5½ x 8½	35 x 45
Books and pamphlets	6 x 9	25 x 38
Postcards	3½ x 5½	22½ x 28½

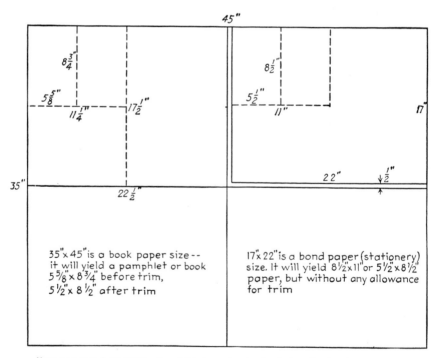

35"x 45" is a book paper size -- it will yield a pamphlet or book 5⅝"x 8¾" before trim, 5½"x 8½" after trim

17"x 22" is a bond paper (stationery) size. It will yield 8½"x 11" or 5½"x 8½" paper, but without any allowance for trim

How two standard sheet sizes fold down to standard sizes for books or pamphlets.

table.) Press sizes also tend roughly to follow standard paper sizes.

One standard article is the business letterhead, or piece of typewriter paper, size 8½ by 11. Another standard article is the book or pamphlet in size 6 by 9. Still another is the postcard in size 3½ by 5½. *Remember these sizes.* Jobs designed in these sizes, double these sizes, or half these sizes, can be printed without waste on stock

papers. Stock envelopes are designed around these sizes too.

Bond paper. Business letterheads and typewriter papers come in size 8½ by 11, except in Federal government service. The sheet used by printers is just four times as big: 17 by 22. This is the basic size to which the basic weight of bond and ledger papers refer. A ream (500 sheets) of ordinary bond paper in size 17 by 22 weighs 20 lb. This is or-

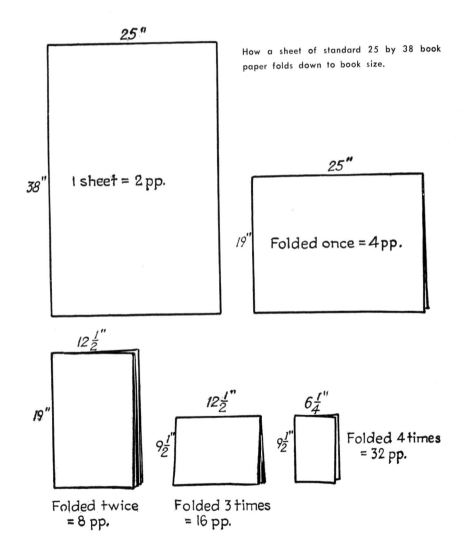

How a sheet of standard 25 by 38 book paper folds down to book size.

25″

38″ I sheet = 2 pp.

25″

19″ Folded once = 4 pp.

12½″

19″

Folded twice = 8 pp.

12½″

9½″

Folded 3 times = 16 pp.

6¼″

9½″

Folded 4 times = 32 pp.

dered as "20-lb bond." A lighter paper would be termed a 13-lb or a 16-lb paper, often written 13# and 16#. A heavier quality of bond would be termed 24#.

It is possible to buy bond paper in other sizes, notably 17 by 28, out of which can be cut four sheets of legal-size typewriter paper (8½ by 14). Naturally a ream of 17 by 28 paper weighs more than a ream of the same paper in size 17 by 22. For identification, however, it is still described as a 20-lb paper, or as being a paper of "substance 20" since it would weigh 20 lb to the ream in the basic 17 by 22 size. All bond and ledger paper is described in terms of basic substance weights, related to the 17 by 22 size. (See also BASIC WEIGHT.)

Book paper. The page size of a printed book or pamphlet is commonly 6 by 9. This folds economically from the standard book-paper sheet size, 25 by 38. To see how this works out, visualize the folding of such a sheet: first, it is 25 by 38, then 25 by 19, then 12½ by 19, then 12½ by 9½, and finally 6¼ by 9½. When the edges are trimmed to even them and to open the folds, the final result is a 32-page pamphlet in size 6⅛ by 9¼, or 6 by 9. *Book-paper*

weights are always based on a sheet 25 by 38. That size is worth remembering.

The next most common book or pamphlet size is 5½ by 8½, which is just half the letterhead size, 8½ by 11. The standard sheet of bond paper will fold from 17 by 22 to a 16-page pamphlet 5½ by 8½. After trim, however, the finished size will be only about 5⅜ by 8¼. The full 5½ by 8½ size can be produced from another standard book-paper size, namely, 35 by 45, one-quarter of which is 17½ by 22½.

Cover paper. Cover paper comes just a little bigger than book paper, since the covers on some pamphlets overhang the text a little. Thus, the basic size on which cover paper substance weights are figured is 20 by 26. (19 by 25 would be exactly one-half standard book paper size.)

Postcard stock. The basic size on which postcard and bristolboard substances are figured is 22½ by 28½. (See CARDBOARD.)

Any given paper may come in many other sizes besides those shown above, but practically all papers come in these standard sizes.

Any size or shape at all is of course possible. There is no law against cutting paper so as to waste some. But by using

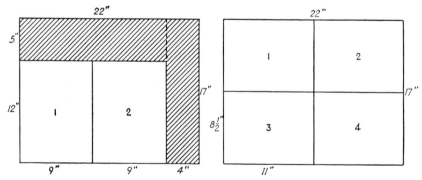

Only two 9 x 12 leaflets can be cut out of a 17- by 22-in. sheet of paper, as against four slightly smaller leaflets, each 8½ by 11 in. In the same way, a small change often permits the printing area of a printing press to be used to greater advantage.

Standard Paper Sizes and Weights

Standard basic substance weights*

	Basic size, and other standard sizes	30	35	40	45	50	60	70	80	90	100	120	140†	150	160	180	200	240	260	300
Coated paper	<u>25 x 38</u>, 28 x 42, 32 x 44, 35 x 45, 38 x 50						60	70	80	90	100	120								
Newsprint	25 x 38 and as above; <u>24 x 36 (in rolls to order)</u>		32	35																
Bond paper	<u>17 x 22</u>, 17 x 28, 19 x 24, 22 x 34, 28 x 34		13	16		20	24													
Ledger paper	<u>17 x 22</u> and as above							28	32	36	40	44								
Cover paper	<u>20 x 26</u>, 23 x 35, 26 x 40, 35 x 46				25		35	40		50		65		80	90	100		130		
Postcard bristol	<u>22½ x 28½</u>												94	100	105					
Printing bristol	<u>22½ x 28½</u>, 24 x 36, 25½ x 30½													100		120	140	160	180	200
Blotter	<u>19 x 24</u>														80		100			140

* Basic substance weights are arranged to show weight relationships between various kinds of paper. Papers of basic substance weights shown in the same vertical column are approximately equivalent in weight per square inch. For each kind of paper, the basic substance weight is that of 500 sheets of the size shown underscored at left.

† Paper is not made heavier than 120 lb. These weights are for comparison only.

standard sizes, the necessary amount of paper will be cheaper to buy, and easier and quicker to locate. The use of standard sizes helps a printer to put the job on a press that it fits instead of on a larger, more expensive press. Folding and bindery machines handle standard sizes most readily. Equally important is the fact that standard-size jobs fit into standard-size envelopes.

A printer should not be asked whether he can handle a job of a certain size. Of course he can, even if he has to print only two pages at a time. The problem is to give him a job that he can handle *most economically* and on which he can quote a good price.

Instead, he should be asked what printing press he would recommend for the job and what is the biggest sheet of standard-size paper it will take. If a sheet of that size is folded down (see illustration), the print user can see whether one of the resulting page sizes is desirable, and whether the resulting number of pages (or half, or double) fills his need. If this size will do, the press will be used at its maximum capacity. Without this kind of planning, double the pressrun may be necessary.

Paper merchants are always glad to supply dummies in any desired size, on any kind of paper. It is well to get several such dummies, to be sure that the right paper is being ordered. Things to check are opacity, mailing weight, "feel," etc. Weighing a dummy of a proposed printed piece has a special advantage: it serves as a check on the poundage of paper that must be ordered. 5,000 copies of a 2-oz pamphlet will obviously require at least 10,000 oz (625 lb) of paper, plus allowance for waste, spoilage, and trim. Without this check, it is very easy, even for experts, to order double or half the right amount of paper, thanks to the always confusing phenomenon of "one leaf equals two pages."

To calculate the amount of paper needed for any job, a dummy should be made to the exact size, then unfolded to show the actual size of the sheet needed. (To this must be added any necessary allowance for trim, bleeds, grippers, etc.) From this one can determine the number of units to be got out of the standard sheet of the nearest size; then the number of sheets needed can be calculated and finally translated into 500-sheet reams. Extra should be allowed for spoilage.

Paper is sold by the quire ($\frac{1}{20}$ ream), the ream (500 sheets), the double ream (1,000 sheets), the carton ($\frac{1}{4}$ case), the case (about 500 to 700 lb), and the skid (about 3,000 lb). Less-than-ream lots cost more per pound than lots of a ream or more. Cutting to special sizes costs extra.

Paper should never be ordered without the printer's approval of every detail of the order. He may want the paper cut in a certain way before delivery. He knows how much extra is needed to allow for spoilage. There may be some reason why he cannot run the jobs as he is expected to, or why he cannot get so many pieces to the sheet as the buyer has figured.

paragraph   See PROOFREADING.

Paraliner   A mechanical ruling device which attaches to a drawing board and makes easy the accurate ruling of evenly spaced lines. A built-in micrometer can be set for any desired spacing, after which each squeeze of the spacing knobs moves the ruler by the preset amount. The Paraliner easily rules business forms, music scales, etc., and does cross-hatching. A built-in protractor permits diagonal ruling. For further information write to Michael Lith Inc., 145 W. 45 St., New York 36.

parcel post   See Appendix 3, Postal Information.

parchment   Genuine parchment is thin skin taken from a calf, sheep, goat, or other animal, and prepared to accept writing. High-grade papers imitating genuine parchment are also called "parchment." The term "vellum" is used in the same way. It originally meant a lambskin parchment, but it is now used generally to describe smooth paper with a good writing surface.

pasteboard See CARDBOARD.

The heavier papers and cardboards get their rigidity and thickness by being built up out of two or more plies, which are either pasted together or pressed together while still wet, or both.

paste-up Material to be pasted up is sometimes given a wax coating on the verso to make it self-adhering. The wax can be applied in advance; it does not stick to the fingers and sticks to the mounting paper only when rubbed down and it can be released and re-stuck when it is necessary to move an element. It also has less tendency than rubber cement to pick up dirt along the edges of pasted elements. A desk-top machine for applying the wax is offered by the Addressograph-Multigraph, Bruning, and VariTyper sales divisions.

paste-up dummy See also PASTE-UP TECHNIQUES; DUMMY; LAYOUT.

The paste-up dummy shows the printer which lines of type and which illustrations go on which pages and how they are to be arranged, spaced, etc.

As soon as galley proofs arrive on the desk of the editor or makeup man, he will have someone separate them into different kinds. Usually at least three sets of galleys are returned by the printer: (1) a master set, which has been proofread by the printer and should be proofread again by the editor and sometimes by the author, (2) a set of numbered galleys, sometimes called "pinks" because frequently printed on pink paper, and (3) an extra set for the files.

Although the second set is generally used for the paste-up, many people prefer pasting up white galleys to get an effect more nearly resembling the finished page. Each galley to be used in the paste-up is first numbered by copying the printed number at the top onto each printed paragraph. (See illustration.) Numbering the galleys tells the printer where to look for the type. It is especially helpful if an item from galley 17 is likely to appear in the paste-up alongside items from galley 5, for example.

The editor or makeup man then has someone "trim" this set of proofs for the paste-up. This means cutting away all margins surrounding each block of text and each major heading.

The makeup man then arranges the trimmed proofs on the dummy (blank pages that have been marked to show margins, columns, etc.). When he is satisfied with the spacing and fit, he pastes them in place with rubber cement.

It is not necessary to show proof-reader's corrections on the paste-up dummy. Corrections must be made on the master set of galley proofs. If corrections promise to shorten a paragraph by one line, it is sufficient for the paste-up merely to snip off the last line arbitrarily. However, the paste-up dummy must take account of corrections on the master galley proofs and allow for changes in length.

To make such a dummy, first paste in the headings, being sure that they fit as planned in the original dummy or layout or can be made to fit an altered layout if desired.

Next, paste in engraver's proofs or photostats of the artwork (trimmed of their margins), or merely leave space for them. Then paste in the captions, checking carefully on the fit. (See CAPTIONS.)

Next try to fit the columns of copy to the space allocated. Before pasting is done, it is often best to pin down the printed columns, using pins like thumb-tacks through the proofs, the page, and into the drawing board. Since the copy may not fit exactly, the next problem is to cut or, if necessary, expand the copy so that the fewest alterations will have to be made by the printer and so that the most effective result may be obtained.

There are many tricks in fitting copy to space although, at first, it may sound like mere cutting and pasting of long strips of paper.

1. If it is necessary to cut several lines, go back to those paragraphs which have a very short last line. Perhaps by omitting a tiny phrase at the end or by substituting "often" for "frequently," a whole line of space can be saved. Whatever corrections are made here must also be made on the master proofs, which will go back to the printer as a guide for corrections. He will not follow alterations made only on the paste-up dummy.

2. Whenever possible avoid dividing a word at the end of a page since it is distracting to the reader to have to remember a syllable until he turns the page and finds the rest of the word.

3. Avoid dividing a paragraph so that the first line of it is alone at the bottom of a column or page, or the last line begins a new column. Better go back to cut out or add a line somewhere so that this wayward line can be brought back to its family. In printer's parlance the single-line carry-over is referred to as a "widow."

4. Watch out for the location of sub-heads. Otherwise a subhead may fall on the last line of a page or column and thus be separated from the copy that it announces. It may be well to go back and "take a tuck" in the preceding copy or, if a single line is involved, expand so that the subhead will be pushed ahead to start the next column or page.

Where a page has several columns, be sure that the subheads do not fall so as to make a distracting pattern on the page. For example, on a three-column page having just two subheads in bold type, it would be unattractive to have these come side by side like a dark streak across two columns of the page. It might be better to remove one sub-head entirely or to move it to another place.

Experience will quickly sharpen the eye so that such items are brought into a harmonious whole.

Finally, when satisfactory cutting and padding have been completed, paste down the copy to make a scrapbook page to guide the printer. Rubber cement is recommended for the pasting because it does not pucker the paper and because the copy can be peeled off if alterations are necessary.

Be sure that all alterations are marked on the master proofs to go back to the printer with the paste-up dummy.

The above procedures for the handling of galley proofs and corrections are standard. However, there are a few printers and publications that follow less orthodox procedures. At least one printer encourages his magazine clients to indicate all corrections right on the paste-up dummy and to return no corrected galleys at all. (This is very uncommon.) It is possible, at least when corrections are likely to be few, to paste up uncorrected galleys, return the paste-up dummy to the printer, and then proofread the galleys. Any corrections discovered in the galleys are held and later transferred to the page proofs. This may mean extra expense, but on the other hand it may also be less expensive to make three corrections in one page proof, than to make two in galley and one in the page proof, provided the corrections in the page proof do not involve changes in other pages as well.

Extreme neatness is not necessary on a paste-up dummy, although it is helpful to the editor in visualizing the appearance of a layout. Dummies need only be clear enough to guide the compositor in "paging" the type and cuts.

There is another kind of paste-up that must be perfect. This is the one made for photographic reproduction. It is on mounting board, not on paper. Galley proofs are not good enough for this kind of paste-up. After all corrections have been made, the printer must supply reproduction proofs pulled with special care. (See REPRODUCTION PROOFS.) These must be trimmed and mounted with painstaking neatness, both to get the alignment exactly right and to avoid any smudging.

There are many tricks to paste-up technique which make the work easier and neater and which are worth learning. (See PASTE-UP TECHNIQUES.)

22–School Exec

Outcomes at the School

Representatives of all subject matter and area committees undertook to survey the desired and attained outcomes of the school. Where test and observational data were not already available as measures of these outcomes, standardized and teacher-made tests were administered.

A thorough investigation was made of the picture-wide activities of the entire student body. Evidence was thus obtained as to the extent to which the school's cultural and technical training was carrying over into the pupil's after-school hours.

Evidence from concrete situations of all kinds was gathered on attitudes, appreciations, and skills at-

A galley proof, numbered and trimmed for pasting on the layout pages or dummy.

paste-up techniques See also LAYOUT; DUMMY; PASTE-UP DUMMY.

Neat, careful pasting must be done in many editorial jobs preparatory to printing, such as pasting up a dummy or mounting a photograph or piece of artwork. Meticulously accurate pasting

must be done on copy—either editorial or illustrative—that is to be reproduced photographically as in offset, photoengraving, or gravure.

There are several equally good ways of getting the same results, but the following paste-up techniques are practical and satisfactory.

The essential tools are rubber cement, a good flexible palette knife for applying and spreading it, a supply of mounting board, layout paper, and tracing paper, scissors, photo trimmer, rulers (including pica rulers and transparent rulers), triangles, T squares, straight pins, a pricker for transferring markings from one page to another, a supply of pencils (hard, soft, black, blue, red, and china-marking), retouching brushes, Chinese white, ruling pen, india ink, erasers, masking tape, Scotch tape—the permanent "mending" kind as well as the white, black, and transparent kinds.

There is no substitute for good rubber cement. It does not stretch or crinkle the paper. It does not soil the paper. When it is dry, any excess can be rubbed off easily with a soft eraser or the corner of a handkerchief. It can be used to make either a permanent or a temporary joint. Substitutes for rubber cement should be avoided. Buy only the kind labeled "rubber cement" or "synthetic rubber cement."

When pasting, it is well to have a good supply of scratch paper handy. Lay the item to be pasted face down on a clean piece of scratch paper. Smear it thinly with rubber cement. Pick it up by putting the palette knife down in the middle of the cemented area so that it sticks to the knife. Position it for pasting. Lay another piece of scratch paper over it, and rub through the back of the other scratch paper. Throw away both pieces of scratch paper rather than run the risk of smearing something else with cement left on them. (Or else put two smeared pieces of scratch paper face to face, and use them again as one piece.)

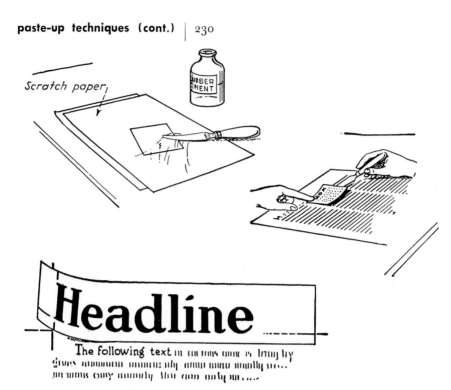

Scratch paper

Headline

The following text in various sizes and in many way...

A good way to apply rubber cement is with a palette knife. The same knife can be used as a handle for positioning the proof on the dummy, since the proof will stick to the knife. It is easy to paste up proofs in exact alignment if guidelines are first drawn in light blue pencil on both surfaces.

To make a temporary joint, put rubber cement on one piece of paper only, and apply when wet. To make a permanent joint, put rubber cement on both surfaces and allow them to dry before joining. (This means using great care the first time in positioning, for once stuck, they will stay stuck.)

In using rubber cement, be careful around reproduction proofs. The cement can smear the ink. When entirely dry, rubber cement can be rubbed off paper with a piece of tissue, but it may take pencil markings on the paper with it.

Trim proofs close before pasting, preferably within less than 1/16 in. This helps to avoid misalignment, or apparent misalignment. Where the alignment is particularly important, rule blue lines both on proof and on the mount, and match them up in the pasting. (See illustration.)

Strive for a paste-up result that will give a good visualization of the actual printed page to come. Use proofs of the same color as the mounting board or layout paper. Reproduction proofs are always pulled on white paper, but printers often send extra proofs on blue, red, or yellow paper. This is a good enough way of distinguishing extra sets of proofs from the master set, but paste-up dummies made with colored proofs do not give the layout man much visual help.

Before pasting, it is customary to arrange the various elements in their proper positions, and pin them there, just to make sure that everything will fit.

pasting See also PASTE-UP DUMMY; PASTE-UP TECHNIQUES; MOUNTING AND FINISHING.

An 8- or 12-page folder can be held together by pasting instead of by wire stitching if desired. The operation is done during the folding process and does not require an extra operation, as stitching does. A thin line of paste is laid on the paper where the fold will come.

Inserts are often pasted into place in books or magazines. (See INSERTS.)

patent base When printing is done entirely from electrotypes or stereotypes, it is common practice to equip the bed of the press with a patent base. This raises the level of the press bed so that the plates need not be mounted on wood but can be clamped directly to the patent base. A patent base looks like a honeycomb, each of the holes providing potential anchorage for a plate clamp.

patents Literary and printed material may be copyrighted but not patented. (See COPYRIGHT.) A patent is a grant of the exclusive right to make, use, and sell, for a limited (17-year) period, the invention covered by the patent.

pebbling Paper may be pebbled either before or after printing. The word "pebble" is a general one covering special finishes such as pebble finish, linen finish, ripple finish, and imitation-leather finish. The process is often referred to as "roller embossing."

Paper is pebbled by passing it under high pressure between rollers embossed with the desired design. Since it is not so easy to print on rough papers as on smooth papers, paper is usually pebbled after printing. A fine-screen half-tone cannot be put on eggshell or antique paper by the letterpress process, but it can be printed on smooth paper that is later pebbled to an antique finish.

Pebbling is often used to improve the appearance, bulk, or pliability of paper so that a less expensive paper may be substituted for more costly stock. It may be used to finish small quantities of paper that could not be purchased with that finish except in excessive quantity.

Among firms handling this work are the Pebbling Co., Inc., 76 Ninth Ave., New York; and Geo. Cassel, Inc., 225 Varick St., New York.

pencils See NOVELTY PRINTING.

pennants See CLOTH PRINTING.

pennysaver Also called "postage saver." (See ENVELOPES; also Appendix 3, Postal Information.)

perfect binding See illustration under BINDING.

perfector press A press that can print paper on both sides in one operation.

perforating Perforating is often done during a printing operation by a sharp steel rule, just enough higher than the type to penetrate the paper. The perforated line is also inked, of course, unless the printer goes to the trouble and expense of cutting away a section of his ink rollers. On cylinder presses a saw-toothed wheel can be used, though it will perforate in only one direction. Perforating can also be done as part of a folding operation.

Perforating is also handled as a separate operation on machines that punch rows of tiny holes or slits. This is considered a finishing operation. (See MOUNTING AND FINISHING.)

periodicals See also NEWSPAPERS.

Periodicals of all kinds—newspapers, magazines, house organs, etc.—present the same variety of printing problems as pamphlets, books, catalogs, and posters. They can be and are printed by every known method, and the choice of a printing process can be made on the same basis as for circulars and pamphlets. (See CIRCULARS; PAMPHLETS.) Letterpress, offset, and rotogravure are the most-used processes.

Where the budget is very small, one of the office-duplicating methods may be indicated. (See DUPLICATING.)

Getting out the first issue of a magazine is exactly like getting out a pamphlet or a catalog. Decisions must be made as to what process, what printer, what size, what paper, what typography, etc. Once made, however, these decisions need not come up again for months or years.

This means that the magazine editor need not ask himself, "Would these illustrations look better in gravure?" His magazine runs in letterpress and that is all there is to it. He need not laboriously specify that a heading be set in "24-pt 20th Cent. Ex. Bold Ital. c & lc flush left on one column." He can just mark it "Style B"—one of several typographic styles worked out in advance and on file with the printer. He need not rule margins and column widths for each issue; he can have layout paper printed up in advance with this information on it. (See LAYOUT.)

Magazine distribution can also become a matter of routine. A decision can be made once and for a long time as to whether to mail in an envelope, in a wrapper, or as a self-mailer. The names and addresses of recipients can be put on plates. (See ADDRESSING.) Second-class mailing privileges can be applied for. (See Appendix 3, Postal Information.)

Only periodicals with a legitimate list of paid-up subscriptions published for the dissemination of news of a public character can get second-class mailing privileges. These are well worth having, since they are much lower than third-class or fourth-class postage rates. (See Appendix 3, Postal Information.)

Designing a magazine. Readers are confronted with dozens of periodicals. Which one they read may be determined by the appearance or design. Seeing the same design gives a feeling of familiarity and at-homeness which is of cumulative benefit.

Since the first design of a magazine will probably be used for a long period, it is worth detailed comparison with similar publications under the guidance of an expert designer. (See DESIGNERS.)

Designing a publication involves such decisions as the following:

1. Size (see PAPER SIZES AND WEIGHTS)

2. Kind and weight of paper (see PAPER)

3. Trimmed or untrimmed paper

4. Pictures or no pictures, photographs, and/or drawings

5. Color or black and white; color on cover or text, or on both

6. One-, two-, or three-column page (professional and scholarly magazines tend to the one- or two-column page, newsmagazines to three columns); width of column; space between columns

7. Size of margins

8. Type face of the text, heads, subheads, photograph legends, by-lines, and credit lines (see DESIGN; also Appendix 1, Type Faces); suitable type sizes for each; alternate type styles for variety in heads

9. Type face and location of the page number, title, and issue of the magazine

10. Placing heads and subheads flush left, centered, or indented

11. Indention; decision on use of nonindented initial capital letter or small caps for the opening paragraph of an article

12. Location for masthead and copyright notice; type, spacing, and regular copy for the masthead

To avoid inconsistencies and to simplify the work, many an editor or production man makes up a typographic style sheet of such information about the design as may be needed for constant reference. It is still more useful if supplemented by pasted-up samples of the type faces, identified as to kind, size, and the average number of characters per column width for text type and one-column heads, and per pica for wider heads. The type face for legends should be marked with the number of characters for a picture of one-, one-and-a-half-, or two-column width. (Remember that a two-column picture is as wide as two columns plus the space between them.)

Planning the contents. A flexible long-range plan should be worked out as to the editorial and advertising content of a periodical. This will set a policy on such questions as the relation of the cover to the content, the desirability of a direct editorial as opposed to indirect editorial comment through pictures and articles, continuing features or departments, the use of signed articles and reprints, the proportion of advertising to editorial copy, etc.

In some instances, the effectiveness of a periodical is enhanced by planning a number of issues on different phases of a single broad theme.

Planning a single issue. An ideal balance and variety of material can be assured more readily with a tentative page plan. This may well be in the form of an editor's dummy with a tentative assignment for every page, even to special features such as boxed announcements, cartoons, and pictures. Or it may be a written outline listing the contents page by page.

Close scrutiny of such a page plan should detect overemphasis on certain subjects; omission of other types of material; lack of balance between factual and human-interest material, between national and purely local or regional news, or between "think" copy and "how-to-do" copy. It should facilitate a closely knit publication with each item contributing to a well-integrated whole.

An annotated list of timely books on newspapers and periodicals is included in Appendix 2, Bibliography. (In addition, see COPYWRITING; COPY PREPARATION; LAYOUT; PROOFREADING; PASTE-UP DUMMY; DISTRIBUTION.)

personalize See LETTERS.
To make a form letter seem like a personal letter.

phonograph records See RECORDINGS.

phosphorescent printing See LUMINESCENT PRINTING.

photo agencies See also PHOTOGRAPHERS; ARTISTS.
Photographs on a huge variety of subjects can be obtained from one or another of the many commercial and noncommercial picture files maintained by:
Commercial photo agencies
Government agencies
National associations (trade, professional, etc.)
Large corporations (care of Public Relations Director)
Advertising agencies (photos used in ads)
Libraries
Some magazines
The following commercial photo agencies will send an assortment of pictures on almost any given subject on request, usually without charge. The recipient is expected to pay for those kept and to return the others promptly. Rates vary from $15 per photograph up, depending on the nature of the use to be made of it. Rates for advertising use tend to be higher.
Donald T. Ballard, P.O. Box 226, Niles, Mich.
The Bettmann Archive, Inc., 136 E. 57 St., New York (historical pictures).
Black Star Publishing Co., 450 Park Ave. S., New York.
Brown Brothers, 220 W. 42 St., New York.
Commercial Museum, 34 St. and Convention Ave., Philadelphia (lends

photos on industrial, commercial, and geographic subjects).

Culver Pictures, Inc., 660 First Ave., New York (historical pictures).

European Picture Service, 39 W. 32 St., New York (photos from United States and abroad).

Fairchild Aerial Surveys, 10 Rockefeller Plaza, New York.

Free-Lance Photographers Guild, Inc., 110 W. 32 St., New York (black-and-white photos and large collection of color transparencies).

Ewing Galloway, 420 Lexington Ave., New York.

Philip Gendreau, 369 Lexington Ave., New York.

Globe Photos, Inc., 67 W. 44 St., New York.

Graphic House, Inc., 280 Madison Ave., New York.

Paul Guillumette, Inc., 59 E. 54 St., New York.

Harris & Ewing Photographic News Service, 155 E. 44 St., New York.

Keystone View Co., 4124 Broadway, New York.

Frederic Lewis, 370 Seventh Ave., New York.

Magnum Photos, Inc., 15 W. 47 St., New York.

Photo-Library Inc., 305 E. 47 St., New York.

Pix, Inc., 236 E. 46 St., New York.

Press Illustration Service, 369 Lexington Ave., New York.

H. Armstrong Roberts, 420 Lexington Ave., New York.

Shostal Press Agency, 545 Fifth Ave., New York (specializes in stock color for calendars, etc.).

Three Lions, Inc., 545 Fifth Ave., New York (photos from abroad).

Underwood & Underwood Illustration Studios, 11 W. 42 St., New York.

United Press International, 220 E. 42 St., New York.

Wide World Photos, Inc., 50 Rockefeller Plaza, New York.

The Federal government has many good photo files. Prints usually cost a dollar apiece. In many cases, however, lack of funds to maintain the files means that Federal departments cannot offer the same service as the commercial agencies and that users may have to visit the files in Washington and then wait one or more weeks for prints to be made, if indeed prints can be made at all.

Good photo files are maintained by the government agencies listed below. The Director of Information for the agency is the man to approach. In some cases the agency itself will have only current material, having been forced to transfer massive collections of important older documentary photographs to the National Archives. Photos may be seen at the Archives if the inquirer knows approximately when the collection was transferred to Archives and by which agency.

Agriculture Department
  Soil Conservation Service
  Bureau of Agricultural Economics
  Farm Security Administration (their outstanding collection has been transferred to the Library of Congress)
Air Force
Army
Coast Guard
Department of Health, Education, and Welfare
  Children's Bureau
  Public Health Service
  Women's Bureau
Interior Department
  Bureau of Reclamation
  Geological Survey
  Office of Indian Affairs
  Bureau of Public Roads
  Forest Service
  Bureau of Mines
Library of Congress, Division of Prints and Photographs
Marine Corps
Navy
Social Security Board
Veterans Administration

Many national organizations, like the American Red Cross, American Library Association, and Amalgamated Clothing Workers of America, maintain files of photographs in their field.

The United Nations in New York also lends photos from its files.

Private corporations are often good sources for photographs within their area of interest. One of the most unusual collections is maintained by the Standard Oil Co. of New Jersey, at 30 Rockefeller Plaza, New York. Photographs are obtainable here free, on every phase of American life in which oil plays a part: oil production, refining, and shipping; oil workers, their homes, their towns, etc.; pictures of oil being used for transportation, etc. The only requirement is publication with a credit line.

Movie stills are another good source of pictures and are obtainable from the motion-picture producers.

Advertisers often grant permission to reprint photographs that have appeared in their ads, provided a credit line is given. Requests for permission should be addressed to the Publicity Director, giving date when the ad appeared, what publication it appeared in, and the purpose for which the picture is to be used.

Public libraries and museums can usually aid in finding good pictures, although once the pictures have been located, permission to reprint must usually be sought from the copyright owners.

An important public picture collection is that maintained by the New York Public Library. It includes millions of pictures and photographs, indexed and classified, on all subjects. The source is given on each. By its very size this collection is a clearing-house of international importance for information on world picture sources and resources. The collection is much used, primarily by artists anxious to find out what the styles looked like at a particular period, how to draw a silo, etc. It consists of both clippings and photos which may be taken out of the library on loan by local residents or through interlibrary request.

Pictures that appear in magazines are sometimes owned by those magazines, and sometimes not. The ownership of them is generally given in the table of photo credits printed at the front or the back of a magazine.

Whether a photograph is borrowed for fee or for free, courtesy demands that the name of the photographer and leading agency be printed alongside.

photochemical stencil See MIMEOGRAPH.

photocomposition See also PHOTO-LETTERING; PHOTOTYPESETTING.

There is a so-called "photocomposing machine" that has nothing to do with type composition. It serves to print an image down on an offset plate as many times as may be needed—as for running a job 2 or more "up." Considerable precision is needed to photocompose the plates required to run a four-color label that is to run 48-up.

photocopying See also PHOTOGRAPHY; and the names of specific processes such as XEROX; VERIFAX; THERMO-FAX; PHOTO-STAT; EKTALITH.

Practically any kind of photographic work could be called "photocopying," but the word is most often applied to those processes that characteristically make copies on paper instead of film. A further distinction should be made between photocopying machines that make only same-size copies and those which can enlarge and reduce. Most of the so-called "office copying machines" do not enlarge or reduce.

The "same-size" processes include the diazo or "whiteprint" processes like Ozalid and Bruning, where the work to be copied must be one-sided and translucent but the materials are inexpensive; the reflex processes like Verifax and Thermo-Fax and diffusion transfer, which are more versatile in what they can copy but use higher-priced materials; and the Xerox process, which can make copies on ordinary paper, from almost any original, but where the manufacturer makes a per-copy charge for the use of the machine. Akin to Xerox, but requiring special paper, are the Electrofax processes. These processes are further described under WHITE-PRINT; VERIFAX; DIFFUSION TRANSFER; THERMO-FAX; XEROX; ELECTROFAX.

Office copying machines differ considerably in first cost, in materials costs, in labor costs, in first-copy costs (as distinct from extras produced at the same time), in space requirements, in the quality of the work produced, in the skill required to get good results, in start-up time, etc. Some will copy only materials (single sheets) that can be fed into a slot and passed around rollers; others will copy pages from magazines and books. Some are better than others at copying from books with small inner margins. Some require that chemical solutions be changed or replenished at intervals; others require warm-up time.

For many years it was the exceptional office that had facilities for making copies on the premises. It was customary to send out for photostats, which cost from 20 cents to $1 per page, depending mostly on the messenger service provided. Then the so-called "diffusion-transfer process" was introduced and popularized by Apeco, and the substantially similar gelatin-transfer process was introduced by Kodak under the name "Verifax." Chemical solutions were involved, copies emerged damp, and the process of making one copy could take a minute or more and cost 10 or 11 cents in materials, but the convenience of on-the-spot copying with relatively inexpensive equipment gave these techniques wide appeal and many competitors.

Another approach to the problem of convenient office copying was the 3-M Company's Thermo-Fax, which brought the cost of copies down to about 5 cents each. The quality of the early copies left much to be desired, and there was some user resistance to the waxy "feel" of the copy paper used, but the process has since been improved on both counts and people liked the fact that no chemical solutions were required and that the copies were dry.

The big breakthrough in office copying was made by Xerox with its introduction of the Xerox 914, which was promptly ordered by almost every office that could afford the minimum charges of about $100 a month. This machine could make a high-quality dry copy on almost any paper from almost any original, including books, for under 5 cents and with minimum operator time required. Later the Xerox 813 was introduced at about half the minimum rental and one-quarter the floor-space requirements; it would do about the same work as the 914 except that it would take only single sheets.

The quick acceptance of the dry copying processes like Thermo-Fax and Xerox was based as much on a reluctance to mix or pour chemical solutions as on a resistance to damp copies—which were usually not very damp—so most of the wet processes have concentrated on providing premixed solutions packaged for ease of handling.

Many of the companies which offer other methods of copying (and Ditto, for example, advertises that it offers them all!) have taken out licenses to offer machines employing the Electrofax principle. Where Xerox creates an image on a special drum and transfers it to any paper, Electrofax equipment creates the image directly on the copy paper.

The Xerox 2400, introduced in 1966, seems likely to obliterate the line between office copying machines and office duplicating machines: it will make a single copy of almost any original for 4 cents, but the rate drops rapidly until the twenty-sixth and succeeding copies of a single original cost only ½ cent a copy. When introduced, this machine commanded a minimum monthly billing charge of $350, against which the customer could have any desired combination of services, ranging from about 9,000 single copies to quantity runs totaling up to 70,000 copies. For information about other processes of possible application to specific office-copying problems, see also KALVAR; ADHEROGRAPHY; IMAGIC; STABILIZATION PROCESS.

All photocopying (as the name implies) depends on light. When the material to be copied is printed, typed, drawn, or written on only one side of a piece of paper that is not unusually thick, this original can simply be held in contact with light-sensitive paper and exposed to light. The result, after suitable development, may be a negative, with white letters on a black background, or (as in the WHITEPRINT processes) a positive.

When the material to be copied is printed on both sides or is opaque, copying obviously cannot be done by sending light *through* it. In such cases, photocopying is done by illuminating the surface and then seeking some resulting effect that can be put to use in making the copy. In so-called "reflex copying," a piece of light-sensitive paper is placed in face-to-face contact with the original to be copied and exposed to light. The light goes through the light-sensitive paper, then hits the image. Where it hits black letters, it is absorbed. Where it hits white paper, it is reflected back. The light-sensitive paper thus gets a double dose of light where it is in contact with white paper and, when the exposure is right, will turn black during development in such areas only. (Twice the exposure would, of course, blacken it all over.)

The direct result of such reflex copying is a wrong-reading (mirror-image) negative. For some purposes this may be satisfactory, but usually it is con-

verted into a right-reading positive by pressing it into immediate contact with white paper. This is the principle of the polaroid camera and the principle underlying the diffusion-transfer and Verifax processes.

The Thermo-Fax, Imagic, and Adherography processes are another application of the reflex-copying principle, but they take advantage of another property of light, namely, the fact that light will heat up a black material faster than a white or transparent material.

Where a lens is used in the copying process, it becomes possible to enlarge or reduce. However, a lens is necessary in the Xerox and Electrofax processes whether or not enlargement or reduction is desired. In these processes, the image projected through the lens is converted into electrical charges than can attract oppositely charged particles of pigment to form an image.

A very simple four-step way to copy a page from a book with practically no special equipment is as follows. In subdued indoor light, lay a piece of sensitized paper face down on the page to be copied. Cover it with a piece of glass (frosted or clear). Snap on a 60-watt bulb held 12 in. above the glass for about 5 sec. Develop and fix the sensitized paper.

The resulting negative will be reverse-reading but can either be read from the back against a strong light, or in a mirror, or can be printed down to make a right-reading positive. Good results require that the sensitized paper be in perfect contact with the page. It helps to put glass under the page being copied as well as on top of it. Suitable paper can be purchased in any photo supply store by asking for high-contrast contact printing paper. (Enlargement paper is too sensitive.)

photoengraving See CUT.

photogelatin Photogelatin, sometimes called "collotype," is a printing process most frequently used to reproduce paintings, photographic posters, displays, and wash drawings in color.

It is a screenless process. Unlike other processes, photogelatin requires no screen for reproducing halftones, whether in black and white or in color. (See HALFTONE.) It is particularly suitable for the facsimile copying of old documents, etc., in that it faithfully reproduces every flaw in the old paper or printing.

Photogelatin reproduction of photographs is generally superior to offset. The cost of making plates is substantially less than in letterpress or gravure. It is likely to be far cheaper than any other process where the problem is to print 100 or a few hundred copies of a very large pictorial subject. On many short-run color jobs, photogelatin will compare quite well with other processes at half the cost.

There are two kinds of photogelatin work: flatbed and rotary. The flatbed process is not much used in the United States, though extensively used in Europe. Production is slow and sizes are limited, though quality can be excellent.

There are at least a dozen firms doing rotary photogelatin work in the United States on modified rotary lithographic presses. These presses are usually large. Most of them can handle a 40 by 60 sheet. They can deliver about 800 impressions an hour, or perhaps 5,000 impressions a day. The plates cannot be rerun a second day. Reruns are possible by saving the negatives and making new plates.

Owing to the large plate size, a very small leaflet must either bear the cost of a large plate or wait its chance to be ganged up on a combination run with other small jobs. (See COMBINATION RUN.) Of course, a small job one-fourth the size of a plate could be run 4-up, thus producing 20,000 copies with 5,000 impressions.

Copy can be prepared for photogelatin in the same way as for offset. Very small type or fine serifs should be avoided.

Because of the fact that new printing plates have to be made for each day's runs, the cost of printing by photogelatin does not go down very much as quantities go up. When quantities go above 5,000 or 10,000, sheet-fed gravure (see GRAVURE) may prove to be a cheaper and equally satisfactory way of printing the same kind of material. For a comparison of photogelatin with other printing processes, see the charts inside the covers of this book.

Photogelatin printing is done on a firm but not coated paper. It is often varnished to give it a gloss. (See VARNISHING.) A photogelatin reproduction of a photograph with two coats of varnish or lacquer is hard to tell from the original photographic glossy print and may be much cheaper. It is even suitable for reproduction, owing to the absence of a screen.

Photogelatin printing begins with a high-fidelity photographic negative made from the original copy. Then a special bichromated gelatin-coated plate is exposed to light through this negative. The gelatin hardens in proportion to the amount of light received. When moistened, the unhardened portions get wetter than the hardened portions. When inked, the wetter portions accept less ink.

Firms doing photogelatin work include New York Gravure Corp., 424 W. 33 St., New York; Black Box Collotype Studios, Inc., 4840 W. Belmont Ave., Chicago 41; and Frederick Photogelatin Press, Inc., 438 W. 37 St., New York. The Meriden Gravure Co., Meriden, Conn., does flatbed photogelatin work, specializing in plates for scholarly books. (Pay no attention to the word "gravure" in the titles of these firms. They specialize in photogelatin printing, not in gravure.)

photographers See also PHOTOGRAPHY; PHOTOGRAPHS: HOW TO SELECT; PHOTO AGENCIES.

Almost every city has commercial photographers who are equipped to take portraits, banquet and wedding pictures, news assignments, etc. Usually they also do copying work and make enlargements. Some, but not all, do retouching of the sort that is necessary to make a satisfactory photograph of an advertised product. (See RETOUCHING.)

To get run-of-the-mill photographic service is not difficult. To get really good work is hard. A good pho-

---

American Society of Magazine Photographers, Inc.

1476 Broadway, New York City

STANDARD FORM MODEL RELEASE

....
DATE

I hereby consent that ....
(Photographer) and/or assignees be authorized to use my name, portrait, picture, photograph, or any reproduction of myself for editorial and/or commercial purposes. Permission is hereby granted to make changes or alterations and/or use my name or any fictitious one for such purposes.

The undersigned warrants that he is over 21 years of age.

....
SIGNED

....
ADDRESS

GUARDIAN'S CONSENT FOR MINOR

The undersigned represents that he is the parent and guardian of the minor named above, and represents that he has the legal authority to execute the foregoing consent and release.

....
SIGNED

WITNESS:
....

tographer is one who will take extra time and trouble and use special lights, film, and flashbulbs when necessary. When outdoor pictures are being taken he may even have to make several attempts to get the right lighting conditions.

$15 will buy a routine news shot at the studios of many commercial photographers. $100 to $125 a day plus expenses is more like what it may cost to get thorough coverage of one situation from a local photographer. The result will, of course, be a selection of pictures, not just one.

Magazine photographers who work for national magazines receive a minimum of $100 a day plus expenses. The American Society of Magazine Photographers, 1472 Broadway, New York 36, can supply names and addresses of members in all parts of the country.

Some photo agencies stand ready to take pictures on special assignment. (See PHOTO AGENCIES.) These include Alpha Photo Associates, Inc., 200 W. 57 St., New York; Wide World Photos, Inc., 50 Rockefeller Plaza, New York; Free-Lance Photographers Guild, Inc., 110 W. 32 St., New York; and UPI Commercial Photography Division, 220 E. 42 St., New York. In almost any city, the photographers who service the local newspapers will accept other assignments.

Agencies specializing in magazine and advertising photography include Black Star Publishing Co., 450 Park Ave. S., New York; Pix, Inc., 236 E. 46 St., New York; and Magnum Photos, Inc., 15 W. 47 St., New York 36. They have correspondent photographers in cities outside New York.

It is often possible to get camera clubs to undertake a photo coverage for nonprofit causes. There are such clubs in most high schools and colleges.

Those unaccustomed to working with a photographer often fail to use his time to best advantage by not planning details in advance. The photographer must know the exact nature of the assignment and the purpose for which the photographs are to be taken so that he can bring the right equipment. All properties should be in readiness, all participants wearing the right clothes.

Often a good photographer will discover picture opportunities that his client has failed to see, and he should be encouraged to do so. It is not fair to the photographer to count on this, however, since the people who are to use the pictures really should know best precisely what will be most useful to them.

A photographer should be responsible for getting the correct names, positions, addresses, etc., of all the people photographed, and for getting written releases from them where necessary. (Where a photographer and a writer work as a team, the writer may do this.)

It is necessary to get written permission from every person shown in a photograph to be used for advertising purposes. A typical form of "release" is illustrated. Usually it is not necessary to get such a release when the picture is not used for advertising. However, a private citizen may bring a civil libel suit if a photograph of him is published that tends to hold him up to scorn or ridicule. A public relief agency will not want to embarrass its clients by permitting recognizable pictures of them to be taken or used for publication.

Photographers retain the ownership of the negatives of any pictures they take, unless other contractual arrangements are made when they take an assignment.

photographs See PHOTOGRAPHY; also the two entries which follow.

photographs: care in handling See also CROP, CROPPING.

A good photographic print should be handled carefully. Even if the negative is available, in case of accident, the original print may be more than just a print—it may be *better* than the negative, thanks to painstaking darkroom work.

Photographs should never be cropped with scissors. This procedure leaves no space for scaling and makes it difficult to correct mistakes. (See SCALING.) Besides, if a photo is to bleed, more of it must appear on the cut than will appear in the printed product. (See BLEED.)

A photo should always be captioned promptly before essential data are lost or forgotten. The best way to do this is to type the caption on thin paper and paste it to the back of the photo with library paste. Rubber cement will in time damage a print.

Typing or writing with a pencil on the back of a photograph should be avoided. A paper clip should be used on a photo only if it is protected by several folds of paper between the clip and the photo. Writing on a thin paper overlay while the photo is underneath is taboo. In all these ways the glossy surface of a photo may be dented or raised in such a way as to catch the light and be spoiled for use in reproduction.

When retouching is to be done on a photograph, it is well to mount it on cardboard lest it curl or crack. First, all captions and credit information should be transferred to the back of the mount before they are lost to view.

The most satisfactory method of mounting photographs is dry mounting. A piece of special dry-mounting tissue, procurable at photo supply stores, is cut to the same size as the photo and placed between it and the mount. Pressure with a hot iron, or in a special heated mounting press, binds the photo to the mount permanently.

Rubber cement is an almost foolproof adhesive since it does not permit puckering and, when dry, can be rubbed off without a trace. It should be brushed thoroughly over both photo and mount and allowed to dry before the two are pressed together. Rubber cement will in time stain a print and should not be used if the print is to be permanently filed. The print may also pucker if it is retouched.

Ordinary flour paste, rightly used, is excellent, but it requires careful handling and drying. It should be free of lumps and should be brushed thoroughly over both photo and backing in each direction, after which the two may be allowed to dry under pressure.

An overlay should always be used to protect a retouched photo. The use of masking tape to hold the overlay in place will eliminate any temptation to use paper clips.

Crop marks are best applied in the margin of a photo with a china-marking pencil or a wax crayon. (See CROP.) In case of mistakes such a mark can easily be rubbed off glossy prints with cleansing tissue or the corner of a handkerchief.

Photos should be filed or stored so that they will not curl or crease. Prints in active use are often kept under a heavy weight. Prints can be most safely stored in the cardboard boxes in which sensitized paper comes.

photographs: how to select See also entry above and PHOTO AGENCIES; PHOTOGRAPHERS; CROP; LAYOUT; PHOTOGRAPHY.

The quality of all photographic reproduction is limited by the quality of the photograph being reproduced, as well as by the printing process used. The effectiveness of a printed photograph is further determined by its size, its content, the way it is cropped, and its placement with regard to other pictorial material.

The 8 by 10 single-weight glossy print is the standard article supplied by professional photographers to newspapers, magazines, book publishers, and advertisers. It is big enough to do justice to most pictures, big enough to be retouched, and a size that engravers and printers are accustomed to working from.

Ordinarily the 8 by 10 print is an enlargement from 2¼ by 2¼, 3¼ by 4¼, 4 by 5, or 5 by 7 film. Occasionally it is a contact print from 8 by 10 film. The smaller film sizes give all the detail and sharpness that may be required for most work if exposed with care, although the 35mm size (1 by 1⅜) is regarded by many photographers as too small to be depended upon for consistently sharp 8 by 10 enlargements.

Photographers often crop (see CROP) their photographs while making prints. They enlarge the image until the essential portion of the picture completely fills the 8 by 10 printing paper. Alternately, they may print everything that is on the negative, and let the editor crop to eliminate unessential areas. The latter procedure gives the editor more control over the proportions of a picture. Otherwise, if he wants to make a wide picture taller, for example, he may have to check back with the photographer to find out whether there is more sky on the negative than shows on the print.

A photograph intended for reproduction by any process should meet the following requirements:

1. It should be sharp. It is permissible and often desirable for nonessential background or foreground elements to be slightly out of focus, but every important detail should be "tack sharp." The vogue for soft-focus pictures has passed except in the portrait field; it is passing there, too.

2. It should have a full range of tonal values, including white, black, and all the gray values between. This means that the brightest highlight in a predominantly dark picture should be white or near-white, not gray; and the darkest shadow in a predominantly light picture should be black or near-black, not gray. However, areas that should contain detail should not be allowed to go white or black. Because a photograph tends to gain slightly in contrast during reproduction, prints made for reproduction may be of slightly lower contrast than prints made for exhibition purposes. A good darkroom operator can often get a usable print from even a poor negative by using a paper of the proper contrast and by giving some areas a longer exposure.

3. It should be free of unessential detail. A photograph should be cropped to eliminate unwanted sky or background, so that the essential elements will reproduce as large as possible. When distracting material cannot be removed by cropping, it can often be grayed down or removed by retouching. (See RETOUCHING.)

4. It should be natural. The people in it should not look posed.

5. It should tell a story. People should be doing something; equipment should be in use. The size of unfamiliar objects should be indicated by comparison with familiar objects. So far as possible it should get its message across with a minimum of caption.

6. It should have human interest. Good pictures of babies, animals, and pretty girls are the conventional "stoppers" because they are so high in human interest and attention value. Pictures with an emotional appeal have the greatest attention value. In general, people are less interested in a picture of the other fellow's product or problem than they are in a picture of "how this might affect me." They like to imagine themselves in the picture.

Large pictures always look better than small ones. Size does something for any picture. Too often an editor asks, "How small can we run this picture?" when he should ask himself, "How large can we run it?"

For help in finding good photographs, see PHOTO AGENCIES. For suggestions on the editorial use of photographs to tell a story, etc., see books listed in Appendix 2, Bibliography.

photography See also COLOR PHOTOG-
RAPHY; NEGATIVE; PHOTOCOPYING; PHO-
TOSTAT; PHOTOGRAPHERS; PHOTO AGEN-
CIES; PHOTOGRAPHS: CARE IN HANDLING;
PHOTOGRAPHS: HOW TO SELECT; MON-
TAGE; FILMSTRIPS.

Photography is now an adjunct to almost all the major printing and duplicating processes. It is also a printing
process in its own right. Those who use
printing, therefore, need to know both
the basic principles of photography and
the major applications of its principles.
The basic principles are reviewed briefly
here. In photographic printing, light instead of ink hits the paper, or film, and
darkens where it hits. In the simplest
techniques of photocopying, an ordinary
business letter is placed over a piece of
sensitized photographic paper, and both
are exposed to light. The sensitized
paper is then "developed and fixed" to
make the image on it permanent. The
result is a duplicate of the letter, but
with white characters against a black
background. Enough light got through
the white paper of the letter to darken

the sensitized paper beneath, except
where the writing or typewriting held
back the light. (See illustration on page
244.)

If a print is now made in the same
way from this negative (white on black)
copy of the business letter, the result
will be a positive print which is black
on white like the original.

The above process, called "contact-
print" copying, works the same way
when sensitized transparent film is used
instead of sensitized paper. In fact, film
works better, since positives made
through paper not only take more time,
but also may show a mottled effect due
to the uneven grain of the paper.

This process is much used for making
same-size copies. It is the principle underlying blueprinting. (See BLUEPRINT.)
It is used in business offices for simple
photocopying. (See PHOTOCOPYING.)
Photographers generally make contact
prints from their negatives before deciding whether or not to make enlargements.

Contact printing does not, however,

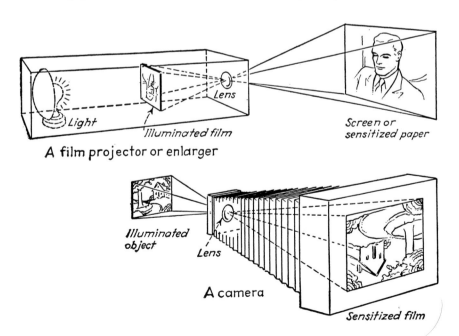

A film projector or enlarger

Light / Illuminated film / Lens / Screen or sensitized paper

Illuminated object / Lens

A camera

Sensitized film

PHOTOGRAPHIC CONTACT COPYING

A piece of sensi-
tized paper(in
a darkened room)

is covered by a
business letter

and exposed to light.

Developer

The exposed, sensitized
paper is put into a tray
of developer for one min-
ute

Developer

and it darkens except
where protected from
the light by the typing.

Water

It is rinsed in water
for five seconds.

Fixer

It is immersed in a
"fixer" for 10 minutes.

Water

It is washed for one hour (prints which
aren't washed enough eventually turn yellow)

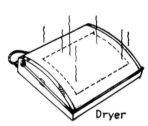

Dryer

and it is
dried.

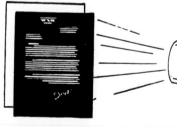

If this "negative"
(white on black) copy
is placed over another
piece of sensitized paper

exposure to light will
darken the paper where
it penetrates

and produce a
"positive" print
like the original.

permit enlargement or reduction of the size of the original. A contact print is always the same size as the original or the film negative from which it is made.

A magic lantern or film projector is a simple form of enlarger. Just as it can throw a picture of any size on a screen or wall, so it can throw a picture on a piece of sensitized paper and thus make a photographic enlargement of the original.

A camera is essentially a magic lantern with a box built around the lens, the beam of light, and the screen. (See illustration on page 243.)

Ordinary cameras are "reducers" rather than enlargers, but large copying cameras can either reduce or enlarge.

Photostat cameras generally use sensitized paper. (See PHOTOSTAT.) Other cameras generally use sensitized film, but film and paper can be used interchangeably.

There are many different qualities of photographic film and paper. Some are very "hard" or of "high contrast," which means that they tend to make everything either white or black. Others are "soft" or of "low contrast" and distinguish between delicate shades of gray.

Most photostat paper is hard and not suitable for making good copies of photographs.

Photographic films and papers differ also in their sensitivity to different colors. Those ordinarily used in photostat and other copying work are called "orthochromatic" and are sensitive to white and blue light but not to red. They will "see" blue as white, and red as black. They should not be used in copying originals that are in color.

In order to make a faithful black-and-white copy of an original which is in full color or which contains blue or red, it is necessary to use a "panchromatic" film that is sensitive to all the colors.

Some good books on photography are listed and described in Appendix 2, Bibliography.

photography: as a printing process See also main entry under PHOTOGRAPHY.

Photography is an adjunct to other printing processes whenever copying, enlarging, or reducing steps are involved. It is also a printing process in its own right. Light instead of ink hits the paper and darkens where it hits.

An example of photographic printing. The light goes through the white part of the paper and darkens the sensitized paper underneath.

Photography and photocopying can also be considered as printing processes in their own right under certain circumstances.

PHOTOCOPYING (q.v.) is however usually a compromise as regards quality and is rarely very useful in making high-quality photographs. Photography itself (the original silver nitrate process) is still the standard by which other processes are judged. It is comparatively expensive for long runs, since it requires the use of relatively expensive sensitized paper, plus additional chemical development and fixing of the image, and drying of the paper.

However, 8- by 10-in. prints can be had for as little as 7 cents each (lots of 100 to 1,000) after an initial investment in a master copy negative of only $2.

The photographic printing process is, therefore, relatively cheap in small quantities. It is also a versatile process. It can make a good black-and-white copy of anything, including type, drawings of all sorts, other photographs, and even originals in color, or any combination of these.

100 photographic copies of a photo can be much less expensive than 100 printed copies and of much higher quality. A caption that is written, typed, or in the form of a proof from set type can, at slight extra cost, be made part of the copy negative and thus print with the photo in the same operation, and can be enlarged or reduced to fit.

The photographic printing process also lends itself to specialized purposes, especially the production of transparent images for use in projection machines. (See FILMSTRIPS.)

It is possible to sensitize almost any surface and print on it photographically—paper, glass, metal, cloth, even a wall or the side of a building. (See also PHOTOSTAT.)

Firms that specialize in photocopying are Copy-Art Photographers, 165 W. 46 St., New York; Howard Photo Service, 155 W. 46 St., New York; and Master Photographers, Inc., 165 W. 46 St., New York. Firms which specialize in full-color photocopying include Moss Photo Service, 78 Fifth Ave., New York; and The Pavelle Corp., 1270 Ave. of the Americas, New York. (Prints in color cost a good deal more than black-and-white prints.)

Photographic Christmas cards can be made from the customer's negative for prices as low as $3 for 25, $10 for 100. Companies giving this service include The Pavelle Corp., 1270 Ave. of the Americas, New York; and Mosscolor Corp., 78 Fifth Ave., New York.

photogravure See GRAVURE.

photolettering The setting of display type by photographic methods. (The setting of *text type* by photographic methods is discussed under PHOTOTYPE-SETTING.) See also LETTERING; ARTYPE; HADEGO; BRIGHTYPE.

Photolettering can cost more than setting display type; it can also be a cheaper substitute. In general, the techniques that aim at high quality also de-mand (or at least reward) considerable skill; others aim at utility, economy, and speed, with a minimum of demands on the skill of the operator.

Photolettering devices, each described under its own heading, include the Linofilm Composer, the VariTyper photocomposing machines, the Typro (made by Friden), the Filmotype, the Monotype photolettering machine, the Photo Typositor, the StripPrinter, and the Morisawa Photo Typesetter.

Important questions to ask in selecting a photolettering machine are: Do you want to make your own decisions about letterspacing, or do you want the machine to do it for you? Will you be content to have to buy a different font for each size you may want to set? Do you care about automatic development? (This may be more of a nuisance than a help if your volume of work is small, considering the problem of keeping fresh developing solutions in the machine.)

photolithography See OFFSET.

photomechanical The usual commercial methods of making printing plates are described as photomechanical, as distinct from "hand" processes. When plates were prepared by hand, the man who prepared a lithographic stone, for example, had to be an artist or at least a copyist. Nowadays lithographic plates are almost always prepared by applying photomechanical techniques, and it is sufficient if the platemaker is merely a good technician.

photomontage See MONTAGE.

Photon The name "Photon" identifies a series of photographic typesetting machines. The first Photon went into successful commercial service in 1954 and was capable of storing 16 type styles on a single spinning disk. The Model 200 "Admaster," utilizing disk storage, is still the most versatile Photon and offers a range of sizes as high as 72 pt and speeds up to 10 characters per second.

The Photon Model 540 has much the same capabilities as the Model 200, except that its input is through punched paper tape only, the keyboard being a separate unit.

The Photon Model 713 utilizes drum storage instead of disk storage of its master alphabets and is capable of setting up to 30 characters per second. It is also tape-actuated. A drum can contain (and mix) eight type styles. The size range is from 5 to 18 pt.

The Photon Model 900 (also called the "Zip") is the fastest of all, being capable of setting lines up to 11 in. long at 2½ lines per second. Its input is magnetic tape which must have been prepared in some kind of computer. In its first application at the National Library of Medicine, it was programmed to set complete four-column pages in one pass.

The Photon (called the "Lumitype" in Europe) was the first real breakthrough in quality type composition since the invention of the Linotype and Monotype. By forming characters through the action of light on photographic film or paper, it opened the way to greater freedom of type design, greater flexibility in type size and leading, greater speed, and increased capacity to intermix type styles and special characters. One interesting possibility was that of producing an accented character by combining the character with the accent in two overlapping exposures.

All Photons operate on the principle of selecting the character to be exposed by flashing a strobe light at just the right microsecond. In the disk and drum models, each revolution brings all characters of a font successively into position in front of the lens. The timing of the flash selects the character, and the motion of the film (like the motion of a typewriter carriage) determines the location of the character on the line.

In the Series 900 Photon, the master characters are stationary, but each has its own strobe light. The film also is stationary during the composing of any

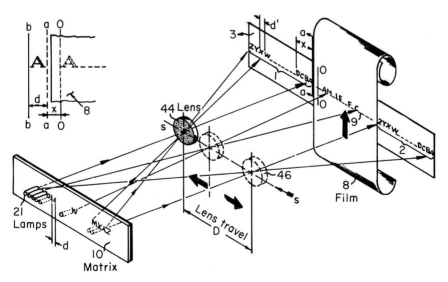

The optical system of the Photon 900 (Zip). During the setting of any given line, nothing moves but the lens.

The Model 200 Admaster is the most versatile Photon.

given line. The lens moves, however, and at *some* time during its motion (which takes 0.4 sec, or 400,000 microseconds) is in the correct position to project any given character into any given location in the line being set. (See diagram.) In operation, the Photon 900 may, for example, determine that the line begins with 1-em space (18 units), then has a cap "A" (12 units), followed by a cap "M." It follows that the "M" must be flashed at the moment when the lens is in a position to project it into position 30 (18 plus 12) in the line. By computer calculation, this may call for the light behind "M" to be flashed when the lens has completed 120,160 microseconds of its travel.

photo-offset See OFFSET.

photoprints See PHOTOGRAPHY: AS A PRINTING PROCESS; PHOTOSTAT; PHOTOCOPYING.

photo retouching See RETOUCHING.

Photostat A photographic copying machine manufactured by the Itek Business Machines Co. of Rochester, N.Y. It will make same-size, enlarged, or reduced photocopies. (The Rectigraph, a substantially identical machine which was introduced prior to Photostat, is made by the Haloid Photo Division, Xerox Corporation, Rochester, N.Y.)

Essentially, a Photostat photocopying machine is a good copying camera, capable of doing anything that the camera will do. However, it is designed to do a limited number of things more quickly and easily than the ordinary camera. It differs from an ordinary copying camera in three ways: (1) It is designed primarily to use photographic paper instead of film. (2) It employs a prism so that its paper negatives will be "readable negatives" instead of being reversed, mirrorwise. (3) It develops, fixes, washes, and dries prints and delivers them ready for use.

The paper copies produced by this machine are called "photostatic copies," "photostats," "stats," or "photocopies." A photostatic copy made from an ordinary business letter is a negative, showing white typing on black paper. For purposes of record, this negative is as useful as a positive. If, however, a positive copy with black type on white paper is required, it is necessary to order two Photostats, first the negative Photostat and then a positive Photostat, which is made from the negative Photostat.

Photostats were once virtually the only practical way of getting copies of business documents short of retyping. There are now many competing copying processes, but few of the "office copiers" will enlarge or reduce, and some of them leave much to be desired in terms of sharpness or blackness. Even organizations with their own office copiers will therefore often fall back on photostatic copies when they need enlargements or reductions or work of "reproduction quality."

Photostatic copies in size 8½ by 11 or less cost from 20 to 50 cents each when ordered from commercial houses. Part of this cost is that of messenger service. A piece of 8½ by 11 photostatic paper actually costs less than 6 cents, to which must be added the cost of developing, fixing, drying, labor, overhead, and profit.

Photostating may be considered a printing process, competitive with Multilith, mimeographing, etc., when quantities are very low. It has the advantage of being very fast. It is not usually so cheap as making 8 by 10 photographic prints in quantities above 10 or so. (See PHOTOGRAPHY: AS A PRINTING PROCESS.) In deciding when to use Photostat rather than some other printing process, consult the charts inside the covers of this book.

Photostats are much used in layout and dummying work for reducing or enlarging the various illustrations or headlines so that they may be pasted up together with the text. The Photostat technique also offers an easy way to reverse type or drawings, black for white. Other uses include copying book pages, charts, clippings, drawings, estimates, records, etc.

In one timesaving technique, photographs, printed illustrations, or even objects themselves are photocopied so that the artist may make a line drawing right over the photocopy, after which the underlying photo image is bleached out.

Photostat machines will usually enlarge to twice the size of the original

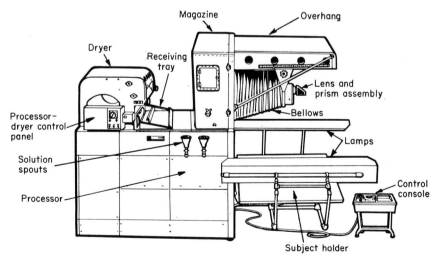

The Photostat 18.24 which produces prints up to 18 x 24 in. without manual processng.

and reduce to one-half the size of the original in one shot. This range can be extended, but only by a skilled operator and by making time-consuming special adjustments. In two successive shots—(1) from original to negative, (2) from negative to positive—it can thus enlarge to four times, or reduce to one-fourth. With four successive shots (original to negative to positive to negative to positive) it can enlarge to sixteen times, or reduce to one-sixteenth. However, a positive copy four times removed from the original is likely to lose so much in the copying as to be unsatisfactory. It is better and sometimes no more expensive (compared with paying for four photostats) to go to a commercial photographer when more than fourfold enlargements or reductions are needed.

Where the majority of the work is layout and dummying with reducing and enlarging, there is a Photostat unit called the "Model Two Special" for making prints 14 by 18 or smaller, which will reduce to 28 percent and enlarge to over 300 percent of original size.

Some photocopying work is of low quality. This is usually due not to any inherent limitation of the equipment, but rather to ignorance or carelessness on the part of the operator. For example, an occasional print may be out of focus in places due to curling of the paper during exposure. This kind of defect (which is prevented in lithographic cameras by the use of a vacuum back to hold the film flat) will be noticed by the careful operator, who will then make another exposure.

While any Photostat machine operator can usually make copies of reproduction quality from black-and-white originals that are not photographs or drawings containing middle tones, not every operator can make good copies of photographs or of originals that are in color.

Photostatic copies of photographs are usually inferior to photographic copies of photographs because standard photostat paper is "hard" or "high-contrast" paper, deliberately designed to record near-white areas as pure white, and near-black areas as pure black. If softer paper or film is not at hand, a skillful operator can produce passable copies by "flashing" his paper before making his copies. He flashes the sensitized paper by exposing it briefly to a plain white surface. This in essence pushes the paper one-third of the way toward complete exposure while stopping just short of actually darkening it. Thus it is put in a condition where even a little more light will start it turning gray. Then he replaces the plain white paper with the photograph to be copied and makes another short exposure (again about one-third of normal).

The copying of colored originals calls for extra skill on the part of the operator because standard photographic papers are orthochromatic, i.e., they see blue as white and red as black. For example, a copy of a business letter may fail altogether to show a blue-ink signature. This can be corrected by making the exposure through the yellow filter that is standard on all machines, but extra exposure time must be allowed. Originals containing red should be copied on special panchromatic paper, which may be used exclusively where a good deal of the copying is to be from colored objects.

Where acceptable photocopies of photographs of colored subjects cannot be obtained because of lack of the proper materials or know-how, such work can of course be obtained from a commercial photographer.

The smallest Photostat machine will produce a finished copy as large as 8½ by 11. Other models will make copies up to 11½ by 14, 14 by 18, or 18 by 24.

phototypesetting   The Fotosetter by INTERTYPE, the PHOTON, the LINOFILM, and the Monophoto (see MONOTYPE) are examples of keyboard typesetting machines that produce a photographic result directly without going through the traditional stages of casting metal type, inking, proofing, etc. See these headings as well as ALPHATYPE; ATF TYPESETTER. See also TYPEWRITER, and for information about the ways in which all keyboard composing equipment has been adapted to set from prepunched tape instead of by direct keyboard action, see COMPUTER TYPESETTING. (Non-keyboard machines for the photographic setting of headlines, etc., are reviewed under PHOTOLETTERING.)

Whereas the traditional metal-casting composing machines could set no faster than hot metal could cool—the practical limit was probably reached in the Linotype tape-driven Monarch, which could cast up to 14 newspaper lines a minute—this speed has now been doubled or better in the Linofilm, the Fototronic, and the Photon 713 and has been increased more than tenfold again in the Photon 900.

Phototypesetting eliminates some of the problems of hot-metal composition while introducing some new problems of its own—notably the problem of making corrections, for which entirely new techniques had to be worked out.

Some of the advantages of phototypesetting may include a variety of type sizes from a single font, greater variety of characters within a font, quicker change of fonts, better fit between characters (full kerning of italics, for example), relief from the storage of large quantities of type metal, relief from the danger of losing or running out of certain characters, faster keyboard action, the ability to set wider lines, the ability to place any accent over any character.

Progress has been slow, however, in finding economic methods of converting photocomposition into the kind of plates needed for printing on letterpress equipment.

Photo Typositor A photolettering machine offering the ability to set type in

The Photo Typositor.

sizes from 9 to 144 pt from a single master font costing $15. Type can also be slanted, condensed or expanded, shadowed, tinted, etc. Scripts can be perfectly corrected because each letter becomes visible to the operator immediately after exposure. 600 fonts are available, and any fonts available on 2-in. film can be used. The Photo Typositor is offered on a rental basis ($17.50 a week) by the Visual Graphics Corporation, 305 E. 46 St., New York.

pi, pie   Type that has been pied is type that has been spilled. Badly pied type must be entirely reset. Occasionally a printer will pi a complete form while lifting it onto the press.

pica   See also TYPE MEASUREMENTS.

Printers measure the width and depth of columns, the length of lines, etc., in picas instead of in inches. A pica is 12 points (see POINT), or almost exactly ⅙ in.

This book has been set in 9-pt type on a 13-pica line, with 1½ picas between columns. The columns are 43 picas deep. Paper, margins, and engravings, however, are measured in inches. The page size is said to be 6 by 9 in., and the one-column illustrations have a maximum width of 2⅛ in.

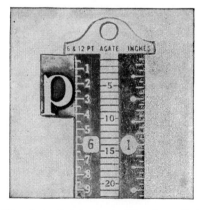

This piece of type is 4 picas deep. It is therefore 48-pt type (4 x 12 = 48).

A pica typewriter is one that writes 10 characters or spaces to the inch. Its name derives from the fact that its letters are 1 pica high, 6 lines to the inch. (What is now called 12-pt type used to be called "pica.") A typewriter with elite type also writes 6 lines to the inch. It differs from a pica typewriter only in that there are 12 elite characters to the horizontal inch as against 10 pica characters.

A pica rule is a ruler with at least one edge measuring in picas and points. A particularly helpful ruler is one that shows picas on one edge and inches on the other, with the calibration of each extended to the middle of the line to permit reading both scales instantly. A sturdy vinylite ruler of this kind is available at $2.50 from The Type Aids Co., 693 Woodbine Dr., San Rafael, Calif.

picking   Papers that are too fluffy or badly made sometimes "pick" on the press, meaning that paper fibers get picked up by the inked type or plates and transferred to the ink rollers. The same result is also caused by the use of ink that is too tacky. Picking forces the printer to wash his ink rollers and form frequently. The chief remedy is to avoid buying highly bulked paper. (See BULK.)

pictograph   See PICTORIAL STATISTICS.

pictorial statistics   When comparative figures must be given about a specific subject, many writers and editors prefer pictorial statistics to the bars, curves, or "wedges of pie" used in more conventional graphs.

Pictorial statistics have several advantages:

1. The subject is immediately apparent because self-explanatory symbols are used. A simplified drawing of a shock of wheat becomes a symbol to represent 100,000 bu.

2. Comparisons are more indelibly impressed on the reader because they

THE WORKER'S DAY
IN MANUFACTURING AND MECHANICAL ESTABLISHMENTS

(Each clock face represents 2 hours of the day.)

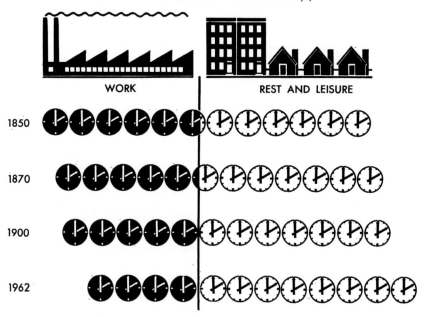

A typical use of pictorial statistics. *(Courtesy of the Pictograph Corporation, 80 W. 40 St., New York.)*

are made by varying the quantities of symbols. A row of 10 easily counted shocks of wheat may represent the crop of one nation and another row of 4 shocks the crop of another nation. Two bars of different length, as used on a conventional chart, might cover the same comparison, but they might also represent a change in railroad mileage, or savings accounts, or production of prunes, since identification depends upon the accompanying caption and description.

Certain warnings should be given in the use of pictorial statistics:

1. Symbols should be simple, self-explanatory, and easily recognized.

2. Larger quantities should be shown by more symbols representing standard units rather than by larger symbols.

3. Pictorial statistics should be used for comparative quantities, not single statements of fact.

4. Only approximate details should be shown pictorially. Symbols do not lend themselves to being sliced into minute fractions.

5. The spaces between rows of symbols should always be greater than the spaces between symbols within a single row.

6. Too many changes, very large changes, very small changes or differences cannot be shown effectively.

Pictographs are available on sheets (Picto-Pak) of pressure-sensitive paper from the Pictograph Corporation, 80 W. 40 St., New York 18, and from Chart-Pak, Inc., One River Rd., Leeds, Mass.

The Pictograph Corporation handles all types of graphic presentation work, including maps of all kinds, and specializes in converting statistical material into pictorial form. The company conducts research through its own staff and also works from material furnished by clients, develops graphic presentations, and executes finished artwork.

pictures See ARTISTS; CARTOONS; CUT; DRAWING TECHNIQUES; ILLUSTRATIONS; PHOTO AGENCIES; PHOTOGRAPHERS; PHOTOGRAPHS: HOW TO SELECT; PHOTOGRAPHY.

pied See PI.

pinks Pink proofs, or pinks, are sometimes submitted by printers for use in dummying. The color serves to distinguish them from the white master proofs on which corrections must be made. The color has the disadvantage of making it hard to get a visual impression of how a paste-up dummy will look when printed. (See PASTE-UP DUMMY.)

planography One of the five basic methods of printing. (See PRINTING.) Its important commercial applications are photo-offset lithography (see OFFSET), photogelatin (see PHOTOGELATIN), hectograph (see HECTOGRAPH), and xerography (see XEROX).

The word "planography" is sometimes applied to cheap offset reproduction work, as though the process in question were somehow different from offset lithography. There is no difference.

"Plane-ography" means printing from a plane (flat) surface. Ink is applied to the entire surface, but because the surface is chemically treated, the ink adheres only where it is wanted. (Since the hectograph process does not follow this procedure strictly, it is sometimes regarded as a sixth basic method of printing, even though it prints from a plane surface. Xerography also is sometimes viewed as a separate method.)

The planographic principle was discovered by Aloys Senefelder in 1796, when he invented lithography. After drawing on a flat limestone surface with a grease pencil, he applied acid to make the stone receptive to water wherever it was unprotected by the grease-pencil drawing. Then he wet the stone and treated the image areas (which had been protected from the acid treatment) to make them receptive to printer's ink. He could now apply grease-based ink to the whole surface, and it would be rejected by the wet areas and accepted only in the image areas.

Paper was now laid on the stone, rubbed, and removed. It picked up ink, exactly duplicating (mirrorwise) the design originally drawn on the stone in grease pencil. Senefelder thus made the first lithograph (from *lithos*, meaning "stone") by the planographic process.

Artists still use this method, although in commercial work, the heavy stones have long since given way to lightweight plates of sheet zinc or aluminum, grained to resemble the surface texture of stones.

The old method of hand copying on the stone with a greasy lithographic pencil has also given way to modern photographic transfer methods. Since the plates wore out quickly when pressed directly against the paper, another improvement has been the perfection of the "offset" technique whereby the ink is first printed on a rubber-blanketed roller, from which it is offset onto the paper.

An example of planography. When ink passes over the plate, it adheres only to the part showing the letter or type.

A later application of the plano-graphic principle came with the discovery of the photogelatin process, sometimes called "collotype." In this process, a film of gelatin is chemically treated so that, where strong light falls on it, it becomes less receptive to moisture than where shielded from light. Thus, the drier areas that received more light accept more greasy ink. Halftone subjects may be reproduced without the use of a screen. (See PHOTOGELATIN.)

plastic bindings. See MECHANICAL BIND-INGS.

plastic plates See also DUPLICATE PLATES.

Plastic plates are often specified instead of mats, stereotypes, or electrotypes in newspaper advertising work. Some of the advantages claimed for them are as follows:

1. They cost less than electros.
2. They give results of high quality and do not stretch or shrink as mats may do.
3. They have a low mailing weight.
4. When they are sent out to newspapers in place of mats, the newspaper can mold its full-page mat directly from them instead of first casting a flat stereo from a mat and then molding from this.

Some printers have been slow in accepting them, perhaps through unfamiliarity with certain peculiarities such as their susceptibility to damage by heat and some kinds of type cleaners. The Government Printing Office has made very successful use of them. Several book manufacturers are using them for printing purposes. Plastic plates can be nailed, sawed, sheared, routed, and drilled like metal plates.

The process of making plastic plates is very similar to that used for making mats and stereos. However, a sheet of thermosetting phenolic plastic is used instead of the paper mat; and granulated thermoplastic molding compound is used instead of melted stereo metal.

The process compares in speed favorably with stereotyping.

plateless engraving Some printers advertise plateless engraving when they really mean "thermography." (See THERMOGRAPHY.)

platen press A printing press in which a flat surface bearing the paper is pressed against a flat surface bearing the inked type. Small handpresses are generally platen presses, as distinct from cylinder presses or rotary presses. (See PRINTING PRESSES.)

plate proofs Proofs taken from stereotypes, electrotypes or other duplicate plates. Usually such proofs are neither requested nor supplied; instead the customer checks only foundry proofs. (See FOUNDRY PROOFS.) Plate proofs are most necessary when the plates are complicated; for example, when halftones and type from different original engravings are to be combined into a single duplicate plate. In such a case the chance for error makes the checking of plate proofs desirable.

plates See also CUT; DUPLICATE PLATES.

All printing is done from a master surface of some sort that determines which parts of the paper are to receive ink. Except when these surfaces are made up of individual pieces or slugs of type, they are called "plates." Thus there are metal and paper offset plates, gravure plates, photogelatin plates, and glass photographic plates.

There are also letterpress (relief) printing plates, but the word "plate" in ordinary letterpress printing usually means a duplicate plate (stereotype, electrotype, plastic plate, rubber plate, etc.). (See DUPLICATE PLATES.) Original plates for letterpress printing are usually called cuts or engravings. (See CUT.)

Some plates are made directly; for example, when an artist cuts a linoleum block or draws with a grease pencil on a lithographic plate. Others are made by more roundabout ways, often requiring that type be set, proofs pulled, proofs photographed, the photographic image transferred to metal, and the metal etched or chemically treated.

The so-called "plateless" printing is really done from an offset plate. It is plateless only in the sense that letterpress cuts and engravings are not required. Plateless "engraving" is done by letterpress from type, instead of by the intaglio process from a subsurface engraved plate. (See THERMOGRAPHY; ENGRAVING.)

point See also LEADING; TYPE MEASUREMENTS.

In measuring type sizes, 1 point is ½₂ pica, or ½₂ in. (0.01384 in. to be exact). In measuring the thickness of bristolboard, mounting board, etc., a point is ⅟₁₀₀₀ in.

These lines are set in 9-pt type, which means that the distance from the top of the highest ascender or capital letter to the bottom of the lowest descender is 9 pt, or ⅛ in. This paragraph is set in 9 pt solid, i.e., with no space between the lines.

This paragraph is set in 9-pt type leaded 2 pt. The same results would have been achieved if the linotyper had been asked to cast 9-pt letters on an 11-pt body—"set 9 on 11."

The text of this book is "set 9 on 10," meaning the 9-pt type is leaded 1 pt.

This is a 1-pt rule:

———————————

This is a 6-pt. rule:

██████████████

Both rules are 72 pt long (1 in.), but it is more common to say that they are 6 picas long.

Postcards are commonly printed on bristolboard which is 6 pt thick, meaning 0.006 in.

positive See NEGATIVE.

postage See Appendix 3, Postal Information.

postage-meter machines See "Metered Postage" in Appendix 3, Postal Information.

postage saver See ENVELOPES; also Appendix 3, Postal Information.

postal information See Appendix 3.

postcards See also Appendix 3, Postal Information.

One good source for picture postcards in natural color is the Dexter Press, Inc., West Nyack, N.Y., which will send samples and price list on request. The price for natural-color postcards, size 3½ by 5½ from your 4 by 5 transparency, is under 3 cents each in lots of 3,000, under 2 cents each in lots of 6,000. Business cards in full color, size 3¼ by 3½, cost a bit less. Giant postcards, size 6 by 9, cost about half again as much.

posters See also OUTDOOR ADVERTISING; TRANSIT ADVERTISING; CIRCULARS; SIGNS.

Posters are most often produced by hand, by silk screen, or by offset, depending on the quantity. (See SILK SCREEN; OFFSET.)

A printer having only letterpress equipment may be able to handle a small poster run satisfactorily if it is possible to use all type (no pictures) and to use only the type that he has on hand. If the poster is to have hand-lettering and decorations or illustrations, silk screen and offset firms can usually prepare the surfaces from which to print more economically than can the letterpress firm. They can usually offer more attractive results for less money.

When 1 to 10 copies of a poster are needed, it is best to consult a sign painter or show-card writer. (See SIGNS; EMBOSOGRAF.)

When 10 to 100 copies of a poster are needed, it is probably most economical to produce them by the silkscreen process. (See SILK SCREEN.) Many sign painters have silk-screen equipment.

When 100 to 1,000 copies are needed, the silk-screen process is probably the best, but offset begins to be a possibility.

Above 1,000 copies probably—certainly above 5,000—offset will be more economical than silk screen. (See OFFSET.)

For example, the car cards used in buses and trolleys are usually done in silk screen if used locally; in offset if used in bigger quantities by national advertisers.

Photographs can be handled by the silk-screen method, but the results leave something to be desired. Posters containing photographs are usually reproduced in offset. (For the highest quality of reproduction of photographs, see PHOTOGELATIN or GRAVURE.) Sometimes it pays to reproduce a photograph by offset, photogelatin, or gravure, and add additional color by silk screen.

Very small type does not reproduce well in the silk-screen process. Silk screen is unexcelled, however, for handling rich, solid colors.

Posters should be planned with regard to the space requirements at the point of display and the problem of shipment or delivery. The size should be such as to cut without waste from standard sizes of poster cardboard, 22 by 28, 14 by 22, 11 by 14, 11 by 28.

It is cheaper to print posters on paper than on cardboard if paper will do. There may be an advantage in printing on paper and then mounting a desired number of posters on cardboard with or without easel. (See MOUNTING AND FINISHING.)

For variety, posters can be built around ad reprints, photographs, photostats, etc. They can be cut into special shapes. (See DIE CUTTING.)

Comparatively low-priced full-color posters can be made by enlargement if the artwork has already been reproduced in a small size. For example, book posters can be enlarged from book jackets in this way. An offset printer makes poster plates by enlargement from black-ink proofs of the plates used for the small-size job.

For simplicity and economy, poster colors should be few, bold, and flat, i.e., not shaded or blended. A poster in full process color is usually prohibitively expensive unless the number to be ordered is very large. On the other hand, it is not very expensive to have a small color print from a circular, book jacket, or ad mounted on a poster.

Help in designing a poster can often be obtained from the firm that is to do the printing. Silk-screen houses are particularly likely to have an artist on the staff, since they make most of their printing surfaces by hand, and not photomechanically like other printers. (See ARTISTS; DESIGN.)

It is often argued that a good poster must be able to get its message across to a commuter sprinting for the morning train. That is not a bad standard to strive for, but unfortunately all messages are not that simple and brief.

A good poster ought to arouse interest at first glance and must be readable over whatever distances are involved in its display, but there would seem to be no good reason why it should not have as much small type as can be kept interesting. It is only necessary that the poster with small type should be displayed where people will have the time to read it and can get near enough to do so.

See Appendix 2, Bibliography, for books on advertising, artwork, and color.

powderless etching A process for making engravings which prevents undercutting without the use of powdered resin.

precanceled postage See Appendix 3, Postal Information.

press book See CLIPSHEET.

pressings See RECORDINGS.

press proofs See PROOFS.

press release See PUBLICITY RELEASE.

presswork The operation of putting the ink on the paper. Most printing jobs consist of (1) composition, (2) presswork, (3) binding. The work of the pressman divides into makeready and running time. (See MAKEREADY.)

prices See ESTIMATING COSTS; SAVING MONEY.

print See PRINTING; PHOTOGRAPHY.

printed indicia See "Permit Imprints" in Appendix 3, Postal Information.

printers: how to choose See also PRINTING.

There are two important elements in choosing a printer: (1) determining the process to be used (see inside front cover) and (2) finding a printer who works in that process, who is skilled in it, and whose equipment, prices, and standards of workmanship are right.

The names and addresses of several printers are given under various entries in this book. Such mention does not imply endorsement of the firms mentioned nor a belief that they are in any way to be preferred to firms that are not mentioned. Names have been given simply for the convenience of readers who may not be able to find a desired specialized service in their own town or who do not have ready access to a Classified Telephone Directory of one of the big printing centers.

The right printer is one who meets the following specifications:

1. He does a lot of the kind of work that you seek and has the right equipment for it. (There are some advantages in dealing with a printer who does not have to give out too many operations to other firms.)

2. His standards of workmanship are acceptable.

3. His prices and terms compare favorably with market prices. (Allowances must be made for differences in service, of course.)

4. He has a union shop. This is important when a union label is desired. (See UNION LABEL.)

NOTE: Printers who run night shifts every night can usually do faster work.

The most satisfactory way to buy printing is to deal consistently with one printer. Printers should be changed no less thoughtfully than employees are changed. If the work is varied, it may not be possible to find one printer who is equipped to handle all printing processes. However, it should still be possible to settle on one letterpress printer, one silk-screen printer, one lettershop, one offset printer, etc., getting competitive bids only occasionally in order to be sure that prices are in line.

The practice of getting bids on every job and taking the lowest is required in some organizations, but it is not a satisfactory way to work, for the following reasons:

1. Letting bids wastes time and slows delivery.

2. In order to let bids, the buyer must specify every detail in advance. He thus cuts himself off from an opportunity to make those minor money-saving changes in the specifications which a good printer might suggest. If the low bidder has made any changes in the specifications, his bid must be thrown out, or bids must be relet, or else there was little point in getting bids in the first place.

3. Printers do not like to do business on a basis of having to bid on every job. Some of the best ones may not trouble to enter such a competition.

4. Printers who get only an occasional job are less inclined to give special service when favors are needed.

5. A printer can give faster, cheaper service to a regular customer than to an occasional buyer for the simple reason that his men have learned that customer's preferences and way of working. This is why periodicals can be printed more cheaply than occasional booklets of similar design.

A good compromise between bids and no bids is to settle on a scale of prices for certain recurrent types of work—so much per page of composition, so much per 1,000 impressions, so much per extra color, etc. This is possible only when the work is very simple and easy to define, or when the printer has had an opportunity to handle several jobs and know his probable average costs for future work.

printers' measurements   See TYPE MEASUREMENTS.

printing   This is an omnibus word. There are so many kinds of printing processes that the beginner may easily get much confused and despair of ever being able to get them all straight in his mind.

Therefore, this book has been arranged on the principle of one thing at a time. For example, the reader who has a poster problem may find by looking under POSTERS that he probably should use the silk-screen process. Then he can look up SILK SCREEN and ignore the other processes for the time being.

Printing as a whole divides itself into three parts: (1) type composition (typesetting, typing), (2) printing (putting the image on paper), and (3) binding.

Type is still set in much the same way that Gutenberg did it 500 years ago. The process has been improved but is basically unchanged. There have been many attempts to find new ways to set type, but despite such recent developments as the Intertype Fotosetter, and other "cold type," most jobs still begin with getting type set by this one basic method—even if that type will do no more than make one perfect copy for further duplication by a new printing process that Gutenberg never dreamed of. (See TYPE for a discussion of how to convert a manuscript into type ready for printing. See also TYPEWRITER; COPYFITTING; COPY EDITING; DESIGN.)

Printing in its more limited sense of getting the desired image on paper (once that image, whether type or pictures, has been created) is done in five different basic ways. Each basic principle has been adapted to still further specialization. (See table on next page.)

For the five basic principles see RELIEF; PLANOGRAPHY; INTAGLIO; STENCIL; PHOTOGRAPHY. For the commercial applications of those principles— the things to remember when printing is ordered—see such headings as LETTERPRESS; OFFSET; PHOTOGELATIN; GRAVURE; MIMEOGRAPH; SILK SCREEN; PHOTOGRAPHY; DUPLICATING.

References to these processes occur under such headings as CIRCULARS; PAMPHLETS; POSTERS; LETTERS; in an attempt to suggest the best process for any given job.

The most important process for the layman to understand is letterpress (relief) printing, which might be called "ordinary printing." This is of first importance because he will probably have type set as if for letterpress printing, even if using offset or some other process.

Anyone with a clear grasp of letterpress printing will have a much easier time understanding the other processes because he will have to learn only how they *differ* from letterpress.

An elementary understanding of photography is an aid to understanding any printing process because photography is not only a printing process in its own right but is also used, or may be used, in every other process, at least in connection with the illustrations.

THERE ARE FIVE BASIC METHODS OF PRINTING

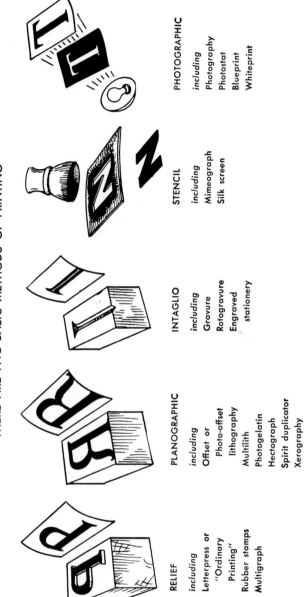

RELIEF

including
**Letterpress or
"Ordinary
Printing"
Rubber stamps
Multigraph**

PLANOGRAPHIC

including
**Offset or
Photo-offset
lithography
Multilith
Photogelatin
Hectograph
Spirit duplicator
Xerography**

INTAGLIO

including
**Gravure
Rotogravure
Engraved
stationery**

STENCIL

including
**Mimeograph
Silk screen**

PHOTOGRAPHIC

including
**Photography
Photostat
Blueprint
Whiteprint**

Information on how drawings and photographs are printed is to be found under HALFTONE; DRAWING TECHNIQUES; etc.

For binding techniques, see BINDING. For books on printing and on specific processes, see Appendix 2, Bibliography. For help in choosing the right printing process, consult the charts inside the covers of this book.

printing brokers Most printers occasionally subcontract work to other printers. They do it when they are too busy to handle a job themselves or when they lack the right equipment but want to help a good customer.

There are some printers, however, who subcontract every job and have no plant of their own. They are not so much printers as brokers. If they know their business, they have the advantage of being able to take every job to a shop ideally equipped to handle it. On the other hand, their work tends, for obvious reasons, to be uneven in quality, and it may not be so easy for them to deliver the miracles that can occasionally be performed for a good customer by a printer having his own shop.

Before starting to deal with a new printer, it is always a good idea to visit his plant and see just what his equipment is.

printing presses The buyer of printing does not have to concern himself with the size, speed, and equipment of the printing presses on which his work will be done, but it may pay him to do so.

There is a perfect or near-perfect printing press for every job. This is true regardless of the printing process used. For greatest economy either the press (and the printer) should be matched to the job, or the job should be designed to fit an available press.

If, for example, a printer has a press that will take a sheet only as large as 17½ by 22½, it would be uneconomical to give him a job 19 by 25 if it could possibly be cut down to 17½ by 22½. He could handle the larger job as two sheets, each 19 by 12½, but would have twice the presswork.

If a printer has a folding attachment for one of his presses, it is well to find out what it can do and plan to use it when possible. Perhaps a 16-page, 6 by 9 unit can be folded right on the press, whereas a 24-page unit would have to be handled as a separate bindery operation.

If a printer has a two-color press, he may be able to offer two-color printing for very little more than the price for one color.

If a printer's presses are all large, it may be foolish to ask him to stop them every few hundred impressions to change an imprint. (See IMPRINTING.) It may be better to give the imprinting work to a printer who has very small presses.

There are two important things to know about any printing press:

1. What is the largest sheet of paper that it will handle?

2. What is the largest area that the printing can occupy on that paper? (Usually, paper cannot be printed right up to the edge, at least not on the gripper edge. See GRIPPER EDGE.)

There is no reason why a small sheet of paper, within reason, cannot be printed on a large press, but the press time will cost as much as for a full-size sheet. Presses are made with capacities varying from label or postcard size up to 52 by 76 in. or even larger.

"Perfector" presses will print on both sides of a sheet of paper in one operation. Multicolor presses will print in two, three, or four colors in one operation. Some big magazine presses will print in four colors on both sides of the paper in one operation.

Many presses have folding attachments so that booklets can be folded and perhaps pasted or stapled as part of the printing operation, thus avoiding separate bindery work. (See BINDING.)

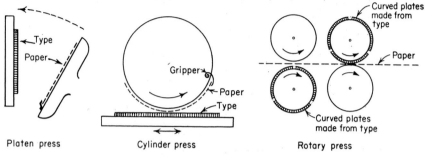

Platen press   Cylinder press   Rotary press

A cylinder press must make two revolutions for each impression. During the second revolution no paper is fed, the cylinder lifts free of the form, and the form slides back to its starting point.

However, trimming the edges of a booklet is usually a separate operation, although some folders will do rough trimming.

Some small presses are hand-fed, but most have automatic feeders. Some presses are "sheet-fed," and some are "web-fed." The sheet-fed presses accept separate sheets of paper. The web-fed presses take paper from a continuous roll and cut it into sheets only after printing it.

Presses are of three types: platen, cylinder, and rotary. Platen and cylinder presses may also be called "flat-bed" presses. Platen presses open and shut like a clamshell. They support the type or plate form on one flat surface and the paper on another, and press them together. Cylinder presses take each sheet of paper, wrap it around a cylinder, and then roll it across a flat surface that supports the inked form. Some cylinder presses hold the form on a horizontal bed; some hold it vertically.

Both platen and cylinder presses run at speeds of 1,000 to 4,000 impressions per hour, with the smaller units capable of the higher speeds.

Rotary presses pass the paper between two pairs of cylinders. In each pair, one cylinder holds curved printing plates while the other acts as an impression surface. Speeds are from 5,000 to 25,000 impressions per hour.

printing-trade customs The prevailing printing-trade customs are listed below. Some points particularly worth noting are as follows:

A printer may decline to release type or plates for use by another printer, e.g., when another printer bids lower on a reprint.

A printer who has furnished ideas but who later loses a job to another bidder may charge for those ideas.

A printer may deliver 10 percent more or less than the amount ordered, and charge accordingly.

If there is any likelihood that a job will have to be rerun, a printer must be specifically instructed to keep the type or plates and may charge for this. However, offset printers usually keep the "flats," from which they can make new plates, for a certain length of time without special instructions.

Printers usually store a customer's paper for a reasonable time without charge, depending somewhat on the extent of the printer's storage facilities.

The trade customs for the printing and lithographic industry as adopted and followed by the printing and lithographic industry of Metropolitan New York are as follows:

Quotations. All quotations are based on work being performed during regular straight-time working hours and conditions prevailing at date of quotations and are subject to amendment or withdrawal at any time prior to the receipt and acknowledgment by the printer or lithographer of any acceptance thereof.

Prices. All prices are based on the written specifications, the work to be begun at once and carried on continuously until completion. Prices on nonestimated work and reprints of both estimated and nonestimated work are subject to change without notice.

Orders. Orders received and accepted by the printer or lithographer cannot be canceled except upon terms that will compensate against loss. The customer guarantees the legal propriety of all matter submitted to the printer or lithographer for production and/or publication; and will indemnify the printer or lithographer against all claims and responsibility arising from the production and/or publication of such matter, including the legal expenses and disbursements incurred by the printer or lithographer in contesting the same.

Experimental work. Experimental work performed on orders, at the customer's request, such as sketches, drawings, composition, camera work, plates, presswork, and materials, whether or not similar to those herein specifically enumerated, will be charged for at current rates.

Sketches and dummies. Sketches, copy, dummies, and all preparatory work created or furnished by the printer or lithographer shall remain his exclusive property, and no use of same shall be made, nor any ideas obtained therefrom be used, except upon compensation to be determined by the owner.

Artwork, type, plates. Including lithographic plates, engravings, electrotypes, negatives, positives, and other items when supplied by the printer or lithographer shall remain his exclusive property.

Proofs. Proofs of type matter, not in excess of two sets, will be submitted with original copy. Corrections, if any, must be plainly written in the margin of the proof and returned with the original copy to the printer or lithographer marked "O.K." or "O.K. as corrected" and signed by the one duly authorized to pass on same. If revised proof is desired, request must be made for the same when the first proof is returned. No responsibility for errors is assumed if work is produced as per customer's "O.K." Lithographic proofs will not be submitted unless specifically enumerated in the proposal.

Alterations. Time consumed by reason of author's alterations of copy, changes in work or materials, delay of presses, and other delays caused by customer will be charged for at current rates. If, through printer's or lithographer's error, work has to be done over, there will be no extra charge, but if, through customer's error or change of instructions, it must be done a second or more times, there will be an additional charge for such extra work. These charges will be made on the basis of current rates for the operation or operations involved.

Standing type matter. All standing type matter held at the customer's request longer than 30 days is subject to a monthly charge for storage. Foundry type cannot be kept standing and will be removed from form after reproduction proofs are pulled and shall be reset, if necessary, at customer's expense.

Press proofs. An additional charge will be made for press proofs when requested unless this form of work is called for when estimate is given. Customer should be present when the form is made ready on the press so that no press time will be lost. Presses standing idle awaiting "O.K." from customer will be charged for at regular production hour rates.

Color proofing. Because of the difference in equipment and conditions between the color proofing and pressroom operations, a reasonable variation in color between color proofs and the completed job shall constitute an acceptable delivery.

Quantity delivered. As it is practically impossible to produce exact quantities, it is agreed that a margin of 10 percent be allowed for over or short count, same to be charged for or deducted at the per-thousand production price, which is the total price of the order, less the preparation expense, prorated per thousand.

Postal cards and stamped envelopes. Since the purchase of postal cards and stamped envelopes involves a cash expenditure, customers must furnish these with their order. If they are not so furnished, an extra charge of 10 percent of their cost will be made to cover additional services in securing them.

Handling paper stock. A charge will be made for receiving, opening, and handling of paper stock supplied by the customer. An additional charge will be made for paper that requires conditioning and/or causes lost time on presses or other equipment because of poor quality or condition of the paper.

Storage charges for paper stock. A monthly storage charge will be made on all stock held by the printer or lithographer longer than 30 days.

Customer's property. All photographs, artwork, engravings, electrotypes, film, flats, and/or plates, paper and other property are held at customer's risk, and printer or lithographer assumes no responsibility for loss or damage by fire, water, or from any other cause, whether or not similar to those herein specifically enumerated.

Plate storage. A monthly storage charge will be made for the storage of all customer's engravings, electrotypes, films, flats, and/or lithographic plates.

Delivery. Unless otherwise specified, price quoted is F.O.B. customer's sidewalk. All estimates are based on continuous and uninterrupted delivery of complete order, unless specifications specifically state otherwise.

Terms. Net cash, unless otherwise

provided in writing. Interest charged on past-due accounts. All claims must be made within five days of receipt of goods.

Agreements. All agreements are made and all orders accepted contingent upon strikes, fires, accidents, war, unusual market conditions, or other conditions beyond printer's or lithographer's control, whether or not similar to those herein specifically enumerated.

Arbitration. All claims, demands, disputes, differences, or controversies and misunderstanding arising under, out of, or in connection with, or in relation to any agreement entered into between printer or lithographer and customer shall be submitted to and be determined by ARBITRATION, pursuant to the Arbitration Law of the State of New York, before the Board of Commercial Arbitration of the Federation of Graphic Arts and Allied Industries of New York City, or in the Tribunal of Justice known as the Court of Arbitration, established and conducted by the American Arbitration Association, and in accordance with its Rules.

process-coated paper   See MACHINE-COATED PAPER.

process color   See also COLOR PRINTING.

Process color, as opposed to "flat color," is the method used to reproduce true-to-life, full-color originals. Although the work is usually done with only four inks—black, yellow, blue, and red—these may be combined by means of the process-color technique to reproduce most of the browns, grays, greens, purples, oranges, etc., that may be in the original. Sometimes more than four colors are used, especially in offset.

Process-color work is expensive, but there is no other way of obtaining faithful reproductions of color photographs and full-color paintings. Not only is the cost of running a job in four colors likely to be at least four times the cost of running it in one color, an even greater expense is involved in the making of the color separations from which the printing plates will be made; and color separations are required, whether they are to be used in making plates for letterpress, offset, photogelatin, gravure, or rotogravure.

In color printing, letterpress has generally been regarded as the most dependable process, that is to say, the process least likely to show variations in quality from the first to the last copies. However, letterpress requires the use of coated paper. This is no particular disadvantage, costwise, since coated paper has long since ceased to cost significantly more than uncoated paper, but the shiny surface is often regarded as undesirable, and *dull*-coated paper does tend to be costly. The other processes can print on uncoated papers.

The quality of color printing varies greatly. In general, you get what you pay for, though it is all too easy to pay for top quality and not get it. And it is possible to pay cut-rate prices and get acceptable results, at least if the original either presents fewer color-correction problems than usual or simply is not of a nature where full fidelity matters.

Although the theory of color separation is fairly easily stated, it is difficult to apply in practice due to the fact that almost none of the printer's materials quite delivers the performance that is theoretically required of them. Even the best inks and filters are less than perfectly monochromatic, and no paper is perfectly white or completely reflective. Even the printer's best blacks are less than totally black. Compromise is therefore inevitable as the printer strives to compress the full range of tones in the original between the limitations set for him by his paper and ink. Color separations made mechanically usually require some further adjustment to the special requirements of the original, usually by means of hand retouching on the color separations prior to the screening of these separations. This handwork is highly skilled and time-consuming, and it is one of the major reasons why process plates cost so much.

A number of approaches have been taken to the problem of reducing or eliminating the work of color correction in separation negatives. Some employ special "masking" techniques. Some, such as the Time-Life scanner, tackle the problem electronically. Essentially, the electronic approach scans the original, splits the light prismatically and converts it into three electric currents representing the three primary colors, causes these currents to modify each other for correct color balance, and finally creates color separations ready for platemaking. Sometimes (depending to a great extent on the nature of the original), the machine-made separations can be used with little if any further correction; usually additional color-correction is called for. Other electronic scanners are the Fairchild and the Klischograph.

Top-quality color separation is expensive, no matter how it is done. In a great deal of work, however, the aim is not so much *fidelity* to the original, which can be elusive, as simply a pleasing result. For example, a shoe advertisement that is slightly off-color may yet be entirely acceptable, where an ad for a slightly off-color beef stew might be repulsive.

A number of firms specialize in supplying low-cost four-color separations "to the trade." A set of four-color screen positives made from a 4- by 5-in. transparency for reproduction in size 6 by 9 can be obtained for about $40 from World Color, Inc., Box 697, Ormond Beach, Fla.; Shelton Color Corporation, 16 Lafayette St., Hackensack, N.J.; and New Horizons Color Corp., 2717 W. Lawrence Ave., Chicago.

A somewhat less expensive but often satisfactory substitute for process-color work is fake process work. (See FAKE PROCESS.)

Special inks are used in process-color

work. The yellow is a bright canary shade. The blue is a rather pale robin's-egg shade. The red is rather bluish. In any form that contains a process-color illustration, it is also possible to use one or more of these inks "flat," perhaps for a border, a headline, or a tint block. The results are often disappointing, however, since only the yellow is the kind of color one would deliberately choose for such purposes. To get a good carnation red or vermilion, it is necessary to print a yellow tint under process red. To get a good blue, heavy enough to use for a headline, it is necessary to add some black or a little red to the process blue.

Most process-color work is four-color work. Some of it, however, is done in as many as 15 colors, or in as few as 3, omitting the black. Theoretically black is not necessary, but it gives added sharpness to the final results.

The procedure for making four-color process-color printing plates is to take four photographs of the original painting, color photograph, or scene. Transparent colored "filters" are placed in the lens barrel of the camera for three of the shots. One lets through all but yellow light, one lets through all but red light, and the third lets through all but blue light.

The resulting photographic negatives are called "separation negatives." From them are made four printing plates, one of which will be printed in yellow, one in blue, one in red, and one in black. (See SEPARATION NEGATIVES.)

In theory, process-color printing can be done on any printing equipment capable of doing just the same kind of artwork in black and white. In practice, it can be quite difficult to do successful four-color work, one color at a time, on offset presses due to the tendency of the paper to absorb moisture and stretch between one impression and the next, which creates an impossible problem of registering one impression with its predecessors. This particular problem is less acute in letterpress and may not be serious when comparatively small sheets are being handled.

process letters   See also AUTOMATIC TYPEWRITER; ADDRESSING; LETTERS.

A process letter is a high-quality printed form letter made to be indistinguishable from a personally typed letter.

Process letters are printed through an inked ribbon on a regular printing press. Then the name and address of the recipient and other personalizing information are added by typewriter. Great care is taken to make the filled-in material align properly with the printed material, to use a typewriter ribbon that matches the ribbon used on the press, and to use identical type styles.

Process letters are considerably cheaper than automatically typed letters (see AUTOMATIC TYPEWRITER), and many users find them just as satisfactory. Furthermore, large quantities can be produced much more quickly.

The producers of process letters pride themselves on turning out a product that will fool experts. They charge accordingly. Cheaper fill-in work is procurable from lettershops having Multigraph equipment, but more often than not it will not really pass for personally typed work.

The term "process letter" denotes a standard of quality, rather than any special process. Most process-letter work is done on flatbed presses, apparently because this kind of equipment has proved more satisfactory in the long run than the Multigraph equipment used for ordinary filled-in letters. Many firms having Multigraph equipment advertise "perfectly matched fill-in work." If their work really is indistinguishable from personally typed work, it hardly matters how they do it. However, many shops that promise perfect fill-in work (also many shops that advertise "process-letter" work, for that matter) do not deliver perfect work.

Many lettershops are beginning to favor the Multilith as a means of putting a facsimile blue-ink signature on a form letter. They claim improved results over the Multigraph method of using a rubber signature plate.

A few firms doing process-letter work include New Era Letter Co., Inc., 495 Broadway, New York; James Gray Hooven-Nahm, Inc., 216 E. 45 St., New York; Doolittle & Company, 320 N. Dearborn St., Chicago; Reuben H. Donnelley Corp., 235 E. 42 St., New York. (For information on prices, see table under LETTERS.)

process plates See PROCESS COLOR.

production A production man, in publishing and printing circles, is one who is responsible for getting things printed, i.e., produced or reproduced. The word "production" is often used interchangeably with "printing."

progressive proofs See PROCESS COLOR.

In process-color printing, four plates must be made: yellow, red, blue, and black. Proofs from these plates, made singly and in combination, are called "progressive proofs."

A set of four-color progressive proofs show (1) yellow plate, (2) red plate, (3) yellow and red plates printed together, (4) blue plate, (5) yellow, red, and blue plates printed together, (6) black plate, (7) yellow, red, blue, and black plates printed together.

This order is not always followed. Sometimes the black plate is omitted, especially in gravure. Sometimes more colors and more plates are used, especially in offset lithography.

proofreading See also COPY PREPARATION; PROOFS.

At the various stages of setting type, making up pages, and producing cuts and plates, the printer sends proofs back to the editor for careful scrutiny, for comparison with the original copy, and for possible corrections and revision.

In most cases, proofs that reach the editor have already been read carefully by the printer's proofreader and bear his marks. Usually there are three sets of proofs, in this order: (1) galley proofs, (2) page proofs, and perhaps (3) engraver's proofs of any cuts. (See PROOFS.)

If the printer is working on a close schedule, he is justified in expecting the corrected proofs to be returned promptly. However, accuracy is of paramount importance in proofreading and should not be sacrificed to speed.

With each set of proofs the printer should return (and may have to be reminded to send) either the original copy or the previously corrected proofs for comparison. When proofreading is completed by the author and editor, all of this same material goes back to the printer as a record of corrections and alterations. The proofreader should be careful never to alter either the original copy or the proofs that have been the basis for the printer's last work. Corrections are made on the new proofs only.

The master set of proofs is the set that will go back to the printer with all corrections. Duplicate sets are retained by the editor or author for his files or, in the case of galley proofs, for use in pasting up the dummy. (See PASTE-UP DUMMY.)

How to read proof. Proofreading usually involves two people: one "to hold," reading aloud from the original manuscript or last proofs, and the other to make corrections on the new proofs. The experienced proofreader sees each letter of a word rather than the image of the word as a whole. This means that he is alert to the possible omission or inclusion of a single letter and catches the slightest error in typesetting.

Although the chief job of the proofreader is to mark typographical errors, he should also be on the lookout for

PROOFREADER'S MARKS

Marginal sign	Mark in text	Meaning	Corrected text
ℐ	Proofreading/	Delete, take out letter or word	Proofreading
ℰ	Legibil/ity is	Delete and close up	Legibility is
first	the‸requirement	Insert marginal addition	the first requirement
◠	of a proof reader's marks.	Close up entirely	of a proofreader's marks.
⌣	Symbols should be	Less space	Symbols should be
⊥	made‸neatly and	Push space down to avoid printing	made neatly and
#	in‸line with	Add space	in line with
eq #	the ˇtext ˇto‸which	Space evenly	the text to which
¶	they refer.⌐ Place	New paragraph	they refer.
no ¶	marks carefully.⌐	No new paragraph	Place marks
	⌐Paragraphs may be		carefully. Paragraphs may be
☐	☐ indented one em	Indent one em	indented one em
☐☐	☐☐ two ems or (rarely)	Indent two ems	two ems or (rarely)
☐☐☐	☐☐☐ three ems. Head-	Indent three ems	three ems.
⊏	⊏ings are flush left	Move to the left	Headings are flush left
⊐	or flush right⎯⎯	Move to the right	or flush right
⊐⊏	⊐ or centered ⊏	Center	or centered
⊔	Mar‿ginal marks	Lower to proper position	Marginal marks
⊓	are ‿separated	Raise to proper position	are separated
X	by vertical	Replace defective letter	by vertical
⃝	lines. ⌐The first correction	Invert this letter	lines. The first correction
w f	in a ⌐line of type	Wrong font; change to proper face	in a line of type
tr	is ⌐beside⌐noted⌐ the	Transpose	is noted beside the
?	nearest ⌐bend of the line.	Is this correct?	nearest end of the line
Sp	and the ⃝2nd⃝ next.	Spell out	and the second, next.
	⃝in this way⃝ both margins	Transfer to position shown by arrow.	both margins are used in
	are used⌐		this way
b f	English Finish	Change to boldface type	**English Finish**
b f ital	English Finish	Change to boldface italics	***English Finish***
rom	*galley* proof	Set in roman type	galley proof
ital	is laid paper	Set in italics	is *laid* paper

PROOFREADER'S MARKS (continued)

Marginal sign	Mark in text	Meaning	Corrected text
u c	Book of type	Set in upper case, or capital	Book of Type
Caps	Book Papers	Set in large capitals	BOOK PAPERS
s c	BOOK PAPERS	Change to small capitals	BOOK PAPERS
c s c	Book Papers	Initial large capitals; other letters, small capitals	BOOK PAPERS
l c	the first Type	Change to lower case or small letter	the first type
x	base-ball player	Broken type	baseball player
Stet	to the editors	Retain crossed out word	to the editors
ᶜ	Water, HO	Insert inferior figure	Water, H_2O
ᵛ	$X^2 \div Y^2 = Z$	Insert superior figure	$X^2 \div Y^2 = Z^2$
≡	printed	Straighten line	printed
‖	The paper / The ink / The type	Align type	The paper / The ink / The type
ld	prepare copy and submit it	Insert lead between lines	prepare copy and submit it
hr #	PAPER	Hair space between letters	PAPER
⊙	to the printer	Insert period	to the printer.
⋏	the proof but	Insert comma	the proof, but
; *or* ;/	excellent it is	Insert semicolon	excellent; it is
: *or* ⊙	to the following	Insert colon	to the following:
ᵛ	authors notes	Insert apostrophe	author's notes
ᵛ/ᵛ	called caps	Insert quotation marks	called "caps"
-/*or* =	halftone	Insert hyphen	half-tone
em	Robert Henderson	Insert em dash	—Robert Henderson
en	1939 1940	Insert en dash	1939–1940
?	"Where" she asked.	Insert question mark	"Where?" she asked.
!	"Stop" he cried.	Insert exclamation mark	"Stop!" he cried.
(/)	author see page 2	Insert parentheses	author (see page 2)
[/]	To be continued	Insert brackets	[To be continued]

errors in grammar, punctuation, capitalization, spelling, word division, indention, and spacing.

An invaluable reference guide for the professional proofreader to have at his side is Joseph Lasky's "Proofreading and Copy-preparation," listed in Appendix 2, Bibliography.

If a manuscript has not had careful copy preparation before being sent to the printer, the proofreading of the galleys is more difficult and correspondingly more important. (See COPY PREPARATION.)

The proofreader is expected to note any differences between the original manuscript, or last proof, and the new proof and to call the author's attention to any unanswered queries on the manuscript. In addition, he should be on guard to correct whatever errors or inconsistencies may have been left uncorrected in the original manuscript and hence appear in the proof. As alterations in proof cost money, changes should be made only after careful consideration and in the most economical way. (See AUTHOR'S ALTERATIONS.)

21—School Execu

School Executive —Editorial
SLUG—MORE NEWS

Film Council Plans
Year's Activities

At a year-end meeting held in Washington, the Film Council of America planned a vigorous program of activities for 1947. Working as an overall organization and through its constituent groups the organization will

1. Continue to support strongly the use of films for international understanding both through the procedures developed by UNESCO and the United Nations.

2. Develop a program of publications and reports through the council and cooperating agencies.

3. Recommend a thorough study by the Library of Congress Motion Picture Project of ways and means to effect better and more expeditious distribution of government-made films and to recommend standardized charges.

4. Effect a close liaison relationship with local and state groups interested in the visual education and adult education fields.

Present at the meeting were representatives of national, government, and private agencies. Film Council President C. R. Reagan, Austin, Texas, was chairman of the meeting.

The careful proofreader would not afflict his printer with the above galley. He would avoid entangling guidelines connecting marginal notes to corrections within the text, and he would write legibly but small enough to get his note beside the line to which it refers. For a neatly marked galley, see *copy preparation*.

How to indicate corrections. Anyone who deals with publications, either in preparing copy for the printer or in proofreading and makeup (see MAKE-UP), must be familiar with the indispensable tools of his trade—the standard proofreader's marks reproduced in the tables on pages 268 and 269. These are specific directions to the printer and hence must be legible and their reference to the text must be absolutely clear. Each alteration requires two marks: one in the text and one in the margin. Textual marks should not obliterate the printing. Marginal signs should be placed at the end of the line containing the word to be corrected. Such signs should be large enough to be legible, but not so large as to invade the space beside other lines.

When two or more alterations must be made within a line, marginal signs may be made in both margins. If there are several marks side by side in one margin, they are separated by a vertical line. The first sign is placed at the edge of the printing and others in order toward the edge of the paper.

When the proofreader is satisfied that he has made all corrections and has answered all queries from the printer, he should initial each page of the proofs.

Correcting page proofs. The corrected galleys should be used as the first check on the page proofs to see that the indicated alterations have been made. Since the correction of even one letter or comma may mean resetting a whole line, it is necessary to scrutinize the entire line, not just a single word, and check nearby lines that may have got out of correct order. If the error is early in the paragraph, the whole paragraph should be proofread as though entirely new copy.

On page proofs where the type from the galleys has been divided into columns and pages, the proofreader may have to expand or cut copy to avoid beginning a column or page with a single short line. (See WIDOW.)

At this stage he must also see that each cut is in the right position with its designated caption and credit line. Page numbers should be inserted in the cross-references and in any lines "Continued from page _____" and "Continued on page _____."

Another special check should be made at this time to see that headings and by-lines have been correctly placed with their own chapters or stories. Every letter of every heading should be scrutinized with a seeing eye since typographical errors take a fiendish delight in creeping into the display lettering or large type of a title and subhead.

Correcting engraver's proofs. The proofreader must be sure that the reproduction is of acceptable quality, of proper screen and free from blemishes, that the size is right, and that crop marks have been followed accurately.

proofs   See also PROOFREADING; DUMMY.

A proof is a trial impression taken from type or plates at each stage of the printing process. There may be

  Galley proofs (of type)
  Revised galley proofs
  Engraver's proofs (of illustrations)
  Page proofs (of type and illustrations)
  Revised page proofs
  Foundry proofs (if stereotypes or electrotypes are to be made)
  Stone proofs (of all pages that are to be printed at once)
  Press proofs

This is the order of business in letterpress printing, although one or more stages may be skipped. In offset, gravure, and photogelatin, page proofs are followed by reproduction proofs (perfect proofs intended to be photographed), and blueprints or vandyke prints may be supplied instead of engraver's proofs or stone proofs if requested.

Small "proof presses" operated by hand are used for the "pulling" of proofs. Ordinarily proofs are made with just enough care to make them legible, but with no attempt to make them perfect. The quality of a job should not be judged by the preliminary proofs, except in the case of engraver's proofs and reproduction proofs, which must be perfect. Printers automatically supply a minimum number of copies of each set of proofs (usually two) and charge extra for additional copies required by the customer.

Galley proofs. Usually called "galleys," these are pulled from type after it has been set but before it has been organized into separate pages. They take their name from the long narrow tray or "galley" in which newly set type is temporarily stored. (See GALLEY.) Galley proofs are usually about 22 in. deep and 9 in. wide. As each shows only one column of type, it will have wide margins on both sides of it, which offer plenty of room for corrections. At the top is shown the number of the galley in which the type is stored.

One master set of galley proofs must be corrected, initialed, and returned to the printer. The duplicate set or sets may be filed, or cut up and used for dummying purposes. (See DUMMY.)

Page proofs. These show the type after it has been arranged in separate pages. It is usually more expensive to make changes in page proofs than in galley proofs. Sometimes the illustrations appear on the page proofs; if not, space is left for them. When halftone cuts are shown on page proofs, they usually are very poor and cause unnecessary alarm to those unfamiliar with the unfinished nature of page proofs.

Stone proofs. These proofs are not often taken; if taken, they show a complete form ready for the press, including all the pages that will be printed on one side of a large sheet of paper. Pages are assembled on a large flat table called a "stone," hence the name.

Press proofs. One of the first copies taken on the printing press that will handle the whole run is called a "press proof." The pressman makes a number of press proofs before completing his makeready and getting a perfect press proof. A press proof is simply a copy of the finished job, though perhaps printed on only one side. This is the time to criticize inking, halftone reproduction, and other details that are not satisfactory. Printers do not like to submit press proofs, because it means holding a valuable press idle while a messenger carries a still-wet proof to the customer. Customers who want to see press proofs are encouraged to come to the plant and stand by during press makeready.

Foundry proofs. Made only if duplicate plates (stereotypes or electrotypes) are to be made from the type pages, a foundry proof is really a final page proof. It shows the page locked up and ready for the foundry that will make the duplicate plates. Sometimes plate proofs are made from the duplicate plates. A foundry proof has heavy black borders around it, called "bearers," which are put there so that the hydraulic presses in the foundry will not crush the type at the ends of the lines. See illustration under FOUNDRY PROOFS.

Engraver's proofs. These are proofs of linecuts or halftones submitted by the engraver who made those cuts. These proofs are carefully made on the finest coated paper and should be examined critically. The printer cannot be expected to improve on them in his final work, and may well get results of somewhat lower quality. When possible, the engraver should be asked to pull proofs of his cuts on the paper that is actually to be used, instead of on deluxe paper.

Engraver's proofs figure only in letterpress printing. (See LETTERPRESS.) In offset, gravure, and photogelatin, press proofs are the only kind of real proofs that can be shown. There are no plates at all until the one big plate is completed, ready for the press. It is possible to see blueprints or black-and-white prints made photographically from the printer's negatives. These are very useful for checking on whether pictures are cropped and captioned correctly, etc., but they do not tell anything conclusive about the quality of the printing plate that will be made from the printer's negatives. (Sometimes it is worthwhile to have the offset printer make a small plate and pull hand proofs—particularly in process-color work—but since a new plate will be made for the pressrun, the result will not be identical.)

Reproduction proofs. Page proofs made with extreme care so that they can be photographed for reproduction in offset, gravure, or photogelatin are called "reproduction proofs." Reproduction proofs must be perfect—if anything, more perfect than would be acceptable in finished copy, since every slightest flaw will be duplicated in the whole run. Good reproduction proofs can be pulled only on the very best proof presses, or else on regular printing presses, and only after painstaking makeready. Corrections on reproduction proofs are costly, since all the work of making the first set is then entirely wasted.

Not every printer will take the time to make good reproduction proofs. The offset or other printer who has to use them should, therefore, be encouraged to reject any proofs that he considers of poor quality and ask for better "repros."

Repro proofs are usually pulled on white coated paper. Occasionally, however, they are pulled on transparent glassine and are then called "glassines" or "bronze" proofs. (The wet ink is dusted with bronze powder to make it more opaque.) Good glassines permit deep-etched offset or gravure plates to be made direct from them, instead of from a film positive, which has been made from a film negative, which has been made from a repro proof on paper.

Proofs on glassine or acetate are also useful in layout work. Type that is to run across a photograph can be shown doing so before the plate is actually made, if proofed on acetate and laid over the layout or the photograph. Transparent proofs for layout work need not, of course, be made with the same care that would be given glassines intended for reproduction. Proofs can be had from some advertising compositors in white or colors on clear acetate and can be ordered with pressure-sensitive adhesive on the back.

Color proofs. Such proofs are simply ordinary proofs rendered in the color or colors in which the job is to be printed. It is a lot of work to mix special colors just to make a couple of proofs and, therefore, expensive; so color proofs should not be requested unless necessary. On the other hand, engravers who are making matched sets of four-color process plates (see PROCESS COLOR) supply six finished full-color proofs and two sets of progressive proofs without extra charge.

Progressive proofs. These proofs show how a set of process colorplates will print, both separately and in combination. A full set of four-color progressive proofs shows (1) yellow, (2) red, (3) yellow and red, (4) blue, (5) yellow, red, and blue, (6) black, (7) yellow, red, blue, and black.

proportional spacing Some typewriters, notably the IBM Executive and the VariTyper, come closer to duplicating the appearance of printer's types than ordinary typewriters. This is because they offer "proportional spacing," which is to say they give space to each letter of the alphabet in proportion to its requirements. See illustration under IBM EXECUTIVE TYPEWRITER. Other proportional-spacing typewriters include the Underwood Raphael and the Hermes Ambassador.

publicity See CAMPAIGN PLANNING; PUBLICITY RELEASE.

publicity release Free publicity is the best publicity if it can be obtained and is favorable. Editors and managers of radio and television stations are naturally reluctant to give away the commodity that they are in business to sell, if they think that the beneficiary can and should pay for it. But they are under constant pressure to give their audience useful and entertaining information, so they welcome publicity of real news value. They are glad to help nonprofit causes whenever they feel that in so doing they are also serving their audience.

To distribute certain information may involve (1) writing, printing, mailing, (2) writing and paying for space or time, or (3) writing only.

When someone else is bearing the entire cost of duplicating and distributing a message, he certainly deserves all possible help from the person or organization pushing that message. One way of helping is to prepare a good publicity release. The publicity release which is likely to be used is that prepared with the recipient's interests in mind at least as much as the sender's interests. There are two recipients whose interests must be watched: the editor, i.e., reporter, newscaster, feature writer, etc., and the reader or listener.

The editor may ask:

1. Is it news? (Today's events must reach a newspaper today, or better yet yesterday in the form of advance write-ups. If it is not spot news, it should at least be feature material that will be new and interesting to his audience.)

2. Is it exclusive? At least is the editor protected by a definite release date against being scooped on the story?

3. Does the release clearly show the origin and the phone number to call if more details are wanted?

4. Does the release contain full background information, including complete and correctly spelled names? (Such a release is of great value to reporters who are attending a press conference,

even though they make their own notes.)

5. Is the release easy to handle? Is it double-spaced, on only one side of the paper, with good margins and space left for inserting a headline? Is the essence of the story put first, so that it will make sense even if later paragraphs are omitted?

On behalf of the reader the editor must also ask these questions:

1. Will this story interest, amuse, or help the reader or listener, or merely bore him?

2. Are its facts presented so as to catch his attention? Is it brief and to the point? Does it raise any questions that it should, but does not, answer?

A publicity release must be delivered in good time. The announcement of a press conference should be delivered the day before, so that the conference can be made part of a reporter's next-day assignments.

A story marked "for release, A.M. papers, date" should be delivered as early as possible the day before. The report of an afternoon meeting should certainly be completed and delivered by the publicity man before he has supper that night. The report of an evening meeting should be phoned in, or delivered as early as possible. (It is better to send in a partial report early, than to send a full report too late.) Both tasks are made easier if an advance release giving the bulk of the information has been prepared and distributed.

The deadline for evening papers varies, but releases should arrive the evening before if possible.

It is a good plan to alternate release dates, by giving the morning papers the break on one release, and the afternoon papers the break on the next. It is poor policy to let TV and radio stations consistently scoop the press, or vice versa. To pay for publicity in one medium and ask for free publicity from the other is equally bad, e.g., when buying newspaper space but no radio time to announce an event.

Release to weeklies or monthlies must take account of closing dates, which may be days, weeks, or months in advance of publication.

A publicity release is normally addressed to the city editor or station manager, but it may also be addressed to the feature editor, sports editor, women's-page editor, etc. If a release is sent to someone by name, a duplicate should be sent to the city editor just in case the other recipient is not at his desk that day.

Releases of national interest may also be sent to the news services, such as AP and UPI. However, news of local origin but national interest may automatically be relayed to those news services by their local member newspaper.

Several excellent books on publicity are listed in Appendix 2, Bibliography.

public-relations consultants Public relations consultants resemble advertising agencies in some ways, especially since the two kinds of firms frequently expand into each other's territory.

However, large firms often hire both kinds of agency. Sometimes, the public-relations men come in at a high policy level and have a certain amount of authority over advertising and the agency that places it as well as over other matters. Sometimes the public-relations assignment is more limited.

The public-relations man seeks to shape public opinion so that it is favorable toward an idea, an industry, an organization, a product, or a man. He

may use free or paid publicity. He may use the standard mass media—press, radio, TV, motion pictures, advertising—or he may work through and enlist the help of schools, churches, clubs, political organizations, trade associations, and the like. He will certainly consider every point where the firm meets the public—packaging, billing, servicing, handling complaints, answering inquiries, etc.

Public-relations services are usually considered to be distinct from advertising and publicity services. However, certain advertising agencies provide their clients with both publicity and public-relations services. In rarer instances, certain public-relations firms provide publicity and advertising services.

Public-relations men believe that the extent and content of advertising and publicity should be determined by a public-relations counselor exercising his independent judgment as to their worth and efficacy in relation to a total program.

Public-relations services are offered either by individuals or by firms, who as a matter of professional ethics do not handle competitive clients. Fees are determined by negotiation, much in the same way that financial arrangements are made between attorneys and clients.

punctuation For rules of punctuation and examples of their application, consult the University of Chicago "Manual of Style," or Lasky's "Proofreading and Copy-preparation" listed in Appendix 2, Bibliography.

Q q

quad A metal blank used for spacing out lines of type. There are em quads, 2-em quads, and 3-em quads. (See illustration under TYPE.) The quads used for filling out the last line of this paragraph have been made type-high so as to print in black.

questionnaires A recognized direct mail technique. Tests show that people both read and answer a questionnaire more quickly than they read and reply to a straight letter.

The questionnaire implies that the inquirer cares what the recipient thinks; therefore, it is inherently flattering. By careful phrasing, the questions can impart as much information as they elicit.

The best results are obtained when a stamped return envelope is enclosed and when those who respond are promised a report on the findings of the survey.

quire One-twentieth of a 500-sheet ream; 25 sheets. Formerly it consisted of 24 sheets.

quoins Wedges used to lock up a form of type in a chase ready for printing. (See illustration under TYPE.)

R | r

radio See also CAMPAIGN PLANNING; TELEVISION; RECORDINGS.

Radio has an important place in many campaigns. The print user needs to understand its possibilities in order to be able to select the best medium for any given purpose.

Printed messages in the form of ads, news items, outdoor displays, pamphlets, direct mail, etc., are often strengthened by repetition through radio announcements and programs.

The different aspects of radio should be understood and evaluated before definite plans are made.

In sheer size and extent, radio is the most pervasive of all the mass media of communication. Nearly 98 percent of all United States homes are equipped with at least one radio set, a total of 228,279,000 sets in use, or four sets per home. More than 50 million of these, or 25 percent of the total, are automobile radios. It is estimated that the average person over the age of 18 makes use of radio for 2½ hr daily at home and for 1 hr a day while traveling in an automobile.

It is important, however, to recognize that this is not one mass audience, but many audiences. There are some 5,500 radio stations (AM and FM) in the United States, and the number is growing by some 100 yearly. (By contrast, at the end of World War II—prior to the growth of television—there were 955 AM stations and only 53 FM stations, the latter reaching a tiny audience.)

Radio programming today consists almost entirely of music, news, sports, and talk, with by far the heaviest emphasis on recorded music. Depending on the proportions of each program type and on the kind of music in which a station specializes, it will tend to attract a particular segment of the audience. Thus, in a large metropolitan market with more than 15 radio stations, perhaps half will concentrate on current popular music, with 5-min news bulletins on the hour or half hour. Such stations tend to attract a teen-age and young adult audience. Advertisers interested in reaching this audience—makers of soft drinks, clothing, candy, cosmetics— would tend to concentrate their advertising on such stations. On the other hand, airlines, publishers, and paint manufacturers would be more interested in stations that program to suit the tastes of more mature listeners.

Time of day is another significant factor. Banks, insurance companies, and investment services tend to concentrate their uses of radio to the hours of 7 to 9 A.M. and 4:30 to 7 P.M., when the chances are greatest that the head of the household will be driving to or from work with the car radio turned on. In like manner, advertisers of food products and detergents are interested in the hours from 9 A.M. to 6 P.M., when housewives are likely to be in the radio audience.

Other significant variables relating to radio use are weekday vs. weekend and winter vs. summer listening patterns. All in all, radio now offers a far higher degree of selectivity in potential audience than was possible in pretelevision days. On the other hand, the media user who wishes to reach a mass audience through radio will have to schedule a large number of messages, at frequent intervals, on many stations throughout the country.

Four radio networks provide programming service on a nationwide basis: American Broadcasting Company (ABC); Columbia Broadcasting System (CBS); Mutual Broadcasting System (MBS); and National Broadcasting Company (NBC). ABC, CBS, and NBC *own* radio as well as television stations. Mutual provides network programming service to stations affiliated with it. In addition, there are several specialized networks, some of which are organized on a regional basis and some for the distribution of certain specific programs. Other groupings of stations function as networks only for the sale of time but provide no program service.

As with TELEVISION (q.v.), radio time is available (1) on a network basis, (2) through national spot advertising, and (3) on a local basis. Unlike television, however, where the ratio of network-spot-local advertising volume is approximately 3:2:1, *local* advertising expenditures on radio are more than twice what

is spent on spot and nearly ten times the network figure. The following chart illustrates the drastically changed position of network radio as an advertising medium vis-á-vis spot and local advertising.

Annual Volume of Radio Advertising in the United States 1948, 1961, and 1964

(Millions of Dollars)

Year	Total	Network	Spot	Local
1948	561.6	210.6	121.1	229.9
1961	682.9	42.8	217.6	422.5
1964	829.5	57.0	240.7	531.8

There has, evidently, been a resurgence of advertiser interest in network radio since the low of 1961, but the growth in radio advertising expenditures since 1948 has been primarily in spot and local buying of time.

Radio time for commercial announcements can be purchased in units as short as 6 sec but is most commonly available in 10-, 30-, and 60-sec units. Advertisers may also purchase complete programs—such as sporting events—that run several hours. Because so many stations provide a music-and-news program format, purchase of a 5-min newscast is a common form of radio sponsorship. The accompanying table compares typical rates for a 1-min announcement and a 5-min newscast in a large, medium, and small market.

City	1-min anncmnt		5-min newscast	
	Highest	Lowest	Highest	Lowest
New York	$185	$40	$250	$150
Des Moines	$20	$10	$30	$15
Astoria Ore.	$5	$5	$6	$6

Many national spot advertisers restrict the purchase of time to the top 30, 50, or 100 markets. One advertising agency estimates the costs of a selective radio-spot campaign according to the following table.

work or on individual stations only—and on the length of time over which the spots are used. Some typical union-scale fees for actors, announcers, and singers recording spots of 1 min or less are (1) for use in New York, Chicago,

Spot Radio Market Coverage and Costs

(Thousands of Dollars)

(Based on 12 60-sec announcements per week for 13 weeks on a single station)*

Markets	% U.S. radio homes in area	Cost per spot		
		Drive time (6–9 A.M. : 4–7 P.M.)	Housewife time (9 A.M.–4 P.M.)	Evening (7 P.M.–mid.)
1–10	37	$ 820	$ 660	$ 440
1–20	49	1,320	1,050	700
1–30	58	1,670	1,330	900
1–40	65	1,880	1,510	1,040
1–50	72	2,170	1,760	1,260
1–60	77	2,350	1,930	1,380
1–70	80	2,600	2,120	1,540
1–80	82	2,750	2,240	1,640
1–90	84	2,880	2,350	1,740
1–100	85	3,010	2,470	1,820

* Note: 12 spots per week—25% discount.
    18–24 spots per week—30% discount.

Source: BBDO estimates.

Network time costs vary widely, depending on the number of stations in the network, their signal strength, and time of day. The range on one network is from $400 for a 6-sec participating announcement to $12,617 for 60 min.

In addition to the cost of commercial time, there are the costs of producing the commercial. Assuming that it is to be recorded on tape for reuse, the creative and production costs can vary from as little as $15 to $1,800 or more for a 1-min spot announcement. To this must be added payments to actors, announcers, singers, musicians, and sound-effects men, which vary depending on the markets in which the recorded announcement is to be used—whether it will be broadcast on a net-

and Los Angeles plus 1 to 25 other cities: actors and announcers, $70 + $9.60 per hour rehearsal; solo singers or duos, $72 + $8.80 per hour rehearsal, with 1 hr of rehearsal minimum in both cases; (2) for use in 1 to 10 cities other than New York, Chicago, and Los Angeles: actors and announcers, $22 + $9.60; solo and duo singers, $24 + $8.80. These fees entitle the advertiser to use the spots for a period of 13 weeks. The same commercials may be continued in use in 13-week cycles beyond the first 13 weeks on payment to each performer of an amount equal to the original recording fee excluding rehearsal time. Fees for network spots are higher.

These fees are, of course, the minimum fees provided for in contracts with the American Federation of Television and Radio Artists. Many "name" actors, announcers, and singers are able to command much higher fees. In addition, fees for musicians must be paid, as well as for sound-effects men when used.

At the local level, both advertisers and public-service organizations have opportunities to participate in radio programming which fits into the station's pattern. For the most part, dramatic programs—once a mainstay of radio—are nonexistent. Certain stations are still interested in live musical performances, round-table discussions on public issues, and feature programs dealing with specialized interests. In large metropolitan areas, radio interview programs are not uncommon, providing opportunities for authors, visiting celebrities, and political figures to discuss issues or to publicize their works. Many stations will broadcast brief announcements of community activities such as amateur theatricals, church bazaars, and fund drives, but they expect that the organization being publicized will provide all necessary information in typescript form. And many communities have at least one program dealing with women's interests on which information about fashions, household hints, and new products is always welcome.

(A useful brochure, *If You Want Air Time: A Handbook for Publicity Chairmen,* is published by the National Association of Broadcasters. Organization chairmen wishing to obtain a copy should communicate with their nearest NAB member station.)

The local radio program, whether commercial or not, has the advantage of being able to appeal to local interests and to feature local personalities. Good results have been obtained by featuring well-known citizens; local sports, plays, and concerts; the history of the city; school activities; an employee barbershop quartet, etc.

Free-lance radio scriptwriters may be located through local advertising agencies, local stations, and neighboring college radio workshops.

Radio programs of varying lengths can be transcribed or recorded, now usually on tape, and syndicated to a number of stations. Recordings may also be rented, purchased, or borrowed through transcription libraries, national manufacturers, foreign broadcasting and information services, national organizations, etc. Some of these provide complete programs; others provide program segments which can be incorporated into local programs. (See RECORDINGS.)

An extensive listing of radio program producers and distributors is published annually in the yearbook issue of *Broadcasting* magazine (1735 DeSales St. N.W., Washington, D.C. 20036).

Live shows are those broadcast with performers at the microphone as contrasted with transcribed programs. The cost of such a show depends on the cost of the performers and the cost of the time.

Typical union-scale rates for commercial network and syndicated radio performers are (1) for actors and announcers: $40 each for a program of ½ hr with 1 hr of rehearsal time required at $9.60 per hr for the first hour; after the first hour, rehearsal time may be computed and paid for in ½-hr periods at $4.80 per ½ hr; (2) for a singer (soloist): $72.60 for each program of 16 to 30 min with 1 hr of rehearsal time required at $8.80 per hr for the first hour and $2.20 per ¼ hr for additional rehearsal time after the first hour; and (3) for a group of two to four singers: $50.80 per person for each program of 16 to 30 min with 1 hr of rehearsal time required at $7.20 per person for the first hour and $1.80 per person for each ¼ hr thereafter.

On individual stations rates vary, depending upon size, unionized personnel, etc.

When a station gets its license, it

Selecting Radio Time

Time	Audience	Cost	Advantages and disadvantages
Early morning "drive time" 7–9 A.M.	Particularly good for reaching the man of the house	Consult station and network rates published by Standard Rate and Data Service, Skokie, Ill.	Little competition with popular television programs; high car-radio use by commuters; good time for announcement of organization activities
Daytime 9 A.M.– 4.30 P.M.	Chiefly housewives		Audience mainly women who often stay tuned in for long periods
Early evening "drive time" 4:30–7 P.M.	Concentration of commuter car radios in use; mainly men		Good time for news, sports summaries, reports on market conditions, etc.
Evening 7 P.M.–midnight	High concentration of teen-agers doing homework		Competition from television is at its highest
Middle of the night midnight–7 A.M.	Small adult audience		Good for reaching night workers, auto and truck drivers

undertakes an obligation to serve the "public interest, convenience, and necessity." Among other things, a radio station is expected to provide "reasonable opportunity for the discussion of conflicting views on issues of public importance." Stations are now permitted to editorialize, and a good many of them do, but responsible representatives of differing points of view have the right to ask for time to respond. In the case of properly certified candidates for public office, the station is required to provide equal time for all candidates if it makes its broadcast facilities available for any one of them.

Any individual, company, or organization can bid for radio broadcasting time at so much per minute or per hour. Most stations ask to see written scripts in advance to eliminate libel or obscenity. Actually a station is not entitled to censor ideas simply because

they differ from those of the station manager. Freedom of speech applies to the airwaves as well as to the printed page.

In addition to commercial radio, there are some 300 stations that operate noncommercially (40 AM, 253 FM). These stations are owned by universities, school systems, church organizations, and other nonprofit groups. For organizations interested in reaching a highly selective audience interested in serious radio communication, noncommercial radio may provide an appropriate outlet. Many noncommercial stations are also members of the National Association of Educational Broadcasters, 1346 Connecticut Ave. N.W., Washington, D.C. 20036, which distributes programs through its tape network. A series of programs of educational interest, produced jointly by a public-service organization and a noncommercial station, can receive nationwide circulation at very low cost in this way.

For further information about radio and its uses, consult your local radio station managers. For further reading, see the books on radio listed in Appendix 2, Bibliography.

radio transcriptions See RECORDINGS.

rag content The most expensive papers are made in whole or in part from cotton or linen rags and are identified as having 25, 50, 75, or 100 percent rag content. Cotton trimmings from clothing factories are the "rags" used, and the long, white fibers make a paper with excellent strength and folding endurance.

It was once supposed that rag fibers had greater permanence than wood fibers inasmuch as rag papers are known to have endured without noticeable loss of strength for more than 500 years. However, even the best rag papers made early in this century are already turning brittle, and it is now known that the early papers endured not so much because they were made of rags, but because they were made by an acid-free process. To get real permanence, with or without rag content, an acid-free paper must also be specified.

railway express See REA EXPRESS.

railway freight See FREIGHT.

raised printing See THERMOGRAPHY; ENGRAVING; EMBOSSING.

REA Express See also SHIPPING INFORMATION.

Both air and surface express are handled by REA Express, the name taken in 1960 by Railway Express Agency. Although it originally moved all shipments by railway, it has become an all-modal carrier using railroads, airlines, steamships, and motor-freight lines—and combinations of these—in this country and overseas as well as its own motor carriers within metropolitan areas.

There is practically no limit to the weight and size of shipments which can move by surface express. Air express is limited in weight (200 lb) and in size (combined weight and girth 132 in.) unless advance arrangements are made. REA has come to specialize in small shipments (LCL and LTL) and speeds delivery by handling same-destination packages of many shippers in unit containers as shown in the photograph on page 283.

Express rates include pickup and delivery in all principal cities and towns within prescribed limits, and insurance on valuations up to $50 for each shipment weighing 100 lb or less, or 50 cents per pound on shipments of over 100 lb. For instance exceeding these allowances, an additional charge of 23 cents is made for each additional $100 or fraction of excess value. Since all express is insured, the recipient must sign on delivery, thus giving a record of time and place of delivery, which may be valuable in case of necessary follow-up. Express may be sent prepaid or collect.

Surface express rates depend upon the weight and distance to point of destination with a minimum rate of $3.40 for 1 lb or fraction. There is no handy chart for express as there is for parcel post. Each shipment has to be worked out on the "rate scale" of REA Express. Further information may be obtained from the local REA Express office.

Surface express generally costs a bit more than surface parcel post (fourth-class mail) which does not include any insurance or local pickup. (See FOURTH-CLASS MAIL in Appendix 3, Postal Information.)

Special express commodity rates apply to advertising and other printed matter. These rates are based on vol-

Unit wire cage containers speed up package handling by REA Express.

ume. Thus, the more you ship the lower the costs.

Air express. Air express is a service of the REA Express and using 39 scheduled airlines of the United States and Canada. Air express directly serves more than 1,800 airport points covering over 115,000 miles of airways, and through closely coordinated rail-truck ground facilities it brings air service to more than 21,000 off-airline communities. Almost every important city in the nation can be reached within a matter of hours. Air express shipments are carried on all passenger and cargo flights. For example, you can air-express a 5-lb package from New York to Chicago for $5.20 and have it delivered the same day. Pickup and delivery are included in the shipping charge. Special delivery is available at extra cost at principal points, if needed, at any hour of day or night and on Sundays and holidays. Air express shipments may be sent prepaid or collect, with insurance included for valuations up to $50; coverage for additional valuation is available at a nominal charge for each $100 or fraction thereof.

All air express rates presuppose a volume of not over 250 cu in. per lb. When the volume is greater, the rates are increased accordingly.

The air express system directly serves Alaska, Canada, Puerto Rico, and Hawaii and extends through connecting air carriers to Central America, South America, and Mexico.

Air express is generally cheaper than air parcel post for parcels weighing over 10 lb. The minimum charge for air express beginning March 7, 1966, is $5.20 which will carry up to 64 lb to cities within 250 miles and proportionately lesser weights for greater distances. (The minimum for air parcel post is 68 cents for one lb.)

For information about REA Express rates—both surface and air—consult *Leonard's Guide* (described under SHIPPING INFORMATION) and your local REA Express office.

ream Printing papers are sold by the 500-sheet ream. Formerly, some papers were sold by the 480-sheet ream, but the 500-sheet size has now become standard. (See PAPER; PAPER SIZES AND WEIGHTS.)

recordings Ideas can be set in motion by sound recordings as well as by the printed word, sometimes even better.

Hence, those who are concerned with publicity and promotion should learn to exploit the rapidly multiplying techniques of sound. Often recorded sound, with or without accompanying pictures and printed words, is used with great effectiveness in sales and fund-raising campaigns as well as in educational programs of all kinds.

Practically all modern sound recording begins with magnetic tape or magnetized film, even when the desired end product is a disk. With tape you can record meetings, speeches, sermons, ceremonies, broadcasts, sales talks, movie commentaries, slidefilm commentaries, interviews, customer comments and complaints, sound effects for dramatic performances, telephone messages, books for the blind, business dictation, etc.

You can make tape recordings in a studio, at a convention, in or from your car, or even with portable equipment carried in your pocket or briefcase.

Some equipment is designed for highest fidelity, some to record voices for hours without attention, some for portability. You can buy or rent equipment according to the qualities you need.

All modern tape recorders use more or less identical tape with a special coating containing minute particles of magnetic iron oxide. The essential magnetic coating can also be applied to new movie film and to some old film.

No visible change occurs in the tape during the recording process, but the pattern of the sound is translated into a pattern of magnetism among the oxide particles. If you should accidentally pass an ordinary horseshoe magnet over the tape, the recording would be erased.

Properly handled, sound on tape can be played hundreds of times without getting scratchy or losing its quality. When you wish to use a tape for a new recording, the old pattern of sound is automatically erased in the reusing. Until then it will retain the last sound recorded on it and can be played back any number of times.

There is a correlation between tape speed and the quality of reproduction obtainable. A tape speed of 7½ ips (inches per second) is quite commonly used in industrial recording. For highest fidelity, a speed of 15 ips may be used, occasionally even 30 ips. For recording of conversation only, 3¾ ips is considered adequate.

However, tape speed alone is not a reliable measure of the quality to be expected of a recording. Equally important are the quality of the tape and recording equipment, the quality of studio acoustics, and the skill with which these are used.

In professional recording studios, disks have been replaced by tape for the initial recording because tape gives better quality, can be edited more easily, and is cheaper. Once a perfect tape is made, perhaps by splicing the best portions of several performances, it can be transferred to disks if desired. However, getting perfect recordings by any medium takes skill. The amateur attempting to make high-fidelity, off-the-air tapes disappoints himself more often than not, even when he has paid dearly for his equipment.

The process of transferring a recording from tape to disk begins by cutting an acetate master from the tape. If less than 700 copies are needed, this acetate master makes a one-step stamper, or "strike off," which is used to make vinyl pressings, commonly called "disks" or "records" by the general public. The one-step stamper is good for 500 to 750 records, but the acetate from which it is made is often expended in the process. This one-step process is less expensive and should be used for small orders and where no reorder is anticipated.

If more than 700 copies are needed, a mold is made from the acetate master by the electroplating process. The electroplated disk, which is made of nickel, is called a "meta master." (It is a negative and therefore cannot be played.) This metal master is used to make a "mother"—also of nickel, but this time a positive. From the mother, a production stamper is made (also of hard nickel), and that is used to make vinyl pressings.

From these stampers, records are pressed much like waffles are pressed in a waffle iron. The label is molded into the record as it is being made.

Before you plunge into record production, careful plans should be made. Begin by asking how the recording is to be used. If a record is for air play, meaning for radio, it will require more careful timing and editing than if it is a printed promotional record on a cereal box.

Time is of prime importance. A 7-in. record plays about 7 min; a 12-in. record about 23 min. Spot announcements can be ganged up on one record, of course—at most, eight on one side of a 12-in. record since spaces between the spots take from the playing time.

In the production and distribution of recordings, the following factors must be considered: studio time, tape, editing time, mastering and pressing, labels, sleeves, and shipping.

Studio time. With one announcer or speaker giving a "stand-up" spot (no sound effects or music), the studio costs about $30 per hour. Setup time in a studio takes about 30 min. Once the wheels get rolling, about an hour is needed to record five or six brief messages. This assumes a good announcer or speaker but also allows for some flubs and repeats.

With a seminar-type program in which several people are participating, it takes about 3 hours to record 2 hours of program. (If you use union musicians, you must pay for a minimum of 3 hours of time anyway.)

The cost of studio setup time can be saved by calling the studio in advance and explaining exactly what is needed—how many people, the time,

etc. Then the setup time is on the studio's time, and there is no extra charge.

Occasionally short promotional spots are recorded at no studio cost by using a name personality who is going to be in the studio on a professional job anyway and who then reads the promotional message, tacked on piggyback to the other job. This arrangement is easier for the personality, too, since he does not have to make a special trip to the studio for the spot recording.

For music, studio rates are higher— up to $50 per hour, including the engineer's time. Using the studio of a local radio station costs less—about half in some cases—but it is less efficient. In general, the independent studios are better than local radio stations for recording. They may charge more, but they also know more about getting good quality.

Tape. At least 30 percent of the problems of recording can be eliminated by the proper selection and use of tape. For the best results, no tape thinner than 1½ mils should be used. This is considered standard and has the heaviest weight base. For home use, tape with a polyester base is satisfactory, but for making a master, tape with an acetate base is essential.

Master tapes should be made at a speed of 15 ips on full track since much professional equipment uses only full track. If full-track tape is not available, use only the upper half of two-track tape.

If the recording is to be all speech, "low-print" tape should be used. If it includes music and other sound effects, special tape is needed to prevent "print-through," or echo effect.

The completely edited master tape is comparable to the mechanical which an artist prepares for the engraver. From this master tape, it is possible to make either tape copies or pressings (disks).

For a 1-min spot announcement to go to radio stations, tape copies should be considered. Most of the larger radio stations are equipped to use tape cartridges. (The cartridge—a transparent plastic box which protects the tape inside—is dropped into the player as easily and quickly as putting a quarter in a slot machine.) A small cartridge for a 1-min tape is practical; larger cartridges are not used because they are too expensive and the longer tape is likely to tangle. The procedure is to send a master tape for a 1-min spot to the radio studio on a reel. The studio makes its own cartridge locally.

The cost of tape for a 1-min spot runs to about $2 if the station has cartridge equipment. Before sending out such a tape, be sure that the station can handle cartridges.

Editing time. Editing and proofreading are done at each stage, and corrections are made. Usually editing costs are about half what studio costs are. The New York rate of $20 an hour is high compared with other cities.

Editing time and costs can be saved by keeping a running tab of the suitability of the various takes when recording is under way. For example, if a speaker reads his script once, then makes a false start on a second reading, the monitor should note which is a false start and which is the better of the two readings. Later, instead of listening to everything, he can spot from his notes the section that is the best bet for the final record.

Mastering and pressing. For stations that do not use tape, it is necessary to send a disk. If 20 or less are needed, use a reference acetate—often called a "dub" or "ref."

A 1-up cut record (i.e., cut one at a time) is a sheet of aluminum covered with lacquer. This kind of record is not so durable as a pressing, but the cost is low—about $6 apiece. If several messages are on one side—1-min spots, for example—the cost may run as high as $15 per side. Thus, if you want five copies, the total cost may run $75 for the lot.

If more than 20 copies are needed, pressings should be made. In all parts of the country, there are pressing plants geared to short runs—less than 500 copies. (For a detailed directory, consult *Billboard Buyer's Guide of the Music-Record Industry,* published annually by *Billboard* magazine, 165 W. 46 St., New York; price $1.) 65 percent of the radio-station transcription pressings in the country are made by Raleigh Records, Inc., 250 W. 57 St., New York. Other major short-run pressing plants are Midwest Record Pressing, Inc., 7007 S. Wentworth Ave., Chicago 60621; Research Craft, 1011 N. Fuller Ave., Los Angeles; Recordings, Inc., 1130 E. Cold Spring Lane, Baltimore, Md.; Houston Record Mfg. Co., 3300 Jensen Drive, Houston, Tex. For long runs (over 1,000), such as promotional albums for sale or giveaway, contact Columbia Record Productions, 51 W. 52 St., New York; or RCA Custom Record Sales, 155 E. 24 St., New York.

Mastering and pressing costs depend largely on the size of the record. For a 7-in. record, mastering and pressing costs are about $30 per side; for a 12-in. record, about $40 per side.

Once the master is made, the charge for pressings depends on both the size of the record and the quantity ordered. Prices charged by pressing plants geared to short runs and giving good service are roughly as follows:

Pressing Cost per Record of Disk

No. of copies	7-in.	12-in.
25	$0.50	$1.25
50	.40	1.00
100	.32	.75
250	.25	.60
500	.15	.45

Sometimes the cost of labels is included in the price of the record; sometimes it is extra. For 1,000 or less, the price is $6 per thousand (single-color ink on contrasting paper stock). If two sides of the record are used, double quantity must be ordered. The price for two sets of 1,000 is $12. Careful editing in advance will prevent additional charges for author's alterations and corrections.

A plain lightweight paper sleeve is sometimes included in the price of the record; sometimes it is extra. If a recording is to go to a radio station, a heavy-weight manila sleeve should be requested.

Most pressing plants will package and mail individual records at a cost of about 25 cents each plus postage. Or they will ship the records in bulk to the customer. If there is to be only one mailing, it may be easier to let the pressing plant handle all shipping details. However, if care is critical, it may be advantageous to handle mailing yourself. If so, be sure to package adequately. Be sure not to fasten a note to the record with a paper clip or write on the sleeve since the wire clip or ball-point pen will damage the record.

Each record sent to a radio station should be accompanied by a printed or mimeographed script so that the engineer can follow it in the studio. It will help him to select the right spot announcement for a special occasion and to know where each spot begins and ends. Scripts should be double-spaced on regular 8½ by 11 typing paper.

Records wanted in quantity for promotional use can be pressed on printed paper. Such records are obtainable from various firms including Auravision® (a service of Columbia Records), Aurapix (a division of General Marketing Corp.), and American Telecard, Inc. On the printed paper, they laminate a transparent plastic coating and press in a disk recording of your message or performance. They can impress recordings of any size and any speed on almost any material, including folders, cartons, book covers, etc. The grooves of the re-

cording can run right through the printing. Charges include perforating (to permit easy separation of the disk) and punching out the center spindle hole. One specialty is a postcard you can put on your phonograph and play.

The price per record is about 8 cents when 25,000 are ordered; 4½ cents each when 100,00 are ordered. It is impractical to order less than 25,000.

In making any recording, you must be very careful about such matters as copyright clearances, written releases from people recorded, and union restrictions. Assume that all book, dramatic, or musical material is copyrighted unless you know otherwise. (See COPYRIGHT.)

When a copyrighted piece of music (or a copyrighted arrangement of a noncopyrighted piece of music) is used (and practically all music less than 56 years old can be assumed to be copyrighted), it is necessary to pay the copyright owner a recording or "mechanical-rights" fee. The basic fee covers use of the music for a limited time only, usually a year. Longer use may involve additional payment. For details on the legal aspects of reproducing music, consult the book "This Business of Music," published by *Billboard* magazine, price $12.

If the recording is to be broadcast, two additional copyright factors must be reckoned with: (1) A fee of varying amounts for each commercial use on each radio station must be paid to the copyright owner. (2) The radio station must be licensed to use the music through ASCAP (American Society of Composers, Authors, and Publishers), BMI (Broadcast Music, Inc.), SESAC, or AMP, etc., whichever of these licensing organizations controls the public-performance rights in the name of the copyright owner. Not all stations are licensed by these agencies.

From those whom you record, get written permission for the use of their voices or performances, and pay at least

$1 for such permission to make it stick legally. Have a clear understanding with professional performers about what rights you are buying and what (if any) you are not buying. Otherwise you may find yourself faced with an additional charge for a use you thought was covered by the first fee.

In most situations you might as well reconcile yourself to paying union rates for talent, for the possibilities of getting around this are almost nonexistent. The Musicians' Union sets the rates for professional musicians. The American Federation of Television and Radio Artists sets the rates for actors and sound-effects men.

Radio programs can be recorded in a studio on tape or disks and sent by mail to any number of radio stations so that those stations can put them on the air at the time agreed upon with the advertiser without the expense of a cross-country network telephone hookup. In the same way, radio programs can be sent to organizations or advertisers, who can make their own arrangements for putting the program on the air locally, together with their own announcement.

A great many schools and some other organizations have facilities for playing recordings on their own public-address systems. Many business firms use tapes and disks in employee training.

In addition, there are many ways to deliver recorded messages automatically. Theaters save operator hours by playing back recorded details of what's showing and when. If you hear a sales message start when you approach an exhibit, you probably triggered the playback equipment yourself, by walking through a light beam, stepping on a footplate, or by mere proximity. (An inductance relay will sense the mere presence of a person.)

There are two machines which combine automatic filmstrip projector and record player. Kodak has one that uses tape with a frequency to trigger an inaudible "beep" and thus move the film-strip forward. DuKane has one using a disk record with inaudible tripping signal which moves the filmstrip to the next frame.

recto A right-hand page, which always bears an odd number. The left-hand page is called the "verso."

register A printed page is in register when the impression is in the correct position on the paper. In book work, correct register means maintaining exactly the same margins from page to page, so that the type area on a right-hand page is exactly backed up by the type area on the following left-hand page.

Jobs printed in two or more colors generally call for close register of the impressions; for example, where a red area meets a black area, there must be neither overlap nor a white space. (See COLOR PRINTING.)

In process-color work, where four or more colors must combine to create the illusion of a color photograph or other full-color subject, exact register is especially important. (See PROCESS COLOR.)

registered mail See Appendix 3, Postal Information.

registration of names and trademarks See TRADEMARKS.

relief One of the five basic methods of printing (see PRINTING). In the relief process, a raised surface (which stands out in "relief" above the surrounding surface) receives a film of ink and then presses this ink onto paper. Applications of the relief principle include the rubber stamp, the Multigraph, and the letterpress process. All daily newspapers and many books and magazines are printed by letterpress. (See LETTERPRESS.)

reprints It is generally cheaper to reprint a given quantity of a piece of liter-

An example of "relief" printing. When an ink roller passes over this letter, only the raised surface receives a film of ink.

ature than it was to print it in the first place. However, this depends on the process used and on whether the possibility of reprinting was foreseen.

The cost of type, cuts, and artwork are nonrecurring items if these were saved. If the type for a letterpress job was not kept standing, it may be cheaper to let an offset printer reprint by photographing a clean copy of the first edition, rather than to set new type. He can duplicate type and drawings without trouble (unless they are on dark-colored paper), but will prefer to work from the original artwork if there are halftones.

Letterpress printers normally do not keep type standing unless instructed to do so, and they may make a charge for doing so. However, when they break up a form, they usually return any cuts or plates to the customer.

Offset printers do not like to keep their plates for very long, but they do keep their "flats" (stripped-up film negatives), from which new plates can easily and quickly be made.

Gravure printers (sheet-fed gravure) can and will keep their copper printing plates indefinitely.

Rotogravure printers do not keep their printing cylinders (they would be extravagantly space-consuming to store) but keep their flats.

Photogelatin printers cannot keep their plates more than a day or so, but they do keep their flats.

Silk-screen printers keep their screens only if instructed to do so. If the screens are not kept, it is usually as expensive to make a reprint as to make the original run.

Photographic services make a practice of retaining any negative that they make on a customer's behalf, unless it is understood that the negative must be returned to the customer. Some photo services are much better equipped than their average customer to file negatives and find them again, but some lose or fail to keep negatives.

Hectograph masters and mimeograph stencils can be saved against the possibility of a rerun, but are not good for a total run of more than a few hundred or a few thousand, respectively. Multilith plates can be saved indefinitely.

reproduction   The printing industry suffers from an almost total lack of creative imagination when it comes to coining needed new words. Such words as "print," "cut," "engrave," and "reproduce" positively stagger under the burden of the work that they are called upon to perform.

Printing is *produced* by means of any one of the various techniques of printing *production*. The quality of the final *reproduction* depends in part on the skill of the *production* man who selected the *reproduction* process.

reproduction proofs   See also PROOFS.

Revised page proofs made on slick paper for photographic reproduction as in gravure or offset. "Repro" proofs should be handled with extreme care, for they smudge easily, and every smudge or mark will be picked up by the camera in the next stage of reproduction. Since they cost more than ordinary proofs, they should not be ordered until it is safe to assume that no further revisions are required.

Many typographers offer many kinds

of reproduction proofs including proofs in black ink on transparent acetate, proofs in white ink on acetate or colored paper, proofs with pressure-sensitive adhesive on the back, etc.

retouching Photographs often benefit by some retouching. Perhaps a distracting background must be grayed down. Perhaps more sky must be added to a horizontal photo so that it may be cropped to print in a vertical shape. Perhaps the details of an advertised gadget should be brought out more clearly.

Some retouching is simple, but some calls for a good deal of skill and experience, not to mention good airbrush equipment. (For an illustration of a photograph before and after retouching, see TYPE.)

Unskilled retouching is usually worse than none at all. Photographers and art studios may or may not be good at it. Photoengravers can handle retouching or recommend a good retoucher.

One branch of retouching covers the coloring of black-and-white photos. A cheap coloring job is worthless for reproduction. A printer can "fake" the color from the black and white better than he can work from a poorly tinted photo. Good coloring can be had, comparable in quality to an original painting or Kodachrome. (See COLOR PHOTOGRAPHY.) It is, of course, expensive, though less so than the color plates themselves.

return of undelivered mail See "Forwarding and Return of Undeliverable Mail" in Appendix 3, Postal Information.

reverse plate See also NEGATIVE.

Lettering or artwork consisting of dark ink on a light background can be made to print light on a dark background through the use of a reverse plate. Reverse plates can be effectively used wherever the type or drawing

The pamphlet cover on the right uses a reverse plate made from the design on the left.

alone would not have enough weight or color on the page.

rewriting See COPY EDITING.

Rex-Rotary A brand of mimeograph duplicator. The same company also makes the Electro-Rex electronic stencil cutter, similar in principle to the Mimeofax. (See MIMEOGRAPH.)

ripple finish see PEBBLING.

rivers of white. This paragraph has purposely been set "loose" with too much space between the words. Careless typesetting like this leads to distracting rivers of white like the one encircled. Legibility and beauty are served when type is set with close spacing and when lines of less than 25 characters are avoided. When rivers of white are noticed in proof, they should be encircled and marginal instructions to the printer should be given to "reset with narrow word spacing."

Robotyper A device for automating a standard IBM electric typewriter, similar in it capabilities to the AUTO-TYPIST (q.v.). (See also AUTOMATIC TYPEWRITER.)

roller embossing See PEBBLING.

rom Proofreader's abbreviation for roman. (See ROMAN; also chart of proofreader's marks under PROOFREADING.)

roman This sentence is set in roman type. *This sentence, on the other hand, is set in italic type.* Both are set in Baskerville.

Roneo Trade name for a machine which resembles the mimeograph.

Ross board See also DRAWING TECHNIQUES.
The Charles J. Ross Company, 1525 Fairmont Ave., Philadelphia, makes a complete line of special drawing boards, all of which are scratchboards and some of which are stipple boards. (See SCRATCHBOARD; SHADING TINTS.)

rotary press See also PRINTING PRESSES.
A rotary press is one in which each side of the paper passes between two cylinders, one of which serves to support the paper while the other prints it. An office mimeograph machine works on the same principle; so do Multigraph, Multilith, and spirit duplicators and offset, photogelatin, and sheet-fed gravure presses. All of the latter print only one side of a sheet of paper at one time.
However, the term "rotary press" is often reserved for rotary *web-fed* perfecting presses like the big, high-speed presses that print metropolitan newspapers, rotogravure sections, and national magazines. (See WEB.)
These rotary presses accept paper direct from a roll and do not cut the web into sheets until after it is printed. Most rotary presses are equipped with folding mechanisms. Paper goes through some of the big rotary web presses at close to 25 miles an hour. Some magazine rotaries print the paper in four colors on both sides, cut it, fold it, put on the cover, and staple it, all in one continuous automatic process.

rotogravure See GRAVURE.

rough See also COMPREHENSIVE.
The first, unfinished sketch of a layout made to give the general effect rather than the exact details. (See illustration under LAYOUT.)

rounding See BOOKBINDING.

routing A method of removing metal from those areas of a cut that are not supposed to print. These areas have, of course, been lowered somewhat by the action of the etching acid, but routing lowers them still more until there is no possibility of the rollers or paper bulging into them and smudging the work. (See illustration under LINECUT.)

rubber plates See also DUPLICATE PLATES; RUBBER STAMPS.
Rubber printing plates are like rubber stamps except that they are precision-made for use on a printing press instead of for use by hand.
Most rubber plates are duplicate plates made from metal type or cuts. Some are cut by hand like linoleum or wood blocks, where the design is simple.
Rubber plates have long been used for printing on rough paper and uneven surfaces. Because they give better coverage with less ink, they are often preferred over metal plates for printing on nonabsorbent materials, such as plastic, foil, or cellophane. They are coming into increasing use in book and job printing; fast, lightweight rotary presses have been designed that will take only rubber plates.
Rubber printing plates are made in much the same way as stereotypes, from previously prepared metal type or engravings. They can be made to give excellent results and can outlast not only stereotypes but also copper electros, much as rubber auto tires far outwear metal-rimmed wagon wheels.
The oil-resistant synthetic rubber plates overcome one difficulty that used to cause trouble, namely, deterioration

and swelling of the rubber through contact with oil-based inks.

Rubber plates can be made of hard rubber for fine ruled work or of soft rubber for printing on uneven surfaces. They have been used for halftone work of 100 screen and higher but not, so far, with quality results. They can be printed alongside metal type and cuts.

Rubber plates are available for patent base as well as for type-high printing. They can be supplied in curved (or curvable) form to fit any rotary press. (For presses specially equipped with smooth rotary cylinders, such as are used in FLEXOGRAPHIC PRINTING (q.v.), rubber plates can be mounted directly on the cylinder by means of a double-sided adhesive tape.)

Unmounted rubber plates can be mailed as easily and cheaply as stereo mats and can be used by printers who do not have stereo casting equipment. They can be used in any ordinary (relief) printing press. However, there is at present no wholly satisfactory way of duplicating a rubber plate except from the original matrix or by pulling a proof of it and making a linecut from this.

One important use for rubber plates is for cuts that are to be run on the Multigraph.

rubber stamps Perhaps the simplest method of printing is rubber-stamping. For a number of purposes it is the best.

Rubber stamps are often used to put a return address on envelopes, to add a dealer's name to manufacturer's literature, to sign letters, to sign or countersign checks, for dating, for receipting bills, and for imprinting such wording as "Special Delivery," "First Class Mail," "Air Mail," "Sec. 562 P. L. & R.," etc.

Special rubber-stamp inks are available in various colors for use on laundry, cellophane, metal, glass, celluloid, checks, meat, etc.

Rubber stamps made to order cost approximately 75 cents per square inch,

or 75 cents per line. Simple dating devices with customer's wording plus changeable dates cost about $4 and up.

Complete rubber-stamp printing outfits can be obtained for as little as $3.39. With this the purchaser can set his own type and make up his own stamps. However, these rank rather as toys than as business tools, since setting the type is very time-consuming.

To make a rubber stamp, type is set, an impression is taken from it in a special material something like plaster of paris, the resulting mold is baked hard, and then vulcanized rubber is forced into the mold.

Customers may supply their own type if they require a style that the rubber-stamp company does not have.

Designs that cannot be set in type, such as signatures or special devices, are first made as woodcuts; then from the woodcuts, the procedure is the same as from type. Signatures should be written in ordinary ink, preferably not india ink. This is because a signature in ordinary ink can be transferred to a wooden block to guide the cutting simply by moistening it and pressing it against the wood.

There are rubber-stamp companies in all large cities. They list such specialties as changeable date stamps, self-inking stamps, time stamps, fonts of loose type, pencil-cap stamps, and a self-inking roller-marker that rolls messages up to 2 by 5 in. onto cartons and crates.

rule Printer's rule is used for printing straight lines, plain boxes, etc. It comes in long strips of brass or type metal, which are cut to order for the job at hand, and in many thicknesses and combinations. Some common styles of rule are shown on page 293.

When rules are made up into boxes and borders, it is important that they fit well at the corners. Mitered corners are preferable to butted corners. (See illustration under MITERED.) Brass rule

Hairline	No. 1402
½ pt	No. M-5099-A
1 pt	
1½ pt	No. 5256
2 pt	No. 5209
3 pt	No. 1434
4 pt	
6 pt	

Dot leader, 2 dots per 8-pt em

. . . .

Dot leader, 4 dots per 8-pt em

....

Hyphen leader, 2 strokes per 8-pt em

- - - - - - - - - - - - - - - - -

Common styles of brass rule and leaders.

is expensive and is cut specially for each use. It is well to keep this in mind when correcting proofs. Corrections requiring recutting of rules cost extra.

It is difficult enough to make rules join perfectly at the corners, and practically impossible to get them to cross each other (as in columns of figures) without the joints showing. Therefore, it is well to try to avoid using both horizontal and vertical rules. However, imperfect joints can be made perfect during the electrotyping process, if electrotypes are made. In fact, one of the most satisfactory ways of handling complicated rules is to omit them entirely during typesetting and have them added "in the wax" by the electrotyper. (See RULING.) However, when electrotypers are very busy, they can be rather slow in getting around to work of this kind.

Alternately, type can be set, repro proofs pulled, rules drawn in with a ruling pen, and a linecut made of type and rules together.

ruling Ruled forms can be printed in the ordinary ways: (1) from brass rule, (2) from offset or other plates made photographically from an original drawn up in india ink. (See also BUSINESS FORMS.)

However, they are often produced on special ruling machines. In these machines, the paper passes under multiple ruling pens which get their aqueous ink from special fountains. Horizontal lines are ruled in one operation, vertical lines in another. The ruling can be done in more than one color simultaneously, without extra cost.

For firms doing this sort of work, look under Paper Rulers in the Classified Section of the Telephone Directory.

When ruled forms must be printed along with type or other material, they may of course be reproduced like any linecut, from printing surfaces prepared by one of the methods listed in the paragraph above. To build ruled forms out of brass rule is difficult since it is almost impossible to make the lines join neatly where they cross or meet.

One device which facilitates the ruling of evenly spaced lines is the Paraliner. (See PARALINER.)

ruling pen Anyone who handles much artwork will find uses for a good ruling pen, even if he is no draftsman. It is often necessary to rule a plain border around a line drawing in order to change its proportions so that it will scale to the desired dimensions.

Ruling pen.

There are a few simple tricks about using a ruling pen which should be borne in mind:

1. Buy a good one (costing $1.50 or more) with polished points of equal thickness.

2. Keep it scrupulously clean, inside and out.

3. Do not expect it to write unless

the points are separated by at least the thickness of a piece of paper.

4. Hold it nearly vertical, with the flat side toward the ruler.

5. Fill it with ink; do not dip it. Use the filler quill in the cork of the india-ink bottle or a dropper. There must be no ink on the outside of the points.

runaround There is a runaround in the text of the above article on the ruling pen. The illustration is cut into the text, and the type lines are run around it.

The use of runarounds increases the cost of type composition and is often avoided on that account. The narrower the type columns, the less need there is for using runarounds. This is one reason for designing this book with a two-column page.

When runarounds are to be used, it is customary to set galleys as if there were to be no runarounds, until their exact location can be worked out. Then the necessary lines are reset to the narrower measure. Needless to say, a given amount of wordage will require more short lines than long lines.

run in To set without paragraphs as a space-saving device; to add new copy without making a new paragraph.

running head See also HEADINGS.

The heading that runs across the top of the page of a magazine, book, or pamphlet giving the title, date of issue, or chapter title.

S | s

saddle stitching   See STITCHING; also illustration under BINDING.

sales letters   See LETTERS.

sans serif   See also Appendix 1, Type Faces.

The words "sans serif" are French for "without serif" and describe those modern type faces that lack serifs, such as Futura, Vogue, Alternate Gothic, and Franklin Gothic. The Monotype Company puts out a type face similar to Kabel (an imported series) which it calls Sans Serif.

THIS TYPE has serifs.
THIS TYPE is sans serif.
THIS TYPE has square serifs.

saving money   See also ESTIMATING COSTS.

There are many real economies to be made in the buying of printing, as well as a tempting array of false economies.

If a 6 by 9 pamphlet will be just as effective as one 7 by 10, if a job in one color will get the same favorable attention and results as a multicolored job, if the omission of illustrations will in no way reduce the effectiveness of the job, then these may be ways to make real savings, not just false economies.

The big economies, though, come from the kind of thinking that not only compares this printer with that, but also inquires whether a form letter might not be even better than a pamphlet, a paid advertisement better than a mailed announcement, or free publicity better than either. (In this connection see the introductory pages in this book, especially the checklist on page viii, and also the entry on CAMPAIGN PLANNING.)

Now look also at the entry on PRINTERS: HOW TO CHOOSE. Next to choosing the right medium to begin with, selecting the *right* printer is more important than anything—much more important than getting competitive bids.

Work with your printer to help him help you save money in the following ways: (1) Call him in *early* enough to take advantage of his suggestions on economies, shortcuts, and ways to greater effectiveness. (2) Prepare your copy *early* enough so you can make your corrections in the copy, not later in type—rewriting in proof wastes more money than any other single thing print buyers do. (See COPY PREPARATION.)

(3) Make or have made a layout (see LAYOUT) comprehensive enough to leave no room for future misunderstandings by anyone. Do not gamble on anyone else "seeing" your squiggles in the same way you visualize them. (4) Deliver your job to the printer complete in every detail and with written instructions, not piecemeal and with oral instructions. (5) Measure your copy to fit before you send it. (See COPYFITTING.) (6) And finally—most important of all—allow enough time for everybody at every step. Haste makes waste. Rush jobs boost costs and lower quality. A poor job of printing is remembered far longer than fast delivery.

In any printing job there are always two costs: the fixed costs and the running costs.

The unit price of printing always drops as quantity increases. To be sure, the second 5,000 copies of a silk-screen job will not be much cheaper than the first 5,000, but a 10,000 order might be noticeably cheaper in offset; in quantities of 250,000 or so, rotogravure might offer substantial economies.

A few additional tips are:

Go to a printer who does a lot of the same kind of work and is equipped for it.

Stick to standard sizes in paper, envelopes, etc.

Avoid expensive paper. A poor job will look better on fine paper, but a good job will look well on any paper. Of course, on very small runs, the cost of the paper is not important one way or the other.

Strive for "press delivery" of the job, i.e., avoid separate bindery operations if possible. Binding costs are often higher than all other costs put together, and may not even go down as the quantity goes up. (See BINDING.)

Use an artist or designer. This may not sound like an economy measure, but it often is. A couple of appropriate drawings can do more for a job than fancy paper or an extra color, and may cost less. This is particularly true of the bigger editions where running costs bulk larger than fixed costs. But warn your artist not to demand close register (see REGISTER) unless he really needs it.

Know the postal regulations. A 24-page booklet mails more cheaply, for instance, than a 12- or 16-page job of the same weight. (See Appendix 3, Postal Information.)

It is worth remembering that printers charge for their services. If you ask them to procure paper, cuts, bindery service, etc., you benefit by being able to hold them responsible for quality and promptness, but you also will owe them a commission on the purchases that they make for you.

sc Abbreviation for small caps. (See chart of proofreader's marks under PROOFREADING.)

It is also the abbreviation for supercalendered. (See CALENDERED PAPER.)

scaling See also CROP, CROPPING.

To scale a photograph or drawing means to calculate how much it must be reduced or cropped in order to fit the layout, and to mark this information on the artwork for the guidance of the engraver or printer.

Some artwork can be reproduced "same size," but usually it must be reduced somewhat; occasionally, it must be enlarged.

If, for example, a photograph 10 in. wide by 8 in. deep is to be reproduced 5 in. wide, the engraver or printer is told that the reduced width of the printed photograph must be 5 in.

This is all he needs to know, because the height will automatically be reduced in the same proportion as the width. The height will be 4 in. The formula is

$$\frac{\text{Width}}{\text{Reduced width}} = \frac{\text{height}}{\text{reduced height}}$$

$$\frac{10}{5} = \frac{8}{4}$$

HOW TO SCALE A PHOTOGRAPH

This layout, left, calls for a 2-column photograph. The photograph to be used, below, is 7½ by 9½ in., excluding the margins.

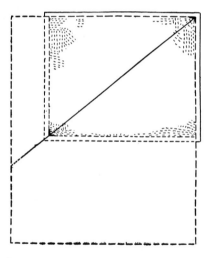

A piece of tracing paper is laid over the photo, two of its edges even with two edges of the photo. The diagonal of the photo is drawn. (It is best to mark just the corner, remove tissue to a hard surface, and then draw the diagonal.)

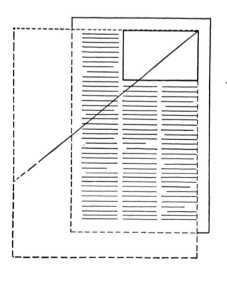

Now the tracing paper is laid upon the layout, the same two edges even with the edges of the space allotted for the photo. *The angle of the diagonal of the actual photo always coincides with the diagonal of any enlargement or reduction of that photo.* Therefore, the space left for this photo on the layout must be made deeper; or the photograph must be made shallower by cropping some sky or foreground to establish a new diagonal having the same angle as the one on the layout.

There is an easier way to scale artwork, however, which requires no mathematics. *Photographs and drawings always reduce or enlarge along their diagonals.*

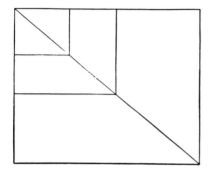

This principle of the diagonal can be applied through the use of a piece of tracing paper. (See illustration on page 297.) The method is completely accurate and will work either way; i.e., the proportions (the diagonal) of the layout can be used to determine the area of the picture to be used, or the proportions of the picture can be used to determine the depth required on the layout for any given width.

The method illustrated is a shortcut, in which only one line need be drawn, the edges of the tracing paper themselves serving as two other lines. If this shortcut seems confusing at first, try tracing the complete rectangle and then extending its diagonal.

If the artwork itself is not rectangular, draw a rectangle around it in light blue (nonphotographing) pencil, just big enough to enclose its highest, lowest, and widest points, and then proceed to scale this rectangle.

Photographs that are to bleed off the edge of the paper offer a special problem. (See BLEED.) At least ⅛ in. will be trimmed off on each bleed edge. They must therefore be scaled to a size ⅛ in. larger than they will be after trim. Thus, a photograph that is to bleed on three sides and be 6 by 9 after trim must be scaled to 6⅛ by 9¼.

Actually, it is not impossible to reduce a 5 by 4 drawing or photograph to 5 by 3 without losing any part of it. It can be done by trick photography. It is often done to make fashion models look taller and slimmer than they actually are. However, this sort of "stretch-squeeze" service must be ordered specially, like lettering or retouching. One firm offering the service is the American Blueprint Company, 7 E. 47 St., New York.

Scan-A-Graver, Scan-A-Sizer By means of the Fairchild Scan-A-Graver, newspapers can make 65-screen and 85-screen halftone engravings more quickly and much less expensively than is possible with conventional methods.

The Fairchild engravings are made on a plastic and can be used for direct printing or for molding stereos and electros. The plastic is strong enough to survive up to 500,000 impressions.

About 20 min is required to make an 8 by 10 halftone; less time for smaller units.

In operation, an electric eye in the machine scans the picture to be reproduced and controls the motions of a vibrating red-hot stylus, which simultaneously scans the plastic surface. Where the picture is light, the needle bites deeply; where it is dark, the needle burns away very little of the surface of the plastic.

To the eye, the dot formation of Fairchild halftones is very hard to tell from results obtained in the conventional way.

The company estimates that the great majority of smaller newspapers now rely on Scan-A-Gravings as their primary source for halftone plates.

The Scan-A-Graver will not enlarge or reduce, but this ability has been built into a later machine called the "Scan-A-Sizer." This latter, according to the company, will enlarge or reduce up to 4½ times, produce finished plates in a choice of screens in any size up to a

It is decided to crop the photo to fit the layout, so a new diagonal is drawn *from the layout.* →

The tissue is now laid back on the photo, with its right edge even with the photo as before. Its upper edge is moved down to eliminate some sky. The diagonal now shows whether some foreground must also be eliminated. ↓

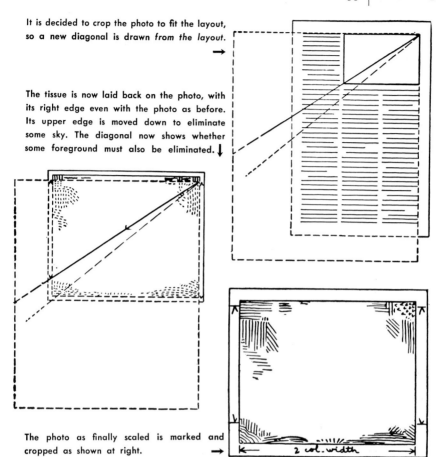

The photo as finally scaled is marked and cropped as shown at right. →

full tabloid page, work 50 percent faster than its predecessor, and even permit a photo to be reduced (or enlarged) more along one dimension so that, for example, short cars can be made longer or square pictures can be made to fit oblong spaces.

The new Scan-A-Graver Illustrator provides enlargements in two fixed ratios up to a minimum engraving of 8 by 10 in.

Fairchild engravers are both leased and sold. For information, write to Fairchild Graphic Equipment, 221 Fairchild Ave., Plainview, N.Y.

A machine called the "Klischograph"

produces halftones by methods somewhat similar to those used in the Scan-A-Graver except that halftones can be made on metal just as easily as on plastic.

scheduling See also DELIVERY; EDITORIAL PLANNING.

Careful scheduling is necessary even on very simple printed jobs if deadlines are to be met. Schedules are usually arrived at by working backward from the date when the material must be delivered or be in the mails. A typical schedule on a sizable job might look as follows:

September 5 (Friday). All copies to be in the mails.

August 21 (Thursday). Mailing must start, since it will require 10 working days to address, fold, stuff, seal, sort, tie, and deliver to post office, and Labor Day intervenes.

August 20 (Wednesday). Completely printed and bound material to be delivered to mail room (at least 25 percent of it), the balance to follow at the rate of not less than 10 percent each working day.

August 20 (Wednesday). Mail room to be ready with addressed envelopes and labels, cardboard backing if needed, the necessary personnel, etc.

August 18 (Monday). Printed sheets must reach bindery, dry enough for trimming.

August 14 (Thursday). Press proofs to be O.K.'d and printing started. Printing to take two working days.

August 13 (Wednesday). Envelopes and labels must be received by mail room, together with the latest mailing-list corrections, mailing instructions as to covering letters, enclosures, lists to be used, etc., since addressing must start a week before mailing starts, if mailing is to be completed in 10 days.

August 12 (Tuesday). Final page proofs to be O.K.'d ready for press.

August 11 (Monday). Corrected page proofs to be in printer's hands.

August 6 (Wednesday). Corrected galley proofs, paste-up dummy, and all artwork to be in printer's hands.

August 4 P.M. (Monday). Printer to deliver balance of galley proofs and engraver's proofs.

July 31 (Thursday). Printer to deliver first part of galley proofs.

July 31 (Thursday). Balance of manuscript copy to be in printer's hands.

July 29 (Tuesday). At least half of manuscript copy to be in printer's hands.

July 29 (Tuesday). Lettering or type proofs for artwork ordered, for completion by Aug. 1.

July 25 (Friday). Artist to deliver finished artwork.

July 18 (Friday). Artist to submit sketches for approval.

July 18 (Friday). Backing cardboard must be ordered, since the paper house cannot promise delivery in less than 4 weeks, and it is needed Aug. 20. August 15 delivery is specified.

July 11 (Friday). Imprinted shipping labels are ordered (see LABELS) since the work requires 4 weeks and the labels are needed Aug. 13. August 9 delivery is specified.

July 2 (Wednesday). Envelopes must be ordered, since the envelope house cannot promise delivery in less than 5 weeks, and they are needed Aug. 13. August 8 delivery is specified.

June 30 (Monday). Paper is ordered, since the mill cannot promise delivery in less than 6 weeks, and paper is needed Aug. 14. August 11 delivery is specified.

The above schedule is a tight one. On large jobs, more time might well be needed for setting type and handling proofs—perhaps a good deal more. The artist may not be able to work so quickly. Notice that the art deadline has been set for almost two weeks before it is due at the printer's to allow for corrections or for delays on the artist's part. Other deadlines have been similarly arrived at.

It is assumed that the above job is printed either on one-color or on multicolor presses. If there must be several separate pressruns, more time must be allowed both for presswork and for drying between pressruns.

If the job involves process-color work, at least a month more must be allowed for preparing the printing plates, making color proofs, correcting the colorplates, etc., regardless of the printing process used.

scoring Scoring is similar to perforating except that the fibers of the paper or cardboard are merely bruised with a sharp steel rule, instead of being intermittently cut through. The purpose of scoring is to make tearing easier. It is done on a regular printing press with a steel rule that is little more than type-high. The rule may or may not be inked.

Creasing, on the other hand, is done to make tearing harder. A blunt rule is used, which compresses the fibers without bruising them. Creasing makes it easier to fold stiff paper or board, and increases folding endurance.

Sometimes the word "scoring" is used as if it meant the same as "creasing." If the purpose of the operation is made clear, the finisher will not go wrong regardless of the word used.

scratchboard See also DRAWING TECHNIQUES.

Scratchboard is a specially prepared clay-coated white drawing board, which helps an artist achieve woodcut effects, or black-and-white-reverse effects, or highlights in dark areas.

It is possible to draw on scratchboard in the ordinary way with pen or brush. It is also possible to use it in such a way as to get white lines against a black background. When an area is flooded with india ink and then "scratched," the scratches show white. Whites produced in this way are pure and solid and easily controlled, which is not the case when white paint or white ink is used for fine work. An artist need not laboriously paint around a highlight; he can boldly rough in the whole area and scratch in the highlights later.

Some scratchboards, often sold as Ross boards, have a stippled surface (see SHADING TINTS) so that any tone can be lightened merely by scratching the tops of the raised dots gently.

screen A halftone is said to have a 65-line screen when it has been broken up into fine dots of which there are 65 to the linear inch. Halftones for use in

newspaper work are made with 65- or 85-line screens. Halftones for use on smoother paper may be made in 100, 110, 120, 133, and 150 screen or higher. (See HALFTONE; also SILK SCREEN.)

scribing A process used in map making. (See MAPS.)

script The kind of type face which imitates handwriting.

Scriptomatic A line of addressing machines operating on the spirit-duplicator principle and specially adapted for use with original addresses on punched or Keysort cards.

The address or other information to be duplicated may be typed by any method, except that special carbon paper must be used to create an image on the underside of the paper or card stock. From this carbon image, from 100 to 200 legible impressions can be taken.

When the addresses are put on IBM or Keysort cards or the like, it becomes possible not only to make a card record which also serves as an addressing plate, but to use machine-sort methods for selecting the addresses to be used.

Fully automatic machines are available which operate at about 6,000 impressions per hour. One will handle envelopes or forms, another will put addresses on tape, Dick strips (see DICK STRIPS), etc. One model will put addresses on tape at speeds up to 40,000 per hour. A special hand model permits easy addressing of packages or addressing on an occasional basis.

Scriptomatic equipment is made by Scriptomatic, Inc., 1105 Vine St., Philadelphia 19107.

seals See also LABELS.

Embossed, metallic, pressure-sensitive, and other specialty seals are obtainable with or without printing from many sources, including the Dennison Manufacturing Co., 300 Howard St., Framingham, Mass., and the Ever Ready Label Corp., 357 Cortlandt St., Belleville 9, N.J.

searchlights Searchlights can be rented to dramatize special events from Publicity Searchlight Service Co., 52 W. 53 St., New York 19.

second-class mail See Appendix 3, Postal Information.

Selectric An IBM typewriter that makes possible quick change of type faces, due to the fact that the characters are all on a single sphere the size of a golf ball instead of on separate typebars. (The type faces available do not, however, include proportional spacing.) The machine costs about the same as the conventional IBM electrics. The new principle completely eliminates jamming of typebars. It also offers faster tab action and faster carriage-return action, due to the fact that there is no heavy carriage to start and stop—the only motion is the lightweight golf-ball assembly.

The Selectric can be obtained with punched-paper-tape capacity. (See DURA; also LETTERITER.)

The Selectric is also available (from IBM) with *magnetic-tape* memory capacity. Special tape reels capable of storing 20,000 characters are used. The reels cost $20 and can be erased and reused indefinitely. This machine is recommended for use where complex documents like legal briefs often go through numerous rewordings. It will store and retrieve the previous version, type out the unchanged parts at 180 words per minute, stop for insertion of the corrections, and insert the corrections into the magnetic record as well as into the newly typed draft. (The magnetic tape used is *not* compatible with that used in computers, having far fewer characters to the inch.)

self-cover See BINDING.

self-mailer See also ENVELOPES; Appendix 3, Postal Information.

Any piece of printed matter designed to be mailed without the use of an envelope. Postcards of all sizes are self-mailers. Letters, newsletters, circulars, pamphlets, and magazines can be sent as self-mailers, provided they will not fall apart in transit. A precanceled postage stamp or gummed seal may be used to fasten the parts of a double postcard or folder.

Self-mailers can be sent at regular first- and third-class rates, under the same rules as to content that govern material to be enclosed in envelopes.

separation negatives See also COLOR SEPARATION; PROCESS COLOR.

In reproducing any artwork that is in more than one color, a separate negative must be made for each color to be used, so that from each separation negative a separate printing plate can be made.

sequential-card cameras Directories and listings which are revised frequently are often advantageously handled by the Compos-o-line (Friden), Fotolist (Vari-Typer), or Listomatic (Recordak) techniques. These machines make it possible to take the information contained in actively maintained card files and reproduce it in catalog form without intermediate typesetting or proofreading. The card files need be out of use only briefly.

The method is most likely to offer useful savings when the information must be maintained on cards anyway. In such a case, the usual costs of composition and proofreading may be entirely eliminated. The method may also offer savings when the cards must be typed specially but when most listings survive unchanged from one edition to the next. In this situation the costs of composition and proofreading may be sharply reduced.

In a typical application, one of the composing typewriters is used to put the

Fotolist sequential-card camera.

information on the cards, which are run through the machine in the desired sequence. The result is a column of type in film-negative form suitable for use in making an offset printing plate. Paper negatives can also be made. The type size may be reduced if desired.

All of the machines will copy one-line entries. One of the Compos-o-line machines will copy entries as deep as 3½ in. The Listomatic will intermix one-line, two-line, or three-line cards, automatically exposing the right amount of film for each kind of entry, provided the cards are prepunched to indicate the number of lines.

Any consideration of the possibilities of sequential-card cameras should probably extend to a comparison of all of them. The limitation of the Fotolist to single-line entries has both advantages and disadvantages. The problem of counting off columns before photographing warrants study, since a great deal of time can be saved if all spacing,

running heads, page numbers, etc., can be photographed in the same pass. In some applications, it could be important to be able to photograph a restricted portion of a card—and perhaps not always the same portion. Compos-o-line features this versatility. Where speed is a consideration, it might be noted that the Listomatic handles more cards per minute, though the Compos-o-line can handle deeper entries per card.

Those whose volume of work does not warrant the purchase of a sequential-card camera (and the darkroom capacity to go with it) might consider working with a printer specializing in this kind of work, such as the Science Press of Ephrata, Pa. Another alternative is the method described under FLEXOPRINT, where cards are hand-shingled on panels and photographed page by page.

Although the Fotolist and the Vari-Typer are specially designed to work as a pair, it is possible to obtain a special platen for the faster, though less versatile, IBM Executive typewriters if it is desired to use these in preparation of cards to be used in the Fotolist.

serif See also SANS SERIF; Appendix 1, Type Faces.

A light line or stroke crossing or projecting from the end of a main line or stroke of a letter. The text type in which this book is set has serifs. The headings at the top of the page, however, are in a sans-serif (without serif) type.

The detached portions of these letters are serifs. Without the serifs, the type becomes sans serif.

serrated edges Roughly cut edges of paper, as in newspapers. The cutting is done on the press as part of the folding operation.

Substantial economies can be made by accepting newspapers, newspaper supplements, advertising broadsides, etc., with serrated edges just as they come from the press, instead of requiring them to be sent to a bindery for trimming.

shade See COLOR.

shading film See SHADING TINTS.

shading tints See also DRAWING TECHNIQUES; SURPRINTING.

Cartoonists, fashion illustrators, and other artists make extensive use of shading tints, often referred to as "benday tints," particularly in work intended for newspaper reproduction. In this way they produce work that is as easy to re-

produce as a line drawing, that has the realism of a wash drawing or photograph, and that looks considerably better than any coarse-screen newspaper halftone. The shading tints are actually made of a pattern of tiny dots or lines, which give a gray effect.

There are five major ways of adding shading to a drawing:

1. The artist may rule in or stipple the shading by hand.

2. The drawing may be made on stipple board having a pattern of raised dots or lines on its surface.

3. The drawing may be made on special paper (Craftint Singletone or Doubletone) having invisible shading tints that can be made visible through the use of a special developing fluid.

4. Shading patterns printed on acetate can be adhered to the basic drawing where they are needed and removed where they are not needed.

5. The photoengraver or lithographer can add the shading in accordance with instructions from the artist, using benday or Tintograph shading mediums.

Typical shading-tint patterns are reproduced on page 306. Specimen stippled and shaded drawings are shown under drawing techniques. (See DRAWING TECHNIQUES.)

When artwork is to be printed in reduced size, care must be taken to use coarse shading tints that will reduce to the desired size without danger of becoming so fine that they will fill in when printing.

It is clear from a glance at the available shading patterns that it would be an interminable task for an artist to duplicate these by hand—although it can be done.

Stipple board. Stipple board has two limitations: (1) Since drawing a clean pen line on it is difficult, it lends itself better to soft effects than to line-and-shading work. (2) Only one screen pattern can be used in the same drawing. On the other hand, the artist can control the darkness or lightness of this screen pattern at will. Other techniques are less flexible in this regard.

Singletone and Doubletone drawing papers. These papers (made by the Craftint Mfg. Co., address below) are widely used by cartoonists and artists

Here the two tones of shading are produced with Craftint developer applied with a brush on Doubletone paper. The solid blacks are done with india ink.

doing newspaper advertising work. The papers are available in a variety of patterns, ranging from very coarse to very fine. The Craftint pattern chart gives for each style not only the number of lines per inch in actual size, but also the number of lines per inch if reduced one-fourth, one-third, or one-half during reproduction. For average newspaper use, the number of lines per inch in the printed result is usually not permitted to exceed 65.

Once the proper paper is selected, the artist first outlines the subject on the Craftint paper. Solid blacks are added with brush or pen, using waterproof india ink. Then where shading is needed, the transparent liquid developer (furnished free with the paper) is applied with a brush or pen, and the

invisible pattern in the paper emerges to give a shaded effect. Singletone paper permits only one shading; Doubletone paper permits light and dark shading, each brought out by a different developing fluid.

Shading tints in sheet form. Such tints (sold under such trade names as those listed below) are easy and economical to use. Patterns in black ink on clear acetate are available for graying white areas. Patterns in white ink on clear acetate are available for lightening black areas. One pattern may be laid over another if necessary for the desired effect. Several patterns may be combined on one drawing.

Some acetate shading sheets have an adhesive on one side so that they will adhere to a drawing when rubbed down firmly. To apply a tint, a piece of film somewhat bigger than the area to be shaded is laid over the artwork. Then the excess film is cut off with a sharp knife, or the pattern is scratched off the areas that are to have no shading. Usually the adhesive is such that film may be peeled off without damage to the artwork.

The same process is used for artwork that is to be reproduced by linecut, photo-offset, or mimeograph with photochemical stencil.

Well-known shading films with name and address of manufacturer are listed below:

Contak Shading Film. Chart-Pak, Inc., 1 River Rd., Leeds, Mass.

Craftint Top Shading Film. Craftint Mfg. Co., 18501 Euclid Ave., Cleveland 12, Ohio.

Tintograph Shading Mediums and Photo-Copy Shading Sheets. The Tintograph Company, Inc., 68 Jay St., Brooklyn, N.Y.

Zip-a-Tone. Para-Tone, Inc., 510 W. Burlington Ave., LaGrange, Ill.

Prices range from 60 cents to $1 for a single 8 by 12 sheet. Sheets can be obtained from almost any artists' supply shop.

Typical shading tints available in adhesive shading film. Note the white patterns in the last two lines to lighten the all-black areas.

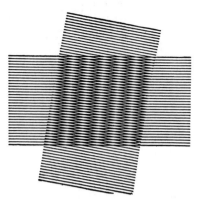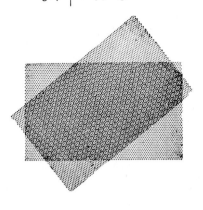

When one shading film is laid over the other, various effects may be obtained.

"Benday" originally meant the process used by an engraver or offset platemaker to add shading tints in accordance with the artist's instruction. Today, however, the term is loosely used to describe any mechanical tint.

To have the benday shading added by the engraver, the editor or his production man should write instructions to "lay a benday" in the areas that have been indicated on the artwork by a blue wash invisible to the camera.

Since there are many benday tints or patterns that approximate different shades of gray, complete instructions should indicate the desired tint by number. For a complete chart of numbered benday tints, consult your engraver.

Having the engraver add shading tints by the benday method is not done so much as it once was, except in color comic-strip work. The work is charged for at hourly rates, in addition to the regular costs of making benday cuts. It tends to be more expensive than when the shading is made a part of the original artwork. The process is, however, a useful resource for the buyer of printing who does not have his own art department.

Cost. The cost of reproducing shaded line drawings by letterpress (but not by offset) is slightly higher than for ordinary line drawings. Both are reproduced

as linecuts, but a line drawing that has added shading will take a special benday rate.

Contrary to a prevailing impression, the cost of an ordinary linecut, or a benday linecut, is higher than the cost of a square newspaper screen halftone of the same size. However, a benday linecut is far cheaper than a highlighted, silhouetted, combination line and halftone cut, which would be the comparable thing.

sheet-fed Printing presses are either sheet-fed or web-fed, depending on whether the paper has been cut into sheets before printing or is fed from a roll and cut into sheets afterward. Generally only large, high-speed rotary presses are web-fed. (See WEB.)

sheet-fed gravure See GRAVURE.

shingling A method of making a column or page of type out of many separate cards or slips of paper, each containing one or a few lines of type. The type must be positioned near the edge of each card, and the cards are then overlapped like shingles on a roof. (See also COLD TYPE.)

shipping information See also FREIGHT; REA EXPRESS; UNITED PARCEL SERVICE;

WRAPPING AND PACKING; Appendix 3, Postal Information.

Unless printed material is shipped properly, the value of the editor's and printer's work may be jeopardized. Material must arrive on time and in good condition if it is to be effective. That is the job of the shipper who must decide two main questions: How shall this material be shipped? How should it be wrapped for such shipment?

Choosing a shipping method. Certain factors must be considered in selecting the most efficient and economical shipping method:

1. The commodity to be shipped. (Rates vary from one commodity to another.)

2. Distance to be shipped. (Almost all rates increase with distance.)

3. The need for speed.

4. Rate for this commodity at this distance and speed.

5. Insurance—whether this is included in the regular rate or is extra; what the limit is.

6. Pickup and delivery service.

7. Return receipt—whether this is needed and, if so, what it costs.

Shipping methods and rates. The chief methods are:

1. The U.S. mail, which includes third- and fourth-class, air parcel post, special fourth-class for books and other educational materials, and special library rates. All have weight and size limitations.

Second-class mail is for periodicals only.

Third-class rates apply only to pieces weighing up to and including 8 oz.

Fourth-class mail (parcel post) is subject to weight and size limitations which vary according to the classification of the post office and the zone to which matter is being sent. The maximum limitations (70 lb in weight and 100 in. in combined length and girth) apply to shipments to or from second- and third-class post offices and to books mailed to any zone. The weight limit on matter mailed between first-class post offices is 40 lb to zones 1 and 2, 20 lb to zones 3 through 8. Insurance is not included in mail charges, but may be secured on payment of an additional fee. No receipt is obtained on delivery of regular fourth-class mail even when insured. The post office does not provide pickup service. (See Appendix 3, Postal Information.)

2. REA Express, which includes both surface express and air express, utilizes trucks, trains, planes and boats to expedite delivery. Both surface and air rates are based on the commodity being shipped as well as weight and distance. (See REA EXPRESS.)

REA Express has almost no limits to the weight and size of the shipments it can handle. The rate includes both pickup and delivery service as well as insurance without extra charge for valuation up to $50 or 50 cents per lb. (Over $50 valuation, insurance is 25 cents in the East and 23 cents in the Mid-West, South, and West per $100 valuation or fraction thereof.) Receipts are taken for all parcels; thus time and place of delivery are recorded as well as the signature of the recipient. Printed matter receives special rates and charges in REA Express Tariff 23. This rate is competitive with the motor freight minimum charge and less-than-truckload class rates.

3. Freight can mean rail freight, motor freight, and air freight, or a combination of these. There are almost no size and weight limits. Each has complex rate schedules based on commodity, weight, and distance. Freight forwarders specialize in choosing the best method of transportation or combination of these and quote a single rate to the shipper although they may use a combination of rail and truck to speed delivery. (See FREIGHT.) In recent years motor freight has spread a vast network of lines into every part of the country and taken over much of what was once rail-freight business, going where rail-

roads cannot give service, and providing both pickup and delivery. For information about freight rates and lines, see *Leonard's Guide* and directories below.

4. Air service is provided by the U.S. mail (airmail and air parcel post); REA Express; and air freight (both passenger and cargo flights). These give the fastest service except to near-by cities or places without direct air service, or under poor flying conditions.

The rate for domestic airmail (weight limit 8 oz) is 8 cents per oz or fraction thereof; for domestic air parcel post (weight over 8 oz and limited to 70 lb) rate varies according to weight, zone, and character of matter. (See AIR MAIL, Appendix 3, Postal Information.)

Air express rates vary with both the weight and distance. The minimum charge is $5.20. Any shipment that would cost more than $5.20 by airmail can be sent cheaper by air express.

Both air services are expedited by delivering the material direct to the airfield. REA Express will pick up matter for air express.

5. Small package shipment is provided by a growing number of services in addition to the U.S. mail, which once had a virtual monopoly in its third- and fourth-class (parcel post) service. Now motor freight and freight forwarders offer special package rates for parcels of less than 10 lb. (See FREIGHT.) United Parcel Service gives repeat service to subscribers paying a weekly charge for service plus a per-package fee. (See UNITED PARCEL SERVICE.) Greyhound, Trailways and other bus lines offer package service which is as quick as passenger service. For information, call the local office of the bus lines in your city. If you have marked copy or proofs to deliver to an out-of-town printer in a hurry, this is worth considering.

Shipping guides. Shippers can get invaluable help from *Leonard's Guide and Service* (G. R. Leonard and Co., 79 Madison Ave., New York 16, and 123 N. Wacker Dr., Chicago 6). *Leonard's Guide,* a loose-leaf, indexed publication kept up-to-date by mail service, gives complete shipping information including rates and regulations for parcel post, REA Express, rail freight, airmail, and air parcel post. A subscriber receives a *Guide* made up for his city, listing rates and routings that apply from that point of origin to the various cities and towns throughout the United States. Every post office and express station in the United States is listed alphabetically, by state, with keys by which to determine the shipping rates by parcel post, rail freight, and REA Express. The subscription price for *Leonard's Guide* is $20 a year in New York and Chicago; $35 a year for the Universal Edition (major cities other than New York and Chicago).

The same firm publishes six motor freight directories (New York, Philadelphia, Chicago, New England, Los Angeles–San Francisco, and Boston) which gives the names of the common carriers of general commodities, the location of the main office of each carrier, and a detailed list of the destinations with the carriers who serve them. Each subscriber to *Leonard's Guide* receives the motor-freight directory for his area as part of the *Guide* service. To those who do not subscribe to the *Guide,* the annual subscription rate for the motor-freight directories is $6. "Bullinger's Postal and Shippers Guide" (Bullinger's Guides, Inc., 63 Woodland Ave., Westwood, N.J. $27 per year rental) lists every United States post office and railroad station or nearest communication point. It is valuable for checking on addresses, since an addressee's post-office address often differs from his express or freight address.

Wrapping and shipping. These are really inseparable problems. For example, the decision to ship by truck may be guided by the fact that printed matter may not require heavy backing and wrapping if the shipment is at least a full truckload, carried directly from the printer to the shipping room. Wrapping a consignment of books to be shipped by parcel post may be guided by the applicable weight limit.

Shipping time. The method of shipping, the weather, and any number of uncontrollable factors influence the time required for shipping. In addition, a number of precautions may be taken by the shipper to expedite his shipment.

1. Businesslike arrangements for prompt wrapping, packing, and shipping frequently mean a saving of several days which not even air service could make up. (See WRAPPING AND PACKING.) The necessary labels, envelopes, and such wrapping material as paper and backing should be ready before

the consignment comes from the printer. Too many times a printer is paid overtime to rush a job that is later held up, at least in part, until minor essentials like fourth-class labels or special mailing tubes can be procured.

2. Careful wrapping and proper marking of matter to be shipped will not only expedite the shipment but will help to assure its arrival in good condition.

3. Advance warning to the consignee that a shipment is on its way will give him time to clear space for it, get his money ready if it is COD, make his own distribution plans, or notify the shipper if the package is not received.

4. Efficient handling of freight receipts, parcel post insurance slips, and

Typical Rates for
Air Parcel Post,* Air Express,† and Air Freight‡
February, 1966

From New York to	5 lb			10 lb			25 lb			50 lb		
	Air P.P.	Air Exp.	Air Frt.	Air P.P.	Air Exp.	Air Frt.	Air P.P.	Air Exp.	Air Frt.	Air P.P.	Air Exp.	Air Frt.
Atlanta	3.02	4.00	7.00	5.82	4.42	9.00	14.22	8.05	10.65	28.22	14.10	13.30
Boston	2.60	4.00	7.00	5.00	4.00	9.00	12.20	4.00	9.90	24.20	4.50	11.40
Chicago	3.02	4.00	7.00	8.62	4.10	9.00	14.22	7.25	10.05	28.22	12.50	12.60
Dallas	3.39	4.17	7.00	6.59	6.34	9.00	16.19	12.85	10.65	32.19	23.70	13.30
Denver	3.71	4.49	7.40	7.31	6.98	9.70	18.11	14.45	13.20	36.11	26.90	18.70
Los Angeles	4.08	5.77	7.40	8.08	9.54	9.70	20.08	20.85	14.40	40.08	39.70	21.90
Seattle	4.08	5.77	7.40	8.08	9.54	9.70	20.08	20.85	14.95	40.08	39.70	22.95

* Air parcel post is limited to 70 lb in weight, 100 in. in combined length and girth. Rates include delivery with regular fourth-class mail but not pickup. Insurance is extra.

† Air express (REA Express) rates include pickup and delivery. The same rate applies to lot shipments (several packages to the same consignee at one time). Thus 10 5-lb packages in a lot shipment get the 50-lb rate. Insurance to $50 included.

‡ Air freight rates are those of a freight forwarder and include door-to-door service and next morning delivery. Insurance is extra.

express receipts will assist in rapid follow-up if any part of a shipment goes astray.

Anyone who orders much printing will be forced to acquire at least a rudimentary knowledge of shipping techniques and requirements. No printing order is complete without shipping instructions, including instructions to the recipients of all bulk shipments.

It is possible for a production man to get pretty well detached from the physical bulk of the items in which he is dealing. Office boys have been sent to pick up by hand quantities actually requiring a truck. Office managers have innocently agreed to accept delivery of quantities too large to fit in their offices.

Anyone making out shipping instructions must create in his mind's eye a picture of the weight and bulk of the items being dealt with in each shipment.

show card A hand-lettered poster. (See LETTERING; SIGNS; POSTERS.)

sidehead See HEADINGS.

side-sewing See illustration under BINDING.

side-wiring See STITCHING and illustration under BINDING.

signature See also illustration under BOOKBINDING.

A folded printed sheet of paper ready for sewing into a book or pamphlet. It usually consists of 16 pages, but may have 8, 12, 24, 32, 48, or 64 pages.

signs See also POSTERS; LETTERING; TRANSIT ADVERTISING; OUTDOOR ADVERTISING.

Sign painters, sign letterers, showcard writers, and neon-sign manufacturers specialize just as printers do. Therefore it is important to go to one who seems to handle a lot of the kind of work wanted. Results will be better and cheaper. A good way to find a good man is to look around for work similar

to what you need and find out who did it. Sign painters often sign their work.

A good sign or show-card man can take a brush and produce finished-looking lettering almost as fast as the layman can write. To pay $2 for a sign that he turns out in 10 min is to pay for his skill. A beginner may work ten times as long over the same sign and turn out an inferior product.

There is a startling gulf, however, between fast hand-lettering that just flows out of the brush or pen and the meticulously finished lettering that appears in advertisements and in gold leaf on store windows. The former may cost $1 a sign, and the latter may cost $1 per letter or more. Hand-lettering on a sign can be much less expensive than actually setting type, or it can be much more expensive. See books on lettering listed in Appendix 2, Bibliography.

A good sign man knows many tricks to gain effectiveness and save money. It is best to tell him what is to be achieved and get his suggestions, not hand him a complete set of specifications.

Some of the myriad kinds of signs are hand-lettering in oil or watercolor on poster board or wood, letters embossed from special type (see EMBOSOGRAF), enamel on metal, gold leaf, neon, and billboards.

When only 3 to 10 signs or posters are wanted, it may be cheapest to make each by hand separately. When larger quantities are needed, the silk-screen process is often used. (See POSTERS.)

silhouette To silhouette a halftone cut means to remove nonessential background in order to produce an outline effect instead of a plain rectangular effect. Silhouette halftones cost extra. The halftone illustration of a mimeograph duplicator at the bottom of page 192 has been silhouetted. (See also VIGNETTE.)

silk screen The silk-screen printing process is one of the simplest and most versatile of the printing processes. It is almost always the best and cheapest way of making from 25 to 1,000 posters, car cards, or billboards, in fact any kind of material except that containing photographs or large blocks of very small type. It can handle photographs (crudely) and fairly small type, but it cannot underbid offset on this kind of work. (See charts "How to Choose the Right Printing Process" inside the covers of this book.) It is often used for printing on felt pennants, glass bottles, metal containers, decalcomanias, etc.

Silk-screen work may be identified by the fact that its colors are usually rich and nonglossy. Under a magnifying glass, one can usually see the pattern of the silk, especially in an area of solid color. The color goes on quite thick, sometimes thick enough to feel. The process lends itself especially well to the reproduction of bold designs with broad, solid areas of color, although very delicate effects may also be obtained by good workmen.

Sign painters were among the first to see the commercial advantages of the silk-screen process and perfect it. It enabled them to offer their customers 25 to 100 posters or show cards for the price of 5 or 10 individually painted ones.

Most sign shops today have silk-screen equipment (see SIGNS), and most commercial silk-screen operators are staffed to do attractive sign lettering. The lettering on silk-screen work is usually done by hand, although sometimes traced from enlarged type proofs or photographically copied from type proofs.

The essential equipment for doing silk-screen work consists of the following:

A wooden frame, like a window-screen frame.

Silk bolting cloth, similar to that used for sifting flour, stretched tightly across the frame.

Ink of semiliquid or paste consistency.

A squeegee, like a windshield wiper or window-cleaning blade, for scraping ink from one end of the silk frame to the other.

In the very simplest application of the process (rare in actual commercial use) a paper stencil (see STENCIL) is cut and laid on a table. (The table top should be protected by several layers of newspaper.) The silk screen is placed over it. Ink is poured onto the silk and spread around so that it goes through the silk and causes the paper stencil to stick to the silk. (Simple stencils will stay in place against the silk through the action of the ink alone, although for safety a few dabs of glue may be used.) The ink also goes through the open spaces in the paper stencil and makes an impression on the upper sheet of newspaper.

With the squeegee, the ink is now pushed to one end of the silk frame, and the frame is lifted. The upper layer of newspaper is removed, and replaced with a sheet of white paper or poster board. The frame is lowered, the ink is squeegeed to the other end of the frame, the frame is raised, and the first poster has received its first impression. After all have received this first impression, or color, another stencil and another run must be made for every other color.

This is the simplest silk-screen method. Another method is to stop up the openings in the silk by brushing glue into it wherever ink is not to penetrate. Still another begins by painting those areas which are to print with a benzene-soluble "tusche" liquid. After this, glue is spread thinly over the whole area with a strip of cardboard, allowed to harden, and then brushed with benzene. The glue that went on over the tusche floats off along with it, leaving the silk porous wherever tusche was applied.

The method most used commercially is the knife-cut film method. This is like the paper-stencil method, except that the film stencil can be chemically adhered to the silk and is supported by a paper backing until firmly adhered. After adhesion, the paper backing is removed. Film stencils can also be prepared photographically when the design is intricate and it would be time-consuming to cut it out with a knife. In fact, halftones have been successfully handled by the silk-screen method.

An excellent description of the whole process is contained in the illustrated book "The Complete Book of Silk Screen Printing Production," by J. I. Biegeleisen (Dover Publications, 1963, paperback, $2). The illustrations in the book are models of clarity and beauty.

Preparing one simple silk screen of medium size may cost $10 to $25 or more, depending on the amount of work involved. Running off impressions from this screen may cost about 3 to 5 cents each, including the paint. On long runs, posters are sometimes run 2-up, so that the running cost is halved, although the cost of preparing the screen is doubled.

Thus, a simple 14 by 22 poster or 11 by 28 car card in three flat colors may cost $30 or so for preparing the screens, and 9 cents per copy to run, plus the cost of the paper or poster board.

If the silk-screen printer has been responsible for creating the design, he may, of course, charge for his services as an artist, as well as for the reproduction work.

Artwork that is to be reproduced in silk screen should be done by an artist familiar with the process. For best results it should be done in a limited number of colors of tempera (show card color), and these colors should be used flat and not mixed. For example, if an artist mixes seven basic colors and sticks to these, then the artwork can be reproduced in seven impressions in silk screen and will closely duplicate the original. One of the assets of silk screen is its ability to make knife-cut film stencils from unfinished artwork.

A process similar to silk screen but

Making a Silk-screen Poster

The upper, hinged, part of the silk-screen frame has a tightly stretched piece of silk tacked across the underside. The stencil design is on the silk, blocking out certain portions for printing.

Now the frame is closed and paint is applied evenly to the silk screen by a squeegee which is pushed by hand from side to side.

Paint goes through the stencil openings in the silk screen, and on the paper positioned on the lower part of the frame. Here the frame is opened to show the design printed on the paper. A new piece of paper will be put in its place for the next impression.

used more abroad than in the United States is the "roller process." This makes use of a fine net of tulle (with no more than 20 threads to the inch) and a paper stencil. The paper stencil is adhered to the tulle both by the ink and by dabs of glue. Then printer's ink is applied with a roller, through the tulle and the paper stencil. The process is much more economical of ink than the silk-screen process, and the screens are cheaper, though they do not last so long. It is mainly used for making rather large posters to be seen from a distance and which can, therefore, be a little rough.

Silvertype A system for making negatives on a proof press. The form is printed on a clear plastic sheet, using a special ink, after which the sheet is sprayed with a regular electrotyper's silver spray solution. The ink is then removed by a solvent.

Singer sewing See STITCHING and illustration under BINDING.

Singletone paper See SHADING TINTS.

size, sizing To "size" paper means to treat it chemically in order to modify its surface qualities. Writing paper is sized so that it will take writing ink satisfactorily. Offset paper is sized so that it will not take up too much dampness from the moist offset cylinder. Gelatin and resin are used as sizings. Such terms as "tub-sized" and "surface-sized" refer to different methods of applying sizings.

skid See also PAPER SIZES AND WEIGHTS.
The cheapest way to accept paper delivery (other than in rolls) is on skids, i.e., simply piled on movable wooden platforms. A skid of paper is usually about 3,000 lb, but the amount varies with sheet size and bulk.

slidefilm See FILMSTRIPS.

slip-sheeting When wet ink on a newly printed page is likely to smear or blot the back of the next sheet, an extra sheet of absorbent paper is slipped between as a kind of blotter to absorb the ink. This slip-sheeting assures a clean job of mimeographing where it is necessary to print on nonabsorbent paper or on both sides of the paper.

slitting Sometimes a book is printed on a 38 by 50 sheet of paper, whereas it is to be folded as two separate 25 by 38 pieces. The larger sheet can be divided by slitting on the press, thus making a later cutting operation unnecessary.

slug A piece of metal used for spacing between lines of type, usually 6 pt thick, but sometimes 12 pt thick. A piece of metal 1, 2, or 3 pt thick is called a "lead." (See LEADING.)
Slug also means a line of type cast in one solid piece on LINOTYPE, INTERTYPE, or LUDLOW machines. (See illustration under LINOTYPE.)

slug-casting machine A machine that casts a line of type as one solid piece of metal. There are four in common use: the Linotype, the Intertype, and (for the larger sizes) the APL (All-Purpose Linotype), and the Ludlow. (See especially LINOTYPE and LUDLOW for further information.)

small caps THESE THREE WORDS are set in small caps, with the initial letter in caps. Most fonts of text type include small caps (but not italic small caps) in sizes up to 14 pt. Display variety can be added to otherwise straight type by using either

EVEN SMALL CAPS

or

CAPS AND SMALL CAPS

Since it is a little more trouble for a Linotype operator to use small caps, composition in which they are used extensively will cost extra. Words doubly underlined in manuscript will be set by the printer in small caps. Words or letters with three underlines will be set in regular caps. (See proofreader's marks under PROOFREADING.)

smashing A binder's term. Paper that has been folded must also be smashed, i.e., stacked and put under pressure to get the air out of the folds, before it can be trimmed. (See illustration under BOOKBINDING.)

Smyth sewing See STITCHING and illustration under BINDING.

soda pulp The soda-pulp method is used to make paper from deciduous trees like poplars. Papers containing a high percentage of soda pulp are very white and soft, with high bulk and opacity but low strength. Soda pulp is often used to give a soft finish to a paper of sulfite pulp base.

solid matter Solid matter may mean extensive areas of small type unbroken by headings or illustrations. It may also mean type that has been "set solid," i.e., not been leaded (spaced between the lines). (See LEADING for examples of both solid and leaded type.)

sound transcription See RECORDINGS.

spacing For spacing between lines of type, see LEADING. For spacing between letters, see LETTERSPACING. Both are illustrated under TYPE.

spatter A drawing technique in which ink or paint is spattered onto the paper, often by running a straightedge along the bristles of a toothbrush that has been dipped in ink or paint. The result is a dotted effect similar to stippling. (See STIPPLE.) Areas that are not to receive the spatter are first masked out.

special delivery See Appendix 3, Postal Information.

special handling See "Special Delivery and Special Handling" in Appendix 3, Postal Information.

Speedaumat See ADDRESSOGRAPH.

Speedball pen A special lettering pen used for show-card writing and lettering.

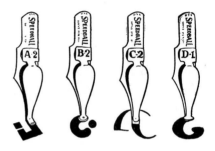

Speedball pens and pen lettering. (*Drawing courtesy of Hunt Pen Co.*)

speeding delivery See "Special Delivery and Special Handling" in Appendix 3, Postal Information.

Speed-o-Print A desk-top addressing machine using embossed metal plates similar to those used in the Addressograph.

spine The back of a book, i.e., the part visible as it stands in a bookcase.

spiral binding See MECHANICAL BINDINGS.

spirit duplicator See also HECTOGRAPH; DUPLICATING.

A spirit duplicator, sometimes called a "fluid duplicator," a "liquid duplicator," or a "liquid hectograph," is an office duplicating machine that can normally produce approximately 300 copies of typed, written, or drawn material at very low cost. In quantities greater than 300, the copies start to grow faint and are progressively harder to read. To get more, it is necessary to prepare a new master.

Up to five colors can be reproduced simultaneously from the same master: purple, red, blue, green, and black. A purple carbon image gives the maximum number of copies. The best results are obtained when special spirit-duplicator paper is used.

The process works as follows: Aniline-dye carbon paper is placed face up beneath a sheet of coated master paper in a typewriter. As the message is typed or drawn with a hard pencil or a ball-point pen, a reversed copy is produced on the back of the sheet. A measurable amount of the dye carbon on the carbon paper is thus transferred to the master. Copies are now printed directly from this master. The paper to be printed picks up a thin layer of the dye because, just before contacting the reverse carbon image, it is moistened very slightly with a special solvent having an alcohol base. The moistening is so slight as not to be detectable in the finished copies. Masters are made for different lengths of run, such as 100, 200, and 300 copies.

On runs below 50 copies, work similar to that produced on the spirit duplicator can be done on a cheaper machine, the hectograph. (See HECTOGRAPH.) Runs of more than 300 copies perhaps could be more advantageously handled by the mimeograph or offset-duplicator process. (See chart on inside of front cover.)

The greatest use of the spirit-dupli-

Spirit duplicator.

cator process is in duplicating business forms.

Systems are available that reproduce all subsequent records from a single original writing of the basic information. Copies required for shipping and billing, bills of lading, tags, labels, and unit media for sales analysis and inventory control can be reproduced from a single writing. For parts and assembly orders, the spirit master is used over and over to reproduce copies required on repeat orders without rewriting.

Spirit duplicators are marketed under the trade names Ditto, Standard, A. B. Dick, Wolber, and Heyer.

A low-cost, portable spirit duplicator weighing 12 lb and costing about $40 is available from the Master Addresser Co., Minneapolis 16, Minn. The price includes carrying case and enough supplies to prepare and run six master letters. It will print a sheet 8½ by 11 inches, or smaller, and will make up to 300 letters or cards from one typing. The same firm offers a "Post Master" at $14.95 for running extra copies of labels and tags from a single original typing.

The Azograph, also manufactured by the A. B. Dick Company, 5700 Touhy Ave., Chicago 60648, employs the spirit-duplicator principle, but with the difference that the masters are brownish in appearance rather than the usual purple, and because there is no dye color in them, they will not stain fingers and clothes. A dark image nevertheless results due to a chemical reaction between the colorless carbon image and the moistening agent on the paper at the moment of impression in the duplicator.

Masters for spirit duplicating can also be made by the thermographic process and are available in teletype-writer rolls, multiple-part sets, computer print-out rolls, etc. A useful catalog containing tips on spirit duplicating is offered free on request by A. B. Dick.

See also SCRIPTOMATIC and MASTER ADDRESSER for the applications of the spirit-duplicating process to the field of addressing.

split fountain Two or more different colors of ink can be run on the same printing press at the same time by means of split fountain.

The trough of ink that feeds the ink rollers of a printing press is called the "ink fountain." This fountain can be split into two or more compartments by means of dividers, and a different color of ink put into each compartment.

To prevent the different colors from running together on the ink rollers, the surface of the rollers themselves is cut away for an inch or so opposite the dividers. It is also necessary to reduce the usual side-to-side vibration of the ink rollers to a minimum. This sometimes leads to streaky inking of large solids. (For a novelty effect, blending of the inks on the rollers is occasionally permitted.)

Of course, any given section of the ink rollers will roll over only certain parts of the typeform. This sets definite limits on which pages of a form can be run in which colors.

The split-fountain technique is often used in magazine work. A form is run in black, and then with only one additional run through the press, one row of pages can receive red as the second color, another row can receive green as a second color, a third row can receive blue, etc.

Since rollers are expensive, it does not pay a printer to cut them unless the run will be very long, or unless the same rollers will be reused a number of times.

split run A method of testing the comparative effectiveness of different mail-order or advertising appeals. Some publications are printed 2-up, i.e., two plates are made from each page or ad, and two copies are printed with each revolution of the press. In such a case, an advertiser can by special arrangement use two slightly differing ads, and test offer A against offer B, knowing that in all other respects the conditions under which subscribers receive the two ads will be statistically identical. Every other copy will contain ad A, alternate copies ad B. Often the term "split run" is also applied to similar testing procedures in the field of direct mail advertising.

spray Krylon is one widely sold brand of spray that is offered in several formulations of special interest to the graphic-arts field. It comes in pressurized cans, and the clear variety is ready to use at a moment's notice as a fixative for drawings, cold-type composition, etc. It gives good protection even when used so sparingly as to be almost invisible, but repeated coatings produce a glossy finish. Krylon can also be obtained in white, black, and colors.

spread See CENTER SPREAD; DUMMY.

square serif A family of type styles sometimes called "Egyptian." (See Appendix 1, Type Faces.)

squeegee A rubber blade similar to the kind used by window washers. Squeegees are used in silk-screen printing to push the ink through the mesh onto the paper. (See illustration under SILK SCREEN.)

stabilization process Films and photographic papers can be developed and fixed in as little as 10 sec by the so-called "stabilization process." Such materials and the equipment to process them in room light are available from Fotorite, Inc., 6901 N. Hamlin, Chicago; and Ilford, Inc., 37 W. 65 St., New York 23, among others.

Although stabilization prints are usable immediately, it may be desirable to fix them and wash them in the ordinary way if permanence is required. This can be done either before or after initial use. Stabilization processing is often used in connection with photolettering to make quick black-and-white proofs from offset negatives and to convert positives into negatives (reverses). Exposure can be either by contact printing or by projection. With the aid of contact screens, continuous-tone originals can be screened for halftone reproduction.

Standard Rate and Data Service See ADVERTISING.

stapling See also STITCHING.

Pamphlets and magazines are usually fastened or "stitched" by stapling. Small ones are saddle-wired with staples. Thicker ones are side-wired with staples. (See illustration under BINDING.)

steel engraving See ENGRAVING.

stencil The stencil method of printing is one of the five basic methods (see PRINTING). Both the mimeograph and the silk-screen processes work on the stencil principle. (See MIMEOGRAPH; SILK SCREEN.)

An example of stencil printing. Ink or paint goes through the open part of the stencil to print on the paper underneath.

A simple stencil looks like the accompanying figure. The letters are simply holes cut in a piece of paper or metal. Ink can be daubed or sprayed through the openings onto any surface, such as a packing case. It is possible to buy an assortment of separate stencil letters and assemble them into any word.

Notice that there are gaps in stencil letters, where it is necessary to support the centers of such letters as "O" and "A" and give extra support to tongues of paper that might otherwise bend during use.

This problem of supporting the inside of an "O" and closed parts of other letters has had to be solved in all stencil processes. In the mimeograph process, a porous lattice of paper fibers supports the inside of an "O." In the silk-screen process, a piece of fine bolting silk gives strength to the open spaces between areas of Stenfilm or glue. In a special "roller process" more widely used abroad than in the United States, paper stencils are supported by a fine net of tulle (with no more than 20 threads per inch) and printing ink is rolled right through the tulle with rubber rollers.

The Stenso Division of Ottenheimer Publishers, Inc., 99 Painters Mill Rd., Owings Mills, Md., offers a variety of stencil lettering guides from 19 cents up, some of which are sold in stationery, department, and five-and-ten-cent stores. (See also LETTERING.)

Stencil machines, both hand-operated and electric, cut shipping stencils in oiled stencil board or in cardboard. Stencils of this type are now used extensively in United States industry for marking shipments of all kinds and sizes. This method for marking is approved and recommended by the Association of American Railroads and the American Trucking Association.

Detailed information about stencil-cutting machines of this type, stencil inks, oiled board, and fountain stencil brushes—all supplies used for stenciling of shipments—can be obtained by writing to Marsh Stencil Machine Company, Belleville, Ill.

Stenafax A device for producing duplicating masters by means of electronic copying from original art-work. It is similar to the Mimeofax, which is described under MIMEOGRAPH.

stereotype, stereo See also CUT; ELECTRO; DUPLICATE PLATES; MAT SERVICES.

Stereotyping is one of the oldest and cheapest methods of making a duplicate metal printing plate from type and/or cuts. A paper matrix or "mat" of special composition is forced down over the type and cuts and made to take an impression from these. The mat then serves as a mold, and molten metal is poured into it. The result is a new metal printing surface duplicating the original surface. This stereo can be used for printing alongside type by mounting it on wood.

The biggest users of stereos today are newspapers. They use the stereo process in making curved plates to fit their rotary presses. (For illustration see NEWSPAPERS.)

Stereo mats, being made of a paper composition, are light in weight and easy to mail. Printers who do any newspaper work are usually equipped to cast metal stereos from mats.

Stereos have the disadvantages, however, of permitting some loss of detail and of being too crude for fine halftone work. They may also show wear even before the type itself begins to wear. They may also stretch or shrink somewhat, both when the mat is made and when the metal is cast.

For longer runs and critical work, electrotypes, rubber plates, or plastic plates are usually ordered. (See ELECTRO; RUBBER PLATES; PLASTIC PLATES.)

Mats are frequently distributed to newspapers by national advertisers, cartoon syndicates, and feature syndicates. The local editor is more willing to include a plug for some worthy cause if he is presented with a mat of a cartoon or feature, ready for stereotyping and immediate printing. His advertising worries are simplified when he receives an ad in mat form, ready for the works. (This use of stereo mats is decreasing as more newspapers convert to offset and can reproduce direct from paper proofs. Unmounted plastic plates also compete with stereo mats, being light to mail and ready to use without casting.)

stet A proofreader's marginal mark meaning "retain crossed-out material." (See proofreader's marks under PROOFREADING.)

stick The receptacle that a hand-type compositor holds in his left hand to receive the type as he sets it. A stick will hold 10 or 15 lines of 10-pt type. Hence, when a newspaper reporter is told to write a "stick" of copy, he knows that he is to write only a couple of paragraphs, or about 2 column in. (See illustration under TYPE.)

stickers See LABELS.

stipple A stippled area in a drawing means an area composed of many fine dots in a random pattern. Stipple board is a kind of illustration board with a pattern of raised dots on its surface. A pencil or crayon drawn across stipple board leaves a dotted or stippled line, not a solid line. (See DRAWING TECHNIQUES.)

stipple board See SHADING TINTS; DRAWING TECHNIQUES.

stitching See also BINDING and the accompanying illustrations.

Most small pamphlets and magazines are saddle-wire-stitched. Two wire staples are generally used and driven from the outside fold through to the center spread. One staple is usually enough for booklets less than 4 in. high. Saddle-wiring is the cheapest method of stitching.

Thicker pamphlets and magazines (96 to 160 pages or more, depending on the thickness of the paper) may have to be side-wire-stitched if they are too thick for saddle-wiring. The wire staples are driven from the first page of text through to the last page, about 3/16 in. from the spine. The cover is usually glued on separately after stitching. This makes a very strong binding, but the pages will not open flat. This is a little more expensive than saddle stitching.

Side-thread stitching, which known as "Singer sewing," is used a good deal for textbook work because of its durability.

Smyth sewing is a method of sewing a thick book so that it will open flat. Most books are sewed in this way. The first 16-page unit of the book is fed into the machine and saddle-thread-stitched. The second 16-page unit is laid alongside the first, saddle-thread-stitched, and also linked to the stitching in the first signature. The third is sewed to the second, and so on.

stock cuts See also MAT SERVICES.

There are a number of firms that specialize in supplying stock cuts for use by job printers and editors of house organs, school publications, etc. They procure humorous and decorative drawings of a sort likely to be adaptable to many uses, and sell these in proof form (for offset), mat form, or in the form of metal cuts. The purchaser usually pays less than he would have to pay to have a similar cut made up specially for his own use, and thus gets artwork virtually free.

Suppliers of stock cuts include Hux Stock Cuts, Inc., 266 W. 71 St., New York; Cobb Shinn, 721 Union St., Indianapolis 25, Ind.; and East Texas Engraving Co., P.O. Box 2038, Tyler, Tex.

"Clip books" containing assortments of stock illustrations are available in art supply stores, and permission to reproduce goes with the purchase of these books.

The A. B. Dick Company offers a monthly assortment of seasonal stock drawings in the form of stencils for use on the mimeograph. (See MIMEOGRAPH.)

stock photos See PHOTO AGENCIES.

stone proof A proof of a typeform taken after it is locked up and ready to go on the press. It shows everything that a press proof can show, except that it gives no indication as to the quality of the press makeready and inking.

The stone proof takes its name from the fact that the pages are assembled on a large, flat table called a "stone" (because its top was made of smooth stone) and are there locked up in a chase ready for press. Nowadays the "stone" is usually made of steel.

streamers See POSTERS.

Streamlined Copy Fitting Method A system for character counting and copyfitting which provides counts on 1,730 faces from 4 to 24 pt, together with tables, scales, and instructions for speeding measurements and calculations. It is manufactured by Arthur B. Lee & Associates, 18 W. 45 St., New York, and offered at $9.75 postpaid.

strip, strip-in, stripping When two or more photographic negatives are used together to make one printing plate, the process of combining them is known as "stripping." The term is used not only in photoengraving but also in offset and in every other process where photography is used.

If, for example, an offset printer is asked to reproduce a form letter, he will photograph it and use the resulting negative to prepare his printing plate. If he is also given a separate illustration and told to reduce it and insert it in a space left for it in the form letter, he must make a second negative of this illustration and then "strip" it alongside the first negative in the proper place before making his plate. He will make an extra charge of $1 or so for this strip-in.

In the stripping process, the film-negative elements of all the pages in a complete form are assembled in openings on a large piece of golden-rod-colored opaque paper called a "flat." A flat must be the same size as the plate that will be exposed through it. The negatives are stuck to the flat with tiny strips of Scotch tape in the exact positions assigned to them on the layout.

The illustration for this form letter was too big for the allotted space, so it was photographed separately and the resulting, reduced-size negative was then "stripped in" with Scotch tape alongside the negative of the letter. The shaded area is opaque paper. The whole assembly is called a "flat." Offset plates are made by exposure to light through such a flat.

StripPrinter A photolettering machine priced in the $300 range which produces lettering on 35mm photographic paper ready for standard developing and fixing. Fonts (including borders) are available in many styles and in sizes from 6 to 96 pt at $5 each. For information, write StripPrinter, Inc., P.O. Box 18-895, Oklahoma City 18, Okla.

The StripPrinter.

stuffer   See CIRCULARS.

style sheet   See also COPY PREPARATION; PROOFREADING.

To prevent inconsistencies, every copywriter and proofreader in an office needs a handy guide to the preferred spelling, capitalization, punctuation, etc., agreed upon by the staff. Such an editorial style sheet need list only those examples that are peculiar to that particular office. It need not duplicate the rules for correct spelling and usage in such a guide as the University of Chicago "Manual of Style" (listed in Appendix 2, Bibliograhy) or the "Government Printing Office Style Manual" (which may be purchased from the Superintendent of Documents).

For example, one editor insists upon streamlined spelling such as "thru" not "through," "tho" not "though." A list of his more common simplifications heads his style sheet.

Another insists upon a comma before the conjunction in such a series as "Bodoni, Caslon, and Garamond" although style books usually leave a choice.

Most offices have some rules of distinctive capitalization or hyphenation, usually relating to their own trade name or product. The Government Printing Office, for example, recommends capitalizing such nouns as "Government" and "State."

No hard-and-fast rules can be given as to the contents of such a style sheet since it is necessarily a distinctive development in each office. Frequent additions and corrections should keep it up to date. Constant use of a good editorial style sheet should help at every stage of copywriting, copy editing, copy preparation, and proofreading.

A typographic style sheet for a periodical is equally valuable for those marking copy for the printer, preparing the layout, or pasting up the dummy. It should enumerate the chosen type faces and type sizes and usages for heads, subheads, titles, etc. (For details see PERIODICALS.)

subhead   See HEADINGS.

subscript   See INFERIOR CHARACTERS.

substance   See BASIC WEIGHT.

sulfate paper   Paper made from wood by the sulfate process is strong but cannot be bleached quite so white as soda or sulfite paper. Kraft paper, used for wrapping and for paper bags, is an unbleached sulfate paper. (See CHEMICAL PULP.)

sulfite paper   See CHEMICAL PULP.

supercalendered   See CALENDERED PAPER.

superior numbers   When the mathematician writes the term x^3 or the writer indicates a numbered footnote, he is using a superior number. (See proofreader's marks under PROOFREADING for the correct way to tell a printer to use a superior number.)

surface express   See REA EXPRESS.

surface-sized   See SIZE, SIZING.

surprinting   Type surprinted on 85-screen tint blocks in both light and heavy values is shown in the accom-

panying illustration. Type can be surprinted on a photograph in much the

same way. Note the loss of legibility
where tone values of type and background are too similar. Note that legibility also suffers when type that is too
small or too delicate is surprinted on tint
blocks of too coarse a screen.

swash letters Letters with unusual
flourishes used for ornamental purposes
in headings, initial letters, or wherever
the designer thinks they would look
well. Swash caps are available for use
instead of regular caps in most fonts of
italic type. Typical swash characters
with their standard counterparts are

$$\mathcal{J} \quad \mathcal{K} \quad \mathcal{N} \quad \mathcal{T} \quad \Upsilon$$
$$J \quad K \quad N \quad T \quad Y$$

sweating See ANCHORING.

T | t

tags See LABELS.

tape Imprinted typing tape for advertising purposes is obtainable from Neuer & Hoffman, Inc., 132 Green St., New York.

Imprinted gummed-paper sealing tape is obtainable from Kraftape Printers, Inc., 148 W. 23 St., New York 11.

Imprinted Scotch tape may be obtained from Transparent Products Co., Inc., 324 E. 24 St., New York 10.

Every editorial room and art department should be familiar with the many special varieties of Scotch tape beyond the omnipresent Scotch *cellophane* tape. There is a Scotch *mending* tape that does not yellow, shrink, or dry out. There is a double-sided tape, in several degrees of stickiness. There is masking tape of the crinkly, stretchable kind. There is white tape, black tape, and colored tape. All are obtainable from art supply stores such as A. I. Friedman, Inc., 25 W. 45 St., New York 36, which will send a catalog on request.

tape recording See RECORDINGS.

television Since 1949 the big development in the communications field has been television. For advertising, publicity, and promotion, television has opened new channels and established new patterns. It cannot be ignored in any campaign and will command a large part of the advertising budget in many situations. Certainly every campaigner or publicity director—from the advertising manager of the largest corporation to the publicity chairman of the local community chest—should explore the possibility of using television time to get his message across. He will need to have information about television and to compare this with information about advertising and publicity through other media. (See CAMPAIGN PLANNING; ADVERTISING; RADIO; PUBLICITY RELEASE; DIRECT MAIL ADVERTISING; etc.)

As in radio, the basic television unit is the individual station. In mid-1965, a total of 563 commercial television stations were on the air in the United States and its territories. Of these, 471 were very-high-frequency (VHF) stations—those operating on channels 2 through 13. Ultra-high-frequency stations (channels 14 to 83) accounted for the remaining 92. Frequencies are licensed to broadcasters by the Federal

324

Communications Commission for renewable periods of up to three years. No more than seven television stations (of which no more than five may be in the VHF band) may be licensed to any individual or corporation.

Nearly all commercial television stations are affiliated with one or more of the three nationwide television networks. These are operated by American Broadcasting Company (ABC), Columbia Broadcasting System (CBS), and National Broadcasting Company (NBC). The networks provide programs to their affiliates, pay the affiliates for time on programs purchased by advertisers, and maintain electronic interconnections for transmission of programs to the affiliates. Responsibility for everything that is broadcast, however, remains with the station licensee and cannot be delegated to the network.

In addition to their network functions, ABC, CBS, and NBC each owns five VHF television stations. Acting as a broadcasting group, these stations combine resources both for the sale of advertising time and for joint programming enterprises. The same is true of other groups such as the Metromedia stations, Group W-Westinghouse, and Corinthian Broadcasting. Particularly in news and public-affairs programming relating to matters of local interest, group pooling is able to provide coverage and commentary that none of the group members could offer on its own.

Certain facts about the use of commercial television are basic and almost universally applicable throughout the United States:

1. Television time is of two kinds: (*a*) sustaining or free time and (*b*) commercial or paid-for time. Sustaining time is available for noncommercial, general-information programs in the public interest and for general entertainment programs of all kinds. Paid-for time may be obtained at rates that are based on the number of TV homes within range of the station.

2. Television spot announcements are usually of 10-sec, 20-sec, or 1-min duration, but 30- and 40-sec periods are also available. Program times vary from 5 min to 1 hr and more.

3. The use of television time may range from the simple word-of-mouth announcement to the elaborate variety show complete with stage sets, costumes, players, and full orchestra.

4. Television costs are of two kinds: (*a*) for station time on the air and (*b*) for the program itself. A half-hour evening program on a full network of nearly 200 stations would cost about $90,000 for the time and anywhere from $40,000 to $85,000 for the program.

By 1965, over 52 million families had television sets. In these homes it is estimated that the TV set is turned on for an average of about 5.5 hr per day, ranging from 6.4 hr in February to 4.5 hr in July. Surveys indicate that the most active viewing is done in households consisting of five or more persons the youngest of whom is under the age of six and the head of which is under 35. Thus it may be said that the "typical" television home is one with a young housewife and a big family.

This is a mass audience which is highly desirable for some information and advertising campaigns. The decision to use television will depend upon the kind of message that is to be put across and whether it is desirable to pay the price to cover such a tremendous audience. If the message is one that affects all ages and all kinds of people, the seemingly high cost of television on a coast-to-coast network during peak evening viewing hours may be cheap for the results obtained. But with certain kinds of technical information or with certain kinds of products, a more carefully selected audience may be much more desirable.

The individual or the organization using television to present its message can select its audience in certain limited ways: (1) by choosing the time of day or night when the audience he wants to reach is likely to be viewing the TV screen; (2) by choosing the type of program that will attract the audience to be reached; (3) by pinpointing the programs to certain areas or localities.

The nighttime television audience is estimated to be 2½ times the daytime audience (64 percent at 8 P.M., 28 percent at 3 P.M.). In some cases, the big night-TV audience may reach a level seven to ten times larger than the morning audience. As might be expected, daytime rates are lower than nighttime, being from 25 to 50 percent of the nighttime rates, depending on a station's location, signal strength, and competition.

Throughout the day the makeup of the television audience varies as shown on the accompanying table.

	9–10 A.M. (%)	2–3 P.M. (%)	5–6 P.M. (%)	7–8 P.M. (%)	11–12 P.M. (%)
Children	47	14	39	26	4
Teen-agers	5	7	13	9	8
Men	13	21	20	29	39
Women	35	58	28	36	49

Also, seasonal variations cause some changes in the audience, as in the summer, for example, when the size of the child audience declines. Sunday afternoon is a time when there are usually many public-service programs, and Saturday morning is largely taken up with children's programs.

Thus you can select your television audience to some extent by selecting the time for a program or spot announcement.

Whether you hold that audience—or attract a particular segment of the potential audience—will depend in part on the nature of the program. For example, sports programs will usually attract an adult male audience, news pro-

grams will attract adult viewers, and a cartoon show or animal performance is more likely to appeal to children.

Basically, there are three methods by which television time is sold to advertisers: (1) On a network basis, which means that the advertiser buys network time plus a program created by the network, by an outside program packager, or by the advertiser. Sponsorship of network programs by a single advertiser is now relatively rare, except for occasional "specials." Sponsorship of regular network series is more commonly on a participating basis, which permits several sponsors to share the costs of broadcasting their messages to a nationwide audience. (2) National spot advertising permits the advertiser to purchase time on any number of stations in any combination of markets that he wants for the presentation of his commercial message as a straight announcement or in the context of a locally originated program. This provides flexibility but limits the advertiser to times not already assigned to network programs. (3) Local advertising permits retail stores and other local business establishments to buy time and sponsor programs on stations serving the communities in which the businesses themselves operate.

Television-time rates are based on the number of television homes within the area reached by a particular station. This figure is the maximum potential for that station; it does not guarantee that the entire potential will view every program any more than the gross circulation of a magazine guarantees that every subscriber will read every advertisement within a magazine.

Various rating services estimate the number of sets which were actually tuned in to certain programs. (For a list of these rating services, see ADVERTISING.)

Although the exact time delimitations vary widely from station to station and from market to market, here is a sample of television-time classification that is fairly representative:

Class AA time:
    7:30 to 10:30 P.M. daily
Class A time:
    10:30 to 11 P.M. daily
    6 to 7:30 P.M. Saturday and Sunday
Class B time:
    5 to 7:30 P.M. Monday through Friday
    5 to 6 P.M. Saturday and Sunday
    11 to 11:30 P.M. daily
Class C time:
    11 A.M. to 5 P.M. daily
    11:30 P.M. to sign-off daily
Class D time:
    Sign-on to 11 A.M. daily

The above station-time classification sample is one of moderate complexity; many are more complicated, some are far simpler. Because the networks do not program for as much of the day as the stations are on the air, network-time classifications are compressed into two or three basic groupings.

Station-time rates vary for these classes of time roughly as follows: Class AA (or prime-time) rates are 125 percent of Class A rates; Class B = 75 percent of Class A; Class C = 60 percent of Class A; Class D = 35 percent of Class A.

Typical station-time rates are given in the accompanying chart. The current rates for each television station in the country will be found in *Spot Television Rates and Data*, published by Standard Rate and Data Service, Inc., of Skokie, Ill.

Perhaps the simplest way for a local advertiser to get his products or his project on the TV screen is to buy time as a participant in an existing local program. He pays for a 1-min announcement, for example, and the star who MC's the program tells about the advertiser's product, holds it up to view, and may even give it his own personal endorsement. Usually the cost is no more than the cost of station time plus a talent fee for the MC. In the context of television programming and with competition from highly sophisticated commercials produced by large national advertisers, the local advertiser may feel that his message is not getting across unless he, too, creates a commercial on film or video tape that makes use of the best production techniques available within his budget.

The production of film commercials is costly and difficult. The cost will depend upon the number of actors, the nature of the sets, the production techniques, the degree of animation, etc. High-quality live-action 1-min filmed commercials can be made for as little as $3,500 or as much as $35,000 and more. The median price range at one New York agency is $8,000 to $16,000. The cost of a 1-min animated commercial will range from $7,500 to $10,000. Commercials (whether live-action or animated) filmed in color tend to run some 20 to 25 percent higher. By careful planning, it is often possible to film three 20-sec commercials for little more than the cost of a single 1-min commercial. By scheduling a large number of showings of the same commercial, the advertiser can reduce his "per-exposure" cost and gain added impact from the repetition of his message.

In contrast to the cost and complexity of producing film commercials, an advertiser may—if he has a very brief message—buy a 10-sec station-identification announcement during which an an-

Typical Television Prime-time Rates

	Network (163 stations)	Large-market station	Small-market station
1 hr	$142,625	$10,200	$330
½ hr	85,575	6,120	198
¼ hr	56,790	4,080	132
20 sec	....	2,850	50

nouncer reads the commercial copy while a slide which shows his product as well as the station's call letters is on the screen.

Program costs are a tremendous factor in television. Writers, artists, actors, musicians, stagehands, and lighting men must be paid; scenery must be designed and built; properties must be procured; and rehearsal time in the studio must be purchased.

Many local stations have solved part of their local program problems by buying syndicated movies, both old and new, to which commercials can be attached. In addition, many former network evening programs are available to stations on a film syndication basis, and a number of series are produced for first-run syndication. Depending on the times at which such programs are scheduled, a local sponsor can frequently tag his message onto such a film program with good results and at comparatively low cost.

Building a local program is a sizable undertaking for the trained professional. Yet there are small cities in which very effective programs have been developed by people with no previous TV experience. In one city of 100,000 the director of the local children's nature museum started a 15-min weekly television program with little more than the free time given by the local station and her own enthusiasm and innately good audience sense. The program has continued for several years and is credited with building tremendous community interest in the museum and with arousing the schools to a broader and more significant program of nature study.

This is one example of a number that could be cited where local TV programs have been developed effectively, despite lack of TV-programming experience, by community leaders who represent organizations and institutions concerned with the public welfare. The success of such programs will depend of course, on the talent and ingenuity

of the volunteer community leader, the cooperation and guidance which can be given by station personnel, the availability of free time, and the response of viewers.

Nonprofit organizations engaged in educational or fund-raising activities that are nationwide in scope may be able to avail themselves of the services of The Advertising Council, Inc., 25 W. 45 St., New York. Every year, the Council, which is supported by the advertising industry, undertakes to assist the campaigns of a number of health, welfare, and educational organizations by providing the creative skills and services that a commercial advertiser would seek from an advertising agency in preparing filmed commercials, slides, announcements, etc. Many television stations contribute free time only to campaigns that have been "adopted" by The Advertising Council.

Like a radio station, a television station receives its license with the understanding that it will be operated in the public interest. This means that station managers will make free time available for certain public-interest and general-information programs. The Communications Act of 1934, which is the basic regulatory statute for the broadcasting industry, requires broadcasters to "afford reasonable opportunity for the discussion of conflicting views on issues of public importance." When a station permits the use of its broadcast facilities (whether paid or free) by a candidate for public office, all other *bona fide* candidates for the same office are entitled to equivalent use of the same terms.

Even more significant as an outlet for information is the increasing coverage of news on television. In addition to subscribing to the news wire services (AP, UPI, etc.), television stations and networks have reporters and mobile camera crews who try to cover the national and community news beats as do journalists working in the print media. (A survey conducted by Elmo Roper and Associates in 1964 found that 58 percent of United States adults named television as their primary news source.) Advance publicity releases about events of local news value sent to television stations as well as newspapers and wire services can often result in coverage on local television.

A relatively recent development on the United States television scene has been the growth of community-antenna television (CATV) systems, through which viewers living in areas where good TV reception is impeded by terrain characteristics can get greatly improved service. A master antenna is erected, often on a hilltop, and the television signals received there are retransmitted to subscribers' homes through coaxial cables that are usually strung on telephone and utility poles. A CATV installation in effect creates a closed-circuit television system within the community in which it functions. At the end of 1964, there were about 1,400 CATV systems, servicing approximately 1.4 million subscribers.

Some CATV operators have been providing special services on one or more of the channels not used for bringing in signals from television broadcasting stations. Typically, the service is utilitarian: the time, weather forecasts, and the like. But sometimes one finds an unused channel being used as a local forum for discussion of community affairs, and it is not difficult to imagine that local programming and advertising may become a regular feature of CATV. If such should be the case, opportunities for low-cost use of television channels on a purely local basis will be greatly expanded in many parts of the United States.

In addition to the commercial broadcasting industry, there has developed in the United States since 1952 a noncommercial educational television (ETV) service. In 1965, 103 such stations were on the air.

Unlike most commercial stations, the primary source of programs for ETV stations is local production. While no advertising is permitted on ETV, it is possible for a business concern to underwrite the production costs of programs on ETV stations in return for a simple credit announcement on the air. In Boston, an insurance company made a grant to the local ETV station to produce a series of programs dealing with preventive medicine, and in New York an oil company underwrote the costs of a nightly news program.

Both businesses and nonprofit organizations can also provide other forms of assistance to ETV stations. Book and magazine publishers may pay the travel costs of an author who appears in a discussion program, a local foreign-affairs study group may cooperate in the production of a series on world affairs, or local appliance dealers may furnish a studio kitchen for a program on *haute cuisine*.

For further information about television possibilities in your community, consult your local television station managers. For further reading about television as a communication medium, consult books listed in Appendix 2, Bibliography.

Tenaplate A patented molding material used in making electros. (See ELECTRO, ELECTROTYPE.)

text paper See PAPER; PAPER SIZES AND WEIGHTS.

Thermo-Fax An office copying machine manufactured by the 3M Company for making dry copies of letters, invoices, price lists, etc. It can copy two-sided, opaque originals in 5 to 6 sec each, at a cost of 4 to 5 cents per copy. No chemicals are needed, copies are made easily and quickly, and the equipment requires little maintenance.

The method uses infrared radiation on heat-sensitized papers now available in a range of colors, including white.

Thermo-Fax Model 47 dry-process copying machine.

Thermo-Fax cannot copy all colored inks. Further, the sensitized papers tend to become discolored in heat or strong light and to grow brittle with age.

The Dual Spectrum copying process, introduced in 1963 by 3M, copies all colors on paper that is not affected by heat in later storage at costs as low as 3½ cents a sheet. It also is a two-step process utilizing both thermal and photochemical principles.

For information, write 3M Company, 2501 Hudson Rd., St. Paul 19, Minn.

thermography Raised printing resembling the genuine engraving used on business cards, wedding announcements, etc.; also called "plateless engraving."

In thermography, a calling card is printed from ordinary type in the ordinary way, but while the ink is still wet, a special powder is sprinkled on and made to adhere to the wet ink. The card is then heated, and the result is raised lettering.

The letters on a thermographed business card are usually shinier than the letters on an engraved card, and not quite so clean-cut. However, a dull surface is also possible in this process.

Typical retail prices for thermographed work are as follows: Business cards, up to 2⁵⁄₁₆ by 3¹⁵⁄₁₆, including the card stock and six lines of composition,

approximately $4 per 100; $6.50 for 500; changes in addresses or salesman's name, $1 per line.

Announcement cards, up to 4 by 5, including stock and up to 50 words of reading matter, approximately $11 per 100; $25 per 500; $40 per 1,000.

One firm specializing in thermography is the Everlast Process Printing Co., 27 W. 24 St., New York 10.

third-class mail See Appendix 3, Postal Information.

three-color printing See PROCESS COLOR.

thumb index Thumb-indexing, step indexing, and tabbing are operations usually handled directly or on subcontract by the binder doing the rest of the work.

In thumb-indexing, markers are first placed in the books to locate the places to cut, then the thumb grooves are clipped out, and finally, half-round labels are pasted into place. Cost is proportional to the number of cuts.

In a typical step-indexing operation, all but the top inch of the right margin of the first section is cut away for ¼ in., all but the top 2 in. of the second section, all but the top 3 in. of the third section, etc. The index headings can be printed along with the rest of the text, or may be added by means of a pasted label. Sometimes (and especially in mechanical bindings) the stepped index pages are made separately on heavier paper and inserted.

Tab indexing implies the use of tabs that project beyond the pages. These can be pasted on or can be part of interleaved sheets on heavier stock. Sometimes they are laminated for greater strength and durability.

Edge indexing is a method of indexing that requires no additional steps beyond normal printing and binding. (See EDGE INDEX.)

tickets The complicated problems of numbering and dating theater tickets, and of running part of them on stock of one color and part on another, make ticket printing something that the specialist can do more economically than the job printer.

Unlike the product of the ordinary printing press, which reproduces any given number of exact copies of the original, a ticket press is designed to accomplish exactly the opposite, depending upon the specific use. This type of press makes each copy in a run of 1 or 10 million different from the first to the last by the inclusion of consecutive numbers, symbols, dates, and codes. For other uses, the numbering may be repeated in duplicate, in series of 5's, etc.

Admission tickets for the motion-picture industry are printed in rolls of 2,000 or fanfolded for issuance through ticket registers, with a different color for each admission price. Reserved-seat tickets for stage shows and sporting events must show section, row, and seat numbers in accordance with individual house seating arrangement.

Admission tickets of every description must be specially printed to show the name and location of the establishment, established price, Federal tax, and total. Because of Federal tax regulations, tickets not so printed and with a face value of more than $1 are illegal.

Imprinted tickets can be had for as little as $15 for the first 10,000, and 22 cents per 1,000 for additional thousands of the same kind or color ordered at the same time.

Among the prominent ticket printers of the country, specializing in cash-control systems through numbering are the Globe Ticket Company, 112 N. 12 St., Philadelphia 7, with branches in Boston, Atlanta, Dallas, Los Angeles, Denver, Pittsburgh, and Tacoma, Wash.; and Weldon, Williams & Lick, Fort Smith, Ark.

time requirements See DELIVERY; SCHEDULING.

tint See SHADING TINTS. For its relation to color, see COLOR.

tint blocks Cuts used to print panels of plain color; or the printed panels themselves. Such panels are often used as a background for type or cuts. Small paragraphs of featured material are emphasized by printing them on a tint block.

Tint blocks are made like cuts, except that, for solid tints, no etching is required. Simple, solid shapes can be sawed, routed, or chiseled out of zinc, copper, rubber, or linoleum. If, however, the tint block is to have an overall screen, it must be prepared like a halftone, or like a benday cut. (See SHADING TINTS.)

A gray tint can be put behind black type or line drawings so as to print along with them, by any of the shading-tint techniques.

It is often more effective to add a spot of color to a page by using a tint block, than by running a line of display type in color. Type often looks weaker instead of stronger when run in color.

When a job contains process-color work and is thus running in black, yellow, blue, and red, the editor may have an opportunity to use one or more of these colors "flat" on pages of the same forms. (See PROCESS COLOR.) None of the process colors looks well when used for printing display type. However, a tint block can be used to put a panel of solid yellow behind some item to be emphasized, and the result will be effective. Panels of blue look best if screened, using perhaps a 30 percent tint instead of the solid color. The red used in process-color work is a sort of magenta and does not usually look well either solid or reduced to a tint. It does, however, look well when black is added to it as, for example, when a rather dark line or scratchboard drawing is printed over a panel of solid red, or when a light tint of yellow is combined with it, to change it toward the vermilion.

tip-ins See also INSERTS.

Halftone illustrations on coated paper or other inserts are often tipped in or inserted at the proper place in books printed on rough paper. The leaf to be tipped in is first given a narrow coating of paste along its inner edge.

A tip-in is not so strong as a wrap. (See WRAP and the illustration under BINDING.)

tone See COLOR.

Tone-Line Process The Kodak Tone-Line Process is a method of converting a continuous-tone image to a line drawing by photographic operations. The result is similar to a pen-and-ink drawing and can sometimes be used without additional artwork. In other cases, a Tone-Line rendering used as a base for further artwork may save much time. It should be said that not all subjects give good results by this method.

In essence, the Kodak Tone-Line Process involves making a film positive from the original film negative, binding them back to back in perfect register, and making a print from the combination. The trick lies in slowly revolving the printing frame during the exposure

under light coming from about a 45-degree angle. A little light leaks around the boundaries of images and creates a line image. Detailed instructions may be obtained on request to the Eastman Kodak Company, Rochester, N.Y.

tr Abbreviation for transpose. (See proofreader's marks under PROOFREADING.)

trademarks See also COPYRIGHT.

Any word, name, symbol, or device, or any combination thereof, adopted and used by a manufacturer or merchant to identify his goods and distinguish them from goods manufactured or sold by others.

Titles of periodical publications and titles of newspaper or magazine columns can be registered under the Federal trademark law.

The right to the exclusive use of a particular trademark grows out of its use, not its mere adoption or registration. Common law recognizes the right to adopt and use a trademark for the purpose of distinguishing the goods or property made or sold by the person whose mark it is, to the exclusion of the use of that symbol by all other persons on the same type of goods.

Federal registration of a trademark is a way of proving when use of that mark began, and also of ascertaining whether the proposed trademark is thought to be defensible in the Federal courts. A trademark must have been used before it can be registered. Federal registration of trademarks is handled by the Commissioner of Patents, Washington, D.C., who will supply a pamphlet on the subject free on request. Registration lasts 20 years and is renewable. The fee for registration of a trademark is $25.

State registration is helpful only where state laws provide more stringent local protection, where they deny common-law protection in the absence of local registration, or where the goods are sold in intrastate commerce.

A trademark that has been registered in the U.S. Patent Office should be used in conjunction with the phrase "Reg. U.S. Pat. Off." This phrase may be abbreviated to ®.

transcription Recording licensed to go on the air. (See RECORDINGS.)

transfer printing See DECALCOMANIAS.

transfer process In certain photocopying processes, such as Xerox and Verifax, the copy is first formed on an intermediate surface and then *transferred* to the surface of the final copy. They are thus referred to as transfer processes, to distinguish them from direct processes such as diazo and Electrofax. See also PHOTOCOPYING.

transparencies Pictures on transparent film that must be viewed by looking through them toward a light. It is relatively easy to produce color photographs of high quality by the Kodachrome, Anscocolor, and Ektachrome processes, but the result is a transparency. Color prints on paper can be made from transparencies. (See COLOR PHOTOGRAPHY.) Printing plates can also be made direct from transparencies.

transit advertising See also POSTERS; OUTDOOR ADVERTISING.

The term "transit advertising" is used to refer to car cards which are placed in the interior of street cars, buses, subways, and suburban trains and to traveling displays which are placed on the outside of similar cars and buses. Both constitute a flexible means of putting a message before commuters and shoppers in specified areas.

Car cards for local use are frequently printed by the silk-screen process in small quantities. National advertisers, needing larger quantities, tend to use the offset process. (See SILK SCREEN; OFFSET.)

In cities where much advertising is done by car cards, there are usually several firms which specialize in their production by the silk-screen process and which are in a position to give designing and lettering service as well as printing service to their customers.

The most popular size for car cards is 11 by 28 in. Other standard sizes include 11 by 14, 11 by 21, 11 by 42, 11 by 56, and 11 by 84 in. Car-card stock comes in 22½ by 42, or 23 by 43. At least ¾ in. must be allowed on either side for steel springs that hold the cards in place.

Transit systems that display car cards can provide the name of the agency through which such space can be purchased. Information about national coverage may be obtained from The Transit Advertising Assn., Inc., 500 Fifth Ave., New York.

Most transit companies will design and produce car cards for advertisers, or supply stock designs ready for imprint.

Car-card advertising space is sold on the basis of a "full run," a "half run," or a "quarter run." A "full run" includes one card in every vehicle. Space rates are quoted on a monthly basis. Minimum rates are offered for 12 consecutive months. Shorter periods are slightly higher. Outside-vehicle space is sold in "showings," ranging from a representative showing to a saturation showing.

Traveling displays may also be placed on the outside of street cars and buses. The sizes most frequently found on the sides of vehicles are 30 by 144, 30 by 88, and 21 by 44 in. The most popular rear sizes are 7½ by 60 and 21 by 72 in.

Most traveling displays are produced by silk screen on waterproof stock.

trim An untrimmed book or pamphlet cannot be read until the pages have been cut open. Trimming opens the folds. Usually about ⅛ in. is taken off during this operation. A pamphlet that is 6¼ by 9½ before trim becomes 6⅛ by 9¼ after trim.

If any illustrations bleed (see BLEED), it is desirable to allow for a trim of ⅛ to ¼ in. (See illustrations under BINDING and BOOKBINDING.)

trimetal plates See BIMETAL PLATES.

trucking See "motor freight" under FREIGHT.

type See also Appendix 1, Type Faces; TYPE MEASUREMENTS; LINOTYPE; MONOTYPE; LUDLOW.

Gutenberg did not invent printing. For years men had printed from wood blocks—one block carved for each page. Gutenberg's contribution was the invention of printing *from movable type*. He invented typesetting. His methods are still used, almost unchanged. Setting type is the first step in every printing job unless the work is to be hand-lettered or typewritten. Type is set or "composed" by men called "compositors," who work in "composing rooms." The customer gets a bill for "type composition."

Type was formerly set by hand, a letter at a time, in even the smallest sizes. It is still set by hand in much display and headline work and on very small jobs. Most type is now set by machine.

Handwork is still the basis of good

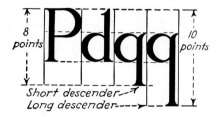

Note how 8-pt type with short descenders may look as big as 10-pt type with long descenders.

typography, since the spacing of headlines and captions and the making of corrections still call for a lot of handwork.

Until recently almost all type composition started with metal type even if this metal type would be used only to make an inked proof to be photographed on film for use in offset, etc. Now there are several ways of going directly to film, including use of the Fotosetter, Photon, Monophoto, Linofilm, VariTyper, Hadego, etc. (See PHOTOCOMPOSITION; also COLD TYPE.) However, the traditional "hot-metal" techniques, still most used, are worth learning first.

Everyone who orders type composition, or works on proofs, should have a mental picture of how the metal type is set and spaced. Otherwise, it is easy to ask for changes that are unnecessarily expensive.

Hand-set **type** is called "foundry type." Printers buy it from typefoundries by the pound in standard assortments, and keep it in "typecases," which provide a compartment for every letter or character. (Printers who have Monotype equipment can cast their own hand type, as needed.)

There are two big problems about foundry type: (1) it wears during printing and (2) it must be distributed after use, i.e., put back in the case for reuse, unless the printer is willing and able to buy more and melt down any that is worn. It is difficult to get good work from type that is partly new and partly

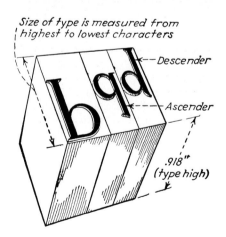

Size of type is measured from highest to lowest characters

Descender

Ascender

.918″ (type high)

Setting type by hand in a "stick." The size being set is 60-pt Lydian Bold.

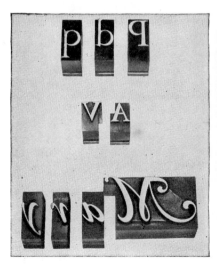

Specimens of hand type, showing how body must be large enough to accommodate both ascenders and descenders and how letters may be mortised for better fit.

After being set, type is stored in galleys like this one. The printer puts a number on each galley proof to tell him in which galley tray that type is to be found.

Basic Methods of Lettering and Type Composition

Direct hand preparation of printing surface	ARTWORK for photographic transfer to printing surface	TYPEWRITER, VARITYPER	Hand-set TYPE	LUDLOW, APL	LINOTYPE, INTERTYPE	MONOTYPE
WOOD ENGRAVING	LETTERING by pen, brush, airbrush, or crayon	Ordinary typewriting for offset and other reproduction	Also called "foundry type"	Instead of setting the type itself, matrices or molds are set. Then a solid line of lead type is cast from the line of matrices. Most used for display sizes	Keyboard action assembles matrices ready for casting solid lines of lead type	Keyboard action to control a machine that casts each letter singly. Does same work as Linotype and Intertype but offers greater flexibility on some kinds of work
LINOLEUM BLOCK	PHOTOLETTERING	Use of carbon-paper ribbon	Some hard-to-replace kinds of display type may be used only to make proofs or DUPLICATE PLATES, to prevent wear of the type itself		This is the most widely used method of setting type for newspapers, magazines, books, and job work	
Copper and steel ENGRAVING		Typing on MIMEOGRAPH stencils, SPIRIT DUPLICATOR masters, MULTILITH masters, ELLIOTT ADDRESSING stencils				
Grease pencil on lithograph plate		GRAPHOTYPE preparation of Addressograph plates				
Stylus or lettering guide on MIMEOGRAPH stencil or SPIRIT DUPLICATOR master						
Brush or knife on SILK SCREEN						
RETOUCHING on photo negative						

Note: Further information may be found by looking up the words set in CAPS. See also PHOTOCOMPOSITION.

worn. Furthermore, distributing the type in the case after use is a time-consuming operation.

Therefore, the history of typesetting has been a continuous attempt to find economical ways to print every job from new type and to avoid the expense of distributing type after use. There are now many such ways.

1. The cost of new foundry type is higher than the cost of distributing type back in the case. Under certain circumstances, however, printers may absorb this extra expense and "throw in" foundry type after a single use. When they prefer not to, or when they cannot do so, as with the rarer display faces, they may refuse to print from foundry type and may limit its use to the making of stereotypes or electrotypes or the pulling of proofs for reproduction. (See STEREOTYPE; ELECTRO.)

2. Text, especially headlines, can be set by the use of matrices (molds) instead of type. A completed line of matrices is then put into a casting machine, molten lead is forced against the matrices, and the result is a line of brand-new type in the form of a leaden slug. (See LUDLOW.)

3. The smaller sizes of type, up to 14 pt, or even larger, can be handled as above. However, the same work on the Linotype or Intertype is much faster. (See LINOTYPE; INTERTYPE.) These machines also assemble matrices and force molten lead against them to produce lines of new type in the form of solid lead slugs. However, they do it automatically by keyboard action, and the matrices are automatically put back in their proper places, after use. All composing rooms of any size either have one or more of these machines, or else have Monotype equipment as described below.

4. The Monotype (see MONOTYPE) also casts lines of new type, but it casts them letter by letter instead of a full line at a time. It can also cast up type for hand composition or corrections.

Characters are sometimes mortised for better fit in headlines.

The Monotype is a little more flexible than the Linotype. On simple matter, it may be a little more expensive; on complicated matter, tabular matter, etc., it may be noticeably cheaper.

Many printers do not attempt to do their own type composition. They send their work out to "trade" composition houses or "advertising typographers" who do nothing but typesetting. These houses serve many printers and advertisers, and offer a greater variety of type faces than the average printer could possibly afford to buy for himself.

Large advertisers usually have their ads set by composition houses, and supply reproduction proofs, stereos, or electros to the magazines or newspapers. (See REPRODUCTION PROOFS; STEREOTYPE; ELECTRO.)

In selecting type faces, it is best to ask the printer what faces he has available and choose from among these, if possible. Delays may otherwise result if he must send out for type or wait until his composing room has finished using a particular type face on some other customer's job. On the other hand, printers who say they do not have the type face requested mean that they do not personally own it. Often they can send out and get it, if urged, and if the customer is willing to O.K. the expense or delay involved.

A page of good composition should

Inking type on a proof press, in order to pull a galley proof.

The same photo as at left, after retouching to sharpen the details.

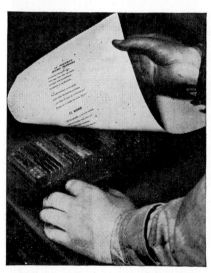

Pulling a galley proof. The impression roller has just pressed the paper against the inked type.

A form of type and cuts locked up in a "chase" ready for printing, showing use of quoins (wedges) and furniture.

CAPS,|lower|case|*Italic,*|p.d.q.

Spacing type

These lines of 24- point Caslon have been set with type-high spaces and leads to show how spacing is done. One lead (2 points thick) was inserted between each two lines.

The paragraphs are indented one em. Between words is the normal "3-em space" (3 to the em). Additional spaces were used as necessary to make the lines come out even.

Some 1½-em and 2-em "quads" were used at the ends of paragraphs. Here is some l e t t e r - s p a c i n g.

show (1) no worn letters, (2) no broken letters, (3) optically pleasing spacing between all elements, (4) correct grouping of elements—no subheads separated from the matter to which they refer, (5) even "color" and word spacing; no rivers (see RIVERS OF WHITE); no widows (see WIDOW).

For further information on the subject of typography, type selection, and layout, consult the books listed in Appendix 2, Bibliography.

type faces For detailed information about the selection and use of type faces and for specimens of text type and display type, consult Appendix 1, Type Faces.

type-high The height of type is 0.918 in. Cuts, stereotypes, and electrotypes to be printed alongside actual type must be ordered blocked on wood or metal so that they are type-high.

Electros and stereos are often left unblocked when no type is to be used with them. In this case, their metal backing is made to a thickness suitable for clamping to a "patent base." Cuts that are to be used only for the making of duplicate plates are left unblocked.

type measurements See also PICA; POINT.

Printers measure type by "points." One point is 0.01384 in., and 72 points are almost exactly 1 in. Actually, 12×72 points fall 4 points short of equaling 12 in.

Points are used in measuring type sizes and leads. These lines are set in 9-pt type. The "pica," equal to 12 points, is used in measuring the length of type lines, the width of margins, the depth of columns, etc. These lines are 13 picas wide. (See illustrations.)

An em is another kind of measurement, being the square of the height of the body of any type size. Thus, a 1-em dash (—) in 9-pt type is 9 pt long. In 12-pt type it would be 12 pt long. These paragraphs are indented 1 em. An en is half an em.

TYPE MEASUREMENTS

One inch = six picas = 72 points.

☐ 8 pt em   12 pt em ☐   24 pt em ☐

One em can be any size. One em is a space as wide as it is high. Thus one em in 12-pt type is 12 pt high and 12 pt wide.

Hair   5-em   4-em   3-em   en   em   2-em   3-em

Spaces for 12 pt   Quads for 12 pt

Spacing between words and letters is done with "spaces" and "quads."

1-pt lead	
2-pt lead	
3-pt lead	
6-pt slug	
12-pt slug	

Spacing between lines is done with "leads" and "slugs." A lead is understood to be a 2-pt lead unless stated to be 1-pt or 3-pt. Leads and slugs do not print; they merely space. Rules print.

typewriter The typewriter is more than a device for overcoming illegible handwriting. It is not only the universal method of writing business letters and other communications but also the preferred method of "type composition" for material to be produced on the spirit duplicator, mimeograph, or Multilith. In the offset field, it is a stiff competitor of Linotype and Monotype. Tape-punching typewriters are also becoming adjuncts to these and other kinds of composing machines.

A typewritten communication that has been well designed can be just as legible and effective as one set in type, and much less expensive.

For these reasons, the capabilities and special attributes of the typewriter as a composing machine deserve study by everyone whose work involves the use of the printed or duplicated word. (See COLD TYPE.) For a discussion of how a typewriter is helpful in making word counts and character counts, see COPYFITTING.

The ordinary typewriter writes six single-spaced lines to the inch, three double-spaced lines. If it has pica type, it writes 10 characters or spaces to the inch. If it has elite type, it writes 12 characters or spaces to the inch. Typewriter type looks different from printer's type because every letter, whether an "i" or a capital "W," must be of the same width, namely, $\frac{1}{10}$ or $\frac{1}{12}$ in. In printer's type, each letter gets as much or as little space as it needs.

The ordinary typewriter prints through an inked ribbon. There are black ribbons and colored ribbons, heavily inked ribbons and lightly inked ones, cotton, silk, and nylon ribbons, and special ribbons for hectograph, Multilith, decalcomania, and other work.

Fabric ribbons tend to thicken the letters. Cleaner, crisper impressions for photographic reproduction are possible through the use of one-use carbon ribbons. Machines not equipped to use a carbon ribbon can produce the same kind of work if the typing is done without a ribbon (i.e., with the ribbon control lever in the nonprint position) directly on the back of a piece of very hard (non-smudging) carbon paper. This cuts the carbon paper to pieces but produces a clean impression on the paper beneath. This procedure is used frequently in preparing copy for offset. (See OFFSET.)

Typewritten lines are ordinarily left unjustified; i.e., they vary in length, producing a ragged right-hand margin. They are not justified to make them all of the same length, as in a book. They can, however, be justified either on an ordinary machine in a somewhat crude fashion or semimechanically by using a special margin-justifier attachment. Both methods require a second typing.

Suppose it is decided to produce a news bulletin having two typewritten columns, each 36 characters wide. To justify the lines on an ordinary machine, the copy is typed once so that no line exceeds 36 characters; many lines will be shorter. Then it is retyped, and in a line that is, say, 33 characters long, two spaces instead of one are placed after each of the first three words, thus filling the line.

A similar procedure will yield even better results when a proportional-spacing typewriter such as the IBM Executive is used. See also VARITYPER and JUSTOWRITER for methods of justifying semiautomatically and fully automatically.

The ordinary typewriter offers more variety than is generally made use of. Headings or words to be emphasized can be put in caps, or in underlined caps, or in underlined lowercase. Headings can be centered, cut in, or put flush left. Text can be single-spaced, double-spaced, triple-spaced, indented, boxed, underlined, etc. Long paragraphs can be broken up into short ones. Certain kinds of information can, to good effect, be taken out of sentence form and put into tabular form.

Short paragraphs (no more than five lines), extra space between paragraphs, generous margins, and frequent sub-heads all help a message to look readable and to get read.

There are some specialized typewriters on the market for specialized jobs. (See VARITYPER; IBM EXECUTIVE TYPEWRITER; AUTOMATIC TYPEWRITER; JUSTOWRITER.)

Electric typewriters are generally preferred to manual machines for reproduction purposes since the work tends to be more even in quality. This is especially important when mimeograph stencils are to be cut.

Electric typewriters range in price from about $140 for the Smith-Corona portable offered by Sears, Roebuck to about $400 to $500 for standard office machines and $600 to $700 for proportional-spacing machines. (VariTypers are up in the $2,000 bracket.)

Typit   A system for providing any typewriter with the capacity to write special symbols as required. When a special symbol like π is required, for example,

it is selected from a case of other commonly used symbols, positioned, and then struck by depressing *any* key. The impression is made when the typebar, acting only as a hammer, comes up and causes the Typit symbol to print through the regular ribbon. Each Typit symbol is held in its own plastic handle and is positioned accurately and automatically by means of a special type guide, which is substituted for the type guide that came with the typewriter as original equipment. Typit symbols cost $3.35 each from stock and can also be made up to special order. Stock symbols include Greek letters, mathematical and chemical symbols, subscripts and superscripts, foreign accents, brackets, fractions, etc. For further information, inquire of Mechanical Enterprises, Inc., 3127 Colvin St., Alexandria, Va.

Typit.

Typograph   See LUDLOW.

typography   See DESIGN; LAYOUT; Appendix 1, Type Faces.

Typro   A photolettering machine for use in office or art department which

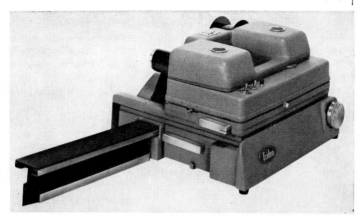

The Typro by Friden.

permits rapid, low-cost composition of display headlines. The operator winds the master film reels in the font magazine to the desired font, then turns the selector handle until the desired letter appears in the viewing window. Each selected letter is then printed down on a strip of photographic paper at the touch of a lever. There is provision for selective letterspacing, centering, multi-line composition, surprinting, mixing of fonts, and use of shading tints.

Fonts are available in many type styles and in sizes from 6 to 144 pt. They cost about $20 each. From 10 to 15 fonts can be housed in a single font magazine, and the change from one magazine to another is quick and easy. Development of the exposed strips can be semiautomatic (where machine is in continual use) or by the hand-dip method. The Typro is distributed by Friden, Inc., and sells in the $1,000 range. See also PHOTOLETTERING.

U | u

u & lc Abbreviation for upper and lowercase. (See proofreader's marks under PROOFREADING.)

undelivered mail See Appendix 3, Postal Information.

union label The printing industry is largely unionized. Particularly is this true of the larger and older plants doing quality work. Printed matter produced under union conditions may, at the option of the buyer, carry the union label.

The union label is always used on political campaign literature as a matter of practical politics. Many other printing buyers require that it appear on their literature in recognition of the fact that about one-quarter of the income receivers of the country are union members, and that they and their families and other supporters of the union movement are likely to be favorably influenced by seeing the union label.

The label, which reads

ALLIED PRINTING

TRADES UNION LABEL COUNCIL NO. 000

Name of City

signifies that the printed matter on which it appears has been produced in unionized plants by AFL-CIO union compositors, pressmen, photoengravers, stereotypers, electrotypers, and binders. The number identifies the actual firm that did the printing. In cities where there is no Allied Printing Trades Council, the labels of the separate unions of compositors, pressmen, engravers, electrotypers, stereotypers, and binders may be used.

The Lithographers and Photoengravers International Union has its own union label which reads as shown below.

United Parcel Service See also SHIPPING INFORMATION; Appendix 3, Postal Information.

A fast, reliable delivery service of

344

small parcels for shippers who have a minimum of several such shipments per week. Weight and size limits are 50 lb and 108 in. in combined length and girth. The shipper pays a weekly charge of $2 for daily pickup service at his premises regardless of the number of packages he customarily ships and whether or not any packages are to be sent out on a particular day. For each parcel there is a fixed per package rate plus a per pound rate determined by the zone. For a package over 84 in. in length and girth, the minimum charge is equal to that for a package weighing 25 lb. There is an additional COD charge of 50 cents per parcel. Rates include automatic protection against loss or damage up to $100 per package without extra charge.

Next-day delivery is provided over extensive territories, second-day to others. Parcels are delivered to the premises of the consignee, even on the upper floor or down a country road. Second and third attempts are made to deliver each package and efforts are made to correct wrong addresses. Parcels are handled exclusively by UPS personnel.

In 1966, UPS was operating in three areas: Eastern (part of Maine south through Virginia and west to include New York, Pennsylvania, and a sliver of Ohio); Midwestern (Ohio and Kentucky west to include Minnesota, Iowa, and Missouri); Western (Washington, Oregon, and California and bits of neighboring states). There is interstate UPS service within each area; intrastate in certain segments of each.

Cross-country services are of two kinds: Brown Label (long-distance service) from New York and Chicago to Los Angeles and San Francisco and vice versa; and Blue Label (air service) from New York, Los Angeles, and San Francisco to seven metropolitan areas. Brown Label provides four-day service between California and Chicago, and five-day service coast to coast. Blue Label service provides two-day delivery service.

For information consult UPS offices in New York, Detroit, and Los Angeles.

uppercase The printer's term for capital letters. Hand type always used to be kept in twin drawers or "cases," the upper one containing the capital letters and the lower one, the small letters. "U & lc" means set in upper and lowercase. Another way of saying the same thing is "c & lc," meaning caps and lowercase. (See illustration under CASE.)

V|v

vandyke See also BLUEPRINT.

Simply a brown blueprint. Offset printers sometimes make a vandyke print from their negatives, to enable the customer to catch any mistakes (e.g., misplaced captions) before the printing plates are made. Vandykes are used primarily as master prints from which to make more blueprints.

VariTyper composing machine The VariTyper composing machine is a typewriter-like device which is employed to compose reproduction copy for photo-offset, direct-image offset and other reproduction methods. Copy produced on the VariTyper machine can be likened to the repro proof produced from metal type. This method is often referred to as "cold type" since it does not involve the use of molten metal, as in conventional typesetting machines.

VariTyper machines are found in offices as well as in printshops. The applications for VariTyper equipment include ruled forms, price lists, catalogs, advertising literature, brochures, house organs, books, and statistical reports.

One of the principal factors in selec-

tion of this composition method is its economy, compared with conventional typesetting methods, and its greater typographic quality, economy of space, and flexibility, compared with typewriter-produced copy.

Operators of VariTyper machines usually are men or women with typing experience. They are given specialized training by the manufacturer, the VariTyper Corporation.

The fundamental distinguishing feature of the VariTyper machine is its *changeable type*. There are over one hundred styles and sizes of type in most of the world's languages—all instantly changeable. Sizes range from 6 to 12 pt. Spacing, both vertical and horizontal, is instantly variable. Vertical spacing (line spacing or leading) is variable in ½-pt gradations from ½ to 18 pt. Horizontal spacing is variable from approximately 14 to approximately 19 characters per inch.

An even right-hand margin can be produced by typing each line a second time, the machine automatically doing the "justifying," with no calculations by the operator.

The VariTyper composing machine.

Many VariTyper Machines are constructed with "differential spacing," the feature which automatically gives the wider characters such as "M" and "W" more space than the narrower characters such as "I" and "J." This paragraph has been composed on a VariTyper with "differential spacing."

Models are also available with "unit spacing," which, like the typewriter, allots uniform space to each character. In other respects, they are basically similar to the differential-spacing models. These are employed, primarily, for internal reproduction work where differentially spaced type may not be required. This paragraph has been composed on a VariTyper with unit spacing. Most commercial VariTyper composition, and that done for external circulation, is done on differential-spacing models.

An optional feature, available on all VariTyper models, is the "forms ruling device." With this device, any style of line or leader is ruled quickly and accurately at the push of a button.

VariTypers with unit spacing range in price from about $1,200 to $1,900. Vari-

Typers with differential spacing range in price from about $2,500 to $3,500. Extra fonts of type cost from $35 to $45 each.

The VariTyper composing machine is a product of the VariTyper Corporation, 720 Frelinghuysen Ave., Newark, 14 N.J. VariTyper Corporation is a subsidiary of the Addressograph-Multigraph Corporation.

For another composing typewriter offering differential spacing, see IBM EXECUTIVE TYPEWRITER.

VariTyper Headliner A photographic composing machine for setting display type in sizes from 10 to 84 pt. It is manufactured by the VariTyper Corporation, 720 Frelinghuysen Ave., Newark 14, N.J., and ranges in price from about $1,100 to $1,900, with extra typefonts at $35.50. It sets type for price books, catalogs, newspaper ads, fliers, signs, nameplates, etc. The machine is designed to be operated on the top of a desk. The copy is set by dialing each desired letter in turn; with practice, speeds of about 30 characters a minute can be attained. The letters are printed in sequence on a strip of sensitized paper or transparent film. The machine is easy to operate, since word and letter

The VariTyper Headliner Model 800.

spacing, exposure time, photographic development, and fixing are fully automatic. The resulting proofs are smudge-proof and of reproduction quality.

varnishing Any printed job will have more eye appeal if it is spirit-varnished or laminated. (See also LAMINATING.) Book jackets are often given a glossy finish in one of these ways.

Quick-drying varnish (or lacquer) can be flowed on over the whole surface of a printed job; or it can be applied like ink to any given area.

For varnishing an average book jacket, one printer charges $10 for the first thousand and $6 for each additional thousand. The thicker the paper or cardboard, the higher the cost.

Even when varnish is flowed on, parallel strips can be left unvarnished if they run from edge to edge. This is often done on can labels and box wraps to leave unvarnished the areas that will later take glue.

As contrasted to the varnishing (or lacquering) which is done on special sheet-coating machines, any letterpress printer can do varnishing work, with varnish in place of ink on a regular press and with rubber plates to apply it. This is called "spot varnishing."

The following companies handle a good deal of varnishing and laminating: John W. Crawford Co., 160 Varick St., New York 13; Greggory, Inc., 1540 Merchandise Mart Plaza, Chicago 54; and Lamcote Division of Arvey Corp., 300 N. Kimball Ave., Chicago 18.

vellum See PARCHMENT.

Velox The trade name of a sensitized photographic printing paper, but the word has come to be used to describe a special process used for reducing the cost of halftone engravings. The process is much used in newspaper advertising work.

In an ordinary halftone, there are very faint dots even in the "white" areas. If an engraver is asked to make a "highlight" halftone, he eliminates these faint dots. This operation does not always improve ordinary photographs, but it can greatly improve the quality of reproduction of pencil and crayon drawings, wash drawings, etc. However, a highlight halftone costs three times as much as an ordinary halftone, and a combination (line and halftone) highlight halftone costs still more.

By the Velox process, these costs can

be greatly reduced. The original art-work is converted into a duplicate pho-tographic print, which is screened and highlighted. The print can be retouched as desired. Near blacks can be painted solid black. Ruling and other line work can be added. Type can be surprinted on the print, or type proofs on acetate can later be laid over the print.

The finished Velox print can then be made into a halftone engraving "dot for dot" at regular benday linecut rates. Very often the cost of a cut made in this way (including the cost of the Velox print) is less than half what the cost would be if the whole job had been done by a photoengraver.

For best results, the screen of the drawings when printed should be no finer than 85 because it is difficult for the camera to "hold" the dots of a finer screen. It is necessary, therefore, to tell the firm that makes the Veloxes the size in which they will be reproduced and the desired final screen.

Varifax An office copying machine (marketed by Eastman Kodak since 1953) which uses a gelatin-transfer pro-cess, also known as the "dye-transfer process." It can make as many as 10 copies from a single matrix and can copy all colors. The approximate first-copy cost is 10 cents, for each copy thereafter, 1 cent. Verifax has the disad-vantage of producing slightly damp copies. The machines are not so com-pletely automated as some of the more expensive office copiers. The Kodak Readyprint copier utilizes the same principle and is a bit faster (25 sec to make a copy), but it will make only one copy from each matrix.

A process very similar to the Verifax gelatin-transfer process is described under DIFFUSION TRANSFER and is em-ployed in a number of other office pho-tocopying machines.

For information about additional office copying processes, see PHOTO-COPYING.

verso A right-hand page in a book is called a "recto," and the back of it, i.e., a left-hand page, is a "verso."

video tape The principle of magnetic tape recording has, since the mid-1950s, been applied to sight as well as to sound through the video tape recorder. After the television camera transforms the light waves it receives into electric cur-rents and the microphone does the same for the sound waves it picks up, both sets of signals are fed to the recording head of a video tape recorder. The re-cording head is essentially an electro-magnet, the magnetic properties of which can be turned on and off accord-ing to the electric signals it receives. Tape passing over the recording head becomes magnetized in a corresponding pattern. When the tape is played back over a playback head, the process is re-versed: the magnetic pattern on the tape generates electric signals, which are reconverted into visual and aural signals on the television screen and loudspeaker.

Video tape recording requires a tape that is 2 in. wide, as contrasted with the ¼-in. tape used in straight sound recording. The most recent recorders operate at two speeds, 7½ in./sec and 15 in./sec, and are capable of recording color. For television, video tape offers higher fidelity than film because it by-passes the intermediary optical steps in-volved in film making. A good video tape recording is often indistinguishable from live television. In addition, mag-netic recording makes instantaneous playback possible; no time need be lost in developing negatives and making prints. On the other hand, film con-tinues to have many advantages where complicated editing or a high degree of mobility in the original shooting is required.

As of Jan. 1, 1965, there were 1,117 video tape recorders at 487 broadcast locations (network, commercial, and ETV stations) in the United States.

vignette To vignette a halftone illustration means to make it fade softly into the whiteness of the paper with no sharp edge. Vignetting used to be done much more than it is today, especially with portraits. Vignetting costs extra. It tends to be a little more successful in offset, photogelatin, or gravure than in letterpress. Vignetted letterpress halftones often show a definite edge when printed, no matter how hard the engraver and the pressman try to avoid this.

vinylite A plastic that is widely used as a substitute for wax, tenaplate, and lead in the electrotype molding process (see ELECTRO). Also used as an unbreakable substitute for shellac in phonograph records and as the essential ingredient of certain plastic printing plates.

W | w

wash drawing   See also DRAWING TECH-NIQUES.

A wash drawing is made with a brush and watercolor. If it is a black-and-white wash drawing, it is made with black watercolor, diluted to obtain the various grays. Since a wash drawing contains grays that are neither white nor black, it must be reproduced as a halftone; it cannot be reproduced as a line drawing. (See HALFTONE.)

watermark   Paper that reveals lettering or a design when held up to the light is said to have been watermarked. Watermarking is not necessarily an indication of high quality.

waterproof paper   See WET-STRENGTH PAPER.

web, web-fed press   Paper pulp is converted into a web of paper as it moves through a papermaking machine. Sometimes this web of paper is cut into sheets; sometimes it is not cut but wound in rolls. Printing presses designed to accept paper from a roll instead of in separate sheets are known as "web-fed" presses. Newspapers are printed on web-fed rotary presses. (See ROTARY PRESS.)

wet-strength paper   Paper is obtainable that does not lose its strength when wet. Such paper is known as "wet-strength" paper. It is indistinguishable from ordinary paper when dry.

Wet-strength paper is not waterproof. Water will pass through it but will not weaken it. In fact wet-strength filter papers have come into wide use in tea bags, coffee filters, etc.

Waterproof paper which will not permit water to penetrate it is also obtainable for special uses.

wf   Abbreviation for "wrong font." (See proofreader's marks under PROOF-READING; FONT.)

whiteprint   See also BLUEPRINT.

The whiteprint, or *diazo*, process is an improved blueprint process. The principle is used in copying machines—made by Ozalid, Bruning, Ditto, and others. As in blueprinting, whiteprinting makes same-size copies of translucent originals. Unlike blueprinting, it makes a positive from a positive, makes copies that do not stretch or shrink in the developing, and can make copies in black, red, or other colors as well as blue.

The cost per letter-size copy is as little as 5 cents commercially, 2 cents where a company operates its own equipment.

Simply by changing from one kind of sensitized material to another, prints can be made on white paper, transparent paper, clear film, frosted film, microfilm, tracing cloth, opaque cloth or film, both sides of the same paper, etc. The process will reproduce photographs, although to duplicate a photograph it is necessary first to make a positive print on film instead of on the usual paper.

Whiteprint equipment is widely used to copy engineering drawings. It can be used wherever the material to be copied has been kept sufficiently translucent.

The whiteprint process is based on the use of light-sensitive dyes that are destroyed when exposed to strong light. When the sensitized paper is exposed to strong light through a master tracing, the dye is destroyed except where protected by the opaque lines of the original. The undestroyed dye is then made permanent by exposure to certain chemicals.

One of the smaller machines costs in the neighborhood of $300 and can make copies up to 9 in. wide and any length at speeds up to 10 ft a minute. With even simpler equipment it is possible to develop prints by inserting them briefly in a covered cylinder containing a bit of ammonia.

For a comparison of whiteprint and other printing processes, see the charts inside the covers of this book.

widow When a column or page begins with the short last line of a paragraph carried over from the previous column or page, this short line is called a

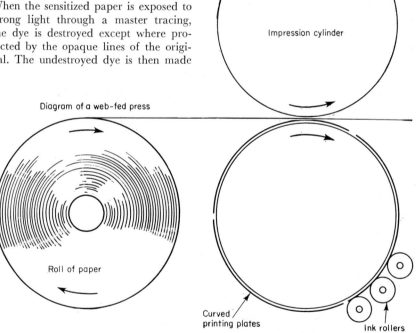

Diagram of a web-fed press

Impression cylinder

Roll of paper

Curved printing plates

Ink rollers

Diagram of a web-fed press.

"widow." The meticulous makeup man, proofreader, or editor will always cut, expand, or adjust the text to avoid widows. In books, they can often be eliminated by making a pair of facing pages one line longer or shorter than the rest of the pages in the book.

window displays   See DISPLAYS.

window envelope   An envelope with a transparent panel in it through which the name and address typed on the enclosure can be read. It is usually cheaper to buy window envelopes than to pay for having a complete name and address typed on both the letter and the envelope. People have come to associate window envelopes with bills, and this militates against their widespread use in direct mail work. Envelopes can be ordered with the window in any desired position. (See also ENVELOPES.)

wire stitching   See STITCHING and illustration under BINDING.

woodcut   See BLOCK PRINTING; WOOD ENGRAVINGS.

wood engravings   Until the invention of the halftone, the wood engraving was the principal method of making illustrations for letterpress printing. Wood engravings were (and are) entirely engraved by hand into the surface of a type-high wooden block and printed, of course, the actual size in which they were engraved.

Wood engravers became highly skilled in rendering objects requiring fine shading and detail, and developed a style (see sample) that has never been surpassed for the reproduction of textures and details on almost any printing surface.

This process has therefore survived in competition with the halftone. More recently it has been imitated with scratchboard drawings, by which artists at-

This illustration was printed from an electro made from a wood engraving.

tempt to duplicate the effective shadings and feeling of the genuine woodcut.

The Sander Wood Engraving Co., Inc., of 542 S. Dearborn St., Chicago 5, is one of the leading firms of wood engravers, and calls attention to the following advantages of the process: (1) The work can be done directly from merchandise or unretouched photos. (2) For a single charge the customer gets both artwork and original printing plate. The artwork is created directly on the printing plate, so that the purchaser has both a cut from which etch proofs and electrotypes can be made and a number of etch proofs, each of which is, in a sense, original artwork. (3) While wood engravings are made to the actual reproduction size, the etch proofs can be enlarged and reduced to meet many size requirements. (4) The single woodcut, in addition to showing textures and detail with a clarity not possible any other way, will print perfectly on any kind of paper, and by any printing process. (Woodcut etch proofs are excellent artwork for offset printing, including rubber-plate printing on corrugated boxes.) (5) Because woodcut proofs are "line" artwork, they frequently eliminate the costs of combination plates when used in newspaper or magazine ads. (6) They do away with problems of suiting screen to medium.

wood pulp Most paper is made from wood pulp, either groundwood pulp or the more expensive but better chemical pulp. (See GROUNDWOOD PULP; CHEMICAL PULP.)

work and turn By means of the work-and-turn technique, a printer can print 1,000 copies of a small pamphlet *on both sides* with only 1,000 impressions. He cuts his paper to double the size re-

quired for each pamphlet and runs the job as shown in the illustration. The phrase "work and tumble" is used when the pile is turned from front to back instead of from left to right. A job too big to run work and turn is run "sheetwise" in the ordinary way. (See illustration below.)

work-up Occasionally a space, quad, or lead that is not supposed to print works up to the height of the type, is inked, and prints. Work-ups are caused when parts of the form are not perfectly square. It is the pressman's job to catch and correct them when they occur.

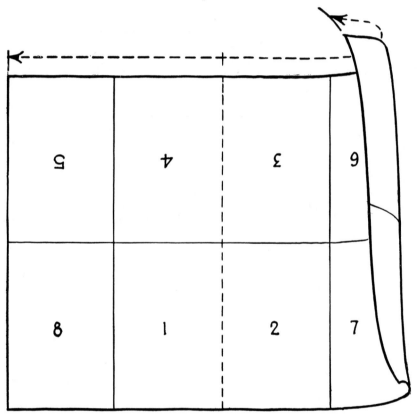

How an 8-page, 6 x 9 leaflet is printed "work and turn." When the pile is turned over as indicated, page 5 will print on the back of page 6, page 8 on the back of page 7, etc. After being printed on both sides, the sheet is cut along the dotted line, and each half folds to make one complete leaflet.

wove paper See LAID PAPER.

wrap See also INSERTS.

A wrap in a book or magazine is an insert that has not been pasted in (tipped in) but has been wrapped around one of the signatures, so that it is stitched into the binding as securely as any other page.

In books printed on antique paper, illustrations on coated paper are often inserted as wraps or tip-ins. (See TIP-INS.) Wraps are stronger, but it is not so easy to get them opposite the desired page of text. (For an illustration, see INSERTS.)

wrapping and packing See also SHIPPING INFORMATION.

Sooner or later everyone who works with words or who must meet deadlines and take responsibility for the movement of printed materials will need to know something about wrapping, packing, and shipping. In some organizations it is safe to leave such matters to the shipping room. In others it is not quite so safe to rely on the shipping-room people, especially if the problem at hand is out of their usual line. In any case, the man who makes plans and places orders involving wrapping and shipping owes it to his shipping-room people to consult them in advance, give them notice of his requirements, and see to it that they have on hand the necessary wrapping materials.

Besides, rare is the executive who does not occasionally have to put some rush proofs, artwork, or samples into the mail after office closing.

When printing and mailing activities are not the main functions of a firm, it may be necessary for a department either to set up its own wrapping table or to procure a place in the regular shipping room and earmark for its own use the special materials that it will need.

For example, stiff cardboard, often in large sizes, is essential for protecting artwork in transit. Cut sizes of cardboard and corrugated board are useful for protecting the contents of envelopes. Mailing tubes are indispensable for protecting posters and other flexible materials that must not be creased. Special rubber stamps or stickers may help packages get the best attention at the receiving end.

Careful packing must precede wrapping and shipping. The following reminders may prevent damage to materials:

1. Use adequate cardboard backing for photographs, artwork, and copy to be reproduced photographically. Tape the artwork to the cardboard backing to prevent its being damaged by slipping back and forth or extending beyond the cardboard.

2. Use ample packing within a box so that printed materials will not be damaged by slipping into the odd crannies. Wadded newspaper makes good packing material.

3. Small pieces, such as cards or pamphlets, will be less easily damaged from shuffling around if they are banded or packaged by the printer in lots of, say, 100. Having them in packages may facilitate distribution also.

Shipping containers will vary according to the product being shipped and whether or not the shipments are standardized. When many similar items are to be shipped, ready-to-use boxes will save time that would otherwise be wasted in cutting board to wrap each separately. Both folding and set-up boxes are available in different sizes and strengths.

If originally packed by the printer in corrugated boxes holding about 35 lb, material is ready for bulk mailing, can be moved easily by a shipping clerk, and is within the 40-lb parcel-post weight limit. (For further information on size and weight limitations, see Appendix 3, Postal Information. See CONTAINER PRINTING for suggestions on printing boxes, tubes, etc.)

Outside wrapping may be unnecessary if the material is in a strong, well-marked package. In many cases, however, the outside wrapping is really the container and as such must be strong and durable. It should be legibly addressed and marked as to contents. (See Appendix 3 for postal requirements on sealing, labeling, and marking for postal inspection.)

Case packing is a science in itself. Let no man assume he can do it until he has taken some lessons from experienced hands. Two or three hundred pounds of printed materials in an up-ended packing case often crush the wadded newspapers that were supposed to wedge them snug, and then slide around and do themselves endless damage. The case packer must assume that any and every element in a case may have to bear the entire weight of all the other items.

The shipping and wrapping room of a firm or department should be located where it is convenient for the delivery of new stock and the shipment of outgoing materials. It should be large enough not only to permit efficient handling of big, rush jobs, but also to allow for storage of materials.

A large table, with space above or below for a roll of wrapping paper and corrugated paper, is a necessity. The following materials will help solve the average wrapping problems:

Gummed tape and dispenser.

Twine.

Scissors.

Mat knife for cutting string, cardboard, and corrugated paper.

Gummed labels, e.g., "CONTENTS: BOOKS: May be opened for postal inspection if necessary."

Scales (the dial-reading kind is a great timesaver over the beam type). It is helpful to have a small scale for letters and a larger one for packages.

Grease stick or felt-tipped pen, for addressing cartons and marking weight or postage required.

Rubber stamps, e.g., "FIRST CLASS," "SPECIAL DELIVERY," "AIRMAIL."

Roll of brown kraft wrapping paper, with cutting blade.

Roll of single-faced corrugated paper. (The standard width is 36 in., but suppliers will slit this, on request, into 10-, 12-, and 14-in. rolls.)

Yardstick and 100-in. tape measure, for checking size limits for parcel post and air express.

Kraft envelopes.

Newspapers for wadding.

Mailing tubes.

Cardboard and double-corrugated backing sheets.

Boxes, set up or knocked down.

U.S. mailbag for bulk shipments. (See Appendix 3, Postal Information.)

Stamps, precanceled stamps, stamped envelopes, or postage meter.

NOTE: Shipping rooms can be a fire hazard unless neatness and care prevail.

Shipping information should be readily available in the simplest and handiest form. One small office found that it was helpful to post such information on a special bulletin board where every part-time helper could get the facts easily.

Since wrapping and packing are influenced by the method of shipping, every shipping clerk (whether a full-time expert, a well-meaning volunteer, or the boss racing for a printer's midnight deadline) should know (1) how best to ship the material and (2) how to wrap it for such shipping.

Help in answering these questions may be given through posting the following:

1. Location of the nearest post office, hours for postal service, time of out-going airmail, etc.

2. Sample rate chart showing comparative costs of shipping by parcel post, by express, and by freight. (See SHIPPING INFORMATION.)

3. Postage rates, and weight limits for

first-, second-, and third-class mail. (See Appendix 3.)

4. Fourth-class postal rate chart and local post-office zone key for use with a "Postal Manual." (See Appendix 3.)

5. Zone map showing an approximation of the fourth-class zones. (See Appendix 3.)

6. Local air-express rate chart available from REA Express.

7. Office rules for wrapping, mailing, packaging, and recording of routine shipments.

Wrapping and shipping are not all. The shipping clerk must have or be a bookkeeper to keep the records of packages sent or received, whether insured, registered, COD, special delivery, special handling, returned for insufficient postage, air or surface express, freight, etc. If the shipment is lost or damaged, these receipts and records must be immediately available.

Wrico Lettering Guides See LEROY.

wrong font The *s*econd word in this sentence contains a letter that is of the wrong font of type. (See proofreader's marks under PROOFREADING; FONT.)

Xerox, Xerography Xerography is a recent and basic development with implications for almost every aspect of photocopying, printing, and the graphic arts in general. It has revolutionized the office-copying field.

The process utilizes the fact that some materials, like selenium, are photoconductive, which is to say that they conduct electricity when illuminated but not in the dark. Thus, it is possible to place an electric charge on an unlighted surface, project an image on that surface, and dissipate the charge wherever the light strikes. Ink powder with an opposite electric charge will then be attracted to the areas that remain charged and can be transferred to an ordinary piece of paper and heat-fused to the paper for permanence.

One limitation of the Xerographic process is its inability to reproduce photographs or solid areas. These normally show up in Xerox copies simply as blank areas defined by a dark-gray edge.

One of the first applications of Xerography was in making paper printing plates for offset duplicators. Then the company introduced the Xerox "Copyflo," a high-speed machine which could make 11-in. wide enlargements

from microfilm at speeds of about 20 ft per min. This machine is priced in the $35,000 range, or it can be rented. It can copy almost anything from book manuscripts to library cards at costs under 5 cents per item.

The Xerox 914 is an office copying machine which will produce up to six same-size copies per minute from bound books, magazines, and documents of all kinds on ordinary paper. The user pays a monthly charge based on the number of copies made. The per-copy cost begins at 3.5 cents, with a $95-a-month minimum, and drops with increasing volume.

The Xerox 813 is similar except that it will not copy books or anything that cannot be fed into a slot and it requires less space. The minimum monthly charge is also lower than that of the 914—about half as much. The copies are slightly reduced in size, about 6 percent.

The Xerox 2400 is faster and more automatic than the 914 and carries a monthly minimum invoicing of $350. Within this minimum, the user can copy 8,750 separate items at the metered rate of 4 cents each or can make 499 copies each of 125 jobs at the rate of 2,400 an hour for ½ cent a copy. The rates are 4 cents each for one to three copies of a single original, 2 cents each for the fourth through tenth copy, 1 cent each for the eleventh through twenty-fifth copy, and ½ cent each thereafter. The machine can be set to produce any number of copies from 1 to 499 and can be loaded with up to 2,000 sheets of paper.

For further information, consult Xerox Corporation, Rochester, N.Y.

For a comparison between the capabilities of the Xerox 2400 and a Kodak Ektalith department, see EKTALITH.

Xograph 3-D printing A process developed by Cowles Magazines and Broadcasting, Inc., for giving an illusion of depth to printed halftone illustrations. A special stereoscopic camera is used which divides the picture into many tiny, vertical parallel strips. These are reproduced in offset with a 300-line screen. The printed picture is then given a plastic coating, embossed to form vertical ridges which act somewhat like half-round glass rods to magnify one vertical stereo strip and hide others, depending on the angle of view. In one of the first uses of the process, 8 million Xograph illustrations for Eastman's Kodak film appeared in *Look Magazine* at a cost of about $200,000.

Z | z

zinc engraving See LINECUT.

Zip-a-Tone See SHADING TINTS.

Appendix 1

Type Faces

Type faces come in hundreds of designs and sizes and weights, but it is possible to classify them roughly as follows:

Text faces	*vs.*	**display faces**
Roman	*vs.*	*italic*
Lightface	*vs.*	**boldface**
Old style	*vs.*	modern
Serif	*vs.*	sans serif
Serif	*vs.*	square serif

Text types, like the one used for the text of this book (9-pt. Baskerville), commonly come in the following sizes (see POINT):

6-pt. Caslon

8-pt. Baskerville

10-pt. Baskerville

12-pt. Baskerville

14-pt. Baskerville

Often they are available in 7-, 9-, and 11-pt. sizes. Text type can be set by hand but is usually set on the Linotype, Intertype, or Monotype. (See LINOTYPE; INTERTYPE; MONOTYPE.)

Display sizes include 18, 24, 30, 36, 48, 60, 72 pt., and sometimes 96 or even 144 pt. Rarer sizes are 16, 21, 42, 54, 84, and 120 pt.

Further information about display faces, along with 106 specimens of display type, is given under the heading "Display Faces" beginning on page 362 of this appendix.

A standard font of text type includes caps, small caps, lower case, figures, punctuation, and special signs. Usually it includes also italic or boldface. (A Linotype operator working with a font of matrices containing both roman and italic letters can mix roman and italic with virtually no loss of speed. But if the matrices contain roman and italic, they cannot contain boldface, and the setting of boldface may put the operator to extra trouble and so slow him down. The setting of small caps also slows down a Linotype operator and thus provides an incentive to the man who will pay the bills not to use small caps any more than necessary.)

Considerable variety can be obtained even within one size and style of type, as shown in the following lines. Often, requirements of display and emphasis can be met without going to another type font, especially if the variations shown here are emphasized further by spacing, indenting, centering, etc.

CAPITAL LETTERS

L E T T E R S P A C E D   C A P S

Caps and Small Caps
EVEN SMALL CAPS
Caps and Lower Case
ITALIC CAPS
L E T T E R S P A C E D   I T A L I C
C A P S
Italic Caps and Lower Case

On the following pages some of the most used type styles are illustrated. Note that the same, or similar, styles are sometimes put out under different names by different companies, and types of the same name may differ slightly in weight or compactness between one company and another, and even within one company, *e.g.,* Linotype Garamond and Garamond No. 3. The best-known type founders are Linotype, Intertype, Monotype, Ludlow, and (for hand-set type) American Type Founders and Bauer Type Foundry.

An important thing about text type is its weight on the page, or "color." Boldfaces, without leading, look very dark on the page. Lightfaces, with leading, have a light color. Boldfaces, generously leaded, have about the same weight on the page as lightfaces without leading, but they have a different texture. Old-style type faces differ in texture from modern faces and from sans-serif faces.

Good design requires that each block of type should have appropriate weight or texture. A block of type constitutes an area of gray. Whether it will be a dark gray or a light gray and whether it will be of unobtrusive texture or of distinctive texture are determined by the choice of type face and amount of leading. Type prints heavier on soft paper than on glossy paper.

Long lines need more leading than short lines and require larger type to be read easily. The most readable lines of type are those whose length is between 1½ and 2½ times the length of the alphabet in the type face chosen, *i.e.,* between 39 and 65 characters in length.

Copy fitting (see COPY FITTING) is the technique of making the words fit into the space available. Sometimes the copy is written or rewritten "to space." Sometimes the type size is chosen to accommodate the copy. Either way it is necessary to know how many words of copy will go into a given space in a given size and kind of type. Information for calculating this is given with each type specimen. This is an alphabet of 10-pt. Granjon:

abcdefghijklmnopqrstuvwxyz

This is an alphabet of 10-pt. Bookman:

abcdefghijklmnopqrstuvwxyz

It is clear that, although they are the same size, 10-pt. Bookman is less compact than 10-pt. Granjon. In fact, a given area of Granjon will accommodate 13 per cent more copy than the same area of Bookman.

Thus, the alphabet length of a given size and style of type is an important piece of information. It is generally given in points. (It is not difficult to measure the point length of an alphabet with an ordinary ruler, if it is remembered that there are 72 points to the inch, 9 points to the ⅛ inch. Alphabet length means lower-case alphabet length unless otherwise stated.)

More useful, however, than alphabet length, is characters per pica (c.p.p.). This is easily figured from the alphabet length (in points). The formula [1] is as follows:

$$\frac{341}{\text{Alphabet length}} = \text{characters per pica}$$

[1] This is sometimes given as 26 (number of letters in the alphabet) ÷ alphabet length in picas, or 26×12 divided by alphabet length in points. However, it will be found that about 28.4 characters fit into one alphabet length in practice since thin letters are used more often than the thicker ones. The formula, therefore, becomes $28.4 \times 12 \div$ alphabet length in points.

For example, 10-pt. Linotype Baskerville has an alphabet length of 129 points. 341 ÷ 129 = 2.64 c.p.p.

The characters per pica are given after each sample of type in the following pages. For example, the notation "C.p.p.: 10 pt., 2.94" as applied to Granjon means that the 10-pt. size of Granjon averages 2.94 lower-case letters and spaces per pica. For character counts of other point sizes see the tables on pages 354 and 355.

From this it is easy to calculate that a line of 10-pt. Granjon 20 picas long will hold about 59 characters. A table for simplifying such calculations is given on page 356.

Note, however, that lines set entirely in capital letters are likely to run half again as long as lines set in small letters, or accommodate one-third fewer letters for the same length.

The ideal type specimen book would show complete alphabets of every style of type in every size, with character counts for each size. This book is not big enough to attempt that, but it does offer complete alphabets of nearly

every popular style in the 24-pt. size on pages 365 to 396 with character counts for the 24-pt. size. These 24-pt. character counts can be converted into character counts for any other size by consulting the tables on pages 362 and 363. The conversion may not be exact, but it will almost always come close enough for practical purposes.

Note that much information about type is contained within the actual specimens of text types shown in the appendix—this seemed a more profitable use of space than the more conventional repetition of the same paragraph over and over again for each type specimen.

If you work much with type you will treasure any type books you can get hold of, and this is often difficult—few printers have adequate ones. If yours is a big account, your compositor will supply you with one at his own expense, but if not you may want to buy one. For $35 you can get one of the best from Howard O. Bullard, Inc., 150 Varick Street, New York 13. (Sample type faces on pages 346 to 396.)

8-pt. Baskerville (Lino), set solid. C.p.p.: 3.22

The following pages constitute a "type book" showing the most frequently used type faces, in both text and display sizes. No printer or composition house will have all the types shown in the full range of sizes. Most will have other types not shown here, *e.g.*, the Cheltenham series, which is no longer in favor with most designers and is not shown here. If possible, type users should obtain a type book from the printer who will be doing most of their composition, showing what types he has. Unfortunately, most printers have no type book, have no copies of it left, or have an inadequate one that does not have large enough samples to help much in the selection of text types. *To make the type showings in the following pages most helpful, marginal notes can be inserted stating which local printers have which styles and sizes.* 1234567890
ABCDEFGHIJKLMNOPQRSTUVWXYZ   abcdefghijklmnopqrstuvwxyz

10-pt. Baskerville (Lino), set solid. C.p.p.: 2.64

A personal loose-leaf scrapbook of type specimens can also be exceedingly helpful. It can be made up of clippings from the printer's publications, labeled for type style, size, and leading. Such a scrapbook is particularly helpful when a periodical is being edited since it can contain samples of the different styles of text, headlines, captions, etc., each marked with name, size, and characters per column. *The abbreviation, C.p.p. stands for "characters per pica." For a full explanation of its use, turn to the entries on* TYPE *and* COPY FITTING. 1234567890
ABCDEFGHIJKLMNOPQRSTUVWXYZ abcdefghijklmnopqrstuvwxyz

12-pt. Baskerville (Lino), set solid. C.p.p.: 2.30

The name of the manufacturer is given beside each specimen. This is an important piece of information for two reasons. First, Linotype Garamond No. 1 is not quite the same face as Intertype Garamond or Monotype Garamont. Second, Linotype, Intertype, Monotype, and Ludlow type faces are cast fresh for each use. ATF (American Type Founders), Continental, Bauer, etc., type faces may or may not be available for actual printing. (See TYPE.) *Sometimes, to prevent wear, printers will use them only to pull proofs, or to make duplicate plates.* 1234567890
ABCDEFGHIJKLMNOPQRSTUVWXYZ
abcdefghijklmnopqrstuvwxyz

14-pt. Baskerville (Lino), set solid. C.p.p.: 2.01

Baskerville is one of the best loved of the so-called "body," or text, types. The specimens on this page are faithful reproductions of the types designed and used by John Baskerville about 1760. *Cuttings of this face have been made also for the Intertype and the Monotype and are virtually identical.* 1234567890
ABCDEFGHIJKLMNOPQRSTUVWXYZ
abcdefghijklmnopqrstuvwxyz

10/11 Times Roman (Lino). C.p.p.: 2.75

These lines have been set in 10 pt., leaded 1 pt. The leading could have been inserted by hand between lines of 10 pt., but as a matter of convenience the 10-pt. type was cast on an 11-pt. slug, or body. (For an explanation of how this is done, see LINOTYPE.) It is therefore correct to say that these lines have been set in 10 on 11. In specifying the type, this would be written "10/11." More leading can easily be added, but removal of the 1-pt. space between lines would necessitate resetting on a 10-pt. slug. *The Monotype, which casts type characters singly instead of in one solid line of type, can also cast 10-pt. type on an 11-pt. or larger body.*

10/12 Times Roman (Lino). C.p.p.: 2.75

These lines have been set in 10 pt. on a 12-pt. body, *i.e.,* leaded 2 points. Long lines like these really need leading if they are to be legible. Short lines can more readily do without it. Sometimes small type, well leaded, is more readable than a larger type set solid. Leading can completely change the appearance of a block of copy. Heavy type appears lighter when widely leaded. Some type, especially the sans serifs, can stand extra-generous leading, at least in the larger sizes, but it is unusual to lead 8- and 10-pt. lightface types more than 2 or 3 points. *Printing a type on soft (antique) paper makes it look heavier than the same type on a coated or hard-surfaced paper.*

10/13 Times Roman (Lino). C.p.p.: 2.75

These lines have been set in 10 pt. on a 13-pt. body, *i.e.,* leaded 3 points. Wider leading demands wider margins. Otherwise the type will not appear as a well-defined block. Mixed leading is considered bad practice. When a story falls short of filling the space intended for it, printers sometimes add enough extra leading to fill the space. When a story runs long, they may take out some leading. The result is to produce a spotty-looking page, with some parts of the text lighter in tone value than others. *The correct remedy is to cut or add copy so as to fill the space while maintaining uniform leading.*

12/14 Times Roman (Lino). C.p.p.: 2.32

These lines have been set in 12 pt. on a 14-pt. body, *i.e.,* leaded 2 points. 12 pt. is the largest type size in common use for large amounts of text matter, although most type faces also come in 14 pt. In selecting a type size it is well to remember that most people read 7- or 8-pt. type every day without complaint of eyestrain. Newspapers are commonly printed in 7-pt. type, leaded 1 pt.; the publishers, however, use a narrow column.

10/10 Granjon (Lino). C.p.p.: 2.94

Eight popular text types are shown on this page and the one following. All are set in 10 pt., unleaded. All are available in 6-, 8-, 10-, 12-, and 14-pt. sizes, and usually in 9 and 11 pt. as well. Granjon is a particularly compact, space-saving type. In fact, 10-pt. Granjon is slightly more compact than 9-pt. Bookman. Since Granjon is small for its point size, it is more often used without leading than are less compact faces like Bookman. *Some printers have Granjon with bold instead of, or in addition to, Granjon with italic.* This is a sample of Granjon Bold.
ABCDEFGHIJKLMNOPQRSTUVWXYZ 1234567890
abcdefghijklmnopqrstuvwxyz   C.p.p.: 8 pt., 3.48; 12 pt., 2.49

10/10 Garamond (Intertype). C.p.p.: 2.92

The most popular type faces are offered by all the type companies. This is true of Caslon, Garamond, Bodoni, and Bookman. Sometimes the different cuttings are almost identical; sometimes they vary noticeably. On one of the following pages the different cuttings of Garamond are compared. Linotype Garamond No. 3, Intertype Garamond, and Monotype Garamont are all similar in weight. Linotype Garamond No. 1 is a little heavier. All the Garamonds have their bold counterparts. *All, including the bolds, have particularly attractive italics.* This is a sample of Intertype Garamond Bold.
ABCDEFGHIJKLMNOPQRSTUVWXYZ 1234567890
abcdefghijklmnopqrstuvwxyz C.p.p.: 8 pt., 3.35; 12 pt., 2.58

10/10 Caslon No. 137 (Mono). C.p.p.: 2.66

Some types are available with either long descenders or short descenders. When 10-pt. type is cast on a 10-pt. body there is room for only short descenders. When the body size is 2 points larger than the type size, it is possible and desirable to ask that matrices with long descenders be used. Type with long descenders is somewhat more attractive and readable than type with short descenders. Occasionally long descenders are standard, with short descenders available only on special order. *This explains the otherwise curious notation in some type books to the effect that a so-called 10-pt. face must be cast on an 11-pt. body.*
ABCDEFGHIJKLMNOPQRSTUVWXYZ 1234567890
abcdefghijklmnopqrstuvwxyz   C.p.p.: 8 pt., 3.32; 12 pt., 2.21

10/10 Bookman (Mono). C.p.p.: 2.58

Bookman, called Bookface in its Intertype cutting, is a big type face for its size. 10-pt. Bookman usually looks as big as 11 pt. in any other type style. This impression of size is obtained by using short descenders and ascenders, thus permitting the central part of the lower-case letters to be somewhat larger than usual. The letters are also a bit heavier than most other faces. Bookman is a versatile face. It will print well on either rough or smooth paper. *It is well adapted for offset or gravure reproduction, having no thin hairlines or delicate serifs to get lost in reproduction.*
ABCDEFGHIJKLMNOPQRSTUVWXYZ 1234567890
abcdefghijklmnopqrstuvwxyz   C.p.p.: 8 pt., 3.10; 12 pt., 2.19

10/10 Cloister (Lino). C.p.p.: 3.10

Cloister, or Cloister Old Style as it is sometimes called, is widely available on the Intertype and the Monotype as well as on the Linotype. There is also a Cloister Bold, and a Cloister Wide. It should not be confused with Cloister Black, which is an Old English style. Cloister is derived from a type cut in 1470 in Venice by Nicholas Jenson. It definitely belongs with the old-style faces like Centaur, Bookman, and Old Style, and not with the modern faces like Bodoni, or the transitional faces like Scotch, Baskerville, and Caledonia. *Note that small caps are available with almost all text types through 14 pt., but not in larger sizes.*
ABCDEFGHIJKLMNOPQRSTUVWXYZ   1234567890
abcdefghijklmnopqrstuvwxyz   C.p.p.: 8 pt., 3.56; 12 pt., 2.75

10/10 Scotch (Lino). C.p.p.: 2.73

Cuttings of Scotch, or Scotch Roman as it may be called, are made by Intertype and Monotype also. Like Baskerville, Scotch is a compromise between the old-style letters of Caslon and the modern letters of Bodoni. Note that figures are classed as old-style and modern just as letters are. The figures shown above under Granjon are old-style figures and have ascenders and descenders. The figures shown below under Bodoni are modern or lining figures because they align at top and bottom like capital letters. Modern figures are preferred for tabular work, and many type faces are cut with both. The Scotch figures, if compared closely with modern and old-style figures, betray their transitional character.
ABCDEFGHIJKLMNOPQRSTUVWXYZ   1234567890
abcdefghijklmnopqrstuvwxyz   C.p.p.: 8 pt., 3.10; 12 pt., 2.19

10/10 Bodoni Book (Lino). C.p.p.: 2.79

Giambattista Bodoni first designed the types that bear his name about one hundred and fifty years ago. He broke away entirely from the old-style types like Garamond and Caslon. These had always imitated the mannerisms of pen lettering to greater or lesser degree. Bodoni designed his letters along formal, geometric lines, with clean hairline serifs, and exaggerated "thicks" and "thins." Where the old-style types were designed to print on rough, antique papers, Bodoni's types looked their best on smooth-surfaced or coated papers that would not thicken his delicate hairlines. *This face, Bodoni Book, is particularly suitable for bookwork.*
ABCDEFGHIJKLMNOPQRSTUVWXYZ   1234567890
abcdefghijklmnopqrstuvwxyz   C.p.p.: 8 pt., 3.31; 12 pt., 2.50

10/10 Bodoni (Lino). C.p.p.: 2.58

The Bodoni series includes Bodoni Book, Bodoni, Bodoni Bold, and Ultra Bodoni, each with its own italic. These faces and related modern type styles are compared on a later page. Bodoni is itself heavy enough to compare with most boldfaces. It looks best when generously leaded. Bodoni shows to best advantage in 12 pt., 14 pt., and larger display sizes. Although typographers often combine two quite different type families, they do not often mix old-style and modern types. *They are more likely to stick to one or the other, or to contrast either with a sans serif.*
ABCDEFGHIJKLMNOPQRSTUVWXYZ   1234567890
abcdefghijklmnopqrstuvwxyz   C.p.p.: 8 pt., 3.13; 12 pt., 2.35

10/10 Excelsior (Lino). C.p.p.: 2.4

In these pages reference has frequently been made to "text type" or "body type" meaning a type suitable for use in a book and in small sizes as opposed to display sizes. However, the word "text" sometimes is used to designate the heavy, broad-pen style of type known as Old English, Black Text, Wedding Text, or Text.
ABCDEFGHIJKLMNOPQRSTU
VWXYZ 1234567890
abcdefghijklmnopqrstuvwxyz

10/10 Benedictine Book (Lino). C.p.p.: 2.53

The Benedictine type family is less popular than it once was, but a good many printers have it. It comes in three weights: Benedictine Book, Benedictine, and Benedictine Bold. It somewhat resembles Goudy Oldstyle. *The most used types today are Caslon, Bodoni, Garamond, Baskerville, Futura, and the square-serif series.*
ABCDEFGHIJKLMNO
PQRSTUVWXYZ 1234567890
abcdefghijklmnopqrstuvwxyz

10/10 Century Expanded (Lino). C.p.p.: 2.40

One of the many points on which printing terminology is confusing is in the use of the word "gothic." The term is sometimes used synonymously with Old English, Wedding Text, etc., to designate the broad-pen, black-letter style used in manuscripts beginning about the twelfth century. It is also used to refer to the modern sans-serif type styles, as for example, Franklin Gothic. *Century Expanded is available on Lino, Intertype and Mono, with italic or with bold.*
ABCDEFGHIJKLMNO
PQRSTUVWXYZ 1234567890
abcdefghijklmnopqrstuvwxyz

10/11 Janson (Lino). C.p.p.: 2.60

This face is also offered by Monotype. The 8-, 10-, and 12-pt. sizes must be cast on 9-, 11-, and 13-pt. slugs, respectively. Since the point size of a type face is generally understood to be the smallest body slug on which it can be cast, *it is not quite clear why these were not called 9-, 11-, and 13-pt. sizes.*
ABCDEFGHIJKLMNOPQRSTU
VWXYZ 1234567890
abcdefghijklmnopqrstuvwxyz

10/11 Caledonia (Lino). C.p.p.: 2.62

This is a recent type designed by W. A. Dwiggins. It is reminiscent both of Scotch Roman and of Bulmer; it is a little more modern in its design than Baskerville. It has become very popular. *The designer took particular care to give the italic the same weight and color as the roman.* **There is also a Caledonia Bold.**
ABCDEFGHIJKLMNOPQRSTU
VWXYZ 1234567890
abcdefghijklmnopqrstuvwxyz

10/10 Linotype No. 21. C.p.p.: 2.62

"This is a printing office—crossroads of civilization, refuge of all the arts against the ravages of time, armory of fearless truth against whispering rumor, incessant trumpet of trade. From this place words may fly abroad, not to perish on waves of sound, not to vary with the writer's hand, but fixed in time, having been verified by proof. *Friend, you stand on sacred ground. This is a printing office.*"—Beatrice L. Warde.
ABCDEFGHIJKLMNOPQRSTU
VWXYZ 1234567890
abcdefghijklmnopqrstuvwxyz

10/11 Fairfield (Lino). C.p.p.: 2.79

Fairfield is another modern type face and was designed by Rudolph Ruzicka. Type designing is a subtle art. The artist must of necessity adapt rather than innovate. Type must never call attention to itself, but rather to its message. Its forms must, therefore, be the old familiar ones.
ABCDEFGHIJKLMNOPQRSTU VWXYZ 1234567890
abcdefghijklmnopqrstuvwxyz

10/11 Electra (Lino). C.p.p.: 2.75

Electra is a modern type face designed by W. A. Dwiggins, who also designed Caledonia and Metro. It has both an "oblique" and a "cursive." Its oblique is often called an "oblique roman," or an "inclined roman." *This sentence is set in Electra Oblique. This sentence is set in Electra Cursive.*
ABCDEFGHIJKLMNOPQRSTU VWXYZ 1234567890
abcdefghijklmnopqrstuvwxyz
NOTE: Electra must be leaded at least 1 pt.

10/10 Garamont (Mono). C.p.p.: 2.71

The type first cut by Claude Garamond about 1530–1540 has been recut for machine composition by all three manufacturers. The specimens in this column show how even the subtlest differences can affect the weight and color of a type. Garamond type tends to identify itself by the very small loop on the lower-case "e." *Note that the Monotype cutting (redrawn by Goudy) is spelled with a final "t."*
ABCDEFGHIJKLMNOPQRSTUVW XYZ 1234567890
abcdefghijklmnopqrstuvwxyz

10/10 Garamond (Lino). C.p.p.: 2.82

The type first cut by Claude Garamond about 1530–1540 has been recut for machine composition by all three manufacturers. The specimens in this column show how even the subtlest differences can affect the weight and color of a type. Garamond type tends to identify itself by the very small loop on the lower-case "e." *All the Garamonds shown here are available in bold and bold italic as well as in italic.*
ABCDEFGHIJKLMNOPQRSTUV WXYZ 1234567890
abcdefghijklmnopqrstuvwxyz

10/10 Garamond No. 3 (Lino). C.p.p.: 2.90

The type first cut by Claude Garamond about 1530-1540 has been recut for machine composition by all three manufacturers. The specimens in this column show how even the subtlest differences can affect the weight and color of a type. Garamond type tends to identify itself by the very small loop on the lower-case "e." *All the Garamonds shown here are available in bold and bold italic as well as in italic.*
ABCDEFGHIJKLMNOPQRSTUVW XYZ 1234567890
abcdefghijklmnopqrstuvwxyz

10/10 Garamond (Intertype). C.p.p.: 2.92

The type first cut by Claude Garamond about 1530–1540 has been recut for machine composition by all three manufacturers. The specimens in this column show how even the subtlest differences can affect the weight and color of a type. Garamond type tends to identify itself by the very small loop on the lower-case "e." *All the Garamonds shown here are available in bold and bold italic as well as in italic.*
ABCDEFGHIJKLMNOPQRSTUVW XYZ 1234567890
abcdefghijklmnopqrstuvwxyz

10/10 Futura Light (Intertype) C.p.p.: 3.05

Everyone who deals with the printed word should sooner or later read "Layout in Advertising" by W. A. Dwiggins, described in the Bibliography. The book was written in 1928, and in it Mr. Dwiggins calls attention to the need for a well-designed sans-serif type. *The Futura designs, imported from Germany during the thirties, met this need.*
ABCDEFGHIJKLMNOPQRSTUVWXYZ
1234567890
abcdefghijklmnopqrstuvwxyz

10/10 Futura Medium (Intertype) C.p.p.: 2.87

Sans-serif types have been in use for more than a hundred years, but the earlier ones lacked grace. Only in recent years have sans-serif types matured into a beauty of their own, thanks to the men who designed the Vogue series, Franklin Gothic, Alternate Gothic, Kabel, Gill Sans Serif, Metro, Erbar, Futura, etc. *The Futura series has perhaps been the most widely copied of all.*
ABCDEFGHIJKLMNOPQRSTUVWXYZ
1234567890
abcdefghijklmnopqrstuvwxyz

10/10 Futura Demibold (Intertype) C.p.p.: 2.59

The Futura types are now distributed by all the leading type manufacturers, but may be called Spartan, Tempo, or Twentieth Century as well as Futura. Furthermore, the weight that one manufacturer calls "bold" may be called "black," "heavy," or "extrabold" by the other manufacturers. *This rather confusing nomenclature may be clarified by comparing samples on page 358.*
ABCDEFGHIJKLMNOPQRSTUVWX YZ 1234567890
abcdefghijklmnopqrstuvwxyz

10/10 Futura Bold (Intertype). C.p.p.: 2.40

Sans-serif types are used more for display headings and in advertising brochures than for the main text of books or magazines. Many people feel that large masses of sans-serif type are somewhat less readable than the same wordage set in roman type. This may be merely a question of familiarity, just as Bismarck is said to have proved to his own satisfaction that the German Fraktur type is much more readable than roman type.
ABCDEFGHIJKLMNOPQRSTUVW XYZ 1234567890
abcdefghijklmnopqrstuvwxyz

10/10 Memphis Light (Lino). C.p.p.: 2.56

Memphis belongs to a family of type styles called "Egyptian" or "square serif." Substantially identical type faces put out by other type manufacturers include Karnak, Stymie, Beton, and Cairo. These are compared on a subsequent page. The serifs on these types are of the same thickness as the rest of the letters.
ABCDEFGHIJKLMNOPQRSTUV WXYZ 1234567890
abcdefghijklmnopqrstuvwxyz

10/10 Memphis Medium (Lino). C.p.p.: 2.56

Square-serif types have become popular because they can be contrasted effectively with either roman or sans-serif styles. They are much used in display work, less used for text matter. The design is rather static and lacks the movement and grace that is obtainable in roman or sans-serif faces.
ABCDEFGHIJKLMNO PQRSTUVWXYZ 1234567890
abcdefghijklmnopqrstuvwxyz

10/10 Memphis Bold (Lino). C.p.p.: 2.56

The profusion of different type faces is bound to be confusing to anyone entering the field for the first time. One of the best ways to bring some order out of the confusion is to study lettering. Type characteristics are determined by the pen or brush or chisel that originally formed the letters. For a few good books about lettering see the Bibliography.
ABCDEFGHIJKLMNOPQRSTUV
WXYZ   1234567890
abcdefghijklmnopqrstuvwxyz

10/10 Memphis Extrabold (Lino). C.p.p.: 2.06

The heaviest cuttings of the square-serif family, like this one, provide the typographer with some of his heaviest ammunition. They pack a terrific wallop, whether for display use, or for small chunks of text. They have a texture all their own.
ABCDEFGHIJKLMNOP
QRSTUVWXYZ 1234567890
abcdefghijklmnop
qrstuvwxyz

10/10 Caslon Bold No. 3 (Lino). C.p.p.: 2.45

The most used text faces come in bold as well as light, each with its matching italic. It would be very uncommon to find a book set in boldface throughout, but many books use a lightface for the text, and the matching boldface for subheads, marginal heads, etc. *The same is true in catalogue work.*
ABCDEFGHIJKLMNO
PQRSTUVWXYZ   1234567890
abcdefghijklmnopqrstuvwxyz

10/10 Garamond Bold (Intertype) C.p.p.: 2.73

A printer who has Garamond Bold may have it on the same matrices as Garamond Light, or he may have it on matrices of its own, along with Garamond Bold Italic. It will be extra trouble for him to mix bold and light on the same line *unless he has both on the same matrices.*
ABCDEFGHIJKLMNOPQRSTUV
WXYZ 1234567890
abcdefghijklmnopqrstuvwxyz

10/10 Bodoni Bold (Mono). C.p.p.: 2.41

Regardless of what other type faces they may have or lack, most good printers have the complete Bodoni series. Advertising layout tends to use the Bodoni oftener than any other type family. *A showing of the complete Bodoni family and related styles is given on page 357.*
ABCDEFGHIJKLMNOPQRSTU
VWXYZ   1234567890
abcdefghijklmnopqrstuvwxyz

10/10 Poster Bodoni (Lino). C.p.p.: 1.99

This heaviest version of Bodoni is variously called ultra, poster, modern or black, depending on which type manufacturer makes it. It compresses large attention value into small space. It looks well in caps, lower case, or italic. It is at its best when generously leaded, on smooth paper.
ABCDEFGHIJKLMNO
PQRSTUVWXYZ
1234567890
abcdefghijklmno
pqrstuvwxyz

CHARACTERS PER PICA

Type face	Size of type face							
	6 pt.	7 pt.	8 pt.	9 pt.	10 pt.	11 pt.	12 pt.	14 pt.
Antique No. 1 w. ital. (Inter, Lino)	3.52	3.2	2.8		2.42		2.08	1.8
Baskerville w. ital. & s.c. (Inter)	3.92		3.2	3.05	2.78	2.63	2.33	2.03
Baskerville w. ital. & s.c. (Lino)	3.8	3.6	3.22	2.95	2.64	2.46	2.30	2.01
Baskerville No. 353 (Mono)	4.08	3.66	3.25	3.06	2.76	2.5	2.3	2.11
Baskerville Bold w. ital. (Lino)		3.57	3.2	2.89	2.61	2.42	2.28	1.98
Baskerville Bold No. 453 (Mono) *			2.97	2.79	2.52	2.29	2.1	
Benedictine	4.08	3.56	3.12	2.82	2.52	2.31	2.12	1.85
Benedictine Bold			2.94		2.33		1.93	1.66
Benedictine Book	4.08	3.56	3.13	2.82	2.53	2.31	2.12	1.85
Beton Medium w. Bold (Inter)			3.48	2.97	2.65	2.35	2.12	1.91
Bodoni w. ital. & s.c. (Inter, Lino)	4.19	3.55	3.13		2.59		2.35	2.1
Bodoni No. 175 (Mono)	3.83	3.33	3.15	2.96	2.66	2.41	2.23	1.89
Bodoni Ital. No. 175 (Mono)	4.25	3.63	3.44	3.22	2.91	2.64	2.43	2.07
Bodoni No. 375 (Mono)	3.95	3.55	3.15	2.96	2.66	2.42	2.23	2.11
Bodoni No. 375 Ital. (Mono)	3.95	3.88	3.15	3.22	2.71	2.64	2.33	2.14
Bodoni Bold w. ital. & s.c. (Inter, Lino)	3.75		2.87		2.44		2.17	1.95
Bodoni Bold No. 275 (Mono) *	3.43	2.97	2.82	2.65	2.41	2.23	2.00	1.96
Bodoni Book w. ital. & s.c. (Inter, Lino)	4.21	3.71	3.32	2.99	2.78		2.5	2.25
Bodoni Book No. 875 (Mono) *	4.3	3.78	3.33	3.15	2.85	2.7	2.58	
Bookface w. ital. & s.c. (Inter)	3.67	3.41	3.10	2.89	2.59	2.36	2.21	1.80
Bookman w. ital. & s.c. (Lino)	3.67	3.38	3.10	2.87	2.58	2.37	2.19	1.84
Bookman Old Style No. 98 (Mono) *	3.68	3.33	3.15	2.98	2.61	2.44	2.23	1.87
Cairo (Inter)	3.57		3.03		2.55		2.09	1.78
Caledonia w. ital. & s.c. (Lino)			3.13	2.87	2.62	2.44	2.26	2.01
Caslon w. ital & s.c. (Inter, Lino)	3.88	3.63	3.17	2.99	2.82	2.42	2.18	1.89
Caslon No. 3 w. ital. & s.c. (Inter, Lino)	3.84	3.45	3.16	2.75	2.46		2.06	1.77
Caslon No. 137 w. ital. & s.c. (Lino)		3.8	3.32	2.95	2.65	2.42	2.18	
Caslon Old Face w. ital. & s.c. (Lino)	4.44		3.67	3.22	3.08	2.80	2.42	2.15
Caslon Old Style No. 137 (Mono) *	4.11		3.32	3.04	2.66	2.41	2.21	
Caslon Bold No. 79 (Mono) *	3.43	3.00	2.82	2.68	2.35	2.19	2.00	1.59
Caslon, New, No. 537 (Mono) *	3.78		3.15	2.69	2.36		2.11	1.75
Century Expanded w. ital. & s.c. (Inter, Lino)	3.6	3.2	2.87	2.67	2.41	2.30	2.11	1.77
Century Expanded No. 20 (Mono) *	3.83	3.35	3.07	2.76	2.56	2.44	2.23	1.79
Cheltenham w. ital. & s.c. (Lino)			3.6	3.2	2.97	2.71	2.54	2.15
Cheltenham Old Style No. 64 (Mono) *.	4.43		3.67		2.97		2.55	2.24
Cheltonian w. ital. & s.c. (Inter)		3.88	3.56		2.97		2.54	2.15
Cloister w. ital. & s.c. (Lino)	4.27		3.56		3.10	2.95	2.75	2.45
Cloister Bold w. ital. (Lino)	3.8		3.13		2.71		2.49	2.18
Cloister Old Style w. ital. & s.c. (Inter)	4.33		3.71		3.16		2.84	2.56
Deepdene No. 315 (Mono) *	4.39		3.62		3.08		2.56	2.31
Deepdene Bold No. 317 (Mono) *	4.02		3.32		2.83		2.35	1.99
Egmont Light w. ital. & s.c. (Inter)			3.63		2.94		2.59	2.25
Electra w. ital. & s.c. (Lino)		3.67	3.28	2.92	2.73	2.54	2.40	2.14
Fairfield w. ital. & s.c. (Lino)			3.21	2.99	2.79	2.61	2.45	
Futura Bold w. oblique (Inter)	3.64		3.1		2.4		1.98	1.74
Futura Book w. oblique (Inter)	4.39		3.88		3.05		2.6	2.22
Futura Medium w. oblique (Inter)	4.21		3.56		2.87		2.42	2.10

* Also comes in italic, which sets a bit narrower than the roman.

CHARACTERS PER PICA (*continued*)

Type face	Size of type face							
	6 pt.	7 pt.	8 pt.	9 pt.	10 pt.	11 pt.	12 pt.	14 pt.
Garamond w. ital. & s.c. (Inter)	3.93	3.64	3.35	3.05	2.92	2.73	2.58	2.3
Garamond w. ital. & s.c. (Lino)	4.27		3.52	3.13	2.82	2.54	2.29	2.05
Garamond Bold w. ital. (Inter)	3.75	3.45	3.20	2.87	2.73	2.50	2.41	2.15
Garamond Bold w. ital. (Lino)	3.84		3.16		2.54		2.02	1.83
Garamond No. 3 w. ital. & s.c. (Lino)	3.93	3.6	3.02	3.08	2.90	2.73	2.30	2.28
Garamond Bold No. 3 w. ital. & s.c. (Lino)	3.65	3.28	3.02	2.78	2.63	2.44	2.31	2.04
Garamont No. 248 (Mono)	4.69		3.41	3.00	2.71	2.44	2.23	2.01
Garamont Bold No. 548 (Mono) *	3.68	3.29	3.01	2.75	2.61	2.47	2.31	2.08
Goudy Oldstyle w. ital. & s.c. (Inter)	4.02		3.35		2.73		2.39	1.99
Goudy Old Style No. 394 (Mono) *	3.99		3.25		2.68		2.34	1.95
Granjon w. ital. & s.c. (Lino)	4.24		3.48	3.16	2.94	2.71	2.49	2.24
Ionic No. 5 w. ital. & s.c. (Lino)	3.27	2.99	2.68	2.49	2.34		2.09	
Janson (Lino)			3.07	2.81	2.60	2.46	2.30	2.08
Kenntonian w. ital. & s.c. (Inter)	4.19		3.25		2.84		2.44	2.14
Memphis Light w. bold (Lino)	3.52		3.28	2.85	2.56		2.06	1.75
Memphis Medium w. ital. & s.c. (Lino)	3.52		3.28	2.82	2.56		2.04	1.73
Metrolite No. 2 w. Metroblack No. 2 (Lino)	3.63		3.16		2.50		2.09	1.8
Metromedium No. 2 w. Metrothin No. 2 (Lino)	3.97		3.52		2.80		2.34	2.02
No. 21 (Lino)	3.80	3.22	3.10	2.96	2.62	2.41	2.20	
Old Style No. 1 w. ital. & s.c. (Lino)	3.75	3.38	3.13	2.89	2.69	2.52	2.28	1.92
Opticon w. boldface No. 2 (Lino)	3.13	2.87	2.63	2.56	2.37	2.24	2.14	
Original Old Caslon No. 337 (Mono) *		3.68	3.34	2.98	2.67	2.44	2.23	2.14
Sans Serif Light No. 329 (Mono) *	4.27		3.39		2.89		2.52	2.55
Sans Serif Medium No. 331 (Mono)	4.23		3.35		2.85		2.49	2.29
Scotch w. ital. & s.c. (Lino)	3.52		3.10		2.73	2.56	2.20	1.84
Spartan Light w. Medium (Lino)			3.67		2.92		2.47	2.16
Spartan Heavy w. ital. (Lino)			3.48		2.61		2.26	2.02
Stymie Light No. 190 * (Mono)	3.92		3.23		2.61		2.18	1.82
Stymie Bold No. 189 * (Mono)	3.43		2.82		2.29		2.02	1.57
Stymie Medium No. 290 * (Mono)	3.92		3.23		2.61		2.20	1.73
Times Roman w. ital & s.c. (Lino)	3.79	3.44	3.14	2.91	2.75	2.56	2.32	2.13
Twentieth Century Light No. 606 * (Mono)	4.68		3.81		3.08		2.61	2.26
Twentieth Century Medium No. 605 * (Mono)	4.68		3.66		2.94		2.44	2.09
Twentieth Century Bold No. 604 * (Mono)	4.00		3.48		2.61		2.26	2.01
Vogue w. Vogue Bold (Inter)	3.97		3.52		2.92		2.44	2.12

*Also comes in italic, which sets a bit narrower than the roman.

TABLE FOR CONVERTING CHARACTERS PER PICA INTO CHARACTERS PER LINE

C.p.p.	Alphabet length, points	10	12	14	16	18	20	22	24	26	28	30
		Characters per line										
0.55	620	5	6	7	8	9	11	12	13	14	15	16
0.60	579	6	7	8	9	10	12	13	14	15	16	18
0.65	525	6	7	9	10	11	13	14	15	16	18	19
0.70	488	7	8	9	11	12	14	15	16	18	19	21
0.75	455	7	9	10	12	13	15	16	17	19	21	22
0.80	427	8	9	11	12	14	16	17	19	20	22	24
0.85	402	8	10	11	13	15	17	18	20	22	23	25
0.90	379	9	10	12	14	16	18	19	21	23	25	27
0.95	360	9	11	13	15	17	19	20	22	24	26	28
1.00	341	10	12	14	16	18	20	22	24	26	28	30
1.05	325	10	12	14	16	18	21	23	25	27	29	31
1.10	310	11	13	15	17	19	22	24	26	28	30	33
1.15	296	11	13	16	18	20	23	25	27	29	32	34
1.20	284	12	14	16	19	21	24	26	28	31	33	36
1.25	273	12	15	17	20	22	25	27	30	32	35	37
1.30	262	13	15	18	20	23	26	28	31	33	36	39
1.35	253	13	16	18	21	24	27	29	32	35	37	40
1.40	244	14	16	19	22	25	28	30	33	36	39	42
1.45	235	14	17	20	23	26	29	31	34	37	40	43
1.50	227	15	18	21	24	27	30	33	36	39	42	45
1.60	213	16	19	22	25	28	32	35	38	41	44	48
1.70	200	17	20	24	27	30	34	37	40	44	47	51
1.80	189	18	21	25	28	32	36	39	43	46	50	54
1.90	179	19	22	26	30	34	38	41	45	49	53	57
2.00	170	20	24	28	32	36	40	44	48	52	56	60
2.10	162	21	25	29	33	37	42	46	50	54	58	63
2.20	155	22	26	30	35	39	44	48	52	57	61	66
2.30	148	23	27	32	36	41	46	50	55	60	64	69
2.40	142	24	28	33	38	43	48	52	57	62	67	72
2.50	136	25	30	35	40	45	50	55	60	65	70	75
2.60	131	26	31	36	41	46	52	57	62	67	72	78
2.70	126	27	32	37	43	48	54	59	64	70	75	81
2.80	121	28	33	39	44	50	56	61	67	73	78	84
2.90	118	29	34	40	46	52	58	63	69	75	81	87
3.00	114	30	36	42	48	54	60	66	72	78	84	90
3.10	110	31	37	43	49	55	62	68	74	80	86	93
3.20	106	32	38	45	51	57	64	70	76	83	89	96
3.30	103	33	39	46	52	59	66	72	79	86	92	99
3.40	100	34	40	47	54	61	68	74	81	88	95	102
3.50	98	35	42	49	56	63	70	77	84	90	98	105
3.60	95	36	43	50	57	64	72	79	86	93	100	108
3.70	92	37	44	52	59	66	74	81	89	96	104	111
3.80	90	38	45	53	60	68	76	83	91	99	106	114
3.90	88	39	46	54	62	70	78	85	93	102	109	117
4.00	85	40	48	56	64	72	80	88	96	104	112	120

THE BODONI FAMILY (Shown in 12 pt. where possible)

Approximate c.p.p. 12 pt.	Approximate c.p.p. 24 pt.	TYPE FACE
2.50	1.43	Bodoni Book, *Bodoni Book Italic* (ATF, Intertype, Lino, Mono)
2.35	1.28	Bodoni, *Bodoni Italic*
2.17	1.21	**Bodoni Bold,** *Bodoni Bold Italic*
1.56	0.83	**Bodoni Ultra,** *Bodoni Ultra Italic* **(ATF, Mono)**
1.86	0.89	**Bodoni Black (Ludlow)** *Bodoni Black Italic* **(Ludlow)**
1.55	0.88	**Bodoni Modern,** *Bodoni Modern Italic* **(Inter)**
1.73	0.83	**Bodoni Poster** *Bodoni Poster Italic* **(Lino)**
	1.51	**Bodoni Bold Condensed (Lino, Mono, Intertype) 14 pt.**
	1.72	**Bodoni Campanile,** *Bodoni Campanile Italic (Ludlow)*
2.14	1.23	**Bodoni Ultra Extra Condensed (14 pt.)**
2.32	1.25	Bodoni Open (ATF)
	1.78	**Onyx (ATF, Mono) 18 pt.**
	1.73	**Bodoni Poster Compressed (APL) (24 pt.)**
1.20	0.62	**Nubian (ATF)**

NOTE: Where no figures appear, the type does not come in that size or else counts were unobtainable.

The Futura Family (Shown in 12 pt. where possible)

Approximate c.p.p. 12 pt.	Approximate c.p.p. 24 pt.	Intertype and Bauer call it *Futura;* Linotype and ATF call it *Spartan;* Ludlow calls it *Tempo;* Monotype calls it *Twentieth Century.* Remember that what one firm calls "bold" others call "black," "heavy," or "extrabold"
2.60		Futura Light, *Futura Oblique Light* (Inter)
2.47	1.29	Spartan Light (Lino)
2.74	1.29	Tempo Light, *Tempo Light Italic* (Ludlow)
2.61		Twentieth Century Light, and *Italic* (Mono)
2.60		Futura Book, *Futura Book Oblique*
2.42	1.31	Futura Medium, *Futura Oblique Medium*
2.47	1.38	Spartan Medium, *Spartan Medium Italic*
2.70	1.29	Tempo Medium *Tempo Medium Italic*
2.44	1.32	Twentieth Century Medium, and *Italic*
2.30	1.23	**Futura Demibold, *Futura Demibold Oblique***
2.26	1.24	**Spartan Heavy, *Spartan Heavy Italic***
2.30	1.07	**Tempo Bold and *Bold Italic***
2.26	1.24	**Twentieth Century Bold and *Bold Italic***
1.98	1.07	**Futura Bold, *Futura Bold Oblique***
1.98	1.07	**Spartan Black, *Spartan Black Italic***
2.00	0.99	**Tempo Heavy and *Heavy Italic***
2.01	0.99	**Twentieth Century Extrabold, and *Extrabold Italic***

NOTE: Where no figures appear, the type does not come in that size or else counts were unobtainable.

The Futura Family (*Cont.*) (Shown in 12 pt. where possible)

Approximate c.p.p. 12 pt.	Approximate c.p.p. 12 pt.	Intertype and Bauer call it *Futura;* Linotype and ATF call it *Spartan;* Ludlow calls it *Tempo;* Monotype calls it *Twentieth Century.* Remember that what one firm calls "bold" others call "black," "heavy," or "extrabold"
2.78		**Futura Bold Condensed**
2.60	1.54	**Spartan Black Condensed, and *Condensed Italic***
2.80	1.48	**Tempo Heavy Condensed**
	1.47	**Twentieth Century Extrabold Condensed and *Italic***
3.11		Futura Medium Condensed
2.97	1.48	Tempo Bold Condensed
2.66	1.34	Twentieth Century Medium Condensed
		Futura Black
1.67	0.97	**Twentieth Century Ultrabold**
2.00	1.18	**Twentieth Century Ultrabold Condensed (14 pt.)**
		Futura Display (14 pt.)
	0.91	**Tempo Black (18 pt.)**
		FUTURA INLINE (18 PT.)
		TEMPO HEAVY INLINE (18 PT.)

NOTE: Where no figures appear, the type does not come in that size or else counts were unobtainable.

Some Other Sans-serif Faces (Shown in 12 pt. if possible)

Approximate c.p.p. 12 pt.	Approximate c.p.p. 24 pt.	Type Face
2.44	1.26	Vogue, *Vogue Oblique* (Intertype)
2.52	1.57	Sans Serif Light and *Light Italic* (Mono)
2.35	1.25	Metrothin (Lino)
2.49	1.61	Sans Serif Medium
2.09	1.13	Metrolite, *Metrolite Italic*
2.37	1.23	Vogue Bold, *Vogue Bold Oblique*
2.49	1.52	**Sans Serif Bold,** *Sans Serif Bold Italic*
2.35	1.25	Metromedium, *Metromedium Italic*
2.03	1.11	**Vogue Extra Bold,** *Extra Bold Oblique*
2.07	1.23	**Sans Serif Extrabold,** *Extrabold Italic*
2.07	1.16	**Metroblack,** *Metroblack Italic*
1.86	0.97	**Franklin Gothic**
		Franklin Gothic Wide
	2.05	Sans Serif Light Condensed
2.99	1.75	Vogue Bold Condensed
	1.73	Sans Serif Medium Condensed (14 pt.)
3.28	1.80	Erbar Light Condensed (Lino)
2.99	1.60	**Vogue Extra Bold Condensed**
	1.45	**Sans Serif Extra Bold Condensed**
2.21	1.20	**Franklin Gothic Condensed (ATF)**
1.75	1.54	**Franklin Gothic Extra Cond. (ATF and Ludlow)**
2.96	1.55	**Alternate Gothic No. 2 (Intertype and ATF)**
3.31	1.79	**Alternate Gothic No. 1 (Intertype and ATF)**
3.28	1.69	**Erbar Bold Condensed (Linotype)**

NOTE: Where no figures appear, the type does not come in that size or else counts were unobtainable.

THE EGYPTIAN (SQUARE SERIF) FAMILY (12 pt. where possible)

Approxi- mate c.p.p. 12 pt.	Approxi- mate c.p.p. 24 pt.	Ludlow calls it *Karnak;* Linotype calls it *Memphis;* Monotype and ATF call it *Stymie;* Intertype calls it *Beton* or *Cairo*
2.12	1.04	Karnak Light (Ludlow)
2.06	1.10	Memphis Light, *Light Italic* (Lino)
2.18	1.14	Stymie Light, *Light Italic* (Mono, ATF)
2.06	1.09	Cairo, *Cairo Italic* (Inter)
2.07	0.98	Karnak Intermediate, *Intermediate Italic*
2.04	1.06	Memphis Medium, *Medium Italic*
2.20	1.08	Stymie Medium, *Medium Italic*
2.12	1.20	Beton Medium *with Italic*
2.07	1.11	Cairo Medium *with Italic*
2.00	0.98	**Karnak Medium**
2.04	1.07	**Memphis Bold, *Memphis Bold Italic***
2.02	1.03	**Stymie Bold, *Stymie Bold Italic***
2.12	1.14	**Beton Bold**
2.05	1.10	**Cairo Bold, *Cairo Bold Italic***
1.80	0.94	**Karnak Black, *Karnak Black Italic***
1.70	0.93	**Memphis Extra Bold, *Italic***
1.86	0.91	**Stymie Extra Bold, *Italic***
1.73	0.93	**Stymie Black *and Italic***
1.67	1.03	**Beton Extra Bold,**
		Beton Extra Bold Oblique
2.52	1.45	Memphis Medium Condensed
2.66	1.46	**Memphis Bold Condensed**
2.46	1.40	**Cairo Bold Condensed**
	1.35	**Karnak Black Condensed (14 pt.)**
2.52	1.44	**Memphis Extra Bold Condensed (14)**
1.69	1.03	Beton Wide
	1.99	Karnak Obelisk (14 pt.)

NOTE: Where no figures appear, the type does not come in that size or else counts were unobtainable.

DISPLAY FACES

106 of the most popular display types are shown on pages 365 to 396. Complete upper- and lower-case alphabets are given for each, in the 24-pt. size. This is by no means a complete listing of existing display types; however, an attempt has been made to show at least one example of each of the most used basic type styles. No one printer will have all the faces shown, and only large advertising typographers will come anywhere near having them all.

The range of sizes given is that available from the manufacturer. Printers often buy only one or a few of the sizes available in any given face.

After each listing is given the characters per pica of the 24-pt. size shown, for both small letters and capital letters. From this information it is possible to calculate approximately how much space any given headline will occupy in any desired style and size of type.

TABLE FOR ESTIMATING THE LENGTH OF A HEADLINE WHEN THE NUMBER
OF CHARACTERS IN THE HEADLINE IS KNOWN

Characters per pica in 24-pt. size as given on pp. 319 to 350	Number of letters and spaces										
	8	12	16	20	24	28	32	36	40	44	48
	Length (in picas) of a headline (in 24-pt. type)										
0.55	15	21	29	36	43	51	58	65	72	80	87
0.60	14	20	26	33	40	46	53	60	66	73	80
0.65	13	18	24	30	37	43	49	55	61	68	74
0.70	12	17	22	28	34	40	46	51	57	63	68
0.75	11	16	21	26	32	37	43	48	53	58	64
0.80	10	15	20	25	30	35	40	45	50	55	60
0.85	10	14	18	23	28	33	38	42	47	51	56
0.90	9	13	17	22	26	31	36	40	44	48	53
0.95	9	12	16	21	25	29	34	37	42	46	50
1.00	8	11	16	20	24	28	32	36	40	44	48
1.05	8	11	15	19	22	26	30	34	38	42	45
1.10	8	10	14	18	21	25	29	32	36	40	43
1.15	7	10	13	17	20	24	27	31	34	38	41
1.20	7	10	13	16	20	23	26	29	33	36	40
1.25	7	9	12	16	19	22	25	28	31	35	38
1.30	7	9	12	15	18	21	24	27	30	33	36
1.35	6	8	11	14	17	20	23	26	29	32	35
1.40	6	8	11	14	17	20	22	25	28	31	34
1.45	6	8	11	13	16	19	22	24	27	30	33
1.50	6	8	10	13	15	18	21	24	26	29	32
1.55	6	7	10	12	15	18	20	23	25	28	31
1.60	5	7	10	12	15	17	20	22	24	27	30
1.65	5	7	9	12	14	16	19	21	24	26	29
1.70	5	7	9	11	14	16	18	21	23	25	28
1.75	5	6	9	11	13	15	18	20	22	25	27
1.80	5	6	8	11	13	15	17	20	22	24	26
1.85	5	6	8	10	12	15	17	19	21	23	25
1.90	5	6	8	10	12	14	16	18	21	23	25
2.00	4	6	8	10	12	14	16	18	20	22	24

NOTE: Be sure to take the caps p.p. count if the headline is to be set in all caps. Take the lower-case c.p.p. count if the headline is to be in lower case. Count incidental caps as two lower-case characters.

TABLE FOR ESTIMATING THE LENGTH OF A HEADLINE (OTHER THAN 24-PT.)
WHEN THE LENGTH OF A 24-PT. HEADLINE IS KNOWN

Length of 24-pt. headline in picas	Approximate length of same headline in type face of other sizes						
	18 pt.	30 pt.	36 pt.	48 pt.	60 pt.	72 pt.	96 pt.
4	3	5	6	8	10	12	16
6	4.5	8	9	12	15	18	24
8	6	10	12	16	20	24	32
10	7.5	13	15	20	25	30	40
12	9	15	18	24	30	36	48
14	10.5	18	21	28	35	42	56
16	12	20	24	32	40	48	64
18	13.5	23	27	36	45	54	72
20	15	25	30	40	50	60	80
22	16.5	28	33	44	55	66	88
24	18	30	36	48	60	72	96
26	19.5	33	39	52	65	78	104
28	21	35	42	56	70	84	112
30	22.5	38	45	60	75	90	120
35	27	44	53	70	88	105	140
40	30	50	60	80	100	120	160
45	34	56	68	90	113	135	180
50	38	63	75	100	125	150	200
55	41	69	83	110	138	165	220
60	45	75	90	120	150	180	240
65	49	81	98	130	163	195	260
70	52	88	105	140	175	210	280
75	56	94	113	150	188	225	300
80	60	100	120	160	200	240	320
85	64	106	128	170	213	255	340
90	68	112	135	180	225	270	360

Example. The headline "PRINT-ING HANDBOOK" is to be set in Memphis Medium caps, to fill a line 28 picas long. The headline consists of 16 letters and 1 space, or 17 characters in all. Under Memphis Medium (see p. 389) is found the information that there are about 0.81 caps per pica in 24 pt. 17 times 0.81 gives 13.7. The headline will therefore occupy about 13.7 picas if set in 24 pt. If set twice as big, in 48 pt., it should occupy about 27.4 picas. If set 2½ times as big, in 60 pt., it should occupy 34.4 picas. 48 pt. is, therefore, the indicated size.

This system does not claim perfect accuracy, but it is usually accurate enough. When working with headlines that are to be set in caps and lower case, one usually counts caps as equal to two small letters. When headlines are short, it may be wise to count "i" and "l" as ½ character, "m" and "w" as 1½ characters, etc.

The accompanying tables make it easy to translate characters per pica into length of headline; and length of a 24-pt. headline into the length of the same heading in another size. First, find the characters per pica in the 24-pt. size of the desired type face (see pages 365 to 396), and find the length of the headline if it was set in 24-pt. type. Then, with the second table, find the approximate length of the same headline in this type in a different size.

The count for characters per pica (c.p.p.) is given only for the version shown. There are likely to be slight differences in character counts as between Monotype Bodoni and Linotype Bodoni, etc. However, these differences are not usually great enough to jeopardize the utility of a calculation; noticeable differences are commented upon below; see Caslon, for example, pages 371 and 372.

Information is given with each type specimen as to whether it is available on the Linotype, Intertype, Monotype, Ludlow, or, as foundry type, from American Type Founders (ATF), Bauer, Continental, etc.

Linotype, Intertype, and Ludlow faces are cast fresh for each use. A printer may or may not be able to cast up more Monotype characters as he needs them, depending on whether he has purchased the matrices or just the cast type.

The machine faces are usually favored if the type itself is to be printed from. This is because printers are understandably reluctant to let their foundry type undergo the wear of actual printing unless they can get more of it, promptly and at a reasonable price. Foundry type is often reserved for the making of reproduction proofs (as for offset) or for making electros.

Alternate Gothic No. 2 (Mono.)
ABCDEFGHIJKLMNOPQRSTUVWXYZ&
abcdefghijklmnopqrstuvwxyz 1234567890

Mono: c.p.p. (24 pt.) 1.55; caps p.p., 1.31. 6-36 pt. ATF: 6-72 pt. No italic. Alternate Gothic No. 1 is slightly narrower; No. 3 somewhat wider.

BALLOON BOLD (ATF)
ABCDEFGHIJKLMNOPQRSTUVWXYZ&
1234567890

ATF: caps only. Caps p.p. (24 pt.) 1.24. Available in 10-96 pt. in Light and Extrabold as well as in the Bold shown here.

Barnum, P. T. (ATF)
ABCDEFGHIJKLMNOPQRSTUVW
XYZ& abcdefghijklmnopqrstuvwxyz
1234567890

ATF: c.p.p. (24 pt.) 1.35; caps p.p. 0.91. 6-36 pt.

Baskerville (Mono No. 353)
ABCDEFGHIJKLMNOPQRST
UVWXYZ&　1234567890
abcdefghijklmnopqrstuvwxyz

Mono:c.p.p. (24 pt.) 1.29; caps p.p., 0.86. 6-36 pt. ATF: 6-72 pt. Lino and Intertype: 6-14 pt.

NOTE: c.p.p. means lower-case characters per pica. Caps p.p. means caps per pica. Character counts may differ somewhat between one typefounder and another for similar faces and between italic and roman.

Baskerville Italic (Mono No. 353)
ABCDEFGHIJKLMNOPQRST
UVWXYZ& 1234567890
abcdefghijklmnopqrstuvwxyz

Mono: c.p.p. (24 pt.) 1.48; caps p.p. 0.91. 6-36 pt. ATF: 6-18 pt. Lino and Intertype: 6-14 pt.

Baskerville Bold (Mono. No. 453)
ABCDEFGHIJKLMNOPQRSTU
VWXYZ& 1234567890
abcdefghijklmnopqrstuvwxyx

Mono: c.p.p. (24 pt.) 1.18; caps p.p., 0.82. 8-72 pt. No italic. Linotype has a Baskerville Bold Italic in 7-14 pt.

Bernhard Modern Bold (ATF)
ABCDEFGHIJKLMNOPQR
STUVWXYZ& 1234567890
abcdefghijklmnopqrstuvwxyz

ATF: c.p.p. (24 pt.) 1.21; caps p.p., 0.80. Available also in a matching italic, and in a lighter Bernhard Modern Roman.

Beton Series (Inter)
See MEMPHIS and also page 361.

NOTE: c.p.p. means lower-case characters per pica. Caps p.p. means caps per pica. Character counts may differ somewhat between one typefounder and another for similar faces and between italic and roman.

Bodoni (Mono)
ABCDEFGHIJKLMNOPQRS
TUVWXYZ& 1234567890
abcdefghijklmnopqrstuvwxyz

Mono: c.p.p. (24 pt.) 1.26; caps p.p. 0.90. 5-36 pt. Every manufacturer offers the Bodoni series in a wide range of sizes. See page 357.

Bodoni Italic (Mono)
ABCDEFGHIJKLMNOPQRS
TUVWXYZ& 1234567890
abcdefghijklmnopqrstuvwxyz

Mono: c.p.p. (24 pt.) 1.28; caps p.p. 0.89. 6-72 pt.

Bodoni Bold (Mono)
ABCDEFGHIJKLMNOPQRS
TUVWXYZ& 1234567890
abcdefghijklmnopqrstuvwxyz

Mono: c.p.p. (24 pt.) 1.15; caps p.p. 0.87. 6-72 pt.

Bodoni Bold Italic (Mono)
ABCDEFGHIJKLMNOPQR
STUVWXYZ& 1234567890
abcdefghijklmnopqrstuvwxyz

Mono: c.p.p. (24 pt.) 1.17; caps p.p. 0.85. 6-72 pt.

NOTE: c.p.p. means lower-case characters per pica. Caps p.p. means caps per pica. Character counts may differ somewhat between one typefounder and another for similar faces and between italic and roman.

Bodoni, Ultra (ATF)
ABCDEFGHIJKLMNO
PQRSTUVWXYZ&
abcdefghijklmnopqrst
uvwxyz 1234567890

ATF: c.p.p. (24 pt.) 0.82; caps p.p. 0.63. 6-120 pt. Ludlow offers a similar face called Bodoni Black (6-72 pt.); Intertype, Bodoni Modern (8-36 pt.); Linotype, Poster Bodoni (8-144 pt.)

Bodoni Italic, Ultra (ATF)
ABCDEFGHIJKLMNO
PQRSTUVWXYZ&
abcdefghijklmnopqrst
uvwxyz 1234567890

ATF: c.p.p. (24 pt.) 0.84; caps p.p. 0.62. 6-72 pt. Ludlow offers a similar face called Bodoni Black Italic with swash characters (12-48 pt.); Intertype, Bodoni Modern Italic (8-24 pt.) Linotype, Poster Bodoni Italic (8-60 pt.)

Bookman (Ludlow)
ABCDEFGHIJKLMNOP
QRSTUVWXYZ& abcdefg
hijklmnopqrstuvwxyz 12345

Ludlow: c.p.p. (24 pt.) 0.99; caps p.p. 0.66. 12-48 pt. ATF: Bookman Oldstyle comes in 6-36 pt. Linotype has it in 6-14 pt. Monotype has it in 6-36 pt. and also has New Bookman in 14-72. Intertype calls it Bookface and offers sizes 6-30 pt.

NOTE: c.p.p. means lower-case characters per pica. Caps p.p. means caps per pica. Character counts may differ somewhat between one typefounder and another for similar faces and between italic and roman.

BOOKMAN ITALIC (ATF)
ABCDEFGHIJKLMNOPQRSTUV
XYZ& 1234567890
abcdefghijklmnopqrstuvwxyz

Same range of sizes as above, except ATF and Intertype have the italic only to 24 pt.
(18 pt. shown here.)

BOUL MICH (ATF)
ABCDEFGHIJKLMN
OPQRSTUVWXYZ&
1234567890

ATF: caps only. Caps p.p. (24 pt.) 0.55. 12-72 pt.

BROADWAY (ATF)
ABCDEFGHIJKLM
NOPQRSTUVWXY
Z& 1234567890

ATF: caps only. Caps p.p. (24 pt.) 0.52. 6-72 pt. Monotype has it in 12-36 pt.

Bulmer (ATF)
ABCDEFGHIJKLMNOPQRST
UVWXYZ& 1234567890
abcdefghijklmnopqrstuvwxyz

ATF: c.p.p. (24 pt.) 1.36; caps p.p. 0.91. 6-48 pt.

NOTE: c.p.p. means lower-case characters per pica. Caps p.p. means caps per pica. Character counts may differ somewhat between one typefounder and another for similar faces and between italic and roman.

Bulmer Italic (ATF)
ABCDEFGHIJKLMNOPQRSTUVW
XYZ& abcdefghijklmnopqrstuvwxyz
1234567890

ATF: c.p.p. (24 pt.) 1.47; caps p.p. 0.94. 6-48 pt.

Cairo Series (Inter)

This comes in the same general range of sizes and weights as Memphis. See also page 361.

Cameo (Ludlow)
ABCDEFGHIJKLMNOPQ
RSTUVWXYZ& abcdefghi
jklmnopqrstuvwxyz 123456

Ludlow: c.p.p. (24 pt.) 0.97; caps p.p. 0.69. 12-72 pt. Similar type styles include Narciss, Goudy Open, Goudy Handtooled, Cloister Bold Tooled, and Caslon Openface.

Cameo Italic (Ludlow)
ABCDEFGHIJKLMNOP
QRSTUVWXYZ&abcdefg
hijklmnopqrstuvwxyz123

Ludlow: c.p.p. (24 pt.) 0.93; caps p.p. 0.65. 12-48 pt.

NOTE: c.p.p. means lower-case characters per pica. Caps p.p. means caps per pica. Character counts may differ somewhat between one typefounder and another for similar faces and between italic and roman.

Caslon (Lino)
ABCDEFGHIJKLMNOPQRS TUVWXYZ& 1234567890
abcdefghijklmnopqrstuvwxyz

Lino: c.p.p. (24 pt.) 1.28; caps p.p. 0.78. 7-36 pt. Every type manufacturer puts out one or more versions of Caslon in a wide range of sizes. ATF Caslon Oldstyle No. 471 is considered by many to be one of the most beautiful cuttings of this type.

Caslon Italic (Lino)
ABCDEFGHIJKLMNOPQRSTU VWXYZ& 1234567890
abcdefghijklmnopqrstuvwxyz

Lino: c.p.p. (24 pt.) 1.42; caps p.p. 0.84. 7-30 pt.

Caslon Bold (Lino)
ABCDEFGHIJKLMNOPQ RSTUVWXYZ& abcdefghij klmnopqrstuvwxyz 12345678

Lino: c.p.p. (24 pt.) 1.02; caps p.p. 0.71. 5-72 pt. Caslon Bold is also called Caslon No 3. Every type manufacturer puts out a version of Caslon Bold in a wide range of sizes.

NOTE: c.p.p. means lower-case characters per pica. Caps p.p. means caps per pica. Character counts may differ somewhat between one typefounder and another for similar faces and between italic and roman.

Caslon Bold Italic (Lino)
ABCDEFGHIJKLMNOP
QRSTUVWXYZ& abcdef
ghijklmnopqrstuvwxyz 123

Lino: c.p.p. (24 pt.) 0.97; caps p.p. 0.64. 5-72 pt.

Century Expanded (Mono)
ABCDEFGHIJKLMNOPQRS
TUVWXYZ& 1234567890
abcdefghijklmnopqrstuvwxyz

Mono: c.p.p. (24 pt.) 1.09; caps p.p. 0.78. 6-72 pt. Lino: 4-24 pt. Intertype: 4-36 pt.; Ludlow: 12-42 pt.

Century Expanded Italic (Mono)
ABCDEFGHIJKLMNOPQR
STUVWXYZ& 1234567890
abcdefghijklmnopqrstuvwxyz

Mono: c.p.p. (24 pt.) 1.12; caps p.p. 0.74. 6-36 pt. Intertype: 4-14 pt. Lino: 4-24 pt.

Century Bold (Mono)
ABCDEFGHIJKLMNOPQRS
TUVWXYZ& 1234567890
abcdefghijklmnopqrstuvwxyz

Mono: c.p.p. (24 pt.) 1.11; caps p.p. 0.78. 5½-72 pt. Lino: 6-72 pt. Intertype: 6-36 pt. Ludlow: 12-48 pt. ATF: 6-120 pt.

NOTE: c.p.p. means lower-case characters per pica. Caps p.p. means caps per pica. Character counts may differ somewhat between one typefounder and another for similar faces and between italic and roman.

Century Bold Italic (Mono)
ABCDEFGHIJKLMNOPQRS
TUVWXYZ& 1234567890
abcdefghijklmnopqrstuvwxyz

Mono: c.p.p. (24 pt.) 1.06; caps p.p. 0.76. 6-72 pt. Lino: 8-48 pt. Intertype: 6-36 pt. Ludlow: 12-72 pt. ATF: 6-72 pt.

Cheltenham Bold
ABCDEFGHIJKLMNOPQRST
UVWXYZ& 1234567890
abcdefghijklmnopqrstuvwxyz

This series, which scored a huge success in the early part of the century, is widely available in Condensed, Wide, Old Style, etc., as well as in Bold. There are cuttings by all the typefounders. However, it is not so much used as formerly, and space will not be taken to give a full showing of it here. C.p.p. (24 pt.) 1.14; caps p.p. 0.79.

Civilite (ATf)
ABCDEFGHIJKLMNOP
QRSTUVWXYZ&
abcdefghijklmnopqrstuvwxyz 1234567890

ATF: c.p.p. (24 pt.) 2.05; caps not used separately. 10-48 pt.

NOTE: c.p.p. means lower-case characters per pica. Caps p.p. means caps per pica. Character counts may differ somewhat between one typefounder and another for similar faces and between italic and roman.

COPPERPLATE GOTHIC LIGHT EXTENDED (ATF)
ABCDEFGHIJKLM NOPQRSTUVWXYZ & 1234567890

ATF: caps p.p. (24 pt.*) 0.54. 6-24 pt.

COPPERPLATE GOTHIC HEAVY (ATF)
ABCDEFGHIJKLMNOP QRSTUVWXYZ& 1234 567890

ATF: caps p.p. (24 pt.*) 0.67. 6-24 pt.

COPPERPLATE GOTHIC BOLD (ATF)
ABCDEFGHIJKLMNOP QRSTUVWXYZ& 1234 567890

ATF: caps p.p. (24 pt.*) 0.64. 6-24 pt.

* The size shown, having no descenders, can be and is cast on an 18-pt. body, and is therefore sometimes called 18 pt., even though it compares in size with any 24 pt. This possibility for misunderstanding must be watched whenever specifying a face that has no lower case.

Cochin, Nicolas (Mono)

ABCDEFGHIJKLMNOPQ
RSTUVWXYZ& 1234567890
abcdefghijklmnopqrstuvwxyz

Mono: c.p.p. (24 pt.) 1.40; caps p.p. 0.70. 14-36 pt. ATF: 6-72 pt.

Cochin, Nicolas, Italic (Mono)

ABCDEFGHIJKLMNOPQ
RSTUVWXYZ& 1234567890
abcdefghijklmnopqrstuvwxyz

Mono: c.p.p. (24 pt.) 1.51; caps p.p. 0.70. 14-36 pt. ATF: 6-48 pt.

Commercial Script (ATF)

A B C D E F G H I J K L M
N O P Q R S T U V W X Y Z &

abcdefghijklmnopqrstuvwxyz 12345

ATF: c.p.p. (24 pt.) 1.28. Caps not used separately. 12-60 pt.
There are too many scripts in too many weights to permit showing even a representative collection of them here.

NOTE: c.p.p. means lower-case characters per pica. Caps p.p. means caps per pica. Character counts may differ somewhat between one typefounder and another for similar faces and between italic and roman.

Cooper Black (Mono)
ABCDEFGHIJKLMNOP
QRSTUVWXYZ&
abcdefghijklmnopqrstu
vwxyz 1234567890

Mono: c.p.p. (24 pt.) 0.83; caps p.p. 0.66. 6-72 pt. ATF: 6-120 pt.
Similar faces are Ludlow Black (8-48 pt.) and Linotype Pabst Extra Bold. These
latter two faces have a matching italic.

Coronet Light (Ludlow)
ABCDEFGHIJKLMNOPQ
RSTUVWXYZ& abcdefghijklmnopqrstuvwxyz
1234567890

Ludlow: c.p.p. (24 pt.) 2.12; caps not used separately. 14-72 pt.

Coronet Bold (Ludlow)
ABCDEFGHIJKLMNOPQ
RSTUVWXYZ& 1234567890
abcdefghijklmnopqrstuvwxyz

Ludlow: c.p.p. (24 pt.) 1.85; caps not used separately. 14-72 pt.

NOTE: c.p.p. means lower-case characters per pica. Caps p.p. means caps per pica. Character counts may
differ somewhat between one typefounder and another for similar faces and between italic and roman.

Corvinus Medium (Bauer)
ABCDEFGHIJKLMNOPQRSTUVW
XYZ& abcdefghijklmnopqrstuvwxyz
1234567890

Bauer: c.p.p. (24 pt.) 1.31; caps p.p. 0.98. 8-60 pt. Corvinus is also available in a Light (8-48 pt.) and a Bold (8-48 pt.)

Corvinus Medium Italic (Bauer)
ABCDEFGHIJKLMNOPQRSTUVW
XYZ& abcdefghijklmnopqrstuvwxyz
1234567890

Bauer: c.p.p. (24 pt.) 1.32; caps p.p. 1.04. Same range of sizes as above. The light has an italic, but the bold has no italic.

Deepdene (Mono)
ABCDEFGHIJKLMNOPQRSTUV
WXYZ& 1234567890
abcdefghijklmnopqrstuvwxyz

Mono: c.p.p. (24 pt.) 1.36; caps p.p. 0.89. 6-72 pt.

Deepdene Italic (Mono)
ABCDEFGHIJKLMNOPQRSTUV
WXYZ& abcdefghijklmnopqrstuvwxyz
1234567890

Mono: c.p.p. (24 pt.) 1.69; caps p.p. 0.96. 6-72 pt.

NOTE: c.p.p. means lower-case characters per pica. Caps p.p. means caps per pica. Character counts may differ somewhat between one typefounder and another for similar faces and between italic and roman.

Deepdene Bold (Mono)
ABCDEFGHIJKLMNOPQRST UVWXYZ& 1234567890
abcdefghijklmnopqrstuvwxyz

Mono: c.p.p. (24 pt.) 1.18; caps p.p. 0.81. 6-72 pt.

Deepdene Bold Italic (Mono)
ABCDEFGHIJKLMNOPQRSTUV WXYZ& 1234567890
abcdefghijklmnopqrstuvwxyz

Mono: c.p.p. (24 pt.) 1.38; caps p.p. 0.88. 6-72 pt.

DELPHIAN OPEN (Ludlow)
ABCDEFGHIJKLMNOPQR STUVWXYZ& 1234567890

Ludlow: caps only. Caps p.p. 0.70. 24-60 pt.

Dom Casual (ATF)

ABCDEFGHIJKLMNOPQRSTUVWXYZ& abcde fghijklmnopqrstuvwxyz 1234567890

ATF: c.p.p. (24 pt.) 1.85; caps p.p. 1.28. 18-72 pt.

NOTE: c.p.p. means lower-case characters per pica. Caps p.p. means caps per pica. Character counts may differ somewhat between one typefounder and another for similar faces and between italic and roman.

Eden Bold (Ludlow)
ABCDEFGHIJKLMNOPQ
RSTUVWXYZ& 1234567890
abcdefghijklmnopqrstuvwxyz

Ludlow: c.p.p. (24 pt.) 1.30; caps p.p. 0.96. 10-72 pt.

Egmont Light (Inter)
ABCDEFGHIJKLMNOPQRST
UVWXYZ 1234567890
abcdefghijklmnopqrstuvwxyz

Intertype: c.p.p. (24 pt.) 1.31; caps p.p. 0.79. 8-30 pt.

Egmont Light Italic (Inter)
ABCDEFGHIJKLMNOPQRST
UVWXYZ 1234567890
abcdefghijklmnopqrstuvwxyz

Intertype: c.p.p. (24 pt.) 1.35; caps p.p. 0.83. 8-30 pt.

Egmont Bold (Inter)
ABCDEFGHIJKLMNOPQRS
TUVWXYZ 1234567890
abcdefghijklmnopqrstuvwxyz

Intertype: c.p.p. (24 pt.) 1.21; caps p.p. 0.77. 8-24 pt. Continental: 8-60 pt.

NOTE: c.p.p. means lower-case characters per pica. Caps p.p. means caps per pica. Character counts may differ somewhat between one typefounder and another for similar faces and between italic and roman.

Egmont Bold Italic (Inter)
ABCDEFGHIJKLMNOPQRS TUVWXYZ 1234567890
abcdefghijklmnopqrstuvwxyz

Intertype: c.p.p. (24 pt.) 1.21; caps p.p. 0.77. 8-24 pt.

Franklin Gothic (Ludlow)
ABCDEFGHIJKLMNOPQRS TUVWXYZ& abcdefghijklm nopqrstuvwxyz 12345678

Ludlow: c.p.p. (24 pt.) 0.98; caps p.p. 0.75. 6-72 pt. ATF: 4-96 pt. Intertype: 18-24 pt. Lino: 18-144 pt. Mono: 4-72 pt.

Franklin Gothic Wide (ATF)

ABCDEFGHIJKLMNO PQRSTUVWXYZ& abc defghijklmnopqrstuvw xyz 1234567890

ATF: c.p.p. (24 pt.) 0.83; caps p.p. 0.62. 14-72 pt.

NOTE: c.p.p. means lower-case characters per pica. Caps p.p. means caps per pica. Character counts may differ somewhat between one typefounder and another for similar faces and between italic and roman.

Futura Light (Bauer)
ABCDEFGHIJKLMNOPQRSTUVW XYZ& abcdefghijklmnopqrstuvwxyz 1234567890

Bauer: c.p.p. (24 pt.) 1.37; caps p.p. 1.04. 6-84 pt. Intertype: 6-14 pt. Virtually identical faces are Linotype Spartan Light, 8-14 pt.; Ludlow Tempo Light, 6-72 pt.; and Monotype Twentieth Century Light, 6-72 pt.

Futura Light Oblique (Bauer)
ABCDEFGHIJKLMNOPQRSTUVWXYZ abcdefghijklmnopqrstuvwxyz& 123456

Bauer: c.p.p. (24 pt.) 1.45; caps p.p. 1.05. 8-48 pt. Intertype: 6-14 pt. Virtually identical faces are Ludlow Tempo Light Italic, 10-72 pt.; and Monotype Twentieth Century Light Italic, 6-72 pt.

Futura Book (Bauer)
ABCDEFGHIJKLMNOPQRSTUVWXYZ& abcdefghijklmnopqrstuvwxyz 1234567

Bauer: c.p.p. (24 pt.) 1.40; caps p.p. 1.09. 8-48 pt. Intertype: 6-14 pt. Intertype has a Futura Book Oblique in 6-14 pt.

NOTE: c.p.p. means lower-case characters per pica. Caps p.p. means caps per pica. Character counts may differ somewhat between one typefounder and another for similar faces and between italic and roman.

Futura Medium (Bauer)
ABCDEFGHIJKLMNOPQRSTUVW
XYZ& abcdefghijklmnopqrstuvwxyz
1234567890

Bauer: c.p.p. (24 pt.) 1.31; caps p.p. 1.02. 6-84 pt. Intertype: 6-18 pt. Virtually identical faces are Linotype Spartan Medium, 6-24 pt.; ATF Spartan Medium, 8-120 pt.; Ludlow Tempo Medium, 6-72 pt.; and Monotype Twentieth Century Medium, 6-72 pt.

Futura Medium Oblique (Bauer)
ABCDEFGHIJKLMNOPQRSTUVW
XYZ& abcdefghijklmnopqrstuvwxyz
1234567890

Bauer: c.p.p. 1.32; caps p.p. 1.01. 8-48 pt. Intertype: 6-14 pt. Virtually identical faces are Linotype Spartan Medium Italic, 6-24 pt.; ATF Spartan Medium Italic, 8-72 pt.; Ludlow Tempo Medium Italic, 8-48 pt.; and Monotype Twentieth Century Medium Italic, 6-72 pt.

Futura Demibold (Inter)
ABCDEFGHIJKLMNOPQRSTUVW
XYZ& 1234567890
abcdefghijklmnopqrstuvwxyz

Intertype: c.p.p. (24 pt.) 1.23; caps p.p. 0.96. Bauer: 8-24 pt. Virtually identical faces are Linotype Spartan Heavy, 6-24 pt.; ATF Spartan Heavy, 6-36 pt.; Ludlow Tempo Bold, 6-72 pt.; and Monotype Twentieth Century Bold, 6-72 pt.

NOTE: c.p.p. means lower-case characters per pica. Caps p.p. means caps per pica. Character counts may differ somewhat between one typefounder and another for similar faces and between italic and roman.

Futura Demibold Oblique (*Inter*)
ABCDEFGHIJKLMNOPQRSTUVW
XYZ& 1234567890
abcdefghijklmnopqrstuvwxyz

Intertype: c.p.p. (24 pt.) 1.24; caps p.p. 0.96. 6-30 pt. Virtually identical faces are Linotype Spartan Heavy Italic, 6-24 pt.; ATF Spartan Heavy Italic, 6-36 pt.; Ludlow Tempo Bold Italic, 12-48 pt.; and Monotype Twentieth Century Bold Italic, 6-72 pt.

Futura Bold (**Bauer**)
ABCDEFGHIJKLMNOPQRST
UVWXYZ& abcdefghijklmno
pqrstuvwxyz 1234567890

Bauer: c.p.p. (24 pt.) 1.03; caps p.p. 0.87. 8-84 pt. Intertype: 6-18 pt. Virtually identical faces are Linotype Spartan Black, 6-24 pt.; ATF Spartan Black, 6-36 pt.; Ludlow Tempo Heavy, 6-72 pt.; Monotype Twentieth Century Extrabold, 6-72 pt.

Futura Bold Italic
ABCDEFGHIJKLMNOPQRSTUV
WXYZ& 1234567890
abcdefghijklmnopqrstuvwxyz

The above specimen lines of Futura Bold Italic are actually set in Mono Twentieth Century Extrabold Italic, since Bauer has no such italic, and Intertype has it only from 6-18 pt. This was done to keep all specimens of the Futura family together and similar. C.p.p. (24 pt.) 1.07; caps p.p. 0.88. Virtually identical faces are Linotype Spartan Black Italic, 6-24 pt.; ATF Spartan Black Italic, 6-36 pt.; Ludlow Tempo Heavy Italic, 12-72 pt.; and Monotype Twentieth Century Extrabold Italic, 6-72 pt.

NOTE: c.p.p. means lower-case characters per pica. Caps p.p. means caps per pica. Character counts may differ somewhat between one typefounder and another for similar faces and between italic and roman.

Futura Medium Condensed (Bauer)
ABCDEFGHIJKLMNOPQRSTUVWXYZ&
abcdefghijklmnopqrstuvwxyz 1234567890

Bauer: c.p.p. (24 pt.) 1.85; caps p.p. 1.58. 8-84 pt. Intertype: 8-14 pt. Virtually identical faces are Ludlow Tempo Medium Condensed, 30-72 pt.; and Monotype Twentieth
Century Medium Condensed, 14-72 pt.

Futura Bold Condensed (Bauer)
ABCDEFGHIJKLMNOPQRSTUVWXYZ&
abcdefghijklmnopqrstuvwxyz 1234567890

Bauer: c.p.p. (24 pt.) 1.60; caps p.p. 1.26. 8-84 pt. Intertype: 6-14 pt. Virtually identical faces are Linotype Spartan Black Condensed, 14-24 pt.; ATF Spartan Black Condensed, 10-36 pt.; Ludlow Tempo Heavy Condensed, 10-72 pt.; and Monotype Twentieth Century Extrabold Condensed, 14-84 pt.

Garamond (Inter)
ABCDEFGHIJKLMNOPQRSTUV
WXYZ& 1234567890
abcdefghijklmnopqrstuvwxyz

Inter: c.p.p. (24 pt.) 1.36; caps p.p. 0.89. 6-36 pt. ATF: 6-72 pt. Lino: (Garamond
No. 3), 6-42 pt. Mono: (Garamont), 6-72 pt. The above cuttings of Garamond are
quite similar in weight and character count. Linotype Garamond (6-36 pt.) (not
Garamond No. 3) is a little heavier, with (in 24 pt.) 1.22 c.p.p. Ludlow Garamond
(8-72 pt.) is a little more compact, with (in 24 pt.) 1.44 c.p.p.

NOTE: c.p.p. means lower-case characters per pica. Caps p.p. means caps per pica. Character counts may
differ somewhat between one typefounder and another for similar faces and between italic and roman.

Garamond Italic (Inter)
ABCDEFGHIJKLMNOPQRSTUVW XYZ& abcdefghijklmnopqrstuvwxyz 1234567890

Inter: c.p.p. (24 pt.) 1.56; caps p.p. 0.94. 6-48 pt. ATF: 6-48 pt. Mono: (Garamont) 6-72 pt.
Also (but see note above) Lino (Garamond) : 6-30 pt. Ludlow: 8-72 pt.

Garamond Bold (Inter)
ABCDEFGHIJKLMNOPQRST UVWXYZ& 1234567890 abcdefghijklmnopqrstuvwxyz

Inter: c.p.p. (24 pt.) 1.22; caps p.p. 0.84. 6-36 pt. ATF: 6-120 pt. Mono: 6-72 pt. Lino: (Garamond No. 3) , 6-144 pt.
Linotype Garamond Bold (6-36 pt.) is a little heavier and broader than the rest; Ludlow Garamond Bold (8-72 pt.) is a little more compact.

Garamond Bold Italic (Inter)
ABCDEFGHIJKLMNOPQRSTU VWXYZ& 1234567890 abcdefghijklmnopqrstuvwxyz

Inter: c.p.p. (24 pt.) 1.36; caps p.p. 0.87. 6-30 pt. ATF: 6-72 pt. Mono: 6-72 pt. Lino: (Garamond No. 3) , 6-72 pt.
Lino Garamond Bold (see above) , 6-30 pt. Ludlow Garamond Bold (see above) , 8-72 pt.

Girder Series
See MEMPHIS and also page 361.

NOTE: c.p.p. means lower-case characters per pica. Caps p.p. means caps per pica. Character counts may differ somewhat between one typefounder and another for similar faces and between italic and roman.

HEADLINE GOTHIC (ATF)
ABCDEFGHIJKLMNOPQRSTUVW
XYZ& 1234567890

ATF: caps only, caps p.p. (24 pt.) 0.83. 24-120 pt. (Note: This face, having no descenders, sets larger on the body than normal.)

News Gothic (ATF)
ABCDEFGHIJKLMNOPQRSTUVW
XYZ& 1234567890
abcdefghijklmnopqrstuvwxyz

ATF: c.p.p. (24 pt.) 1.20; caps p.p. 0.94. 6-72 pt.

News Gothic Condensed (ATF)
ABCDEFGHIJKLMNOPQRSTUVWXYZ& abc
defghijklmnopqrstuvwxyz 1234567890

ATF: c.p.p. (24 pt.) 1.55; caps p.p. 1.25. 12-48 pt.

News Gothic Extra Condensed (ATF)
ABCDEFGHIJKLMNOPQRSTUVWXYZ& 1234567890
abcdefghijklmnopqrstuvwxyz

ATF: c.p.p. (24 pt.) 2.40; caps p.p. 1.99. 6-72 pt.

NOTE: c.p.p. means lower-case characters per pica. Caps p.p. means caps per pica. Character counts may differ somewhat between one typefounder and another for similar faces and between italic and roman.

Hauser Script (Ludlow)
ABCDEFGHJJKLMNOPQRSTUVW
XYZ& 1234567890
abcdefghijklmnopqrstuvwxyz

Ludlow: c.p.p. (24 pt.) 1.57. Caps not used separately. 24-72 pt.

Kabel Series

See SANS SERIF and also page 360. Mono Sans Serif series is substantially identical with the Kabel Light, Kabel Bold, and Kabel Black faces imported by Continental and European.

Karnak Series (Ludlow)

See MEMPHIS and also page 361.

Kaufmann Bold (ATF)
ABCDEFGHIJKLMNOP2RSTU
VWXYZ& 1234567890
abcdefghijklmnopqrstuvwxyz

ATF: c.p.p. (24 pt.) 1.37. Caps not used by themselves. 10-96 pt. There is also a Kaufmann Script which is lighter. Similar faces include Gillies Gothic Light and Bold, and Signal Light, Medium and Black.

Lydian (ATF)
ABCDEFGHIJKLMNOPQRSTUV
WXYZ& 1234567890
abcdefghijklmnopqrstuvwxyz

ATF: c.p.p. (24 pt.) 1.22; caps p.p. 0.92. 10-96 pt.

NOTE: c.p.p. means lower-case characters per pica. Caps p.p. means caps per pica. Character counts may differ somewhat between one typefounder and another for similar faces and between italic and roman.

Lydian Italic (ATF)
ABCDEFGHIJKLMNOPQRSTUVWX YZ& abcdefghijklmnopqrstuvwxyz 1234567890

ATF: c.p.p. (24 pt.) 1.35; caps p.p. 0.98.

Lydian Cursive (A C F)
ABCDEFGHIJKLMNOPQRST UVWXYZ& 1234567890
abcdefghijklmnopqrstuvwxyz

ATF: c.p.p. (24 pt.) 1.47; Caps not used by themselves. 18-72 pt.

Lydian Bold (ATF)
ABCDEFGHIJKLMNOPQRSTUV WXYZ& 1234567890
abcdefghijklmnopqrstuvwxyz

ATF: c.p.p. (24 pt.) 1.19; caps p.p. 0.91. 10-96 pt.

Lydian Bold Italic (ATF)
ABCDEFGHIJKLMNOPQRSTUV WXYZ& 1234567890
abcdefghijklmnopqrstuvwxyz

ATF: c.p.p. (24 pt.) 1.25; caps p.p. 0.94. 10-96 pt.

NOTE: c.p.p. means lower-case characters per pica. Caps p.p. means caps per pica. Character counts may differ somewhat between one typefounder and another for similar faces and between italic and roman.

Memphis Light (Lino)
ABCDEFGHIJKLMNOPQRS TUVWXYZ& 1234567890
abcdefghijklmnopqrstuvwxyz

Lino: c.p.p. (24 pt.) 1.10; caps p.p. 0.82. 6-24 pt. See page 361 for a list of virtually identical faces by other typefounders.

Memphis Medium (Lino)
ABCDEFGHIJKLMNOPQRS TUVWXYZ& 1234567890
abcdefghijklmnopqrstuvwxyz

Lino: c.p.p. (24 pt.) 1.06; caps p.p. 0.81. 6-144 pt. Virtually identical faces are Karnak Intermediate, Stymie Medium, Beton Medium. Cairo Medium is similar. See page 361.

Memphis Medium Italic (Lino)
ABCDEFGHIJKLMNOPQRS TUVWXYZ& 1234567890
abcdefghijklmnopqrstuvwxyz

Lino: c.p.p. (24 pt.) 1.08; caps p.p. 0.80. 6-48 pt.

Memphis Bold (Lino)
ABCDEFGHIJKLMNOPQRS TUVWXYZ& 1234567890
abcdefghijklmnopqrstuvwxyz

Lino: c.p.p. (24 pt.) 1.07; caps p.p. 0.81. 6-144 pt. Virtually identical faces are Karnak Medium, Stymie Bold, Beton Bold. Cairo Bold is similar. See page 361.

NOTE: c.p.p. means lower-case characters per pica. Caps p.p. means caps per pica. Character counts may differ somewhat between one typefounder and another for similar faces and between italic and roman.

Memphis Bold Italic (Lino)
ABCDEFGHIJKLMNOPQRS TUVWXYZ& 1234567890
abcdefghijklmnopqrstuvwxyz

Lino: c.p.p. (24 pt.) 1.08; caps p.p. 0.80. 6-24 pt.

Memphis Extra Bold (Lino)
ABCDEFGHIJKLMNOPQ RSTUVWXYZ& abcdefg hijklmnopqrstuvwxyz 1234567890

Lino: c.p.p. (24 pt.) 0.93; caps p.p. 0.71. 8-144 pt. Virtually identical faces are Karnak Black, Stymie Extra Bold, Beton Extra Bold. Cairo Heavy and Stymie Black are similar. See page 361.

Memphis Extra Bold Italic (Lino)
ABCDEFGHIJKLMNOP QRSTUVWXYZ& abcde fghijklmnopqrstuvwxyz

Lino: c.p.p. (24 pt.) 0.87; caps p.p. 0.66. 8-24 pt.

Metro Series (Lino)

This Linotype series includes Metrothin, Metrolite, Metromedium, and Metroblack. See page 360 for a comparison between it and other sans serif faces.

NEULAND (CONTINENTAL)
ABCDEFGHIJKLMNOPQRSTU VWXYZ& 1234567890

Continental: caps only. Caps p.p. 0.81. 14-72 pt. Europ Type: 14-72 pt.

NOTE: c.p.p. means lower-case characters per pica. Caps p.p. means caps per pica. Character counts may differ somewhat between one typefounder and another for similar faces and between italic and roman.

NEULAND INLINE (CONTINENTAL)
ABCDEFGHIJKLMNOPQRSTU
VWXYZ& 1234567890

Continental: caps only. Caps p.p. 0.85. 14-72 pt. Europ Type: 14-72 pt.

Old English (Ludlow)
ABCDEFGHIJKLMNOPQRS
TUVWXYZ& 1234567890
abcdefghijklmnopqrstuvwxyz

Ludlow: c.p.p. (24 pt.) 1.25. Caps not used by themselves. 8-48 pt. Similar faces include Cloister Black (ATF and Mono), Engravers' Old English (Inter and Mono) and Caslon Text (Lino).

Onyx (Mono)
ABCDEFGHIJKLMNOPQRSTUVWXYZ&
abcdefghijklmnopqrstuvwxyz 1234567890

Mono: c.p.p. (24 pt.) 1.74; caps p.p. 1.44. 24-72 pt. ATF: 18-120 pt.

Pabst Extra Bold (Lino)

See COOPER BLACK

Park Avenue (ATF)
ABCDEFGHIJKLMNO
PQRSTUVWXYZ&
abcdefghijklmnopqrstuvwxyz 1234567890

ATF: c.p.p. (24 pt.) 1.64. Caps not used by themselves. 12-72 pt. Inter: 12-18 pt. Similar faces are ATF Piranesi Italic and Raleigh Cursive, and Ludlow Mayfair Cursive.

NOTE: c.p.p. means lower-case characters per pica. Caps p.p. means caps per pica. Character counts may differ somewhat between one typefounder and another for similar faces and between italic and roman.

Post Roman Light (Amst.)
ABCDEFGHIJKLMNOPQRST
UVWXYZ& 1234567890
abcdefghijklmnopqrstuvwxyz

Amst.: c.p.p. (24 pt.) 1.08; caps p.p. 0.82. 6-48 pt.

Post Roman Medium (Amst.)
ABCDEFGHIJKLMNOPQR
STUVWXYZ& 1234567890
abcdefghijklmnopqrstuvwxyz

Amst.: c.p.p. (24 pt.) 1.15; caps p.p. 0.70. 6-48 pt.

Post Roman Bold (Amst.)
ABCDEFGHIJKLMNOPQRS
TUVWXYZ& 1234567890
abcdefghijklmnopqrstuvwxyz

Amst.: c.p.p. (24 pt.) 1.08; caps p.p. 0.75. 6-72 pt.

Radiant Heavy (Ludlow)
ABCDEFGHIJKLMNOPQRS
TUVWXYZ& abcdefghijklm
nopqrstuvwxyz 123456789

Ludlow: c.p.p. (24 pt.) 1.00; caps p.p. 0.79. 10-72 pt. There is also a Radiant Bold Condensed (12-72 pt.) and a Radiant Bold Extra Condensed (14-72 pt.).

NOTE: c.p.p. means lower-case characters per pica. Caps p.p. means caps per pica. Character counts may differ somewhat between one typefounder and another for similar faces and between italic and roman.

Sans Serif Bold (Mono)
ABCDEFGHIJKLMNOPQRSTUV
WXYZ& abcdefghijklmnopqrstuvwxyz
1234567890

The Monotype Sans Serif series includes Light, Medium, Bold, Extrabold (each with matching italic) and Light Condensed, Medium Condensed and Extrabold Condensed. This series is substantially identical with the imported Kabel series and is often used interchangeably with Vogue, Futura, Metro, etc. See page 360 for a comparison with similar faces. C.p.p. (Bold 24 pt.) 1.50; caps p.p. 0.94.

Studio (Amst.)
ABCDEFGHIJKLMNOPQRST
UVWXYZ& abcdefghijklmno
pqrstuvwxyz 1234567890

Amst.: c.p.p. (24 pt.) 0.99; caps p.p. 0.83. 8-72 pt.

Spartan Series (Lino)

See FUTURA and also pages 358-359.

STENCIL (ATF)
ABCDEFGHIJKLMNO
PQRSTUVWXYZ&
1234567890

ATF: caps only. Caps p.p. (24 pt.) 0.62. 18-60 pt. Ludlow: 36-pt. caps only.

Stymie Series (Mono)

See MEMPHIS and also page 361.

NOTE: c.p.p. means lower-case characters per pica. Caps p.p. means caps per pica. Character counts may differ somewhat between one typefounder and another for similar faces and between italic and roman.

Tempo Series (Ludlow)

See FUTURA and also pages 358-359.

Trafton Script (Bauer)
ABCDEFGHIJKLMNOPQ
RSTUVWXYZ&

abcdefghijklmnopqrstuvwxyz 1234567890

Bauer: c.p.p. (24 pt.) 1.96. Caps not used by themselves. 14-84 pt.

UMBRA (LUDLOW)
ABCDEFGHIJKLMNOPQ
RSTUVWXYZ&
1234567890

Ludlow: caps only. Caps p.p. (24 pt.) 0.69. 24-72 pt.

Venus Extra Bold
Extended (Bauer)

ABCDEFGHIJKLMNOPQR
STUVWXYZ&1234567890
abcdefghijklmnopqrstuv
wxyz

Bauer: c.p.p. (18 pt.) 0.75; caps p.p. 0.52. 8-84 pt.

NOTE: c.p.p. means lower-case characters per pica. Caps p.p. means caps per pica. Character counts may differ somewhat between one typefounder and another for similar faces and between italic and roman.

Vogue Series (Inter)

See page 360 for a comparison of the various weights of Vogue with similar faces.

Vogue (Inter)
ABCDEFGHIJKLMNOPQRSTUV
WXYZ 1234567890
abcdefghijklmnopqrstuvwxyz

Intertype: c.p.p. (24 pt.) 1.28; caps p.p. 0.90. 6-60 pt.

Vogue Oblique (Inter)
ABCDEFGHIJKLMNOPQRSTUV
WXYZ 1234567890
abcdefghijklmnopqrstuvwxyz

Intertype: c.p.p. (18 pt.) 1.28; caps p.p. 0.90. 6-18 pt.

Vogue Bold (Inter)
ABCDEFGHIJKLMNOPQRSTUV
WXYZ 1234567890
abcdefghijklmnopqrstuvwxyz

Intertype: c.p.p. (24 pt.) 1.24; caps p.p. 0.88. 6-60 pt.

NOTE: c.p.p. means lower-case characters per pica. Caps p.p. means caps per pica. Character counts may differ somewhat between one typefounder and another for similar faces and between italic and roman.

Vogue Bold Oblique (Inter)

ABCDEFGHIJKLMNOPQRSTUV WXYZ 1234567890

abcdefghijklmnopqrstuvwxyz

Intertype: c.p.p. (24 pt.) 1.24; caps p.p. 0.88. 6-24 pt.

Vogue Extra Bold (Inter)

ABCDEFGHIJKLMNOPQRST UVWXYZ 1234567890

abcdefghijklmnopqrstuvwxyz

Intertype: c.p.p. (24 pt.) 1.11; caps p.p. 0.83.

Wedding Text (Mono)

ABCDEFGHIJKLMNOPQRSTUVW XYZ& abcdefghijklmnopqrstuvwxyz

1234567890

Mono: c.p.p. (24 pt.) 1.78. Caps not used by themselves. 8-36 pt. ATF: 6-48 pt. There are two sizes each of 18 and 24 pt.

Weiss Roman (Bauer)

ABCDEFGHIJKLMNOPQRSTUVW XYZ& 1234567890

abcdefghijklmnopqrstuvwxyz

Bauer: c.p.p. (24 pt.) 1.56; caps p.p. 0.95. 16-60 pt. (also Intertype)

NOTE: c.p.p. means lower-case characters per pica. Caps p.p. means caps per pica. Character counts may differ somewhat between one typefounder and another for similar faces and between italic and roman.

Appendix 2

Bibliography

There are some basic books and working tools that every user of print will want to keep at hand. These include the following:

Dictionary. Popular desk dictionaries include the Merriam-Webster "Collegiate Dictionary," the "American College Dictionary," and the "World Dictionary." Probably the most widely used unabridged dictionary is "Webster's New International Dictionary."

Classified Telephone Directories for New York and Chicago. These are invaluable for locating firms offering specialized services.

Type books of printers who are being dealt with.

Paper sample books from paper merchants.

Ink sample books from ink manufacturers.

Most of those who have to plan, produce, and use the printed word will also want to be familiar with as many as possible of the other books listed below, consulting some of them at the public library and buying those which are needed for repeated reference. The list is a selected one, including only those books that the authors of the present volume have found to be readable,

authoritative, and helpful in their everyday work of planning, editing, and buying printing of all varieties.

The books are grouped as follows:

General Reference
Advertising
  (See also Layout and Design)
Artwork
Book Publishing
Color
Copyright
Direct Mail
Displays
Fund Raising
Layout and Design
Lettering
Newspapers and Magazines
Packaging
Paper
Photography
Printing Processes
Publicity and Public Relations
Shipping
Television and Radio
Typography
Visual and Audiovisual Aids
Writing, Editing, and Proofreading

Note that many of the books listed under General Reference and Printing Processes have chapters on art, layout, paper, photography, etc. There is considerable overlapping among the groups. Because much valuable material is issued by the trade magazines, they are listed along with the books. Older books, even a few out-of-print books, have been listed where their presentation of basic principles remains as valid as ever and is hard to equal elsewhere.

GENERAL REFERENCE

Production in Advertising and the Graphic Arts, by Donald Hymes. New York: Holt, Rinehart and Winston, Inc., 1958. 389 pp. $8.75.

Basic information on photoengraving, typography, duplicate plates, paper, ink, printing, lithography, gravure, silk screen, binding, and die cutting.

The Penrose Annual, edited by Allan Delafons. New York: Hastings House, Publishers, Inc. About $14.50.

This British annual contains excellent summaries of the new developments in the graphic arts and includes also essays on design and many specimens of printing. Though British, its coverage of progress in the United States is excellent.

Sales Promotion Handbook, by John C. Aspley. Chicago: Dartnell Corp., 4th ed., 1964. $17.50.

Although this bumper reference book is designed primarily for sales managers of large firms seeking detailed help on promotion techniques, it contains valuable pointers and extensive reference material for advertising men, promotion directors, buyers of printing, and those who are responsible for direct mail letters, mailing lists, distribution, styling, and proofreading. The book includes extensive tables listing parcel-post rates, air and surface express rates, circulation and rates of principal magazines and newspapers, advertising rates of principal radio and television stations, principal business directories, business-paper editors, etc.

The Technique of Advertising Production, by Thomas B. Stanley. Englewood Cliffs, N.J.: Prentice-Hall, Inc., 1954. 214 pp. $11.

Good chapters on visualizing the appeal, focusing attention by layout, illustrating ads, understanding color, using photoengraving, gravure, and lithography, learning to recognize type, putting type to work, getting acquainted with paper, and planning printed matter.

Graphic Arts Procedures, by R. Randolph Karch. Chicago: American Technical Society, 3d ed., 1965. 388 pp. $5.25.

This is a basic text for students of the graphic arts, originally published in 1948, revised in 1957, and revised again in 1965. The latest edition contains a good, 24-page review of recent progress in graphic-arts technology and a chapter on careers in the graphic arts.

Careers in Graphic Reproduction, by Earl L. Bedell. Princeton, N.J.: D. Van Nostrand Company, Inc., 1965. 169 pp. $6.95.

Although addressed to young people deciding on a career, this book gives valuable information for all who are concerned with printing and promotion. It describes the tools of modern graphic reproduction (typewriters, duplicating and copying machines), the techniques (duplicating by stencil, offset, and electrostatics), and the related skills of drafting, illustration, photography, color, and reproduction and enlargement of graphic materials.

Printing Purchasing Manual. Oradel, N.J.: Walden, Sons & Mott, Inc. About 200 pp. $2. Published annually in September.

A comprehensive buyers' guide to printing services and materials with reference information on postal rates and regulations, copyright and patent laws, trade associations, and supplementary lists of new equipment and supplies as well as new books, movies, and slide films on the graphic arts.

THE LITERARY MARKET PLACE. New York: R. R. Bowker Company. About 650 pp. $7.45. Published annually.

A directory of firms, organizations, and individuals actively engaged in the production, marketing, or use of literary material. The key personnel in each organization are named. The listings cover book publishers (with notes on specialties of each), major magazines, book clubs, newspapers and news services, radio and TV stations and programs, motion-picture studios, literary agents, book reviewers, columnists and commentators, literary awards and prizes, clipping bureaus, book wholesalers, photographers, free-lance designers, artists, indexers, editors, etc.

ADVERTISING AND SALES PROMOTION. Published monthly in Chicago. $3 per year.

A down-to-earth magazine, filled with material that the advertising or promotion man can apply directly to his work, including art and photography, labeling and packaging, shows and exhibits, window and store displays, radio and TV production, layout and typography, paper, printing, and platemaking.

ADVERTISING

(See also LAYOUT)

PRINCIPLES OF ADVERTISING, by Philip W. Burton. Englewood Cliffs, N.J.: Prentice-Hall, Inc., 1955. 608 pp. $11.95; text ed., $8.95. Illus.

A review of the whole field of advertising, with chapters on the structure of advertising, how advertising is regulated, market research, where to advertise, layout, copy, budgeting, etc.

PRINCIPLES OF ADVERTISING, by The Committee on Advertising, Woodrow Wirsig, Editor. New York: Pitman Publishing Corporation, 1963. 560 pp. $8.50.

Sixty-four professors of journalism, business, and marketing have jointly produced this all-inclusive compendium of information about advertising: the economic and social aspects, market research and analysis, media selection, copywriting, layout, processes of reproduction, agencies, the advertising campaign, and tests for effectiveness.

ENCYCLOPEDIA OF ADVERTISING, by Irvin Graham. New York: Fairchild Publications, Inc., 1952. 622 pp. $3.

A reference book organized in very much the same way as the "Printing and Promotion Handbook" except that it provides rather fuller coverage of advertising and somewhat less coverage of such topics as direct mail, duplicating, type, and paper.

ADVERTISING HANDBOOK, edited by Roger Barton. Englewood Cliffs, N.J.: Prentice-Hall, Inc., 1950. 1015 pp. $10.

Although somewhat dated, this jumbo volume by 39 advertising men contains a vast store of information on every aspect of the subject.

TESTED ADVERTISING METHODS, by John Caples. New York: Harper & Row, Publishers, Inc., rev. 1961. 308 pp. $6.95.

This timeless classic, first published in 1932, remains one of the most readable primers in successful copywriting ever published. A veteran advertising executive explains how to get favorable sales results from headlines, illustrations, and copy, with innumerable examples of good and bad, right and wrong.

ADVERTISING COPYWRITING, by Philip Ward Burton and Bowman Krerr. Englewood Cliffs, N.J.: Prentice-Hall, Inc., 2d ed., 1962. $11.95.

A practical handbook of suggestions for those who plan and write advertising copy of all kinds including retail selling, fashions, mail order, business papers, outdoor displays, radio, and television.

HOW TO WRITE ADVERTISING THAT SELLS, by Clyde Bedell. New York: McGraw-Hill Book Company, 2d ed., 1952. $10.95.

This is a real how-to-do-it book which provides a systematic and methodical approach to creative advertising. It discusses in detail the problems of the advertising copywriter, the tools with which he works, the elements of selling strategy, and the methods of applying them to produce effective ads.

WHICH AD PULLED BEST?, by Carroll J. Swan. New York: Funk & Wagnalls Company, 1951. 163 pp. $7.50.

139 tests of such elements as headline, copy, illustrations, layout.

VISUAL THINKING IN ADVERTISING: A WORKBOOK, by Edith Heal Berrien. New York: Holt, Rinehart and Winston, Inc., 1963. 118 pp. Paper, $2.95.

An advertising and promotion specialist with magazine experience gives pointers on layout techniques, idea hatching, intriguing materials, and design for such specialities as packages, booklets and folders, and posters. Many photos of rough layouts and finished ads.

VISUAL PERSUASION: THE EFFECT OF PICTURES ON THE SUBCONSCIOUS, by Stephen Baker. New York: McGraw-Hill Book Company, 1961. Unpaged. $13.50.

With over 1,000 photographs and convincing text, an experienced advertising consultant explains how pictures can sometimes be more effective than words in the art of advertising persuasion.

ADVERTISING—CREATIVE COMMUNICATION WITH CONSUMERS, by Harry Walker Hepner. New York: McGraw-Hill Book Company, 1964. 692 pp. $8.95.

An advanced textbook which is also a valuable source book for those who plan, create, and buy advertising. The emphasis is on being creative.

MEDIA IN ADVERTISING, by Roger Barton. New York: McGraw-Hill Book Company, 1964. 559 pp. $12.50.

Detailed information for all who buy advertising of any kind. Covers publications, TV and radio, outdoor, point of purchase, direct mail, etc., with special attention to trends.

PROFITABLE NEWSPAPER ADVERTISING, by Edmund C. Arnold. New York: Harper & Row, Publishers, Inc., 1960. 136 pp. $4.95.

A practical guide for the retailer on the preparation of newspaper ads, including planning, copywriting, layout, type selection, and artwork, with more than 60 illustrations of ads in various stages.

HOW TO INCREASE ADVERTISING EFFECTIVENESS, by Richard D. Crisp. New York: McGraw-Hill Book Company, 1958. 120 pp. Paper, $2.65.

Information for the corporation executive on budgeting, selection of an agency, measuring effectiveness, and test marketing.

INDUSTRIAL ADVERTISING: PLANNING, CREATING, EVALUATING AND MERCHANDISING IT MORE EFFECTIVELY, by Fred R. Messner. New York: McGraw-Hill Book Company, 1963. 314 pp. $9.

The Account Director of the Industrial, Technical and Scientific Marketing Division of McCann-Erickson gives step-by-step directions for planning, creating campaigns and selecting media, communicating with the prospect, evaluating advertising effectiveness, and merchandising to both management and field forces.

INTERNATIONAL HANDBOOK OF ADVERTISING, edited by S. Watson Dunn. New York: McGraw-Hill Book Company, 1964. 788 pp. $19.50.

This reference volume, written by 76 international advertising experts, gives detailed information about principles and procedures of marketing common to all areas of the world, articles about the unique characteristics and facilities of 56 countries and areas, and extensive appendixes of expenditures, agencies, and audience-measurement services throughout the world.

ADVERTISING AGENCY OPERATIONS AND MANAGEMENT, by Roger Barton. New York: McGraw-Hill Book Company, 1955. 348 pp. $9.50.

An authoritative guide to effective methods of operating an advertising agency, this book will also be of interest to those who work with agencies as clients, consultants, free-lance artists, etc. Noteworthy case material reveals how particular accounts have been handled for various objectives.

STANDARD DIRECTORY OF ADVERTISERS. Skokie, Ill.: National Register Publishing Company.

This covers about 17,000 national and regional advertisers, giving address, products, personnel by name, agency handling the account, and media used. It is published in two editions, one arranged under 47 product classifications, the other arranged by state and city. A single copy of either edition sells for $35. The basic volumes plus cumulative monthly supplements are priced at $65 a year. There is also a separate STANDARD DIRECTORY OF ADVERTISING AGENCIES, priced at $15. (These two directories incorporate the old McKittrick's directories.)

Printers' Ink: The Weekly Magazine of Advertising. Printers' Ink Publishing Co., Inc., New York. $6 per year.

Latest news in the advertising field: new techniques, trends in business, pointers on preparation of copy and artwork, developments in radio and TV advertising, and an annual advertising index.

Advertising Age: The National Newspaper of Marketing. Published weekly in Chicago. $5 per year.

News of the advertising market, leading advertisers, market surveys, trends, etc.

ARTWORK

COMMERCIAL ART TECHNIQUES, by S. Ralph Maurello. New York: Tudor Publishing Company, 1952. 126 pp. $3.50; paper, $1.95.

A practical handbook telling how to develop art techniques for 18 different media. Specific materials and equipment are discussed and evaluated for the commercial artist.

COMMERCIAL ART AS A BUSINESS, by Fred C. Rodewald and Edward M. Gottshall. New York: Viking Press, Inc., rev. ed., 1960. $4.95.

Although written for the commercial artist to assist him in the business of selling, making contracts, etc., this book will also be helpful to editors and art directors who plan and purchase commercial art.

CAREERS AND OPPORTUNITIES IN COMMERCIAL ART, by J. I. Biegeleisen. New York: E. P. Dutton & Co., Inc., 1963. 263 pp. $4.95.

Chapters on sign painting, show-card writing, lettering, typography, trademarks, book jackets, illustrating, posters, fashion work, textiles, cartooning, industrial designing, packaging, window display, stage designing, government jobs, and how an ad agency works. Vocational guidance is the purpose of this book, but art buyers will find invaluable its hints on the prices charged for various kinds of artwork.

SCIENTIFIC ILLUSTRATION, by John Livesy Ridgway. Stanford, Calif.: Stanford University Press, 1938. 173 pp. Out of print.

Although the illustrations under discussion are technical ones, this book goes so thoroughly into the objectives and techniques of illustration that it will interest any artist, draftsman, author, or editor. It contains a useful section on how and where to get base maps and the permission to use them.

TECHNICAL ILLUSTRATION, by T. A. Thomas. New York: McGraw-Hill Book Company, 1960. 149 pp. $6.50.

The basic requirements and techniques, including exploded drawings; the mechanics of perspective, shading techniques, and photo retouching; inking methods; special tools; and materials.

BOOK PUBLISHING

BOOKMAKING: THE ILLUSTRATED GUIDE TO DESIGN AND PRODUCTION, by

Marshall Lee. New York: R. R. Bowker Company, 1965. 416 pp. $12.75 net postpaid.

A generously illustrated volume covering every step in designing and producing a book, from both the creative and the practical point of view. Partial contents: "The Profession" —background, function, requirements, opportunities, "Basic Knowledge"—composition, plates, printing, paper, illustration, binding, etc.; "Procedure"—analysis, the text plan, galley proofs and cast-off, layout of illustrations, front matter and back matter, etc. The author has been for 18 years head of the Design Department at H. Wolff Book Manufacturing Company and has taught a course in book design at New York University for some 12 years.

THE BOOK, THE STORY OF PRINTING AND BOOKMAKING, by Douglas C. McMurtrie. New York: Oxford University Press, 1943. 676 pp. $12.50.

The history and development of a book from the origin of the alphabet and paper to current practices in typography, design, binding, and illustration.

THE BOOKMAN'S GLOSSARY: A COMPENDIUM OF INFORMATION RELATING TO THE PRODUCTION AND DISTRIBUTION OF BOOKS. New York: R. R. Bowker Company, 4th ed., 1961. 212 pp. $5.

Definitions of about 1,200 printers' and editors' terms.

Publishers' Weekly. Published by R. R. Bowker Company, New York. $15 per year.

The trade journal of the book-publishing and book-selling industries.

Book Production Magazine. Published monthly, New York. $10 per year (U.S.).

Journal of the book-manufacturing (as distinct from book-publishing) industry.

COLOR

BASIC COLOR, by Egbert Jacobson. Chicago: Paul Theobald, 1949. 207 pp. $14.75. 460 illus.

Through text, color charts, color illustrations, and diagrams, this book gives a very practical and understandable interpretation of the Ostwald color system.

COPYRIGHT

A MANUAL OF COPYRIGHT PRACTICES FOR WRITERS, PUBLISHERS, AND AGENTS, by Margaret Nicholson. New York: Oxford University Press, 2d ed., 1956. 273 pp. $7.

For the layman seeking information in a specific situation involving copyright. Simple, readable, and authoritative. Some 49 of the major problems that arise are dealt with in detail.

A COPYRIGHT GUIDE, by Harriet F. Pilpel and Morton David Goldberg. New York: R. R. Bowker Company, 1963. 40 pp. $3.

Ninety-three questions and answers give the basic information about copyright, assignment of copyright, renewals, public domain, infringement, fair use, and international copyright provisions. Bibliography. Index.

DIRECT MAIL

SUCCESSFUL DIRECT-MAIL ADVERTISING AND SELLING, by Robert Stone. Englewood Cliffs, N.J.: Prentice-Hall, Inc., 1955. 320 pp. $6.50.

A discussion of the factors that make direct mail an effective method of selling, along with specific suggestions for writing selling letters, developing and using mailing lists, profiting from direct mail tests, and applying direct mail mathematics.

PLANNING AND CREATING BETTER DIRECT MAIL, by John D. Yeck and John T. Maguire. New York: McGraw-Hill Book Company, 1961. 387 pp. $7.95.

A valuable guide to direct mail advertising—how to increase readership, how to keep lists up to date, how to prepare copy, how to select the best format, how to buy art and layout, how to solicit funds and sell by mail.

HOW TO SELL THROUGH MAIL ORDER, by Irvin Graham. New York: McGraw-Hill Book Company, 1949. 443 pp. $7.75.

This practical guide to mail-order advertising through mass media and direct mail to special lists gives particularly good suggestions on precampaign planning and postcampaign analysis.

HOW TO INCREASE SALES WITH LETTERS, by Earle A. Buckley. New York: McGraw-Hill Book Company, 1961. 182 pp. $5.95.

A useful handbook of information about kinds of letters for different purposes, mailing lists, special offers, and methods of handling inquiries.

THE ROBERT COLLIER LETTER BOOK, by Robert Collier. Englewood Cliffs, N.J.: Prentice-Hall, Inc., 6th ed., 1950. $10.

This book is one of the classics of the profession and should be read and reread by everyone who has to move people to action by mail. It includes literally hundreds of letters and sales approaches of proved effectiveness in getting attention, arousing interest, convincing, and getting action.

GUIDE TO AMERICAN DIRECTORIES FOR COMPILING MAILING LISTS, B. Klein, Editor. New York: McGraw-Hill Book Company, 6th ed., 1965. 110 pp. $25.

This directory contains extensive information on available directories, yearbooks, annuals, etc., that can be used for market research or sales-promotion work. It is valuable in finding sources for compiling up-to-date mailing lists in all fields.

The Reporter of Direct Mail Advertising. Published by Henry Hoke, New York. $7.50 per year.

The trade paper of the direct mail advertising industry. Published monthly.

DISPLAYS

HANDBOOK OF WINDOW DISPLAY, by Nestor Castro. New York: Hastings House, Publishers, Inc., 1954. 194 pp. $8.50.

With many illustrations to amplify the text, the author gives practical and detailed instructions on how to make the best use of window space.

MODERN SIGN PAINTING, by Edward J. Duvall. Chicago: Frederick J. Drake & Co., 1959. 160 pp. $5.

How-to-do-it book for the commercial sign painter with directions for such varied techniques as sprayed signs, gold leaf, neon repaints, cut-in signs, silk-screen signs, etc.

FUND RAISING

FUNDRAISING MADE EASY, by Edwin S. Newman and Leo J. Margolin. Dobbs Ferry, N.Y.: Oceana Publications, Inc., 1954. 158 pp. $2.50.

A valuable manual for volunteer fund raisers in social-service organizations, including information about special events, soliciting special gifts, and public-relations campaigns.

LAYOUT AND DESIGN

THE BUTLER CLINIC HANDBOOKS. Mendota, Ill.: The Butler Clinic. $4 each, except No. 6, which is $5. Order by number.

This useful series offers special help to the one-man publication staff. It includes (1) "Effective Illustrations"; (2) "Headline Design"; (3) "101 Usable Editorial Layouts"; (4) "Double-Spreads"; (5) "101 More Usable Layouts"; (6) "Display Typefaces"; (7) "Back-of-the-Book Layouts." Also available: Harry Coffin's *Art Archives,* a clip book of 500 royalty-free illustrations, price $5.

ADVERTISING LAYOUT AND ART DIRECTION, by Stephen Baker. New York: McGraw-Hill Book Company, 1959. 326 pp. $15.

A veteran advertising agency director explains how graphic advertising ideas are created and produced, with copious illustrations showing thumbnail sketches, roughs, final art, and finished ads. There are useful chapters on "Designing for Television" and "The Knack of Buying Art."

ADVERTISING LAYOUT AND TYPOGRAPHY, by Eugene de Lopatecki. New York: The Ronald Press Company, rev. ed., 1952. $4.25.

For those who purchase printing and those who make the actual layouts, this book offers helpful pointers on the principles of design, use of the thumbnail sketch, type selection, and visualization.

LETTERING

THE ABC OF LETTERING, by J. I. Biegeleisen. New York: Harper & Row, Publishers, Inc., 2d ed., 1958. $9.50.

An excellent manual for artists, show-card writers, poster artists, display letterers, or students, with notes on equipment, exercises, and 105 pages of alphabet styles.

THE ELEMENTS OF LETTERING, by John Howard Benson and Arthur Graham Carey. New York: McGraw-Hill Book Company, 2d ed., 1950. $7.75.

Theoretical, practical, and historical elements in the art of lettering are given here, primarily for the artist and letterer who will create but also of interest to those who will plan, design, and finally evaluate lettering as a part of design.

SPEEDBALL TEXTBOOK FOR PEN AND BRUSH DRAWING, by Ross F. George. New York: London Book Co., Inc., 18th ed., 1960. Paper, 75 cents.

Over 100 styles of lettering are given with illustrations showing exactly how to use pen or brush to form every letter. This is perhaps the most practical, explicit, and thorough brief book on the subject. Suggestions on poster design are included.

LETTERING TODAY: A SURVEY AND REFERENCE BOOK, edited by John Brinkley. New York: Reinhold Publishing Corporation, 1965. 143 pp. $12.75.

Critical essays on modern trends in calligraphy for advertising and packaging, books and magazines, and architecture, with 300 illustrations gathered from England, Europe, and the United States.

NEWSPAPERS AND MAGAZINES

FUNCTIONAL NEWSPAPER DESIGN, by Edmund C. Arnold. New York: Harper & Row, Publishers, Inc., 1956. 340 pp. $9.95.

How to solve layout and typography problems on every kind of newspaper, from the masthead and front page to classified ads and from the sports page to the women's section. 200 illus.

MAGAZINE PUBLISHING, by Lenox R. Lohr. Baltimore: The Williams & Wilkins Company, 1932. 328 pp. Out of print.

From the working notes that one editor compiled for his successor. Elementary facts about the organization and management of a magazine, how to secure and edit articles and write editorials, the mechanics of reproducing illustrations, steps in production, advertising, etc. This editor's view of the problems of buying printing contains many tips of value to other editors of business papers. Although obtainable only at libraries or in the secondhand book market, this book is well worth whatever effort may be involved in seeing a copy. It is one of the best for the beginner.

Editor and Publisher. Published weekly in New York. $6.50 per year.

The trade paper of the newspaper world, with news of editorial and advertising affairs and ventures.

PACKAGING

MODERN PACKAGING ENCYCLOPEDIA ISSUE. Sold as a part of the magazine *Modern Packaging.* Published by Breskin Publishing Div., McGraw-Hill, Inc., New York. Magazine subscription, $13.

The Encyclopedia Issue of the magazine is a basic reference work, textbook, and buyer's directory of the packaging industry, with well-indexed material on package planning and design. It tells how and where to buy plain or printed cans, tubes, cartons, boxes, glass containers, aerosols, and plastics. It covers package printing methods, displays, adhesives, waterproofing, wet-strength papers, etc. It contains a great many advertisements by package manufacturers and printers and by materials suppliers, with samples of papers, films, foils, flock printing, etc. The emphasis is on packaging for sales, but shipping and industrial packaging are also covered.

PAPER

THE PAPER YEARBOOK. Duluth, Minn.: Ojibway Press, Inc. Published annually in January. $10.

This encyclopedia of the paper industry describes, explains the special properties and uses of, and gives the sources of supply for more than 1,500 different kinds of papers and paper products. It is well illustrated and indexed.

PHOTOGRAPHY

PICTURE EDITING, by Stanley E. Kalish and Clinton C. Edom. New York: Rinehart & Company, Inc., 1951. Out of print.

How to develop a feeling for pictures, how to create good picture ideas and work with photographers, and how to cope with the specific problems of scaling, cropping, determining print quality, retouching, caption writing, making layouts, and using color.

PRINTING PROCESSES

REPRODUCTIONS REFERENCE GUIDE, Third Edition. New York: Wolf Business Publications, Inc., 1963. 268 pp. $2.50.

Essential technical information on reproduction for business and industry personnel; articles on the major reproduction processes, along with specification charts of certain types of equipment and an extensive buyer's guide.

THE COMPLETE BOOK OF SILK SCREEN PRINTING PRODUCTION, by J. I. Biegeleisen. New York: Dover Publications, Inc., 1963. 252 pp. $2.

Includes chapters on the history of the process, basic techniques, photo-stencil methods, screen fabrics, paints and lacquers, color matching, printing on special surface (paper, board, plastic, decalcomanias, cylindrical surfaces, textiles), silk screen as a fine-art medium, price estimating, sources of supply, bibliography.

SCREEN PROCESS METHODS OF REPRODUCTION, by Bert Zahn. Chicago: Frederick J. Drake & Co., 1956. 252 pp. $5. 179 illus.

Detailed description of methods, materials, and equipment now in use in reproduction by the screen process, including such widely varied techniques as silk-screen stenciling, paint press method, flocking, photographic methods, zinc-plate emulsion method, and automatic screen process.

PHOTOGRAPHIC REPRODUCTION: METHODS, TECHNIQUES, AND APPLICATIONS FOR ENGINEERING AND THE GRAPHIC ARTS, by Harold Denstman and Morton J. Schultz. New York: McGraw-Hill Book Company, 1963. 187 pp. $9.

Detailed information on the techniques of line, halftone, and continuous-tone reproduction, by the photographic diazo, blueprint, and silk-screen processes. Primarily for the technician. Does not cover Xerography.

Reproductions Review (incorporating *Office Duplicator Review*). Published monthly by Wolf Business Publications, Inc., New York. $5 per year; 50 cents a single copy.

A valuable digest-size magazine which is packed with timely articles and reviews of recent booklets, samples, catalogs, and audiovisual materials, as well as reviews of new products of interest to the reproductions field. Of particular value to lettershop operators.

PUBLICITY AND PUBLIC RELATIONS

THE NATURE OF PUBLIC RELATIONS, by John E. Marston. New York: McGraw-Hill Book Company, 1963. 393 pp. $7.95.

The author defines public relations and gives a working pattern of procedure with the formula "Research-Action-Communication-Evaluation," which he illustrates with actual case studies of specific public-relations problems.

EFFECTIVE PUBLIC RELATIONS, by Scott M. Cutlip and Allen H. Center. Englewood Cliffs, N.J.: Prentice-Hall, Inc., 2d ed., 1964. $11.95.

A basic public-relations guide and reference book for business firms, professional organizations, welfare agencies, and school systems.

PUBLIC RELATIONS HANDBOOK, edited by Philip Lesly. Englewood Cliffs, N.J.: Prentice-Hall, Inc., 1962. $12.50.

An exhaustive discussion of every aspect of public relations by 36 experts in the field.

THE TECHNIQUES OF WORKING WITH THE WORKING PRESS, by Hal Golden and Kitty Hanson. Dobbs Ferry, N.Y.: Oceana Publications, Inc., 1962. 232 pp. $6.

Detailed guidance for achieving maximum newspaper coverage of special events and important promotions of corporations, clubs, churches, and civic groups: what editors want and need in the way of information and cooperation, what types of photography are suitable, how stories should be planned and written, and deadlines for submission.

HOW TO PLAN, PRODUCE AND PUBLICIZE SPECIAL EVENTS, by Hal Golden and Kitty Hanson. Dobbs Ferry, N.Y.: Oceana Publications, Inc., 1960. 256 pp. $6.

Information about staging and publicizing every type of special event, including sales meetings, parades, flower and fashion shows, open-house or plant visits, company outings, conventions, luncheons and banquets.

SHIPPING

POSTAL MANUAL. Washington, D.C.: U.S. Government Printing Office. $4.

The authoritative source of postal information in brief form and simple language for the lay reader. It includes information about both domestic and foreign mail service.

LEONARD'S GUIDE AND SERVICE. Leased, not sold, by G. R. Leonard & Co., 79 Madison Ave., New York 16, and 123 N. Wacker Dr., Chicago 6. $20 a year each for New York and Chicago guides; $35 a year for the Universal Edition (major cities except New York and Chicago).

A loose-leaf, indexed book kept up-to-date by mail service, which gives complete shipping information, including rates and regulations for parcel post, REA express, rail freight, airmail, and air parcel post. A subscriber receives a "Guide" made up for his city listing rates and routings that apply from that point of origin to the various cities and towns throughout the United States.

The same firm publishes six motor-freight directories (New York, Philadelphia, Chicago, New England, Boston, and Los Angeles-San Francisco)—each available at $6 per annum.

BULLINGER'S POSTAL AND SHIPPERS GUIDE for the United States, Canada, and Newfoundland. Westwood, N.J.: Bullinger's Guides, Inc. Published annually. About 1,200 pp. $21.

Lists every post office, railroad station, landing (200,000 names), or nearest communicating point, with county, and whether or not there is a telegraph office. Contains a digest of postal rate information but nothing on express or freight rates.

TELEVISION AND RADIO

TELEVISION AND RADIO NEWS, by Bob Siller, Ted White, and Hal Terkel. New York: The Macmillan Company, 1960. 227 pp. $6.25.

A practical guide to the exacting techniques of news broadcasting with examples of news scripts and advice on writing and delivering them.

SUCCESSFUL TELEVISION AND RADIO ADVERTISING, by Gene F. Seehafer and Jack W. Laemmar. New York: McGraw-Hill Book Company, 1959. 648 pp. $10.75.

A practical guide for those exploring the field of television and radio advertising: creating programs and commercials, research for advertising, TV and radio campaigns, and station management.

HANDBOOK OF BROADCASTING, THE FUNDAMENTALS OF AM, FM, FAX, AND TV, by Waldo Abbot and Richard L. Rider. New York: McGraw-Hill Book Company, 1957. $9.95.

This guide gives nontechnical explanations of FM, AM, TV, FAX, recording, etc., discussing not only the "before the microphone or camera" aspects, but also the business and production techniques used most effectively in actual practice for each. Covers every aspect of broadcasting in all media.

TYPOGRAPHY

DESIGN WITH TYPE, by Carl Dair. Toronto, Canada: University of Toronto Press, 1965. $7.50.

A practical and at the same time stimulating analysis of the principles underlying good typographic design, with some 90 working layouts employing only type elements and requiring no artwork.

HOW TO RECOGNIZE TYPE FACES, by R. Randolph Karch. New York: Taplinger Publishing Co., Inc., 1952. 265 pp. $7.50.

A practical reference book which is intended to assist the reader in identifying close to 1,500 type faces, which are grouped in this book by certain distinguishing features.

INTRODUCTION TO TYPOGRAPHY, by Oliver Simon. Hollywood-by-the-Sea: Transatlantic Arts, Inc., 1949. 137 pp. $7.50.

A concise and informative handbook dealing with the fine points of typography in book production. Many examples of type are given with an explanation of their particular uses in bookwork.

GRAPHIC ARTS TYPEBOOK: MACHINE COMPOSITION; vol. I, "Serif Faces"; vol. II, "Sans Serifs, Square Serifs, and Miscellaneous Faces." New York: Reinhold Publishing Corporation, 1965. Vol. I, 289 pp.; vol. 2, 256 pp. $5.95 per vol.

Over 300 type fonts are included in the two volumes. For each size of each type face, there is a two-page spread with full display of alphabets of the font (roman, italic, oblique, medium, bold, or small caps); a character-count chart showing 10 through 30 pica counts for lowercase, caps, and small caps; and four separate paragraphs set with different leading of both roman and italic to facilitate choice of proper type and leading. Four more volumes are to be published in the series: three on hand composition and one a glossary of terms. Prepared and produced with the cooperation of the Graphic Arts Typographers, Inc.

THE WESTERN HERITAGE OF TYPE DESIGN, by R. S. Hutchings. New York: Hastings House, Publishers, Inc., 1965. 127 pp. $7.95.

Complete alphabets and numerals of 70 type faces in use in the Western world today are arranged in sequence of development. With each is a concise commentary on its origin or derivation.

A MANUAL OF DECORATED TYPEFACES, by R. S. Hutchings. New York: Hastings House, Publishers, Inc., 1965. 96 pp. $6.95.

Complete alphabets and numerals are given, with notes, for 72 decorated type faces in current use, including in-line, outline, shaded, three-dimensional, stencil, cameo, halftone, two-color, and embellished designs.

VISUAL AND AUDIOVISUAL AIDS

THE PREPARATION AND USE OF VISUAL AIDS, by Kenneth B. Haas and Harry Q. Packer. Englewood Cliffs, N.J.: Prentice-Hall, Inc., 3d ed., 1955. $8.

This book covers motion pictures, sound and silent filmstrips, slides, the use of the opaque projector, the preparation of maps, charts, graphs, diagrams, post-ers, photographs, etc. Much of its information is hard to find elsewhere. It contains valuable lists of sources of visual materials.

SIMPLIFIED TECHNIQUES FOR PREPARING VISUAL INSTRUCTIONAL MATERIALS, by Ed Minor. New York: McGraw-Hill Book Company, 1962. 124 pp. $3.95.

Generously illustrated presentation of the techniques of mounting, lettering, tracing, enlarging and reducing, and making projection transparencies by various methods. It includes a good directory of sources.

PLANNING AND PRODUCING AUDIO-VISUAL MATERIALS, by Jerrold E. Kemp and others. San Francisco: Chandler Publishing Company, 1963. 169 pp. $6.50.

Detailed information for planning and producing picture series, slide series, film-strips, overhead transparencies, motion pictures, and television materials. Of particular value is the section on the fundamental skills required for photography, graphics, and sound recording.

WRITING, EDITING, AND PROOFREADING

THE ART OF READABLE WRITING, by Rudolf Flesch. New York: Harper & Row, Publishers, Inc., 1949. 237 pp. $3.95; paper, 95 cents (Collier).

Copywriters and copy editors will get concrete help from this book. It shows how short sentences, simple words, and personal references make nonfiction more readable. It explains how to sample, test, and measure the readability of copy and then classify it scientifically according to the grade level of the readers. The author's common-sense approach and keen humor help make this book a perfect illustration of the lessons that it teaches.

THE CAREFUL WRITER, A MODERN GUIDE TO ENGLISH USAGE, by Theodore M. Bernstein. New York: Atheneum Publishers, 1965. 487 pp. $7.95.

This is an excellent desk reference by the assistant managing editor of *The New York Times*. More than 2,000 alphabetized entries answer questions of use, meaning, grammar, punctuation, precision, logical structure, and color.

A DICTIONARY OF MODERN ENGLISH USAGE, by H. W. Fowler, revised and edited by Sir Ernest Towers. New York: Oxford University Press, 1965. 725 pp. $5.

Since 1926, Fowler's *Modern English Usage* has been an indispensable guide for all who use the English language. The alterations and additions of this new edition bring the book abreast of present-day usage.

A STYLE MANUAL FOR AUTHORS, by Edward D. Seeber. Bloomington, Ind.: Indiana University Press, 1965. 96 pp. Paper, $1.25.

This concise handbook explains acceptable principles of typescript preparation, styling, and proofreading, with illustrations of footnotes, bibliographical entries, and foreign-language problems. It includes advice on obtaining illustrations and permissions.

THE COMPLETE REPORTER, by Stanley P. Johnson and Julian Harriss. New York: The Macmillan Company, 1942. 424 pp. $6.95.

General textbook in news writing and editing with exercises and problems. Detailed "how-to-do" on writing the news lead and news story, simple items such as personals, complex stories about business and politics, special stories or features.

PROOFREADING AND COPY-PREPARATION: A TEXTBOOK FOR THE GRAPHIC ARTS INDUSTRY, by Joseph Lasky. New York: Mentor Press, 1954. 656 pp. $7.50.

Excellent reference book for the proofreader and copy preparer, with problems illustrated by actual examples. Gives authoritative principles for compounding English words, division of words into syllables, capitalization, punctuation, and abbreviations, as well as extensive reference lists of compound words, words divided into syllables, abbreviations, homonyms, etc.

THE MASS MEDIA: REPORTING, WRITING, EDITING, by William L. Rivers. New York: Harper & Row, Publishers, Inc., 1964. 531 pp. $5.95.

Although prepared as a journalism textbook, this volume will be invaluable to those interested in newspapers, magazines, and radio-TV. The bulk of the book deals with the specifics of reporting, writing, and editing for each medium, with case histories, reference lists, before-and-after examples of manuscript writing and copy editing, stylebooks, and trade terms. Equally interesting is the story of the development of the modern mass media and the emerging role of each.

EDITOR AT WORK, by Julie Eidesheim. New York: Rinehart & Company, Inc., 1939. 231 pp. Out of print.

This is one of the best and most readable books on what an editor's work consists of and how to do it. Long experience as an editor (defined as "one who prepares the work of others for publication") qualifies Miss Eidesheim to give concrete advice on the technique of editing, the tools of the editor, how to do library research, sentence construction, punctuation, spelling and capitalization, the mechanics of composition, and style.

EDITING THE SMALL MAGAZINE, by Rowena Ferguson. New York: Columbia University Press, 1958. 271 pp. Paper, $1.95.

A practical guide for the editor with little or no staff and limited experience. It includes helpful information on editorial planning, processing manuscripts, making layouts, and printing requirements.

WORDS INTO TYPE, based on studies by Marjorie E. Skillin, Robert M. Gay and other authorities. New York: Appleton-Century-Crofts, Inc., 1964. 596 pp. $7.50.

A guide to modern form, style, and usage for writers, editors, proofreaders, and printers. It includes detailed information on manuscript preparation, copy editing, proofreading, typography, printing style, correct grammar, and effective use of words.

MANUAL OF STYLE. Chicago: The University of Chicago Press, 11th rev. ed., 1949. 394 pp. $6.

This authoritative guide for authors and editors gives rules for capitalization, punctuation, word division, footnotes, etc., as well as directions for the preparation of manuscripts and copy estimating. The emphasis is on book publishing. Specimens of type used at the University of Chicago Press are included.

THE NEW YORK TIMES STYLE BOOK FOR WRITERS AND EDITORS, edited and revised by Lewis Jordan. New York: McGraw-Hill Book Company, 1962. 124 pp. $3.75.

A desk manual of rules or guides designed to ensure consistency of spelling, capitalization, punctuation, and abbreviation, arranged alphabetically for easy reference.

HEADLINES AND DEADLINES: A MANUAL FOR COPY EDITORS, by Robert E. Garst and Theodore Bernstein. New York: Columbia University Press, 1961. 237 pp. Paper, $1.75.

This valuable handbook, written by two managing editors of *The New York Times,* gives practical advice on editing copy, writing headlines, and proofreading, with a reference list of abused words, a headline vocabulary of related words, and a glossary of newspaper terms.

Appendix 3

Postal Information

Certain facts about postal regulations are well worth memorizing, as a handy guide to efficient distribution.

The first-class postage rate is 5 cents per oz; postcards 4 cents. (For details see FIRST-CLASS MAIL below.)

Second-class privileges apply only to periodicals, but rates are much lower than on any other class. (For details see SECOND-CLASS MAIL below.)

Third-class postage applies to circulars and other miscellaneous printed matter, also to merchandise weighing up to but not including 16 oz. The regular rate is 4 cents for the first 2 oz and 2 cents for each additional ounce. Bulk mailings made under post-office permit cost only 18 cents per lb with a minimum of 2¾ cents per piece for circulars, printed matter, and merchandise, and 12 cents per lb for books, catalogs of 24 or more pages (at least 22 of which are printed), seeds, cuttings, bulbs, roots, scions, and plants; minimum charge—2⅞ cents each piece. (For details see THIRD-CLASS MAIL below.)

Fourth-class postage is parcel post, beginning at 16 oz and over, consisting of merchandise, printed matter, and all others not in first-, second-, or third-class matter, with rates depending both on the weight and the zone to which

it is to be delivered. Rates range from 29 cents for local delivery of a 2-lb package to $12.26 for eighth-zone delivery of a 70-lb package.

Note that the weight limit on most shipments is 20 or 40 lb—not 70 lb as formerly, and as now allowed only in certain circumstances. (For details see FOURTH-CLASS MAIL below.)

Books of 24 pages or more, permanently bound, and containing no advertising matter other than incidental announcements of books may be mailed to any part of the United States and possessions for 10 cents for the first pound or fraction, 5 cents for each additional pound up to and including 70 lb. (See BOOK POSTAGE RATES below.) Library materials retain the old rate of 4 cents for the first pound and 1 cent for each additional pound.

The post office goes much further than simply fixing rates for certain classes of mail and then getting that mail to its destination. In addition, the following services are offered:

COD service is ideal where the shipper does not wish to extend credit or the customer does not wish to pay in advance. (See COD below.)

Insurance. Insurance up to $200 may be taken out on third- and fourth-class mail within the United States and its possessions and certain foreign countries. (See REGISTERED MAIL, page 447, for comparison of insured and registered mail.)

Registered mail. This service provides special handling for valuable articles and indemnity therefor. (See REGISTERED MAIL, page 447.)

Certified mail. For a 30-cent fee over and above the regular postage, the post office will obtain a receipt for delivery of a letter to the addressee or his representative. This is somewhat the same service offered under "registered mail," but without the indemnity and at a lower rate. (See CERTIFIED MAIL below.)

Postal cards. Both single and double postal cards, separate or in sheets of 20 (double) or 40 (single) for printing, may be secured for the price of the postage, 4 cents per card. (See POSTCARDS below.)

Envelopes. Envelopes with postage stamp embossed on the paper of the envelope itself may be purchased through the post office. For small extra charge the post office will print them with return name and address. In 1965, 1,000 size 6¾ envelopes with 5-cent stamp embossed, unprinted, cost $56.40; printed, $58.90. (See ENVELOPES below.)

Business reply cards, envelopes, and labels. Forms permitting the addressee to pay postage may be printed by special post-office permit. (See BUSINESS REPLY CARDS AND ENVELOPES below.)

Mailing-list corrections. These can be assembled readily by printing the endorsement "Return Requested" on second-, third-, or fourth-class mail that the sender wishes returned if undeliverable. The post office will mark all such mail either with the new address or the reason for nondelivery, and charges the sender return postage or a minimum fee—8 cents for third- and fourth-class mail, 10 cents for second-class. (See MAILING-LIST CORRECTIONS below.)

Payment of postage. To avoid the labor of affixing stamps and, in the case of third-class bulk mailing, to take advantage of the cheaper postage rate, a permit may be obtained to use permit imprints, often called "printed indicia," in place of stamps (paying for the postage at the time of mailing), or the imprint of a postage-meter machine. (Third-class bulk-rate economies are offered only on condition that the mail is handled in such a way as to save the post office the labor of canceling and sorting. See THIRD-CLASS MAIL below.)

Precanceled postage. This is used chiefly on third- and fourth-class matter. (See PRECANCELED POSTAGE below.) Permission must be obtained from the postmaster; no fee is required.

Permit imprints. Such a permit for permit-imprint, nonstamped mail may be obtained from the postmaster. The fee is $15, no part of which may be applied as postage. (See PERMIT IMPRINTS below.)

Postage-meter machines. These may be used for all classes of mail. (See METERED POSTAGE below.)

Transit time. No guarantee can be given as to the exact time required for collection, transportation, and delivery of mail. City post offices frequently issue a local schedule of transit time to certain points for first-class mail. Usually this does not include time allowance for mailbox pickup, post-office sorting, or delivery at point of destination.

Additional time for these may be estimated to some extent as follows:

1. Approximately 1 to 2 hr elapse between the time when mail is received in a post office and the time when it is put on the train.

2. Collections are made from train mailboxes located in railroad stations about 15 min before train departure time (for small quantities only).

3. From 1 to 3 hr are required for sorting at the station or post office of destination, depending on quantity of mail on hand before delivery begins. This is shortened in the case of special-delivery mail. The time of delivery of

regular mail depends upon the established delivery schedules.

4. The earlier mail is dispatched in the afternoon the more likely it is to make overnight trains and be delivered in the morning.

5. First-class mail and that marked for special handling usually requires about half the transit time required for regular second-, third-, and fourth-class mail.

Almost any business office or its mailing room will profit by posting the table of transit time of the local post office; or by assembling this information and posting it for easy reference if a printed table is not available.

(For information about transportation of all kinds, see SHIPPING INFORMATION in the main text of this book.)

Unmailable matter. The following articles are among those listed as unmailable: poisons, explosives, matches (except safety matches packed as pre-scribed by postal regulations), intoxicating liquors, obscene and indecent matter, matter involving lottery or fraud, with certain exceptions, firearms capable of being concealed on the person, libelous matter on the outside of the mail. In addition, stringent regulations govern the mailing and packaging of meat and meat-food products, plant and plant products, live animals, fowls, insects, and reptiles.

The "Postal Manual," Chapters I and II, is the authoritative source of postal information. Copies may be obtained from the Superintendent of Documents, Government Printing Office, Washington 25, D.C., $4, including supplementary service for approximately two years.

airmail Airmail, carried by air and the fastest connecting surface carriers, is given the most expeditious handling in dispatch and delivery. Airmail is not

AIRMAIL RATES
DOMESTIC RATES (WITHIN CONTINENTAL UNITED STATES AND TO AND FROM ITS POSSESSIONS)

Weight		Rate

8 oz or less	Air postal or postcards
	Business reply cards
	Letters and packages
	Airmail in business reply
	  envelopes not over 2 oz
	Over 2 oz
		6¢ each
		8¢ collected when delivered
		8¢ an ounce
		8¢ an ounce plus 2¢ per piece,
		  collected when delivered
		8¢ an ounce plus 5¢ per piece

Air parcel post	Zones 1, 2, 3	Zone 4	Zone 5	Zone 6	Zone 7	Zone 8
Over 8 oz and not exceeding 1 lb	$0.68	$0.73	$0.78	$0.83	$0.83	$0.88
Each additional pound.......	0.48	0.50	0.56	0.64	0.72	0.80

First-class air parcels	8¢ per oz for the first 8 oz and 5¢ for each additional oz or the applicable zone rate if it is higher.

given special delivery to the addressee unless a special-delivery fee is paid in addition to the airmail postage.

It is limited to 70 lb in weight and 100 in. in combined length and girth, and may be left sealed or unsealed without affecting the rate.

Airmail outside of continental United States and possessions may be sent for rates that vary from 13 cents per ½ oz to Central America, Bermuda, and the Caribbean area; 15 cents per ½ oz to South America, Europe, and Mediterranean Africa; 25 cents per ½ oz to the U.S.S.R. and the rest of the world.

Registered, insured, and COD mail may be sent by air on payment of the proper fees. (See REGISTERED MAIL and COD.)

Material of unlimited weight may be sent by air express (not a post-office service). Rates depend upon the nature, weight, and volume of the material being shipped. (See REA EXPRESS in the main text of this book.)

air parcel post A term sometimes applied to airmail weighing over 8 oz. (See AIRMAIL.)

book postage rates Books consisting of at least 24 pages (including cover), permanently bound, and containing no advertising matter except incidental announcement of other books may be mailed at a special fourth-class rate.

Books are an exception to the usual fourth-class-weight limits, in that up to 70 lb may be sent to or from all zones or post offices within the United States, not just some of them. (See SPECIAL FOURTH-CLASS RATE.)

A special library-materials rate applies to books loaned or exchanged between schools, colleges, or universities and public libraries, nonprofit organizations, etc. For details, see LIBRARY-MATERIALS RATE.

business reply cards and envelopes A business reply card, envelope, or label requires no postage from the sender since the addressee (who originally sent it out) agrees to pay return postage. This is not to be confused with the stamped postcard or envelope which may also be sent out for reply.

The advantage of a business reply card, envelope, or label over one that is prepaid is that the addressee pays postage only on those cards which he receives instead of paying postage on all that he sends out, many of which may never be returned. However, the rate is 2 cents higher for each piece received than on regular mail. That is, the business-reply-card postage rate is 6 cents collected on delivery, and a business reply envelope is 2 cents in addition to regular postage for up to 2 oz.

Application for permission to send out business reply cards, envelopes, and

COMPARISON OF BOOK RATES

	Weight limit	Class	Rate	
			1st lb	Each additional lb
Special fourth-class rate	70	Fourth	10¢	5¢
Library-materials rate	70	Fourth	4¢	1¢

Note: Same rate to all zones.

labels must be made to the postmaster at the office where they are to be returned, by filing post-office Form 3614. No fee is required to accompany this application.

The permit number, address, and other stipulated information must be imprinted on the address side of a card, envelope, or label in one of the forms supplied by the post office when the permit is issued. No illustrations, trademarks, or advertising may be printed on the address side. No stipulation is made regarding the reverse side.

Business reply cards, like postcards, may be no smaller than 3 by 4¼ in. and no larger than 4¼ by 6 in. (If larger, they are charged at the rate applicable to business reply envelopes.)

Double reply cards. When the reply half of a double reply card is imprinted as a business reply card, the address side carrying the permit number, etc., must be folded inside when the double card is originally mailed.

certified mail See also REGISTERED MAIL below.

In the past, registered mail has ac-

complished two functions: (1) certification that the piece of registered mail is delivered to the addressee in person and (2) indemnity against loss or damage. Certified mail, a new type of service inaugurated in 1955, accomplishes the first of these two functions at a lower rate than registered mail.

Certified mail is used to make sure that a piece of first-class mail of no intrinsic value is delivered in person to the addressee or his representative. If certified mail is lost in transit, no insurance or indemnity may be collected.

The fee in addition to postage is 30 cents; for return receipts showing to whom and when delivered, 10 cents extra, or showing to whom, when, and address where delivered, 35 cents extra. The fee and postage may be paid by ordinary postage stamps, or meter stamps.

You may mail certified mail at the post office or in a street letter box provided you follow specific directions as to the use of certified-mail coupons and blank return-receipt forms if those are needed. For details see the "Postal Manual" or consult your local post office.

This is one of three forms prescribed by the Post Office for a business reply card.

The sender of a certified letter retains a receipt. If he does not request a return receipt at time of mailing, he may later request one from the addressee's post office by accompanying his request with his receipt and a 25-cent fee.

COD Through its COD (collect-on-delivery) service, the post office helps solve the problem created when a shipper does not wish to extend credit or the customer does not wish to pay in advance. For a fee the post office delivers a package and collects the money, which is returned to the shipper by postal money order. The addressee may not examine the COD parcel until charges have been paid and a receipt given. A COD shipment must be a bona fide order for the contents or be in conformity with an agreement between the sender and the addressee.

Fees for collection include automatic insurance against loss, rifling, or damage in an amount equivalent to the actual value or the cost of repairs, or against nonreceipt of COD collections. The maximum amount collectible on a single parcel is $200.

If a COD shipment is sent by registered mail, it is assured the extra care in handling that is given all registered mail. Since fourth-class mail may be registered only if first-class postage is paid, it would be superfluous to add a special-handling stamp.

Shipments valued at more than $200 must be registered. No more than $200 can be collected from the addressee, but indemnity in case of loss greater than this can be secured through registration.

COD tags. These must be attached to parcels sent COD. Each tag must be filled in by the sender to show the complete name and address of the sender and of the addressee, the amount of charges to be collected upon delivery and remitted to the sender by money order, and the money-order fee charged the addressee for the amount involved. Consult the local postmaster for infor-

mation about the four styles of COD tags that are used for the service.

Advance notice of the shipment of a COD parcel is recommended so that the addressee may know its contents and may be ready with the exact change when it is delivered. Such notices cut down the instances where addressees refuse delivery and the sender must pay return postage.

For further details, consult the local postmaster or the "Postal Manual."

COD FEES (IN ADDITION TO POSTAGE)

Amount to Be Collected or Insurance Coverage Desired	COD Fees
$0.01 to $5	$0.40
$5.01 to $10	0.50
$10.01 to $25	0.70
$25.01 to $50	0.80
$50.01 to $100	0.90
$100.01 to $200	1.00

COD (maximum amount collectible is $200) may be registered at the regular registered rates plus an extra fee of 40 cents.

educational-materials rate In 1964, the Post Office Department abolished this term and replaced it by the term "Special Fourth-class Rate"—followed by the specific category: Books, Manuscript, Printed Music, and so on. For details, see SPECIAL FOURTH-CLASS RATE.

envelopes The U.S. Post Office sells envelopes at very low rates and will imprint them with return name and address. For example, in 1965 the Post Office was supplying a stamped 3⅝ by 6½ commercial envelope made from 24# white sulfite bond at $56.40 per 1,000. For $2.50 additional per 1,000, the customer's name and return address could be imprinted in a standard form in the corner. Imprinted regular envelopes (meaning envelopes which have no window, are not for airmail, and are not precanceled) were available in two sizes in lots of 500 and 1,000.

Unprinted regular envelopes were available in any quantity with 4- or 5-cent stamp imprinted.

Unprinted window envelopes and precanceled envelopes were available only in box lots (500 per box).

first-class mail (See table below.)
First-class mail includes:

1. *Written and typewritten matter* such as letters (including carbons), postcards (both government and private

mailing cards), business reply cards, and letters in business reply envelopes.

2. *Matter partly in writing* like printed cards or letters with added handwritten notes, printed forms filled out by hand, drawings and artwork that are hand-lettered.

3. *Sealed matter* except certain sealed third- or fourth-class matter that may be opened for postal inspection.

Registered mail. For special registry rates, surcharges, indemnity limit, and

RATES FOR FIRST-CLASS MAIL (DOMESTIC)

Kind of mail	Rate
All first-class mail except postal and postcards and drop letters (United States and possessions)	5 cents per oz or fraction of an ounce
Single postcards (United States and possessions)	4 cents each
Double postcards (reply portion does not have to bear postage when originally mailed)	8 cents (4 cents each portion)
Business reply cards (good only in United States and possessions except Canal Zone)	6 cents each, collected when delivered
Mail enclosed in business reply envelopes (good only in United States and possessions except Canal Zone)	5 cents per oz plus 2 cents per piece not over 2 oz, collected when delivered; 5 cents per oz plus 5 cents per piece over 2 oz
Airmail letters and packages (United States and all possessions)	8 cents per oz (8 oz or less); over 8 oz, use air parcel post

RATES FOR FIRST-CLASS MAIL (INTERNATIONAL)

Kind of mail	Rate
Letters to Canada and Mexico.................	5 cents per oz
Letter to all other countries..................	11 cents for the first oz, 7 cents for each additional oz

LIMITATIONS ON FIRST-CLASS MATTER

In United States and possessions..	Maximum weight limit is the same as for fourth-class mail (see FOURTH-CLASS MAIL). No size limit.
To Canada....................	Maximum length, 24 in. Maximum length, breadth, and thickness combined, 36 in. Weight limit, 60 lb,
To all countries except Canada...	Maximum length, 24 in. Maximum length, breadth. and thickness combined, 36 in. Weight limit, 4 lb 6 oz.

return receipt, see REGISTERED MAIL below.

Certified mail. A service for first-class mail to certify delivery to the addressee without providing insurance or indemnity in case of loss. For rates see CERTIFIED MAIL above.

Return to sender. When marked with name and address of sender, undeliverable first-class mail except postcards is returned to sender without additional postage, provided the original postage was paid in full. For information about return of postcards, see POSTCARDS.

Forwarding. Unopened first-class mail is forwarded without additional charge, provided postage was fully prepaid at the first-class rate.

Speeding delivery. First-class mail moves faster than any other class except airmail since it is handled first and on the fastest trains. The same speed may be purchased for third- and fourth-class mail in either of two ways: (1) by "special handling," which guarantees that fourth-class matter will be handled and transported as first class but will be delivered on scheduled parcel-post trips, and (2) by paying for "special delivery," which guarantees the parcel's being expedited with first-class mail as well as being delivered by special messenger at the point of destination between 7 A.M. and 7 P.M. In larger cities special-delivery matter is delivered from 7 A.M. to 11 P.M. (See SPECIAL DELIVERY AND SPECIAL HANDLING below.)

forwarding and return of undeliverable mail Mail will be forwarded to another post office under certain conditions and at certain fees given below:

First-class mail: Forwarded; no charge.

Second-class mail: Forwarded when forwarding postage is guaranteed by addressee.

Third-class mail: Forwarded only if it is of obvious value or when forwarding postage is guaranteed by the addressee.

Fourth-class mail: Forwarded to addressee from whom additional postage is collected.

Airmail weighing 8 oz or less: Forwarded without additional charge. Air transportation is used when available to the new address.

Airmail weighing over 8 oz: Forwarded by air at the applicable air zone rates to be collected on delivery unless the article bears sender's instructions to forward by surface mail. Forwarding postage is collected from addressee on delivery.

Registered, insured COD mail: Forwarded without payment of additional *fees,* but the ordinary forwarding *postage* charges, if any, must be paid.

Mail that cannot be delivered because of incomplete or incorrect address, or which is unclaimed or refused by the addressee, is handled in various ways:

First-class mail except postcards and postal cards: Returned to sender without additional charge.

Second-class mail: Returned to sender if it bears a pledge to pay return postage.

Third-class mail: Returned to sender if it is of obvious value or bears the sender's pledge to pay return postage.

Fourth-class mail: Returned to sender and return postage collected.

Airmail weighing 8 oz or less: Returned by surface transportation at no additional charge.

Airmail weighing over 8 oz: Returned by surface transportation unless it bears the sender's instructions to be returned by airmail. Return charges are collected on delivery to sender.

fourth-class mail See also SPECIAL FOURTH-CLASS RATES; COD; REGISTERED MAIL in this appendix.

Fourth-class mail, commonly called "parcel post," is used for matter that is not first-, second-, or third-class, that weighs at least 16 oz, but that does not exceed the limitations shown in the accompanying table.

	Size limit (combined length and girth)	Weight limit
Between first-class (large) post offices: In local zone and Zones 1 and 2.....	72 in.	40 lb
In Zones 3 through 8	72 in.	20 lb
Mailed at or to any second-, third-, or fourth-class post office............	100 in.	70 lb
Books mailed to any zone............	100 in.	70 lb

Parcels weighing less than 10 lb and measuring over 84 in., but not exceeding 100 in. in length and girth combined, are chargeable with a minimum rate equal to that for a 10-lb parcel for the same zone.

For further **details, consult the** "Postal Manual."

Larger or heavier packages may be shipped by REA express, rail freight, or motor freight. (See SHIPPING INFORMATION in the main text of this book.)

Fourth-class parcels may be sealed without endorsement. If books are being shipped at educational-materials rate, they should be so labeled.

Postage rates on fourth-class matter. Domestic rates are charged according to the distance, or zone, of the point of destination, and the weight. When the zone and the weight are known, the postage can be computed from the chart of fourth-class (parcel-post) rates on pages 439 and 440.

To determine the zone of a post office, look it up in the "Directory of Post Offices," where a unit number is listed by each city or post office. Then on a local "zone key," which the local postmaster will supply on request, find the zone number that corresponds to the unit number.

For easy reference in a shipping room, a large zone map of the United States can be made for the wall with the zones marked off in concentric circles around the local shipping point.

Overseas rates. For the exact rate to a particular country, consult the local postmaster.

Catalog rates apply to individually addressed catalogs and similar printed advertising matter in bound form of 24 or more pages and weighing 16 oz to 10 lb. Zone rates apply beginning at 21 cents for up to 1½ lb for local.

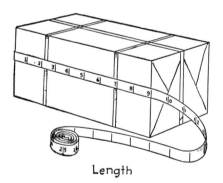

Length

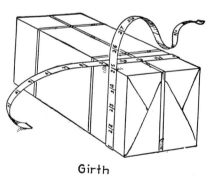

Girth

The way to measure combined length and girth is shown above. This package measures 25 in. in combined length and girth, being 9 in. long and 16 in. around.

FOURTH-CLASS (PARCEL-POST) ZONE RATES EFFECTIVE APRIL 1, 1964

Weight, 1 lb and not exceeding	Zones							
	Local	1 and 2	3	4	5	6	7	8
2 lb............	$0.29	$0.40	$0.42	$0.46	$0.52	$0.59	$0.66	$0.72
3 lb............	0.31	0.46	0.49	0.55	0.64	0.73	0.83	0.93
4 lb............	0.33	0.51	0.55	0.64	0.75	0.88	1.01	1.13
5 lb............	0.35	0.57	0.62	0.72	0.87	1.02	1.18	1.34
6 lb............	0.37	0.62	0.68	0.80	0.97	1.15	1.34	1.53
7 lb............	0.39	0.68	0.75	0.88	1.07	1.28	1.50	1.73
8 lb............	0.41	0.73	0.81	0.95	1.18	1.41	1.66	1.92
9 lb............	0.43	0.78	0.87	1.03	1.28	1.53	1.82	2.12
10 lb............	0.45	0.83	0.93	1.10	1.38	1.66	1.98	2.31
11 lb............	0.47	0.88	1.00	1.18	1.48	1.78	2.14	2.48
12 lb............	0.49	0.93	1.06	1.26	1.58	1.90	2.29	2.66
13 lb............	0.51	0.98	1.12	1.33	1.69	2.02	2.44	2.83
14 lb............	0.53	1.03	1.18	1.41	1.79	2.14	2.60	3.01
15 lb............	0.55	1.08	1.24	1.48	1.89	2.25	2.75	3.18
16 lb............	0.57	1.13	1.30	1.56	1.99	2.37	2.90	3.36
17 lb............	0.59	1.18	1.36	1.64	2.09	2.49	3.06	3.53
18 lb............	0.61	1.23	1.42	1.71	2.20	2.61	3.21	3.71
19 lb............	0.63	1.28	1.48	1.79	2.30	2.73	3.36	3.88
20 lb............	0.65	1.32	1.54	1.86	2.40	2.85	3.51	4.06
21 lb............	0.67	1.36	1.59	1.93	2.48	2.96	3.65	4.23
22 lb............	0.69	1.40	1.64	1.99	2.57	3.07	3.79	4.40
23 lb............	0.71	1.44	1.69	2.06	2.65	3.18	3.93	4.57
24 lb............	0.73	1.48	1.73	2.12	2.74	3.29	4.07	4.74
25 lb............	0.75	1.52	1.78	2.18	2.82	3.40	4.21	4.91
26 lb............	0.77	1.56	1.83	2.25	2.91	3.51	4.35	5.08
27 lb............	0.79	1.60	1.87	2.31	2.99	3.62	4.49	5.25
28 lb............	0.81	1.64	1.92	2.38	3.08	3.73	4.63	5.42
29 lb............	0.83	1.68	1.97	2.44	3.16	3.84	4.77	5.59
30 lb............	0.84	1.71	2.01	2.50	3.25	3.95	4.91	5.76
31 lb............	0.86	1.75	2.06	2.57	3.33	4.06	5.05	5.93
32 lb............	0.88	1.79	2.11	2.63	3.42	4.17	5.19	6.10
33 lb............	0.90	1.83	2.16	2.70	3.50	4.28	5.33	6.27
34 lb............	0.92	1.87	2.20	2.76	3.59	4.39	5.47	6.44
35 lb............	0.94	1.91	2.25	2.82	3.67	4.50	5.61	6.61
36 lb............	0.96	1.95	2.30	2.89	3.76	4.61	5.75	6.78
37 lb............	0.98	1.99	2.34	2.95	3.84	4.72	5.89	6.95
38 lb............	1.00	2.03	2.39	3.02	3.93	4.83	6.03	7.12
39 lb............	1.02	2.07	2.44	3.08	4.01	4.94	6.17	7.29
40 lb............	1.03	2.10	2.48	3.14	4.10	5.05	6.31	7.46
41 lb............	1.05	2.14	2.53	3.21	4.18	5.16	6.45	7.62
42 lb............	1.07	2.18	2.58	3.27	4.27	5.27	6.59	7.78
43 lb............	1.09	2.22	2.63	3.34	4.35	5.38	6.73	7.94
44 lb............	1.11	2.26	2.67	3.40	4.44	5.49	6.87	8.10
45 lb............	1.13	2.30	2.72	3.46	4.52	5.60	7.01	8.26

Fourth-class (Parcel-Post) Zone Rates Effective April 1, 1964—Continued

Weight, 1 lb and not exceeding	Zones							
	Local	1 and 2	3	4	5	6	7	8
46 lb............	1.15	2.34	2.77	3.53	4.61	5.71	7.15	8.42
47 lb............	1.17	2.38	2.81	3.59	4.69	5.82	7.29	8.58
48 lb............	1.19	2.42	2.86	3.66	4.78	5.93	7.43	8.74
49 lb............	1.21	2.46	2.91	3.72	4.86	6.04	7.57	8.90
50 lb............	1.22	2.49	2.95	3.78	4.95	6.15	7.71	9.06
51 lb............	1.24	2.53	3.00	3.84	5.03	6.26	7.84	9.22
52 lb............	1.26	2.56	3.05	3.90	5.11	6.37	7.97	9.38
53 lb............	1.28	2.59	3.10	3.96	5.19	6.48	8.10	9.54
54 lb............	1.30	2.62	3.14	4.02	5.27	6.60	8.23	9.70
55 lb............	1.32	2.65	3.19	4.08	5.35	6.70	8.36	9.86
56 lb............	1.34	2.69	3.24	4.14	5.43	6.81	8.49	10.02
57 lb............	1.36	2.72	3.28	4.20	5.51	6.92	8.62	10.18
58 lb............	1.38	2.75	3.33	4.26	5.59	7.03	8.75	10.34
59 lb............	1.40	2.78	3.38	4.32	5.67	7.14	8.88	10.50
60 lb............	1.41	2.81	3.42	4.38	5.75	7.25	9.01	10.66
61 lb............	1.43	2.85	3.47	4.44	5.83	7.36	9.14	10.82
62 lb............	1.45	2.88	3.52	4.50	5.91	7.47	9.27	10.98
63 lb............	1.47	2.91	3.57	4.56	5.99	7.58	9.40	11.14
64 lb............	1.49	2.94	3.61	4.62	6.07	7.69	9.53	11.30
65 lb............	1.51	2.97	3.66	4.68	6.15	7.80	9.66	11.46
66 lb............	1.53	3.01	3.71	4.74	6.23	7.91	9.79	11.62
67 lb............	1.55	3.04	3.75	4.80	6.31	8.02	9.92	11.78
68 lb............	1.57	3.07	3.80	4.86	6.39	8.13	10.05	11.94
69 lb............	1.59	3.10	3.85	4.92	6.47	8.24	10.18	12.10
70 lb............	1.60	3.13	3.89	4.98	6.55	8.35	10.31	12.26

Exceptions

Parcels weighing less than 10 lb, and measuring over 84 in., but not exceeding 100 in. in length and girth combined, are chargeable with a minimum rate equal to that for a 10-lb parcel for the zone to which addressed.

Book rates apply to books containing 24 or more pages, permanently bound, and containing no advertising except incidental announcements of other books. (See special fourth-class rates.)

Speed in delivery of fourth-class mail can be requested by paying a special-delivery or special-handling fee. Either of these assures the parcel's being handled on fast trains or trucks along with first-class mail. Special delivery also provides local delivery by special messenger. (See special delivery and special handling.)

insured mail Third- and fourth-class mail may be insured for a maximum of $200. For details, see information given in chart "Comparison of Registered, Insured, and Certified Mail" on page 448.

library-materials rate For the extremely low rate of 4 cents for the first

FOURTH-CLASS CATALOGS, SINGLE-PIECE MAILING*

Weight, 1 lb and not exceeding	Zones							
	Local	1 and 2	3	4	5	6	7	8
	Cents	Cents	Cents	Cents	Cents	Cents	Cents	Cents
1.5 lb.............	21	25	26	28	29	32	34	38
2 lb..............	22	27	28	30	32	36	38	43
2.5 lb.............	23	28	30	32	35	39	43	48
3 lb..............	24	30	32	35	38	42	47	53
3.5 lb.............	25	32	34	37	41	46	52	59
4 lb..............	26	33	35	39	44	49	56	64
4.5 lb.............	27	35	37	41	47	53	60	69
5 lb..............	27	36	39	43	49	56	64	74
6 lb..............	29	39	42	48	55	63	73	84
7 lb..............	31	42	46	52	61	70	82	95
8 lb..............	33	45	49	57	66	77	90	105
9 lb..............	35	48	53	61	72	84	99	115
10 lb.............	36	50	56	65	77	91	107	125

* Note: These rates apply to individually addressed catalogs and similar printed advertising matter in bound form, weighing 16 oz or over, but not exceeding 10 lb, and consisting of 24 or more pages.

FOURTH-CLASS CATALOGS, BULK MAILING OF 300 OR MORE*

Weight	Zones							
	Local	1 and 2	3	4	5	6	7	8
	Cents	Cents	Cents	Cents	Cents	Cents	Cents	Cents
1 lb to 2.5 lb, *piece rate*............	14.0	17.0	17.0	17.0	17.0	17.0	17.0	18.0
1 to 2.5 lb, *bulk pound rate*.........	2.2	3.2	3.8	4.8	6.0	7.6	9.0	10.7
Over 2.5 lb to 10 lb, *piece rate*......	15.0	18.0	18.0	18.0	18.0	18.0	18.0	19.0
Over 2.5 lb to 10 lb, *bulk pound rate*..	1.8	2.9	3.5	4.4	5.6	7.0	8.6	10.3

* Note: These rates apply when separately addressed identical pieces are mailed in quantities of not less than 300 at one time. The total charge for each bulk mailing is the sum of the charges derived by applying the applicable pound rate to the total number of pounds and the applicable piece rate to the total number of pieces.

pound and 1 cent for each additional pound or fraction, certain library materials can be mailed when loaned or exchanged between schools, colleges, universities, public libraries, certain nonprofit organizations, and their members or borrowers. These materials include books which contain no advertising other than incidental announcements of books, printed music (bound or in sheet form), periodicals, sound recordings, 16mm films, filmstrips, slides, microfilms, scientific or mathematical kits and instruments, and catalogs of

FOURTH-CLASS CATALOGUES AND SIMILAR PRINTED ADVERTISING MATTER

Weight, 1 lb and not exceeding—	Zones							
	Local	1 and 2	3	4	5	6	7	8
	Cents	Cents	Cents	Cents	Cents	Cents	Cents	Cents
1.5 lb	14	16	18	20	22	24	26	28
2.0 lb	16	20	22	24	26	29	32	35
2.5 lb	18	23	25	27	29	33	37	41
3.0 lb	18	24	26	28	31	36	40	45
3.5 lb	19	25	28	30	34	39	44	50
4.0 lb	20	27	29	32	36	42	48	54
4.5 lb	20	28	31	34	39	45	51	59
5.0 lb	21	29	32	36	41	48	55	63
5.5 lb	22	30	34	38	43	51	59	68
6.0 lb	22	31	35	40	46	54	62	72
6.5 lb	23	33	37	42	48	57	66	77
7.0 lb	24	34	38	44	51	60	70	81
7.5 lb	25	35	40	46	53	63	74	86
8.0 lb	25	36	41	47	55	66	77	90
8.5 lb	26	37	43	49	58	69	81	95
9.0 lb	27	39	44	51	60	72	85	99
9.5 lb	27	40	46	53	63	75	88	104
10.0 lb	28	41	47	55	65	78	92	108

Exception: In the first or second zone, where the distance by the shortest regular practicable mail route is 300 miles or more, the rate shall be the same as for the third zone.

NOTE—These rates apply to individually addressed catalogues and similar printed advertising matter in bound form, weighing 16 oz or over, but not exceeding 10 lb, and consisting of 24 or more pages.

such materials. Rates are computed on the basis of weight regardless of zone to which addressed. Weight limit: 70 lb.

For special rates on similar materials shipped by or to those not eligible for the library-materials rate, see SPECIAL FOURTH-CLASS RATE.

mailing-list corrections See also MAILING LISTS in main text of this book.

Two valuable allies for keeping mailing lists up to date are the post office and the addressee.

Help from the post office. The post office provides various methods for getting correct information about changes of address on third-class mail. (See THIRD-CLASS MAIL and FORWARDING AND RETURN OF UNDELIVERABLE MAIL in this appendix.)

On envelopes being mailed third class, most mailers print the phrase "Return Requested" below their return address in the upper left corner. Without such notice, undeliverable mail of no obvious value is destroyed. With it, any change of address or the fact that addressee has moved and left no address is marked on the undelivered item, which is then returned to the sender. The sender is charged either return postage or the minimum fee for such return, whichever is higher. The minimum fee for third- or fourth-class mail is 8 cents per piece.

The minimum fee for second-class or

controlled-circulation publications is 10 cents per piece. Return postage for such mail is computed at the transient rate for second-class, or the applicable third- or fourth-class rate for controlled-circulation publications.

The old legends "Forwarding Postage Guaranteed," "Return Postage Guaranteed," and "Form 3547 Requested" are obsolete and should not be used when preparing new envelopes or mailing pieces. Old stocks may be used until exhausted, however. The post office will treat the legends "Return Postage Guaranteed" and "Form 3547 Requested" as if they actually read "Return Requested." The legend "Forwarding Postage Guaranteed" will, however, be disregarded.

Help from the addressee. The addressee may help keep a mailing list correct if he is asked to do so and if it is made easy for him. Naturally, he can help only if the mailing piece reaches him; so such corrections eliminate only minor errors.

By printing on the envelope a request for corrections in the name and address as shown, many firms have been able to correct errors in spelling and street number and get the names of new personnel. Enclosing a postage-paid envelope will increase the returns as well

as the good will of the addressee. Two popular forms for requesting this information are shown below.

metered postage A postage meter may be used for printing and recording postage. The postage imprint may be put directly on the letter or package or it may be put on paper tape and pasted to the article.

Metered postage must show the date of mailing on first-class mail, special delivery, special handling, or airmail, and on all mail sent registered, insured, or COD. The month and year must be shown, but the day may be omitted on tapes on second-, third-, and fourth-class mail. When tapes are *not* used, the date may *not* be shown in meter stamps on second-, third-, or fourth-class mail.

Metered mail must be mailed from the post office shown in the meter postmark, but you may deposit first-class metered mail in street or building letter boxes. All other metered mail must be deposited in the post office.

Unless packages are too irregular, all metered mail must be separated by class of mail, faced, and bundled.

Small mailings as well as large mailings can be expedited, with considerable saving in time, through the use of a postage-meter machine, which is a sort

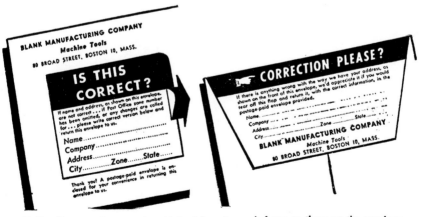

Mailing-list corrections may be obtained by using such forms as these on the envelope.

of mechanical post office capable of printing postage of any denomination, for any class of mail, directly on the envelope (or on a gummed tape to be affixed to a package).

There is a variety of hand and electric models capable of stamping, postmarking, and sealing from 2,000 to 15,000 pieces per hour.

Postage is paid in advance, as when buying ordinary postage or making a deposit for "permit mail." The meter is checked at the post office and is set to print meter stamps up to the value paid in. Instead of buying and keeping track of loose stamps in various denominations and quantities, you simply have your meter set for the sum paid in, from which you "dial" and print any stamp value as and when needed. Postage can be added to the meter at any time before the prepaid value runs out.

Advantages. Nearly all postage-meter machines provide the following features:

1. Meter stamps can be printed by a single machine in many denominations, from 1 cent up.

2. Mail can be sealed and postmarked when it is stamped, or sealing can be omitted.

3. Postage labels for fourth-class mail can be printed by using a separate attachment on some postage machines. Other machines only print labels instead of printing directly on envelopes.

4. Metered mail saves time at the post office, since it is already postmarked and needs no facing or canceling there.

5. The meter provides accurate postage records of the postage used and the amount of authorized postage on hand.

6. The meter can be locked against unauthorized persons.

7. "Postmark ads" (see illustration below) can be printed with the meter stamp at no extra cost except for the printing plates.

Securing postage-meter machines. Postage-meter equipment generally consists of two parts (except for a new small desk model available from one manufacturer, which is in a single unit). One part is an office mailing machine, and the other is its detachable postage meter, licensed for use by the Post Office Department. Since meters print U.S. postage and account for government revenue under official lock and seal, they cannot be sold outright, as the mailing machines are, but are leased from an authorized manufacturer who is held responsible for their location, operation, and servicing.

In recent years the Post Office Department has liberalized metered-mail regulations with new conveniences for the small mailer. These include the elimination of the former daily statement of mailing, the ability to deposit first-class metered mail in any regular mailbox within your post-office jurisdic-

A postage meter for first-class mail shows the amount of postage, the date, place, and meter number. The Cancer Society notice at the left is a "postmark ad" which may be changed or omitted as desired. (*Imprint courtesy of Pitney-Bowes, Inc.*)

tion, and faster procedure for dispatching metered mail through the out-going post office.

Postage-meter machines are made by

Commercial Controls Corp., Division of Friden, Inc., 31 Prince St., Rochester, N.Y. 14607.

Friden, Inc., 2350 Washington Ave., San Leandro, Calif. 94577.

International Postal Supply Co., Division of Friden, Inc., Lewiston, Pa. 17044.

National Cash Register Co., Dayton, Ohio 45409.

Pitney-Bowes, Inc., Pacific and Walnut Sts., Stamford, Conn. 06902.

Tele-Norm Corp., Postalia Division, 32–31 57 St., Woodside, Flushing, N.Y. 11377.

parcel post See FOURTH-CLASS MAIL above.

permit imprints Neither stamps nor the imprint of a postage meter is necessary when permit imprints, often called "printed indicia," are used. Application to use the permit imprint must be made to the post office in advance, accompanied by an application fee of $15.

Postage must be paid at the time the mail is brought to the post office unless the sender has set up a credit account with the post office in advance by depositing a sum of money large enough to cover postage for the mailing. Many firms that frequently make third-class bulk mailings keep a working cash balance at the post office so that postage for any mailing may be taken care of without delay. (Deposits may also be used for all classes of mail sent under nonmetered permit.)

The permit imprint must be made by printing press, handstamp, lithography, mimeograph, Multigraph, Addressograph, or similar device, not typed or hand-drawn. It must conform with those illustrated.

All classes of mail may be sent with printed impressions provided each mail-

One of these three permit indicia must be printed on third-class bulk mail which is mailed, without stamps affixed, as nonmetered mail.

ing consists of certain minimum quantities, as follows:

First-class mail: 300 pieces of identical weight

Second- and third-class mail: 300 pieces of identical matter, except with third-class bulk mail which must weigh at least 50 lb or consist of 200 identical pieces

Fourth-class mail: 250 pieces of identical mail, except bulk catalog mailings require 300 identical pieces

For information about exceptions to these minimum quantities, consult your local postmaster.

Mailing procedures. Before mailing, all classes of mail carrying a permit imprint must be faced, separated into classes, and, in the case of second-, third-, and fourth-class mail, sorted by cities and states. Such mail must be deposited at the post office that issued the permit or at a deposit point designated by the postmaster. Each mailing must

be accompanied by a Mailing Statement, Form 3602.

postage meters See METERED POSTAGE
above.

postcards Government postal cards, or
private mailing cards which conform to
the same general specifications, are ac-
corded the special privilege of being
handled as first-class mail even though
they mail for 4 cents instead of the 5
cents minimum charged on first-class
envelopes or outsized private mailing
cards. Of course, private mailing cards
that contain no writing and can qualify
as third-class matter can be mailed at
third-class rates, which may be lower.
(For example, a double reply, government postal card costs 8 cents; a private
double reply card of the same size,
mailed third class, may require only 4
cents outgoing postage, and provide for
return either under stamp supplied by
recipient or under a business-reply-card
permit.)

The fact that true postcards are first
class of course insures that they will be
forwarded where necessary. The 4-cent
rate applies in the United States and
its possessions, Canada, and Mexico; the
rate to other countries is 7 cents.

Government postal cards. For domestic use these cost 4 cents each for both
card and imprinted stamp. Double
(reply) postal cards are 8 cents each.
Cards purchased from the post office
may be imprinted with advertisements
and illustrations on the back and left
third of the face. For printing purposes
both single and double cards may be
obtained as shown in the accompanying
table.

Kind of card	No. of cards to a sheet	No. of cards to a case
3¼ x 5½ single.....	40	10,000
3¼ x 5½ double....	20	5,000

Private mailing cards. These cannot
be smaller than 3 by 4¼ in. or larger
than 4¼ by 6 in. They must be of
cardboard similar to that of the government postal card and may carry advertising and illustrations on the back and
left half of the face. The postage rate
is 4 cents each.

Double reply postal cards. These must
be folded with no enclosures. They
may be obtained from the post office
at 8 cents each with stamp imprinted
on each card. Privately printed double
cards within prescribed size must carry
4 cents postage, with reply half subject
to the same when mailed. The stamp
may be used to hold the card together
only if precanceled stamps are used.

Business reply cards. These are the
ones for which the sender guarantees return postage of 6 cents each by filing
Form 3614 and securing permission
from the postmaster of the office where
the cards are to be returned. (See
BUSINESS REPLY CARDS AND ENVELOPES
above.)

Return to sender. Undeliverable postal
cards, single or double, will be returned
to the sender, provided his name and
address are given in the upper left
corner of the address side along with
the statement "Return Requested,"
pledging payment of return postage of
4 cents each.

precanceled   postage Precanceling
means the cancellation of postage stamps,
stamped envelopes, or postal cards in
advance of mailing. The use of precanceled postage reduces the time and costs
of mail handling. Because precanceled
mail is sorted and tied in packages by
the mailer, it requires less processing
time in the post office and is therefore
dispatched more quickly.

Precanceled stamps may be used to
pay postage on third-class cards (not on
first-class mail, unless specifically authorized by the postmaster on Form
3620), and on second-, third-, and
fourth-class mail.

Precanceled postage may be of two kinds: (1) adhesive postage stamps which may be canceled only by the post office, and (2) postage which may be canceled by any individual or organization which has secured a post-office permit to precancel stamped envelopes or postal cards with its own precancellation mark. Your canceling mark must include the name of the post office and state, your permit number, and (for first-class mail only) the date of the mailing. (See illustration on page 444.)

Any number of pieces of precanceled mail may be mailed at the same time regardless of whether they are identical, except for pieces of third-class bulk mail which must be identical and have a minimum of 200 pieces, or 50 lb, in each mailing. (See THIRD-CLASS MAIL below.)

BULK RATE

With precanceled stamps, third-class bulk mail must be marked with this inscription, with or without box rule, either printed or hand-stamped in the upper right corner.

printed indicia See PERMIT IMPRINTS above.

registered mail You may obtain added protection for your valuable and important mail and evidence that it has been delivered by having it registered with a return receipt requested. Because registered mail is always carried in locked bags and a record is kept of every person who handles it, it is less likely to be lost or rifled. The registry fee (paid in addition to regular postage) provides indemnity against loss, damage, or rifling up to $10,000 of declared value. When the declared value exceeds this $10,000 maximum indemnity, an additional charge (surcharge) is made. (Insured parcels can be protected only to $200. Certified mail does

not provide any indemnity or insurance if the mail is lost in transit.)

Registered mail is recommended for money and articles having a monetary value. Note that registered-mail service is the only service that provides indemnity for first-class mail. (Only third- and fourth-class mail can be insured.) Certified mail is recommended for those items which have no monetary value. (See CERTIFIED MAIL above.)

Requirements for registry. All registered mail must be sealed and requires postage in addition to the registry fee and possible surcharge.

Return receipt cards. A return receipt, showing to whom and when registered mail was delivered, will be mailed to sender for a fee of 10 cents if requested at the time of mailing; if requested after mailing, the fee is 25 cents. For a return receipt showing to whom, when, and where registered mail was delivered, a fee of 35 cents is charged. Such a receipt must be requested at time of mailing.

return of undeliverable mail See FORWARDING AND RETURN OF UNDELIVERABLE MAIL above.

second-class mail Newspapers, magazines, and other periodicals may be sent for extremely low rates when mailed by the publisher or registered newsagents under second-class mailing privileges. For example, under certain circumstances a four-page newsletter weighing $\frac{1}{4}$ oz mails for a minimum rate of $\frac{1}{8}$ cent per copy.

Eligibility for second-class rates. A newspaper or periodical must be printed (not duplicated in imitation of a typewriter) and published at least four times a year from a known office at stated intervals, numbered consecutively with date of issue, have a legitimate list of paying subscribers totaling 65 percent of total circulation, and be issued for the dissemination of information of a public character or devoted to litera-

COMPARISON OF REGISTERED, INSURED, AND CERTIFIED MAIL

	Registered mail	Insured mail	Certified mail
What safety provisions are made?	Handled separately from other mail in locked bags with record of each person handling en route	Handled with other mail. Record made only on delivery, but no delivery record on minimum-fee parcels	Handled with regular first-class mail. Record made of delivery
To what classes of mail can it apply?	First and airmail	Third and fourth	First
What is the maximum that will be paid in case of loss, damage, etc.?	$10,000	$200	Nothing
What are the requirements about sealing?	In all cases it must be sealed	Parcels may be sealed	Must be sealed

What does it cost?	Requires first-class postage fee plus a registry fee as follows:
	
	Declared value Fee
	$ 0.00–$ 100.. 0.75
	   100.01– 200.. 1.00
	   200.01– 400.. 1.25
	   400.01– 600.. 1.50
	   600.01– 800.. 1.75
	   800.01– 1,000.. 2.00
	Increasing gradually to
	$9,000.01–$10,000.. 4.25
	If mailer has commercial or other insurance, the registry fee for declared value of over $1,000 is slightly less than that given above, and postal liability is $1,000 maximum or prorated
		Requires third- or fourth-class postage plus insurance fee as follows:
		
		Insurance Fee
		$ 0.01–$ 15...... 0.20
		  15.01– 50...... 0.30
		  50.01– 100...... 0.40
		100.01– 150...... 0.50
		150.01– 200...... 0.60
			Requires 30¢ fee in addition to first-class postage

Is a receipt returned to the sender?	Yes, if requested and additional fee paid	Yes, if requested and additional fee paid (not available for mail insured for $15 or less)	Yes, if requested and additional fee paid

ture, the sciences, arts, or some special industry. It must not be designed primarily for advertising purposes, for free circulation, or for circulation at nominal rates. Application for second-class entry must be made through the postmaster on Form 3501 accompanied by payment of an application fee. Fees are graduated according to the circulation of the periodical.

Rates of postage on second-class matter. These vary according to the kind of publication (daily, weekly, or otherwise), whether or not delivery is to be made within the county of publication, and the ratio of reading matter to advertising matter contained therein.

Within the county of publication, postal rates range from 1¼ cents per lb to 2 cents per copy for periodicals published less often than weekly and weighing over 2 oz.

Outside the county of publication, rates are charged as follows: (1) 1.8 cents per lb for publications issued by nonprofit religious, educational, scientific, philanthropic, agricultural, labor, or fraternal organizations; and (2) 2.8 cents per lb for publications other than nonprofit with no advertising.

With advertising in the publication, zone rates per pound are charged for the advertising portions as shown in the accompanying table.

SECOND-CLASS MAIL, RATE PER POUND

Published outside of county

	CENTS
Nonadvertising	2.8
Advertising:	
Zones 1 and 2	4.2
Zone 3	5.2
Zone 4	7.2
Zone 5	9.2
Zone 6	11.2
Zone 7	12.0
Zone 8	14.0

For further details regarding envelopes, wrappers, payment of postage, sorting, and mailing, consult the local postmaster or see the "Postal Manual."

special delivery and special handling
For greater speed, the post office provides two special services: special delivery and special handling.

Special delivery may be provided for all classes of mail. A letter or package carrying a special-delivery stamp is expedited with first-class mail, which is handled first and on the fastest trains. In addition, special delivery guarantees that a letter or parcel will be delivered by special messenger at the point of destination between 7 A.M. and 7 P.M; in larger cities between 7 A.M. and 11 P.M. Special-delivery services are not available to rural routes.

Special handling applies only to fourth-class mail. It guarantees that fourth-class matter will be handled and transported as speedily as first-class mail, but will be delivered on regular parcel-post trips, not by special messenger.

Thus, 10 lb of books or manuscript, art, and photos for a book can be mailed at the speed of a first-class letter for 90 cents. (Special fourth-class rate for 10 lb = 55 cents; plus special handling fee, 35 cents.) This is the greatest bargain in the U.S. mail and the one most frequently overlooked. Nothing is gained by putting a special-handling stamp on an item also bearing a special-delivery stamp, since the latter alone entitles the item to both kinds of service.

special fourth-class rate A special rate of 10 cents for the first pound and 5 cents per pound thereafter applies to educational materials. These are defined as books and manuscripts for books (including art and photos), periodical articles and manuscripts for same, printed music and manuscripts for music, 16mm films and 16mm film catalogs (except when mailed to commercial theaters), printed objective-test materials, printed educational reference charts, and loose-leaf pages and binders for medical information to doctors, hospitals, medical

FEES FOR SPECIAL DELIVERY AND SPECIAL HANDLING, CENTS*

	Weights		
	2 lb or under	Over 2 lb and not over 10 lb	Over 10 lb
Special delivery, first class and air mail....	30	45	60
Special delivery, all but first class........	55	65	80
Special handling, fourth class (only)......	25	35	50

* The above fees are in addition to regular postage.

schools, and medical students. Weight limit: 70 lb.

Packages should be marked "Special Fourth-class Rate"—followed by one or more of the following specific categories: Books, 16mm Films or 16mm Film Catalog, Printed Music, Objective Test Materials, Sound Recordings, Manuscript, Educational Reference Charts, or Medical Information. When two or more articles described in this section are mailed in the same package, the terms are simply combined; for example: "Special Fourth-class Rate—Books and Sound Recordings."

An even lower rate (4 cents for the first pound and 1 cent for each additional pound or fraction) applies to similar materials when loaned or exchanged between schools, colleges, universities, public libraries, and nonprofit organizations and their members or borrowers. (See LIBRARY-MATERIALS RATE.)

special handling See SPECIAL DELIVERY AND SPECIAL HANDLING above.

speeding delivery See SPECIAL DELIVERY AND SPECIAL HANDLING above.

third-class mail See also FOURTH-CLASS MAIL above.

Third-class postage applies only to nonpersonal matter weighing up to but

not including 16 oz that is either unsealed or subject to postal inspection if sealed.

This includes form letters, circulars, catalogs, books (see BOOK POSTAGE RATES), printed matter not in the nature of personal correspondence, proof sheets, manuscript copy accompanied by corrected proof sheets thereof, drawings that have no handwriting or hand-lettered captions, photographs, and merchandise.

Fully sealed envelopes (all sizes) are encouraged by the post office. Sealed envelopes containing third class must be marked with the words "Third Class." These words cannot be abbreviated, but can be placed anywhere on the face or back of the envelope. The marking may not be within or part of a meter stamp or permit imprint.

The table at the top of page 451 gives comparative rates for regular third class and for third-class bulk mailings. Bulk rates, i.e., rates for mailing at one time 200 or more identical pieces or enough to weigh 50 lb, are applicable only to specially authorized mailings.

To mail at third-class bulk rates:

1. A permit must be obtained from the local postmaster.

2. A fee of $30 each calendar year is required. A receipt on Form 3544 is issued for each fee paid.

3. When there are 10 or more pieces

THIRD-CLASS POSTAL RATES

(Limit up to, but not including, 16 oz)

Types of material	Single rate	Bulk rate
Circulars, books, catalogs, and other printed matter, merchandise	4¢ first 2 oz, 2¢ each additional ounce or fraction	Rate dependent upon nature of piece, weight, etc. 2⅞¢ minimum charge. Annual bulk fee of $30 required, sorting and tying by mailer. Minimum rate to authorized non-profit organizations is 1¼¢.

for one post office or state, pieces must be sorted by cities and states and tied in bundles. Consult your postmaster for details about sorting.

4. Matter must be mailed in the post office, *not* in a letter box.

Payments of postage on third-class bulk mailings may be made in any of three ways:

1. By metered postage impressions. (See METERED POSTAGE above.)

2. By precanceled stamps or precanceled stamped envelopes. (See PRECANCELED POSTAGE above.)

3. In cash for mail with permit imprints (printed indicia). (See PERMIT IMPRINTS above.)

Postage-saver envelopes. Also called "penny savers," these are frequently used for third-class mail since they have one loose flap that permits postal inspection if necessary. Although this tucked-in side flap sometimes carries a ⅛-in. spot of gum to hold it a bit tighter, the envelope is still considered unsealed and is, therefore, acceptable for third class.

Forwarding and return of undeliverable mail. Both of these services for mail of various classes are described under FORWARDING AND RETURN OF UNDELIVERABLE MAIL above.

Mailing-list corrections. These can be greatly facilitated if the sender takes advantage of the post-office service in supplying (1) the reason why mail is undeliverable or (2) the new address to which mail has been forwarded. (For details, see MAILING-LIST CORRECTIONS above.)

undeliverable mail See FORWARDING AND RETURN OF UNDELIVERABLE MAIL above.

HOW TO CHOOSE THE RIGHT PRINTING PROCESS
for "line" work where there are no photographs or other halftones

| COPIES | 10 | 25 | 100 | 500 | 1,000 | 2,500 | 5,000 | 10,000 | 50,000 | 100,000 | 250,000 |

CARBON COPIES

PHOTOSTAT

BLUEPRINT, WHITEPRINT

XEROX

SPIRIT DUPLICATOR

MIMEOGRAPH

SILK SCREEN

MULTIGRAPH

MULTILITH*

OFFSET (Photo-offset lithography)

LETTERPRESS

ROTOGRAVURE

line

*The Multilith is a small offset press